Post-traumatic Culture

Post-traumatic

Culture

INJURY AND
INTERPRETATION
IN THE NINETIES

Kirby Farrell

THE JOHNS HOPKINS UNIVERSITY PRESS

BALTIMORE AND LONDON

PS
228
.P74
F37
1998

The Johns Hopkins University Press
2715 North Charles Street
Baltimore, Maryland 21218-4363
The Johns Hopkins Press Ltd., London
www.press.jhu.edu

Library of Congress Cataloging-in-Publication Data will be found
at the end of this book.
A catalog record for this book is available from the British Library.

ISBN 0-8018-5786-4
ISBN 0-8018-5787-2 (pbk.)

For Helen Farrell and Merrick Johnson

Contents

Preface

STRANGE TO SAY, this book grew out of an essay on Sherlock Holmes that discovered violent ambivalence toward children and colonial "children" in *The Sign of Four*. Like Holmes injecting cocaine, I had a nagging sense of unfinished business after criticism had closed its case. Then I noticed that Holmes's antagonist is named Small, that his henchman is a murderous black dwarf from the colonies small enough to be mistaken for a child, and that Holmes anguishes over the ultimate smallness of death. At that point, with a sort of crystalline naiveté, the novel fell open to the hammer tap of analysis, revealing obsessive connections between death anxiety and the cultural prejudices of late-Victorian England. In effect, the peculiar social world of the novel unfolds from a hidden injury associated with childhood and death.

A similar pattern caught my eye in a recent American novel marketed for young readers. In Virginia Hamilton's *Sweet Whispers, Brother Rush* (1984), a ghostly figure leads a young black girl into a trancelike state in which she recovers her lost childhood and confronts her fear of death. The novel's upbeat ending appears to celebrate the girl's hard-won autonomy and a vision of racial and feminist solidarity, and yet—astonishingly—it answers her disabling fears by silently borrowing heroic values from 1980s America, so the girl ends up in solitary triumph with nearly all the other characters marginalized or doomed.

Eventually Sherlock Holmes led me to investigate a cluster of late-Victorian fantasies, among them Rider Haggard's *She*, H. G. Wells's scientific romances, and the stories of Jekyll and Hyde, Dorian Gray, and Bram Stoker's predatory patriarch. Then an essay I wrote on the Disney film *Beauty and the Beast* (1991), of all things, spurred my interest in a group of recent American films that included, among many others, Michael Moore's *Roger and Me* (1989), some post–Vietnam War sagas, and Spielberg's *Schindler's List* (1993).

The present book crystallized when I realized that what had drawn me to these stories from the ends of two centuries—what they all share, suffusing and energizing them, latent and yet formative—was a mood of cultural crisis: a sense that something has gone terribly wrong in the modern world, something that we can neither assimilate nor put right. The mood's special poignancy comes not only from life's usual struggles and sorrows, but also from a sense that the ground of experience has been compromised. Implicitly, that is, these are fantasies about trauma. But they are also particular *uses* of trauma to interpret and adapt to the world, and that is the central concern of this book.

Late-Victorian physicians created the clinical concept of traumatic neurosis in an era when "modern life" was routinely categorized as sick, degenerate, and stressful. That clinical concept has interacted with a host of ideological concerns outside the doctor's office, from the defeat in Vietnam to massive layoffs. The term has become metaphorical even as its clinical significance persists, contributing to increasingly psychologized and medicalized explanations for behavior.[1]

These days, journalists and screenwriters routinely use the trope of childhood trauma to account for the behavior of serial killers, superstars, and even corporate executives. On another level, recent novels and films such as Don De Lillo's *White Noise* (1986) and John Sayles's *Passion Fish* (1992) argue that modern life is inherently crippling. Although neurological evidence points the other way, conventional wisdom—as in the movie *Look Who's Talking* (1989)—assumes that birth itself is traumatic. In the 1970s Dr. Frederick Leboyer's crusade for the soothing treatment of newborns echoed Otto Rank in attributing adult anxiety to birth trauma.[2] It would be hard to overestimate the plasticity and the elemental power of the concept. People use trauma as an enabling fiction, an explanatory tool for managing unquiet minds in an overwhelming world. But it has that explanatory power because, however overstated or implausible the concept sounds, people feel, or are prepared to feel, whether they are aware of it or not, as if they have been traumatized.

To recognize representations of trauma in stories is easier than to see how those fictions may express the world that created them. What spurred me to that second step was a moment's insight in a schoolyard in Kazakhstan, in the former Soviet Union, where I was doing some work in 1993 for the Peace Corps. One Monday morning I was about to enter a grammar school near the Chinese border. The Tien Shan Mountains to the east had scarcely changed since the days of Marco Polo, but on the human scale, cultural forms were shivering from the psychic quake that had ended the Cold War. The flat-roofed brick school building could have been in Abilene, Kansas, were it not for the junked Soviet fighter-bomber playing the role of jungle gym in the playground. Watching the kids clamber over the rusty jet, I suddenly thought of my own childhood in postwar America; I remembered playing heroic war games in sunny New England backyards, dimly aware of the satanic Communists supposedly hiding under every bed. The fighter-bomber brought to mind a school trip in the 1950s, a Cold War propaganda junket to a battery of pretentious and probably incompetent Nike missiles that had been installed across town in order to shoot down Soviet bombers and their nuclear payloads over the suburbs of Boston. The offspring of those hospital-white Nike missiles are with us today in the Patriot missiles hyped in Gulf War press releases, and in "Star Wars" pipe dreams.

Pausing in that schoolyard in Central Asia, watching children at play with a modern military-industrial tool for mass killing, I savored the deep current of insanity that courses smoothly through everyday life. In that moment I could feel the power of dissociation—Orwell called it "doublethink"—that had invisibly tyrannized the world of my childhood as it does the present. In a flash of associations, the jet fighter in the playground evoked for me a sense of menace that had haunted my neighborhood in those days of Ike and sunshine: Korean War comic-book heroes slaughtering "gooks" and "yellow devils" with a stylized rage that eventually exploded for real in Vietnam; but also insidious threats hovering around the subjects of money, jobs, race, and the "battle of the sexes"—conflicts that flare up in today's headlines. With a pang I saw more clearly than ever that I had grown up in a world of public illusions and disconnected emotions. Nor did the associations stop there. When I went to write about that morning, weeks later, my thoughts went back to my own childhood again, this time even closer to the unsettled ground of experience, when I was nine years old and suddenly understood that one day I was going to die.

The death of a grandfatherly neighbor shocked me. My father broke the news with the gentle but resolute manner he admired in Gary Cooper, but my father had lost his parents when he was about my age, and I sensed his own dread. That night, while my mother was out visiting, I lay in my bed in a state of gathering panic. It wasn't dying that terrified me, it was the idea of not being, of being dead forever. In the wisdom of slang, the idea "got to" me. A storm of adrenaline shook me. One by one I called up a thousand arguments to save my mind, and one by one they fell to shreds. When I tried to think of religion, I realized that I couldn't imagine heaven: I couldn't believe in it. Heaven was a word, something people said to calm each other. The feeling of utter helplessness was as much a shock to me as the idea of imminent death. Finally in a spasm of horror I leapt out of bed and ran into my father in the kitchen. I was sweating anguish, leaking tears, and I couldn't talk. And the fear was contagious. In his brusque confusion I felt my father's own invisible, helpless fear.

Standing there in my pajamas, stammering evasions, struggling to swallow my panic, I was undergoing an initiation. My father too was afraid; on some deep level everybody was. We had to stay calm, everybody had to, because there is no remedy and panic is contagious. When my father sent me back to bed, I lay awake in a state of heart-pounding vigilance, envying the family mutt her innocence, trying various mental tricks to compose myself. In my terror I was look-ing for other people, for culture, to rescue me from death. I can remember the shock of realizing that nobody had an answer. And when I realized how helpless we are, I saw how invented the human world is, how wishful and counterfeit. Much of my terror came from the shock of discovering that my mind was not its own master but trapped in a body fighting for its life like a hunted animal. Gripped by survival panic, my body became part of the threat. In my struggle for composure, my mind seized on the threat with paralyzing obsessiveness that made me feel even more helpless and panicky.

For months afterward I suffered from anxiety and memories of that first rush of terror. I slept badly, startling awake during the night to a sense of dread, and dragging through the days feeling exhausted and too queasy to eat. From time to time dread would break in on my thoughts and threaten another spiral of panic. The everyday world took on a sinister coloration, stained by a sense of danger. At one point my mother took me to the family doctor, the practical Dr. Bier, who looked like Peter Lorre and prescribed "the green medicine"—some sort of sedative. By then I suspect my mother had made out my death anxiety, al-though she had no idea what to do about it. Dr. Bier's exam turned up nothing physically wrong. But he recognized that the patient was an imaginative child with a sensitive nervous system, and he knew enough to prescribe not only the green anodyne but also the cultural remedy of denial. "Ziss boy," he told my mother, "he has a type of mind, always he muss be kept very busy."

A Victorian doctor would have associated my symptoms with hysteria. Dr. Bier probably thought of my distress as anxiety; for my parents it was "nerves." In fact, my experience had many characteristic features of trauma.

I BRING UP this story because it illustrates so plainly what can happen when, for whatever reason, we blunder outside the magic circle of everyday life. Nat-ural catastrophe or human violence readily breaks the circle, but under the right conditions any pileup of stresses, any mortal terror, can do it. In trauma, terror overwhelms not just the self, but the ground of the self, which is to say our trust in the world. In this way trauma is an injury not just to the central nervous sys-tem or to the psyche, but also to the culture which sustains body and soul. Pre-scribing busyness, Dr. Bier was wisely prodding the child to resume spinning a cultural cocoon that could safely enclose an imagination that had somehow gone too far.

What Dr. Bier did not say, what took me years to see, is that terror made the world around me feel false and ungrounded, a tissue of interpretations. But the reverse was also true. Something about that particular world had contributed to my vulnerability in the first place. I had grown up sensing fear around me as I sensed it in my father that night, yet the world denied—disconfirmed—all that terrible inner experience. Much of the terror came from that isolation. In part my experience was a contagious effect of trauma in my parents' early lives, and in a nation that had been maimed by the Great Depression: an America still mourning its dead from World War II and Korea, and spooked by the new Soviet H-bomb and by spectral Communist spies. Prosperity and the neurotic-sounding military-industrial "complex" presented totally incompatible realities. Like a shaken war veteran, the nation reassured the neighbors that it felt on top of the world, yet it slept badly, with the light on, one eye open, and a pistol under the pillow.

In the Vietnam era those gathering contradictions surfaced. Would the Great Society invest in the lives of marginal Americans: women, racial minorities, the young, the desperately poor—people who might otherwise have reason to feel victimized? Or would resources go into military-financial triumphalism? The Vietnam debacle shook the nation's self-esteem, discredited its leaders, and bankrupted efforts at social progress at home. By the 1980s and 1990s there were no "evil empires" left to make sense of Cold War sacrifices, and a growing gap between rich and poor, institutional power and everyday people, had recreated the grinding contradictions of the Gilded Age. As a sense of disorientation spread, the idea of trauma flourished too.

This interplay of injury and interpretation distinguishes the texts explored in these pages. The book has been subdivided in various ways to allow readers access to particular themes, writers, books, and movies. But its basic aim is to unfold a continuous if wide-ranging argument. Dr. Bier's green medicine, whatever it was, anticipated Dylar, the drug invented to calm the fear of death in Don DeLillo's queasy, comic *White Noise* (1986)—a novel unimaginable in Ike's America. Once you see through the conventional world to the vastness of things, never again can you wholly screen out the white noise of background dread. But then, the same loss of certainties—the same letting go—can spur imagination to new creativity. I suppose this is why, as the old Soviet world dissolved around us, a sunny moment in a schoolyard in Kazakhstan could lead my imagination back to a long-ago crisis of childhood insight, and now a step further, into the clusters of stories I described above, and into this meditation on the cultures that gave them being.

Acknowledgments

THIS BOOK PROMISED to be a short scientific expedition among misty peaks, sudden villages, and unknown lives. The actual trek included a fair amount of heartsick swamp and ignominious lost bearings. The truth is, I was encouraged in this enchanted folly by my dearest friends, especially Kathy Conway and Bruce Wilcox, who looked at a map doodled on a napkin and uncorked the bon voyage champagne. Kay Smith, Frank Brownlow, and Steve Helmling kept the expedition going with brilliant talk, buckets of coffee, and timely crocodile sightings. On the frontier I was fortunate to find Neil Elgee manning the Ernest Becker Foundation's hospitable outpost. Dan Levy, Les Gasser, Mimi Sprengnether, Mary Sue Moore, Jean Boase-Beier, Brian Grant, Bill Perry, Sybille Heintz, Uli Martzinek, Jules Chametsky, and Chris Williams have helped in more ways than I can say. My family was wondrously good-natured about having the expedition's camels tethered in the house. Finally, the University of Massachusetts at Amherst and the Department of English deserve special thanks for supporting new research in an era of penny-wise management philosophy.

In different forms some of the book's arguments have appeared in *Arizona Quarterly* 52, no. 1 (1996); *Contemporary Literature* 31, no. 2 (1991); *Massachusetts Review* 34, no. 2 (1993), and 37, no. 2 (1996); *Pictures of a Generation on Hold*, edited by Murray Pomerance and John Sakeris (Toronto, 1996); and *Studies in the Novel* 16, no. 1 (1984).

Post-traumatic Culture

Introduction

TRAUMA AS INTERPRETATION OF INJURY

> Individuals with hysterical symptoms are found in all cultures. Indeed the form that the hysterical symptom assumes seems to be culturally defined. This suggests that the forms are learned and have symbolic meanings.
>
> *Hysterical Personality*, edited by Mardi J. Horowitz

> Severe trauma explodes the cohesion of consciousness. When a survivor creates a fully realized narrative that brings together the shattered knowledge of what happened, the emotions that were aroused by the meanings of the events, and the bodily sensations that the physical events created, the survivor pieces back together the fragmentation of consciousness that trauma has caused.
>
> Jonathan Shay, *Achilles in Vietnam*

AN AIRLINER HAS CRASHED. A few survivors stagger through a cornfield escaping the wreckage. Near-death brings out a rapturous, almost superhuman calm in one of the survivors, a family man and architect. Like the high that sometimes gives soldiers a sense of invulnerability under fire, this ecstasy enables the architect to overcome his terror and save others. In the aftermath, experts minister to the survivors; ambulance-chasing lawyers browbeat them. The architect goes home but feels alienated from his old life and even his lovely wife. Flashbacks and nightmares harass him. Before long he develops a powerful bond with another survivor, a young mother immobilized by the loss of her child in the disaster. Surrounded by insensitive people, the two traumatized survivors come to feel that American society itself has crashed. To face down his terror and prove his immortality, the architect keeps compulsively daring death, at one point making himself walk the parapet of an office building. Finally he straps the young mother into his Volvo with him and recreates the plane crash by plunging them into a concrete wall. This suicidal—and potentially homicidal—

smash-up breaks the spell of disaster and frees both survivors to go back to their families.

This is the plot of Peter Weir's film *Fearless* (1993), and a particularly forthright example of what I call post-traumatic culture. The screenplay gives the crash survivors clinical symptoms of trauma, but the entire culture is figuratively afflicted. As the anguished mother laments, "The U.S. is falling apart." Like the late Victorians, who invented the term *traumatic neurosis, Fearless* registers the shock of radical historical change. At the end of the nineteenth century, when railroad accidents could produce thousands of deaths in a year, the flood of passenger litigation included many psychosomatic injuries, which doctors began to call traumatic neurosis.[1] In *Fearless* the passengers are now airborne and death may be broadcast nationwide, as the *Challenger* explosion was, with contagious post-traumatic effects on spectators, including children. The architect in *Fearless* returns to a society in which numbed and alienated strangers are eager to exploit in lawsuits a sense of victimization. The film assumes that its audiences will find this post-traumatic behavior realistic, either from personal experience or from conventional ideas about trauma.

In contemporary culture, as in *Fearless*, trauma is both a clinical syndrome and a trope something like the Renaissance figure of the world as a stage: a strategic fiction that a complex, stressful society is using to account for a world that seems threateningly out of control. Historically, a post-traumatic mood makes sense as an aftershock of the great catastrophes of midcentury, the Great Depression and World War II. The postwar years advertised compensatory serenity, but they also inaugurated the Cold War, the Korean War, McCarthyism, threats of nuclear annihilation, and new racial and socioeconomic tensions.

With President Eisenhower's departure, grim new injuries followed. A list could begin with the Kennedy assassination, encompass the Vietnam War, urban riots, Watergate, the savings-and-loan scandals, and race on. In their symptomatically titled *America: What Went Wrong?* Donald L. Barlett and James B. Steele show how technological change, Machiavellian financiers, and corporate muscle have wrecked the postwar economic compact. As the battered labor movement picks through Rust Belt rubble, new economic forces are "tending to split society in two," says Paul Krugman, and "may eventually trigger a social crisis," the "impending collapse of the social order" that Christopher Lasch and survivalist groups have foreseen.[2] A survey of graduates of Bucknell University's class of 1970 concludes that "most are experiencing a complete breakdown of the society they once thought they could conquer."[3] For the young, the split marks "the first generation of Americans since the Great Depression that can expect to have a *lower* standard of living than its parents." For them, "this experience of downward mobility is terrifying."[4] After "the trauma of defeat" in the Vietnam War,[5] American middle-class incomes began a steady decline. The massive entry of women into the work force partially masked that slippage, although not without putting additional stress on families and children.[6] During the 1980s the world's greatest creditor nation became its greatest debtor.[7]

The Cold War has shriveled up like a vampire in the sunshine, and so have the stories that gave it purpose. This is the end of "victory culture."[8] And yet the headlines still shudder over a "war" on drugs, holocausts in Bosnia and Rwanda, and epidemics of AIDS, rape, domestic battering, teen violence, and child abuse. As the rain forests go up in smoke, environmentalists deplore global climate change and species extinctions. These shocks haunt Harry Angstrom after his heart attack in John Updike's *Rabbit at Rest* (1990), when he leads a local Fourth of July parade dressed as Uncle Sam, queasy with fatality and rue. As if traumatized, Harry keeps reliving old moments of anguish, trying to give his life coherence.

A particular disaster may immediately cripple some survivors, but most will begin repairing their lives. By contrast, the mood I am describing is post-traumatic—belated, epiphenomenal, the outcome of cumulative stresses. It reflects a disturbance in the ground of collective experience: a shock to people's values, trust, and sense of purpose; an obsessive awareness that nations, leaders, even we ourselves can die. In a popular diet book published in 1993, a doctor explains our evolutionary "fight-or-flight response" in terms that imply post-traumatic victimization: "If a saber-tooth tiger jumps out in front of you, then these changes help you survive. . . . However, in modern times, there are 'tigers' everywhere, and these mechanisms are chronically activated. Because of this overstimulation, the blood may clot and the arteries may constrict. . . . This can lead to a heart attack."[9]

Change exacerbates the mood by undercutting social consensus and the stable transmission of values from one generation to another. Its most prominent symptoms express anxiety about loss of control and decline or degeneration, along with the death anxiety these symptoms often mask. "To a majority of conservative leaders and pundits, moral and cultural decline far outweighs economic slippage as an explanation of the nation's 1990s trauma."[10] In the ivory tower, postmodern theory has rediscovered the instability of meanings and the constructedness of human reality as if for the first time. Bookstores display *The Decline of American Empire*, *The Withering of the American Dream*, and *The Decline of Intelligence in America*. Publishers light the night sky with the funeral pyres of heroic verities: *The Death of Literature*, *The Death of Intimacy*, and *The Death of Meaning*, to name only a few.

Historically, when a millennium slouches to a close, Western imaginations have begun apprehensively summing up, and Norman Cohn's classic study of millennial thought demonstrates how readily its doomsday themes assume new guises.[11] Closer to hand is the precedent of the last *fin de siècle*, when Victorians thronged to buy Max Nordau's thrilling indictment of contemporary degeneration and, crash-landing in the future, H. G. Wells's Time Traveller came face-to-face with hidden rot in the present and cosmic annihilation to come (1895). A century later, mutations of apocalyptic thought surfaced in President Reagan's bizarre references to Armageddon, and have played out in group delusions such as the September 1994 doomsday that Harold Camping touted on forty family-owned radio stations.[12]

However perfect the world to follow may be, apocalyptic visions are rooted in fantasies of exterminatory rage. They remind us that reactions to traumatic injury can be violent as well as depressive or anxious. Doomsday ideation regularly invokes cosmic warfare and rage akin to what is called "combat berserking." In *The War of the Worlds* (1898), Wells threatens humankind with cosmic cannibalism. A "Christian thriller" called *The End of the Age* (1995), written by the politician and preacher Pat Robertson, "describes the events preliminary to the second coming of Christ, among them a meteor falling on Los Angeles and the Antichrist at large in the White House."[13] By calling his social criticism *Slouching towards Gomorrah* (1996), Supreme Court nominee Robert H. Bork threatened a disobedient nation with a cosmic death sentence.

Juxtaposed, the 1890s and 1990s can provide a vivid, stereoscopic view of modernism. Part 1 of this book explores the post-traumatic imagination in some late-Victorian writers, principally Arthur Conan Doyle, Rider Haggard, H. G. Wells, and Oscar Wilde. Part 2 turns to some American films and texts created a century later, in the process examining mutations of earlier themes. Histories of the *fin de siècle* regularly spotlight the imagery of a crash. G. M. Young pictures the 1880s "struggling for a foothold in the swirl and wreckage of new ideas and old beliefs."[14] Men in particular shuddered that modern life would prostrate Western civilization at the feet of barbarian hordes and domineering women. The terrorist bombings of the World Trade Center (1993) and a federal building in Oklahoma City (1995) could have headlined newspapers a century ago, when Fenians and anarchists resolved to shake the social order. "Doomsday" plagues such as HIV and the Ebola virus had a counterpart in hereditary syphilis. Late-Victorian periodicals published a profusion of articles "announcing the decline or decay of such phenomena as cricket, genius, war, classical quotations, romance, marriage, faith, bookselling, and even canine fidelity."[15]

Hindsight helps clarify the role played by belief and interpretation in post-traumatic behavior, and criticism can try to assess the imaginative shocks encoded in texts. To some extent such analyses are always provisional and hypothetical. Although Darwinism plainly helped hollow out Victorian religion, for instance, we have no precise way of measuring the effects of those developments on particular groups. Like other visions of "progress," such shifts in collective belief both swelled and deflated human self-esteem. They could feel liberating or poisonous. Criticism can identify developmental patterns of belief. Criticism can also examine the uses to which beliefs are put in a particular cultural moment, as when alienated people construe the immolation of David Koresh's apocalyptic Branch Davidians in Waco, Texas, as an injury that justifies retaliatory mass murder in a government office building in Oklahoma City.

This sketch makes the post-traumatic mood a fairly straightforward response to the slings and arrows of recent history. People are shaken and it shows in their thinking about the world. The reality is more complex than this doodle. In the concatenation of motives and agents that makes up history there is always more causality than we can process. From one point of view every generation's experience is potentially traumatic because no era wholly avoids misfortune, battered idealism, and reminders of death. When has urban decay in America *not* been appalling? Why should trauma be a hot topic now? And if everyone is traumatized, does the concept have any useful meaning at all? Or is it culturally significant but clinically as superficial as the star-spangled plastic bandages parents put on a child's sore finger? And if berserk violence in life and onscreen represents one sure method of settling scores and relieving the stress of an excruciatingly competitive society, can trauma exercise a sinister attraction?

Post-traumatic stress does help explain some cultural behavior, and the mood sketched above does reflect a collective experience of historical shock. Having made that claim, I have to begin a long process of qualifying it—a process that is, in effect, this book.

Clinical Trauma

Clinically, trauma is an acute injury. The term comes from the Greek word for a wound, and the analogy to a physical wound has influenced thinking about psychological trauma. Clinical definitions posit overwhelmed psychic defenses and a destabilized nervous system. "Traumatic events generally involve threats to life or bodily integrity, or a close personal encounter with violence and death. They confront human beings with the extremities of helplessness and terror, and evoke the responses of catastrophe."[16] *The Comprehensive Textbook of Psychiatry* defines the core experience as "intense fear, helplessness, loss of control, and threat of annihilation."[17] From the standpoint of existential psychology, the *Textbook* is describing stress that impairs lifelong defenses against humankind's primary terror of death, which helps explain its effect on all areas of psychic life.[18]

Traumatic stress overwhelms the body's autonomic fight-or-flight response. Theories usually construe the result as a shock or freeze that leaves the stress unassimilated and induces changes in the central nervous system. In effect, the short circuit imprints the triggering event, leaving the victim in a state of neurological hyperarousal and vulnerable to distress that may emerge long after the crisis is past. This is Post-traumatic Stress Disorder (PTSD). Therapy usually tries to help the victim complete the blocked process of integration by reexperiencing the crisis in a safe environment. Most theorists "speculate that the repetitive reliving of the traumatic experience must represent a spontaneous, unsuccessful attempt at healing."[19] PTSD interferes with the natural processes of relearning by which the brain ordinarily goes about extinguishing a conditioned fear; therapy works to structure and support that relearning.[20]

The variety of post-traumatic suffering makes clear how capacious a concept trauma can be. Symptoms may range from paralysis to frantic, disorganized action. They may be intrusive, as when flashbacks, nightmares, or troubling thoughts haunt the victim. Life may feel meaningless and futile, and the victim may become alienated from others. Numbness or depression may constrict feeling, or hyperalertness may produce impulses to aggression, startle responses, panic reactions, and a feeling of losing control. The victim may suffer mental confusion or have trouble with concentration or memory. Dissociative and personality disorders may be attributed to the catastrophic event, as may neurotic conditions, atypical psychoses, and many impulse-control and substance-abuse disorders. And all these symptoms may play out against a ground of anxiety, with physical problems such as digestive disorders or fatigue, or with chronic dread.

To bring some order to this array of symptoms, theories of trauma have had to be elastic. The paradigm of combat neurosis has been expanded and analogized far beyond the battlefield. But causality has always been debatable. Has a traumatic memory produced the patient's psychiatric problems, or have those problems shaped or even caused the memory? If the effects are post-traumatic, operating at some remove from any unequivocal etiological source, the ground for doubt is expanded. Like the medical ethnographer Allan Young, I believe that "the disorder is not timeless, nor does it possess an intrinsic unity. Rather, it is glued together by the practices, technologies, and narratives with which it is diagnosed, studied, treated, and presented by the various interests, institutions, and moral arguments that mobilized these efforts and resources." Yet the experience can be real even if the explanation for it is untrue. In Young's words, "the reality of PTSD is confirmed empirically by its place in people's lives, by their experiences and convictions, and by the personal and collective investments that have been made in it."[21]

For this reason I emphasize post-traumatic *themes*. There are three principal modes of coping with traumatic stress: social adaptation and relearning, depressive withdrawal or numbing, and impulsive force (berserking). In the movie *Fearless*, the therapist models the effort to reestablish social bonds. Following traditional gender roles, Carla withdraws into depression. By contrast, the hero defies God and death. In the crash and in bonding with Carla, he experiences a messianic sense of purpose and invulnerability. When he smashes his car to restore Carla's conviction, his behavior is a benignly intended form of berserking. This is only one of many contemporary uses of berserking to serve supervening cultural, ideological ends.

Conditioning these modes of coping are two other basic themes. From the beginning, the idea of traumatic neurosis has been accompanied by concerns about compensation. In *Fearless* the crash survivors enter a robust subculture centered on legal and therapeutic compensation. Much of the psychiatric science of PTSD has evolved through the Veterans Administration Medical System and government support for Vietnam veterans. In a larger sense the idea of trauma also "compensates" for distress that may otherwise be impossible to focus or control. Ultimately, trauma is a radical form of terror management. The plane crash in *Fearless* offers the survivors—and the movie audience—a framework within which to locate fears that "the U.S. is falling apart" and that each of us will die someday.

Whatever the physical distress, then, trauma is also psychocultural, because *the injury entails interpretation of the injury*. I emphasize that phrase because terror afflicts the body, but it also demands to be interpreted and, if possible, integrated into character. In an effort to master danger the victim may symbolically transform it, compulsively reexperience it, or deny it. And those interpretations are profoundly influenced by the particular cultural context. Evolution gives everyone a survival drive, but combat stress would probably have had different effects on a Roman centurion than on a suburban teenage conscript in Vietnam. A culture may make terror and loss heroically meaningful and so diminish its damage, but a culture may also contribute to psychic ruin. For exactly this reason—because trauma can be ideologically manipulated, reinforced, and exploited—it calls for critical analysis as well as psychiatric intervention.

Although traumalike pathologies have been recognized for centuries, the concept began to find its modern form a century ago, in "the idea of a memory that is embedded in the neurophysiology of pain and fear rather than in words and images."[22] In 1866 the British surgeon John Erichsen published *On Railway and Other Injuries of the Nervous System*, which held that physical shock to neural tissue could result in mental injury. In the 1870s, with a shift of emphasis, the neurologist Jean-Martin Charcot discerned a relationship between fright and neurosis. Terror of death or crippling injury, he hypothesized, "was translated into an electrical shock that spread through the nerves and so brought down the nervous organization. The moment of looking death in the eye had jarred the nervous system, toppling it like a house of cards. So hysteria had broken out."[23] Charcot recognized that trauma not only represents a specific threat; it also breaches defenses against death anxiety that form the ground of personality. In turn, as Ernest Becker and others have shown, those defenses are profoundly cultural as well as individual.

The medical fantasy of electricity overwhelming the nerves reapplies ideas from science and industry, even as late Victorians more generally focused on the stress of modernism, what Matthew Arnold called "this strange disease of modern life." The scale of the new was itself shocking, comparable in psychic impact to the inhuman vastness of the first atomic bombs. When Isambard Brunel's iron steamship the *Great Eastern* was being built in a Thames shipyard in 1854, "the huge black shape slowly rising above the marshy Isle of Dogs was so immense it defied comprehension. It seems, wrote one observer, to 'weigh upon the mind as a kind of iron nightmare.'"[24] As technologies such as the telegraph and railway overcame the resistance of time and space, they thrilled but also frightened people, and that ambivalence is still deeply embedded in cultural imagination. Sigmund Freud and the composer G. A. Rossini suffered railway phobias; a major wreck left Charles Dickens with post-traumatic symptoms. From their inception in the 1830s the railroads inspired an anxious folklore about their debilitating effects on nature—not unlike twentieth-century consumer anxiety about microwave ovens and cancer-causing electrical fields. We have largely forgotten the lore of Victorian industrialism, in which the steam engine was the iron horse but also the iron monster. Such fears were psychosomatic and psychocultural, because they combined direct experience of pollution, noise, and accidents with a traditional, highly moralized worldview alarmed at Faustian tampering with nature, and led to worries that the overwhelmed nervous system would sicken with scientific-sounding "nervosity."

But there is an existential dimension to the railway syndrome, too. As tools for magnifying human freedom and power, technologies destabilized self-image just as Darwinism did. What kind of creatures are we? Jules Verne could envision people on the moon. Thomas Edison could turn night into day and make a voice live forever on a wax cylinder. Such self-enhancement made poverty, failure, and death harder to accept, as reformers kept rediscovering. Railway travel created a particular double bind. In his *Journal*, Julien Green observes that most people travel "to deceive ennui," and that ennui "quite simply is one of the faces of death, and . . . it is death that many people flee when they travel."[25] Home is safe but deadening, yet escape through technology (the railway) can also be fatal. If travel relieves and arouses death anxiety, that magnifies any threat to safety on a train or plane.

Railway travel brought an epidemic of symptoms such as anxiety reactions, phobias, and the specific conversion hysteria—paralysis or loss of responsiveness in part of the body—called "railway spine." Doctors and attorneys promptly rushed in to alleviate this crisis. An influential treatise by Herbert Page, a surgeon for the London and Northwest Railway, cites more than two hundred cases of possible hysteria. What Charcot called "traumatic hysteria" the Berlin doctor Hermann Oppenheim renamed "traumatic neurosis," keeping the idea of "psychic shock" but expanding the range of symptoms and elaborating a theory of "molecular alternations" to give his amorphous term a more authoritative basis in physiology.[26] In lawsuits, where fraud and neurosis had to be sorted out, doctors struggled over truth as they do today in the controversy about "false-memory syndrome" in child sexual abuse. "Once they had names such as 'hysteria,' 'railway spine,' and 'traumatic neurosis,' doctors—armed with the theories of Charcot, Oppenheim, Page, and others—believed that the railways were causing profound injuries to many unsuspecting persons."[27] In 1846 the Campbell Act mandated compensation for families of victims killed in accidents caused by the negligence of a second party. In 1864 Parliament broadened the Act to include compensation for victims of railway accidents.[28] "According to Page, the British public was fully aware of the provisions of the Campbell Act, and people involved in railway accidents were now unable to think of injuries in isolation from their possible monetary significance."[29]

In the nineteenth century investigators surrounded and attacked trauma and hysteria, but without closure. Theories failed, and still fail, to meet the test of parsimony, as the volume of recent studies attests.[30] To be sure, there were advances. Not only did physicians come to recognize the psychological dimension of hysteria, but they gradually sorted out some psychosomatic and iatrogenic ambiguities. Twentieth-century studies have clarified cultural influences such as gender roles, medical ideologies, and conditions within the medical profession. An overview of the studies, however, makes plain how profoundly interpretive hysteria is. Feminist approaches alone present a complex assortment of disagreements, with differing methods and assumptions driving toward interesting, usually plausible, yet partial accounts.[31]

As in the 1890s, these ambiguities can strain the composure of the most judicious researcher. Elaine Showalter contends that the cultural narratives of hysteria, which she dubs *hystories*, "multiply rapidly and uncontrollably in the era of mass media, telecommunications, and e-mail."[32] She compares them to alarming diseases such as Ebola and Lasa fever, warning that "in the 1990s, the United States has become the hot zone of psychogenic diseases, and mutating forms of hysteria amplified by modern communications and fin de siecle anxiety." In turn she counts herself among an "informal international network of scholars" she calls "the New Hysterians," who track these "psychological epidemics" much as the Centers for Disease Control in Atlanta monitors lethal threats to public health. But this heroic medical model presupposes a normative "healthy" sanity not always evident in history. As Richard S. Lazarus reminds us, "illusion is necessary to positive mental health." Hysteria sharpens the everyday paradox that "illusion or self-deception can both be adaptationally sound *and* capable of eliciting a heavy price. . . . The paradox can be resolved by shifting to the more sophisticated question: What kinds and degrees of self-deceptions are damaging or constructive, and under what conditions? Or, as Becker (1973) has put it, 'On what level of illusion does one live?'(p. 189). Alternatively, perhaps some illusions work better than others."[33]

Rather than try to unfold a history of hysteria from a set of universal laws, Mark S. Micale adopts what amounts to a symbolic interactionist stance:

> The conclusion, it seems to me, is that once a disease concept enters the domain of public discussion, it effectively becomes impossible to chart its lines of cultural origin, influence, and evolution with any accuracy. Rather, visual, dramatic, and medical theories and images become inextricably caught up with one another. Eventually, this criss-cross of ideas, information, and associations forms a single sociocultural milieu from which all authors—professional and popular, scientific and literary—may draw. Ultimately, in writing the cultural history of medicine, I believe it will prove most appropriate and productive to work toward a model of influence that is neither one- nor two-directional but *circular*.[34]

In *Shattered Nerves*, Janet Oppenheim uses just such dynamic circularity to interrelate a prodigious store of sources.[35]

Victorian theories of trauma deepened considerably when World War I sent home a generation of "shell-shocked" men. The victims suffered a host of torments from catatonic immobility and suicidal depression to fits of rage. During World War II, psychiatry gave trauma theory its modern form in texts such as Abram Kardiner and H. Spiegel's *War, Stress, and Neurotic Illness*.[36] Kardiner and others grasped the crucial role played by bonding in protecting soldiers from terror, an insight that in some post–Vietnam War thinking foregrounds the critical relationship between combat breakdowns and soldiers' disillusionment with the moral integrity of their culture.[37]

At the same time, as bitterly satirized in Joseph Heller's *Catch-22*, military psychiatry borrowed techniques from industrial management to return soldiers to combat expediently. To explain hysteria, Victorian "alienists regularly invoked 'the spirit of the age,' the pace of contemporary life, the 'wear and tear' wrought by modern pressures," blaming a "vast and amorphous causative agent" and deflecting criticism "from specific abuses in the living and working conditions of the masses."[38] The "wear and tear" of war is no less a cultural creation. If a culture denies responsibility for the foxhole and the slum, dissociating or

limiting their reality, then the culture itself—not just modernism or warfare—
contributes to traumatization.

Post-traumatic Injury

Post-traumatic Stress Disorder first became widely familiar after the Vietnam
War, when journalists reported on its use as a legal defense for veterans in trouble with the law, and veterans demanded that it be included in the American
Psychiatric Association's *Diagnostic and Statistical Manual of Mental Disorders*
(1980).[39] The term posits that even long after a soldier's return home, stress can
reactivate disturbances that originated in combat. Mentally, neurologically, the
veteran is still at war, in a survival mode, unable to come to terms with that original horror. Similar dynamics are assumed in more-recent syndromes that spring
from the same family tree, such as "battered persons' syndrome" and "parental
abuse syndrome."

There are four characteristics of post-traumatic stress that make the concept
useful for thinking about culture. The first is the proposition that an injury can
continue to influence behavior long after the initial impact. Symptoms may surface belatedly and in disguised, often somatic, forms. From this point of view, a
given behavior need not be a direct reaction to a massive injury, but may represent the cumulative effect of a number of small but synergistic shocks. Such a
view is akin to the ego psychologists' premise that adult personality is shaped by
an accretion of potentially neurotic defenses or character armor.

Closely related to the discontinuous persistence of symptoms is the fre-
quency of dissociation in post-traumatic stress. In Judith Lewis Herman's account, "traumatized people [may] alternate between feeling numb and reliving
the event. The dialectic of trauma gives rise to complicated, sometimes uncanny
alterations of consciousness, which George Orwell, one of the committed truth-
tellers of our century, called 'doublethink,' and which mental health professionals . . . call 'dissociation.'"[40] Orwell's *1984* envisions the postwar world as a
nightmarish post-traumatic culture in which traumatic dissociation is Big
Brother's basic tool of social control. Most of the time dissociation goes unre-
marked or seems natural, and we continue to feel in control of our thoughts
even if we become aware of screening things out. By contrast, traumatic dissociation represents a loss of control, panic in the face of what is unthinkable. For
more than a century researchers have tried to clarify the relationship between
switched-off or locked-up cognitive processes and the emergence of somatic
symptoms such as paralyzed limbs and phantom pain. When job "termination"
means loss of self-esteem and fear of social death, the pain is predictably somatic

as well as psychic. As one management study sums up the "high stress costs" of downsizing, "Disability claims mirror rising job cuts."[41] The neat fiscal formula both clarifies and obscures the psychosomatic mysteries.

The third significant quality of post-traumatic stress is its contagiousness. Herman describes in detail the "vicarious traumatization" that may afflict therapists when working with victims.[42] Explicit symptoms such as phobias or rage are likely to disturb people around the victim. And as the etymology of the word *panic* witnesses, and as Victorian doctors acknowledged in one meaning of the diagnostic term *hysteria*, we are creatures susceptible to infectious fear and arousal. But even when symptoms are latent, we unconsciously communicate emotions such as anger and sorrow. Because of our capacity for suggestibility, post-traumatic stress can be seen as a category of experience that mediates between a specific individual's injury and a group or even a culture. A vivid example is the way Hitler, who was nearly killed in World War I, infected an entire nation with his post-traumatic symptoms. In a sense, all his policies obsessively attempted to undo that earlier calamity through fantastic aggression. In cultural applications, then, it is useful to see post-traumatic experience as a sort of critically responsive interface between people: a space in which patterns of supremely important, often dangerous symbols and emotions may reinforce one another, gaining momentum, confirmation, and force when particular social conditions and historical pressures intersect. This model offers one way to understand the rapid coalescence of lynch mobs in the American South when a white woman reported a traumatic sexual assault.

The fourth salient characteristic of post-traumatic experience is the way in which it destabilizes the ground of conventional reality and arouses death anxiety.[43] A catastrophe "blows" the mind. In a different way childhood sexual abuse may subvert the stability of the world when lies and denial create conflicting realities. The problem is not simply a victim's loss of trust in particular guarantees, but the recognition that no life can be absolutely grounded. As Ernest Becker, Zygmunt Bauman, Jonathan Shay, and others demonstrate, cultural integrity and death anxiety are closely and reciprocally related. The centrality of terror management in trauma relates it to the basic developmental project of coming to terms with mortality. Post-traumatic symptoms, that is, are related to the coping processes of everyday life.

Despite its ambiguities, I use the term *post-traumatic* because it is widely current today, and because its expanded scope has allowed people to fill it with fantasies. It is the most serviceable term I can find for trauma understood as an interpretive process. I don't expect readers to be able to make absolute distinctions between post-traumatic and traumatic symptoms: much of the time clinicians cannot either.[44] The truth is, it would be hard to invent a more comprehensive problem than trauma. It enfolds organic and psychic disorders, with causality capable of moving in both directions, and engages fundamental defenses against death anxiety. Given the feedback loop of self-awareness, the psyche contends not just with death anxiety but also with the fear of being—in the immemorial phrase—scared to death. Not only do defenses and thresholds vary from one individual to another, but the injury is also an assessment of the injury, subject to all the contingencies of interpretation.

Stress, then, is not self-evident. Neurobiological studies continue to refine charts of a brain circuitry that supports fear and its expression, and the expanding literature abounds with tantalizing speculation about such structures as the amygdala and the hippocampus.[45] But stressors do not come in standard units, and in some cases clinical inquiry may reify a phantom. Even what common sense calls physical pain is an interpretive construct, as studies of dental patients show, especially when juxtaposed with studies of tribal people who happily file their teeth with primitive tools or scarify themselves for an extra touch of beauty. Like pain, threat entails interpretation—choices—as does any conflict of values presented by crime or taboo or violation.

In turn, interpretation is anything but self-contained, because a victim builds on past experience and anticipates a future outcome—a process that depends on cultural meanings. As Jonathan Shay emphasizes in *Achilles in Vietnam*, injustices in the war and in American culture exacerbated the combat breakdown of troops in Vietnam. Soldiers began berserking not only out of terror and loss, but also because they felt betrayed by their own culture. How you construe your suffering determines how likely you are to feel the ground of your existence undermined. The *New York Times* (February 13, 1995) reported the murder of an Amish housewife by a teenage farm hand, and implied amazement that the grieving widower and the community calmly accepted the horror as God's inscrutable plan. The family and the community used a truly profound fatalism to calm one another and repair psychic damage. This is one mode of managing trauma: deliberately using social and ideological controls to train people to reinforce one another's self-control. It has roots in ancient religious techniques for calming the central nervous system to prevent or to relieve terror.

In sharp contrast, the nation at large is confused and ambivalent in its attitude toward victims.[46] Official and popular perceptions entangle victims in complex ideological and emotional toils. The homeless are pitiful victims of a ruthless economic system and an inept social-welfare system, or they are conniving parasites—welfare queens, in President Reagan's sneering anecdote. In a Christian culture, intense competition radically destabilizes attitudes toward victimization, because it can be impossible to square casualties and "losers" with a theology of compassion. This dissonance can be seen in witchcraft persecutions in the early-modern period, and it resounded jarringly in the nineteenth century.[47] The idea of trauma may help put a problematic victim safely beyond blame.

My argument examines trauma both as a clinical concept and as a cultural trope that has met many different needs. As an interpretation of the past, trauma is a kind of history. Like other histories, it attempts to square the present with its origins. The past can be personal or collective, recent or remote: an artifact of psychoanalysis or an act of witness; a primordial myth or a use of ancestral spirits to account for misfortune or violation. Because not everybody in a given culture is likely to be neurologically afflicted, or affected the same way, trauma is always to some extent a trope. In the early-modern period, people used the trope that life is a play to come to terms with changing subjectivity and social possibilities. The notion of role-playing affected their outlook and even their behavior; Elizabethan sumptuary laws tried to regulate clothing styles by class in an effort to keep upstarts from "acting like" their betters. Trauma resonates in a similar manner. People may use it to account for a world in which power and authority seem staggeringly out of balance, in which personal responsibility and helplessness seem crushing, and in which cultural meanings no longer seem to transcend death. In this sense the trope may be a veiled or explicit criticism of society's defects, a cry of distress and a tool grasped in hopes of some redress, but also a justification for aggression.

Trauma and Cultural Controls

The core experience of trauma is violence. Judith Lewis Herman contends that the study of psychological trauma "provokes such intense controversy that it periodically becomes anathema" and is "forgotten" or repressed. More than once in the past century the subject has languished, she thinks, because to study it is "to come face to face with human vulnerability in the natural world and with the capacity for evil in human nature."[48] Because perpetrators are often dangerous, because victims ask us to identify with pain and unbearable terror, and because we have the bystander's option of doublethink, it is tempting to do nothing. "The systematic study of trauma therefore depends on the support of a political movement" that challenges, for example, "the sacrifice of young men in war" and "the subordination of women and children."[49]

As Herman forcefully reminds us, the clinical term returned to public awareness in America when the antiwar movement bore witness to the problems of Vietnam veterans afflicted by combat neuroses. The women's movement likewise brought before the public conscience the reality of violence against children and women, which Herman calls "the combat neurosis of the sex war." "Women were silenced by fear and shame," she declares, "and the silence of women gave license to every form of sexual and domestic exploitation. Women did not have a name for the tyranny of private life. It was difficult to recognize that a well-established democracy in the public sphere could coexist with conditions of primitive autocracy or advanced dictatorship in the home."[50] Herman's "sex war" alludes to this century's struggle against fascist dictatorship, with women as victims and feminists as the forces of democracy. She invites the reader to bear witness against evil as Holocaust survivors have taught us to do, for "the conflict between the will to deny horrible events and the will to proclaim them aloud is the central dialectic of psychological trauma."[51]

Underlying this argument is another massive historical change: the nineteenth century's awakening sensitivity to human rights—meaning not only the abolition of slavery but also a new awareness of children and the developmental integrity of childhood. These emerging ideals painfully conflicted with entrenched hierarchies and, no less, with aspirations to rise in the world through dog-eat-dog competition. I will return to this stressful awareness again and again, because a fundamental premise of this book is that the specter of social death can be as traumatic as literal death. Not that social death is merely a figure of speech. In modern society, as among our primate cousins, those at the top of the hierarchy enjoy better health and live longer than marginal members and their offspring. News stories about teen gang murders or fatal child abuse in poor urban neighborhoods tacitly remind us that children in affluent suburbs are comparatively safe, whether we acknowledge it or not. Similarly, media images of starving refugees around the world solicit sympathy but also warn viewers that people at the bottom—people who lose their place, who don't belong—die.

Herman sums up the tricks American society has used to deny aggression against women and children, and the murderous compulsion of warfare. To her brief we could add racial persecution and, more generally, economic violence. And yet although the denial of atrocity is unquestionably a moral question, it is also much more than that. One of the core paradoxes of trauma is that "the greatest confrontation with reality may also occur as an absolute numbing to it, that immediacy . . . may take the form of belatedness."[52] Researchers since Freud have agreed that in traumatic experience, neurophysiological processes often keep an overwhelming threat from registering in memory. This dissociation shades into everyday forms of self-protective denial. In this sense trauma is a particular degree and form of our creaturely denial of death.

Post-traumatic culture registers the dissonance—the shock—of meeting long-denied realities that threaten our individual and collective self-esteem. The unwilling "discovery" of military and gender atrocities may be among the deepest of seismic tremors in recent American culture, but as researchers have shown, erosion of self-esteem directly increases vulnerability to death anxiety. Denial, then, is part of a complex feedback loop that implicates not only immediate victims but potentially a wide circle of witnesses and others. And a crucial problem for cultural studies is that people do not simply ignore or become numb to death, but seek to tame it and ultimately heal its wounds through symbolic transformations.

The present cultural mood reflects the contagious effects of clinical and political trauma, with predictable spasms of anxiety and rage, depression and mourning. Despite the chest-thumping military budgets of the 1980s, the comic-opera invasions of Grenada and Panama, and the exultation over the demise of the Soviet "evil empire," the Vietnam War continues to perplex the nation. Kali Tal argues that American culture turned Vietnam veterans from agents of genocide into victims of trauma, and thereby rehabilitated the military for the Gulf War in 1991.[53] Brutality against women and children haunts the headlines, exacerbated since the 1980s by economic strain, including unprecedented competition between men and women in the work force. In a direct allusion to the Vietnam War memorial in Washington, the September–October 1994 issue of Ms. magazine displays on its cover, against a black background, the names of more than 250 women and girls—out of 1,500 annually—who were killed by male partners or former partners. This salience has incalculable effects, from the hypnotic spell cast by the O. J. Simpson trial (1995) and the celebration of heroic female killers in Hollywood films to the most incidental social relations.[54]

When the idea of trauma moves out of the psychiatrist's office and into the surrounding culture, its clinical definition recedes and its explanatory powers come to the fore. When a group suffers a trauma as, say, European Jews did in the Holocaust, the survivors create new cultural forms to repair the fabric of reality. New meanings enfold the alien terror and influence the evolving identity of the group, as in Israeli military culture and the cry "Never again." Cultures not only report but classify traumatic events: a train "wreck" may be a "catastrophe" or a "tragedy" or merely an "accident." The interplay of publishers, editors, reporters, and audiences determines the meaning of an injury and the nature of our involvement.

We not only tolerate daily accounts of catastrophe, we are drawn to them; 53 percent of television news is devoted to crime and disaster coverage.[55] Just as capitalism exaggerates the pleasures of consumerism to provide escape from a repressive "work ethic," so journalism and mass entertainment market traumatic themes to relieve the cramped ennui of workaday discipline. Violence sells, as media executives remind us, because it serves a sharpened appetite for stimulation. Like obsessive headlines about illicit drugs and sex, tamed violence is an important means of regulating our needs for excitement and security. But then, Becker would argue that in our obsession with work we are invoking sacrifice and heroic productivity to ease lurking anxieties about death and futility, "earning" a conviction of being worthy and invulnerable.

In this context, disaster stories model a range of human relationships to misfortune and keep our defenses exercised. They may function as a reality check even as they frame, and distance us from, horror. As a form of post-traumatic repetition, our obsessiveness about disaster headlines may represent an effort to assimilate what has frightened us since childhood, desensitizing us to the shocks that all flesh is heir to. In a complementary way the headlines invite momentary low-grade worry that, like worry beads, superstitiously promises to buy off big trouble if we submit to a little ritualized distress every day. Mundane accounts of a distant ferryboat catastrophe or earthquake both are and are not real to us. We engage them in a spirit of doublethink, registering the data with safely mediated feeling. Auto accidents command attention because their dangers and consequences are closer to us, and statistically their victims are likely to suffer post-traumatic symptoms.[56]

In existential terms such tamed deaths have a purpose. Like the gladiatorial games the younger Pliny praised "for preparing the spectators for death and suffering," headline disasters model what is unthinkable.[57] They vaccinate the skittish human animal against crippling dread. The news regulates doses of adversity and death, mediating horror through dissociation—embedding the story between, say, a romantic toothpaste smile and the muscular bonhomie of a beer ad. But the news also offers survival pleasure. As Aristotle remarks, luck is the moment of survival, when the soldier next to you is felled by the arrow.[58] "Better you, alas, than me." Disaster stories appeal to deep and deeply disguised motives in us: to pity and terror perhaps, but also to a magical sense of our own immunity, our own ransom from death, our ability to "beat" adversity and outlive others. At bottom, a heroic disaster is preferable to a lonely, messy, vegetative death in a nursing home.

We often deny the addictive potency of survival ecstasy and berserking, but consider Richard Rubenstein's bracing observation that for many World War I veterans "real living" was a memory of intoxicating death arousal. "It was a war of mass death in which massed men were fed for 1500 days to massed fire power so that more than 6000 corpses could be processed each day without letup. When it was over, 10,000,000 soldiers and civilians had been killed and mass death had become an acceptable part of the experience and values of European civilization. Worse still, after the war Europe was filled with men who looked back nostalgically to their war experience as the only period of real living they had ever known."[59]

At the same time, as Kai Erikson observes, "trauma is normally understood as a somewhat lonely and isolated business," yet it often elicits "revised views of the world that, in their turn, become the basis for communality."[60] Responses to trauma may be a means of creating social bonds. What complicates that salutary bonding is the human propensity to manipulate it by engineering injury. Perversely, as Otto Rank, Ernest Becker, René Girard, and others have demonstrated, people may create solidarity by scapegoating and sacrificing others.[61] However controlled it may appear, however hedged by rules and social apparatus, trauma destabilizes the ground of experience, and therefore it is always supercharged with significance and always profoundly equivocal in its interpretive possibilities. Like a traditional religious-conversion experience, it can signify rebirth and promise transcendence, or it can open onto an abyss.

How does culture act to tame trauma?

As I write, my local newspaper is reporting a USAir crash in Aliquippa, Pennsylvania. It could have been the crash in *Fearless*, although there were no survivors. In a sidebar, in prominent type, the newspaper quotes a clergyman at the site: "[People will ask] why, and I'll tell them I can't answer that. It's very traumatizing and a very terrible thing to see—the remains of a human being in a pile, with no way to identify him except for a belt and a piece of clothing." A paramedic concludes that "once people witness something like that, they never forget it, no matter how many crash victims they've pulled out of crumpled, flame-scarred planes."[62] What imprints the experience is the annihilation of meaning and identity. That psychic violence suddenly exposes—and compromises—the processes of terror management at the center of all culture. The newspaper story is one way in which culture goes about assessing and repairing the damage.

And so USAir flight 427 crashes in Aliquippa, Pennsylvania, and under the caption "Investigators at a Loss," the journalists describe federal investigators sorting bits of flesh and mechanical evidence, trying to reconstitute causality and identity. The prospects are daunting but not hopeless. The officials are detectives, Sherlock Holmeses, armed with tenacious logic, and they are "reviewing the plane's black boxes," which always promise to yield the secret.[63] Like a paperback mystery novel, the newspaper looks for signs of foul play—a bomb, a terrorist Cain, a devil—that could supply a purposeful enemy to explain nothingness. The detectives are incipient rescuers. Although thwarted by death this time, their labors will presumably save others like us from a similar fate in the future. The investigators bear the burden of looking directly at horror in an effort to rescue the future.

Among the rescuers (and quoted twice on the same page) is the clergyman, who witnessed "a hand with a ring on it. . . . They think it was an airline stewardess because her uniform was close by."[64] Because the shock of nothingness is unbearable to us, the post-traumatic imagination grasps at the hypothetical stewardess offered by the detectives and the consoling symbols of the competent human hand, the artistic, eternalizing ring (as opposed to heaps of other body parts), and the uniform "close by" that substantiates her official status in society as someone who served others. The clergyman's response to death is an act of imaginative value making. Because the values are those of his culture, death triggers a creative act of value affirmation. What he chose to see and to recount, and the editors chose to print, is grisly and grievous but no less packed with heroic meaning.

One of those meanings is, again, the ring. It evokes marriage, which customarily encloses couples in a culture as the airliner encloses travelers and a walled medieval city enclosed its citizens. As society's basic means of perpetuating itself, marriage is arguably the most important institution in a culture. The ring symbolizes marriage, and through it posterity, the future—ultimately, nothing less than immortality. The wife is gone but the ring endures, and with it the promise of renewal. The clergyman implies a consoling, even happy, ending. In another perspective, the ring points to a supporting framework of religious doctrine and emotions; implicitly the clergyman's focus on the ring makes an argument for the claims of religion against the bitter treachery of the material world.

The newspaper trauma is both an individual and a collective fantasy. It poignantly illustrates the way in which fantasy injures and recuperates, threatens and reassures, tests and denies and accommodates reality. This potent equivocation may help explain why, at a time when communications technology and unprecedented capacities for self-consciousness are producing a surfeit of supercharged and unassimilable symbolic forms, a rapidly changing society of several hundred million people like 1990s America should fantasize so much about trauma. It can represent not only a paranoid posture, with exaggerated defenses always anxiously in need of renewal, but also a defining stimulus for healthy engagement with identity themes and the future. In a paradoxical way the idea of trauma can function as an organizing or focusing tool for a creature that must constantly balance conflicting needs for stability and change, defense and creativity.

In the above example, trauma is associated with a radical, momentary change in perspective that creates an imaginative gap that compensatory cultural materials try to fill. Trauma is a "mind-blowing" experience that destroys a conventional mind-set and compels (or makes possible) a new worldview. This is why practices as diverse as brainwashing and mysticism may manipulate the dynamics of trauma,[65] and why those dynamics may also play a part in conversion experiences. In the aftermath of shock, a person may move toward numbness and derangement or toward deeper insight and reintegration.

As in the account of the Aliquippa plane crash, culture readily interprets recovery as a kind of play-death and rebirth. One anthology of memoirs by "incest survivors" proclaims, for example, "The women in these pages have transformed themselves, like phoenixes rising from the ashes, through their own words."[66] The injury is not simply a psychic wound, but a fractured or double perspective created by the shock of near-death. Now on the edge of conventional social reality, the victim is able to look outward into chaos and death, and inward, with a fresh eye, toward the protective, systematic illusions of cultural heroism. In Daniel Petrie's movie *Resurrection* (1980), as in shamanism, this position is frankly magical. After a spectacular auto accident, a woman (Ellen Burstyn) "returns" from near-death with uncanny healing powers. The screenplay adapts Elizabeth Kubler-Ross's fantasy of dying as a tunnel of light opening toward heaven, in which departed souls act as greeters.[67] As in *Fearless*, traumatic symptoms are converted into "spiritual" healing powers, and death-anxiety gives force to messianic wishes.

At first glance technology appears to be a wholly different mode of coping with disaster. Accident investigators seek to isolate and eliminate the "malfunction," using scientific controls to ensure accuracy. Correction of a given mechanical anomaly—say, the famous O-rings on the space shuttle Challenger—is supposed to "return" life to a naturally safe state. But life is not naturally safe, and complex systems can be expected to produce what Charles Perrow calls "normal accidents"—failures resulting from the unpredictable interrelation of complex parts or subsystems.[68] As in evolution or cancer biology, a particular outcome can be so richly overdetermined that no analysis can tame mutability. Technology is not magic, but technological cultures regularly accommodate magical thinking. In human behavior, magic and technology complement each other, covering different ends of the cognitive spectrum, as it were. But they also interact.

Even specialized technological cultures like NASA may unwittingly normalize risk in their routines.[69] Like the military, business and engineering cultures often accommodate risk in order to maximize morale and performance. In his analysis of accounting practices, for example, Trevor Gambling argues that accounting "contains all the elements of pre-scientific thought: magic, scholasticism . . . and above all humanism, in the sense that human satisfaction is the final end—indeed a specious and easy philosophy 'to serve civic ends.' The renaissance could be viewed as a general raising of men's morale to the point where they could face the rather uncomfortable view of the natural world of modern science, and a similar uplift is needed before men can be brought to cope with a really hard-edged approach to the management of human relationships as well."[70]

Lest we forget, morale is ambivalent: a function of our expansive drives and fear as well. Changes in morale affect both our creative and defensive behavior, sometimes in unexpected ways. In the drive to maximize efficiency, profits, and purchasing power, people may use safety innovations to justify cutting corners in other parts of a system or to rationalize greater risk taking.[71] This seems to have happened when the boom mentality of the 1980s smashed up the supposedly foolproof postdepression financial system, creating the epochal savings-and-loan catastrophe. Similar dynamics have crashed airliners. Paradoxically, relief from threat may lead to greater risk exposure. The obsessive pursuit of longer life may arouse a conviction of immortality that blocks prudent fear even as it increases real danger. These dynamics are salient features of modernism. They can seem especially significant when they conflict with traditional moral concerns—think of all the warnings in Shakespeare about the engineer hoist with his own petard; the limed soul, that struggling to be free, is more engaged; the man to double business bound. This anxiety becomes all the more nightmarish when cultures deliberately try to objectify and regulate controls on morale—and sometimes inevitably fail. The trope of trauma can be viewed as a corrective or cautionary device that modern culture uses in its efforts to regulate morale in the face of new kinds of stress. In this perspective, it seems to me, the trope has developed as one component of the increasingly complex systems of managing motivation that made modern culture possible.

The Uses of Trauma

People not only suffer trauma; they use it, and the idea of it, for all sorts of ends, good and ill. The trope can be ideologically manipulated, reinforced, and exploited. As a result this book has several overlapping aims: to take account of clinical trauma and its cultural correlates, but also to sort out, where possible, some of trauma's strategic uses. Beyond its immediate therapeutic purpose, for example, Judith Lewis Herman's popular book *Trauma and Recovery* uses trauma to muster a moral campaign against violence. Hitler, by contrast, made a policy of terror. The Romans strategically killed and maimed captives to instill lasting inhibitions.[72] In this respect the infliction of trauma resembles the use of torture, as Elaine Scarry describes it, to create physical pain "so incontestably real that it seems to confer its quality of 'incontestable reality' on that power that has brought it into being. It is, of course, precisely because the reality of that power is so highly contestable, the regime so unstable, that torture is being used."[73] In this account, that is, torture is another technique for invoking a ground of being.

Many cultures have systematically induced trauma or near-trauma in an effort to reinforce the conviction of a ground of experience and to strengthen group bonding. When an entire Huron or Iroquois village gathered to torture and eventually cannibalize a captive warrior, taking turns in the torments and actively socializing with the victim, who was expected to sing throughout the ordeal to prove his courage, the calculated, ritualized trauma likely served to reinforce the group's control over its own potentially dangerous vulnerabilities by demonstrating a mastery of terror. The shared arousal of threat, mastery, and relief powerfully bonded the survivors. The ritual murder of a scapegoat affords tormentors a conviction of mastery over their own terror, helplessness, guilt, and directed rage. In the Vietnam War, officers sometimes ordered new soldiers to kill enemies who were then revealed to be innocent civilians, deliberately using traumatic guilt to promote bonding among the new men.[74] In ritual ordeals such as the periodic self-mutilation of Mayan rulers and the solitary, strenuous magic of Siberian shamans, people deliberately induced pain and dissociation in an effort to confront death and acquire special powers.[75]

These different ritual experiences shared a drive to violate and expand the boundaries of conventional life. Through states of altered consciousness, even trance, people sought to open up the realm of death in order to tap some transcendent and transformative power that would imprint identity. The processes seem to have been dangerously equivocal, liable to kindle aggression and panic rather than exaltation if the controls failed. The fundamental control is the underlying metaphor of initiation and rebirth. Experiences that we might associate with trauma mediated a kind of play-death, and the subsequent psychic reintegration signified a renewal or rebirth.[76] And this is by no means a remote fantasy. In the 1990s, Serbs have not only used terror as a weapon against others, but also made the legendary trauma of the Serbian defeat at Kosovo in 1389 the ground of their "resurrected" ethnic identity and the justification for genocidal berserking. Ideology turns repetition-compulsion into heroic fidelity to a transcendent identity.

The effort to heal psychic wounds invariably involves a need to substantiate or reconfirm the self, which often entails convictions of transcendence. In *Resurrection*, Senator John Danforth describes the confirmation hearing of his protégé Clarence Thomas as a trauma of messianic persecution. The Supreme Court nominee exhibited clinical symptoms of traumatic stress, including fits of uncontrollable weeping and paranoia.[77] During the summer of 1991, "Clarence lived in fear that people would kill him," says Senator Danforth. "In all but the strictly physical sense, the person I saw on Wednesday afternoon, Oct. 9, [1991,] was dead." But "on the morning of the third day Clarence Thomas walked into the Senate Caucus Room, took a seat at the witness table and commenced his testimony. Clarence had risen." Danforth's book closes with this resurrection and a cry of "Alleluia."

Insofar as Senator Danforth makes trauma a polemical weapon like the hideous ecstasies in John Foxe's *Book of Martyrs*, his book is typical of many arguments in the 1990s that are grounded in the authority of victimization. Overreliance on this strategy perverts it and also threatens to blunt its effectiveness. The law professor Alan Dershowitz has attacked what he calls "the abuse excuse," in which victims justify their own violence against someone else as a reprisal for alleged earlier abuse.[78] This problem loomed vividly in British courtrooms in the 1890s. Not only was trauma bound up with tort law from the start in the railway lawsuits mentioned above, but an explosion of libel suits dramatized a complex ideology of (mostly male) victimization that implicitly defined an "assault" on one's "reputation" as traumatic. Self-esteem and the sort of heroic immortality Ernest Becker describes depended on comprehensive yet often insecure cultural relations whose disruption was felt to be a grave injury.

The ends of the nineteenth and twentieth centuries have in common a pervasive insecurity about systems of heroic value. Trauma has provided one mode of coping. Journalists commonly ground heroism in fantasies of survival magic. Mary, Queen of Scots used this ancient idea as her motto: *virescit vulnere virtus*— "Virtue thrives on injury."[79] In profiles of celebrities, childhood injury functions as the motive engine for heroic ambition. In the August 1994 issue of *Vanity Fair*, Cathy Horyn explains that after leukemia killed supermodel Cindy Crawford's four-year-old brother, she "strove to be the perfect child—'to make up,' as she says, 'for a dead brother.' In high school, after her parents were divorced, she pushed herself to . . . graduate first in her class." Overcoming the threat of death, the supermodel seeks to be larger than life—"the All-American entertainment icon of the future," a messianic "model" for a culture dazzled and disoriented by change.[80] This formula flourishes today as it did in Horatio Alger's tales and in the Book of Job's notion of suffering as God's test of heroic belief. The dynamic of play-death and rebirth is plain to see. Surviving Troy, Aeneas gives life to glorious Rome. The ancient rhythm shapes conventional accounts of the economic postwar economic "miracle," the "rebirth" of Germany and Japan.

More perplexing is journalism that routinely discovers traumatic abuse in a criminal's childhood, predicating a moral economy in which crime is revenge that somehow balances out past injustice. However clinically accurate, this application of trauma invites ideological distortions and Oedipal feelings to rationalize disturbing material. Comparable is the use of the suffering of crime victims to justify popular policies of "getting tough" on crime, including capital punishment.

As a trope, trauma helps account for a world in which power and authority may seem overwhelmingly unjust. The trope may be a cry of protest as well as distress and a tool grasped in hopes of some redress. When competition is fierce and consolations are inadequate, a claim of trauma can be a signal of submission like the bared throat that stops a fight among wolves. Trauma can be invoked to substantiate claims on the empathy of others, as a plea for special treatment, or as a demand for compensation.

In Victorian railway lawsuits, plaintiffs used trauma to substantiate emerging ideological conflicts over the claims of modern and traditional values, corporate responsibility to the public, and workers' compensation. In the post-Vietnam era trauma has served as a courtroom exhibit in more explicitly ideological contests over victimization. Although the antiwar and women's movements have prominently used trauma to give weight to legal arguments, the phenomenon has expanded into many areas of tort and criminal law and public policy. The 1990s brought challenges to the reliability of victims' memories in numerous lawsuits over sexual abuse, and deep divisions appeared among researchers and therapists over what has become the "false-memory controversy." When it is associated with ambulance-chasing shysters, trauma can be an object of satire, as in an episode of the cartoon series *The Simpsons* in which a sleazy doctor points to a cranial x-ray of Bart Simpson and announces gravely, "See that smudge that looks like my fingerprint? It's a trauma."[81] Dr. Page identified the problem a century ago: "The knowledge of compensation . . . tends, almost from the first moment of illness, to colour the course and aspect of the case, with each succeeding day to become part and parcel of the injury in the patient's mind, and unwittingly to affect his feelings towards, and impressions of, the sufferings he must undergo."[82]

Add to these problematic instances the range of symptoms and pseudosymptoms of trauma, and its puzzles can be baffling. A woman jogger nearly stomped to death by "wilding" teenagers in Central Park contributed something fairly explicit to the national mood. But what of the mother and her family on the *Sally Jessy Raphael* show who won audience sympathy with their report that spirits had sexually abused them, in bed and out, in their house?[83] What of patients whose "recovered-memory" therapy leads them to conclude that their parents long ago subjected them to satanic rites in which, among other abominations familiar to historians of medieval delusions, the participants cannibalized infants? In the 1990s so many adults have recovered memories of childhood sexual abuse in therapy and sought redress in the courts that some psychologists (and accused parents) have formed a movement to counter what they call "false-memory syndrome."[84]

Because cultural memory is necessarily overdetermined, past injury can be ambiguous or even apocryphal and still be damaging. William Faulkner's *The*

Sound and the Fury dramatizes repercussions of the Confederacy's defeat fifty years after the fact. For Serbs, even after six centuries, Kosovo remains a "nightmare," obsessively conjured up and yet also ambiguously intrusive. Summing up the Vietnam War as America's "loss of innocence," commentators carelessly draw on the Edenic story of overreaching ambition and demonic seduction to moralize the war's far-reaching psychic consequences. Latent in the facile phrase "loss of innocence" is the idea of rape. Ancient catastrophes continue to shape us like the vestigial gills and tails paleontologists can see in our bodies. The Fall of Rome colors thinking today as it did in the Renaissance, though our memory of that expiration can only be virtual.[85] Moralized Roman ruin frightened the late Victorians, who felt that "progress" was in conflict with Darwinian struggle and was sapping Western manliness. Their guilty dread about barbarian invaders swarming out of the colonies is echoed today in business alarums about the "rise" of international (usually Asian) competition and America's decline.

The *Atlantic Monthly*, for example, has engaged its affluent readers with Robert Kaplan's warnings about "The Coming Anarchy" (February 1994). As Charles Sugnet observes, "*Atlantic* readers know the slums of Abidjan are [horrible] . . . because they've seen Chicago or South Central L. A. on television. . . . They know that global anarchy is coming, because they feel the U.S. is falling apart."[86] The trope of cultural crash links third world hordes, the American underclass, and the barbarians who sacked Rome, while silently exalting the affluent civilization cherished by the magazine's readers. In stimulating fear, the trope can refresh the audience's values and self-esteem. "Memory" in this instance is an ideological artifact that rationalizes the anxiety of an elite and its efforts not only to police boundaries between classes and continents, but also to justify heroic, often harsh countermeasures. That said, the precedent of Rome, like that of the Great Depression, can have a real traumatic impact.

Fantasies about Rome point indirectly to another source of threat. Insofar as post-traumatic symptoms are maladaptive, they constitute part of an ongoing process of injury. Aor. Konrad Brendler argues that in Germany "the legacy of silence within the family [about the Holocaust] may have a traumatizing effect on the psyche of the generation of the grandchildren."[87] In the aftershock of World War II, Soviets and Americans continued obsessively fighting a cold war that climaxed in Soviet collapse and an America militarized to an extent once unthinkable. Post-traumatic imagination may spin compensatory dreams that risk grave deflation. In the eighth century, the Mayan city-state of Copan was shaken when one of its last kings, known to archaeologists by his glyph-name, Eighteen Rabbit, was captured during a raid on a rival city-state and probably tortured to death. Copan was badly stricken. Eighteen Rabbit's successor countered this shock by building a ceremonial staircase that contains the longest script of Mayan glyphs in Mesoamerica. The propaganda staircase advertised the glory of Copan and its past, striving to ground the kingdom once again and restore its sense of symbolic immortality.

Coming as it did when Copan was on the edge of extinction, the staircase project has an air of futile grandiosity like the proclamations of the later Roman emperors. As a coping strategy it is ambiguous. Does it signify a decadent, compensatory waste of resources in a time of crisis? Or a wise—if in this instance unlucky—technique for transforming survival anxiety into adaptive energy? Because we too are experiencing a historical shift colored by survival anxiety, the question is anything but frivolous. Our own New Jerusalem was founded by English Puritans who had left behind a world they believed due for an apocalyptic scourging, but their vision of traumatic violation aroused in them a rage to start anew, with an astonishing indifference to hardship and death. This equivocal potential for constricting or enlarging life-space is why it can be useful to view post-traumatic behaviors not primarily as symptoms or products of stress, but as ongoing symbolic interactions.

Trauma and the Nineties

I have no master narrative that could map all the interactions of trauma and culture; the primary work of this book lies in each chapter's engagements with particular texts. Although the book attempts no methodical comparison of *fin de siècle* Britain and 1990s America, the play of analogies between the two cultures can be revealing, and I have tried to calibrate my instruments to catch some of them. Trying to test strict scientific hypotheses against a changing culture is akin to measuring a developing weather front with a stepladder and a yardstick. Meteorologists do measure weather with radar and mathematical models, but the results justify that emergency umbrella you keep in your car. Films and novels are something like radar sweeps of the social atmosphere, sensitive to patches of turbulence and the movements of large air masses. The essays that follow develop interpretations of the blotchy, heuristic maps that radar's scanning generates. Their predictive powers are minimal, but they may usefully locate unsettled imaginative conditions and identify their paths of development.

Throughout I have tried to select radar-texts that sweep the culture in a number of different directions. Some of these sweeps overlap here and there; others are more isolated and fragmentary than I would like. Every reader is destined to find that my argument scants, distorts, or overgeneralizes some aspect of these teeming cultures. The writers in part 1, for example, are mostly professional-class white males and compose a narrow sample of evidence. I focus on their fantasies because they spoke to such a wide audience—letters still arrive at Baker Street for Sherlock Holmes—and their texts are most likely to be familiar to readers today, having never gone out of print.[88] Not only did their middling status make professional men peculiarly sensitive to shifting social boundaries and shocks to identity; they also had and still have a special relationship to trauma. Doctors, lawyers, scientists, journalists, writers—and now many feminist and antiwar activists—have actively sculpted the public idea of trauma. In the 1890s doctors faced the additional stress of trying to substantiate their social status and expertise with limited powers; they were often helpless to relieve the distress they saw in daily practice. At the same time I have tried to avoid retracing the paths established by the many recent feminist and medical studies of hysteria and trauma.[89]

Narratives are not the same thing as raw experience, although what we like to call raw experience is also an imaginative construction. As a result, criticism is always a negotiation among inexhaustible variables. In fiction, signs of trauma can change shape, function, and coloration with any shift of perspective. When *The Time Machine* climaxes in the Time Traveller's rampage against the Morlocks, H. G. Wells is describing behavior much like berserking in combat neurosis. Yet that violence is also, ambiguously, a convention of the literary genre. It may express traumatic stress in Wells and his culture, and also, through play and objectification, embody efforts to master that stress. For genteel readers, the novel may supply an intuitively regulated dose of desirable stimulation. But it may also strategically evoke symbolically mediated stress to structure and desensitize aroused fears and make mastery possible.

I think of modernism as a cumulative series of upheavals that are spikes in a rising baseline of stress: markers for massive, disorienting storms of new information and technology. The level rose steeply in the early-modern period, and again in the nineteenth and twentieth centuries, even as living standards and longevity were improving. Lynn White Jr. calls the Renaissance "the most psychically disturbed era in European history."[90] The accounts in courteous textbooks aside, the rise of the European nation-state in the early-modern period is a bloody saga of factional violence, religious holocaust, and lawlessness, in societies wracked by intermittent famine and plague. Survival anxiety and exterminatory fury fed on each other with consequences such as the witchcraft mania, the Hundred Years War, and New World genocide, which are comparable to the atrocities of the twentieth century.

The next great spike of change—the French and American Revolutions, the abolition of slavery, women's suffrage, industrialism—sent out shock waves that not only palpably changed people's lives, but transformed the conceptual building blocks and frames of reference with which people constructed their worlds.

Out of a larger project of cultural self-examination that spurred Marx, Darwin, and Freud came a radically modified conception of human identity that complicated the radical alterations in self-image brought about by new contrivances such as the electric light and the telephone.

For all its Faustian allure, this new plasticity in human nature set the self adrift in vertiginous possibilities. Like Oscar Wilde, "Henry Adams was aware of a 'subconscious chaos' of multiple inward selves, described by a 'new psychology' that had 'split personality not only into dualism, but also into complex groups, like telephonic centres and systems.' For Adams, the coherence of individual identity became a precarious balancing act, not a given."[91] Such drastic change could be energizing or crippling, ecstatic or terrifying. It reached new levels of synergism and instability in the nineteenth century and has not let up since. Defenses against this incremental pandemonium ranged from vigilant respectability to robust innovation, from numbness and mourning to iconoclasm and anarchistic rage. Seen through the lens of trauma, what leaps into focus is a change in attitudes toward subjectivity that is the outcome of processes underway since the early-modern period. Self became an object of thought, its scope expanded and yet also, it seems, more fluid, problematic, and ephemeral. In a period of rapid transformation, social death was a real threat, but anxiety about loss or deformation of subjectivity could also be traumatic.

This is why radical existential thinkers such as Rank and Becker are central to this book. They make it possible to see that in different ways people at the top and also at the bottom of society have used the trope of trauma to manage the disorientation of changing subjectivity. Ordinary people have experienced the "pandemonium" of identity and social flux, even though it was—and still is—usually defined from the top down by the professional and privileged classes. My suspicion is that *because* people high and low experience different forms of survival anxiety and rage—and because those different experiences may meet in the trope of trauma—we can better understand convulsions such as the two world wars by exploring the post-traumatic ideation surrounding them.

The cumulative pressure of a rising baseline change produced traumatic effects. But there is another dimension of change that can be isolated as well. Richard Rubenstein has proposed that the "demographic explosion that began in Europe during the eighteenth century" initiated "the modern, worldwide phenomenon of mass surplus population" and an "age of triage." Few problems "have been as insidiously corrupting or as destructive of the common good as the phenomenon of mass surplus population."[92] As episodes of wrenching modernization and genocide witness, governments and dominant economic powers tend to suppress or remove surplus populations.

In the 1890s and 1900s, when Cecil Rhodes was lamenting that "the world is nearly all parcelled out,"[93] the closing of frontiers threatened to choke off emigration as a painless solution to the problem of surplus population. Consolidation in agriculture swept rural multitudes into the cities even as machinery was displacing human labor everywhere at a worrisome rate. Generally, the intensive rationalization of economic life—the invention of the corporation and trusts, the utilitarian obsession with efficiency and the "bottom line"—created an appearance of inexorable, "natural" order while depersonalizing work and diluting loyalty and responsibility. The twentieth century came to speak of "the corporation" or "the system" as if these were actual individuals whose overriding needs could justify brutal triage whenever necessary, as recorded in John Steinbeck's novel *The Grapes of Wrath* (1939) and Michael Moore's film *Roger and Me* (1989).

One way of conceiving of the resemblance between the decades is to see it as the return of the repressed. In this account the conflicts endemic to modernism and capitalism led to—and were masked by—the twentieth century's world wars, global depression, broad government economic regulation, and finally the lingering, obsessive Cold War, whose dissolution in the late 1980s allowed basic contradictions and disequilibrium to reemerge in the industrial democracies.[94] From this perspective it is no coincidence that the concept of trauma is flourishing now as it did a century ago when it was invented.

Nor are the analogies only structural; they are matters of cultural values—of the interpretation of injury—affected by shifting frames of reference. "One factor making this period so traumatic," said the *New York Times*,

> is that since World War II people have expected that their lives . . . would steadily improve. "It's important to recall that throughout American history discontent has always had less to do with material well-being than with expectations and anxiety," David Herbert Donald, a social historian at Harvard said. . . . "What we are reacting against is the end of a predictable kind of life, just as the people who left the predictable rhythms of the farm in the 1880's felt such a loss of control once they were in the cities."[95]

The unpredictability reflects disjunctions in cultural imagination. In Michael J. Sandel's words, "the gap between the scale of economic life and the terms in which people conceived their identities" has created confusion, alarm, and anger.[96]

Expectations can also be used to argue that people have become spoiled and unreasonably demanding of a subtly improving world.[97] Such critiques tacitly participate in the current sprawling debate about the ideological implications of trauma and victimization. In parodying the title of Freud's great meditation on civilization, for example, Robert J. Samuelson's *Good Life and Its Discontents* not only justifies the status quo and discounts people's distress signals as "mere" hysteria or misjudgment, but also implicitly mocks the therapeutic, antiutilitarian worldview associated with Freud. Samuelson rightly senses that people may need to invent or ground their "discontents" in a construction such as "trauma." But the deeper problem is that "the good life" is so full of unexamined conflicts, injustices, and deceptions that people's "discontents" are often less foolish than they seem. Gumption matters, but so does a clear head and candid discussions with the neighbors.

In both decades of the nineties, whichever model we use, there is a shift in emphasis as survival becomes a theme more prominent than those of nurture and self-fulfillment, and trauma emerges as a means of connecting—as well as euphemizing and taming—an increasingly wider-ranging competition for status and resources. To put it starkly: although people had far less reason to struggle over subsistence than in earlier centuries, they faced far more comprehensive and acute competition for the symbolic materials of subjectivity, the markers of status and autonomy that prevent social death. At the turn of the century, the Social Darwinist doctrine of the survival of the fittest fed anxieties about individual, class, and race "suicide." In conventional wisdom, migration to the cities turned (supposedly) independent yeoman farmers into (supposedly) faceless degenerates. In the Reagan era, Social Darwinism and the fear of decline again roared loudly.

In both decades of the nineties, not always for the same reasons, people felt insecure. Late-Victorian society shuddered at the fate of "down-going men," and downward pressures have lost none of their terrors.[98] Great Britain was already moving away from manufacturing and toward a service and finance economy, not unlike Rust Belt America weathering the information and cybernetic revolutions a century later. The disproportionate beneficiaries of change in both eras were society's elite. The Gilded Age put a smiling, haughty face on stunning concentrations of power and wealth. Yet anxiety affected those at the top, too. They took militantly conservative positions on social issues and economic justice. They hardened their views of the world into the "upper-class paranoia . . . which was to erupt with such violence in England between 1910 and 1914."[99] In the 1996 American presidential primaries, similar class tensions churned in Pat Buchanan's threatening vision of the working poor "storming the castle walls."

If stable hierarchies reduce aggressiveness and foster cooperative bonds, as research indicates,[100] then episodes of perceived pandemonium and paradigm shifts are likely to arouse dangerously polarized wishes and dread. This principle operated in 1960s America. Accompanying dramatic if uneven progress in civil rights, long overdue and underfunded antipoverty initiatives raised such hopes and articulated such distress in decaying cities that when concrete improvements came only fitfully, urban rioting resulted. The Great Society programs raised the possibility of relief from distress, and those expectations proved to be tragically volatile. Promising improved lives, the nation tacitly confirmed that the poor had been victims, and that made it harder for the poor to remain resigned or numb to their status. By the 1990s, the conventional wisdom had again turned against collective remedies for poverty, raising the potential for trauma by cutting the social "safety net" and blaming the poor and the young for their failures.

But there is another dynamic to consider. When change is conventionalized as a departure from, or rebellion against, tradition, innovation is usually schematized as a contest or battle. In Robert Louis Stevenson's paradigmatic *Strange Case of Dr. Jekyll and Mr. Hyde*, scientific aspiration rebels against Respectability, and strife leaves both belief systems untenable. In Rider Haggard's *She*, the assertive woman overreaches and withers to nothing. Oscar Wilde conjured an aesthetic revolution and ended up in Her Majesty's prison, afraid of going mad. H. G. Wells's Time Traveller throws off the shackles of conventional reality and discovers a dying universe. Although both periods were marked by resurgent conservatism, the crucial motive may rather have been a growing sense of being trapped in a double bind. These are historical moments doubly uneasy about the guttering candles of "traditional values" and a century of "failed" rebellions. Pundits in the "mature" 1990s dismissively label recent social ferment "the sixties," and deride the self-indulgence of "baby boomers," folding it into the "trauma" of an ever-dimming Vietnam War. The mood of enervated opposition aches in the self-conscious nihilism—the ready-to-wear trauma—of novels and films such as Brett Easton Ellis's *Less than Zero* and Tony Scott's *True Romance*.

In both eras fantasy responses to injury oscillate between aggression akin to berserking and numbed withdrawal. Images of Faustian aggrandizement alternate with images of helpless exhaustion and paralysis. The paradigm is Sherlock Holmes, one moment godlike, the next abjectly depressed. The masters of empire slaughter mutinous natives, yet simultaneously complain of "neurasthenia" and fearfully await robust barbarian invaders.[101] A century later Americans cheer as the abused Vietnam veteran John Rambo takes on an entire province of the "evil empire" in a berserk rampage, while the documentary *Roger and Me* shows American "big business" decimating its work force and scattering numbed refugees to the winds like the Okies of the Great Depression.

These extremes express not only survival anxiety, but also a lack of faith in the efficacy of conventional roles. Although the everyman "me" of *Roger and Me* searches high and low, the agent of havoc—nominally the callous chairman of General Motors, Roger Smith—remains as unaccountable as Orwell's Big

Brother or the Mafia Godfather. Every walk-on hero interviewed in the film reveals shabby motives. The film's images conflate class and family conflict. The paternalistic corporation brushes aside its importunate "children"—both the filmmaker "me" and the literal preschoolers whom the camera tracks as they are evicted from their house at Christmastime while their helpless mother panics.

Compare Havelock Ellis recalling his youth in the 1880s: "I had the feeling that the universe was represented by a sort of factory filled by an inextricable web of wheels and looms and flying shuttles, in a deafening din. That, it seemed, was the world as the most competent scientific authorities declared it to be made. It was a world I was prepared to accept and yet a world in which, I felt, I could only wander restlessly, an ignorant and homeless child."[102] In *The Island of Dr. Moreau* (1896), H. G. Wells evokes the same experience of radical disembeddedness and psychic dislocation. The doctor's surgical engineering has turned animals into "Beast People" no longer instinctually adapted to their surroundings. "Now they stumbled in the shackles of humanity, lived in a fear that never died, fretted by a law they could not understand." As in Ellis's imagery, this is a factory world: "A blind fate, a vast pitiless mechanism, seemed to cut and shape the fabric of existence," and its inhabitants "were torn and crushed, ruthlessly, inevitably, amid the infinite complexity of its incessant wheels."[103] The image is as powerful and apt today as it was a century ago.

Recognizing the human animal's disembeddedness, Wells's narrator is traumatized. He "fell into a morbid state . . . alien to fear, which has left permanent scars upon my mind. I must confess I lost faith in the sanity of the world."[104] The narrator's "morbid reaction" is the traumatic "freeze response" of Edvard Munch's *Scream*. Numbing gives way to berserking when rebellion wrecks the factory island, just as anarchists tried—and still try—to explode the factory universe or the cosmic-sounding World Trade Center. Once home, the survivor enters a post-traumatic phase that requires psychiatric treatment:

> With my return to mankind came, instead of that confidence and sympathy I had expected, a strange enhancement of the uncertainty and dread I had experienced during my stay upon the island. No one would believe me. . . . They say that terror is a disease, and anyhow I can witness that, for several years now, a restless fear has dwelt in my mind, such a restless fear as a half-tamed lion cub may feel. My trouble took the strangest form. I could not persuade myself that the men and women I met were not also another, still passably human, Beast People, animals half-wrought into the outward image of human souls. . . . But I have confided my case to a strangely able man [who] seemed half to credit my story, a mental specialist—and he has helped me mightily.[105]

Finally, the imaginative excess of cannibals and superpredators should remind us that all interpretations of trauma are to some extent conditioned by our cognitive limits. Controlled overexposure can gradually desensitize a patient to a painful stressor. A corollary, however, is that efforts to objectify and express distress require the renewal or even the escalation of narrative conventions because overfamiliarity may dull the perception—and reception—of an injury, even though its pain persists. As a result, imagination keeps trying to devise a more forceful and convincing vocabulary. Today's horror is tomorrow's cliché—in life as well as art. In the 1990s as in the 1890s, for example, there is an uneasy consciousness of excess—"decadence"—in the artistic vocabulary of sensational effects. The evolution of new cinematic technologies, especially computer simulations, has made onscreen violence in the 1990s more compelling and profitable than ever, especially since the creation of international entertainment markets, which favor violent films because they need little editing for other cultures and languages. Like many other aspects of trauma, the problems of cognitive fatigue and escalating hyperbole can create baffling ambiguities, not least of all because sooner or later they point back to the fundamental role of psychic defenses in our lives.

Part 1 begins with the fantasies of traumatic rescue associated with the Victorian superman, Britain's legendary Saint George, whose rescue of maiden fertility functions like the triumphal staircase at Copan to overshadow awareness that in the end his enemies captured, tortured, and killed the saint as they had the Mayan warrior-king Eighteen Rabbit. Like the bombastic staircase at Copan, the saint's story illustrates the compensatory nature of decadence at the end of Victoria's reign, when wishful medievalism flowered and faltering faith erected stupendous Victorian cathedrals. Late Victorians praised manly aggrandizement, but they also obsessively depicted the fallen knight, and implied that an invisible injury—the seed of futility—was latent even in the dragon-slayer's moment of glory.

Part I

The Sorrows of the Gay Nineties

Strange though it may seem, in 1870 a small group of islands off the mainland of Europe dominated a large part of the world. . . . Their influence was ubiquitous. A century later, with a few small exceptions, the British were confined to their islands. No other people in the modern world has experienced such a dramatic change.

Keith Robbins, *The Eclipse of a Great Power*

A sense of vagueness, of incoherence, and indirection, grows on us as we watch the eighties struggling for a foothold in the swirl and wreckage of new ideas and old beliefs.

G. M. Young, *Victorian England: Portrait of an Age*

Fig. 1. Saint George and the Dragon (Scuola di S. Giorgio degli Schiavoni), by Vittore Carpaccio, Venice, Italy. Courtesy of Alinari/Art Resource, New York.

ONE

Traumatic Heroism

> We all fail to do what we want here on earth. We all fail to be the
> persons we dreamed and wanted. . . . Who ever gets enough life????
> (i.e., fucking, fame, joy).
>
> Ernest Becker, letter of January 5, 1972

Traumatic Rescue

As an opening to the post-traumatic mood of the 1890s, here is Max Nordau's diagnosis of *fin de siècle* "morbidity." "Christendom," he reports, "is held
to be a creature reeling to its death presumptively in dire exhaustion." A mil-
lennialist "horror of world-annihilation has laid hold of men's minds," and
"more highly developed" imaginations dread that "mankind with all its institutions and creations is perishing in the middle of a dying world." This is the mood
of "a sick man, who feels himself dying by inches . . . the envy of a rich, hoary
voluptuary, who sees a pair of young lovers."[1]

Degeneration blasted celebrity Decadents such as Oscar Wilde, as well as
misfits, criminals, and lunatics, for subverting conventional values. Nordau's
moral tonic may look quaint or neurotic now, but his attack on pessimism and
panic electrified the public. *Degeneration* exorcises anxiety by repudiating "morbid" thoughts labeled irrationality, perversity, anarchism, pessimism, nihilism,

and so on. As a behavior, the book is a rallying cry for its readers, bonding "us" into a sensible vigilante crowd that can rout degeneracy from "our" midst. Whatever their particular sins, morbid types compromise our defenses against the fear of chaos and death and against unhealthy appetites. Presumably, morbid people are not actually "rich, hoary voluptuaries," but only feel exhausted and doomed, so their envy of young lovers means that they cannot feel desire and have nothing to live for. Their "horror of life," as the Decadents called it,[2] is real, but it is a disease that must be isolated and managed lest spreading panic overwhelm our natural "fight-or-flight" responses and destroy "our" will too.

In its dynamics and core themes, *Degeneration* has much in common with late-Victorian studies of trauma. Nordau believes that "every great war is a cause of hysteria among the multitudes," and Europe's wars have made nervous systems "susceptible to the pernicious influences of the city and factory system." He employs the idea of post-traumatic stress, for "'Traumatic hysteria,' 'railway spine,' the nervous maladies consequent on a moral shock, are . . . frequently unobserved until months after the event occasioning them" (207). This indirection has induced the hysteria of the age and yet also obscured its particular traumatic origins.

Once underway, "morbidity" is a disease process that induces helplessness, a traumatic "freeze," and the loss of will. Nordau invites "us" to counter panic with a surge of adrenalized militancy—the nervous system's "fight response." His book can be seen as a highly sublimated form of mob action for the respectable classes; a prescription for measured arousal; a nerve tonic to cure feelings of ennui, alienation, faltering self-esteem, and dread. In the newspapers and in everyday use, the term *morbidity* identified "an enemy within, an internal threat to the organism."[3] Like all scapegoats, the supposed enemy is a cognitive trick that enables us to explain psychic dissonance and sharpen our definition of "healthy" values. In policing culture with this medico-military trope, critics such as Nordau operated as part of a semiofficial public-health campaign. The underlying metaphors surface in a cartoon of 1882 that depicts a savior of public health, the medical scientist Robert Koch, as the chivalric warrior Saint George trampling the dragon tuberculosis.[4]

At first glance the mounted saint evokes optimism. John Singer Sargent used it to organize his group portrait of the four medical heroes who founded the Johns Hopkins School of Medicine. The four men wear academic robes and grave, priestly expressions. But behind the four, at the center of the composition, hovers a fifth figure, in a painting within the painting: El Greco's *Saint Martin on Horseback*. As George Frederick Drinka observes, El Greco "shows the Roman Christian soldier Saint Martin of Tours tearing his robe and giving half to a beggar. So like the medical men to see themselves this way! They saw themselves as a sainted class, helping the poor, the starving, and the distressed of the world with their knowledge."[5]

But the mounted saint also focuses deep conflicts. "Like Saint Martin," says Drinka, "medical men stayed on their chargers, safe in their hospitals and laboratories. A widening chasm began to separate the doctors from their patients. . . . Indeed, medical men saw this chasm, this ignorant hero worship, as a benefit" (64). The soldier-saint expresses the "medical imperialism" of the period, for Americans seemed to be conquering not only "a decaying Spanish civilization" but also infectious disease (64). In Britain and America the jingoism of warrior and saint provoked strong criticism, some of it profoundly "morbid." After all, the greatest triumphs of medical science can only postpone inescapable death. As a character in a novel by John Davidson puts it, "Is there anything that is not morbid? Life is a disease: the moment we are born we begin to die."[6] Or as *Punch* captioned a cartoon showing worms evolving into the eminent, soon to be dead Darwin: "Man is but a worm."[7] And food for worms.

Saint George makes a useful marker for the conflict between heroic will and morbidity. The popular tableau shows the saint rescuing the daughter of a prince whose walled city is besieged by a dragon associated with Satan and death (fig. 1).[8] Because the maiden's fertility objectifies the city's future and the knight wins her and comes to rule the city, his triumph is effectively the act that grounds civilization and identity. Yet Saint George is doomed. After governing successfully, according to the canonical story, he enlisted in the Crusades and was martyred by his enemies—boiled in lead and sawn in half, among other horrors. Folk tradition portrays the saint springing back to life so irrepressibly that in his *Praise of Folly* Erasmus mocks those who use him as a magical talisman.[9] By contrast, the undersong in the story insinuates that no triumph is enough, and sooner or later restless heroism will prove futile.

In the course of the nineteenth century the sense of heroic doom rose fitfully in meditations on fallen knights, from the memorial cult of Prince Albert and Alfred Tennyson's *Idylls of the King* to Pre-Raphaelite elegies;[10] from Oscar Wilde's dismembered Happy Prince to Richard Wagner's twilight of the gods. Paradoxes and double binds confounded the hero's will. Passion could doom him to a Liebestod, yet manly self-control could lead to "race suicide."[11] In his "Briar Rose" series Burne-Jones dramatizes not the rescue of the princess but the knight's discovery of a world frozen in play-death, his futile predecessors felled in a state of traumatic paralysis (fig. 2). When King Arthur confronts a visionary dragon (fig. 3), Aubrey Beardsley places him in an impossible landscape whose paradoxical planes illustrate dissociation and baffled will. The florid setting evokes an "overwrought" culture in which subjectivity is idealized, sublimated, and trapped. Beardsley's imagery evokes the tragic futility in Tennyson's *Idylls*.

Fig. 2. The Briar Rose Series: The Prince Enters the Briar Wood, by Sir Edward Burne-Jones, Coll. Faringdon, Buscot, Oxfordshire, Great Britain. Courtesy of Bridgeman/Art Resource, New York.

Not that the knight suffered alone. The public also sorrowed for Dante's doomed Beata Beatrix, the Lady of Shalott, expired Elaine, and many desolated Ophelias. In berating Sir Edward Burne-Jones for the "indescribable sadness" of his women, art critics were working out fears of sexual futility and blocked will. The painter's Venus seemed to them traumatized and numbed. "The very body is unpleasant and uncomely," one critic growled, "and the soul behind it, or through it, is ghastly. It is a soul that has known strange tortures; a body that has writhed with every impulse of sickness."[12] As an artistic genre, deathbed illness could be implacably idealized, as in Henry Peach Robinson's popular photograph *Fading Away* (1858), but by the end of the century a painter like Edvard Munch could define authenticity through the horror of the sickroom. After Albert's death, Queen Victoria ritualized futility with a funereal spell that transfixed the nation for years and kept women like H. G. Wells's mother Sarah in widow's black for much of their lives.

Although it is vivid in its own right, the mood of heroic futility is also implicated, like a virus stimulating antibodies, in different compensatory reactions: not only the Decadents' misogyny, aestheticism, and consuming irony, but also the drumbeat of philistine criticism and more literal-minded militarism. Broadly speaking, in post-traumatic terms, Decadent figures withdraw from the horror of life and attempt to overcome numbness through aestheticism, while surrogate warriors—think of Wells's Time Traveller slaughtering Morlocks—run amok. As a kind of Saint George attacking "morbidity," Nordau rallied considerable sup-

Fig. 3. How King Arthur Saw the Questioning Beatrice, by Aubrey Beardsley, London, Great Britain. Courtesy of Victoria & Albert Museum/Art Resource, New York.

port. Yet even this success reflects the conflicting attitudes toward heroic will. His readers believed, or wanted to believe, in the crusade. Yet Nordau's vehement alarmism also suggests how strong some people felt the enemy to be.

Like Nordau, the writers of "invasion novels" were also tacitly crusading to reinvigorate heroic will. The genre of invasion or future-war novels developed in reaction to the German conquest of France in 1870.[13] Colonel George Chesney's *Battle of Dorking* (1871) imagined the Germans crushing England; it so alarmed the public that William Gladstone himself had to caution against hysteria in terms that sound like President Eisenhower's warning against America's mushrooming military-industrial complex.[14] In these novels Britain's defeat or near-defeat confirmed Nordau's diagnosis of fatal decay and loss of will. And like Nordau, Chesney and his imitators sought to rouse public morale. In this context Saint George is a contested symbol in a debate about group morale, the relative claims of hardiness and comforts, sacrifice and affluence, defense budgets and commerce.

The tragic paradox of the post-traumatic Saint George is that debate about heroic will seems to have become polarized into "morbid" and warrior-superman attitudes. In seeking to wake the public to a menacing reality, the fantasists of future war contributed to the mood of dread and messianic aggrandizement that armed Europe to the teeth and exploded in World War I. One proof of this is what I. F. Clarke calls "the first great legend of the war."[15] After British sharpshooters stopped the German advance at Mons in August 1914, Arthur Machen published a short story called "The Bowmen" in which British soldiers find a visionary host of heavenly warriors fighting on their side. One soldier "heard, or seemed to hear, thousands shouting":

"St. George! St. George!"
"Ha, messire; ha! sweet Saint, grant us good deliverance!"
"St. George for merry England!"
"Harow! Harow! Monseigneur St. George succour us."
"Ha! St. George! Ha! St. George! a long bow and a strong bow."
"Heaven's Knight, aid us."

At this point the soldier saw "a long line of shapes, with a shining about them. They were like men who drew the bow, and with another shout, their cloud of arrows flew singing and tingling through the air toward the German hosts."[16]

Clarke sees this story as the end product of half a century of imaginary wars. He points out the irony that all the writers' efforts to rouse the nation's military will culminated in a wishful popular fantasy. The Saint George of 1914 evokes Agincourt, but also Shakespeare's self-deluded Richard II, with his frightened boasts that God has "in heavenly pay" glorious angels who will fight Richard's enemies.[17] The legend of 1914 was still reacting against the undersong of futility in the 1890s: the legacy of bloody revolts in the colonies, General George Gordon's sensational death in the Sudan (1885), and the Boer War. Like the 1914 war itself, the legend promised group transcendence of the creeping death anxiety that Nordau had targeted for his thrilling scorn.

Although Saint George never enjoyed the same veneration as Ireland's Saint Patrick or Scotland's Saint Andrew, in the time of Edward III he became the patron saint of England, and I regard his story as one of Britain's basic accounts of its identity and destiny. Like the "pacification" that created Great Britain, the nation's imperialism justified its predatory violence—its heart of darkness—as a civilizing crusade against bestial others, on behalf of tender maidens, executive nobility, and immortal posterity. In this context Saint George represents something like "victory culture" in America.[18] And as with victory culture, the decay of the dragon-slayer's story meant pain and disorientation—and presaged what Tom Engelhardt would call a crisis of "storylessness." The historical forces that outlawed slavery, challenged imperialism, extended suffrage, and gave maidens other career options than captivity by dragons also made Saint George an ambivalent and increasingly irrelevant figure. At the same time, not surprisingly, his "injury" and the collateral cultural damage seemed in some quarters to justify redoubled imperial ambition as a regimen to prevent "race suicide" and "impotent, decadent manhood."[19]

The tableau of the triumphal dragon-slayer often omitted his eventual defeat, torture, and martyrdom. To think of the hero's ultimate futility as traumatic might suggest a concern less with *post*-traumatic reactions to earlier events than with a dread of future doom. But this is the century-old puzzle described in my Introduction. It begins to be solved if you think of trauma as an interpretive event that breaches our basic defenses against death anxiety, because trauma necessarily entails dread of the future. For a survivor the past may be safely past, but survival also cues the now vigilant imagination to the death sure to come someday. In this respect, the idea of trauma can allow existential terror to be displaced into the past and reassuringly (if painfully) contained in a specific "injury." At the same time, even the triumphs of scientific progress could entail psychic injury because they undercut traditional immortality systems and read the eventual extinction of humankind in the fossil record.

Late-Victorian invasion novels foretell traumas that straddle the past and future, because the catastrophe to come originates in existing and individually irremediable faults. In its vision of world-annihilation, H. G. Wells's *Time Machine* implies a future doom that has already begun—already happened—in the present. Terry Gilliam's film *Twelve Monkeys* (1995) dramatizes the paradox of "future trauma" by having a plague-stricken twenty-first-century society force a "volunteer" to return through a time machine to the 1990s in order to search out the source of the trauma. The hero suffers an injury that is simultaneously past, future, and present, and he is pointedly diagnosed in the 1990s as a madman. His attempt to save his civilization is finally a traumatic rescue. To *be* Saint George in the unfolding moment is one thing. To be compelled to emulate his example, knowing his eventual doom, is another. Cognitively, this is a condition like combat stress, because even if the immediate rescue from death succeeds, futility darkens the larger horizon.

Traumatic Heroism as a Cultural System

Western culture is grounded in traumatic stories.[20] In Genesis, divine light rends the primordial void. Creation, like the division of cells, ruptures and differentiates categories. Born perfect in paradise, Adam degenerates into mortal growth. He and Eve acquire self-awareness through the brutal alienation of the Fall. Expelled from Eden, humankind discovers itself outside the natural world and sentenced to death. Seduced by the serpent's invitation to compete with the Lord ("ye shall be as gods"), Adam and Eve aspire to overleap a forbidden boundary, only to fall.

The crash of the first couple produces the curse of consciousness: alienated will (labor), painful childbirth, and the awareness of death. Adam and Eve react with post-traumatic symptoms: anxiety and guilt ("I heard thy voice in the garden, and I was afraid"); withdrawal ("I hid myself"); aggression (the Lord "will put enmity between thee and the woman, and between thy seed and her seed"); intrusive reexperience of the trauma ("Because thou hast . . . eaten of the tree . . . in sorrow shalt thou eat of it all the days of thy life"); discovery of the conventional nature of reality and the possibility of deception (invention of clothing, names, role-playing, and identities); self-alienation (lest Adam live forever, "the Lord drove out the man"); and the core symptom, poisonous death anxiety (Gen. 3).

The Genesis stories make history itself post-traumatic: an original injury endlessly reexperienced, so that all being is stained by that originary guilt and dread, and rescued through divine grace. Many Victorians had a keen appreciation of original sin, and conceptions of childhood were evolving away from an Augustinian vision of the child as a polluted creature in need of purifying discipline.[21] When Cardinal Newman looked out his window, he saw suffering and confusion as an aftershock: "The human race is implicated in some terrible aboriginal calamity. It is out of joint with the purposes of its Creator."[22] Although the scientific reappraisal of geological evidence shattered Christian Europe's conceptions of space and time, it perpetuated the sense of originary trauma. In his influential *Époques de la nature* (1778), for example, Georges Louis Leclerc,

Comte de Buffon, concluded that humans had emerged some six to eight thousand years ago. "Naked in mind and body, defenceless against the elements, they underwent calamities which left an indelible mark on human consciousness. These included local inundations, which were transformed in memory into a universal catastrophe."[23]

Nor has the conviction that there was a traumatic fall disappeared. It flourishes not only in fundamentalist Christianity but in all sorts of sophisticated secular thought as well.[24] In Christianity the Savior heals the trauma of the Fall. Medieval theology allegorized Christ as the perfect knight, the model for ambiguously secularized warrior-heroes such as the legendary Saint George, whose exploits mingle venerable folk tales with the myths of Perseus and Heracles, wrestlers of monsters and liberators of maidens.[25]

The saint's rescue condenses many levels of meaning. Among other things, it can represent Christ's liberation of the Church from Satan; spirit's ascendancy over the flesh; culture's defense against death; the recovery of fertility from a lord of the underworld akin to Hades; a suitor's defeat of a rival to win a wife; an aristocratic hunter's triumph over nature's tooth and claw; and European civilization's conquest of barbarian Others. The story of Saint George illustrates the human need for enemies in order to consolidate group identity and political organization. In effect, the dragon as predator causes humankind to band together and develop those skills—rhetoric, hypocrisy, diplomacy—by which the city controls explosive civic rivalry.[26] In novels of the 1890s, Dracula effectively creates the "band of light," even as the cannibal Tonga brings together the genteel "family" Sherlock Holmes takes under his wing.

But there is another aspect of this system worth exploring. As psychic topography, the walled city recalls some clinical definitions of trauma, including psychoanalytic metaphors that envision the ego under siege: "A postulated stimulus barrier or protective shield is breached, and the ego is overwhelmed and loses its mediating capacity."[27] In this formulation, despite the elusive passive verbs, the assault on a fortified self makes the ego akin to a citizen of a walled city. In this topography the warrior-hero functions as the ego's "mediating capacity," defending against encroaching death. Our term for a blow or sudden impression on the mind that radically alters perspective—"shock"—developed as a metaphor out of the military terminology for a clash of armed forces (a meaning still with us in the expression "shock troops"). The word appeared in English as a term for the collision of armies or two jousters (*Oxford English Dictionary*, 1565), then expanded to denote any blow, and more specifically a sudden, usually painful disturbance of the mind or feelings (*OED*, 1705), on its way to its nineteenth-century medical application to conditions of nervous exhaustion and overstimulation (*OED*, 1805), and finally its designation of electrical stimulation of a nerve

(*OED*, 1818). The nervous-system response we call "fight or flight" likewise takes its terminology from violent conflict. The etymologies suggest that in combat, trauma is never far away. And in fact trauma may spur panicky flight, an immobilizing "freeze," or a berserk rage capable of destroying a dragon.

Given trauma's robustness as a trope, especially in early medical lore, it is only a short step from these military images back to the Lord's curse on Adam and Eve. Treating hysterics in his clinic at the Salpêtrière, for example, Jean-Martin Charcot hypothesized that "a fear of imminent death, of crippling injury[,] was translated into an electrical shock that spread through the nerves and so brought down the nervous organization."[28] Charcot was impressed by a veteran whose symptoms had seized him when a peal of thunder that he associated with cannon fire had terrified him. The resemblance to the ancients' fear of Zeus's thunderbolts has prompted one medical historian to call this "the Zeus myth" of neurosis.[29] The Zeus myth links military metaphors (cannon shot, breached psychic defenses) with the dread of a god's annihilating wrath in Greek myth and in Genesis. They express a terror rooted in infantile experience and the ground of being. Like the city, the dragon-slayer himself is enclosed. The knight's armor is akin to the neo-Freudian metaphor of "character armor" or defenses.

The tableau implies a social drama that sheds light on this paranoid imagery. As God's soldier, the youth is vulnerable to combat trauma. Even the quasi-religious code of courtly love shows the dynamics of trauma, because in Platonic theory, love at first sight imprints or stamps the lover's imagination, with a sense of the body being shocked and invaded and the will overthrown. To "fall" in love, stricken by love's arrow, is to suffer an obsession as consuming as any illness. But the knight is also a suitor fighting a bloodthirsty rival for the woman. He can defeat a projection of his own evil potential, or he can be an ogreish father-figure expressing the envious rage that Nordau personified in the "rich, hoary voluptuary, who sees a pair of young lovers making for a sequestered forest nook."[30] Even the Virgin could contribute to the implied Oedipal conflict, since she is both maiden and mother of Christ/Saint George.[31] This triangle echoes the strife in the Garden of Eden, in which the outraged father confronts a rebellious young couple. In evolutionary terms, both Genesis and the Saint George stories describe the division of a family group when a clash over dominance leads a rivalrous son to start a new family or tribe. Within the walled city of traditional society the father is law. The dragon can be seen as his mirror image, a tyrant of appetite, who jealously seizes the fertile daughter for himself in what today might be called an act of incestuous abuse. Fear of death makes the father a predatory monster feeding on the vitality of others, like Stoker's patriarchal vampire.

In this context Saint George dramatizes generational antagonism and social competition. However insidiously, the rival's ambivalence shadows the hero's project, potentially crippling his will. Heroic rescue can be seen as a strategy for controlling this conflict. The dragon-slayer is messianic. As a martyr, he is the loyal, self-sacrificing son. The ancient world, from which the Bible takes its roles—Lord, servant, and the like—polarized authority into extremes of dominance and submission. In such systems succession is not a gradual transition but a reversal. The patriarch falters and dies, and the suddenly empowered youth takes his place. Until that moment the tension of parental suspicion and youthful impatience threatens social stability. Greek and Roman myths register that stress in stories of familial atrocity, as when a predatory parent such as Saturn or Laius tries to destroy his potentially parricidal children. The fear of death and usurpation tempts the father to identify with death, increasing the polarization and peril.

The Christian story handles the problem by making the supreme Father an unmoved mover, an incontestable conscience figure or judge actively defended by the sacrificial Son. This system redirects competition, delegating to the Son the struggle against enemies. The Son not only resists Satan's temptation to fulfill his personal ambition; he projects onto him, and kills, the antagonism of the Father. By sacrificing himself in a climactic rescue, the Son saves humankind—the other children of the Lord—and dies reconciled with the Father, identifying with him and sharing his power. The rescue absolves the Son of suspicion as a rival, and his submission earns the Father's love.[32] Just as God resurrects the crucified Son, the Leicestershire mummers' play makes Saint George's father, the "king of England," witness his son's death and then summon the doctor, who saves him.

Christianity reconciles these conflicts by fusing the resurrected Son with the heavenly Father. The residual tension in the solution can be seen in the millennial themes that the dragon-slayer also allegorizes.[33] Christ's second coming as apocalyptic warrior undoes the original crucifixion in another "final" triumph over demonized rebellion and death. Once victimized by the bloodthirsty mob, the scapegoat comes to rule the world. Triumphal mastery preempts sacrificial love, celebrating a righteous cosmic slaughter akin to traumatic berserking. At Judgment Day, in an echo of the traumatic Edenic curse, the Father will separate his children into the saved and the damned, the beloved and the spurned. Then the militant Christ will once more rejoin the cosmic Father. This vindictive nightmare makes sense as an effort to impose closure on life, especially at historical moments of great uncertainty, irrationality, and injustice. In the 1890s, when the old boundaries of time and space were in flux, speculation about ultimate ends was rife. H. G. Wells's mother was devoutly obsessed with millennial themes, for example, and her son's popular Time Traveller actually drops in on the end of the world.

The saint's story attempts to balance self-aggrandizement and effacement. The son saves the father-prince, marries the maiden, and rules the walled city until a crusade (for the Father) summons him to pay his debt to the Father. But in practice, messianic heroism crowded out the epilogue. In Britain, through the Order of the Garter, George harnessed aristocratic youth to the discipline of government.[34] Even in the nineteenth century, for a culture nervous about change, nostalgic for medieval verities, and ambitious for chivalric refinement, the warrior-saint was a veritable engine of idealization.[35] As hybrid warrior-saint, son and hero, he met a crucial Victorian need to civilize instinct. In effect, his self-effacement made manly violence respectable.

The saint flourished in Anglophile American culture too. After the trauma of the Civil War and the collapse of Southern aristocracy, Saint George lent his equivocal authority to vigilante berserking on behalf of injured self-esteem and white womanhood in the fantasies of the Ku Klux Klan and D. W. Griffith's *Birth of a Nation* (1915).[36] Reform-minded organizations and fraternal orders styled themselves knights of Pythias or of labor. In *The Gospel of Wealth and Other Timely Essays* (1900), the ruthless Andrew Carnegie turns the millionaire into a self-sacrificing Saint George who expires during his life's project of "bettering" the world.[37] In the epic mural Carnegie commissioned in Pittsburgh, the knight is an idealized steelworker. The poor man's model was the Aspiring Young Rescuer of Horatio Alger's novels and of stage melodrama, who routed and saved disguised versions of the father.[38] As in Britain, the aristocratic mystique of chivalry made it useful as an instrument for "civilizing" the middle and lower classes, even as the unresolved status of the warrior-son could make the story's aura of gentility seemingly democratic.

And yet the myth was decaying. During the Renaissance, Saint George was already a nostalgic consolation for changes that had shrunk the scale of aristocratic heroism and made the armored knight a pompous sitting duck on the battlefield. In Shakespeare's day, English nobles still pumped up their heroic self-esteem by jousting, but the cult of chivalry was already becoming an exercise in bravura histrionics and solemn doublethink.[39] The longer the cult of Saint George persisted, the more it became an ornament of class privilege and an empty gesture.[40] Mark Twain ridiculed it. In stained-glass windows and namesake schools at home and throughout the empire, the saint lent his emblematic shield to the service of a declining church. His impersonality gave him utility as a universal tool even as it reduced him to a generic abstraction. Like his lineal descendants, Superman and the 1990s Mighty Morphin Power Rangers, the hyperidealized warrior became progressively less able to hide his roots in infantile wishes. By the end of the century the conviction had mostly drained out of Queen Victoria's cult of Albert as a fallen knight.

For a society "nerved up" by the stress of individualistic competition and the early skirmishes of the "sex war," the trope of the dragon-slayer was especially equivocal and unstable. With his impressive steed and armor as intimidating as the horns of a stag, the knight put on a courtship display for the benefit of the damsel and the spectator, just as paintings of Saint George advertised the patrons who could afford to display them. In evolutionary terms, male adornment in sexual displays "has an imposing and aggressive, not just a seductive meaning. Male dances are typically war dances. Male ceremonial tends to serve another general interest that can also get out of hand—the competitive taste for impressing, terrifying, and outdoing possible rivals. Where this taste takes charge, people may . . . be caught in an inconvenient and unbalanced pattern of life."[41]

The perfunctory character of chivalry for the late Victorians made its decay as myth also a sign of the impotence and marginality of men. Like the lamia or Stoker's white worm, the demonized lineaments of the erotic woman in Gothic romance signaled depths of ambivalence the categories of heroic rescue could not manage. *Dracula*'s paladins save Lucy Westenra from her own vampire appetite by driving a stake through her heart like Saint George skewering the dragon.[42] In his scandalous white-slavery report, "The Maiden Tribute of Modern Babylon," the journalist W. T. Stead invoked the blood sacrifice of maidens to the Minotaur, with himself tacitly in the role of Theseus–Saint George, although that did not prevent him from serving three months in prison for abduction.[43] Brother knights, Pre-Raphaelite and Wagnerian, came to fascinate male homosexuals of the day.[44] Even without the complications of feminism or romance scenarios that dispatch the maiden to rescue the knight,[45] or, in Amazon variations, master him, the knight was already mired in paradox. After all, although the maiden remains passive in the dragon-slayer tableau, she indirectly dominates the scene, not only as the embodiment of fertility and immortal posterity but also as the justification for the knight's glorious, immortalizing violence. Without the maiden to valorize civilization, Teddy Roosevelt's noble imperialist would be merely another predator, just as the subject of Sir Frank Dicksee's painting *Chivalry* (1885) could be fratricidal competition between Cain and Abel.

Put the courtship-rescue in a Darwinian context and the disenchantment becomes all the more unmanageable. Saint George's triumph is no longer a celebration of noble will but an evolutionary compulsion. As in Oscar Wilde's nightmare image of the puppet theater, the knight is slave to a ruthless determinism. The discovery of our creatureliness has post-traumatic impact, for in the dragon Saint George attacks the mortal body that must devour other living creatures in order to live—in Victorian iconography, the savage beast, cannibal, Martian, Morlock, and stealthy vampire. These images dissociate the awareness that we are "naturally" predators: that, in Ernest Becker's unsparing account, "life on this planet is a gory spectacle, a science-fiction nightmare in which digestive tracts fitted with teeth at one end are tearing away at whatever flesh they can reach, and at the other end are piling up the fuming waste excrement as they move along in search of more flesh."[46]

The fantasy of Saint George is a cultural effort to deny that reality by affirming the primacy of symbolic immortality. Even the *Punch* cartoon of Darwin as an evolved worm sanitizes this terrifying reality by euphemizing the coiled, predatory, fanged digestive tract as the lowly, "friendly" worm. For late Victorians the dragon-slayer's perfunctory, honorific status had become a sign of his defeat. This is one reason that Oscar Wilde's "Soul of Man under Socialism" (1891) seems not simply subversive but desperately ingenious in identifying nihilist heroism with "real Christianity." Few of his contemporaries could look the traumatic Medusa in the eye—any more than people could in the 1990s, when the Darwinian shock was beautifully euphemized in Steven Spielberg's *Jurassic Park* (1993), for example. The film's Darwinist-grandfather, manipulating evolution, recreates the voracious dinosaurs that drive the hero's family from the Edenic island park.

Saint George suffered grave injury at the end of the century, and the shock registered widely, although it took another decade before chivalry succumbed in the carnage of World War I. Heroic conviction is finally a social behavior. To be substantiated, for its energy to be synergistic for others, heroism needs to be witnessed. For two decades (1881-98) Burne-Jones worked over his painting of women grieving for King Arthur on his bier (fig. 4). Like many other Victorian laments for lost heroes, this unfinished project of bereavement seems to signify not only parent-child mirroring (the figures posed as a Pietà, women and king substantiating each other as parent and child), and not simply the power of pain and eulogy to confirm passing values, but also a fear that the lone maids' witness is poignant *because* heroism is "dead" and consensus gone. After all, Burne-Jones's farewell to Arthur was, among other things, a feat of deadpan repression, screening out both implacably "healthy-minded" critics and the throngs of unruly ironies that were disturbing sentimental life everywhere outside his studio in the 1890s. The year he began the painting (1881), the *Magazine of Art* was already deploring his art's "effeminacy" and its "union of pessimism and laxity."[47] In Vietnam-era America, public voices fired off the same sort of moral salvos in denial when the American victory story was going the way of Saint George.[48]

One sign of the impairment in heroic conviction is "the craze of suicide," which more than one newspaper reader felt was "palpably on the verge of breaking out among us."[49] The "craze" rushed into the void between impossible ideals and baffled will. As the alarum in the *Daily Chronicle* added, "the conditions of life are daily narrowing the relationship between the imagination and the will, with a too obvious consequence, namely the subjugation of the latter to the sensuous and mysterious potency of the former."[50] This coded attack on

Fig. 4. The Dream of Arthur in Avalon (detail), by Sir Edward Burne-Jones. Courtesy of Museo de Arte de Ponce, The Luis A. Ferré Foundation, Ponce, Puerto Rico.

Decadent "genius" anticipated Nordau's protest that too much imagination was unraveling everyday "healthy" repression. This is another way of disconfirming public worries that cultural models like the dragon-slayer story were collapsing under the weight of contradictions. At the same time the protest ambivalently excused readers too distressed for wholehearted repression by flattering—in the dragon-slayer vocabulary—the imagination's "mysterious potency" and heroic drive to "subjugation."

The feeling of being suicidally overwhelmed by uncontrollable forces was exacerbated, as John Stokes points out, by the massive scale of scientific studies such as Henry Morselli's *Suicide: An Essay on Comparative Moral Statistics*, which seemed to confirm a frightening determinism at work. "The sense of panic that pervaded the coming of the *fin de siècle* was by no means unconnected with the way that statistical categories tended, in the hands of scientific enthusiasts like Morselli, to proliferate almost beyond control."[51]

The preoccupation with new orders of scale and causality registered in the stories of naturalists like Zola and aroused sharp ambivalence in the public. In "Locksley Hall Sixty Years After" (1886), Tennyson had his speaker groan that "Zolaism" was plunging civilization "into the abysm!" Even as it attracted an im-

Fig. 5. Anxiety (1894), by Edvard Munch, Munch Museum, Oslo, Norway. Courtesy of Erich Lessing/Art Resource, New York.

perialistic rhetoric of exploration and conquest, science sharpened a sense of human futility. Technological society evolved a psychological double-bind which is still acute. The same order that tamed menacing forces through data-bases, graphs, insurance tables, and highly rationalized social codes could also suffocate the spirit and make life's inevitable terrors more plainly unmanagable.

Technological imagination thrived by abandoning fatalism—and the consolations of fatalism. In Edvard Munch's scenes of pedestrians, social forms regulate life, but subjectivity and heroic purpose have drained out of the faces and left behind hollow-eyed anxiety (fig. 5).

Not that we are done mourning the ideal knight today. By the late 1990s the king and queen of the Kennedy "Camelot" were both dead, but in "assassination theories" and journalism's idealizing obituaries for the cancer-stricken Jackie Kennedy Onassis, the nation nourished a cult of injury. In a more adrenalized mood a 1990s "Christian thriller" could imagine Saint George's dragon literally scourging the landscape of a depraved America.[52] Any number of dragon-slayers have followed Flash Gordon into outer space. In George Lucas's *Star Wars* (1977, 1997), Luke Skywalker obeys the benevolent father Obi-Wan Kenobi and uses a laser sword to defeat the predatory parent Darth Vader. In Roland Emmerich's Pyrrhic, post-traumatic *Independence Day* (1996), the warrior-knights have to annihilate the walled city (Houston) in order to stop the alien invader. Like these bracingly moralized scenarios, the 1990s fantasy of traumatic satanic abuse is a version of the saint's story inasmuch as it imagines predatory parents sacrificing children to the devouring demon as the walled city's inhabitants do, while the trauma victim, carried by a therapist-steed, takes the knight's role.[53]

Saint George serves as one index against which to measure historical change. Sherlock Holmes, for example, acts out a version of the knight's rescue, recovering a treasure chest with connotations of social power and absolute value. But the chest is empty. And just as Saint George's triumph implies his martyrdom, so the novel concludes with its hero fighting despair with drug addiction, like Nordau's "sick man, who feels himself dying by inches" in a dying world.

TWO

Empty Treasure

SHERLOCK HOLMES IN SHOCK

> "It is a romance," cried Mrs Forrester. "An injured lady, half a million in treasure, a black cannibal, and a wooden-legged ruffian. They take the place of the conventional dragon or wicked earl."
>
> Conan Doyle, *The Sign of Four*

IN A SENSE, all detective stories are post-traumatic because they presuppose some violation. Conan Doyle's *The Sign of Four* (1890) gathers together a representative sample of post-traumatic themes of the 1890s, which is one reason to scrutinize the novel in some detail. The book opens with Sherlock Holmes using his cocaine addiction to fight depression. Preparing an injection, he brushes aside Watson's objections. His mind "rebels at stagnation";[1] the drug is a "transcendently stimulating" (*SF* 3) substitute for the "mental exaltation" of detective work that he "craves" (5). Crime, that is, makes heroic exaltation possible, and Holmes needs that heroism as a relief from the threats of addiction and, at root, "stagnation."

But why is stagnation so menacing in the first place? Asked if he has a new case to inspire him, Holmes responds with an anguished "tirade":

> None. Hence the cocaine. I cannot live without brain-work. What else is there to live for? Stand at the window here. Was ever such a dreary, dismal, unprofitable world? See how the yellow fog swirls down the street. . . . What could be more hopelessly prosaic and material? What is the use of having powers, doctor, when

one has no field upon which to exert them? Crime is commonplace, existence is commonplace, and no qualities save those which are commonplace have any function upon earth. (20)

Like the word *stagnation*, with its suggestion of entropy, this eloquent world-weariness euphemizes the fear of death. Holmes echoes Hamlet's numbness: "How weary, stale, flat, and unprofitable / Seem to me all the uses of this world."[2] His tirade plays on Hamlet's suicidal meditation in which the "sullied flesh" and the "hopelessly material" world (Hamlet's "unweeded garden") are meaninglessly "commonplace." In Hamlet's terms, "brain-work" makes man "noble in reason . . . infinite in faculties . . . how like a god," yet also "the paragon of animals," and the "quintessence of dust."[3]

Holmes is identifying with a son made suicidal by his father's death. Hamlet exhibits familiar post-traumatic symptoms, from the intrusive hallucinatory Ghost to the impulsive rage in which he stabs Polonius. Hamlet despairs because the Ghost demands not just revenge but self-effacement: he is to kill the "abuser" Claudius without claiming anything for himself.[4] Like Hamlet and Saint George, Holmes sacrifices himself when attacking criminal desires yet is mysteriously paralyzed in willing for himself. This is what leads Nicholas Meyer's *Seven-Per-Cent Solution* (1976) to postulate a childhood trauma in which the young Holmes watched his father murder his unfaithful mother.

Holmes also takes a cue from Marlowe's Faust, since the "transcendently stimulating" cocaine (*SF* 3) suggests magical omniscience and the idea of detection as "mental exaltation" (5). "Crime is commonplace, existence is commonplace" (20), and guilt poisons all values. The underlying assumption points back to the originary trauma of God's curse on Adam. If "the reward of sin is death" and "we must sin," Faust reasons, "then we must die an everlasting death."[5] Like Faustus, Holmes would rival the cosmic judge, boasting that "I am the last and highest court of appeals in detection" (*SF* 5). But unlike the magus, he cannot see or feel the source of his compulsiveness.

Watson complements Holmes. To Hugh Kenner the two characters are facets of a single persona, the "split-man," since they "epitomize humanity dissected into ratiocinative violence and sentimental virtue, the latter avid of absorption into the former."[6] Why should Watson want to be absorbed into Holmes? For one thing, the death anxiety dissociated in Holmes is more overt in Watson. Combat trauma has marked him. Injured in "the Afghan campaign," the doctor's body cannot stand "any extra strain" (*SF* 3). During Holmes's "tirade," Watson sits "nursing [his] wounded leg" which "ached wearily at every change of the weather" (7). As Holmes will be "limp as a rag" and suffer a "black mood" at the end of an episode, so Watson "wearily" suffers periodic aches of mortality. Faustus fantasizes a solution in his wish to be "eterniz'd for some wondrous cure."[7] If sin is death, then the obsessive heroism of Holmes and Watson—the compulsion to "cure" sin by exposing it—expresses the same wish for immortality.[8]

There is another analogy at work too. Faustus would have his demonic spirits "fly to India for gold,"[9] and the novel likewise dispatches its villain to India, where greed for "gold moidores" (SF 247) produces the traumatic murder that supports its heroic fantasy. The novel projects onto its villains the Faustian criminal motives that it discovers and yet denies in its heroes. With its rebellious "black fiends" (234) and "black devils" (232), not to mention its injury to Watson, colonial India expresses the traumatic experience dissociated in the novel's England, even as the criminal Jonathan Small acts out dark motives masked in the heroes.

Traumatic Smallness

As his name suggests, Jonathan "Small" is a nonentity from a village containing "a heap of Smalls" (SF 229). Like Holmes, he has rebelled against the commonplace, stagnant world. In India, desperate to make something of himself, he murdered "the merchant Achmet" (246) for a rajah's treasure. His career caricatures Victorian dreams of "making it" through imperialism and ruthless "merchant" competition. Imprisoned for the murder, he bribes a British officer, Major Sholto, who absconds with the stolen treasure to respectable London. Small escapes to England and is trying to reclaim "his" treasure when his black cannibal "mate" Tonga kills Sholto's son with a poison dart while retrieving the twice-stolen treasure. Enter Holmes. Hired by Mary Morstan, the daughter of the other bribed officer (who has disappeared seeking his share of the loot from Sholto), Holmes kills Tonga and captures Small. For Victorian readers Small's punishment presumably justified "legitimate" imperialism and "respectable" new money. But his obsessive hunt through London for "his" treasure is also a search for "stolen" autonomy and an effort to overcome a sense of injury and futility that relates him to Holmes and Watson.

Small's life is a series of traumas. As a young man he fled from his roots in "a mess over a girl" (229). In India he tried out the heroic role of soldier, only to lose a leg to a crocodile swimming in the Ganges (compare Watson's leg injury), which brought to the surface the threat of death (and Freudian castration), as well as basic anxiety about power and identity. Shaken and crippled, Small leaves the army for a compromise role as foreman for a successful planter, the aptly named Mr. Abel White. Although he must defer to Mr. White, he also polices the plantation's "coolies." Half servant and half surrogate master, Small is able to tolerate this compromise because the planter "would often drop into my little shanty and smoke a pipe with me, for white folks out there feel their hearts warm to each other as they never do here at home" (231). This relationship, even down to the pipe, mirrors Watson's situation in Baker Street.

But then comes rebellion. The mutinous "black devils" prefigure Small's "faithful mate" Tonga, who acts out Small's "dark" motives. Given this symbolic logic, the Sikh rampage expresses Small's impulse to run amok. Mr. Abel White is killed and "blacks" supposedly compel Small to join their murder plot in order to gain a treasure that could make him a "Mr. Abel White" himself.[10] Proposing their plot to Small, the Sikhs define a crisis in his life. So far he has been a loner. Now "you must either be with us . . . or you must be silenced for ever. . . . Either you are heart and soul with us . . . or your body this night shall be thrown into the ditch, and we shall pass over to our brothers in the rebel army" (SF 241–42). Provoking a ferocious British reaction, the mutiny effectively exposes the potential for violent social control in Small's England. "There is no middle way," the Sikh rightly insists: either you dominate or are dominated (242).[11] The death threat is also a threat of rejection. Cast into a ditch, with its associations of rubbish and shame, Small would be "for ever" a nobody. To be somebody he must identify "heart and soul" with "brothers in the rebel army." The Agra treasure presents a fantasy solution to this conflict, permitting a bond with the "black" brothers and also a vicarious triumph for Small among his countrymen: "How my folks would stare when they saw their ne'er-do-well coming back with his pockets full of gold moidores" (SF 247).[12] Eventually the psychic bond between Small and the Sikhs takes palpable form in the treasure map and the pact sealed by the "sign of the four" conspirators (SF 272).

For Small, then, murder for jewels is a means of controlling a berserk rage that would otherwise pit him against his own society and perhaps destroy him. In the actual ambush of Achmet, Small claims, he merely tripped the victim while the others killed him. Later, Tonga will assassinate a man (Bartholomew Sholto) whom Small has cause to hate. Again Small professes innocence (280). This systematically dissociated rage helps account for the swimming accident that crippled him. In India and the army largely against his will, Small is attacked by a crocodile, which suggests projected rage, as in childhood nightmares about wild animals. The crocodile expresses dissociated anger: both the wrath of those he has hurt back home and also his own post-traumatic rage. Hence he feels the loss of his leg to be "a blessing in disguise," because it renders him safely impotent, a "useless cripple" (230) but eligible for Mr. Abel White's companionship.[13] Identification with the plantation owner requires that Small suppress "coolies" (SF 231), so his service—shared pipe-smoking and warm hearts notwithstanding—can only be superficially humble. Eventually these shadowy brothers retaliate by killing Mr. Abel White. Because the uprising is presumably part of the Sepoy Mutiny, and the sepoys were "black" soldiers in British service, it is as if the rage Small suppressed as a soldier—that voracious crocodile—has surfaced again with redoubled fury to carry him "heart and soul" to murder and visions of lordly power.

Convicted of slaying Achmet, Small and his confederates suffer twenty years on a prison island. Although Small bribes two British officers to free him, Major Sholto betrays him. In despair Small meets his own dissociated rage again, this time in the form of Tonga, the "venomous" Andaman Island cannibal (274). Because he is "sick to death, and had gone to a lonely place to die" (273), Tonga objectifies the trauma of Small's imprisonment. The prisoner is able to doctor the savage because, like Watson, he "had picked up something of medicine" (273). As a primitive, infantile will, unhindered by conscience, Tonga becomes the force that enables Small to escape the island, freed to kill a guard who had "never missed a chance of insulting" him (275) and to seek revenge against Sholto.

Significantly enough, Major Sholto has fulfilled Small's dream in his stead. An alcoholic gambler and therefore another ne'er-do-well of sorts, the major has absconded to England with the twice-stolen treasure and become respectable. Small finally tracks him down on his deathbed, and at the sight of his face at the window Sholto dies of fright. As his sons watch at the bedside, they see at the window "a face . . . looking in at us out of the darkness. We could see the whitening of the nose where it was pressed against the glass. It was a bearded, hairy face, with wild, cruel eyes and an expression of concentrated malevolence" (62).

In this scene Small tacitly relives his original traumatic exclusion from the family. The face he presents momentarily fuses himself and Tonga and dramatizes his sense of victimization and rage. The darkness outside suggests the savage dark that haunts the imperialistic mind. Sholto has achieved respectability by inheriting "a fortune" from his uncle (272) even as he was stealing the treasure from his fellows. Symbolically, elite England, as represented by the uncle's legacy, has rewarded the major for breaking his pact with his outcast "brothers." Although he is rich now, "yet he could stoop to treat five men as he . . . treated us" (272). As the Sikhs warned Small: join your "black" brothers or be killed, for "there is no middle way" (241–42).

For the first time Small reacts with open hatred. Tainted though his past is, he attacks parasitical privilege: "Where is the justice that I should give the treasure up to those who have never earned it!" He then recounts the hardships of prison, protesting that he has been "bullied by every cursed black-faced policeman who loved to take it out of a white man" (227). His imagery effectively describes the psychology that privilege uses to exercise control over society's no-bodies. He sees himself stripped of will ("take it out of") by a policing con-science that pretends to serve instinctual needs ("black-faced") while reducing him to nothing for the "love" of dominance. Deviously, Small comes at last to hate respectable England. He has become a renegade and gone over to the dev-ilish "black" brothers. Hence Sholto, who has been a Small himself and denied it, sees that "wild, cruel" renegade face at his window and dies of fright (62). The treasure finally cannot secure a heroic life in England because it produces an alienating vision of justice and revenge. And this is why Tonga, and implicitly Small himself, must be killed by Holmes and Watson.[14]

Holmes continually flirts with the dangerous vision Small dramatizes. "It is of the first importance," he warns Watson at one point, "not to allow your judg-ment to be biased by personal qualities. . . . I assure you that the most winning woman I ever knew was hanged for poisoning three little children for their in-surance-money, and the most repellent man of my acquaintance is a philan-thropist who has spent nearly a quarter of a million upon the London poor" (32). These are the sorts of insights that, if felt deeply, could lead to maddening dis-trust and revolt against the sham of respectable life. Like Small, Holmes is an outsider, ambiguously above the law, at risk for obsession and despair. For these reasons Watson must break with him in the end. Yet the rich connections be-tween Watson and Small, not to mention Watson and Holmes, mean that per-ilous knowledge is in the air now, worrisomely close to awareness. And therefore no love, least of all Watson's wishfully innocent love, can put the uneasy mind at peace.[15]

Although the symmetry of hero and villain is a structural gimmick that helps Conan Doyle control his materials, I think it also expresses a deeper imaginative process by which a core of traumatic materials expands in the novel as a spatial analogue of post-traumatic flashbacks and repetition compulsion. In remarkable detail the novel's villains parody its heroes. They develop different possible out-comes of the same core disturbance, even as the novelist imposes a resolution on them. The "sign of 4" has the obsessional force of a traumatic curse or proph-esy, like the "sherd of Amenartas" in Haggard's *She*. But it also corresponds to the "case" that binds Holmes to a past injury. Like the detective, Small exposes society's sham by obsessively tracking a criminal (Sholto) and seeking "lost" au-tonomy. He aspires to supremacy in "a palace" (*SF* 261), just as Holmes wishes to be the "highest court of appeal in detection" (5). Similarly, with his "half-animal" instincts (205), the "stanch and true" Tonga (274) grotesquely mirrors the emotional, hero-worshiping Watson. Like the heroes, the villains constitute a "split-man." Small is a rational plotter, whereas Tonga is all impulse and sen-timent. The dynamics of one split persona mirror those of the other, although not always in the same pairing. Just as Watson in his "brochures" presents Holmes to the public as a model, so Small has "earned a living . . . exhibiting poor Tonga at fairs and other such places as the black cannibal. He would eat raw meat and dance his war-dance" (278–79). Holmes dramatizes the fantasy that pure mind can rise above the threat of death and meaninglessness; Tonga acts out onstage the "savage" attempt to surmount death by ritual killing: by cannibalism. Holmes presents a sublimated, genteel version of the savage's forbidden ritual heroism. The cannibal would literally devour others to incorporate more life and control death,[16] the detective mentally strives to take in all the world, down to the minutest ash (9–10), putting himself in the criminal's shoes in order to grasp his motives and capture him. And in the final chase on the river Holmes proves to be as efficient a killer as Tonga. Like Tonga, that is, Holmes cannot be accommodated in conventional, domestic London.

Predatory Parent, Cannibal Child

The novel, then, develops out of post-traumatic anxiety about death. Unpack that distress and a cluster of traumatic disturbances emerges: a sense of alienation, numbness, and loss of autonomy; victimization and compensatory aggression. For many of the characters the treasure comes to signify a stolen birthright, a disturbance in the ground of identity. Unwittingly Conan Doyle provides a means of probing the novel's traumatic core: a pattern of submerged details concerned with struggles for identity and power within the family. On this level Small is "small" as a child dreaming of triumph over a family that has rejected him: "How my folks would stare when they saw their ne'er-do-well coming back with his pockets full of gold moidores" (SF 247). The triumph depends on aggression, which the novel associates with children. "Small" joins in the murder of the childlike Achmet, "a little, fat, round fellow" (250). The "unhallowed dwarf" Tonga (205) kills Major Sholto's son Bartholomew, twin of "our little friend" Thaddeus (84). Small himself blames Tonga for having been "a little, bloodthirsty imp" (280), as if he is grumbling about a mischievous child. Because Tonga objectifies infantile energy with his unconditional love and hate, Watson is both wrong and right when he concludes of Bartholomew's murder that "a child has done this horrid thing" (96).

The novel presents an ambivalent view of children, in terms that look back toward ancient sources: the New Testament's image of the child as holy innocent, as modeled by Christ the wise child teaching in the temple, and the Augustinian view of the child as the demonic or brutish embodiment of original sin in need of severe discipline.[17] As they approach the scene of Bartholomew's murder, for instance, Miss Morstan reveals "the instinct to turn to me for comfort and protection. So we stood hand-in-hand, like two children, and there was peace in our hearts for all the dark things that surrounded us" (79). With its religious echoes, this passage makes Mary Morstan's "instinct" a source of redemptive, childlike innocence.

By contrast, Tonga is an Andaman Islander, "one of the *smallest* race upon this earth." These figurative children are demonic, being "naturally hideous," according to Holmes, "having large, misshapen heads, *small*, fierce eyes, and distorted features" (159–60; emphasis added)—characteristics that caricature the exaggeratedly cerebral, fiercely observant Holmes. Moreover, these savages are "so intractable and fierce . . . that all the efforts of the British officials have failed to win them over" (160). The childish "black" and the "black" child can never be brought into civilization. The cannibal child is a monster of infantile appetite. Similarly, the "black devils" who attack their British masters in India, "dancing and howling round the burning house" (234), are akin to rampaging children. The paternalistic metaphor that governs imperialistic doctrine makes the Augustinian view of the child the basis for righteous exploitation, even as it vindicates a punitive attitude toward the suspect young at home.

At first glance the novel appears to justify paternalism. As they approach the scene of Sholto's murder, for instance, all the characters but Holmes regress. Watson and Miss Morstan become "like two children." Thaddeus acquires "the helpless, appealing expression of a terrified child." All the while Holmes acts the parent, giving "firm, crisp" orders (79–80). He has no compunction about employing "a dozen dirty and ragged little street Arabs" with "naked" feet as "Baker Street irregulars." On the contrary, "they instantly drew up in a line" for him, with a military air reminiscent of Indian sepoys. Watson smugly notes that one of them adopts "an air of lounging superiority which was very funny in such a disreputable little scarecrow" (154–55). His tone holds affection and callousness in suspension, rather like "the new convention for representing waifs as jaunty streetwise rogues" in painting and photography, which contrived sexual and class voyeurism for the viewer.[18] But then, the entire novel disguises the traumatic parent-child abuse at its core. After all, in shooting Tonga, the masterful symbolic father Holmes is killing a renegade son.

Meekness makes the weak eligible for surrogate parental love. Yet such love owes its pathos to its rarity. In the larger world of the novel, the young face coldness and hostility. The pattern of detail is telling. The man who lends Holmes his bloodhound threatens to sic his dogs on strange callers because "I'm guyed at by the children, and there's many a one comes down this lane just to knock me up" (117). The "most winning woman" Holmes has ever known was the mother who poisoned her children for their insurance money (32). Miss

Morstan grew up "placed . . . in a comfortable boarding establishment" (25) by a distant father. But for their amusing pluck, the street Arabs might be starving beggars. Certainly their resourcefulness is meant to allay a reader's worry about their destitution, even as the "motherly" Mrs. Forrester compensates for exploitative British paternalism in India and the harshness of lower-class London. At the sight of her doorway Watson rhapsodizes that "it was soothing to catch even that passing glimpse of a tranquil English home . . . in the midst of the wild, dark business which absorbed us" (114). "Wild" and "dark" suggest that Watson looks into this enviable English home from the psychological vantage point of the colonies, where the empire's "children" are "kept up to their work" (231)—as if, like Small with Tonga, Watson harbors in his heart a child capable of great devotion.

Indirectly, then, the novel sympathizes with the young, even the monstrous Tonga, who "was always hanging about [Small's] hut" (274) after Small saved him. Still, the sympathy tends to be sly and wary. When the boatman's son defies his mother's command to "come back and be washed"—that is, to stop being "black"—Holmes asks the "rascal" what he would like. The boy retorts: a shilling. When Holmes coaches him ("Nothing you would like better?"), the "prodigy" quips: "I'd like two shillin' better." Whereupon Holmes makes a cynical joke that acknowledges (and tops) the boy's wit, mocks his greed, and applauds his self-interest: "A fine child, Mrs. Smith" (142–43).

Young Smith has an analogue in the young Jonathan Small, for whom the Agra jewels are "gems such as I have read of and thought about when I was a little lad" (256). The source of Small's obsessive anger and greed is his striving to make something of himself among "a heap of Smalls" who presumably sought to humble him (229). At home, as among the empire's "children," self-assertion amounts to defiance, and defiance leads to traumatic rejection or even death.

As a criminal, Small acts out the rage of an excluded child. Nowhere is this more striking than in the scene of Major Sholto's death. Looking in from the darkness upon the major's deathbed, that quintessential tableau of Victorian family piety, Small presents a face convulsed by envy and anger, his nose "pressed against the glass" (62) like a child gazing in a shopwindow. In this scene of inheritance the outsider sees a privileged patriarch hoard his treasure even in death, keeping the secret even from his own sons. When Bartholomew eventually does find the treasure, he becomes a rival, and it makes sense that the infantile Tonga should kill him so Small may at last possess the jewels.[19]

The model for this rivalry over inheritance is the account of Watson's eldest brother in the first chapter. While Watson served in India like Small, suffering a traumatic wound and returning to uneasy poverty, his brother "was left with good prospects, but he threw away his chances . . . and, finally, taking to drink, he died" (*SF* 16). Although Watson at last inherits his father's pocket watch, he is peculiarly distressed when Holmes deduces the inheritance and the brother's shameful death from the watch, as if it is a sign of troubling or even guilty feelings.

Even the original murder and theft in India comes about in a context of wrongful inheritance and exclusion. Small and his "black" brothers steal the gems from a rajah of undeserved wealth. "Much has come to him from his father," they argue, "and more still he has set by himself, for he is of a low nature and hoards his gold rather than spend it" (244). Like the "low" Major Sholto, who inherited an uncle's fortune yet nevertheless swindled and then hoarded the Agra treasure, and perhaps like Watson's eldest brother, who squandered his patrimony, the rajah is a selfish hypocrite. He is implicitly a patriarch too, insofar as his messenger is a childlike "little, fat, round fellow" (250) who resembles Sholto's son Bartholomew and, like him, is slain for the jewels. Because, as Holmes remarks of Watson's watch, "jewellery usually descends to the eldest son" (16), a son like Watson can claim his patrimony only through the death of the intervening brother. Small's seizure of the Agra jewels from Achmet and then from Bartholomew Sholto symbolically enacts a wishful, forbidden solution to Watson's marginal status.

For Watson's brother, the rajah, and the major, a legacy leads not to sharing with brothers but to arrogant self-indulgence and even vice. They are variously drunkards, gamblers, liars, and swindlers. The rajah has tried to feign loyalty both to the British and to his rebellious brothers, so that Small and his confederates can disingenuously conclude that "his property becomes the due of those who have been true to their salt" (245). Psychologically, again, there is no middle way.

Although Holmes has been a sporting pugilist (75) and is efficient with a pistol, neither hero is permitted to be personally aggressive. For Watson the taboo is overwhelming. Flustered by love, for example, he tells Miss Morstan how "a musket looked into" his tent one night in Afghanistan, and how he "fired a double-barrelled tiger cub at it" (44). In this anecdote yet one more child (the cub) wanders out of the wild darkness like Tonga, seeking nurture or, like the cannibal, someone to devour. Watson's nervous reversal of cub and musket, however, dissociates him from his gunshots and excuses his violence.[20] But there is a further twist. The reversal also has the effect of allowing Watson to assimilate the menacing child (he "fired a . . . tiger cub at" the musket) even as Small assimilates and expresses his aggression through Tonga. Moreover, Watson's "cub" explodes at an intrusive sign of intimidating adult (specifically military) power: the musket. Only thus circuitously is Watson associated with rebellion. In the end it is Holmes who shoots Tonga. Firing from a distance during the chase down the Thames, the detective executes the childlike rebel. That cold execution leads back to visions of stagnation and the cocaine syringe.

This crippling inhibition begins to explain the "morbid" mood of the novel. For the "small" child who is not self-effacing, growing up means a traumatic clash with parents. There is not enough autonomy for everyone. The novel's families deviously traumatize children by betraying them, hoarding love, and preying on the children's vitality. The children associate this rejection with death. Rebelling, Small impregnates a girl in a sorry parody of a father's role. Fleeing abroad, exploited along with native "children," he runs amok trying to reclaim his "rightful" place at home. Symbolically, the murders of the "obstinate" Mr. Abel White (SF 232) and Major Sholto are parricides, while the assassinations of Achmet and Bartholomew are fratricides. Overtly the novel punishes the renegade son. Beneath the surface, however, simmers an apology for rebellion that associates it with post-traumatic symptoms.

Trauma as Prison Island

As I read The Sign of Four, then, the novel is generated out of intolerable cultural conflicts that intensify a crippling death anxiety. From the opening line, in which Holmes reaches for his hypodermic needle, death haunts Watson's thoughts. He euphemizes about the drug's "morbid process" (SF 4), but his fear is plain. Each of the main characters objectifies a possible solution to that basic threat, just as such a threat undoubtedly figured in Conan Doyle's own desperate credulity about spiritualism.[21]

Yet the novel's conclusion is queasily pat. Watson abruptly breaks with Holmes and the autonomy he represents in favor of Miss Morstan and the Victorian ideal of moral selflessness. This marriage has something compulsive and self-disabling about it. For one thing, the lovers' renunciation is perfunctory. Although they gladly give up the Agra jewels, the chest turns out to be empty after all, not only producing a smug irony about the vanity of riches but also leaving the lovers' appetites or "smallness" untested. Watson then sums up with an economic equation that calls to mind the have-and-have-not conflicts that led to murder elsewhere in the novel: "Whoever had lost a treasure, I knew that night that I had gained one" (SF 222). It could be argued that he rejoices not only for love gained, but also for an irresistible temptation luckily removed. With Small subdued, Watson can relinquish a treasure that implies triumphal greed in favor of one that promises heavenly self-surrender. Yet as the degraded ambiguity of "heavenly" indicates, the spiritual treasure may have less potency than at first appears, while the worldly loot has more.

For the Agra treasure also promises immortality. As a means to power over others—power to command their labor and devotion—the treasure focuses a fantasy of consuming the energy of others, of sacrificing others to achieve personal apotheosis. In an evil irony of history, it is a fantasy apt to seem more readily corroborated by everyday social experience than a faith that the meek shall inherit. The implied dynamic is cannibalism. If others do a master's bidding when awed by treasure, they become subsumed in, and magnify, the master's will. Small himself goes directly from dominance over Mr. Abel White's "coolies" to seizure of the treasure proper. Paired with Tonga, Small murders his enemy's son and steals back the treasure. The cannibal child becomes a predatory parent figure.

In its submerged preoccupation with traumatic conflict in family and society, the novel half-perceives that the root of evil is not simply money, but the covert belief that the powerful can use money and other lives to gain more and more life for themselves. Fathers and siblings hoard their power and impoverish others in hopes of guaranteeing their own survival. In his dying confession, Major Sholto curses his own greed and dimly senses the fetishistic nature of the treasure he has stolen: "I have made no use of it myself, so blind and foolish a thing is avarice. The mere feeling of possession has been so dear to me that I could not bear to share it" (58). The unshared "it" is ambiguously both the treasure and the "feeling of possession" or power. In a deathbed tableau epitomizing the family's closeness and its mastery of death anxiety, the respectable patriarch Sholto imagines his crime to have been greed. Utterly repressed, only to surface later in Small's own confession—itself a sort of deathbed—is the source of the fetish: power amassed through murder, theft, treachery, and the sacrifice of servile "coolies" such as the orphaned employee Miss Morstan herself might be were she not sheltered by Mrs. Forrester and Sherlock Holmes.

In such a sinister world selflessness would seem to court destruction. And to be sure, with her "singularly spiritual" eyes and a "refined and sensitive nature" unlike any Watson has ever seen on "three separate continents" (23), Miss Morstan is not altogether of this earth. She enters wearing a plain dress of "sombre greyish beige, untrimmed and unbraided," and a "small turban of the same dull hue, relieved only by a suspicion of white feather in the side" (22). There is something funereal or ghostly about her, with perhaps a "suspicion" of Christian symbolism as well. In her otherworldly passivity she expresses that sublime worship of death by which Victorians so often converted horrifying necessity into a reward chosen and thereby apparently mastered.[22] To embrace sweet resignation is to dream of preempting death.

These disquieting intimations about the future add to the pathos of Watson's farewell. They lead back to the earlier question: what does the separation from

Holmes mean? In a sense this question haunted Conan Doyle, because he became captive to his hero's extraordinary popularity. Eventually, trying to be done with him, he killed Holmes off, only to grudgingly resurrect him later to placate his devotees. Having conjured a demigod, the conjuror found himself trapped into subservience long after his own disenchantment had set in. So in part, Holmes represents a fantasy that threatens to overmaster the imagination it engages. As the echoes of Faust indicate, the fantasy opens toward wishes for omnipotence that are as frightening as they are seductive. And being ultimately illusory, like Faust's magic, the fantasy demands an increasing commitment to remain satisfying.[23] Predictably enough, Conan Doyle gradually magnified Holmes until he matched the universal master criminal Dr. Moriarty in a struggle with cosmic overtones.

More immediately, the bond Holmes invites, the spellbinding transference, draws Watson and his creator toward erotic taboo, as it does in the romance between Small and his "faithful mate" Tonga, who is not allowed to survive their adventure. The novel counters this forbidden intimacy by closing with proper Victorian renunciation. For all his egotism, Holmes is made to serve others. Having liberated the lovers, he must relinquish them both, substituting the compensatory cocaine for unacceptable feeling.[24]

As an ecstatic substitute for experience, the cocaine calls attention to the vicarious nature of detection itself, and so points to the final quality that makes it impossible to live with Holmes or without him. Ordinarily his substitute for intimacy is the act of detection: specifically his imaginative penetration of clients' and criminals' thoughts. He combines scrutiny of outward signs with intuition about personality to unfold the "plots" of other people's lives. In this respect he resembles a fortuneteller or a medium—or a novelist. But there is another analogue to consider. Listening to confessions, bringing about a climactic abreaction that releases the client from crippling mystery and repressed trauma, Holmes functions as a crude sort of psychoanalyst. For Freud, says Philip Rieff, "'repression,' psychologically understood, is 'secrecy' morally understood."[25]

Holmes could be quoting Freud himself when he philosophizes about "how small we feel, with our petty ambitions and strivings, in the presence of the great elemental forces of Nature!" For "the chief proof of man's real greatness lies in the perception of his own smallness. It argues, you see, a power of comparison and of appreciation which is in itself a proof of nobility" (SF 134). This passage tries to justify the novel itself. By tracking down Small, the novelist-detective acts out the discovery of human smallness. He brings us to acknowledge our limits and enlarge our awareness. Yet Holmes's conjuration of nobility rings hollow when he is reaching for a loaded syringe.

The ultimate "smallness" is mortality. To know one's own smallness would be to "appreciate" one's own death. This Holmes cannot do. Instead he conventionalizes smallness by reducing people to cases, from "the most interesting woman" to the stereotypical natives he adduces from his encyclopedia (159–60). Although he feigns scientific objectivity, he compulsively judges, using moral leverage to gain control over the world. Whereas Freud at least believed that he wanted to increase his clients' autonomy, Holmes dominates. He lives through his clients' experiences. Even though his vicariousness looks like vigor, Holmes's detection actively controls, and substitutes for, experience. Holmes's reckless obsession with demystification makes him distinctively modern and post-traumatic. The sleuth labors to disintegrate everything in order to analyze it, turning it into facts and laws. Like factory discipline, his mental work produces power, yet it also risks disenchanting culture's crucial symbolic immortality, revealing the futile smallness of humankind and inviting the desperate compensation of drugs.

In Holmes's obsessiveness the secularization of Victorian life has reached a poignant critical stage, and religious and industrial modes of thought precariously intermingle. While honoring the grandeur of nature, he minimizes the ultimate mystery of things. Nature is a glorified machine whose rules anyone can master, as he is forever demonstrating like a bossy schoolmaster to Watson. Underneath its mystique, detection is drudgery not unlike the toil of coolies. Holmes assumes behavior serves some ulterior lawful but instrumental use. Devotion to nature's order may be a life-giving form of worship, but if devotion is compulsive and nature is mechanistic, the worship opens toward a life-denying fatality. Emptied of criminal mystery, the world would reveal endless commonplace lawfulness, a grim moral economy that drives, like the detective himself, toward exhaustion—or, to use the trope that opens the novel, stagnation.

Watson's farewell attempts to mediate between Mary Morstan and Holmes—between incompatible and potentially deadly ideals. Reaching for his cocaine, Holmes is trapped. Like Small on the prison island, he needs an illicit and quasidemonic energy to restore to him a semblance of freedom and vitality. Although the novel celebrates truth and love, its vision of both is shadowed by a furtive, deadening despair. At the same time its vision of evil—of smallness—is imbued with an instinctual passion for life as crucial as it is inadmissible.[26]

Modern Trauma

Having examined *The Sign of Four* with the detective's magnifying glass, I want to step back and put things in a larger context. In particular, I want to identify a cluster of concerns that are related to the conditions that have brought trauma back to prominence today.

To begin with, the novel plays out the ancient conflicts of traumatic rescue, with Holmes and Watson in the position of Saint George—or with Holmes mounted, as it were, on the faithful Watson.[27] The cannibal Tonga holds the place of the voracious monster threatening the city, prefigured by the crocodile that devours Small's leg. Whereas Renaissance paintings elide the saint's eventual martyrdom, the novel calls attention to Holmes's compulsion to self-sacrifice. Destroying split-off mirror images of himself, seeking a drugged "transcendence," Holmes is engaged in a futile repetition compulsion.

This sense of traumatic alienation prefigures post-traumatic themes prominent today. Judith Lewis Herman finds the Vietnam War and domestic violence behind the recent rediscovery of trauma; Conan Doyle has Watson nursing a war injury, Small joining in murder under wartime stress (a form of berserking), and Holmes behaving as if his life is a war against crime. Although the New Woman makes no appearance in its pages, *The Sign of Four* registers the day's much-publicized gender conflicts in Holmes's misogyny, and Conan Doyle's preoccupation with parent-child violence is peculiarly obsessive. The two themes merge in Small's account of the Sikh mutiny. The first sign of "two hundred thousand black devils let loose" is Small's discovery of his coworker's wife "all cut to ribbons, and half-eaten by jackals and native dogs," who are symbolical stand-ins for the cannibal child-man Tonga (*SF* 232). The following chapter looks more closely at this rage against women, especially mothers, who can be alluring and yet, as Holmes warns, poison "children for their insurance-money" (32).

Conan Doyle was not writing at a moment of manifest historical crisis. True, London was tense with the economic unrest that erupted in the Bloody Sunday mayhem of 1887. But between the 1850s and the 1890s, Britain experienced increasing domestic stability and a rising standard of living. Political rioting became notably infrequent and all forms of crime declined—"an extraordinary development in a rapidly-expanding population, firmly contradicting the adage that industrialization and urbanization necessarily lead to higher rates of criminality."[28] The upper classes had reason to feel invincibly complacent about the nation. Nevertheless, the novel is the product of a disturbed social world. Angus McLaren quotes a contributor to the *Lancet* who "lumped together the era's most sensational crimes as evidence of some mysterious contagion of irrationality. 'The future historian of the latter part of this nineteenth century cannot fail to note the present epidemic of homicide; in the foreground of his picture he will place the dynamiting anarchist, and in the deepest shades of horror the crimes of Deeming, the Whitechapel "ripper" and of this last, the poisoner of prostitutes; and he will comment on them probably as phases of a curious morbid and dangerous mental phenomenon.'"[29]

Contrast Holmes's cool dread of "stagnation" with the torment and turmoil of Dickens's world, and the full-blown traumatic symptoms that afflict Dickens's characters—nervous tics, obsessions, amnesias, severe withdrawal. If Dickens registered the shock of social change, Conan Doyle's generation was coming to terms with its aftershocks. Death and poverty are brutally familiar in Dickens, and victims look for relief in an intense religiosity and a fatalism that lost conviction as the century of "science and progress" unfolded.

Despite the long upward curve in living standards, the end of the century felt the misery of economic injustice and insecurity as keenly as ever. Some reformers perceived a crisis of relative expectations. J. A. Hobson's *Problems of Poverty: An Inquiry into the Industrial Condition of the Poor* (1891) argued:

> If by poverty is meant the difference between felt wants and the power to satisfy them, there is more poverty than ever. The income of the poor has grown, but their desires and needs have grown more rapidly. Hence, the growth of a conscious class hatred, the "growing animosity of the poor against the rich," as [the Reverend] Barnett notes in the slums of Whitechapel. The poor were once too stupid and too sodden for vigorous discontent, now though their poverty may be less intense, it is more alive, and more militant. The rate of improvement in the condition of the poor is not quick enough to stem the current of popular discontent.[30]

As Americans saw in the late 1960s when Lyndon Johnson's antipoverty programs raised hopes and frustrations among the poor that helped set Detroit and Los Angeles ablaze, relief from despair can energize shocking demands for change as "Small" desires are released from prison, so to speak, and come home.[31]

One sign of colliding expectations is the way in which reform became more "scientific" even as reformers were conjuring moral outrage in tracts such as the Reverend Andrew Mearns's *Bitter Cry of Outcast London* (1883). Charles Booth's *Life and Labour of the People of London* (in thirty-three volumes) appeared in four editions between 1889 and 1903. Like Seebohm Rowntree's *Poverty: A Study of Town Life* (1901), Booth's massive study for the first time defined poverty as a social phenomenon rather than as a legal and moral category. Rowntree found nearly 30 percent of York's population living in poverty.[32] Systematic data may well inspire faith in rational solutions to problems, but its initial effects are likely to be, and to a great extent are, shock. There is a further likelihood that, as with improving medical care, faith in an ever more potent technic of well-being inadvertently strengthens narcissistic expectations of safety and control, tacitly lowering thresholds of pain. These paradoxes may help account for the fears of ennui and death that jar in Holmes's word "stagnation."[33]

If the period suffered a crisis, it was a crisis of awareness: the dissonance of suddenly knowing more than the culture could process. As Shearer West recognizes, in the nineteenth century a millenarian sense of doom with ancient roots "spread like a plague throughout the western world, fueled by the growth of journalism and a larger circulation of published work. The prospect of an extended readership and the need to 'create' issues in order to satisfy this growing demand resulted in a wider comprehension of international concerns and a greater self-consciousness about the problems and potential of modern society."[34] Holmes nearly caricatures that darkening mood. As he amasses an ever more vast data bank, he becomes ever more emotionally alienated. He sees into the sordid corners of London with a mix of rationalization and dissociated dread. The more he knows, the more superficial it seems, and the more compulsively he concentrates the global sense of disaster on the particular, slightly mechanical criminal cases he solves one after another.

This sort of awareness tends to be self-intoxicating. It effectively propagates problems and escalates demands on the available solutions. As crime becomes a supposed "epidemic," it calls forth the period's "epidemic" of detective and spy novels. As awareness threatens to undermine the usual heroic values, it summons the superhero Holmes, who "transcends" mere police and politics and family like the ultimate-weapon fantasies that have hypnotized the modern world, from Wells's Martian rays to today's neutron bombs and laser blasters.

In this context, imagination increasingly recognizes the irrationality of the social order. After all, this is the Gilded Age. Production may increase, but the force-multiplier effect of capital and new technology still makes the rich richer and the poor handicapped. Hard work alone will never raise a Jonathan Small out of nonentity. Too much depends on luck, the vicissitudes of competition, the fraud of a Major Sholto, or the advertising flimflam H. G. Wells burlesques in *Tono Bungay*. Naturally the contented interpret their good fortune as virtue rewarded, while justifying cruel privilege as the ancient Romans did, by pronouncing the poor morally defective.[35] For those without resources, the "criminal" pursuit of "treasure" begins to look like risky but justifiable self-interest. The emptiness of the chest seems to bring home the irrationality of society with a climactic futility, not only for the criminal nobody but also for the chest's new "rightful" owner, Miss Morstan, as if confirming women's traditional self-sacrificing role.

The looted chest, then, dramatizes anxieties about irrationality, illegitimacy, and fraud.[36] And the detective's superrationality is a futile attempt to police a world felt to be ever more perverse. After all, Sholto hoarded the treasure even after inheriting a legacy, and Small pitched the jewels into the Thames rather than let others have them. Conan Doyle could imagine no way of reconciling past and future in the unhappy present. Nor was this merely a function of his temperamental conservatism and genteel circumstances. By the 1890s, social reformers had already formulated many of today's ideological positions, and social thought had a familiar quality of irreconcilable religious schism that pitted moral, individualistic explanations of poverty, say, against structural analyses of hopeless living conditions and a culture of poverty. The distress of the 1890s, then, came from frustration with real problems and frustration with available conceptual tools, but also from "morbid" existential distress as more and more people were in a position to recognize the irrationality—the irremediable perversity—of the culture. This is the mood that culminated on the eve of World War I when the reform-minded Teddy Roosevelt despaired at the imminent "general smash-up of our civilisation."[37]

Conflicted awareness helps explain why imperialism became so charged with trauma. Emigration and colonial enterprise had long provided an escape from claustrophobia within British society. During the so-called Great Depression nearly three million farm workers may have migrated to the cities or, like Jonathan Small, to the colonies.[38] As the empire reached its zenith, however, the frontier was closing.[39] The Sikh rebellion was symptomatic, as was the nation's suspenseful anguish in 1885 over General Gordon's entrapment and death at Khartoum. In Rudyard Kipling's story "The Man Who Would Be King" (1888), two adventurers much like Jonathan Small become messianic rulers of "Kafiristan" until the natives revolt, beheading one and crucifying the other. The sadomasochistic potential of the Saint George fantasy reaches megalomaniac proportions as Kipling's heroes become intoxicated with power. Just as the infidel headsman finally brought down the saint, so Kipling's devastated survivor wanders back into British India with his partner's severed head in a sack.

The Sign of Four discovers London implicated in this alien trauma. The dragon has already penetrated Saint George's walled city by the time Watson finds a cannibal's footprint at the scene of a murder and shudders at London's "monster tentacles" extending into the country (SF 45–46). The hackneyed trope of the city as monster links fears of modern industrial society, Darwinian degeneration, economic predation, and disease. "To look at our enormous cities, expanding day by day . . . and running out their suckers, like giant octopuses into the surrounding country, one feels a sort of shudder come over one, as if in the presence of some strange social malady."[40] The city was "frequently seen as a consumer of men," or in the phrase Jack London used to describe the East End slums, "a huge man-killing machine."[41] Figuratively, the metropolis is a sort of cannibal. London is the "modern" (young) cannibal child feeding on the traditional countryside, but also the head of the country, the predatory parent feeding on the empire's "children." The conflict is everywhere; there is no safe place to stand. Instead of being a heroic struggle against an external enemy, life feels queasily ungrounded, and the result is a mood of depression that seeks relief in paranoid rage. This, after all, is exactly what happens when Small nurses the lost, desperately sick child-man Tonga, restoring him to his "natural" canni-bal self.

Like canaries in a mine, children are especially sensitive to dangerous con-ditions in the ground of society. Jonathan Small and the street Arabs only faintly evoke the abuse, neglect, and early death Victorian children faced.[42] Between 1868 and 1925, thousands of children were packed off to Canada and the colonies as laborers and servants. In 1893, the *Daily Chronicle* did an investiga-tive series called "Our Dark Places," which criticized the penal system for turn-ing "criminals into machines" (like the East End slums), and noted at one point that you might discern "a strong well-set-up boy with a face on which all sorts of good qualities were written . . . sent to prison simply because he had been found in the streets at night and had nowhere to lay his head"—and no Sherlock Holmes to employ him for a few pence.[43] Reformers such as Lord Shaftesbury increased public awareness of the plight of children, and ancient prejudices began to evolve into the modern conception of childhood as a distinct develop-mental phase. Yet childhood was still a "sink" for all sorts of ambivalent projec-tions.[44] Children were, among other options, incipient angels or filthy brutes to be disciplined. Even a leisurely stroll through child-rearing manuals of the day turns up abundant expert "evidence" that children are as unruly as "black devil" mutineers. Lower-class children were thought to be particularly precocious and inclined to depravity. As James R. Kincaid reminds us, puberty was construed as a "revolution," with sexuality "awakened" and violent. Sexual maturation is a fall comparable to the traumatic curses of Eden, so "puberty-as-flood became an awesome catastrophe, the invasion of sexual need and interest."[45]

This psychic riot was the more horrific when it erupted in, or was projected onto, the empire's fiendish "children." In some circles the colonies were con-sidered an Ali Baba's cave of erotic as well as economic treasure.[46] Fleeing a scandalous pregnancy at home, Jonathan Small makes a "faithful" mate of the childlike Tonga in India. Small shared his itinerary with a number of Victorian adventurers, real and fictional, who sought to escape the confines of respectable marriage and regulated intimacy.[47] The exotic Orient allowed Europeans to dis-sociate and thereby escape from paralyzing erotic conflicts "at home."

Small's empty treasure chest dramatizes not only the vanity of riches, but also the illusory desires of empire. As far back as the mid–eighteenth century, Dr. George Cheyne warned that "since our wealth has increased and our Navigation has been extended, we have ransacked all the Parts of the *Globe* to bring to-gether its whole stock of materials for *Riot, Luxury* and to provoke *Excess.* The Tables of the Great (and indeed of all Ranks who can afford it) are furnished with Provisions of Delicacy, Number, and Plenty sufficient to . . . gorge the most large and voluptuous Appetite."[48] Cheyne's qualms about social pretense ("of all ranks who can afford it") and greed (indulgence equals illness) show his commitment to moral therapy rather than to social reform, although conflicts between wealth and poverty likely troubled him as a physician attuned to suffering.

The physicians Conan Doyle and Watson are also conservative, but they are troubled about the "excess" of Holmes's drug addiction, and about Small's craving for "treasure" (social status and autonomy), which Conan Doyle never really understands. A novel like Thackeray's *Vanity Fair* analyzes money's actual relation to status. Conan Doyle, by contrast, implies an irrational gulf between labor and an unreachable, practically invisible executive supremacy. Criticism could account for this disconnection by analyzing class structure or economic changes such as Britain's shift during these decades away from manufacturing and toward a finance and service economy. In one way or another, however, the disconnection decouples action from desire, and the break underlies the sense of sham and death anxiety in Conan Doyle's novel and in the period.

Kipling's conniving "man who would be king" gains ruthless personal power over "his" natives; this parody of British monarchy culminates in atrocious revolution. Small tastes this power in the work gangs that he polices for Mr. Abel White. But as in the factory system, ultimate executive control is dissociated from labor, hoarding power in London; Small exists at the critically unstable boundary between executive will and labor. During the revolt, the Sikhs warn Small that he must choose one extreme or the other. In truth he has no real freedom to choose, and literally spends much of his life in prison. Once radically alienated, "criminalized," half-aware of society's sham, you cannot easily belong again.

This is Holmes's dilemma as well. In his professionalism the detective functions at the unstable interface between official executive authority and the supposedly unruly mob, policing the criminal mass of humanity. However lofty his work, Holmes *serves* the state and a range of clients, including nobility, but always from the outside, without passionate allegiance. In his drug addiction he is confined, like Small, to a psychic prison. He escapes into action through the "exaltation" of detection, yet even that can be imprisoning. In the coldly impersonal work of extirpating the criminal will, detection works like the prison system, in the words of the *Daily Chronicle*, turning "criminals into machines." Watson himself calls Holmes an "automaton" and "a calculating machine" (*SF* 21).

Positioned at the managerial interface between executive authority and brute action, Holmes's superrationality anticipates some of the fantasies in Frederick Taylor's first paper on "scientific management" (1895), which was a harbinger of the twentieth century's drive to rationalize ever-increasing productivity from workers. Similarly, Holmes's database mentality naively reflects the intensifying pace of technological integration that would make possible universal conscription and the industrial scale of carnage in World War I. "After seeing Soissons," says his biographer, "Conan Doyle wrote perhaps the most savage remark he ever made: 'May God's curse rest upon the arrogant men and the unholy ambitions which let loose this horror upon humanity.'"[49] In facing up to the horror, he rebelled against official authority (arrogant men, unholy ambitions), but still he personalized causality rather than recognizing the intersection of larger forces such as nationalism and industrialism.

Even apart from any British chauvinism, the Holmes fantasy was implicated in the mood that eventually led to the war. In the 1880s and 1890s, invasion panics incited paranoia about spies and enemy armies dressed as tourists.[50] The occasional Fenian or anarchist bombing kept public insecurity alive. Le Queux's novels obsessively flog the theme of espionage,[51] and Joseph Conrad sardonically depicts the resulting atmosphere of official surveillance in *The Secret Agent*. In ferreting out aliens such as Tonga and Small and systematizing criminal data, Holmes personalizes the armies of police spies, Pinkerton-style security agents, and private detectives that flourished in the 1890s and into the new century. One strain of development links industrial and nationalistic obsessions, and runs through Andrew Carnegie's and Henry Ford's corporate secret police and the Nazi-Stalinist police states into the National Security State and the delusional maze of George Orwell's 1984.

The Holmes fantasy must have been especially fascinating to middle-class readers because it positioned him at the critical dividing line where people most acutely felt invisible forces splitting society into the few moving upward and others headed, like Small, toward social death. Conan Doyle keeps Holmes aloof from conflicts over status by making him both an independent amateur and an autonomous professional true to his own code. It would be revealing to regard the splitting of Holmes and Small as a fantasy solution to conflicts facing Doctors Watson and Conan Doyle at a time when their rapidly expanding profession was under great pressure to magnify its promises, ambitions, and liabilities.[52] Holmes serves respectability as the amateur doctor Small saves the marginal instinctual child Tonga. Through their respective forms of social invisibility, both "doctors" transcend mundane English life, but at the cost of alienation. Holmes compartmentalizes such violent contradictions as his gallantry, his judicial impartiality, his vigilante execution of Tonga, his musical sensitivity, his emotional frigidity, and his drug addiction. Pride in professional autonomy—call it the Holmes fantasy—focuses an overstressed, incoherent subjectivity. The fantasy *depends on* his alienation. In the world of real social power, Holmes would be "small."

To a great extent the fantasy of professional autonomy derives directly from the detective's command of information. Holmes anticipates the late twentieth century's information revolution. He combines the physician's observational acuity with an encyclopedic database, and his diagnoses treat the world as a vast structure of finite information. Conan Doyle's criminals have none of the inexhaustible perversity of Fyodor Dostoyevsky's, and none of the manic inventiveness of Oscar Wilde's speakers. Like the social science of the day, with its data grubbing and its endlessly elaborated classificatory schemes and syndromes, Holmes's "method" actually produces crude motivation and simplistic causality. Plug in the right information—the characteristics of Andaman Island cannibals, for instance—and the output will restore order in London. The origin and fate of the captured criminal are moot. As in a video game, Conan Doyle keeps attention riveted on the action, dissociating the ultimate framework of death and loss. These are reasons why Holmes's detection prefigures current fantasies about the executive mind's cybernetic control over reality—or reality transformed into a vast database out of which, as from God, foolproof instructions and plans issue. To the extent that Holmes's detection does uncover irrationalities such as Small's treasure mania, Holmes and Watson hear the confession like clinicians recording a new case, anticipating the vigilant detachment of modern professionalism.

Insofar as the empty treasure chest focuses the novel's contradictions and psychic stress, it reinforces Holmes's sense of the world as a nest of deceptions. Detection is one expression of the sense of sham about which so many people in the period complained.[53] In turn, sham is as close to suicide as Holmes's detection is to his addiction. Consider the rash of suicides headlined in the popular press about the time *The Sign of Four* appeared.

John Stokes reprints from the *Daily Chronicle* of August 16, 1893, the suicide note of one Ernest Clark, who shot himself after making resolute, systematic preparations worthy of the strategic Sherlock Holmes. On many levels his voice echoes Holmes's opening despair in the novel: "I resolved long ago that life is a sequence of shams. That men have had to create utopias and heavens to make it bearable; and that all the wisest men have been disgusted with life as it is. Carlyle and Voltaire advise hard work, but only as an anaesthetic. . . . Only the transcendental and aesthetic in life are worth our thought. Only a life following beauty and creating it approaches any degree of joyousness, but the ugliness and vile monotony in my life have crowded beauty out."[54] Two days later a reader's letter opined in equally relevant terms that "a scientific age has . . . proved that 'he who increases in knowledge increases in sorrow,' and in a commercial age has superadded that to fail in the race for wealth, renders unworthy of life." On August 23, another reader commented that "deliberate suicide is simply the ultimate expression of moribund individualism—of the competitive system of production and distribution. . . . Within a comparatively brief period ten men of good culture, with whom I was more or less intimately acquainted, have committed suicide."[55]

To try to understand those anguished voices at this distance is to risk patronizing or scolding them mostly to protect ourselves. But some responses are worth suggesting. The new acuteness of economic and social awareness magnified the need for—and difficulty of—action. The newspaper suicides routinely allude to a sense of sham and futility in everyday life, often blaming the stress of competition.[56] The *Pall Mall Gazette* of January 21, 1895, printed the suicide note of a young plumber, recently converted to socialism, whose drug overdose failed: "I have retired from the battle of life, weary of its selfishness, its cant, and its shams, weary of its brute struggle for existence, its misery, poverty and degradation; the crushing of what is noble and good, the fostering of what is ignoble and bad. For many years I have had the opinion that the life of the wage earner, under the present economic conditions, was not worth living."[57] Workers competed not only against their compatriots but increasingly against foreign labor. In an article headlined "The Suicide Season," *Reynolds's Newspaper* of September 8, 1895, reports the suicide of a watchmaker whose unemployment was the result of the "sale, as English watches, of inferior Swiss and American watches, which bore the brand names of presumably respectable shopkeepers."[58] This sort of deception is figuratively at work in the careers of Small and Major Sholto in Conan Doyle's novel, and the foreignness ties in with imperial anxieties.

The crucial issue is not "the economy" but relative or contextual meanings. As A. Alvarez insists, "external misery has relatively little to do with suicide. The figures are higher in the wealthy industrialised countries than in the underdeveloped."[59] The journalist's melodramatic clucking about the dangers of "inferior" goods, say, contributes to the larger constellation of concerns about degradation, degeneracy, and sick values. Rhetoric about transcendence and aesthetic degradation served the period as a lightning rod for a storm of concerns over meaning and the quality of life: an artificial ground, as it were, for atmospheric worry about the ungroundedness of experience. What sounds like philosophy could be a polite gasp of pain, or a way of diluting disappointment and anger. For all its prescriptiveness, Nordau's *Degeneration* is an angry book. The taboo against making a scene is striking in *The Sign of Four*, where the closest Small comes to a confrontation with his lifelong antagonist is to peer in like a child at the major's deathbed. All the violence in the novel is peculiarly indirect and perfunctory. Holmes effectively wishes Tonga away with one distant pistol shot, and Small, mired in mud, simply confesses everything.

The excitement in the newspapers over suicide frequently reveals tensions between parent and child. In *Reynolds's Newspaper*'s report on the "suicide season," the journalist recounts a double suicide of young lovers. The girl's father found chalked on his door a note reading: "You will find me and Fred in the pond up the field. You are the cause of all this.—From your broken-hearted daughter." The journalist concludes with sly delicacy: "The girl was *enceinte*."[60] Parental control, I think, tacitly relates to the transcendence-degradation scheme, because the perfect obedience of the child would give the parent a sort of transcendence, both by magnifying the parent's power and by extending his or her will beyond death. The connection between disobedience and degeneration speaks for itself.

Let me try to connect these themes by turning to the suicide of the child Father Time in *Jude the Obscure*, which Hardy composed between 1890 and 1894. Stokes calls it "the most sensational fictional suicide of the nineties."[61] Overcome by poverty and psychic crisis, Jude's family self-destructs. Young Father Time murders his even younger stepbrother and stepsister, then hangs himself, leaving a note that reads, "Done because we are too menny." Here is Jude's explanation for his son's tragedy: "It was in his nature to do it. The doctor says there are such boys springing up amongst us—boys of a sort unknown in the last generation—the outcome of new views of life. They seem to see all its terrors before they are old enough to have staying power to resist them. He says it is the beginning of the coming universal wish not to live. He's an advanced man, the doctor."[62]

The child's death raises fears of deep sickness or weakness of will that affect the survivors' sense of the ground of being. This is the sort of dread Schopenhauer famously identified, but it was in the air in Baker Street also. Jude's explanation, which amounts to a diagnosis of traumatic neurosis, unwittingly implies the sort of fatal generational antagonism that lies at the heart of Holmes's England. Father Time's stepmother Sue blames herself for having confessed that she was pregnant again, and as Stokes observes, the suicide note ("Done because we are too menny") "suggests an unconscious Malthusianism."[63] The threat to survival presented by too many mouths to feed fosters overwhelming guilt, raising the specter of the cannibal child. In addition, the suicide note resonates with the anxious self-hatred latent in the trope of the city as a ravenously proliferating monster. With its associations of lives out of control, the monster-trope reached into the farthest corners of late-Victorian culture. The monster is "progress" but also all the new lives displaced from the family home into the world, including the Jonathan Smalls. And the sense of guilt directly plays out in Small's loss of his leg, Tonga's near-fatal illness, and the pair's eventual destruction.

But there is another aspect of little Father Time's behavior that deserves attention too. The child's name implies that he has assumed an adult role; he has become father to a family in which the actual parents can no longer cope. Lloyd deMause calls this "projective reversal."[64] It is mirrored in Holmes's paternalistic treatment of Watson and Miss Morstan, who feel like children around him. The reversal is significant inasmuch as it reflects a culture that ambivalently neglects and places severe demands on children, with the likely result the sort of suicidal despair evident not only in young men like Ernest Clark, but also in the addicted Holmes and the distraught Father Time. They behave as if they are responsible for everyone else, and for meaning, too ("Done because . . . "). Holmes keeps compulsively trying to explain an evil world to his clients and to himself. The resulting stress leads to aggression against the self (depression) and against others. After all, both Father Time and Holmes are literally killers.

In different ways Hardy's novel and *The Sign of Four* each describe a society in which real autonomy is in short supply and is relentlessly contested, so that children may become passively demoralized or develop a "cannibalistic" appetite for power and identity, in which case they are apt to be punished or killed. If they survive, they turn into predatory parents, dominating others because they continue to harbor in themselves voracious children. This survival appetite connects not only with *The Sign of Four*'s atmosphere of inexhaustible criminality, its aura of fog, pollution, and illness, but also with its pervasive, self-intoxicating—in Victorian terms, "hysterical"—dread of impending death.

There is a final characteristic of post-traumatic culture that Father Time suggests. Staggered by the child's death, Jude can find no solace or credibility in traditional explanations. He appeals instead to the authority of medical science. "He's an advanced man, the doctor," Jude reassures himself. The remark could apply to that other "advanced man," the split man Holmes/Watson. Whereas Watson is officially a practitioner, Holmes behaves as a protopsychoanalyst, drawing out confessions that enable a sick society to cope. Small actually uses stolen scraps of medical lore to heal the sick Tonga and win his devotion—a taboo intimacy made acceptable for polite readers, like the annihilation of Jude's family, by the trope of traumatic illness. Holmes and Watson will in turn put Tonga to death, freeing Small to confess.

Seen this way, Small's confession "empties" the obsessional strongbox. The association evokes the faith in abreaction popular among neurologists in the 1890s, as well as ancient religious psychology, with its wish to undo the Edenic curse and start afresh. Dispel a traumatic past and the unblocked social world thrives again, no longer addicted to fantasies of "treasure." One of the most prominent features of post-traumatic cultures, especially the Freudian twentieth century, is just this wish to undo the obsessional grip of injury. But there is another side to this resolution. Emptied of obsession, the self may be free to play, but it may also discover a horror of its own nothingness. Walt Whitmans are genuinely rare. "Stagnation" may reveal its association with the second law of thermodynamics, which so rattled the Victorian public with its prediction of a universe winding down to terminal entropy. H. G. Wells memorably dramatizes that prospect at the end of *The Time Machine*, but Sherlock Holmes unwittingly reveals the source of much of its terror in the paralyzing conflicts and the denial of the social world outside his window.

IN THE STRUGGLE to restore lost autonomy and ground himself again in the world of his childhood, Jonathan Small makes a criminal grab for treasure. In the most symptomatic scene, Major Sholto lies on his deathbed as Small's enraged face presses against the window. The sons inside the room are piously mourning the patriarch, while the excluded "son" curses him as a fraud. Instead of mourning, Small wants to seize his "rightful" patrimony, and he causes Sholto's death through shock just as he in effect murders one of his "brothers" over the legacy.

By contrast, *The Sign of Four* opens with Mary Morstan mourning her lost father and appealing to Holmes for help. A decade before, her father had vanished, and every year since then she had inexplicably received a valuable pearl. Captain Morstan, we later learn, died of a heart attack while seeking his share of the Agra treasure from Major Sholto, which explains why the cryptic note his daughter shows Holmes calls her "a wronged woman" (*SF* 20).

In the first of these two fantasies a child is expelled into the world feeling traumatically aggrieved. The second fantasy supposes a mysteriously "wronged" or abused child who has suffered traumatic abandonment. But as she selflessly mourns her lost parent, she is "magically" compensated with a small treasure of pearls. By the novel's end, mourning has tacitly restored her losses when she marries the tenderly paternal Watson.

The following chapter explores fantasies of post-traumatic mourning. In one direction, like those uncanny paths to lost civilizations in late-Victorian romance novels, mourning leads to the sense of doom Sherlock Holmes shared with so many others at the turn of the century. In the opposite direction it promises a way back to life. As we stumble across the path in the wilds of history, the problem is how to tell which direction is which.

THREE

Post-traumatic Mourning

RIDER HAGGARD IN THE UNDERWORLD

WHEN TEDDY ROOSEVELT commiserated with Rider Haggard about the impending "general smash-up of our civilization,"[1] the ex-president and the novelist were mourning a loss of traditional verities. In particular they lamented the traumatic expulsion from an agrarian Eden that had forced sturdy yeomen into modern urban squalor. And social rot at home today, they agreed, meant barbarian hordes at the gates tomorrow—forebodings that ironically came to pass two years later in the Great War. Although propaganda caricatured the "Huns" as the long-dreaded barbarian invaders from the east, the carnage took place in the local, murderous heart of the European family. Running in biblical grooves, Haggard's imagination decried "all the great nations of the world arming themselves to the teeth for that Armageddon which one day must come."[2] The trauma of modernity had deranged "our civilization" and would lead to annihilation. At the turn of the century this cluster of ideas was as commonplace as it was tenacious—as anyone growing up in the nuclear age can testify. In *The Sign of Four*, Jonathan Small is the displaced yeoman whom Roosevelt and Haggard deplore, rootless in the hallucinatory confusion of the city, even as Tonga heralds the feared barbarian horde.

This crisis mentality is a function of traumatic mourning. Haggard's *She* (1886) and his autobiography *The Days of My Life* (1912) exemplify the period's sense of loss—especially, in a time of closing frontiers, a lost future. Haggard naively dramatizes a range of mourning behaviors that his culture used to manage post-traumatic distress. Mourning can mean fixation on what has been lost: *possession* in the sense of trance and of grasping. Miss Havisham's decaying wedding cake in Dickens's *Great Expectations* illustrates the perversity of fixation, as does Queen Victoria's retreat from reality after Prince Albert died, which hardened her implacably reactionary views. In a healthier mode, mourning can be a de-idealizing process of transforming what has been lost, including cultural verities, into new meanings. This is how Peter Homans understands Freud's creation of psychoanalysis: as a mourning process that allowed him to recreate in secularized forms traditional values whose vitality was expiring in the nineteenth century.[3]

Where Conan Doyle projects oscillating fantasies of rebellious expansiveness and depressive withdrawal, Haggard tries to reconcile them in mourning. He grew up in a kingdom ruled by a funereal Queen Victoria, who was everybody's mythic mother and yet as life-denying as a Greek Fate. The analogous situation in *She* calls up a scenario of traumatic rescue that tries to resolve childhood conflict and loss. This effort to undo an originary injury, and its fusion of personal and cultural themes, may help explain why the novel was sensationally popular—why Freud recommended it to a patient and Jung saw it as the anima incarnate. Although Haggard's romances drive outward into exotic regions, by the indirection of mourning he tries to reconcile the now-stale world of his father and the lost paradise of mother love with the rebellious passion he projected onto the "east" and the frustrated religiosity that mesmerized him and so many of his readers.

Like other post-traumatic fantasies, *She* is notably self-involved, with constricted empathy in its social vision. Mourning represents one way of trying to unblock feeling. Like formal Victorian rites of bereavement, it is both strategic and naive, with one eye on others' reactions. Indirectly, the novel's mourning is a collective act. In loving, killing, and then grieving for the doomed queen of a lost world, the mild London legal servant conjures and shapes otherwise "dead" feelings in the bustling culture around him.

Living to Mourn: Mourning to Live

Haggard's heroes, Leo Vincey and Horace Holly, discover Queen Ayesha—She—in her second millennium of grieving for a dead lover, Kallikrates, inside a mortuary mountain, at the center of a lost kingdom (Kôr) in remotest East

Africa.[4] I read Queen Ayesha first in terms of Haggard's autobiography, *The Days of My Life*, and then against Queen Victoria, who created a new standard of sepulchral stamina after Prince Albert's death in 1861. But first a quick reprise of the novel's plot:

> Leo Vincey is an orphan whose father, while he lived, could not bear to look upon the boy's face because his appearance had caused his wife to be taken from him (she died in childbirth). What Leo and Holly find inscribed on the sherd of Amenartas is a message from another woman who died in childbirth. It exhorts her son to grow up and compensate for his father Kallikrates' death by taking revenge on his murderer, Ayesha. After Leo does grow up and find the woman, however, he does not murder her. Instead he replaces his ancestor in her affections. Haggard makes the identification between Kallikrates, the ancestral father, and Leo concrete by having Vincey confront his own image in mummified form in chapter XXI, "The Dead and Living Meet." No sooner does Leo appear on the scene than Ayesha escorts Leo to the magical fire, which will enable him to be her spouse forever. When she kisses him just before stepping naked into the fire [to renew her tacit immortality], she presses her lips to his forehead "like a mother's kiss." Finally, the impossible incestuous mating is halted by Ayesha's disintegration.[5]

The novel supposes an ancient trauma, Ayesha's murder of her lover, that still drives events in the present. Suffering a sort of psychic splitting, Ayesha mourns her slain lover, punishing herself with remorse, yet she also keeps reliving the original violence, putting to death rebellious subjects, killing her latest rival, Ustane, and seducing Leo, "with the corpse of his dead love for an altar, [to] plight his troth to her red-handed murderess."[6] Leo experiences the trauma as a "command" to "seek out the woman and learn the secret of Life, and if thou mayest find a way to slay her" (*She* 37). For Leo, the novel is a process of recovering what is tacitly a dissociated memory of injury. Because the dead Kallikrates is Leo's forefather and alter ego—his mirror image—we can read the plot as Leo's attempt to recover, reenact, and magically undo his own catastrophic past. Alternatively, Leo is recovering a dissociated childhood memory of an ancestral (parental) quarrel.

The novel's incidental catastrophes, such as Leo's near-death from fever, culminate in the master trauma on which its heroes will brood for the rest of their lives. Ayesha's death represents not only their loss of all that she stands for, including "the secret of Life" and a conviction of heroic purpose, but also their failure to get control over parent figures and in turn over their own lives. The novel projects a trauma and a state of mourning that ambiguously contains it. The result is a narrative that promises transcendent meaning to the mourners even as it dissociates them from life.

For Leo and Holly, the original shock is basically the discovery of an overwhelming anger and need for power in women. Ayesha amplifies characteristic

Victorian ambivalence about women to mythic proportions. She is quasi-immortal and maternal in her life-giving powers, yet she is also She-who-must-be-obeyed: sister to Venus Victrix, the femme fatale, *la belle dame sans merci*, and Leopold von Sacher-Masoch's cruel Venus in Furs. And Ayesha frankly tells us as much, in sententious speeches that mix the Victorian matriarch with the mythic paramour, as when she informs Holly that "it is so hard for woman to be merciful" (*She* 186). Critics have emphasized Haggard's misogyny, showing how "his plot neutralizes Her powers."[7] But that misogyny is part of a larger histori-cal and anthropological context. Cultures have long projected angry mythic queens, from Medea to Shakespeare's Titania and Cleopatra, and *She* reworks some venerable conventions. More immediately, Haggard's generation wit-nessed some of the first organized feminism, and Ayesha must have fascinated readers as a marker for emergent instabilities in gender relationships. Like Jung's "anima" and feminist invocations of "the goddess," the novel conjures a super-human mother with a religiosity that has excited readers from the start. More in-timately, the novel expands upon a wounding love Haggard experienced as a young man, and the Oedipal entanglements of his own childhood. All these cir-cumstances called for new ways of coming to terms with women.

But there is another framework for Haggard's "misogyny," which emerges when we begin to think about trauma. In a radical existential context, the novel dramatizes struggles to manage death anxiety and to recreate immortality guar-antees that were losing vitality in the nineteenth century. Like Cleopatra, Ayesha dramatizes immortal longings. Supposedly "Age cannot wither her, nor custom stale/Her infinite variety."[8] She represents one solution to Sherlock Holmes's dread of "commonplace" mortality, although pillars of fire explain her life-giving potency less convincingly than transference or hero worship do.[9]

Identifying with a powerful other—a parent, lover, or monarch—people feel they transcend weakness and death. Ideally, hero worship is symbiotic: the wor-shipers make a hero larger than life by carrying out the master will with collec-tive strength; the group shares the conviction of superhuman vitality that results. But hero worship is inherently ambivalent. Efforts to merge or ground the self in heroic others always risk disillusion, if only because sooner or later every Elvis or Cleopatra does die, and in the meantime adoration is likely to be colored by fear of displeasing or losing the all-powerful other. The pressure of unconscious motives may create a sense of sham; ambition or a suspicion of ultimate futility may abort the relationship, sometimes violently.

Transference is also historically conditioned. In a Renaissance English household the master "subsumed" the identities of his dependents, even as pa-triarchal ideology was inconsistently calling for the father to be as tender as a mother to his child.[10] During the Reformation, Protestants felt so profoundly ambivalent toward the icons of the old religion—loving, hating, and fearing them as objects of supernatural hero worship (or idolatry)—that they smashed up churches in the hope that this iconoclasm would authenticate the worship of the true supernatural Father. Haggard's Ayesha resembles one of those revered saints who incarnates everlasting life and is finally pulverized in dismay. Her aura catches sublime rays from many angles, then: from religion and monarchs such as Victoria and Cleopatra, but also from less neatly defined historical sites such as courtly love, the nineteenth-century stage, and above all, Victorian motherhood.

As a hero-worshiper, Leo Vincey has—like Jonathan Small—lost his family and been "in trouble over a woman" inasmuch as he caused his mother's death in childbirth. Leo is also "small" in his relation to his adoptive father Holly and to Ayesha—in the manuscript, he gushes with adolescent-sounding slang.[11] Like Bottom in Titania's bosom, Leo tastes Edenic, pretraumatic bliss. No less than Titania, Ayesha "will purge thy mortal grossness."[12] Mourning for more than two millennia, she has preserved her lover Kallikrates until he can be revived in his descendant Leo. Reciprocally, Ayesha recreates for Leo the mother he killed in childbirth, grounding his identity in love as the lost mother would have. In their bond the lovers substantiate each other, (re)creating an originary ground for their identities.

At the same time this bond is a cultural fantasia, a means to revitalize fading convictions. In 1886, Britain's queen, however beloved, was a dowdy, selfish old woman nominally presiding over an empire shadowed by fears of decline. Making love to the queen of Kôr is a dream of renewal.[13] Ayesha tacitly critiques "stagnant" Victorian values. In the often stilted dialogues in which Holly and Ayesha try to picture her in a British-European context, the novel is evaluating her and foregrounding the British materials out of which Haggard has fabricated her. The "position papers" she delivers to Holly and Leo catalog many of the shocks modern Britain faced. Ayesha is a Social Darwinist justifying violent competition (*She*, 197); a eugenicist tampering with human breeding (151); a scientific "materialist" (188); a Machiavellian tyrant and exponent of realpolitik.[14] She is a cultural relativist—"The religions come and the religions pass, and civilisations come and pass" (*She*, 187)—and a type of the "New Woman," proudly independent and unencumbered by the large family of old. She casually draws her imagery from hard-nosed Victorian commerce, seeing desire as an economic transaction, as when she "cynically" remarks that "passion is to men what gold and power are to women," and "man can be bought with woman's beauty" (196). Advocating self-fulfillment, she is a Nietzschean existentialist who can expostulate, "Ah, if man would but see that hope is from within and not from without—that he himself must work out his own salvation! ... Thereon let him build and stand erect, and not cast himself before the image of some unknown God, modeled like his poor self, but with a larger brain to think the evil thing, and a longer arm to do it" (187).

In promising more life, Ayesha is as intimidating and beguiling as modernism itself. But the conservative Haggard was at most half-aware of his own contradictory motives. He could never live with Ayesha, or without her either. Mourning enables him to worship her yet contain her, and finally to possess her at one remove, in imagination, as a sort of mummy. In effect, mourning is an intermediate reality that blurs the rigid categories of consciousness, allowing an interplay of desire and renunciation, ambition and righteous humility, life and death. Although *She* restores conventional order by incinerating Ayesha, mourning partly recuperates the lost dream. For Haggard and for Conan Doyle, waking into the faithless modern world was nerve-racking. Conan Doyle tried to believe in fairies, and Haggard's romances are obsessive excursions to colonial fairylands.[15] Mourning opens up a play space in which conventional and uncanny values can interact, policed by renunciation.

What Peter Homans says of Freud's later analyses of culture applies as well to Haggard. They share "a profound and mournful sense that the past of Western culture—the common cultures of the West—has been lost."[16] For Homans, "secularization has been an ever-so-gradual kind of mourning for the lost symbols and the communal wholeness they organize in the West. . . . Like so many other cultural achievements in the West—modern literature and modern art both immediately come to mind—psychoanalysis is a creative response to this loss. It seeks to replace what is lost with something new."[17] Trying to reintegrate his world, Haggard created Ayesha. When trauma disturbs the ground of experience, cultural values lose their life-supporting conviction. Reciprocally, when change disrupts heroic value systems, trauma and fantasies about trauma ensue. The process can become self-reinforcing, as it does in Haggard's late-Victorian obsession with mummies and lost civilizations, and in his autobiography, where on page after page he decorously grieves over cultural decay and personal loss, keeping tight control over a deep undercurrent of panic.

Haggard in the Underworld

Was there trauma in Haggard's own life? His memoir hints that he was a lonely and anxious child. His mother was continually pregnant and apparently remote, his father overbearing and stormy. Unable to sleep, the child had to have placed under his head a folded napkin, which he called "an ear." "To this day," he says, "I have dim recollections of crying bitterly until this 'ear' was brought to me." He calls this the behavior of a "whimsical child" (*DML* 1:5), and makes nothing of the consoling presence of a symbolic listener on the fearful edge of sleep. The denial of pain is a recurring pattern, as when he apologizes for "my dear mother declaring that I was heavy as lead in body and mind" (ibid.), and makes light of the family nursemaid's use of a rag doll named "She" to frighten the children into behaving—which indirectly gave the novel and She-who-must-be-obeyed their names.[18]

The middle-aged man who excuses the pain adults caused him as a child seems to have been an obedient son, fairly rigidly self-controlled, isolated in the middle of a bustling family. To use John Bowlby's term, the family probably "disconfirmed" the pain and anxiety to which neither his parents nor his siblings could respond. A sense of abandonment and fear of punishment shudder in his discovery of death:

> Of those early years . . . few events stand out clearly in my mind. One terrific night, however, when I was about nine years old, I have never forgotten. I lay abed . . . and for some reason or other could not sleep. Then it was that suddenly my young intelligence for the first time grasped the meaning of death. It came home to me that I too must die; that my body must be buried in the ground and my spirit be hurried off to a terrible unfamiliar land which to most people was known as Hell. In those days it was common for clergymen to talk a great deal about Hell, especially to the young. It was an awful hour. I shivered, I prayed, I wept. I thought I saw Death waiting for me by the library door. At last I went to sleep to dream that I was already in this hell and the peculiar form of punishment afforded to me was to be continually eaten alive by rats! Thus it was I awoke out of childhood and came face to face with the facts of destiny. (*DML* 1:28–29)

The core ("Kôr") of *She* is a vast underworld of death; Haggard recovers there a mother figure who can draw him into the intimacy he missed as a child, replenishing the empty "Kôr" of his own identity. As he mourns her in later life, his mother "seems to be much nearer to me now that she is dead than while she still lived. It is as though our intimacy and mutual understanding has grown in a way as real as it is mysterious" (1:24). A simpler explanation might be that once gone, the mother who had judged the child "heavy as lead in body and mind" (1:5) could be loved without so much ambivalence. "No night goes by that I do not think of her and pray that we may meet again to part no more." And with the insecure child's urge to win over once and for all the all-powerful mother-who-must-be-obeyed, he fantasizes about self-sacrifice. "If our present positions were reversed [i.e., if he were the one dead], this would please me, could I know of it, and I trust that this offering of a son's unalterable gratitude and affection may please her" (1:24). If mother and son were to swap roles as he envisions, she would be in Ayesha's position, endlessly mourning the lost son and lover.

The association of mother and mythic queen is apt, but only part of the story.

Haggard's mother, however judgmental, had less of Ayesha's passion than did his father, who "reigned at Bradenham like a king, blowing everybody up and making rows innumerable" (1:17), especially with his sons (1:23). One reason for looking beyond schematic misogyny in Haggard is his peculiar ambivalence toward his father. He attributes to this "extraordinarily popular," explosive "king" qualities that fit She-who-must-be-obeyed with eerie exactness:

> His mind had certain feminine characteristics. . . . He jumped to conclusions as a woman does, and those conclusions, although often exaggerated, were in essence very rarely wrong. Indeed I never knew anyone who could form a more accurate judgment of a person of either sex after a few minutes of conversation, or even at sight . . . though I am sure that he did not in the least know upon what he based his estimate. It must not be supposed, however, that he was by any means shallow or superficial. In any event his nature revealed an innate depth and dignity; all the noise that he was fond of making ceased and he became very quiet. Nobody could be more absolutely delightful than my father when he chose, and, *per contra*, I am bound to add that nobody could be more disagreeable. (1:20–21)

The memoir depicts a parental "ruler" capriciously terrifying and delightful, but ultimately remote, irrational, and unapproachable. Like his sometimes mournful wife, who deliberately whispered at times to get her noisy family's attention,[19] the Russian-born William Maybohm Rider Haggard could be indecipherably quiet.

The Haggards were minor country gentry of a traditional sort. Unable to afford the university education his two older brothers had received, Haggard personally felt a contraction of opportunity in England at a time of rising expectations. For his first job his parents found him a position as an administrative assistant in Africa. His mother wrote a valedictory poem for him, expressing noble sentiments with a heartfelt, stilted gravity much like Ayesha's. "Rise to thy destiny!" she commanded. "Awake thy powers!/Mid throng of men enact the man's full part!/ No more with mists of doubt dim golden hours, . . . And make God's gift of life a treasury." Dispatching him into "her [life's] troublous sea," she vowed, "I love thee well:/How well, no heart but mother's heart may know" (*DML* 1:46–47).

While Haggard was happily at work in Africa, his father caused a revealing clash of wills. In order "to bring a certain love affair to a head by a formal engagement," Haggard temporarily resigned his post and started back to England. Misinterpreting the resignation, his father fired off "a most painful letter. . . . Evidently he thought or feared that I was abandoning a good career in Africa and about to come back upon his hands. . . . What I hold even now was not justified was the harsh way in which it was expressed. The words I have forgotten, for I destroyed the letter many years ago, immediately upon its receipt, I think, but the sting of them after so long an absence I remember well enough, though some four-and-thirty years have passed since they were written, a generation ago." The rebuke "hurt me so much that . . . I withdrew my formal resignation and cancelled the passage I had taken. . . . As a result the course of two lives was changed. The lady married someone else, with results that were far from fortunate, and the effect upon myself was not good" (1:21–22).

Typically, the "traditional" side of Haggard denies the conflict by obediently reducing it to a trite lesson: "The moral is that people should be careful of what they put on paper."[20] Writing in middle age, he still could not admit that in this Oedipal crisis he not only lost his nerve but also suffered lasting hurt. Only a hundred pages later, without mentioning this loss of his beloved, did he allude to a blow that he suffered—"so crushing that at the time I should not have been sorry if I could have departed from the world. Its effects on me also were very bad indeed, for it left me utterly reckless and unsettled. I cared not what I did or what became of me" (*DML* 1:116). Some critics identify this lost beloved with Ayesha, and Haggard's wife with the faithful, tamer Ustane.

Indirectly the Oedipal pattern repeated itself after Haggard married a few years later. He returned to the Transvaal to farm a large estate—a squire rivaling his father—only to have Gladstone's anti-imperialists give the territory to the rebellious Boers in 1881. Like the father who had failed to provide a university education and then bullied him about his dependency, Gladstone "betrayed" the dutiful son by giving his patrimony to rebellious "brothers." Haggard was outraged, but he again capitulated, returning with his new wife to England, where he took up a legal career without relish.

Insecurity about parental love and a sense of alienation kept Haggard obsessively digging for something solid beneath the surface of life. He weathered lifelong bouts of depression and a dread of apocalyptic collapse. John Bowlby argues that distorted communications between parents and children may lead the children to distrust other people and their own senses.[21] This sounds like the sense of sham and nullity that Ernest Clark lamented in his suicide note to the *Daily Chronicle*, and the chronic suspicion of Sherlock Holmes. With its codes of respectability, late-Victorian culture itself behaves like a disconfirming parent, conditioning its "children" to control conflicted social realities through dissociation or dutiful sublimation. Even as a young man in Africa, Haggard tells us,

> I was subject to fits of depression and liable to take views of things too serious and gloomy for my age—failings, I may add, that I have never been able to shake off. Even then I had the habit of looking beneath the surface of characters and events, and of trying to get at their springs and causes. . . . I despised those who merely floated on the stream of life and never tried to dive into its depths. Yet in some ways I was rather indolent, that is if the task at hand bored me. I was ambi-

tious and conscious of certain powers, but wanted to climb the tree of success too quickly—a proceeding that generally results in slips. (*DML* 1:49)

Like Holmes, he swung between "fits of depression" and heroic, inquiring "ambition," trying "to climb the tree of success" like a young Adam defying the prohibitive Father. The same oscillation keeps Sherlock Holmes reaching for the cocaine syringe. Not only can the grown man not recognize how substantial his own motives had been, but he scolds himself with parental moralizing about unwise ambitions.

Haggard's life followed Jonathan Small's pattern insofar as he was a younger son pushed out of pastoral England to make his fortune in the colonies, got in "some sort of trouble about a woman," and lost a "treasure" through the treachery of a father figure (Sholto/Gladstone/Haggard *père*). In 1912, several decades after the fact, he still invoked "this great betrayal, the bitterness of which no lapse of time can ever solace or even alleviate" (1:194). For all his success, he still feels robbed of purpose and meaning. Small's rage works through his murderous alter ego; Haggard has Ayesha kill the rival Kallikrates. Most importantly, despite the happy sublimation of romance writing, Haggard suffered a post-traumatic sense of self-disablement and doom not unlike Holmes's addiction and Small's final immobility.

The pattern is stark in *She*. In seeking out Ayesha in Africa, the heroes solve a two-thousand-year-old crime. But just as She is freeing Leo from the chains of the past, the pillar of fire—that outsize symbol of the father—betrays her to dust and nearly blasts Leo and Holly too. From regal erotic dreams the son flees back to commonplace England. Haggard's autobiography follows the same rhythm of self-assertion and elegiac retreat. He titles a chapter "Marriage" but then uses it to eulogize an old school friend who became a Trappist monk. Marriage, the fulfillment of manhood, turns into a valediction. Oedipal self-assertion collapses into grief for a sexually innocent, monastic alter ego, as if to deny or punish Haggard's own desire. But then death in turn spurs him to fantasize about immortality: "Since I for one cannot believe that he and all mankind are the victims of a ghastly delusion, or are led forward by mocking marsh-fires of self-evolved aspirations to be lost in some bottomless gulf of death, I will *not* add—farewell" (*DML* 1:162). Memorializing his friend, he is in part mourning for himself.

Haggard never stops dreaming of winning love through heroic self-sacrifice. Writing about telepathy, he reports having a series of hypnagogic reveries that he recognizes as "subconscious imagination," although he suspects they may be memories of a previous incarnation or "racial memories of events that had happened to forefathers" (*DML* 2:169–72). These "pictures" reveal a personality gripped by fantasies of sacrifice as a resolution to trauma. The sets vary—prehistoric England and Africa, a Viking hall, archaic Crete—but the themes are all related. In a typical reverie Haggard is a black man who defends a woman from "attackers" and then falls "into the arms of the woman and die[s]." In another, a cruel overseer is about to kill "as useless" an injured slave and to take "his" woman because the victim—"once an individual of consequence"—"has been reduced to slavery by some invading and more powerful race" (*DML* 2:169–72). These variations of traumatic rescue echo the central preoccupations of Haggard's romances and his social world. Social Darwinism and the fall of empire, erotic sacrifice and familiar Oedipal themes, all fuse in these reveries with the galloping hoofbeats and martyrdom of the dragon-slaying Saint George. When an ancient Egyptian beauty "with violet eyes" opens herself to him (2:169), the rescuer renounces desire just as he has abjured hate (1:xviii). In the end of this account, Haggard maintains his renunciation through another valediction: "And now farewell to the occult. Mysticism in moderation adds a certain zest to life and helps to lift it above the level of the commonplace [as do cocaine and heroic romance]. But it is at best a dangerous sea to travel before the time" (2:172).

Haggard began writing *The Days of My Life*, he tells us, after he learned that a mistaken rumor of his death was circulating in the press. But one day, he sighs, elemental forces "like the storm that I hear raving outside the windows as I write" actually will sweep him away (1:xvii). He imagines that the memoir may distill "some essence" of his life "worthy of preservation"—not unlike the mummies of Kôr—"at which eyes unborn may be glad to look" (1:xviii), as Leo and Holly gaze on the progenitive Kallikrates.[22] Haggard's autobiography embodies mourning like an everlasting funeral monument, a literary version of the Albert Memorial Chapel at Windsor, with its effigy of the princely husband dressed up as the slain knight of chivalric romance.

Victoria's Funereal Empire

The century's unrivaled mourner was Queen Victoria. Like the spellbound Queen Ayesha, the empire's queen managed her husband's death in 1861 by making mourning "a sort of religion."[23] Because her mother had just died too, Victoria was doubly stunned. Haggard was a child of five when the nation went into shock. Hitherto somewhat ambivalent about the German prince consort, the public clamored for *carte de visite* photographs of him (seventy thousand sold in one week) and evinced such hysteria that Dickens—that connoisseur of funeral sentiment—growled they were making "Jackasses" of themselves.[24] A monument-building campaign ensued. The queen kept more or less in seclusion for nearly a decade. "To her subjects," presumably including the young Rider Haggard, "it increasingly seemed as if their sovereign had lost all interest in life, and was concerned exclusively with the commemoration of the dead."[25] For a while, rumors circulated that she was ill or even mad. By the time Haggard wrote *She,* the cult of the prince had faded in the public mind, so that "if there were any cult figure, then it was Queen Victoria herself."[26]

Like Ayesha's, Victoria's mourning combined passionate aggrandizement and trancelike abnegation, vehemence,[27] and implacable resolve. She sought to freeze time by having every object in her possession photographed from three angles and catalogued so that its place in her rooms could be everlastingly fixed. With Albert's visage affixed to the headboard of their bed and his clothes laid out for him every night for forty years, the royal apartments cultivated illusion, using the cognitive tricks of ritual and mummification by which the Pharaonic tombs created an ambiguous sense of ongoing life. The queen was a compulsive hoarder, stuffing cupboards and wardrobes with all the clothes and accessories she had ever owned. With Albert's death the compulsion became a votive ritual. Yet this mentality resonates elsewhere in the culture, in the overstuffed rooms and the acquisitiveness that fascinated novelists. Like the immutable apartment, property promises to substantiate the self. In trying to materialize her evanescent life with Albert, Victoria was grasping at treasure like a Jonathan Small, countering the terror of nonentity and nothingness. For that matter, Holmes himself is similarly counterphobic. After all, the detective has amassed information about every item in the world, as if he too can freeze the flux of reality. The queen had her world captured in fat, richly bound albums; Holmes has his encyclopedias and his files on such minutiae as types of cigar ash. Even more literally than Holmes, the queen took the whole world as her province, yet looked out gloomily on a dead landscape that had to be recharged with heroic meaning through the intoxication of mourning.

To create that meaning, Victoria became an artist of sorts, using the technic of hero worship to create not only monuments but also a superhuman hero to inhabit them. In some ways her task was straightforward enough. Coming from a family of "wicked" uncles (her own father was forced out of his army command for sadistic abuses), Victoria had good reason to worship her kindly husband. Having been thoroughly sheltered all her life, Victoria could logically regard herself after Albert's death as a "poor forlorn, desolate child—who drags on a weary, pleasureless existence!" In this well-known letter to her uncle Leopold, king of the Belgians, she vows that Albert's "wishes—his plans—about everything, his views about every thing are to be my law! And no human power will make me swerve from what he decided and wished. . . . I am also determined that no one person, may he be ever so good, ever so devoted among my servants—is to lead or guide me or dictate to me. I know he would disapprove it. And I live on with him, for him; in fact I am only outwardly separated from him, and only for a time."[28]

Like most systems of hero worship, this one was richly equivocal. Even as Victoria's idolatry personifies Necessity to give life absolute meaning, she appoints herself arbiter of the superhuman will, thus magnifying her own autonomy. Her fortified will emerges in an earlier letter to Leopold complaining that "the poor fatherless baby of eight months . . . is now the utterly heartbroken and crushed widow of forty-two! My life as a happy one is ended! The world is gone for me! . . . Oh! to be cut off in the prime of life—to see our pure, happy, quiet, domestic life, which alone enabled me to bear my much disliked position, cut off at forty-two—when I had hoped with such instinctive certainty that God never would part us . . . —is too awful, too cruel!"[29] Lytton Strachey drily comments that "the tone of outraged Majesty seems to be discernible. Did she wonder in her heart of hearts how the Deity could have dared?"[30] She sounds like She-who-must-be-obeyed, as she does in her lament that "I am on a dreary sad pinnacle of solitary grandeur."[31]

Such intoxication removes the self to an exotic never-never land not unlike the ones Haggard visited in his romances. Peering into Albert's sarcophagus at the Frogmore Mausoleum as it neared completion, the devoted wife sighed, "Oh! could I but be there soon!"[32] By projecting a mythic Albert who in turn substantiated her being, Victoria became tacitly self-created. Leo Vincey—and his creator—do the same thing by projecting the quasi-immortal Ayesha, who then redefines Leo as a creature of heroic destiny. Conjuring up Albert's presence year after year, Victoria created a male paradigm for her autonomy: a supreme father to the "poor fatherless baby." In her letter to her uncle she sees herself not only stricken by Albert's loss, but also, drawing on childhood sorrows, as the abandoned infant traumatized by her father's death and her widowed mother's distress. Like Ayesha presiding over a vast interior kingdom of mummies and sepulchral remains, Victoria experienced trauma as a repetition and proliferation of losses. "The dead, in every shape—in miniatures, in porcelain, in enormous life-size oil-paintings—were perpetually about her."[33] While her symptoms were emergent, the queen created a mythic Albert, and her trauma was contagious; it moved others to consecrate cult memorials throughout the nation and the empire. She was like many of her subjects in using trauma to conjure up complexly escapist idealism, charged with a fervent, sublimated eroticism and an ambivalent rigidity of will.

At first the public found relief from shock in the cult of the fallen prince. Albert was ambiguously cast as a loving father and husband, a wise statesman and youthful warrior. In effigy and in Victoria's favorite portrait, for example, he was depicted in medieval armor and associated with the sacrificial "son" Saint George; the iconography of the Order of the Garter also linked him to fantasies of traumatic rescue. The ambiguity made the gentle Albert a congenial tutelary spirit, able to relate to competing fantasies of martial, diplomatic, and commercial heroism, and to reconcile in mourning the sort of generational antagonism that bares its teeth in *The Sign of Four* and many other narratives of the period.

In actual families, Oedipal rivalry was more problematic. The dutiful Albert, for example, had left his sickbed to scold his son Edward for his most recent sexual escapades while at his military quarters. The queen believed the trip hastened Albert's death, and for the rest of her life she kept Edward from power. In those years many—Haggard no doubt among them—thought the queen should vacate the throne for her son. This may be one of the Oedipal fantasies fulfilled in *She*, because in chapter 21 the novel unites the young hero and the motherly queen over the body of the estimable but inhibiting father figure. Freed from mourning, the queen promptly reduces Kallikrates' mummy to dust. But then, at the moment of Oedipal consummation, her own death frees the young hero to return to England and manhood, empowered and yet ghostly too—exactly as Haggard later took Edward to be when he watched the new king following Victoria's coffin to her burial at Windsor: "A picture never to be forgotten. And now, after a few brief years, the mourning monarch who formed its central living figure [is] himself the mourned!" (*DML* 2:215).

Edward's frustration is emblematic of a much larger cultural pattern. As the queen's generation consolidated its power and control over access to its fortune, the generation following seems to have felt blocked like the Prince of Wales, deflected abroad like Small and Haggard, preyed upon like Dracula's young adversaries, or driven to provocation like Oscar Wilde or to revolt like Wells's Invisible Man.[34] The conflict was sharpened by pressures from below, including feminism and labor. But especially as refracted in *She*, the aging Victoria is emblematic of a hardening of privilege against change and the claims of the young. Personally she was despotically selfish and hostile to every form of democratic progress. In court life she demanded obsequious toadies. Contrary to public myth, she was no lover of children.[35] Haggard never came to terms with his ambivalence. Like Conan Doyle, Wells, and Wilde, he fantasized about murderous confrontation, but in the end turned his anger depressively inward.

In preserving stability, mourning is conservative. It displaces parental power into the play space of memory and imagination, defusing antagonism. At the same time, mourning compensates for loss by generating vital cultural beliefs, as in the rich mixture of religious, aesthetic, and military conviction derived from Victorian—and Wagnerian—medievalism. In an implied psychic economy, Queen Victoria and her subjects invested devotion (hero worship) in the cult of the prince consort, which gave back a conviction of heroic purpose and symbolic immortality. This economy in turn relates to the old colonial system in which laboring "natives" are supposed to send raw materials such as gold to the "mother" country, where they are transformed into the higher forms of civilization—crowns, crosses, gold plate, and the like—that embody law and religion and other cosmic meanings. In this fantasy exchange, crude earth—clay, dust, death—is refined into symbolic "treasure."

The problem is that in time all mourning becomes—in Holmes's terms—commonplace. The minute Ayesha finds new love in Leo, she disposes of Kallikrates' mummy. When Victoria eventually found solace in her Scottish retainer John Brown (in some circles she was snickeringly referred to as "Mrs. Brown"), her dedication to Albert's memory relaxed.[36] For the public, as time went on the monuments to the prince consort became disenchanted. Like the Christlike statue in Wilde's fairy tale "The Happy Prince," they lost much of their meaning and devolved to raw materials, scrap metal and marble—analogous to the ruins that Haggard associated with lost civilizations in his travels. This is the spirit of "Recessional," which Kipling wrote for the queen's jubilee (1897).[37]

As in *The Sign of Four*, disillusion entails an awareness of sham. When the spell of mourning is self-intoxicating, as it is for Dickens's Miss Havisham (Have-a-sham), awakening from it can mean confronting long-denied anguish and a much greater death anxiety. The spell is a sort of play-death that promises to keep deferring real death as long as the spell can be sustained. But nobody can remain entranced forever. When Ayesha awakens to Leo, she destroys Kallikrates' remains and then suddenly needs a rejuvenating recharge from the Pillar of Fire, which—like the flames that incinerate Miss Havisham—proves lethal.

Despite an aura of sensational violence, Ayesha has survived for millennia as a lone woman ruler by cunningly playing groups off against one another. She has been living in a vacuum of desires, as it were, not personally living so much as manipulating life. Only when she acts to fulfill her desire with Leo does the Pillar of Fire annihilate her. After two thousand years, time finally catches up to Ayesha, and she shrivels to a wizened, hideous monkeylike animal, a puppet of biological destiny, and then is gone. As children ground themselves in their mothers, mothers may ground themselves through mourning in their husbands and fathers, mystic shamans (Noot), and Pillars of Fire. For the novel's eyewitness heroes as for its author, the loss of that groundedness and the resulting sense of sham threaten to confirm the terrifying nothingness of things.[38]

Something like that queasiness haunted the end of Victoria's reign as well. After reminding us of the doomsday angst that traditionally shadows the ends of centuries, Karl Beckson notes that in 1889, the Reverend Michael Paget Baxter, the author of books of prophecy and editor of the *Christian Herald*, was expecting the end of the world in 1901. Beckson points out that the apprehensive Reverend Baxter was "not entirely wrong in his . . . prediction, for Queen Victoria's world did come to an end in 1901, when she expired."[39] Alone at night in his room back in England, with Leo now white-haired from shock, Horace Holly concludes *She* by converting the lost past into fantasies of what will happen when "that *final* development ultimately occurs, as I have no doubt it must and will occur, in obedience to a fate that never swerves and a purpose that cannot be altered." The sentimental nod to kismet and the woozy dream of reincarnation unfold in the mourning imagination, so that as the book ends consolation buffers the deadly vision of romantic self-sacrifice and Kallikrates once again flees "down the coast of Libya to meet his doom at Kôr" (*She*, 300–301). As a romance convention the moment is high hokum. As a form of traumatic repetition it is the cry of a paralyzed soul trapped in its own compulsions and looking to the trappings of apocalypse for relief.

Mourning Mother and Mortality

Like table manners and other social codes such as respectability, mourning can be a strategy for controlling competition. Whereas Doyle imagines mirroring heroes and criminals implicated in a murderous economic struggle, Haggard presents the world as a maze of Oedipal entanglements. As Norman Etherington points out, if Ayesha is associated with the desired but unattainable mother, "then she is the rival of *all* other women. . . . By the same token the image of the mother is reflected in the eyes of all lovers. . . . [The] Chinese box structure of the novel . . . allows the triangular rivalries to be presented over and over without ever being precisely duplicated."[40] The same multiplicity applies to the novel's father figures. Endless triangular rivalries add up to a society obsessed with competition.[41] In such an environment the transition from infant nurture to "mature" competition and survival anxiety is likely to be traumatic. The child must cope with implicit threats of annihilation that have profoundly unsettling effects the more evident they become. The shock of Darwinism—the Social Darwinist's reduction of natural selection to a zero-sum rage for survival—is one sign of that traumatic transition. For the nine-year-old Rider Haggard, a crucial stage of the transition must have been his discovery of death fantasies about hell, because hell is a patriarchal police state, dedicated to the punishment of unruly wills, superintended by God's despotic archrival—not unlike the underworld regime of She-who-must-be-obeyed. It is the antithesis of the infantile paradise of the mother's breast.

One solution to a brutal world is the radical self-effacement of mourning. Queen Victoria venerated Albert as a nurturant mother-father, and she protected that ideal from challenges by effacing herself and all "children." Accordingly, the most powerful woman in the realm vehemently submitted to "Albert's will" while condemning "Women's Rights" as a "mad, wicked folly" through which "woman would become the most hateful, heartless, and disgusting of human beings were she allowed to unsex herself; and where would be the protection which man was intended to give the weaker sex?"[42] Because the premier woman of the empire was also only a political figurehead who insisted on personally signing boxes of memos day after day in the absence of more practical powers, it makes sense that she would minimize discordant claims to autonomy in herself and competition with female "siblings." At the same time, her concern about maximizing "the protection which man was intended to give the weaker sex" makes a different kind of sense in an era when, as John Stuart Mill protested, many husbands regularly "indulge[d] in the utmost habitual excesses of bodily violence towards the unhappy wife," and an area of Liverpool known for grisly domestic violence was popularly called the "kicking district."[43]

Haggard's mourning likewise manages competition. This is what makes so poignant his terrible grief over the death in 1891 of his nine-year-old son Rider—"he was by his own wish called Jock, to avoid confusion between us." The doting father praises the boy's "singular sweetness" and then innocently adds, "even while he was still in his frocks I have known him attack with his little fists someone who made a pretence to strike me" (DML 2:41). In his love, Haggard is keenly attuned to the ambivalence of the father-son bond, moved by his child's loyalty to him. He vows that he would gladly have sacrificed his own life to spare his son.

The colonial world magnified these dynamics. Looking back in 1912, Haggard envisioned meeting his Zulu "man" Mazook in a desegregated heaven. Like Billali in *She*, Mazook is by turns father and son to the Englishman, who cherishes Mazook as Small does Tonga: "I do not know that I felt anything more in leaving Africa than the saying of good-bye to this loving, half-wild man" (1:202). This eulogy in effect apotheosizes the spontaneously affectionate (dead) native "son." Haggard dreams of a reconciliation with split-off parts of his own childhood self. And yet, as in his lament for his son, this love for Mazook is also counterphobic. The native "children" who don't love you may eat you. In his vision of the hot-potting Amahaggar, as in the culture's thrilling lore about cannibals, British imagination projects its own frightening "dog-eat-dog" social experience onto exotic others, where it can be more safely acknowledged.

Fathers are no less split than sons. They may be as violently unfathomable as the Pillar of Fire, or as nurturant as the "native" father-mother Billali—"my nominal parent" (She, 297)—who nurses the traumatized heroes after their escape from the fire, and then has to spirit them off because he cannot protect them against the cannibalistic Amahaggar "siblings" who are also "my children" (295).

In thinking about these contradictions, it is easy to focus on particular roles and prejudices, and to overlook the way they work to control basic death anxiety. The novel plays out an inner life not simply misogynistic but appalled at the treacherous emptiness of all parental guarantees. As a son, Haggard half-saw the hollowness of patriarchal claims, even as he recognized some of his father's personal limitations. But to confront that weakness would be to risk exposing the emptiness of the guarantees that ground society, so instead he pays little attention to Kallikrates and mourns for an ideal strength. In witnessing Ayesha in her bedroom with the corpse of the forefather Kallikrates, a son may be living out a Freudian primal scene. But when Leo meets this dead alter ego in chapter 21, the moment reveals not only Leo's triumph in Oedipal rivalry, but also his own death mirrored in the mummy. To win the struggle against one's parents is to de-idealize them and acknowledge their puny, creaturely limits. But to survive them is to feel abandoned in the universe. This is one source of the pathos readers are supposed to feel at the spectacle of Ayesha grieving for two thousand years. It may also help explain why Ayesha dissolves Kallikrates' mummy and then immediately decides that she and Leo must be reinoculated against death in the Pillar of Fire.

Ayesha's destruction in the fire certainly plays out male anxieties about "superhuman" motherhood. So ambivalent are Ayesha's motives that the novel even makes her a vegetarian to deny the possibility of cannibal aggression that is elsewhere so menacing.[44] But critics are apt to make a melodrama of Haggard's punishment or control of "Her" power, as if Ayesha's defeat empowers Leo or Holly. Playing on the Pillar of Fire, Gilbert and Gubar conclude that "she must be fucked to death by the 'unalterable law' of the Father,"[45] but although this spirited aphorism offers us a satisfying glow of righteousness, it ignores the depth of the novel's disenchantment and dread. In its symbolic logic, She makes Ayesha's death justify the gratifying survival-escape fantasy and visionary mourning that finally suspend the plot. But the moment of her death is harrowing in its disenchantment: "Her face was growing old before my eyes!" (She, 279). Few novels find such a condensed metaphor for the collapse of the psychic ground of conventional reality. However misogynistic it may be, the moment demystifies romantic love and motherhood as systems of symbolic immortality, and without recuperating "the 'unalterable law' of the Father" either. On the contrary, the woman's death reveals the "law" that grounds experience to be sinister and paralyzing.

The result can be seen as an anxious child's—or more patronizingly, a boy's—stance toward the world. The novel justifies obedience as a consoling sacrifice, as when the beloved, dull Ustane proves woman's benevolence through her compulsive self-sacrifice. Ayesha, by contrast, would lead the rebellion the young Rider always flirted with (literally in his courtship) and renounced, even though he kept returning to the theme of native peoples revolting against oppressive tyrants.[46] And in the end, fantasies of self-sacrifice control Ayesha too. In a version of traumatic rescue she plays Saint George, dispatching the demon-father Kallikrates, who for two thousand years, like the dragon, has held an entire kingdom in sepulchral thrall. As a mummy, a semblance of life, he evokes Dracula in his coffin and the vampire's insidious thirst for life. Rebelling against the compulsion to mourn and against Kallikrates' embodiment of death, Ayesha would rescue Leo and redeem the walled city—the "dead" worlds of Kôr and England. If she had her way, "strong and happy in her love, clothed in immortal youth, [Ayesha] would have revolutionised society, and even perchance have changed the destiny of Mankind." But then, as in Saint George's later career, she too is soon martyred by the unfathomable fire. "Thus she opposed herself against the eternal law, and, strong though she was, by it was swept back to nothingness—swept back with shame and hideous mockery!" (*She*, 281–82). Like all saints and angels—and children—she is a potential rival to the cosmic Father, as Lucifer was.

The renunciation is at once Ayesha's, the heroes', and Haggard's—and tacitly the reader's as well. The novel offers consolation by assimilating the martyred queen to the lost mother, as the music of mourning swells to a climax. Haggard promotes the dream of infantile reintegration with the rescuing, sacrificial mother by improbably having the wind blow Ayesha's cloak onto Leo like a baby's blanket at the moment of her death, "so that it covered him almost from head to foot. We could not at first make out what it was, but soon discovered by its feel, and then poor Leo, for the first time, gave way, and I heard him sobbing there upon the stone" (289). Leo relives the sorrows of the little boy who needed a substitute mother's napkin-"ear" in order to find sleep and withstand the "death" of separation from her (*DML* 1:5). The blanket recapitulates the childhood napkin, and again the child's comfort comes from the sublimation of mourning.

Beyond dread, grief, and the perverse exhilaration of survival, readers can also find in Ayesha's death a rage at the woman who leads her "children" to the fount of life, only to reveal incomprehensible horror. As the ground of our experience, mothers also sooner or later focus the insoluble problem of death. This is, after all, one reason why cultures divide up the project of guaranteeing immortality and self-esteem between parents. In fantasies of traumatic rescue, for example, the idealized Saint George/Christ rescues from death a maiden who, as the Holy Virgin, is also his mother. Queen Victoria looked to the fatherly (and distinctly maternal) Albert to secure herself in "everlasting" belief.[47] Ayesha, like Haggard *père*, combines maternal and paternal qualities, but in the end the novelist can believe in neither father nor mother as a reliable ground. On this level mothers sacrifice, while fathers are grim cosmic abstractions such as destiny or eternal law or a scenic underground blast furnace.

One effect of this dread—and it is also present in the epidemic anxiety about child abuse and abortion in our own day—is a painful, often tragic tendency to scapegoat parents, especially women, for intolerable levels of death anxiety in the culture. The later Victorians were widely apprehensive and censorious about women's fitness for motherhood. In the atmosphere of post-traumatic tensions I have described, with its sense of decadence and degeneration—of something gone wrong—"bad" mothers were easily associated with the damaged ground of life. Sherlock Holmes cites the mother who poisoned her children for their insurance money. In period newspapers, novels, and medical tracts men blamed unnurturing women for all sorts of grave distress. The core fantasy was a dread of annihilation. They attacked "baby-killing" mothers who sought to control their fertility through abortion or birth control. "The press was full of violent denunciations of women who had recourse to abortion," reports Angus McLaren. "The respectable referred to it as murder and to women who sought abortion as murderers."[48]

This righteous fury seems partly a transformation of real childhood rage and distress, but it probably reflects even more a post-traumatic conviction of childhood injury and has strong powers to account for lives beset by conflict. But the fury had proximate material causes as well, for "in the last decades of the nineteenth century women's need for assistance in terminating pregnancies had taken on a special urgency. Social pressures to restrict family size had increased, but adequate contraception was simply not available."[49] Furthermore, new laws were criminalizing the termination of pregnancy,[50] even as the self-aggrandizement of the medical profession as supreme arbiter in matters of health reinforced society's fantasies that it could rationally control (that is, police) its own fertility and, symbolically, immortality.

Individual anxieties about infantile trauma interacted with group beliefs. The sense of individual abuse readily spilled into cultural fears of decadence, sterility, and collective annihilation—a hysteria that gathered force up to World War I, and in fact has never fully subsided since. The feminist Frances Swiney complained that "persons, totally ignorant of physiology, write diatribes on the declining birth-rate; and equally hysterical effusions on the fearful mortality of infants fill magazines, reviews, and papers, the onus in each case being thrown on the incapable and ignorant mothers of the race, who are, first blamed for not producing more infants, and secondly, upbraided with the loss of those produced."[51]

This dread of exhaustion and sterility grips the correspondence between Teddy Roosevelt and Haggard. They fear the modern urban world will collapse like the Tower of Babel or Kôr.[52] Its fallen bricks will be "crumbled to powder by . . . everlasting sun"—a sun akin to the Pillar of Fire. From those ruins Haggard gazes on annihilation: "An ultimate dearth of Life: the woman who will not bear children on the one hand; the woman who may not bear children on the other. A destruction: with a vision (for those who can see) of the East once more flowing in over the West and possessing it" (DML 2:188). As Western motherhood deteriorates, oriental sexuality "flows," which is one reason he fears the annihilation of the race "(I speak of the white Nations)."[53]

Sympathizing with Roosevelt about urban poverty, alluding to a magazine photograph he has seen, Haggard focuses on "a number of your New York women (members of the upper 400 . . .) feeding their lap-dogs, adorned with jewelled collars, off plates of gold. Elsewhere I have read and seen pictures of New York poor starving in the snows of winter" (DML 2:188). He seems not to connect these society "queens" pampering pet "children" with She-who-must-be-obeyed dominating Leo and Holly—"the lion" and "the baboon." Neither does it occur to Haggard to blame the elite "fathers" whose economic systems have created irrationality and survival torment in New York. Instead he obliquely scolds the callous "mothers" and reverts to the pastoral-agrarian fantasy of emptying out the corrupt cities and repopulating the countryside. In effect, reform is a shadow of rebellion, and the mourner seems careful that the one should not lead perilously into the other.

To a great extent this is the comfortable paralysis of privilege, because serious reform would challenge the gentleman-writer's own class. At some moments *She* naively registers the injustices and cruelties of class. The explorers find in a huge vault "bodies of the poorer citizens of Imperial Kôr. These bodies were not nearly so well preserved as were those of the wealthier classes . . . in some instances being thickly piled one upon another, like a heap of slain" (*She*, 207). The imagery here finds in the funereal shadows the usually hidden truth that wealth buys symbolic immortality. People compete to escape not only deprivation but death itself. In the hierarchical structure of hero worship, Ayesha has access to the life-giving Pillar of Fire and in turn would initiate Leo and Holly. By contrast, only tenuous life is possible for the faceless Amahaggar or the "blur and splotches" of faces that the servant Job sees when he thinks of his seventeen siblings (208)—as anonymous as "the heap of Smalls" in Jonathan Small's village.

The "command" of immortality rests on worship and, failing that, on physical violence. Ayesha holds sway by violent cunning; the mummies of the anonymous poor are "piled one upon another, like a heap of slain" (207)—like the cannon fodder and expendable slaves of history. This is the vicious economy implied by the human sacrifices ritually mimed at Kôr (212), and it draws on the same associations as Small and Tonga do. The most significant difference is that here the rage for life is projected not onto the cannibal child but onto a "large, powerful woman," frenzied and bloodthirsty, who calls for a black (scape)goat until dancers dressed as animals oblige her with a saucer of blood (210–13).

This ogre caricatures Ayesha, "savages," and the hateful appetites of the devouring mother who would kill a "kid." Like the bloodthirsty Lucy in *Dracula*, the woman is also a sort of vampire from among the dead, literally possessed. Her appetite for sacrificial, bloody immortality reveals the terror masked by Ayesha's nonchalant counsel: "Endeavor not to escape the dust which seems to be man's end" (211). The central truth is that the kingdom, like the entire novel, is an effort to "escape the dust." Woman embodies not only fertility and the future, but also a symbolic promise of escape. Even in *The Sign of Four*, Miss Morstan, like a ghostly Ayesha, tacitly commands the plot by spurring Holmes to seek the missing "treasure," a search that scapegoats the black Tonga and Small to produce the novel's heroic excitement.

The sacrificial festivities at Kôr are structured by post-traumatic mourning. The Amahaggars' "minds seem to have taken their colour from the caves in which they live, and [their] jokes and amusements are drawn from the inexhaustible store of preserved mortality" (*She*, 212). Burning mummies to celebrate, they take energy from the dead; in the ancient logic of sacrifice, death fertilizes life. Reveling among corpses piled "like a heap of slain," they resemble those warrior kings whose monuments depict them victorious over mountains of slaughtered captives.[54] Their festivities are driven by veiled dread and aggression, in the service of a mourning queen. The close of chapter 20 reveals the desperate instability of Haggard's world. The moment Ayesha finds Leo and new life, her rival Ustane appears, and suddenly jealousy threatens to literalize the mechanisms of scapegoating and sacrificial killing that are precariously sublimated in the Amahaggar festivities.

The novel associates Ayesha's capacity for rebirth with the spiritualism that consoled the later nineteenth century. And spiritualism is another form through which mourning tames sacrifice to summon life from death. Its rites reduce the bloody commerce of ancient sacrifice to a hypnagogic reverie in a hushed, genteel parlor, with (usually) a motherly guide. Like the novel, it is a marker for the countless surrogate religions that have proliferated since the nineteenth century, supplementing or displacing orthodox belief.

In his adolescence Haggard attended séances in London with a medium named Mrs. Guppy, on whom the irreverent guest played a few pranks. But just when Haggard might seem to be winking slyly, he defends the occult. At one séance, he tells us, he met the spirits of "two young women of great beauty," one of whom, though presumably dead, he tried to kiss ("I think she remarked that it was not permissible"). This naive fantasy of necrophilia focuses the wish to overcome death through the central immortality rite of culture: courtship. "To this day," he writes, "I wonder if the whole thing was illusion, or, if not, what it can have been." But he sidesteps his skepticism: "I do not believe it was a case of trickery; rather am I inclined to think that certain forces with which we are at present unacquainted were set loose that produced phenomena which, perhaps, had their real origin in our own minds, but nevertheless were true phenomena" (DML 1:37–39).[55] As a fantasy of undoing death, a séance directly engages post-traumatic themes in an atmosphere of religiosity and suggestibility. As a rite of mourning, Haggard's ghostly brush with desire at the séance is a preview of his heroes' later assignation with the queen of the dead.

Mourning and Modernism

Recall the anguished mixture of apocalyptic dread and militant reform that preoccupied Haggard and Teddy Roosevelt. Roosevelt was by far the more ro-bust reformer, though Haggard volunteered some public service in his later years (DML 2:190–230). To the extent that their reform was motivated by wishes to undo a traumatic past, it looks irresolutely backward, not toward innovation. Reform in this mood dreams of pastoral simplicities and spiritual sublimation. The post-traumatic anxiety that reform cannot control emerges dissociated in fantasies of the ultimate trauma, apocalyptic collapse, which is paradoxically not simply ultimate cosmic annihilation but also the ultimate purifying reform. This peculiar combination of themes still flourishes in post-traumatic culture today, as in the *Rambo* films, whose hero emulates the noble savage in his bat-tle against apocalyptic military-industrial evil.

Variants of mourning shaped other reformers also, including the great Victo-rian philanthropist and reformer Lord Shaftesbury, whose version of the Saint George paradigm was his dogged rescue of children and working people. Al-though he "was the leading political champion and public spokesman for legis-lation aimed at eliminating the abuses to which children were subjected," Lord Shaftesbury also "viewed his work as a losing battle against irresistible, evil forces."[56] With an orthodox, Augustinian imagination and what seems to me post-traumatic obsession, he kept returning to the plight of the child. "Behind his efforts," says Robert Pattison, "lay a mystical, apocalyptic view of society and religion, a marriage of Tory gloom and evangelical piety." He looked at the misery and vice about him, "saw that it was hopeless, and changed it anyway."[57] In this context, mourning manages guilt at the world's injustice by transforming loss into reparation.

However grave and dignified this mentality, the pressure of the hysteria behind it is palpable. The word "hysteria" itself points revealingly toward the famous clinic at the Salpêtrière in Paris, where in the last decades of the century Charcot was beginning to understand the "disorder" as a function of psychic trauma.[58] Culturally, the clinic's male doctors and their most famously tormented patients were unexpectedly in a relationship something like that of Haggard and his heroes to his sacrificial queen, Ayesha, in her spectacular final throes. In their seizures some of Charcot's patients used to fall into poses of flagrantly erotic or religious ecstasy. With special intensity—and like Ayesha—they acted out the radically split image of woman as saint and whore that Freud described in "The Most Prevalent Form of Degradation in Erotic Life."

Charcot's patient Geneviève emulated the possession of a stigmatized Belgian saint who was much celebrated in the Parisian press. Like the roughly contemporary American women who had conversion experiences,[59] the French women drew upon the repertory of religious feelings available to poor women in order to express their plight in a society with limited sympathy for them. Their Christian body language of "praying" and "crucified" seizures "unconsciously" gave them a heroic role that countered myths associated with sordid illness, degeneracy, despair, and death, even as Christ was supposed to undo original sin in the redemptive trauma of the crucifixion. This sacrificial ideation, shared in different ways by patients and physicians, is related to the theme of reform and the ultimate reform implied in millennial fantasies. It is possible to see the sacrifice of Ayesha in the Pillar of Fire as analogous to the sacrificial behavior of the women patients that so fascinated Charcot and his fellow clinicians. It suggests not simply misogyny or "fear" of women's power, but a complex of cultural fantasies. All those involved were caught up in versions of traumatic rescue. In their unconscious management of power relations, the period's gender and class expectations assumed grotesque forms. Like the stricken Queen Victoria, the "crucified" women were at once radically self-effacing and self-aggrandizing, as were the heroically "objective" doctors. In a sense all concerned were unwittingly competing to be saviors.

Nor was this all. Like Ayesha, the teasing, vain, fiery-tempered Geneviève had suffered the traumatic loss of a lover in her youth. Her young man had died of "cerebral fever" (from which Ayesha rescues Leo in *She*). "When her foster father refused to let her go to the funeral for fear of her nervousness, the young Geneviève escaped from home and ran to the cemetery at night. Trying to dig up the remains of Camille, she was overcome with a crisis and was found unconscious by his grave. She remained in this state for twenty-four hours. For the next year [cf. two millennia] she was sad, withdrawn, refusing to talk, often angry."[60] After her foster mother died she was hospitalized in Poitiers and eventually at the Salpêtrière, where in her "career as a professional hysteric" she wooed and captured the attentions of the heroic doctors rather as Ayesha is "reunited" with Leo and wins over the university "doctor" Holly.

As the doctors and their patients played different sorts of heroic roles, they were tacitly renegotiating power relations. The physicians were genteel authorities, while the women patients were indigent nobodies. For complex political and intellectual reasons, the scientists were eager to demystify religious superstition and "neurotic" saints, and as a result, in his public lecture-demonstrations Charcot inadvertently reinforced the patients' predilection for religious symbolism.[61] In fact, as we can now appreciate, the patients' "heroic" seizures were unwitting collaborations between the masterful doctors and their suggestible, helpless patients. Only when the doctors finally kept the patients separated and stopped reinforcing their symptoms did their iatrogenic hysterical symptoms subside and more-concrete conflicts in the patients' lives get needed attention.[62]

Unconsciously, the seizures in Charcot's clinic became a mediating theatrical zone in which the wishful heroic roles of male doctors and female patients could meet and, in bursts of synergistic fascination, focused in part by the mourning for lost health and childhood integrity, produce new meanings. For people who now sought in science the ultimate answers no longer convincing to them in religion, the potency of the saint was slipping into other roles, including the hysteric and the physician. Original sin took on a different significance when identified as a "hereditary taint."[63] Mourning was reshaping the world, generating a new faith in professional and institutional medicine, in secular models of illness, and ultimately in the emergence of psychology, of mind—that is, of the modernism so richly implicated in post-traumatic culture.

FOUR

Traumatic Prophecy

H. G. WELLS AT THE END OF TIME

> In our days there have arisen in more highly developed minds
> vague qualms of a Dusk of the Nations, in which all suns and stars
> are gradually waning, and mankind . . . is perishing in the midst of
> a dying world.
>
> Max Nordau, *Degeneration*

WHEN TRAUMA DISRUPTS the magic circle of everyday life, the effort to restore psychic integrity may entail a renewal of social bonds or withdrawal and
numbing. The work of H. G. Wells illuminates the conceptual space—I call it
a rift—between radical individualistic and social modes of post-traumatic coping. Wells's prophetic imagination projects into the future, magnified as if on a
movie screen, the shocks of modernism. Like one of the railway accidents that
contributed to the formulation of traumatic neurosis in the 1880s, *The Time Machine* (1895) presents a psychocultural crash. As he soars into time, the Time
Traveller panics. Losing control of his vehicle, he is flung some 802,701 years forward into a landscape of "ruinous splendor" that caricatures the modern world
he has left behind.[1] As Roosevelt and Haggard feared, "civilization as we know
it" has decayed and "we" have been supplanted by degenerate "others." Society's
aristocratic masters have devolved into infantile victims or—to give the joke its
proper bite—livestock. Faustian aspiration has devolved to "ape-like" Morlocks
akin to savages such as Tonga, "our cannibal ancestors of three or four thousand
years ago" (77), and an alienated, vengeful proletariat (57).[2] The two species or

social classes are locked into a murderous economy and traumatized by "the Great Fear" between them (*TM* 76).

While the Time Traveller presides over a comfortable social circle at home in London, the "Great Fear" of death anxiety lies just under the surface there. Sherlock Holmes's "stagnation" has become cosmic entropy. In Haggard's terms, the formidable She has shrunk to the flirtatious juvenile Weena, and the dying sun now threatens to consume not only the Pillar of Fire but the entire solar system. The immediate shock comes with the Traveller's demonstration to his dinner guests of his model time machine, whose amazing dematerialization is only the acceleration of ordinary time to reveal, like Ayesha suddenly aging, the death in store for everyone. In turn the full-scale time machine promises a means of transcending creaturely limits, only to deliver awareness into a nightmare future.

The traumatic nature of this awareness comes through poignantly in the earlier, *National Observer* version of the novel, which ends with the Time Traveller back home regaling his circle of friends. He is describing the extinction of life to them when he "stop[s] abruptly. 'There is that kid of mine upstairs crying. He always cries when he wakes up in the dark. If you don't mind I will just go up and tell him it's all right.'"[3] The irony here is mordant, because the Traveller's story wakes up childlike humanity to its terrifying cosmic futility. Because Wells himself suffered childhood nightmares and intermittent "anxiety dreams" throughout his life,[4] the child's distress in the novel may be seen as a direct representation of post-traumatic experience. In the final version of the novel the post-traumatic reaction is far more severe; the Traveller behaves like a berserk soldier, dashing graphically into the face of cosmic extinction.

In *The Time Machine* social and individualistic modes of coping with shock are in conflict. Time traveling involves a process of dissociation just as Holmes's drug visions do: a process of going out of the conventional mind and seemingly beyond creaturely limits, on a voyage to discover the ground—literally, the end—of life. At first the process brings a reassuring revelation, because the Time Traveller lands among the childlike, communal Eloi. But almost at once he begins to reexperience trauma more intensely than ever. "The Eloi . . . had decayed to a mere beautiful futility" (*TM* 71), and the Morlocks incarnate the predatory horror of Social Darwinism. The Traveller reacts with hypervigilance and, in his climactic rage against the Morlocks, a frenzy of berserking akin to combat breakdown. In a panic he flees back to London and then once more into time. As in the works of Conan Doyle and Haggard, psychic shock can find relief neither in other people nor in heroic individualism. As Holmes retires into a drugged torpor and Ayesha shrivels to dust, so in the end Wells dispatches his Traveller into the oblivion of time.

Wells offers a useful perspective on the rift between social bonding and visionary dissociation. Victorian ideas of progress seemed to record the natural evolution of ancient feudal-aristocratic social structures toward a middle-class ideal of individual freedom and democratic cooperation. Yet Wells's generation saw intractable inequities, with "robber barons" exploiting "wage slaves," and industrial culture aggregating and dehumanizing populations. In Wells's satiric *Tono-Bungay*, consumers are figuratively herd animals. In *The Island of Dr. Moreau* the Beast People are each unique yet cruelly bound by a "human" code that stands for culture and denies them autonomy. At the other extreme, Sherlock Holmes, Wells's Time Traveller, and the Invisible Man—or the industrial magnate Andrew Carnegie—grasp at godlike autonomy because the force-multiplier effect of knowledge and capital invites dreams of executive mastery.

Even Victorian science split humankind into the mass categories of technological, social-scientific culture in one direction and radical individualism in the other. What sort of creatures are we? Victorian Darwinists conceived of humans as solitary predators endowed with superior mental faculties. Only gradually did evolutionists acknowledge that we are highly sociable primates characterized by lifelong juvenile traits such as adaptive flexibility, cooperativeness, and curiosity. In the course of his early career Wells glimpsed that post-Victorian Darwinism without quite being able to grasp its significance. Again and again in his work, fantasies of cooperation and despotic violence melt into one another.

That conceptual conflict is directly related to post-traumatic culture. Familiar fantasies of traumatic heroism permeate *The Time Machine*. Slaughtering monsters, trying to save the maiden Weena, the Traveller brings back a cosmic revelation to the city, only to disappear in another sally, perhaps forever this time. Wells's personal and cultural situations, shaped his thinking, especially his poignantly limited evolutionary understanding. These conflicts matter because in novels such as *The Island of Dr. Moreau* (1896), *The Invisible Man* (1897), and *The War of the Worlds* (1898), as well as in Wells's prophetic books, they prefigure the traumatic themes of the twentieth century. This is after all the same imagination that in 1914, as Europe was dropping into the abyss, predicted nuclear warfare.[5]

In an era of stressful change, *The Time Machine* enabled readers to probe the boundaries of conventional Victorian reality and relieve the pressure of the unthinkable. As readers expanded the magic circle of everyday life by entertaining "the future," they could vicariously take the role of explorer-scientist, which was an important source of heroic values and consolation in the 1890s.[6] Like Haggard and Conan Doyle, Wells softens the pain of loss, even as he makes bearable the distant horror to come. In this way *The Time Machine* functions as a form of magical worry: an effort to neutralize dread by giving it a manageable form. Like allergy shots, the novel provokes anxiety to desensitize our responses.

Mourning among the Cannibals

Stranded in "the future," the shaken Time Traveller tries to contemplate the lost ground of experience: "All the activity, all the traditions, the complex organization, the nations, languages and literatures, aspirations, even the mere memory of Man as I knew him, had been swept out of existence" (TM 76). This is only partly true. For one thing, the Traveller readily identifies the Eloi as an aristocracy in decline. His interpretations of this new world suggest that for him the missing ground is not simply the dynamic 1890s but also the vanished England of great patrician estates such as Up Park that Wells idealized as a child. To make the point another way: Wells constructed his future out of materials at hand. *The Time Machine* satirizes topical concerns such as vegetarianism, flower-bedecked aesthetes such as Oscar Wilde, dilettante upper-class "communists" and utopians, and alienated proles. As in all satire, this implicit scorn also implies unstated values, and for Wells those values look backward as well as forward. In important ways, like Haggard, he generates his exotic otherness out of traumatic mourning.

The clearest sign of this is the novel's central fantasy of failed rescue. If the Traveller did save Weena from the Morlocks, what would he do with her in 1890s London? Exhibit her until she succumbed like Pocahontas? Given his painfully disproportionate power, how could he erase the suggestion of kidnapping? The rescue must fail for the same reason that the ideal mother, Ayesha, must die: you can't go home again. What's more, the effort to recreate the past alienates him from the present. Hence the mourning that closes the book. Returning from his ordeal, the Time Traveller echoes Holmes-Watson motifs. His brain has gone "stagnant" and he is now "limping" (108), and his restlessness to be off again has some of the detective's suicidal obsessiveness, just as the novel ends on an elegiac note.

The traumatic "crime" he unearths in the future is fratricidal rivalry. "Ages ago, thousand of generations ago, man had thrust his brother man out of the ease and the sunshine. And now that brother was coming back—changed!" (72). The originary traumas of the fall of Lucifer and of humankind evolve through Cain and Abel, and now "the Capitalist and the Labourer" (60), into the nightmare future of Eloi and Morlock. Like many Victorian Christians and Social Darwinists, Wells moralized evolution by focusing on merciless competition and analogizing it to Judeo-Christian originary trauma.[7]

Against this deterministic "curse" Wells sets a traumatic rescue fantasy. Beset by death anxiety, the Traveller turns the alien future landscape into a fantasia of cultural heroism, exploring sources of late-Victorian ideology and symbolic immortality. Mounted on the time machine like Saint George on his charger, he would deliver a maiden, the embodiment of fertility, from underworld monsters besieging the "ruined palaces" of the "upper" world and devouring the innocents. Surviving his messianic mission, ambiguously triumphant yet defeated, the hero entertains but cannot redeem the mentally walled-in city (London), and ultimately—like Saint George—rides offstage to his righteous doom. Late-Victorian novels about future wars tend to divide into fantasies of triumph and disaster, although even the disasters often function as a bracing call to arms. Wells's imagination has roots in the genre but is more complexly disturbing.[8]

Wells assembles his deliverer out of ideologically compatible ingredients. The Traveller first casts himself as scientist and detective, scholar and colonial explorer, gathering data and theorizing. But panic overcomes him. When he first misses his time machine, he suffers "a kind of frenzy" (TM 43) in which he falls and smashes his face bloody. Before long he begins to find the Eloi's terror of darkness contagious. As he tries to "find signs of the old constellations in the new confusion" of the heavens (76), he suddenly understands the cannibalistic economy around him. Instantly he shifts from astronomer-scientist to atavistic warrior-hero. He turns his mind to chivalric military technology—fortification (the walled city) and weapons (his improvised mace). At the climax of the novel he rampages like a combat soldier. In the symbolic vocabulary of imperialism the Traveller is the civilizing white man subduing prolific "ape-like" cannibals with a fury that anticipates Kurtz's cry in Joseph Conrad's *Heart of Darkness*, "Exterminate the Brutes!" Given the contemporary debate over that most vicious form of traumatic rescue—saving white women by lynching alleged black rapists in the American South—the Traveller's ferocious defense of Weena enjoys the freedom of indirection if not overt euphemism.[9]

Saint George's sally is finally a traumatic rescue because in a larger—veiled—context it cannot control the death anxiety that motivates it. In *The Time Machine*, rescue disintegrates into ambiguities and contradictions just as the constellations move into "new confusion." It can be argued, for example, that the novel supplies no clear evidence that the Morlocks are cannibals.[10] If persuasive, such a reading would relate the Traveller to the destructively suspicious European explorers of the New World,[11] or mad scientists such as Dr. Frankenstein. Even if we accept the Traveller's judgment, his heroism becomes progressively more futile, as if it too obeys the inexorable law of entropy that governs Wells's cosmos.

In part, rescue fantasy fails because it is always potentially a disguise for the sort of homicidal rivalry that terrorizes the novel. Almost from the start the Traveller seems to be looking for a justification for chivalric violence. At times his voice is an irrational mix of sadistic war cry and judicious technical report, as when he breaks apart a machine in the museum: "I had judged the strength of the lever pretty correctly, and I rejoined [Weena] with a mace in my hand more than sufficient, I judged, for any Morlock skull I might encounter. And I longed very much to kill a Morlock or so" (*TM* 83). The same tension between science and heroic aggression contributes to Holmes's drug use, even as fear of the conflict lies behind the self-destructive psychic split of Dr. Jekyll and Mr. Hyde, not to mention the anguish of J. Robert Oppenheimer after Hiroshima. To the end of his life, as demonstrated in *The Shape of Things to Come* (1933), Wells was fascinated by the idea of a benevolent despotism of samurai-scientist-executives subduing unruly humanity in order to rescue it.

The Time Machine directly dramatizes the counterphobic function of rescue fantasy: the Traveller's rescue of Weena from drowning "drove [dread of the Morlocks] out of my head." Weena, he explains, "was a pleasant substitute" (55). He saves her as Small saves Tonga, and like the "faithful mate" Tonga, she becomes a child-wife, a cultural "substitute" created to relieve the distress of "real" survival anxiety. As a surrogate wife, "the little doll of a creature presently gave my return to the neighborhood of the White Sphinx almost the feeling of coming home" (53). Domesticity maps the landscape, taming its terrors. At the same time, however, Weena is like the repudiated Morlock "others" she substitutes for insofar as rescue requires her inferiority—her closeness to death—in order to make the rescuer larger than life. It is partly to keep her from sliding back into "otherness," and partly to keep reinforcing his conviction of heroic immortality, that the Traveller must escalate his campaign against the Morlocks.

There is an element of child's play about this domesticated chivalry. The surrogate wife is "a little doll," a toy, a child, a lovely, vacuous Lolita who would initiate "a miniature flirtation." As a caricature of the upper-class lady, she exists to substantiate her savior while he "masters" the world's problems.[12] Yet this system of hero worship so infantilizes the idealized victim that she holds no interest for him outside the rescue fantasy. The Traveller is patronizingly impersonal with Weena. As a scientist he never seriously tries to enter into the strange lives around him, and in the last analysis we learn almost nothing about Weena. The traumatized scientist may well be less curious than the unseeing Morlocks who probe his face as he sleeps.

Superficially, the Time Traveller does play at inquiry. When he first meets the Eloi, he tries to learn their language like an anthropologist-explorer. But almost at once Victorian obsessions about production, utility, and authority distort his roles. Among these "little people" (*TM* 33), "I felt like a schoolmaster amidst children" (32). But instead of being disciplined model pupils, the Eloi prove to be distractible and playful. Like "children they would stop examining me and wander away after some other toy" (33). The self-appointed Gradgrind expects the natives to be the ambitious scholarship students that the young, upwardly mobile H. G. Wells wanted to be. Like the first European explorers in the New World, he is ambivalent about the natives' freedom from repression and character-building drudgery. He faults them for a "lack of interest," but that turns out to be their indifference to the drill that he associates with power and problem solving.

The Eloi's indifference to work seems to reflect the tensions created as Wells's generation became disenchanted with Victorian piety toward sacrificial labor, heroic ambition, and progress. Even the Time Traveller mocks his "absurd assumption that the men of the Future would certainly be infinitely ahead of ourselves" (68). In the 1890s leisure was finally changing the meaning of work in England, and reformers were freeing children from the work force into something like the modern developmental conception of childhood. Instead of signifying heroic or even cruel necessity—and symbolic immortality—labor could now be a cause of suicidal ennui, as many letter writers proposed during the newspapers' suicide "epidemic" about the time Wells was writing *The Time Machine*.[13] Leisure called into question a cluster of basic assumptions about social hierarchy, divine purpose, and finally the nature of subjectivity itself. For the Time Traveller, work is fundamentally a survival fantasy. Compared to the sober households guided by Mrs. Beeton, the Eloi palaces are slovenly: everything has a "dilapidated look," windows need reglazing, and curtains are "thick with dust" (*TM* 31). Their housekeeping violates a code that assumes that if you relax your vigilant self-control, "filthy" predators will grab you. In the Social Darwinists' terms: attend to business or die.

The Time Traveller heralds a favorite self-delusion of the twentieth century: praising science but practicing industrial technology and atavistic heroism. And just as his science is compromised, so his industry comes to nothing. Like Wells, the Traveller is a solitary inventor ill suited to cooperative productivity. Although he laments the Eloi's failures of mastery, his own heroic aggrandizement would make him a potentially murderous rival to them. He behaves as if his vision of universal bloodshed has traumatized him, leaving him unable to relate to others. He withdraws from the social bonds that humans most depend on to manage rivalry and bloodshed. The Eloi make an acceptable but "futile" (*TM* 71) compromise insofar as their infantilism prevents any fatal competition, but that infantilism also precludes the intimacy and cooperation that might help allay death anxiety. In effect, competition presses Wells to see others as "children," a maneuver that creates ambivalence in them—and that in turn splits them into beautiful, futile dependents and mutinous brutes. This imaginative maneuver fetishizes children and has much to do with the "epidemic" awareness of child abuse in our own time.

In the context of post-traumatic symptoms, the Traveller vacillates between flight and fight responses. He flees from death anxiety into a future that promises consoling scientific glory (and interest on prepaid investments!), but instead he finds repressed symptoms erupting in panic and berserking. The Eloi and Morlocks likewise caricature post-traumatic flight and fight. The Eloi's behavior suggests the dissociation and inhibition to be expected among people disempowered and chronically victimized. Distracted by day, they are gripped by anxiety at night, and easily startled at any time, as when the Time Traveller mimics a thunderclap.[14] As victims they suffer not only cannibalism, but also suggestively sexual probing in their sleep, as when the Time Traveller wakes to find Morlocks probing his face with hands like "the soft palps" of sea anemones (TM 54). In the air shaft's dark depths, feeling "the throb of the great pump" (69), he reacts as if to a threat of rape when the Morlocks' unseen hands begin "plucking at [his] clothing" and he is finally "grasped from behind, and . . . violently tugged backward" (69–70).

The Morlocks, by contrast, have been dehumanized, exploited, and driven underground, and have fixated on survival aggression. They seem hypervigilant—on the move night and day—and appear to carry out their depredations in a dissociated state. As former victims of the once-dominant Eloi, the Morlocks dramatize a widely held conviction among trauma psychologists: that predatory abusers often prove to have been abused themselves as children. Their role reversal suggests not only vindictiveness but a repetitive, obsessive-compulsive effort to undo past injury.

From this perspective, Wells creates his future by intensifying the post-traumatic symptoms latent in the conventional world around him. In the 1890s, as The Time Machine illustrates, he shared the widespread anxiety that "bad nerves" were progressively limiting people's autonomy. A world in the grip of post-traumatic symptoms was figuratively suffering a version of the relentless entropy so shocking in The Time Machine. The novel plays out the decade's fear that society was ill and decaying, or even "post-cultural."[15] At the same time, crucially, Wells's anxious reaction to that prospect reinforced some of the conflicts that contributed to the symptoms in the first place. Like the hysterical violence that climaxes it, the novel reacts to cultural distress with a vision that turns out deviously to be part of the problem.

The Child as Father to the Prophet

One way into the web of traumatic stress in Wells's early life is through his mother's shock over the death of his sister Frances. Wells attributed his mother's depression to her loss of that fervently idealized child. At his birth two years later, she "fixed her fears as well as her hopes on the new baby," or as he put it, she "decided that I had been sent to replace Fanny and to achieve a similar edification."[16] Wells was born into a scenario of traumatic rescue, but his lifelong fantasies of deliverance take on even more significance given the mournful, judgmental, and apocalyptic strains in his mother's religiosity. Like Conan Doyle and Haggard—and in a grimmer way, his mother Sarah—Wells coped with oppressive death anxiety through complex mourning behaviors. Sarah Wells modeled herself after the "supreme widow," Queen Victoria, whom Wells called "my mother's compensatory personality, her imaginative consolation for all the restrictions and hardships . . . imposed on her" (*HGW* 18).

Sarah Wells believed in an "unquestionable hierarchy" dominated by God the Father and Victoria. "From these two points in Sarah's firmament," Norman and Jeanne MacKenzie conclude, "all the lower ranks descended. It was an order that seemed threatened only by the harassments of the Devil, the temptations of sin, and the dangers of falling into the hell-fire of Victorian poverty" (ibid.). It would be hard to overstress the way in which modernism's prophet kept recreating in book after book the basic dynamics of his mother's social and religious imagination. *The Time Machine*, for instance, brilliantly and naively dramatizes its hero's hysterical dread of being pulled down into the Morlocks' demonic and socially degraded depths. In the MacKenzies' resonant phrase, this is "the hell-fire of Victorian poverty." The novel's imagery richly evokes the snobbery and apocalyptic terror mixed in his mother's depressive personality. Wells grew up on the outskirts of London's sordid slums, with no personal experience of their residents' suffering. "Just as my mother was obliged to believe in Hell, but hoped that no one would go there, so did I believe there was and had to be a lower stratum, though I was disgusted to find that anyone belonged to it. I did not think the lower stratum merited any respect" (*HGW* 32).

Yet like Dickens shuddering over his brief boyhood stint in the blacking factory, Wells was marked by his early struggles with poverty. His parents came from the equivocal world of upper servants in country houses, ambiguously managerial and yet below-stairs persons. His father was a failed shopkeeper, an ineffectual person with a sharp temper. The Oedipal rage in novels such as *The Invisible Man* (1897) and *The Holy Terror* (1939) suggests the fear and hostility Joe Wells inspired in his youngest child. The son was fourteen when his parents separated and he was "hastily pitched out of his home . . . caught up by the whirling fringe of a social revolution and whipped away into a new phase of life full of uncertainty and fear. His memory of that time was of an invading and growing disorder" (ibid.).

His mother became housekeeper at Up Park, a country house essentially bypassed by time and therefore a sort of museum of early-nineteenth-century culture (6, 37). The young Wells idealized the country-house system for nurturing the gentlemen-scientists of an earlier day. "The great estates, ruled by order and owned by enlightened guardians of scientific intelligence, provided him with the pattern for his utopian societies and cultivated elites which were to control them" (38). As a museum, Up Park resembled the palace of green porcelain where the Time Traveller seeks shelter and weapons. His panicky discovery of Morlock footprints there suggests Wells's lingering fear of being snatched back into the below-stairs darkness of the servants' world.[17]

The MacKenzies construe Wells's insecurity as a function of the psychic and social topography of his childhood. "Until he went up to London in 1884, he moved from one false start to another in towns and villages around its edge, hovering between the older, rural and in some ways more secure world in which his parents had grown up and the machine civilisation, full of uncertainties, tension and relentless change" (HGW 33). In all of his work Wells also "hovers"—as if on a time machine—between two worldviews: one sardonic, pessimistic, and modern; the other pastoral, romantic, nostalgic, and patrician. Like Sherlock Holmes, he would mediate between worlds, interpreting one to the other with the help of the all-embracing encyclopedias he advocated. After a zealous first year studying science at South Kensington, he nearly lost his scholarship when he backed away toward fiction and journalism; the earliest draft of The Time Machine dates from this period. Poverty and illness oppressed him in those years, but he also withdrew from a marriage to science as he was later to do from his wives and lovers.

As Arnold Bennett observed, Wells tended to see people as types or groups. He was an onlooker, an outsider. The Time Traveller typically finds himself between two species, "a position isotopic with the position of the petty bourgeois Wells."[18] But that compulsive distancing can also be seen as a habit of dissociation from painful intimate emotions, and The Time Machine caricatures that distancing, trying to repudiate it, in the depiction of the monstrous crabs on the final beach with their displaced "evil eyes . . . wriggling on their stalks" (TM 103). At the close of his life Wells countered his fear of dissociation and his dread of extinction with a consoling theory of collective immortality—a rhapsody of belonging.[19]

Like the prototypical Saint George, and many of his protagonists who go beyond the boundaries of the conventional world, Wells projects messianic roles that promise to anchor and integrate the self. Charging into the uncanny future, for example, the Time Traveller meets two split-off possibilities of Wells's childhood self that defined—and plagued—him all his life. In this psychic plot, Wells's creative imagination tries to rescue a playful, erotic aspect of himself from his own vindictive "subterranean" rage. The Traveller is unable to extricate the carefree, open-hearted "aristocratic" child he might have been from the clutches of the overworked, deprived, resentful child that he fears he may have become. Failing to pull himself together, he flees further ahead in time, shocked to encounter in the crabs a still more monstrous condensation of his motives: the grotesque eyes of the alienated "onlooker" at life, the mouth "all alive with appetite," and the "vast, ungainly claws" of overdeveloped defenses (*TM* 103). As a mode of self-analysis, ambiguously self-aware, this psychic plot half-recognizes but cannot confront the appalling monster potential in the self. Like Georg Groddeck and Freud, among others, Wells imagined subjectivity at a time when science and art were rapidly de-idealizing humankind's self-image, revealing "animal" motives and insoluble conflicts.

Wells countered by trying to recuperate messianic plots. In related ways the Time Traveller and the Invisible Man disappear into superhuman roles, while in *The Holy Terror*, Rud Whitlow becomes World Dictator and carries out a program borrowed without evident irony from Wells's utopian prophecy *The Shape of Things to Come: The Ultimate Revolution*. In the novel Wells subjected his own infantile fantasy to reality testing by following Whitlow's career past its wishful apex into suicidal decline. He described Whitlow as "the man who was so terrified by life that he could not feel safe until he was dictator of all mankind."[20] This scenario of terror and compensatory aggrandizement is quintessentially post-traumatic. On a personal scale, the scenario envisions obsessive-compulsive motives taking over behavior. Culturally, as in European fascism after World War I, world-building megalomania magically compensated for threatening change by naively conjuring up total—and totally controlled—change. In the event, perversely, the conjuring brought totalitarian world war and the total change of ruin.

Wells's messianism is the upper-world equivalent of the conflation of hell and poverty in the Victorian—and Sarah Wells's—imagination. Inasmuch as his messiahs are often scientist-sages, the wishful conflation of religion and science is also characteristic of Victorian compromises with modernism. But messianic rescue has a dark side too. In his *Experiment in Autobiography* (1934), Wells sought to objectify and exorcise the childhood syndrome of terror and compensatory omnipotence, not quite recognizing it as the motive energy behind the prophetic voice in his books. "Adolf Hitler is nothing more than one of my thirteen year old reveries come real," he confesses. Poignantly he dismisses this infantile aberration as "my Hitler phase."[21] As in some other forms of traumatic rescue, the Hitler analogy reveals the drive toward love and deliverance that masks rage. Because even righteous omnipotence cannot finally dispel death, the Hitler-child dreams of buying love and immortality by killing scapegoats. In a traumatic crisis Griffin, the Invisible Man, physically and emotionally effaces himself. Out of savage poverty he robs his own father, causing his suicide. Whereupon Griffin begins a reign of terror—with intentional allusions to the French Revolution—that would relieve his own trauma by making trauma a strategy for subjugating the world. But in the end, like the self-confounding Rud Whitlow, he is hunted down by implacably conventional folks and put to death, with the narrator's irony insinuating a sort of martyrdom.

Wells's ambivalence about this rage makes more sense in the context of the illness that imperiled him for a decade or more as a young man. At age twenty-one he was diagnosed with tuberculosis and "filled with a fear and resentment of death" (HGW, 71). A year later (1888), still unwell and depressed, he pictured himself as a wounded soldier who has "dropped out of the marching column." He wrote to a friend, "My life work will be to give as little trouble as possible in an uncongenial universe while I stay therein and try not to leave too big a hole in anybody else's world when my creation terminates" (75). The goal of dying and leaving "not too big a hole" in others' lives suggests fantasies of invisibility such as those Griffin pursues, although the invalid had apparently not yet discovered or faced up to his alter ego's murderous rage for immortality.[22] But that rage pursued Wells to the end of his life. In his last decade, as the MacKenzies feelingly point out, the aging prophet was still trapped in a nightmare. "Though he powerfully expressed the underlying anxiety of his times he offered no acceptable means of discharging it, and he became increasingly isolated and frustrated. Behind the rhetoric of his repeated appeals for the salvation of mankind there was a cry for help, for personal salvation from the nightmare of extinction" (HGW 412–13).

This vulnerability also helps explain the young man's attraction to science; even as science was supporting fantasies of irresistible material progress in the 1890s, its disenchantment of traditional doctrines also focused suicidal motives. Cruel scientists such as Wells's Griffin and Dr. Moreau played to Victorian fears that Darwinism would dethrone the cosmic Father and license revolt among his children. Like Lucifer, Griffin and Moreau usurp legitimate authority and grasp at power. But in their invisibility and isolation, they also dramatize post-traumatic numbness and dissociation. Regarding all creatures as "mere" animals, they no longer feel any bonds. The Darwinian vivisectionist Moreau no longer registers the howls of pain he causes. In moralizing science in such figures, Wells shared his culture's need to assimilate a new worldview that was truly overwhelming to the extent that it foregrounded the prospect of individual annihilation and ultimate human extinction.

Wells's childhood and cultural distress help explain why he seized on some aspects of Darwinism and not others—and reciprocally, his particular grasp of evolution sharply illuminates the world that formed him. At the end of his life

Wells was intrigued by the idea of neoteny in human evolution—that evolving primates have preserved juvenile characteristics and the adaptive flexibility of the young into their adult lives. In hopeful moods, Wells seized on the idea of neoteny and the sociable behaviors that follow from it. Yet he was never able to shake off his personal, late-Victorian conception of evolution as a progressive hardening of traumatic symptoms.

Traumatic Evolution

The Victorian reception of Darwinism is, among other things, a record of cultural efforts to come to terms with death. Besides controverting traditional religious doctrine, Darwinism disrupted the magic circle of personal and cultural narcissism by situating humankind among the animals in an adaptive struggle doomed to end in meaningless extinction. *The Time Machine* represents one effort to assimilate this cognitive shock. The culture vigorously rationalized the threat. Some openly repudiated Darwinism, while others massaged it into conformity with existing verities and consolations. Some agile churchmen tried to maintain that natural selection was only a technical term for the benevolent hand of God. But philosopher-scientists could be limber too. From "the survival of the fittest," Social Darwinism recuperated old-fashioned notions of hierarchy and warrior-heroism and mated them with modern enthusiasms for progress and productivity.[23]

Conservative tamers of Darwin minimized the role of chance and the play of genetic possibilities in evolution while promoting a reassuring sort of determinism. "Survival" became an absolute value, for example, and "proved" the absolute worth of the "fittest." Andrew Carnegie used this rhetoric to praise millionaires in his *Gospel of Wealth*, raising a cathedral of sanctimonious capitalism that still defies the laws of gravity in Washington and elsewhere today.[24] Nor was "survival" merely rhetoric; the great philanthropist had just crushed the last union at his Homestead mill in 1892, leaving some steelworkers as dead as any Morlock. As R. A. Rappaport succinctly puts it, "Sanctification transforms the arbitrary into the necessary, and regulatory mechanisms which are arbitrary are likely to be sanctified."[25]

Pseudo-Darwinian determinism implicitly sanctified the status quo, grounding society's inconsistencies and irrationality in a new conviction of natural authority. The varieties of pseudo-Darwinism worked to rebuild cultural morale and to substantiate puny humans—especially rich puny humans—in the world. In this sense the theories were a cultural technology for converting survival anxiety into a new, robust conviction of power and symbolic immortality.[26] Andrew

Carnegie ends his sermon on wealth by rhapsodizing about the rich man's ability to squeeze through the eye of the needle into heaven. From the biblical text Carnegie extracts—I am tempted to say "extorts"—the faith that the rich will be accepted into God's neighborhood and live forever. He never mentions that economic failure symbolically and sometimes literally means death. Even the upbeat plutocrat needed to warp Darwinism away from death.

But determinism could console the poor too, just as fatalism supported the ancient Egyptian peasant. Even a painful destiny may be co-opted to serve an apparently submissive human will. This was Queen Victoria's strategy for controlling death anxiety and grief when she sacralized and fixated on Albert's death. And it was a characteristic maneuver of the age. It is a subtle step from accepting God's will to identifying with—sharing in, codirecting—God's will. Emulating the queen, even dressing like her, Wells's mother Sarah managed adversity by trying to spy out divine necessity and conform herself to it. And in a different but related way, so did her ostensibly rebellious son H. G. The essence of the behavior is passive assertion, or even passive aggression. It is evident in the way the prophetic Wells submitted to an apocalyptic vision and used it to support messianic fantasies of saving the world through his superior insight. One model for this imaginative maneuver is the idea of Christ the crucified Son submitting to, and sharing in, the will of the Father, so that by his self-sacrifice he comes to command and deliver humankind. Almost always in Wells's work, meditations on extinction are matched by fantasies of self-aggrandizement. Even his most rigorous thinking about evolutionary possibility usually reveals some sort of determinism at work, and shows the vestigial outlines of Victorian ideologies. His distortions matter because half-unwittingly they anticipate many of the twisted shapes science and evolution have taken in the twentieth century.

One way of getting at these distortions is to look at the evolutionary concept of neoteny. Wells alludes to neoteny in the final pages of *The Shape of Things to Come*, one of his later prophecies of world catastrophe and therapeutic scientific despotism. As first defined by J. Kollmann (1884), neoteny is the evolutionary process in which the regulatory system retards ancestral developmental rates so that in humans—in fact, in the whole primate order—neotenates still look and act like juveniles when they are reproductively adults. The process of retarded allometric development produces adult animals that retain the increased adaptive flexibility of the young.

The Shape of Things to Come pretends to be a dream diary kept by a League of Nations official. Like the time machine, the dreams supposedly have penetrated time. The dreamer has been able to read a future textbook that recounts history from the actual early twentieth century, through a calamitous world war, a reconstructive period of "Puritan Tyranny," and finally a sort of millennial near-utopia. This future advertises Wells's belated fervor for eugenics and a familiar Lamarckian wishfulness about the heritability of desirable cultural traits.[27] With artistic sleight of hand he salts his visionary rhetorical stardust with daring statistical nuggets—"the Behaviour Control Report for [the year] 2104," his dreamer tells us, "records 715 cases of stealing for the whole world."[28] With an old man's doggedness he revisits his favorite themes: the menacing "abyss of extinction" (STC 426), deliverance by an oligarchy of military-scientific wise men, integrated world government, a world encyclopedia even more promising than the Internet,[29] and a revolutionary "new pattern of living" to be "imposed" upon "our race" (STC 431).

Where this sibylline exercise turns a fresh corner is near the end, when the narrator describes near-utopian humankind as neotenic. He announces a "difference in the age cycle between ourselves and our ancestors, which has prolonged the youthful phase and shifted on the valid years towards the thirty-five to eighty period" (426). In the remote past "our ancestor species [was] in a phase of almost fundamental individualism." While early man "was as solitary an animal as the tiger," he passed "through stages of increasing sociability. The onset of these stages was made practicable by the retention of immature characteristics into adult life. The same thing is happening to the remnant of lions today. They remain cubbish and friendly now to a much later age" (427).

A split soon develops in this train of thought. "The history of mankind . . . is a story of ever increasing communication and ever increasing interdependence" (ibid.). "What has happened during the past three and a half centuries to the human consciousness has been a sublimation of individuality" (428). Yet almost in the same breath Wells insists that "the history of mankind is also a history of education and compulsion. . . . Man almost up to the present day has remained at heart still the early savage, caring only for himself, for his sexual life, and during the few years of their helplessness, his children. He has been willing to associate for aggression or for defence, but only very reluctantly for a common happiness. He has had to barter his freedom for the advantages of collective action, but he has done so against the grain, needing persuasion, pressure and helpful delusion" (427–28).

Humankind is somehow both profoundly sociable and individualistic. In Wells's imagination these two possibilities are disconnected at a deep level, just as they were in his culture. Victorian sensibilities celebrated the power of a childlike purity of heart in social life, and reformers drafted blueprints for socialism and communism. Yet in Victorian political and economic ideology, not to mention masculine survival fantasies, the hallowed virtues are "adult" characteristics: individual fitness, competitive strength, discipline, fixity of purpose, and the like.

Neoteny occurs when the environment changes rapidly and profoundly enough to render some of a species' adult genetic traits less adaptive than its youthful ones. Over many generations neoteny results in a species that retains its ancestral youthful characteristics throughout its life history.[30] Most writing on neoteny concerns the evolution of physical or anatomical traits, yet the same argument can be extended to inherited behavioral or psychological traits. By this argument, the human species not only looks more like youthful than adult chimpanzees or gorillas, but in some important ways also behaves more like them. Coppinger and Smith, for example, have argued that neotenic mammalian species such as humans continue throughout life to display typically youthful propensities to play, to be curious, to solicit care, to be timid and docile.[31] If humans have inherited "the extremely social instincts of youthful primates" rather than "typical adult animal behaviors such as territoriality or dominance hierarchy,"[32] neoteny can help to explain how early humans became fitted for their migratory way of life during the last few million years. The same qualities have probably diminished much species-specific recognition behavior and supported the youthful care-soliciting behavior that since the last ice age has brought humans and all their various domesticated animals into an alliance so prolific that it is "threatening the extinction of all wild species that are habitat-specific, highly specialized and independent."[33]

Throughout his life, Wells's interests kept bringing him close to the idea of neoteny. The Eloi and Morlocks have many juvenile traits, for example, but the novel scorns them as maladaptive. In the 1930s Wells wrote *The Science of Life* with Julian Huxley at a time when Huxley was exploring neoteny. Yet Wells only began to grasp the concept at the close of *The Shape of Things to Come*, the year after Huxley's *Problems of Relative Growth* came out. To ask why he missed or resisted the idea is to unpack some of Wells's distinctive prejudices, but also some of the major cultural shifts of his lifetime.

For the early Wells, neotenic traits signified not adaptive advantage but liability. With "their little pink hands," hairless faces, "little chins," and "large and mild" eyes, the Eloi present conspicuously juvenile proportions (*TM* 28). But the Eloi are helpless, and the Morlocks rigidly predatory, each imprisoned in a specific environmental niche. The Eloi's "social paradise" (38) disguises nature red in tooth and claw. In part this is Wells the susceptible young journalist echoing Max Nordau (*Degeneration*, 1892) and other fashionable Jeremiahs. But invasion novels and a shifting balance of international power justified some disquiet. By 1896, "faced with the ominous rise in German militarism and the recalcitrant tendencies of British society," Herbert Spencer had become pessimistic enough to foresee in the conclusion of the third volume of *The Principles of Sociology* "at least the possibility of a catastrophic 'bursting of bonds,' a tragic return to war which would constitute 'extinction' not 'progress.'"[34] The sinister underside of Germany's modernization resonates with the Morlocks' subterranean menace.

But Wells's conception of Darwinism also reflects a much wider array of influences. His teacher T. H. Huxley carefully preserved a moral dimension in evolution. For Huxley, intelligence and culture placed man "as on a mountain top, far above the level of his humble fellows, and transfigured from his grosser nature by reflecting, here and there, a ray from the infinite source of truth."[35] Such tacitly religious rhetoric grounded the new science in the ancient hierarchy of patriarchal values. He modifies Christianity's dualism and conviction of cosmic purpose without relinquishing them. For all his iconoclasm, Huxley's mountaintop rises into a Victorian Christian sky, lifting his superior humans toward visionary immortality.[36]

Whereas neoteny finds adaptive value in juvenile traits, many Victorian Christians and Darwinians shared ancient prejudices about childhood.[37] Augustinian theology saw the child as a chaotic, excremental creature akin to the brutes and in need of firm adult discipline. The Augustinian child is close to the lowly origins that Christians—and even the skeptical Huxley—sought to transcend. Social Darwinism especially resonated with Augustinian fantasies by making virtues out of supposedly "adult" traits such as competition, self-discipline, tenacity, muscular strength, and individualism—characteristics that in neotenic terms are fixed and potentially maladaptive. Darwin, by contrast, "argued that the moral sense or conscience was derived from a feeling of dissatisfaction at the non-fulfillment of an innate tendency to sociable behavior."[38] Only in *Mutual Aid* (1902) did Peter Kropotkin make his famous case for the adaptive benefits of cooperation.

As James Kincaid has pointed out, adult projections and the internal contradictions of the period made childhood endlessly plastic.[39] Like women, children were objects of polarized feeling, complexly idealized and degraded. The Victorian cult of the child spun an enchanted aura of tender, often erotic pathos. In the 1890s, for example, the Pre-Raphaelite Thomas Cooper Gotch was painting portraits and allegories "in which the idea of childhood is treated as something mystical, even holy."[40] Those tutelary spirits of the household, Mrs. Beeton and Mrs. Ellis, anticipated the twentieth century's Dr. Spock in urging the parent "to make her child feel that home is the happiest place in the world," and that "a happy childhood is the best preparation possible for the realities and hardships of later life."[41]

Yet this idealization countered Augustinian assumptions that persisted (in bewildering mutations) throughout the century, as visions of individual fulfillment, industrial efficiency, and pastoral traditionalism clashed in bewildering ways. Some enlightened medical authorities and parents deliberately delayed the exposure of young children to educational rigors in order to prevent over-taxed young nerves. But as contemporary sources attest, old attitudes yielded slowly. Sarah Wells's religion and many medical commentaries tangled children in a net of prescriptive controls. Some doctors tended to medicalize cultural alarm over defective training and infantile rebelliousness, devising morally charged treatises on bedwetting and harnesses to restrain or punish erotic be-haviors in children. Economic life stressed not the fluent give-and-take of chil-dren's play but industrial efficiency, bureaucratic order, and above all profit. On yet another level, racial chauvinism identified "lesser breeds" both with chil-dren and with the apes popularly imagined to be our ancestors.

The reaction against Augustinian values and the improved quality of nurture by no means signified that people had grasped the idea of neoteny as an evolu-tionary justification for changes in child rearing. In the early 1890s, Wells ex-plored educational issues in articles for the *Educational Times* and the *Pall Mall Gazette*, in sympathy with developmental views of childhood such as those of Johann Heinrich Pestalozzi. But like Wilde's cry in *De Profundis* that we are all childlike, the idea of "childlike qualities" remained morally and ideologically charged. Increasing insight into child development set the stage for a revalua-tion of evolution, but the idea of neoteny seems to have required too many breaks with the past to be readily assimilated.

The process of change produced teasing paradoxes and fitful insights. Late Victorians worried volubly about a fatigued white race falling back into the beautiful, futile childishness that debilitates Wells's Eloi. The fear that the stress of modern life was sapping manliness inspired an ambivalence toward primitive men, who seemed disturbingly barbaric and yet full of impressive vitality. One result was a not always coherent educational movement that prescribed a boy-hood of natural, healthy savagery. Instead of prematurely constraining the boy to be a "little man," education was supposed to develop a boy's "savage" vigor. Although such theories gave "natural" childhood a place in the lives of men, they continued to focus on the adult man, even a superman, as the ultimate goal.[42]

Although Wells agreed with many of its underlying concerns, the belief in healthy primitivism contrasts with his conviction in *The Shape of Things to Come* that contemporary man was still "an early savage" in his "selfishness" and willingness "to associate for aggression or for defence, but only very reluctantly for a common happiness" (427). Perilously ill himself as a young man, Wells seems to have coped with the threat of physical enervation through faith not in therapeutic savagery but in rational controls and technology—especially in so-cial schemes for the provision of nutrition and shelter. When he associates the primitive and the child, as he does with the Morlocks, for example, he finds the resulting vitality sinister and degenerate. If they come together he imagines that the primitive will overcome or adulterate the qualities of the child.

Victorian fantasies about childhood and race are unthinkable apart from assumptions about gender. Wells's audience would have classified most neotenic characteristics as feminine, subject to the culture's ambivalence toward women. Insofar as the revered mother was the model of respectability and domestic management, neotenic qualities were probably most evident in girlhood, in courtship behaviors, and in relations among women, where culturally sanctioned "adult" characteristics were less important than sociability, care soliciting, play, and the like. Exactly these qualities hover about the clusters of nude water nymphs in Pre-Raphaelite paintings. The coquettish, pathetic Weena exhibits some excusable care-soliciting behaviors in coaxing the Time Traveller into "a little rubbing of limbs" (*TM* 52). By comparison, neotenic traits actually signal danger as stereotyped in the seductive aggression of the femme fatale. But then, to explain original sin, Augustinian tradition focused on the juvenile qualities in Eve—on her curiosity, impulsiveness, and indiscriminate sociability, especially toward strangers.

In *The Time Machine*, pseudoneoteny reflects many Augustinian assumptions about childhood and gender, all of them intensified by an apocalyptic dread that owes much to Sarah Wells's religious zeal. Wells stressed the Morlocks' morphological changes and their adaptation to meet material needs. Why then should they become fixed in such inefficient predation?[43] The Time Traveller moralizes their behavior as revenge, evoking Cain and Abel. "Generations ago, man had thrust his brother man out of the ease and the sunshine. And now that brother was coming back—changed!" (*TM* 72). The fantasy of revenge owes its power to conflicts over competition that the novel assumes its readers will share.[44] At the same time, these distressing adult issues are displaced onto ancient "brothers" and the Morlocks are characterized as half-civilized and immature "things." As abused, angry inferiors, the Morlocks fill an ideological niche in Victorian culture that had been inhabited by rioting apprentices in early-modern London, and is inhabited in today's media and film lore by depraved juvenile gangs, neo-Nazi skinheads, and drug-crazed teenage psychopaths. Wells's treatment of them suggests the pressure of repressed guilt.

The Time Traveller's pity for the victimized Eloi and his outrage at the predatory Morlocks expresses a parental ambivalence toward the young. Unlike their forebears, Victorian parents were increasingly concerned not to break the spirit of their children in order to extinguish "the old Adam." The Eloi reflect anxieties about the dangers of inculcating too much submissiveness or not enough self-discipline, just as the Morlocks suggest fears of arousing uncontrollable hatred through too much severity. The novel imagines a parent figure among pseudochildren who are beyond the parent's control. Authority and nurture are alike in crisis. Even in depicting Weena's childish female dependency, the Traveller makes affection a liability. The Eloi are generally erotic, but they pay for it on Morlock dinner tables.

The Traveller's obsession with parental authority signals his anxiety about regulating competition within as well as between families. He has landed in a world in which individual autonomy is dangerously scarce, a world in which the Victorian parent must strike out at alienated children to recover the stolen time machine that stands for adult autonomy and the freedom to move. With Morlocks constantly menacing him for food, the Traveller defends his desire "to go killing one's own descendants! But it was impossible, somehow, to feel any humanity in the things" (TM 83–84). The parent-child competition here expresses a wide range of generational, class, and gender conflicts.

To complicate matters, although the Traveller rages at hostile youth, the child in him fears shadowy, hostile parents. When he first sights "white, ape-like creatures . . . carrying some dark body," he feels premonitory dread and thinks of them as ancestral "ghosts."[45] A moment later his anxiety about predatory parents reminds him that, as "the younger Darwin" speculated, "the planets must ultimately fall back one by one into the parent body," the sun (TM 56). Like the shafts that house the Morlocks and can suck in a scrap of paper, these images suggest parental reabsorption or cannibalism. But this infanticidal ideation is also compatible with the late-Victorian trope of vampirism. The vampire usurps the victim's will and dramatizes the dread that, in a world without enough autonomy to go around, powerful others may capture you. A parent or parent figure may usurp or "take back" the child's will. Marx envisioned capital as a vampire preying on labor.[46] The Time Traveller fears that the Morlocks will probe and in effect master him as he lies sleeping like a child, feeling "drowned" (TM 52). During the climactic mayhem, he experiences the Morlocks as vampire children, their "little teeth nipping at my neck" (92). But it is significant that the minute he recovers from his ordeal the Traveller attacks his dinner "with the appetite of a tramp" (108), smacking his lips over "good wholesome meat" (108).

These infantile fantasies implicate another pattern of anxieties that the Morlocks and Eloi evoke. In different ways, both groups exhibit the morphological and behavioral sexual ambiguity of children that is characteristic of neoteny. The Time Machine debuted in an England horrified and fascinated to have Oscar Wilde and homosexuality on trial. In a letter to a Tory journalist in 1894, Wilde identified the fin de siècle with artistic achievement as opposed to cultural decadence: "All that is known by that term I particularly admire and love. It is the fine flower of our civilisation: the only thing that keeps the world from the commonplace, the coarse, the barbarous."[47] Wilde puts flowers in opposition to barbarity just as Wells does in opposing the flower-bedecked Eloi and the Morlocks. Moreover, the Eloi are passive and androgynous; the Morlocks' stealthy probing of sleepers and groping aggression in the tunnel imply a fear of homosexual rape and submission. Given Oscar Wilde's use of the Parisian homosexuals' dyed-green carnation as an icon, it is at least suggestive that the routed Time Traveller loses Weena and narrowly escapes back to London with a telling exotic flower that focuses all the excitement and awe of his homosocial dinner circle.

As Robert Pattison points out, English culture has balanced Augustinian pessimism about the child with a tradition he derives from Pelagius, which centered on Christ the wise child teaching in the temple.[48] This tradition expands the trope of the sacrificial, innocent lamb and supports a nurturant parenting ethos. It is symptomatic of conflicted Victorian attitudes that Wells shifts the Pelagian traits onto the feeble, beautiful Eloi with a mixture of pathos and scorn. Although he chivalrously defends them, the Time Traveller is nonetheless ambivalent toward the Eloi, rather as public opinion was toward "degenerate" hippie "flower children" in the 1960s.[49]

In disparaging children's fascination with toys, the Traveller perpetuates older ideas of children as economic instruments to be harnessed into social fitness. He never recognizes that play is basic in human development, important to adults and children. The hostility to play is revealingly keyed to the Traveller's fear of the Eloi's dependency, his resentment of their lack of productivity, and his fear of their incapacity for self-defense (TM 52–53). Although he is an inventor, he shows no appreciation of the heuristic, improvisatory nature of play as a means of mastering an environment. On the contrary, childhood means the loss of self-control, as when he reacts to the loss of the time machine by "bawling like an angry child" (44). The loss of autonomy also figures in his fear of being "examined" in his bed while asleep, like a child under a parental gaze—a fear that accords with the proverb that "children should be seen but not heard." Indirectly the child's diminished autonomy helps account for the Eloi's alarming loss of individuality and gender difference as well as their "communism."[50]

By the 1930s, other voices were qualifying Victorian Darwinism by emphasizing the adaptive values of cooperation and social life. To Freud's argument in *Civilization and Its Discontents* that aggression is an original, instinctual disposition in humankind, Havelock Ellis replied, echoing Peter Kropotkin, "As regards the primary impulse of aggression, I would not object to this if you insisted equally on a primary impulse of mutual help. If the primary aggressive impulse was predominant,—we should not be here! A species can only survive by the predominance of the impulse of mutual help."[51] In July 1929, in marginal comments to Wells on the early, serialized version of *The Science of Life*, G. B. Shaw ridiculed the persistence of old ideas: "All this dreadful dead wood must be cut out when you republish in book form, and replaced by modern Creative Evolutionary theory. . . . A good deal of [recent theory] may be rubbish; but at all events it is undetected and unexplored rubbish, and more amusing than the Victorian dust heap you are raking up. And it is at least full of hope and encouragement, whereas your stuff leads to nothing but cynical pessimism, despair and Schrecklichkeit."[52]

As Wells tried to come to terms with old age in the 1930s, he began pushing the consoling idea of "collective immortality." The fantasy tacitly draws on neotenic social bonding. Given his lifelong anxiety about extinction, Wells may have been attracted to neoteny partly because it enabled him to rationalize an existential refusal to accept the finality of fixed roles and ultimately death itself. In *The Time Machine*, pseudoneoteny focuses Wells's fear of death on decadence and compensatory fantasies of heroic aggression. By contrast, neotenic socialization and plasticity offered Wells in his last years a consoling vision of cooperation, nurture, and symbolic immortality.

In addition, because juvenile behavior relies so much on play, it implies a value system that may have given Wells some relief from the grimly competitive— "predatory"—values of the young man who had struggled up from poverty half a century earlier. In glancing at neoteny he may have been trying to get beyond the workaholic survival motives of his youth. Perhaps it would be more accurate to say that Wells periodically rebelled against "adult" fixity all his life—not only in his self-renewing love affairs, but even in the irresolute retreat from the discipline of laboratory science at South Kensington that turned him into a journalist and indirectly brought *The Time Machine* into being. In this sense, neoteny provided a "scientific" justification for his own characterological need for gregarious, heuristic play. It offered him a means to rethink and resist the obsessive, traumatic doctrines that had formed him, from apocalyptic entropy to chivalric violence.

It is symptomatic of Wells and of his time that he was unable to make more of neoteny. *The Shape of Things to Come*, after all, enlists the concept to serve a familiar prophetic program. Its rhetorically driven arguments are closed to the sorts of insights that have led to post-Victorian Darwinism: specifically to the new skepticism that a particular gene produces a particular cultural effect, and to the shift in emphasis away from biological determinism to biological potentiality.[53] Perhaps most threatening of all to an animal that substantiates itself in the world through symbolic order and meaning, post-Victorian Darwinism is open to the role of chance in evolution. A century after *The Time Machine* was published, evolutionary theories make more room for stochastic change. Eric White puts it succinctly:

The "postmodern" stance toward the natural world . . . entails an alternative emplotment of evolutionary history. If themes of *intelligibility, transcendence,* and *purpose* are prominent in narratives based on the Modern Synthesis, many recent evolutionists from the 1970s at least, would sooner highlight in their depictions of the course of biological evolution themes of *complexity, finitude,* and *freeplay.* These critics of the Modern Synthesis have argued that Darwin did not himself support what Stephen Jay Gould and Richard Lewontin have labelled the "Panglossian paradigm" of adaptive optimization.[54]

Recent humanistic analyses of Darwinism have stressed its historical particularity and its constructedness.[55] Every generation faces the problem of how to find language and theories more adequate to the ineffable complexity of evolutionary possibilities. But there is a second problem too, as Wells's use of neoteny illustrates: how to overcome the creaturely denial that defends us against death anxiety and the world's overwhelming complexity at the cost of restricting our vision. The idea of intelligibility is a consoling anodyne, as handy and irresistible as a Victorian headache powder. Today as in Wells's day, science readily devises intellectual maneuvers that attempt, in Davydd Greenwood's words, "to domesticate Darwinism's randomized, liminal world in motion and render it less fearsome."[56] In *Climbing Mount Improbable* (1996), Richard Dawkins still uses Thomas Henry Huxley's idealizing metaphor of the mountain to describe evolution.[57]

So many basic evolutionary processes remain unfathomed that it makes no sense to fault Wells for his peculiar angle of vision. We are transitional creatures, in the middle of something, not atop a peak with a telescope in hand. In the 1930s, the world depression amplified unresolved survival anxiety and paranoia from World War I. Although Keynesian "pump-priming" metaphors are closer to play than is the prevailing ideology of sacrifice and grim perseverance, the connection with neoteny was bound to seem far-fetched. And the shock of irrationality has by no means dissipated. Modern industrial warfare herds masses of obedient, gregarious young soldiers together like sheep and then describes the slaughter with a heroic vocabulary borrowed from Homer. What kind of animals are we? The problem cries out for more thought and fewer bugle calls.

In this context it does matter that in *The Shape of Things to Come,* Wells cannot see that his prophetic dream of an oligarchy of wise men is retrograde. Nor can he recognize the need for a revolution in feeling away from the sadistic-triumphal themes of punishment and industrial might that shaped European culture—as they continue to distort ours. After all, we too compulsively overestimate our "adult" traits.

In a perverse way, despite his transparent sentimentality, Wells was not merely shrewd but emotionally coherent in the speech he gave at a seventieth-birthday dinner organized by PEN to honor him in October 1936. After the guests' tributes, Wells said he felt like "a little boy at a lovely party, who has been given quite a lot of jolly toys and who has spread his play about on the floor. Then comes his Nurse. 'Now Master Bertie,' she says, 'it's getting late. Time you began to put away your toys.'" Wells added: "I hate the thought of leaving. . . . Few of my games are nearly finished and some I have hardly begun."[58] This valediction catches some of the great themes of his life, including his transformation from below-stairs poverty to "Master Bertie" of the jolly toys and doting nurse. But it also sums up his intellectual life as child's play, with a sort of humility and candor that puts in a healthy and moving perspective some of the anxious distortions of his prophetic self.

Wells's messianic fantasies are moving to behold in his old age because they still defend against the traumatic themes of his youth: terrors summed up in the Invisible Man's nightmare that as he stands among the mourners at his father's funeral, a homeless child, unseen and helpless, "overwhelming forces" are crowding him into the open grave, about to bury him alive.[59] The symbolic logic of that graveside nightmare affected Oscar Wilde as well, and Wilde also balanced between fantasies of messianism and immobility tantamount to burial alive, although he sought to cope in a strikingly different way.

FIVE

Post-traumatic Style

OSCAR WILDE IN PRISON

> Oscar Wilde . . . was the superb comedian of his century, one
> to whom misfortune, disgrace, imprisonment were external and
> traumatic. His gaiety of soul was invulnerable.
>
> G. B. Shaw, letter to H. G. Wells

> He was prisoned in thought. Memory, like a horrible malady, was
> eating his soul away.
>
> Oscar Wilde, The Picture of Dorian Gray

ON NOVEMBER 21, 1895, while serving his two-year sentence for "indecent acts," Oscar Wilde was transferred to Reading prison. "Handcuffed and in prison clothing, he had to wait on the platform at Clapham Junction from two to half past two on a rainy afternoon. A crowd formed, first laughing and then jeering at him. One man recognized that this was Oscar Wilde and spat at him. 'For a year after that was done to me,' Wilde wrote in De Profundis, 'I wept every day at the same hour and for the same space of time.'"[1] Wilde's post-traumatic reaction—the sort of intrusion Freud called "repetition compulsion"—dramatizes the social ground of identity. For the supreme individualist and champion of Epicurean self-control, rejection was devastating.

The incident at Clapham Junction is especially significant because Wilde had earned his celebrity—and paid his bills—by ministering to the unsettled mood of the time. From the start, as the aesthete *terrible* on the lecture circuit in America in 1882, he rebelled against philistinism and extolled self-fulfillment to a clientele caught between Victorian staleness and nerve-racking change. In his prison letter De Profundis (1897), he still exhorted that "whatever is realised is right."[2] As part of an uneasily tolerated Uranian (homosexual) subculture, he lived by a daring, imaginative doubleness. As a freelancer in a marketplace choked with inspirational tracts, medical counsel, fashion philosophy, and the arts, he used his solvent wit to mix do-it-yourself initiative with values that were basically aristocratic in their emphasis on leisure, refinement, and liberality. He was a high priest of transcendent beauty and a Shakespearean clown, a daring innovator and a derivative mechanic,[3] relentlessly mercurial.

Wilde cries out for attention because his imaginative style held in precarious suspension so many post-traumatic themes: generational competition, vexed expectations, mourning, and alienation. Even in prison, Wilde could sound like Sherlock Holmes, the "last and highest court of appeals in detection," when he referred to himself as "the supreme arbiter" of style in art (DP 909), or waved a Faustian magic wand: "I awoke the imagination of my century. . . . I summed up all systems in a phrase and all existence in an epigram" (913). Like Holmes unfolding a criminal history out of a single cigar ash, he boasted that he had made the trivial "the keystone of a very brilliant philosophy" (880–81).

This infantile self-inflation directly counters the same sort of traumatic dread that finally immures the drug- and art-intoxicated Holmes in a comparable psychic prison. In rejecting philistinism, Wilde and Holmes both recoil against "stagnation" and dread.[4] All his life, Wilde felt oppressed by a sense of doom (OW 436). As his mentor Walter Pater says of Jean-Jacques Rousseau at the close of The Renaissance, "an indefinable taint of death had clung always about him."[5] In Wilde's art, the worship of youth and beauty counteracts a consuming fear of death. As Lord Henry gravely quips in The Picture of Dorian Gray, "The basis of optimism is sheer terror."[6] Wilde was adept at gallows humor, and the term calls attention not only to wit's management of terror but also to themes of punishment and martyrdom central to Wilde's character. Even his most festive style—his post-traumatic optimism, as it were—has a counterphobic quality.

In prison, Wilde claimed that "the gods had given me almost everything" (DP 912) in a charmed life interrupted by "Doom" (889). The reality was not so simple. All along, despite his celebrity, he was an outsider in England, an iconoclastic, sexually dubious Irishman on the make.[7] With a streak of self-dramatizing grandiosity that her son shared, his mother styled herself "Speranza" and became a literary champion of Irish independence. Beguiled by legends of Irish martyrs, she urged her son to brave courtroom martyrdom in 1895 rather than slip off to France, as his friends and even the prosecution expected.[8] His father was a prominent Dublin physician and scientist who sexually abused a patient and plunged the family into a courtroom scandal when Oscar was ten. Three years later, Oscar's much-loved younger sister Iseult died. There were other grave shocks: a probable venereal infection; alienation from his wife and children when he was thirty-two years old and Robert Ross finally seduced him into a confrontation with his homosexual desire. His passionate obsession with Lord Alfred Douglas ("Bosie") half a dozen years later destroyed him. Accused of being a "sodomite" by Bosie's pugnacious father, the Marquess of Queensberry, Wilde was goaded into suing for libel. The trial backfired. Convicted under the Criminal Law Amendment Act of 1885 at the height of his success, then imprisoned, bankrupted, and alienated from his family and later his country, Wilde never recovered his creativity.

A rhythm of post-traumatic repetition links these episodes. As a child Wilde weathered his eminent father's trial for sexual misconduct; as a man he plunged to ruin by the same route. More than once he carried out in life risky behaviors presaged—"prophesied," he thought—in his writing. Richard Ellmann calls *The Picture of Dorian Gray* "premonitory of his own tragedy" (OW 313). Melissa Knox claims that his fatal love for Douglas was "in many ways a recapitulation of his love" for his dead sister.[9] In his novel Wilde embraced contemporary beliefs about traumatic inheritance, in which the sins of fathers steer a son toward doom. He imagined self-realization as "multiplying personalities"—a phrase that echoes in today's fascination with trauma and "multiple-personality" syndrome.[10] In the years leading up to his disaster he navigated a surging tide of successes with increasing recklessness.

But self-destructiveness and victimization by the mob form an incomplete picture. Like other post-traumatic writers, Wilde was in rebellion, yet deep inhibitions in the historical moment and in his personality made his opposition finally self-confounding. His velvet provocations triggered Max Nordau's retaliatory snarl at his "ego-mania": "He who has not learnt to impose some restraint upon himself in order not to shock others is called . . . not an Aesthete, but a blackguard."[11] Nordau diagnosed Aestheticism or Decadence as a disease. Because Wilde had given society a traumatic "shock," the critic justified his own aggression as a medical regimen. The place to "impose" self-restraint is prison.[12]

Wilde's sense of injury, his rebellion, and the psychic disablement brutally concretized in his imprisonment were all connected. In "The Happy Prince," *The Picture of Dorian Gray*, and *De Profundis*, Wilde's use of style turns a post-traumatic sense of disembeddedness into a form of personal freedom—an impossible freedom that looks in one direction toward messianic sacrifice and in the other toward prison.

Post-traumatic Style

In his image of the universe as a nightmarish factory and himself as a homeless child, Havelock Ellis struck a resonant note. This is the scientists' post-Christian universe of death, but also the world of factory-philistinism against which the young Wilde rebelled. In *The Importance of Being Earnest* a foundling uncovers his true identity, which enables him to belong to a clockwork society of self-involved puppets while retaining some comic freedom. In "The Happy Prince" a statue-child beholds a world of "grinding" poverty and sacrifices himself to win a home in paradise.[13] *De Profundis* depicts Wilde as childlike and "absolutely homeless" in a prison world (DP 914).

The climactic drama in Wilde's life also has roots in this imagery. Wilde was sexually attracted to "homeless boys," including the "rent boys" whose prostitution contributed to his downfall. He delighted in rescuing them for a night from deadness into the "golden land" of sumptuous imagination. Even the aristocratic Bosie—a childhood nickname for "Boysie"—was a footloose child dependent on Wilde for food, shelter, and heroic purpose, and Wilde fatally clashed with the law thinking that he was saving him from his father's despotism (OW 460).

The purest form of factory-philistinism is the prison, with its treadmill, regimentation, and meaningless work, governed by "the inflexible laws of an iron formula" (DP 904). The image crystallizes some of Wilde's deepest feelings, as in his protests to the *Daily Chronicle* about the homeless children among his fellow inmates. In the letters he tries to confront—to sensitize others to—the effects of trauma: "A child can understand a punishment inflicted by an individual, such as a parent or guardian, and bear it with a certain amount of acquiescence. What it cannot understand is a punishment inflicted by society. It cannot realise what society is." And therefore "the terror of a child in prison is quite limitless"—that is, traumatic (CW 959). Figuratively speaking, the child overwhelmed by the factory world ends up stricken.

Conan Doyle generated *The Sign of Four* out of the homeless Jonathan Small's prison experience. Suffering behind bars, Wilde came closer to seeing the reality latent in Havelock Ellis's image: that the factory and the orphan represent social death, and that in a hierarchical, dog-eat-dog society, social death disables the weakest competitors even as it confirms the symbolic immortality of those with power. In truth, the socially ambitious Wilde was more rebellious than Conan Doyle. His imaginative style evolved to resist the "iron" fixity of factory and prison. He relied on irony, paradox, equivocation, and wordplay—multiplicity, indeterminacy, negative capability. They can allow a speaker to criticize the inadequacy of things without specifying a solution; to invoke ineffable ideals; to honor complexity and change while deferring judgment. They can also distance the self from menacing reality, as in Lord Henry's gallows-humor comment about optimism and terror. Play and illusion counter the awareness of living under a sentence of death, as Pater put it in *The Renaissance*. By contrast, prison "makes one see people and things as they really are. That is why it turns one to stone."[14]

The plenitude of meanings in verbal play prevents meaning from being exhausted. Multiplicity promises more life. It forestalls reductive judgment and disenchantment. This principle is one of Wilde's core immortality fantasies, as seen in the idea of "realizing" an inexhaustible self through role-playing. "Is insincerity such a terrible thing?" asks *The Picture of Dorian Gray*. "I think not. It is merely a method by which we can multiply our personalities." Dorian Gray "used to wonder at the shallow psychology of those who conceive the Ego in man as a thing simple, permanent, reliable, and of one essence. To him, man was a being with myriad lives and myriad sensations, a complex multiform creature" (*PDG* 111). In this scheme the self is fragmented into "myriads." Like the implied meaning of riddling wordplay, identity is somehow definite yet ungraspable and inexhaustible—deathless.

The problem is that open-ended imaginative forms are radically equivocal and can be chaotic as well as liberating. The early-modern trope of the world as a stage shows an awareness of this phenomenon. The idea of role-playing opens up freedom, but also deception and instability. Analogously, Shakespeare's sonnets systematically compound ironies and multiple meanings, creating an ineffable surplus of sense that may evoke an ecstatic conviction of love or delusion.[15] Wilde protected his innermost identity by aggressive play and the use of illusion. But when the prosecutor smashed through his equivocations and the court's judgment demolished his equilibrium, Wilde suffered an agonizing disorientation. The qualities that had sustained him turned thinking into a hall of mirrors, a compulsive reflexivity that led him to messianic fantasies and, between times, fear of madness.

To control irony's nihilistic potential, Wilde relies on formalism—not only literary form but also social codes and ritual. Playing the Shakespearean fool, he systematically subverts platitudes, freeing up riddling possibilities. But he also reins in anarchic meanings by playing the philosopher-priest, as when he cultivates "the trivial" and then claims it constitutes a philosophy. In practice, his credibility depended not on playing one role or the other, but on his ability to maneuver between them. As a priest he could enchant a jaded audience, and as a fool deflect criticism.[16] His magic depended on his chimerical quickness: on irony being quicker than the eye. Loss of that freedom—judgment, deadlock, paralysis, imprisonment—meant deflation and death. Yet the poseur's ironical knowingness implicitly opens onto the abyss, and that can make fixity a perversely desirable ground. His ambivalence about freedom was not only typically modern but also compulsive.

It is easy to forget that Wilde's iconoclasm had a conservative subtext. His drive toward subversive play is itself oftentimes subverted by his impulse to be sententious, prescriptive, and categorical. In "The Soul of Man under Socialism" (1891), with thrilling moral boldness, he applauds the poor for being "ungrateful, discontented, disobedient, and rebellious," yet the bulk of the essay promotes values that are basically aristocratic in their emphasis on leisure, aesthetic refinement, and liberality.[17] In making a career niche for himself, he sidestepped direct competition with powerful patrons by advertising himself as a unique purveyor of beauty and critical judgment.[18] Like Sherlock Holmes, he wanted to be an autonomous professional detecting "smallness" to protect superior values or "treasure" for a superior clientele. He extolled the new without actually confronting modernism, as social reformers tried to do. Like Pater, he conjured the future on the authority of classical civilization, projecting an oxymoronic future/past such as Wells's Eloi epitomize. Looking ahead, he emulated the Romantic heroes Lord Byron, Percy Bysshe Shelley, and John Keats. In this context, Wilde's heroic aggrandizement seems childishly conflicted because—like his culture—he clings to the past with one hand while pointing toward the treacherous future with the other.

This is not to deny Wilde's promotion of tolerance and creativity.[19] Like Rider Haggard pursuing forbidden childhood obsessions in a lost African kingdom, he was not so much seeking new worlds as trying to loosen formative inhibitions. His compulsive risk taking says as much about his past as it does about his goals. "By a dextrous transvaluation of words," says Richard Ellmann, "Wilde makes good and evil exchange places," opening up new possibilities. Yet he keeps "looking back to conventional meanings like sin, ignoble, and shameful."[20] Subtract the transvaluation of taboo, and his love letters to Douglas sound embarrassingly conventional, and his daring "sins" have an air of escapism and competitive boyish hijinks.

Wilde's famous doubleness did more than protect his risky sexuality. It registered tensions that deeply destabilized and depersonalized his society. That social atmosphere comes into focus in Ellmann's account of Wilde's first meeting with the novelist Olive Schreiner (to whom Haggard had been much attracted). Wilde asked her why she lived in the East End. "'Because the people there don't wear masks.' 'And I live in the West End because the people there do'" (OW 258). In this celebrity skirmish, Schreiner issues a moral challenge, and Wilde stylishly bests her. His retort operates not by refuting but by comprehending her point of view, as if to say that he recognizes her moral claims but also sees them as naive and inadequate. More insidiously, the skirmish dramatizes Schreiner's complaint about insincerity, for Wilde is not really listening to her or relating to her. The joke sweeps aside all resistance and closes off conversation. Instead of validating each other, the speakers become more isolated. Even as Wilde criticizes the world of masks, he is embracing it, putting on a performance, competitive, convinced he could master the illusions.[21]

The West End in this anecdote is symptomatic of a world in which, for reasons I call post-traumatic, people do not substantiate one another. Instead society fosters mistrust, dissociation, competition, and other expressions of survival anxiety. The Time Traveller turns up marooned in a future that caricatures London insofar as neither the atrophied Eloi nor the hostile "underclass" Morlocks can mirror a self back to him. In desperation the Traveller undertakes a futile warrior-rampage against the Morlocks and finally, after his polite London friends disconfirm his traumatic story, he plunges recklessly into nothingness one final time. Despite its romantic gestures and gay subtext,[22] even the sunny *Importance of Being Earnest* depicts an eerily depersonalized society. In a post-traumatic world, personality risks being caught up in self-consuming reflexivity and doubt. The more frantic the search for a ground of experience, the wider the abyss opens. Dorian Gray's attack on himself in the uncanny mirror of his portrait epitomizes this process.

Louis Sass has linked this self-consuming mentality with schizophrenia and with modernism.[23] In the extreme, the dizzying perspectives of implacable irony and multiplied selves become an "inextricable web" as nightmarish as the factory universe itself. Even the favored Victorian term *breakdown* is an industrial metaphor. A plenitude of selves can imply that traumatic conflict has shattered the personality, as in the dissociation that afflicts Dr. Jekyll and Dorian Gray.[24] The conventional medical model of psychic economy attributed hysteria to personal excess, which could induce a nervous breakdown. In the metaphorical terminology of the day, a breakdown implied "ideas of descent (ultimately madness), of a decline in health, of downward movement, not merely to a lower level of vitality, but to the very loss of selfhood." For "breakdown also means, as it meant to the Victorians, fragmentation into small pieces—the same image at work in 'shattered nerves.' Nervous breakdown, at its most terrible, signified the complete destruction of the personality."[25]

Operating in this metaphorical system, the physician-husband in Charlotte Perkins Gilman's story "The Yellow Wallpaper" (1892) calms his own fears of death by prescribing fixity—confinement, total bed rest—for his wife's supposed nervous exhaustion. Like Wilde, however, the wife feels imprisoned and becomes urgently fascinated—and oppressed—by artistic excess. She imagines the wallpaper's "sprawling flamboyant patterns committing every artistic sin," for when she follows the pattern's curves, "they suddenly commit suicide—plunge off at outrageous angles, destroy themselves in unheard of contradictions."[26] Isolated from the natural world, both prisoners try to substantiate identity by writing "forbidden" things. Neither can effectively answer the juggernaut authority that pushes them toward breakdown to "save" them.

This anxiety about disintegration can also be seen as the product of a historical moment in which expansive expectations and severe ideals clashed with unruly reality. Looking out into the world, Cardinal Newman experienced the same derealization as others of lesser faith: "The world seems simply to give the lie to that great truth, of which my whole being is so full; and the effect upon me is, in consequence, as a matter of necessity, as confusing as if it denied that I am in existence myself. If I looked into a mirror, and did not see my face, I should have the sort of feeling which actually comes upon me, when I look into this living busy world, and see no reflexion of its Creator."[27] Newman divided his identity between a chaotic world and a divine voice within him that could not be confirmed in social reality. Newman looked into society and feared the loss of his identity ("if I looked into a mirror, and did not see my face") because the gap between the ideal spiritual self and the degenerate world is too great. This is a version of Wilde's—and the culture's—impasse. Anxiety about the substantiation of identity was widespread enough to affect the suicide "epidemic" of the early 1890s and to spur Émile Durkheim to coin the term *anomie*.

Wilde was much intrigued by mirrors and self-portraits, trying to find himself corroborated there. But at times he tried to counter nullity as Newman did, by trying to cherish a superhuman voice within. He had a lifelong fascination with messianic and sacrificial figures, notably Christ and the homoerotic Saint Sebastian. In *De Profundis* he muses on a Christ modeled on the persecuted, heroic sinner Oscar Wilde. This is a *fin de siècle* Christ, humanized as in Rider Haggard's mourning. In this Galilean peasant lad who literally achieves heroic immortality, the imprisoned Wilde sees an alter ego who compensates for his damaged self-esteem and his appalling losses. "Christ . . . seems to have always loved the sinner as being the nearest possible approach to the perfection of man," for "in a manner not yet understood of the world he regarded sin and suffering as being in themselves holy things and modes of perfection" (*DP* 933). This Christ is "the supreme Individualist" (926), a great sinner, as superbly beautiful as Dorian Gray. And like Dorian—and his alter egos Adonis, Saint Sebastian, and Saint George—he is a traumatic figure.

Messiah and Martyr

Wilde's messianic fantasies deserve a closer look. Modernism's dream of imaginative freedom through infinite perspectives promised inexhaustible vitality. But its open-endedness could also cause the jitters that led to repression. In *De Profundis* the imprisoned Wilde tried to join Newman in a return to Christ as a model. Yet in his meditation he repeated the same imaginative behavior that had led him to psychic prison in the first place. Although he aspired to humility, his identification with the Messiah was self-expansive; he grasped at an impossible transcendence while brooding on Christ's martyrdom with dangerously self-destructive feelings.

In his writing, Wilde plays out two different resolutions to the conflicts of messianic thinking. In the "innocent" scenario, a Christlike hero such as the Happy Prince sacrifices himself in a traumatic rescue and earns love and translation into paradise. In the more ambivalent resolution modeled by Dorian Gray, the hero puts up a superhuman struggle against disenchantment and death. He becomes a Faustian sinner consumed by "a wild desire to live, most terrible of all man's appetites" (*PDG* 143)—the mad hunger of the cannibal dwarf Tonga, Count Dracula, and the messianic Kurtz in the Congo. In his meditation on the sinner Christ, Wilde urgently tried to synthesize these conflicting scenarios.

"The Happy Prince" emphasizes its innocence by evoking Christian myth and fairy tale. Like Saint George, the Prince relieves a suffering city. But instead of going on to rule the city, he avoids direct competition with the city "fathers." Sacrificing himself and the swallow who serves him, he wins the heavenly Father's praise. The story imagines earning ultimate parental approval and a sanctioned place in paradise for the homosexual love of the Prince and his faithful servant. As we might predict, this apotheosis is a reaction to traumatic conflict.

The Prince, we are told, was a sheltered, carefree child who died young. The adult world has recreated him as a statue on a high pedestal from which, like Cardinal Newman, he stares helplessly at the misery of humanity. He beholds the wretched but cannot personally connect with them—just as Newman fears he cannot see his face mirrored in the world. Where the Cardinal cultivates a divine voice within, the Prince bonds with an adoring swallow who sacrifices himself in the winter cold in order to carry out the Prince's good works for him. Piece by piece, the Prince commands that the swallow carry off parts of his body—jewel eyes and gold-leaf skin—to sick, starving, and despairing strangers in the city. The tale closes as an angel brings the dead bird and the Prince's broken heart of lead to the heavenly Father, who decrees eternal life for the two. As Ellmann notes, Wilde presents his fairy tales "like sacraments of a lost faith" (*OW* 299). As such, they play out the same mourning process evident in Haggard.

As I read it, this plot is charged with death anxiety and a familiar ambivalence toward children. The statue itself objectifies symptoms of trauma, especially the nervous system's propensity to "freeze" when overwhelmed. This kind of "virtual death" may signify an attempt to forestall or buy off real death.[28] But other symptoms include paralysis (conversion hysteria), numbness (feeling no cold, no pain), intrusion (memories of childhood, visions of suffering), and compulsive weeping. What is the source of this shock?

On the surface, the fairy tale celebrates the tenderhearted child as a secular Christ, a young Saint George with a ruby-hilted sword, presenting gifts of new life to the city's wretched souls and then rewarded in paradise. Yet the story is also a cultural fantasia full of sublimated conflict. For one thing, the death of the child who "did not know what tears were" can be seen as God the Father's punishment of his selfishness ("HP" 107). Turned into a statue, the Prince actually undergoes a sort of play-death that breaks his selfish will. Otherwise he might become a Dorian Gray. After all, the depraved Dorian is also a narcissistic child and is subjected to an analogous hideous fate, disintegrating in the portrait as the Prince does on his pedestal. Justifying his own punishment in *De Profundis*, Wilde defines himself as "so typical a child of my age, that in my perversity . . . I turned the good things of my life to evil, and the evil things of my life to good" (*DP* 915). The association of the statue with prison is evident in Wilde's comment that prison "turns one to stone."[29] A "too happy" child faces tacit death, both from the judgmental adult world and from self-punishing guilt over his own dark motives. On this level readers can identify with the child, the better to control the conflicts of the children in themselves. Both as a sentimental role model ("and a little child shall lead them") and as a scapegoat for adult guilt, the child enables imaginations—Wilde's among them—to give shape to some of late-Victorian culture's most painful tensions.

In the symbolic logic of the tale, then, the trauma originates in a symbolic death: a crisis of radical self-effacement that is both a punishment imposed on the child from outside and a suicidal wish. But this pattern is part of a cultural system that needs unpacking. In a practical way, the child's self-sacrifice can reduce the parent generation's fears of its offspring's aggressive neediness and eventual rivalry. This is an ancient model of social stabilization. In the New Testament, Christ the Son voluntarily gives up his life in suffering in order to prove his submission to the Father and earn everlasting life and atonement for humanity. The Christian story projects a social system in which the young efface themselves, often through a play-death, and thereby earn autonomy from a patriarch.[30]

"The Happy Prince" dramatizes a late-Victorian variant of this pattern. Adult authority (the palace, elite society) sacrifices other "children"—the poor—to create a conviction of power and immortality for itself. More prosaically, the tormented labors of people such as the poor seamstress and the match girl in the city generate comforts and security that permit the elite society to escape from Adam's curse of work and death. The palace relieves its guilt by projecting it onto the "too happy" son, who dies and is recreated as a statue instilled with a guilty compulsion to make reparation to the otherwise invisible poor. The privileged culture of the palace "where suffering is not allowed to enter" harbors an unconscious, punitive guilt about its survival greed, and takes out that guilt on the "too happy" child by instilling in him a traumatically severe self-control and self-disabling idealism ("HP" 107).

Historically, the "too happy" child's ambiguous guilt and punishment may reflect the late-Victorian clash of heightened expectations of control and comfort with cruel social realities. Genteel society limits the shock through sacrificial reparation and by recreating the child as an icon of happiness. Wilde lampoons the hypocrisy of the city "fathers" when they consign the derelict remains of the statue to the trash heap. Their dismay confirms the horror of the Prince's slow-motion suicide and suggests how deeply ambivalent is the belief in sacrificial giving to others. To a competitive commercial culture enjoined by Christianity to give up worldly goods and trust in God, the Prince's "fatal charity" could reinforce survival anxiety and Social Darwinist defenses against sharing.[31]

On his pedestal, the Prince is sentient but paralyzed. He can relate to no one because in the city, people are alienated. The palace excludes all distress, and the city "fathers" are blindly disgusted by the decrepit statue and the dead swallow. But even the innocents misinterpret life and cannot respond to the Prince. The match girl, for example, mistakes his sapphire eye for a "lovely bit of glass" ("HP" 110). Despite Wilde's charming irony, the lack of mirroring relationships creates a world of masks such as Wilde found in the West End: artificially merry for the privileged, full of death anxiety for the poor. The city is akin to Jonathan Small's London, the shadowy underworld of Kôr, and the Eloi's ruined, incomprehensible civilization. In addition, poverty destroys the will; the Prince sees sick and "starving" children. There is no sign of the protest advocated in "The Soul of Man under Socialism," because the Prince's radical effacement is in part a symbolic execution, and the ultimate official—and parental—threats are rejection and death. As soon as the Prince strips down to a humble form, the town councillors find him "little better than a beggar" (111) and order his ruined body destroyed. When God finally rescues him, the Prince and the swallow are discarded body parts on a dustheap. At the comparable point, forced to choose between ending up a corpse on a rubbish heap or joining the Sikhs, Jonathan Small revolts. By contrast, the Prince's self-mutilation begins when he takes apart his sword, his capacity for anger. As a result he is a Saint George without a weapon or a dragon, bypassing the Saint's youthful triumph for martyrdom.[32]

The Prince's bond with the swallow offers a fantasy solution to his paralysis. The swallow reanimates the statue, carrying out the Prince's will and substantiating him in a mirroring relationship. Like the seamstress's sick boy, the swallow is an alter ego of the Prince, and their love-death reintegrates the Prince in paradise. This is a scenario of magical undoing, fulfilling and yet sanitizing the earlier narcissism through mutual self-sacrifice. In Ellmann's telling phrase, "their love is perfected, and disinfected, in death" (OW 269). Transported to paradise, the lovers do not die so much as undergo a play-death, out of the repressive city, into a tacitly homosexual play space akin to Tangier but now blessed by the Father. The tale's magical undoing is potent because it allows the Prince to play the redeemed older brother or even surrogate father to a world of figurative children, working out his reparation. This consummation may help explain Wilde's attraction to lower-class boys, and suggests that eros for him was partly a reparative economy of sexual and material gift giving. It may also shed light on his staggering misperception of Alfred Douglas's dangerous personality, and his compulsive profligacy with his spoiled lover. Frantically sifting the past in *De Profundis*, Wilde cannot understand why his generosity brought not ecstatic fulfillment but ruin.

Traumatic Childhood

The traumatized Prince "goes to pieces" and finds love and reintegration in death. *The Picture of Dorian Gray* follows a similar course, but Wilde glosses its meanings more searchingly. A traumatic childhood freezes Dorian into a "statuesque" model of perfection. For a time he strives to live up to a messianic ideal as an object of hero worship. The "eternal youth" embodies symbolic immortality; the painter Basil Hallward finds him uncannily "pure" to the eye (*PDG* 99), and feels his personality could "absorb my whole nature, my whole soul, my very art itself" (11). But when this platonic freeze fails, Dorian begins to go to pieces. Few novels are so gripped by death anxiety. As survival rage overtakes him, Dorian splits off illicit selves, not sacrificing himself but preying on others. In a sort of devil's pact, he grasps at immortality by displacing all the evil effects of his greed for life onto Basil Hallward's portrait of him. While Dorian blazes with "eternal youth," using up lovers like a vampire, his painted double secretly decays. When he finally stabs himself, his body suddenly withers as Ayesha does in the Pillar of Fire, revealing a long-denied death. Yet his aggression turns out to be a sacrifice after all, insofar as it restores his alter ego's perfection. Like the Happy Prince, this fallen "Prince Charming" arrives at a messianic apotheosis, but in a scenario of torturous ambiguity.

What is the source of Dorian's messianic aura? For one thing, the novel turns Havelock Ellis's vision inside out. Here the homeless orphan has displaced the factory world and become the center of meaning for others. Wilde accomplishes this magic by making Dorian a site of intoxicating idealization. The novel constructs Dorian as a catalog of incantatory, adjectival "perfections." However outlandishly narcissistic and preposterous his dandified tastes, Dorian brings out a sacramentalizing impulse in others. That aura of larger-than-life significance dispels death anxiety and its symbolic equivalents: failure, rejection, isolation, "stagnation," and the like. The "eternal youth" is also akin to the archrebel Lucifer, that hyperbolical "morning-star of evil" (146). His aura is related to the hypnotic force that charges figures such as Haggard's She-who-must-be-obeyed and George du Maurier's demonic Svengali. Like mesmerism in the 1890s, it ministers to traumatic anxieties. It is also Faustian aggrandizement in dandy's dress: a grandiose credulity that cannot be sustained.[33]

The novel dramatizes a struggle to sustain that intoxication. It resembles stories about alcoholism or drug addiction in which the personality deteriorates as exaltation fails. Disenchantment unleashes survival anxiety. Dorian loves Sibyl Vane's "immortal Juliet," for example, until her artistic spell lapses and he panics as if witnessing Ayesha's face "growing old before my eyes!" (*She*, 279). The episode is especially resonant because *Romeo and Juliet* presents a sublime version of Dorian's mother's star-crossed marriage. Night after night in the theater he compulsively reexperiences the loss of a larger-than-life woman, mourns for her, and tries to recover her in loving Sibyl—much like Rider Haggard's project.

But this is where intoxicating perfection begins to fail. Sibyl Vane renounces "immortal" art for the traditional immortality system, family love (*PDG* 69–71), which projects life into the future as posterity but also means submission to the fatality of birth and death. Dorian panics as Wilde did when pregnancy made his wife's body "loathsome" to him.[34] Their terror and their homosexual desires are hard to disentangle. At first Dorian is numb: "So I have murdered Sibyl Vane!" (*PDG* 78). And then: "Why is it that I cannot feel this tragedy as much as I want to?" (79). Thereafter he begins grasping at "eternal youth" through sexual conquests, just as the increasingly pederastic Wilde did after his anguished retreat from Constance. As a love of youth, this homosexual desire foregrounds the counterphobic function of sexuality. Society condemns libertinism not only because it is heartless toward partners and offspring, but also because its obsessiveness may reveal an underlying survival mania. Although the novel advertises Dorian's sins with adjectival vehemence, his desires are most vividly associated with transgression, loss, and death. Women acutely embody mortality for him. Sibyl's suicide echoes his mother's early death and provokes a spasm of denial. Basil Hallward forces Dorian to face the unspeakable reality: "Why, man, there are horrors in store [in the grave] for that little white body of hers!" (85). Whether this terror relates to Wilde's loss of his young sister Iseult, as Knox maintains, or to his sensitivities as a doctor's child, it has traumatic force. Dorian's dissolution in the magic portrait records not only the ravages of age and evil but also the progress of post-traumatic obsessions "eating away" at him. Ayesha's horrific death creates the post-traumatic spell that transfixes Horace

Holly and becomes the novel *She*. Likewise, dissociated, unfelt death—as in Sibyl's suicide and in the decay in the painting—intensifies Dorian Gray's furious intoxication.

Just as Sherlock Holmes demonstrates superhuman powers by exposing the "Smallness" around him, so Dorian deflates virtually everyone he touches. When Dorian and Lord Henry exercise their dazzling scorn, they not only reproduce the aggressive idealism of fathers, but also compulsively act out a competitive society's struggle over meaning and status. But no matter what ineffable ideals it serves, mockery makes a barren triumph, and sooner or later dread returns. Hence Dorian and Holmes both periodically collapse. This is the neurasthenic dead end Des Esseintes reaches in Joris Karl Huysmans's "fatal" book *Against Nature* when he broods on flowers and jewels in self-hypnotic isolation.[35] Dorian's "treasures, and everything that he collected," were "modes by which he could escape, for a season, from the fear that seemed to him at times to be almost too great to be borne" (*PDG* 109).

Conventional life would be a "stagnant" prison for Dorian, as it would for Holmes. But then, withdrawal is also imprisoning in the end. Hence the pressure on Dorian to multiply himself to "realize" new roles. But because the roles are taboo, his fragmentation turns out to entail the suicidal psychic splitting epitomized by Jekyll and Hyde. It is analogous to the statue-prince disintegrating himself, but without the redemptive love-death. Dissociation becomes one of the only ways to escape from the obsession with perfection. Little wonder that Wilde sought to lose himself in sex with lower-class "nobodies." Yet in the end, despite the defiant praise of self-realization through sin, Dorian's knife attack on his painted image acts out overwhelming self-hatred and guilt—just as the Prince's self-sacrifice is a reparation for his having been "too happy," and just as Wilde broods on redemption through his imprisonment. Wilde imagines the discharge of guilt bringing an intoxicating apotheosis: the Prince and the swallow united in the Father's paradise; Dorian's portrait miraculously restored to ideality. Dorian celebrates expansive life but his behavior also dramatizes a perverse urge toward self-containment—and prison.

Although Dorian Gray and the Happy Prince implicitly share the same traumatic guilt, the novel casts a much stronger searchlight on its childhood origins. The novel opens with Dorian frozen in "statuesque" perfection. As that magic wears off and Dorian unfolds other selves, childhood distress suddenly surfaces in his mind. Humankind, he believes, is "a complex multiform creature that bore within itself strange legacies of thought and passion, and whose very flesh was tainted with the monstrous [inherited] maladies of the dead" (111). This formula attributes the sense of being multiple selves to the inherited presence of "monstrous" ancestral character traits. "Multiform" personality is conditioned by intrusive voices from the past. It suggests a culture in which powerful others constantly impinge on the individual. If Dorian's motives are partly ancestral and shaped by their ideals, then the self-made dandy can never really be master of his own house. Likewise, if social life overvalues the demands of others, then internally the proud individualist may be a child struggling for scarce autonomy. Exactly this structure is implied by the late-Victorian obsession with reputation and respectability.

The self haunted by ancestral motives is Wilde's version of the sepulchral psychic kingdom of Kôr, in which actions that occurred two thousand years earlier determine present behavior. Kôr is a "whole mountain peopled with the dead, and nearly all of them perfect" (*She*, 179). Haggard's peculiar sentence yokes the wreckage of a civilization and the idea of the "perfect" dead to a static (frozen) mental world. This could be a probe of Dorian Gray's depths, with his internalized mania for perfection, his psychic numbness, and his oppression by an invisible or unconscious past. It is only a short step to images of the remote, undead Dracula presiding over an invisible kingdom of living-dead minions. Like the fin de siècle fascination with "hereditary taint" and eugenics, these images express fears about the ground of experience. They read a particular upper-class Victorian family structure as a biological imperative. The parental will that can immortalize children in paradise can also destroy them. And the judge may also be a criminal. In a Lamarckian process, the "sins of the fathers" are passed on through increasingly degenerate offspring. This is the persecutory underside of messianic wishes.

Dorian's grandfather sums up the parental threat. Wilde caricatures him as an "old-fashioned," brutally jealous patriarch who had his son-in-law assassinated in order to "recapture" his daughter. This incestuous greed for life has tainted the old man's descendants, including Dorian. Thinking about "multiform" identity in the passage above, Dorian imagines in himself ancestral voices assimilated or introjected in childhood. These monstrous voices are tantamount to an unresolved childhood trauma with continuing intrusive symptoms. And Dorian is literally a child of trauma because his mother rebelled against her father, who then had her commoner husband, Dorian's father, murdered. In this disguised Oedipal struggle the son (Dorian) identifies with the passionate husband-lover slain by the father-grandfather. Because the grandfather has raised Dorian from an icy distance, he is virtually the boy's father. But we are looking at a social system. Oedipal rage has warped the grandfather because *his* father "hated" him as he hates Dorian (*PDG* 31).

In this fantasy, sons are the traumatized victims of fathers who are in their own right traumatized sons. In the idiom of 1990s therapy, the abused grow up to be abusers. Instead of escaping into paradise on a sacrificial kiss, the child turns into a predatory parent—one reason Dorian fears growing older. Dorian associates his childhood with the playroom in which he hides the picture of his flawed, mortal self.[36] In "those dead days" his remote, hateful "father" kept him virtually imprisoned in the "lonely" playroom. Wells's harrowing analogue of this imprisonment is the Invisible Man's dream of mourners crowding him into his father's open grave and burying him alive. Like Kôr, Dorian's state of "stainless purity" (PDG 95) combines perfection and death. In this scenario the father freezes the Oedipal antagonism by trapping the son in a statuelike play-death ("those dead days") of frigid "stainless purity." Growing up, the "young god" Dorian has internalized this cold idealism, which combines with (his mother's) beauty to mesmerize others.

This obsessiveness shapes family life. Parents instill it in the young to regulate them. The young internalize it in an effort to integrate childhood shock. It becomes a superficial ground for self-esteem and a substitute for intimate bonds blocked by conflict. For Dorian it makes the playroom of childhood a prison. One treacherous feature of such a system is that, however different their specific values, the young are apt to identify with the position of parent-judge. Wilde seems not to appreciate how much the ostensibly defiant Dorian identifies with his censorious grandfather's ruthless idealism, disposed to self-hatred. The voices in Wilde that resist such obsessiveness belong to Sibyl—whose suicide suggests thwarted idealism—and to Lord Henry, whose compulsive deflation of ideals speaks for itself.

Dorian Gray never really fathoms his own dividedness. As he watches himself deteriorate in the picture, he invokes an "ancestral trauma" to explain it. He dissociates his own forbidden desires, attributing them to his forebears, judging them even as he embraces them, so that they become not negotiated conflicts in his own nature but sins of the fathers: the "doom" of "some strange poisonous germ" infecting him from the past (111). Like the splitting-off of taboo selves and the search for sex with workingmen, this compromised evasion of self-judgment entails self-loss. The effort to be thoroughly "insincere" or "indifferent" in desire amounts to a symbolic suicide. It is as deadly as the factory world.

When he does finally try to break out of his psychic prison, Dorian blindly attacks his surrogate father, Basil Hallward, first by repudiating his judgment in a "boyish insolent manner" (119), then in a murder that amounts to parricide. Wilde insists on Dorian's perverse motivation. But the murder makes sense as an assault on the father-judge. Presumably Dorian is enraged by his conviction that fathers are hypocrites who use idealism to mask their own sins. In the serialized version of the novel especially, Hallward's homosexual feelings are plain. To Dorian he is potentially a seducer, and in his righteous homophobia a sham.

This complexity opens into another. The murder is also a traumatic rescue.

In painting Dorian, the surrogate father with "stern eyes" (119) is judging him, with a threat of exposure that would mean social death. The picture is akin to blackmail, the epidemic vice of late-Victorian Britain, which actually did ensnare Wilde. Hallward tries to extort conformity by indirectly threatening to reveal Dorian's secret life. Attacking him, Dorian is rescuing his alter ego from social death.[37]

In messiahs, not to mention perfect gentlemen, idealism is supposed to inhibit aggression. Certainly it was so for Wilde. In *De Profundis* he calls the laws that imprisoned him "wrong and unjust" (915), and his outrage at Alfred Douglas smoulders on every page. At the same time, with self-consciously Christlike forbearance, he intones hypnotically against anger and hatred (893-94). *The Picture of Dorian Gray* illustrates the depth of the impasse, for Dorian does act out his anger. After murdering Basil Hallward, he feels himself "swept towards" an abyss. His impulse is denial—to blind himself as the Happy Prince does. But blinding would be useless, because he cannot escape his terrified imagination. "Then, suddenly, time stopped for him," and horrible thoughts "dragged a hideous future from its grave, and showed it to him. He stared at it. Its very horror made him stone" (*PDG* 129). In his guilt Dorian is paralyzed like the Prince, staring at his own annihilation "dragged from the grave." At the climactic moment of self-assertion or self-sacrifice, trauma stops life. He—and his creator— are caught between post-traumatic options: berserking or a psychic freeze; fragmentation or prison. In fact, the freeze saves him from further rage—from a rampage such as Wells's Invisible Man undertakes. No wonder, as Ellmann remarks, "his sense of doom had been present since childhood" (*OW* 436).

In a Perfect Prison

Imagery of psychic freeze and paralysis haunts these writers from the 1890s: Jonathan Small pinned in the mud by his wooden leg; Holmes nodding on cocaine; an empty treasure chest; Ayesha mourning for two millennia; the Time Traveller stranded in time; Dr. Jekyll immured in his laboratory; Dracula lying in his coffin. All of the writers oscillate between obsessive compensatory idealism and disillusion, aggrandizement and collapse. Wilde dramatizes the social dimensions of this rhythm. Like post-traumatic vigilance, his compulsive idealism grasps at order and defends against threat, change, and chaos. When it mixes with carnival mockery, as in Wilde's comedies, the result is a highly charged mood, giddy with ironies, pleasurable but unstable. For the middle-class public, but also for Wilde himself, that mood was susceptible to hysteria: the moral panic that sent Dorian Gray to his doom and his creator to prison.

This imaginative instability begs to be schematized. But moral panic is only one expression of a phenomenon that was pervasive and plastic. As "an inextricable net" of rules and expectations, punishments and rewards, compulsive idealism contributed not only to the cult of respectability but also to the "stagnation" Sherlock Holmes dreads and the grim factory world that oppressed Havelock Ellis. On another scale, the violent idealism of the Happy Prince evokes the hysteria that froze some of Charcot's famous patients in religious poses, and the related urge to self-mutilation. *The Picture of Dorian Gray* shows idealism not only as a route to rapture, but also as a widely used social instrument of intimidation, control, and competition.

This perspective by no means discounts other historical forms of idealism. Linda Dowling has demonstrated, for example, that at his first trial Wilde defended the nobility of love between males in language that "belongs to a strategically revived idiom of Greek ideality" that engaged the prosecution in a serious contest of ideas that had been unfolding for at least two centuries in England.[38] Significantly, the war of ideas was grounded not so much in questions about sexual preference as in ancient concerns that "effeminacy" rendered males unable or unwilling to fight and die for the polis.[39] In the bowels of the debate, so to speak, Dowling locates another example of the survival anxiety that underlies so much post-traumatic ideation.

It seems to me that Wilde became trapped in the force fields of idealism. As his conflict with Queensberry sharpened, he half came out from behind his ironic masks. As Ellmann observes, others were pushing him into battle, and he seems to have needed to prove his courage (OW 443–44). He saw the combat as a heroic rescue scenario. Bosie's bullying father resembled the father-figures Dorian Gray despises, and *De Profundis* attributes to Bosie's father a strain of inherited madness such as Dorian fears.[40] Defying the monstrous marquess, Wilde sounded like a Victorian knight: "The tower of ivory is assailed by the foul thing" (OW 458).

Had he defeated the foul thing, he could have claimed the role of life-giving father to his culture, as the allegorical Saint George does. At his first trial he tried to claim the role when he defined the "love that dare not speak its name" by identifying with cultural fathers such as King David, Plato, Michelangelo, and Shakespeare, and their guarantees of immortality. For Oedipal strife he substituted the idea of "a great affection of an elder for a younger man" (463). To justify himself, however, he had to attack Queensberry, who was the manly father of the rules of boxing, at least nominally a family man, and a well-connected aristocrat. The prosecution sided with Queensberry and made Wilde the monster. Trying to express his disgust, the marquess saw the chivalric dragon as a Darwinian beast, calling Wilde an "iguanadon." Inflamed ideals increasingly polarized options until the outcome had to be prison for either Queensberry or Wilde.

Wilde came to grief not only because of sexual taboos, but also because of generational tensions that magnified male conflicts over autonomy and hierarchy and recast them as family dynamics. "Loathing" between fathers and sons, Wilde insisted, is "very common in English domestic life" (DP 949). It not only blocked personal fulfillment, it undermined the ground of experience. In seeking a judgment against Queensberry, Wilde was tacitly arguing that the traditional patriarch who once conferred a conviction of immortality had become a greedy competitor. Even if his homosexuality *had* evoked Shakespeare instead of the sinister Dorian Gray, it would still have challenged the image of the paterfamilias as a benevolent progenitor. Nor was Wilde alone in unsettling the psychic guarantees of family; witness the misogyny unleashed by women's use of contraception and abortion to increase control over their lives, and the parricidal fantasies that *Dracula* supported. As insults to ancient, always fragile immortality beliefs, these role changes also resonated with the metaphorical shift that turned "mother" nature and "the heavenly Father" into the dehumanized factory world.

In short, Havelock Ellis was not alone in feeling like a victimized child. In the 1890s, as in the 1990s, for example, public opinion was sensitive about the abuse of children. As in W. T. Stead's sensational report on white slavery, "The Maiden Tribute of Modern Babylon," with its inflammatory accounts of evil mothers selling virgins to upper-class libertines, adult exploitation of the young captured widespread attention.[41] Class inequities further sharpened feelings; Wilde aroused lower-class hostility as a figure of the upper-class sexual predator. To his horror, he turned into the figure of the sinister father he had indicted in *The Picture of Dorian Gray*.[42]

Ironically, the fluidity of Wilde's identity resulted in part from his unconscious assumption of a middle-class status. Although Wilde was no conventional Victorian burgher, Barbara Charlesworth rightly sees in him "an 'ordinary man' who felt terrible guilt for the sins of that part of him represented by Dorian Gray."[43] He anticipates a twentieth-century style of middle-class identity, which assumes that nearly everyone is in the middle. Today this practice works to deny class tensions. A consumer democracy can put furniture styled after French aristocracy in a suburban ranch house. Newspapers at least pretend to believe that the homeless could be "just like us." Wilde shows an early form of that strategy. For all his snobbery, he could be relaxed about class boundaries in his actual behavior. In his work he wanted to sympathize with the militant poor, and he indulgently mocked the rich. This undercurrent unquestionably supported his popularity with middle-class audiences.

To be sure, it was an undercurrent. Wilde's sense of the middle developed less out of politics than out of democratic grandiosity. He imagined himself, like the humanist Shakespeare and Walt Whitman, containing all types and conditions of people. He gave Dorian Gray a version of this dream. At times Dorian felt "that the whole of history was merely the record of his own life, not as he had lived it in act and circumstance, but as his imagination had created it for him" (*PDG* 113). In Whitman such expansiveness is rhapsodic. For Dorian Gray it is more a means of stuffing or fortifying the self against a sinister world and an inner darkness, as it is in the encyclopedic Holmes, the self-sufficient Time Traveller in the Porcelain Palace, and the kingdom enclosed by female topography that Ayesha rules.

But the sense of the middle is even more problematic because its egalitarian convictions were—and still are—working to contain undying fantasies of aristocracy. In his heart, Wilde half-accepted Alfred Douglas's unspoken criticism that he was a parvenu. The truly elite, Wilde gushed to Bernard Berenson, have more of everything. They "are more alive" and "breathe a finer air" than mere mortals (*OW* 283). Wilde loved this aura in the young Lord Douglas. Yet it was dangerous to love it too openly, because the elite punished upstarts.[44] Worse, although Bosie was full of class conceit, as his memoir shows, he was in a weak and confused position: improvident, self-involved, and alienated from his family. These passionate confusions inflamed Wilde's devotion and also fatally undermined him. In a related way, he loved exercising erotic mastery with lower-class males, although those encounters were out of his control, as became clear in his second trial when they were systematically used to destroy him.

Significantly, these class dynamics are by no means simply a function of Wilde's homosexuality. Time travel crash-lands Wells's imagination in the problematic middle. Bosie needed rescue as did the Eloi; the furtive "renters" resembled Morlocks. Not only did the rent boys have to operate underground, as it were, but Wilde deliberately depersonalized them, flirting with the risks they presented, exploring the disinhibiting effect of their illiteracy, ugliness, and dirtiness.[45] In calling his sexual encounters with them "feasting with panthers" (*OW* 387), he equates them with cannibals like the Morlocks and Tonga. Like the Time Traveller, when Wilde cut loose from the conventional world of his day, he "found himself" between a childish aristocratic love and dangerously exciting sexual animals he could not seem to avoid—and the split nearly killed him as it did the Time Traveller. A similar argument could be made about Conan Doyle and Haggard.

As the grandson of a patriarch and the son of a defeated, lower-class father (*PDG* 85), Dorian Gray projects a version of Wilde's situation. As in Renaissance changeling lore, his genealogy supports fantasies of discovering one's long-lost "real" nobility. And downward mobility is a lurking worry. When Dorian spurns the glamorous Sibyl Vane for revealing her "common" humanity, Wilde has him stalk off into a paragraph-long tour of "evil-looking" slums, with drunks like "monstrous apes" and "grotesque children huddled in doorways" (*PDG* 71). This is the poverty and childhood helplessness that Wilde confesses he dreaded in his youth.[46] It also implies class competition and guilt. Like Small's face at the window by Major Sholto's deathbed, Jim Vane's visage in the conservatory window shocks Dorian Gray into a "death-like swoon" (*PDG* 152). The specter of the rejected, vengeful, "colonial" other "freezes" the guilty "brother" as the city's misery does the "too-happy" Prince.

While a public atmosphere of moral panic destabilized Wilde's identity, the panic worked on his own real contradictions. In his multiplicity he was not only a noble father, a visionary artist, and a daring sinner, but also at times a guilty child. In *De Profundis* he sympathizes with Queensberry, outraged that Bosie had pushed so hard "to get [his] father into prison" (*DP* 896) and ruin him. With self-confounding ambivalence he also indicts himself as "so typical a child of my age that in my perversity . . . I turned the good things of my life to evil" (915).

The supposedly ruthless Dorian Gray illustrates the paralyzing effects of a discordant ego ideal and severe controls on anger. As Dorian spies Jim Vane's face in the conservatory window, guilty panic literally floors him. Instead of defending himself, he faints, acting out compulsive self-punishment (*PDG* 152). In their face-to-face confrontation on the docks, the social controls are more explicit and perverse. Trying to kill Dorian, Jim Vane is in the position of a child retaliating against an upper-class libertine, a figure of the predatory parent. But Dorian escapes by feigning youth. In this fantasy role reversal, Dorian allies himself with innocent youth while using against Jim Vane the voice of a censorious parent: "Let this be a warning to you." He berates Jim Vane for his anger, and Vane instantly becomes angry at himself and begs his enemy for forgiveness (147). Parental and class inhibitions freeze the marginal Jim.

Internalized social controls inhibited Wilde's protests against laws whose injustice he saw plainly. His monotonous warnings against anger and hate in *De Profundis* are urgent efforts at self-policing as well as noble sentiments for Bosie's benefit. In his letters to the *Daily Chronicle*, Wilde is far more genteel and placatory in his protests than, say, Max Nordau was toward him in print. His inhibition compares tellingly with the confinement of the "neurasthenic" wife in Charlotte Perkins Gilman's "Yellow Wallpaper" (1892), who only begins to recognize herself as the woman trapped "in" the wallpaper pattern, "behind bars," as she begins to lose her conventional mind.

Gilman's story dramatizes some of the invisible regulatory mechanisms of late-Victorian society. The narrator's "illness" and her husband's medical authority focus the familiar themes of death anxiety and immortality. Like Dorian Gray hiding the portrait of his soul in a locked attic nursery, the wife discovers her "mad" alter ego in an upstairs nursery with barred windows and the scars left by rebellious children. Like Wilde among West End masks, she is in a velvet prison. At one point she wishes to visit relatives, and the prose briefly highlights the invisible repression: "But [my husband] said I wasn't able to go, nor able to stand it after I got there; and I did not make out a very good case for myself, for I was crying before I had finished."[47] At stake is a silent judgment against which the tacit offender must "make a case." Her reaction resembles Wilde's compulsive weeping on the railway platform at Clapham Junction insofar as her tears preempt self-assertion or anger in what she experiences as a "natural" and irresistible reflex. In the 1990s her compulsive self-disablement would readily feel like a symptom of abuse. In fact, her husband controls her with nothing more palpable than a "stern, reproachful look,"[48] like the "stern" looks of Dorian Gray's grandfather (PDG 95) and Basil Hallward. The dissociated fear and anger at this aggression appear in Bram Stoker's account of the invisible depredations of the patriarchal Dracula—and in his victims' extravagant revenge. At bottom the hidden threat is social death, which is why Dorian retaliates by killing Hallward, and why Gilman's narrator ends up crawling over her husband's body in a "mad" parody of murder.

The extent to which Wilde was struggling against his own anger may be seen in his protests to the *Daily Chronicle*. The system's cruelty to children is either "madness" or "stupidity," and he takes it to be stupidity because like the imprisoned child, he "cannot realize what society is." Given the forces that crushed him, he was misguided in his sense of threat.[49] "The despot . . . being an individual, may have culture," he maintains in "The Soul of Man under Socialism," "while the mob, being a monster, has none."[50] Yet it was neither despot nor mob but the machinations of elite England that felled him and hounded his family out of the country. *De Profundis* smoulders with rage at Douglas and the legal system, yet Wilde strains to keep the composure of a gentleman. "Every day I said to myself: 'I must keep love in my heart to-day, else how shall I live through the day?'" (DP 899). Anger implies traumatic danger and social failure, and he numbed himself against it. In a practical way prison, like psychic paralysis, was a desperate solution to desperately insoluble anger.

When he thinks of proper society, Wilde shows little sense of its capacity to do evil. And unlike the other post-traumatic writers, he has no Morlocks or colonial cannibals to deflect his rage. In prison he sentimentalized the poor as "wiser, more charitable, more kind, more sensitive than we are" (911). Possessing nothing, expecting nothing, his fellow convicts may have been more inured to abuse. They seemed to know who they were. Wilde had less survival training in the cruelty of his culture, and farther to fall.

Prison recapitulates the condition of the statue-child, the Happy Prince, overwhelmed by "paralysing immobility" and a broken flow of time in which "suffering is one very long moment" (904). The prisoner resists by multiplying possibilities. In *De Profundis* Wilde constantly rehearses new roles in the theater of his mind. He scourges his sins and then vows "fresh mode[s] of perfection" to come (918–19). But because "passion makes one think in a circle" (943), these roles proved chimerical, it became impossible to disentangle life-sustaining hope from repetition compulsion, and at times Wilde feared he was losing his mind.

To be everyone is finally to be no one. Endless multiplicity leads to alienation and derealization. Sooner or later the overextended self becomes a host of spectral roles, implying a distinctively modern emptiness at the core of personality that frightened and inspired Wilde.[51] It links him with Haggard, Conan Doyle, and Wells, who in related ways also worked obsessively at managing nullity, and with Joseph Conrad, who mapped that emptiness onto twentieth-century culture in the unforgettable image of the dying Kurtz's voracious mouth and heart of darkness. For Wilde it was finally not the suffering of prison but emptiness that left him stricken, without a voice.

Reconnaissance

BECAUSE TRAUMA IS PARTLY a function of expectations, who can be surprised that American culture took on post-traumatic coloration at the end of the volatile twentieth century? In this brief reconnaissance I want to sketch some of the stories the nation developed to manage not only its changing sense of identity but also its acutely unstable expectations, because especially after the Vietnam War those stories helped create conditions conducive to ideas of trauma. For practical reasons I have had to de-emphasize some important stories—of developments in psychology, the practice of psychotherapy, health insurance, and the law, for example. Instead, I look at stories that constitute a cultural environment in which post-traumatic themes flourished.

Many of these stories assume a life-cycle plot of the sort that made Max Nordau's *Degeneration* so alarming in the 1890s. The youthful United States grew to heroic preeminence in the middle of the century, and is now declining toward a humiliating decrepitude. In this narrative the Vietnam War and the emergence of feminism evoke traumatic themes, as Judith Lewis Herman demonstrates, because whether you support or deplore them, they can be taken to confirm the nation's decay. Seen from above, they signify a loss of heroic power and conviction; from below they focus on themes of oppression and victimization. At both extremes the changes labeled "decline" imply increased polarization, competition, and awareness of injury.

The stories I call post-traumatic reflect the radical disorientation of the century. After all, whole classes of people—farmers and servants—have nearly vanished in the course of the century. An urbanized industrial work force has coalesced and in its turn begun to disappear into a service economy, its jobs usurped by machines or captured by the "barbarian hordes" of immigrants that worried Teddy Roosevelt. Where Roosevelt's bully America was expansively imperial, after the Vietnam War the country became, like Britain a century earlier, anxious about its "loss" of frontier, empire, status, and vitality. President Reagan tried to reinflate warrior heroism. But with the collapse of the "evil empire" there was once again, as in the 1890s, a shortage of enemies to support warrior self-esteem, even as globalized economic competition was sharpening survival anxieties.

Tom Engelhardt calls this "the end of victory culture."[1] From the beginning, he argues, America's national identity was grounded in a tale of expanding democratic freedom and manifest destiny that euphemized a history of exploitation. In effect, Saint George signed the Mayflower Compact and the Declaration of Independence, pacified the frontier in a coonskin cap, and made the world safe for democracy in more than one war. Like imperial Britain's slaughter of eleven thousand dervishes with Maxim machine guns and forty-eight British casualties at the Battle of Omdurman in the Sudan,[2] the American expansion brought an exterminatory force to bear on Native Americans and colonized people such as the Huks in the Philippines. The octopus that came to dominate commerce required an elaborate architecture of prejudices and doublethink to rationalize its antidemocratic aggrandizement.[3] World War II substantiated the victory story and rescued the nation from the Great Depression, and classic Westerns and war movies prolonged the triumphal note. But the Vietnam debacle, the Soviet collapse, and giddy shifts in gender and class relations have undercut the victory culture, even as the World War II generation is dying out. In the 1990s the Holocaust took on new prominence in accounts of the war, a change symptomatic of a shift in emphasis from victors to victims. The outcome has been a moment of incoherence that can signify opportunity (as in Ronald Reagan's "morning in America") or a doomsday loss of purpose (as in Robert Bork's *Slouching towards Gomorrah*). The historical turn has compromised a venerable immortality system, shaking collective self-esteem and arousing an end-of-empire morbidity of the sort Rider Haggard took to heart.[4]

Engelhardt thinks of this "triumphalist despair" as a "societal crisis" of "storylessness,"[5] and I take his point. But the victory story has not vanished; rather, it has evolved into new forms and opened up spaces in cultural imagination for compensatory tales. Although "storylessness" constituted a shock in its own right, some of the narratives that were developed to manage it actually heightened the atmosphere of crisis and reinforced the sense of injury. It can be difficult to describe these post-traumatic stories because they are really a cluster of loosely interrelated, often competing narratives, sometimes as powerful yet inchoate as moods. In addition, as an improving economy began to soften some post-traumatic themes toward the close of the 1990s, memories dimmed of the bizarre emotions of the post-Vietnam period when an elderly Iranian ayatollah had America "held hostage," and anxiety about increasing homelessness, child abuse, and family breakdowns coincided with demands for sacrifice and Spartan hardness.

A cross section of these clustered narratives can be seen in the story that took official form in the speeches of President Reagan during the early 1980s, even as the post-Vietnam awareness of trauma was beginning to crystallize. Not only was the Reagan version representative and widely sanctioned, it also remained the nation's "life story" into the 1990s. It had a strong mythic-religious coloration, and it functioned as both a response to and a source of post-traumatic themes. Ronald Reagan did not invent the story he told. Still, his childhood in the Midwest during the Great Depression did give the story resonance, and it helps explain why the nation elected him to tell it. Much of the story's material came from the corporate and financial elites that used Reagan as their ideological spokesman for many years; some came from the religious right; and some originated in traditional Midwestern or "hometown" ideas about America. No less important are the *fin de siècle* themes that the story naively recycles. Reagan's speeches echoed Max Nordau's *Degeneration* and the Time Traveller's admonitory vision, even as his military alarums resembled the outcry about the British decline after the Boer War and his budgets promoted a compensatory arms race like the buildup that culminated in World War I.

In the story Reagan told, America had suffered traumatic injuries. Externally, from Vietnam to Nicaragua, the Soviet "evil empire" was the ultimate perpetrator. But the nation had been vulnerable because it had degenerated into a self-indulgent "compassionate state." The president would have to take the budget ax to sacrifice enfeebling social programs while pumping up military-industrial investment. Because "big government" had become a dragonlike or vampirelike monster devouring "our" vital capital resources, and because welfare had bred greedy dependence, a perverse generosity was fatally weakening us all, even the healthy.[6] Accordingly, political cartoons pictured President Reagan taking over a sinking ship or slashing at reptilian budgetary monsters poised to devour him and the nation.[7] Spartan "cuts" would have to hurt some parasitical people, but that suffering would restore vitality. In the sports slang of the day, "no pain, no gain." In an Election Day broadcast during the severe 1982 recession, one unemployed voter told an interviewer, "Well, Reagan said it was going to be painful. It *is* painful, but the pain will do some good." Another believed that "this recession has been a cleansing thing."[8]

The Reagan story's post-traumatic quality lies not only in its aura of injury, but also in its internal conflicts. The story hardened group boundaries again after the ferment of the 1960s and Vietnam War protests, and it did so by scapegoating "enemies" inside and outside the country. Unlike Franklin Roosevelt's famous reassurance during the Depression—the only thing we have to fear is fear itself, and "our" government can help us all—Reagan's speeches countered fear by prescribing self-punishment in the service of urgent self-idealization. In practice the result was a splitting, as in the heroic aggrandizement of Holmes and his circle accomplished through the sacrifice of Small and the insubordinate black "child" Tonga.

In the 1980s the sacrifice and social death of the nation's parasites, from "welfare queens" to the homeless, confirmed the survival of the righteous— Main Street America, but especially yuppies, daring entrepreneurs, and warrior-heroes.[9] Like hysteria, such a system is self-intoxicating. Reduced support for the poor contributed to a new Gilded Age for the affluent, who relieved their sharpened guilt about their own greedy appetites by projecting them onto "greedy" welfare parasites and a grasping "evil empire." Much of the windfall for the affluent resulted from tax and deregulatory "revolts" against "big government," policies that fanned resentment against the institution embodying the national identity—another form of symbolic self-division and self-hate. In this atmosphere of psychic conflict, the concept of traumatic victimization helped the losers explain and seek redress for their battered self-esteem, and helped the elites justify their aggressive appetites as lifesaving discipline. The preoccupation with traumatic sacrifice and deflation in the early 1980s laid the ground for the compensatory binge of berserking—deregulation, federal indebtedness, speculative mania, and downsizing—that followed. Although the savings-and-loan scandal broke historical records, the memory of it dimmed in the 1990s partly because the new gambling mentality actually grew stronger.

It is easy to overestimate Ronald Reagan's responsibility for the demonstrable harm this fantasy system caused. He personified the widespread frustration and anger in American society after the Vietnam defeat, and also the folksy good humor and "misspoken" casualness about facts that enabled Americans to deny their aggressive feelings. But Reagan was more a facilitator than a source for the mood, just as Victoria sparked but by herself could never have "caused" the mourning that gripped "her" subjects after Albert's death. And although it is true that particular political, economic, and religious interests fostered the story he told, in varying degrees both political parties collaborated in it, and the story resonated widely in the nation. Even in the face of unnecessary hardship, many vulnerable people acquiesced in the belief that sacrifice would bring increased vitality. The "Teflon president" could do no wrong because so many Americans shared his fantasies.

Among those approving Americans were conservative Christians, whose apocalyptic themes had close affinities with Reagan's tale. As a traumatic rescue scenario, the tale's "triumphalist despair," to use Engelhardt's term, is akin to the grim subtext haunting Saint George. In the middle of the century, Uncle Sam liberated the walled city from fascism and communism, as it were, only to suffer agony in Vietnam as Saint George did at the hands of the infidel. Unless the warrior-saint could restore his righteous strength, the "evil empire" would put him to death. In one direction—in the *Rambo* films or General Westmoreland's public speeches—this crisis supported scenarios of betrayal in Vietnam. Policymakers had carried an ambivalent nation into the war, and the grief, anger, and guilt at its defeat were so painful that many people blamed some form of treachery. Two decades later, some veterans' groups could still become apoplectic at the mention of "Hanoi Jane" Fonda.

In another direction the crisis of heroism led to religious parables of apocalyptic punishment and martyrdom. The doomsday struggle was a vital part of President Reagan's message. In 1982 the *New Yorker* commented that "'the first thing people want to know when they put on the news is . . . whether World War III has started.' Books on the coming apocalypse began selling in the millions, and *Esquire* would soon report that 'most Americans, says the Gallup poll, now think World War III may break out in the Eighties, that they themselves may not survive the attack, and that they would rather not think about the prospects.'"[10]

It is difficult to disentangle realpolitik from post-traumatic symptoms in this crisis mood. In hindsight, the rhetorical flirtation with World War III appears to have been a largely contrived adrenalin rush, wasteful but bracing. The exorbitant military buildup and the clashes in Libya, Grenada, and Panama had some therapeutic effects on self-esteem, with a modest if unnecessary loss of life. Yet the post-traumatic mood was real. The comic-opera invasion of Grenada, planned for months and executed on the flimsiest of pretexts, was so excessive that it functioned as a kind of ritualized berserking. While sunbathers and joggers watched, seven thousand troops and a supporting arsenal pounded the little island and "blew away" its one hundred Cuban combatants. ABC's *Nightline* (October 27, 1983) crowed that the nation had "snapped the tentacle of the Russian octopus [cf. dragon] that threatened us," and the exultant military handed out eight thousand medals.[11] "YANKS SEIZE TERROR ISLAND," trumpeted the *New York Post* (October 26, 1983), as if celebrating America's conquest of trauma itself.

As in the 1890s, stories like President Reagan's grew out of a familiar cognitive conflict. The twentieth century witnessed staggering atrocities and disorientation, yet standards of living improved for most Americans. The nuclear age lowered the threshold of terror by making annihilation seem a real possibility. It came to symbolize the incalculable promise and peril of modernism. Yet after World War II, paradoxically, heightened expectations of security and fulfillment increased people's sensitivity to shock. For here was a nation in which, for nearly the first time in history—at least according to conventional wisdom—women, children, and workers had recognized rights, and nobody had to fear starvation. The New Deal had introduced disaster relief and retirement insurance. But President Johnson's Great Society programs, though underfunded and sometimes hastily improvised, actually represented the first attempt at a comprehensive national effort to improve the lives of ordinary people.

With its debts, dissension, and unresolved inner furies, the Vietnam War ended the idea that well-being for everyone was a national project. The post-traumatic character of people's responses developed not only from the war's palpable damage, but also from a sense of betrayal. Veterans, policymakers, antiwar protesters, grieving relatives—each group could point to some nemesis to explain the loss. However fair the blame, betrayal models the same dynamics as traumatic abuse. Feeling victimized, people believed they had been unjustly manipulated by unaccountable forces. In different groups ambivalence toward the war split off a reproachful conscience that in turn called up equally angry defenses against guilt. To the extent that stabbing consciences and guilt remained alienated, they gave shape, in a variety of combinations, to the roles of abuser and victim.

In this way the war is emblematic of the shock that rising expectations met as the nation tilted toward its supposed decline. Stories like President Reagan's aimed to relieve this shock. "We" had been betrayed by enemies but also weakened by our affluence. "We" had become a "pitiful, helpless giant," but through sacrifice (lowering expectations) and an investment in the fighting spirit (taming threats, chastening parasites, redeeming self-esteem) we could heal this trauma.[12] It is a measure of how inadequate this account was that it so readily merged with the apocalyptic imagery of the Christian right. The conflicts within the story limited its ability to relieve psychic distress, and so the potency of the imagery had to be increased.

One basic reason for the story's poor fit with reality is that, as in the 1890s, anxiety produced a rhetoric of sacrifice—recall the Happy Prince literally giving himself away—and messianic ambition. But what actually came into play was a doctrine of Social Darwinist competition that inevitably favored the powerful, and frightened or actually injured others. In this sense the Vietnam War shifted to the domestic sphere, and a tacit war against the poor supplanted Johnson's War on Poverty. Although it is easy to exaggerate or sanitize it, much of the survival dread and messianic renewal of the post-Vietnam decades reflected unresolved vindictive feelings. Rarely, if ever, for example, did President Reagan express sympathy or nurture in his speeches. And his chief theoretician, George Gilder, was openly scathing about the harm caused by "the compassionate state."[13] The Reagan story was organized around fantasies of struggle, not pleasure, discovery, or empathy.

The Reagan policies demanded sacrifices at the bottom while redirecting major economic benefits toward those at the top, creating an unprecedented federal deficit. When an interviewer asked George Gilder if it was not true that "the rewards of supply-side economics are given right now, to the wealthy" while "the penalties are imposed right now, on working-class, low-income, welfare citizens," the inventor of Reaganomics "replied, with a grin, 'That's life, folks.'"[14] During the severe economic slump of the early 1980s these policies seriously hurt the poor, especially women ("welfare queens") and children.

In this climate the idea of traumatic victimization called attention to the power of—and fear of—the nation's vindictive feelings. As the Reagan story invoked trauma to justify "slashing" and "cuts," some groups—feminists and the helping professions, for example—tried to use trauma as a control signal, a brake on dangerous aggressiveness. The diagnosis of trauma and the focus on children—who could be *for* child abuse?—gave medical and "natural" authority to moral conflicts being finessed by some of the most powerful, sanctioned voices in American life. "The more children Reagan sacrificed," says deMause, "the more local newspapers discovered such group-fantasies as 'an epidemic of child abuse sweeping the city.'"[15] Although real child abuse was scarcely new, this painful sensitivity to it was. The acute emotions of that period are registered in the child-abduction hysteria that swept the country in 1983. Inflamed by false data, opportunistic media, moral panic, and fears of parental helplessness or neglect, the public imagined child molesters swarming through America's neighborhoods like vampires or "the enemy within."[16] In 1985 the *Denver Post* won a Pulitzer Prize for exposing the false alarm, showing that "official" abduction figures were being inflated at least tenfold, though this did not curb the delusion. "By the spring of 1986, pictures of miss-ing kids had appeared on three billion milk cartons."[17] A similar scare imag-ined razor blades and poisons in Halloween treats and charged the holiday with suspicion and dread. The idea of trauma flourished in this atmosphere of panic about the vulnerability of children—and the child in every adult—to malevolent "perpetrators."

Those who contributed to this overwrought atmosphere, including some politicians, therapists, and television evangelists, could fan the flames while plausibly striving to bring relief. Cognitively there is a strong link between the confessional dynamics of being "born again," "recovering" forgotten abuse, and exposing the stealthy machinations of the "evil empire." In each case there is a split-off devil to fight to redeem self-esteem. Those who benefited from encouraging the escalating alarm and stern measures could also justify their behavior by pointing to their own or the nation's injuries. Trauma could support opposite scenarios. In the 1980s, military-industrial elites began justify-ing "lean and mean" discipline "at home"—massive layoffs, attacks on housing and school lunch subsidies—as a lifesaving reaction to perceived threat and loss, even as officers in Vietnam had urged soldiers to fight traumatic bereave-ment through vindictive rage: "Don't get sad. Get even!"[18]

But executive anger in this scenario is equivocal. Although it is meant to fire up wounded or lax morale, it can also backfire, catching up managers in the fear and guilt experienced by those they "discipline." The latent metaphor that best captures the obsessional perversity of "lean and mean" policies is anorexia. As a *Los Angeles Times* article reported, "Corporate anorexia may wind up being fatal," inasmuch as "massive layoffs and corporate restructur-ings harm employee morale and prevent effective team building."[19] In busi-ness culture as among some adolescents, the logic of sacrifice depends on the self-intoxicating fantasy that shedding guilty "fat" creates more life.

The real and symbolic attacks directed at "welfare queens," and in the 1990s at "feminazis,"[20] created a polarized environment in which feminist criticism could scarcely avoid seeing analogies between gender violence—in Herman's phrase, the combat trauma of the sex war—and official "patriarchal" policy.[21] And yet for men the attacks were not only self-serving, but also a post-traumatic response to fears of lost manhood going back to the turn of the century.[22] In the 1890s the sexual revolution seemed destined to produce androgynous, enervated Eloi or despotic Amazons such as She-who-must-be-obeyed. The press was "full of violent rhetoric denouncing women who aborted as murderers."[23] Like contraception, abortion threatened to increase women's autonomy and encourage them to betray their motherly instincts. George Gilder's *Wealth and Poverty* (1981) thinly disguises its impassioned and characteristically late-Victorian social prejudices. Gilder maintains, for example, that men have been "'cuckolded by the compassionate state' which had encouraged women's sexual and career independence to such an extent that a man 'could no longer feel manly in his own home.'"[24] In the extreme, this panic about emasculation is survival dread and blurs into—for example—the misogynistic rhetoric of the 1890s that depicted abortion as the slaughter of a fetus "always presented as male, as a 'potential man.'"[25] In the 1990s it found pseudoscientific outlets in fears about "chemicals" in the environment causing male sperm counts to plummet and hormonal changes to threaten gender integrity. The tropes of trauma and cultural crash fuel this death anxiety, as when a spokeswoman for the World Wildlife Fund told a CBS interviewer that unless we keep chemicals from affecting reproductive capability, "we are headed for extinction."[26]

Now, as in the 1890s, guilt underlies many post-traumatic symptoms. In killing Tonga, Sherlock Holmes acts out British anger and guilty dread toward the colonial "children" and "barbarians" who could be expected to come storming out of the heart of darkness in retaliation for British mistreatment. And so the renewed "lean and mean" ethos of the 1980s lifted the regulatory restraints on the already powerful, weakening those with few resources to compete. The "culture of contentment," as John Kenneth Galbraith termed it, understandably preferred to attribute its own guilty appetites to greedy, "degenerate" parasites at home and hordes of greedy immigrant peasants at our borders. Competition for status and profits has knocked apart the postwar social contract, sharpening the conflicts between rich and poor, exacerbating crime, and undermining the consensus about the value of work and family.

Those suffering or fearing social death defended themselves by embracing a rhetoric of traumatic victimization. But America's elites have also invoked trauma to explain the economic windfall they served themselves. These opposite versions of the trope meet in some stories of the 1990s, especially Hollywood's mass-market fables. Not that trauma is new on the movie lot. Films about traumatic amnesia, for example, are staples of the late show. But consider a more particular connection: Sam Wood's *King's Row* (1942), the tale of traumatic amputation around which Ronald Reagan organized his autobiography *Where's the Rest of Me?* (1965).[27]

In the film, Reagan plays a young man (Drake) who had "inherited a good deal of money" but lost it and his status when "the head of the bank had absconded with it" (WRM 4). The symbolic father-son rivalry evolves into a grisly shock when Drake is injured in a railroad-yard accident. "Taken to a sadistic doctor (who disapproved of my dating his daughter and felt it was his duty to punish me), I recovered consciousness in an upstairs bedroom. I found that the doctor had amputated both my legs at the hips" (4). The scene obsessed Reagan the actor; in shooting it, "the affair began to terrify me" (5).

Through the ordeal of preparing to shoot the scene he "found that part of my experience was missing" (3).

The movie's Oedipal antagonism asks to be read in relation to Reagan's ambivalence toward his own parents.[28] Once, he remembers, his highly religious mother lost her temper "and stood as a figure of righteous wrath" while his abusive, alcoholic father "clobbered us" (WRM 11). Another time his father kicked him "a foot in the air with the flat side of his boot . . . my first sample of adult injustice" (8). Compare his description of the movie doctor who "felt it was his duty to punish" him. In part, then, "the rest of me" is the rage and pain the child must have felt, but that the grown man had "lost." In a way, Reagan's entire career was shaped by a post-traumatic numbness toward childhood conflict. The symbolic castration scene dramatized how, during a dissociated "blackout," an authority figure could cut a young man down to size, so to speak. In effect, amputation turned Reagan's character into a Jonathan Small dissociated from a helpless, angry "dwarf" alter ego. In the movie, Drake has post-traumatic nightmares whenever he hears trains at night; threat persisted in Reagan's real life also. The several years of emotional turmoil following this scene climaxed in a period of suicidal depression during a bout of pneumonia.

The castration scene was the beginning of a conversion process that would transform Reagan from a defiant Democratic labor activist into a prosperous spokesman for an anticommunist, union-busting corporate elite.[29] Interrogated by three agents from the Federal Bureau of Investigation during his involvement in the Screen Actors Guild, in the first years of the postwar Communist witch hunt, he describes not powerful governmental police powers capable of destroying his career and his new affluence, but three gentlemen "I came to admire" (WRM 170). Reagan's cryptic account of the meeting says little about his change of heart. The FBI made it intimidatingly clear that "national security" was at stake ("You know what spies and saboteurs are"); that "the Communists hated [him]"; and that the government was aggressively spying on his suspected fellow actors ("For a long time . . . we've known exactly where he has been and who he has been with"), and probably on Reagan as well (WRM 170). On the spot, Reagan turned informer. Before long he became a dutiful son to corporate power, excoriating his former allies as Communist dupes. The Reagan who spent most of the war in Hollywood became the champion of military might, yet carefully chose as adversaries only weak, insubordinate "children" such as Grenada, Panama, Libya, and, at home, protesting students and the air traffic controllers' union. In practical terms he found (and was given) roles that allowed him to restore coherence to his personal and cultural identity by suppressing in surrogate rebels dangerous motives close to his heart.

Reagan's life story reflects the dynamics of the 1980s' concern with child abuse. "Where's the rest of me?" is the basic question behind "recovered memory" therapies. Searching for the missing "rest of me," the man could not bear to blame (and perhaps felt it unfair to blame) an abusive father and social world.[30] Instead, the star who had suffered abuse as a child converted to become one of the patriarchal abusers that feminists and liberals deplored, redirecting his residual wrath at the phantom of big government. This is the opposition of predatory parent and cannibal child familiar to us from the 1890s, and the familiar pattern of the abused child becoming an abusive adult. It helps explain how the rhetoric of victimization and "me first" affluence can be functions of survival competition in the Reagan story, even as they point to deeply rooted generational antagonisms.

But the same conversion experience also spotlights the crucial ambiguity that has always shadowed trauma studies: the degree to which the behaviors are strategic. There is consternation when defendants in court justify their aggression by claiming to have been victimized. But in the 1980s, post-traumatic themes served different interests, and not always consciously. In joining the nation's affluent elite, Ronald Reagan needed a forcefully defined sense of injury and anger to reconcile his privileged status with his sense of decency and his doubts about his personal worth. After all, the "rest of me," he says in his memoir, is the political persona he discovered after his conversion, and it was something missing because he felt that the life of an actor was insubstantial. Growing up with a confusing and simplistic ideology in hard, contentious times, he—like many Americans—badly needed a means to substantiate himself.

On a larger scale, in the 1980s the go-go culture licensed by Reaganomics likewise had use for the trope in its efforts to substantiate a sense of heroic purpose. The ambiguity is always problematic, because in every phase of these stories huge sums of money and prestige were—and still are—at stake. Among other things, sacrifice and survival discipline, further rationalized as "lean and mean" management, supported the frenzy of speculative buyouts and downsizing that by the mid-1990s the press was comparing to battlefield slaughter.[31] The factory of pulleys and gears that Havelock Ellis feared was arbitraged into a "rust belt" and superseded by a computer-driven global financial system akin to the fabled octopus of a century ago. Donald L. Barlett and James B. Steele summed up the harmful effects on the nation's work force and its families in *America: What Went Wrong?* (1992), whose title points to a traumatic accident. As earning power declined, people worked longer hours, women entered the work force in greater numbers, and terms such as *single-parent family* and *latchkey children* became commonplace. During the 1980s the Reagan story so dominated national life that newscasters seemed to be reporting a natural disaster when they itemized new layoffs, liquidated careers, and the occasional suicide of foreclosed farmers.[32] To preserve a sense of perspective, listeners would have had to remind themselves how bizarre it is that the nation could land humans on the moon and yet could not, or would not, protect its own citizens from catastrophe in their working lives.

Recycling the Victorians

Stories like the one President Reagan assembled can be seen as attempts to come to terms with injuries caused by historical change. But they also served to rationalize the stress of new (or renewed) economic and status competition. Reagan campaigned for President in an atmosphere of fears about modernism and cultural crash that naively recreated 1890s hysteria. "A strange new disease has found its way into the lives of Americans and . . . people in other highly industrialized nations of the world," warned Karl Albrecht in *Stress and the Manager* (1979). Stress "is now reaching epidemic proportions, yet it is not transmitted by any known bacterium or other microorganism. The range of symptoms is so broad as to bewilder the casual observer and to send the typical physician back to the textbooks. The symptoms range from minor discomfort to death." For a remedy Albrecht prescribed a healthy lifestyle and a program of "humanizing the business organization" through "human resource development" or "preserving and developing human beings." In his prognostications Albrecht warned that "oppressive overcontrol on the part of top managers could well trigger widespread employee revolts," and that public resentment could even bring about the abolition of corporations.[33]

As it turned out, the 1980s was a decade not of humanized corporations but of "lean and mean" ruthlessness and the "corrective" demolition of rust-belt industries. The Reagan stories and the trope of trauma played a crucial role in this development. They "explained" the violent contradictions of a democratic society operated as a business oligarchy and driving toward a new Gilded Age, and in the process they helped defuse any "widespread employee revolts." No wonder that the stories revisited the post-traumatic themes of the late Victorians, especially degeneration and the righteous judgment of the elect and the "down-going." Ronald Reagan's personal story spotlights the rags-to-riches conflicts that drew him to self-justifying Social Darwinism, traumatic rescue, and apocalyptic struggle. As at the turn of the century, the loosened social guarantees and controls that "liberated" heroic ambitions also inescapably sharpened insecurity, not only for the abject but also for those at the top who now had much more to lose. As Saint George illustrates, once you finally triumph over adversity, there is no place to go but down—hence the suspicions of degeneration and the lure of martyrdom or apotheosis.

This dilemma haunted the late Victorians, not only Nordau and Haggard, but also Oscar Wilde and Richard Wagner. In echoing their stories, President Reagan tacitly opposed the midcentury liberal vision of social justice based on negotiation and binding arbitration.[34] Attempts to impose order on a tumultuous society through appeals to the authority of God and "the bottom line" created a strong sense of dissociation. Although headlines about terminated employees gone homicidally berserk had become commonplace by the 1990s, Judge Bork, in his jeremiad *Slouching towards Gomorrah* (1996), still sounded like Max Nordau. Those who, like the judge, recycle the Reagan story endorse its faith in a paramilitary buildup. In our post-traumatic drift, Adam Walinsky admonishes, "we" have lost "our" will to defend ourselves. Unless we send many more police into the "war" against disorder, we face a "long descending night" of crime.[35] When a woman jogger was mauled in Central Park in 1989, the millionaire deal maker Donald Trump bought a full-page ad in the *New York Times* that demanded the return of the death penalty in one-and-a-half-inch capital letters and proclaimed that "what has happened is the complete breakdown of life as we knew it."[36]

The reliance on the stories of the 1890s compensates for the incompatibility and dissociation of stories in the present. The hurricane of information that battered Renaissance Europe has not let up, even though Sherlock Holmes has metamorphosed into magical computer chips and satellite surveillance technology. Temperance—now the "war on drugs"—mounts paramilitary actions against barbarian invaders even as it defers to Tono-Bungay, Prozac, and what might reasonably be called the neurasthenia industry. As in the 1890s, the courtroom and the clinic continue to preside over traumatic injury. The struggle over suffrage continues in feminist and civil-rights discourse, while anarchism has resurfaced in militia groups and headline terrorism. The post-traumatic mood magnetizes discordant themes into unexpected alignment, as in the 1990s genre of "Christian thrillers," which imagine righteous believers betrayed by a nation in the clutches of Satan, and reveal affinities with militia doctrines.[37]

America's civic religion, consumer capitalism, is no less conflicted. Newly invented consumerism began restructuring expectations and flogging desire in the 1880s and 1890s, at about the time that trauma was being formulated. Oscar Wilde anticipated the veneration of consumer choice, and crusaded against lifeless philistinism to preserve the magic of "true" taste.[38] But in Ernest Becker's innocent, shattering words, "We *all fail* to do what we want here on earth. We *all fail* to be the persons we dreamed and wanted. . . . Who ever gets *enough life????*"[39] To the extent that consumer culture tries to fulfill immortality fantasies with visions of endless plenty, it is quixotic. And when resources and expectations are tied to the factory world and out of phase with each other, shock waves radiate, as they did in the two decades of the nineties.

Among the plentiful consumer goods of the 1990s are recycled stories of the 1890s. Versions of the time machine are still blasting off in *Star Trek* sequels and in Terry Gilliam's film *Twelve Monkeys* (1995), while the war of the worlds has become sumptuously hackneyed in films such as Roland Emmerich's *Independence Day* (1996). Sherlock Holmes has proved to be as undead as Count Dracula, and both have spawned swarms of imitators. Ingenious equal-opportunity variants of Holmes now include women, minorities, clairvoyants, and hard-boiled, morally ambiguous Jonathan Smalls. Hollywood has remanu-factured *Dr. Jekyll* and recolonized *The Island of Dr. Moreau.*

To a great extent, late-Victorian story models fill the void of "storylessness" left by victory culture. But they are also a manufactured taste, promoted by the structure of mass-industrial culture, which always needs something fresh but familiar and standardized to sell to a world market.[40] They are just distant enough from the 1990s to tame their troubling content with an edge of self-parodic stylization. Television in particular makes its relentless borrowing seem fresh by fragmenting, recontextualizing, and winking at everything. In this way television models style as an end in itself, reflecting a mentality that looks back to Oscar Wilde. The resulting dissociation ambivalently signifies a liberating coolness, but also the vacancy of "plastic" culture and anxiety about "amusing ourselves to death."[41]

Like Wilde, the entertainment industry promotes chic knowingness, be-cause it is continually flirting with the exhaustion of its story models. Holmes's and Dorian Gray's dread of "staleness" still fogs the windows of the soul. Al-though the multichannel airwaves are thronged with "characters," and movies made with video release in mind replace landscape shots with close-up faces, screen narratives show little interest—little belief—in interior life. Narrative action or celebrity glamour routinely crowds out subjectivity, so that when ex-citement or charisma flags, a queasy dread of depersonalization emerges, as in fantasies about robots, aliens, and traumatic victimization. Prozac epitomizes the way formula has replaced Freud's endless analysis of character as a "fix" for neurasthenia. The promise of narrative riches keeps threatening to be a "pan-demonium" of possibilities,[42] or worse, like the Agra treasure, an empty box.

Remanufactured late-Victorian narratives are popular because they give definitive form to the mood of traumatic rescue. When the sirens screamed in the 1990s, they summoned heroic technico-medical intervention—which looked back to the analytical Holmes and empathetic Dr. Watson. In a supposedly scientific era, wearing a lab coat or a badge, Saint George still "fights" disease, crime, and other ills. Zygmunt Bauman points out that by medicalizing life—a maneuver the late Victorians first mastered—we turn death anxiety into particular manageable problems, and cycle among infallible specialists until we drop dead.[43] Technical protocols and the authority of the database operate to calm the central nervous system and manage panic. This is the style of the encyclopedic Holmes. Yet the monster is still ultimately death, and every rescue ends in eventual futility. In post-traumatic culture, that awareness becomes poisonous. Just as Holmes feels healthy only when absorbed in a particular case, so the technological fix shrinks life to a self-contained microscope slide. Medical soap operas usually feature an arrogant doctor who dramatizes this constriction.

Where there is post-traumatic constriction, we find compensatory behavior too. Lewis Lapham relates the nation's bloated medical-industrial complex to the wishful self-deception of victory culture: "Over the past fifty years the volume of superstition in the country has expanded at almost the same rate as the achievement of our science, and I suspect that both variants on the theme of immortality followed upon the American victories in World War II. Prior to 1945 few Americans imagined themselves masters of the universe and therefore entitled to immunity against the evils afflicting the lesser nations of the earth, and the medical professions performed very few miracles."[44] Religion has always managed cosmic death with the miracles of intercessory gods, angels, and saints. In the 1990s the fundamentalist Christian savior and secular figures such as Batman embodied that personalized intercession; even a modest fad for angels developed, Victorian in its sentimental iconography and feminine in its market orientation. But generally, heroic agency has continued to split into superheroes and antiheroes, dragon-slayer and martyr, with queasy ironies negotiating the chasm between them.[45]

The Old in the New

In a courtroom or a clinical setting, or in a novel, today as in the 1890s, trauma invariably radiates assumptions that need examination. This is especially true in contemporary popular narratives in which the victims—women, children, and minorities, for example—are often explicitly protagonists of ideological change. Even though culture may recycle Victorian imaginative materials, a new world is coming into being, but we cannot grasp much more than a line here and a patch of color there. Although contemporary post-traumatic narratives often advertise progressive or feminist values, for example, their use of trauma sometimes disguises the persistence of old triumphalist cultural forms and their subversion of the new. Similarly, the berserking in some Hollywood films dramatizes the expectable outrage of underdogs, but it can also disguise the economic violence of elites. Many of the examples I analyze have been chosen because they illustrate the complexities of trauma as a trope, and repay attention precisely because they are so often deceptive.

Chapters 6 and 7 explore psychocultural identity and traumatic abuse; chapters 8 and 9 focus on the traumatic legacy of black slavery and of the Holocaust; chapter 10 considers traumatic undercurrents in romance narratives; chapters 11 and 12 examine different forms of berserking. Throughout, I have tried to keep in sight the socioeconomic shifts that affect all these representations of violence, injury, and reaction. The factory world, for example, drove events in the Vietnam War in profound ways. The secretary of defense, former Ford executive Robert McNamara, rationalized the military on corporate lines, and his strategy assumed that lavish technology and matériel would prevail over a rustic enemy.[46] In the post-Soviet 1990s, victory culture lived on in corporate capitalism's story of world conquest, even though—as in the Vietnam War—there are self-confounding distortions in this myth, and it has many dissenters.

This should not surprise us. Trauma and triumph have been complementary masks in America from the beginning. The nation was founded as a haven for victims of old-world oppression *and* as a business venture. Misfortune, homesickness, and death racked the Puritan founders of the New Jerusalem. In facile praise of the early settlers' spiritual fortitude and in facile moralizing about their atrocities it is easy to overlook how profoundly terror shaped their culture. From witchcraft hysteria to outbreaks of genocidal frenzy against Native Americans, a good deal of early American history can be productively understood in terms of post-traumatic behavior.[47] Often symptoms—the witchcraft persecutions, for example—appeared just as living conditions seemed to be stabilizing. The security that settlement brought was continually undercut by the poisonous tensions of slavery, schism, and class conflict. As Toni Morrison puts it, "For a people who made so much of their 'newness'—their potential freedom, and innocence—it is striking how dour, how troubled, how frightened and haunted our early and founding literature truly is."[48] One of the central tropes of that "founding literature" is the protean captivity narrative in which Saint George appears in a coonskin hat or, in D. W. Griffith's *Birth of a Nation*, in Klan regalia.

The triumphalism in American stories was developed to justify the acquisitive, consolidating project of settlement. It was designed to recruit support, define group identity, and sort out a mob of values. Even so, the familiar lineaments of traumatic rescue are rarely out of sight. Repeatedly the cavalry must gallop onstage because demonic "savages" have ambushed peaceable Christian families who have drawn their covered wagons into a defensive circle like the medieval walled city. In Hollywood Westerns and war films, victimization justifies the rescuers' exterminating fury against the bestial other. The enemy invariably threatens to capture a maiden or a pregnant wife, stripping off scalps just as Saint George's dragon strews body parts about. The ideological emphasis may be on triumph or on terror, but in either case injury and aggrandizement are synergistic. In Horatio Greenough's sculpture *Rescue* (1837–43), for example, "a superhuman pioneer . . . wrests the tomahawk from an all-but-naked savage who is about to brain the Caucasian mother and child at his feet. The Indian warrior is as helpless in the grip of the backwoodsman as that baby is in its mother's arms. . . . The Indian brave stands no chance and does not, Greenough seems to imply, deserve one, either."[49] Greenough's "superhuman pioneer," often associated with the Indian-hater Daniel Boone, stood dealing death on the steps of the Capitol until 1958. A decade later, when Arthur Penn's *Little Big Man* appeared (1970), the Vietnam War was looking futile, and a complex of guilt, sympathy for victimized Indians, and shock had undercut stories like Boone's.

As in imperial Britain in the 1890s, the stupefying obsessiveness of rescue and triumph has compensated for guilt and dread. In 1880, Pierton Dooner wrote a disaster novel about the conquest of the United States, the first of many knockoffs of Chesney's *Battle of Dorking* (1871). Dooner's *Last Days of the Republic* "is an early example of the mortal blow dealt by the enemy from within, then a novel device that would become a universal stereotype before the end of the century. On this occasion Chinese labourers combine to take over the United States; the Imperial Dragon flag of China is raised over the Capitol; Washington falls to the merciless yellow men."[50]

In a 1919 magazine story titled "One Awful Night," the Chinese threat has literally gone underground and the rescue has a strongly post-traumatic cast. The story's detective heroes descend into "the famous Chinese tunnels" under San Francisco's Chinatown to kill "Chinese crooks gobbling up the girls by the wholesale and shipping them to the Chinese foreign markets."[51] The story appeared during a period of immigrant-bashing after World War I, a time of civil unrest (including the Boston police strike), Red scares, and labor strife. Its maidens are passive icons of fertility, in trouble because they went out "in party dresses," without their protective white menfolk. They have been nabbed by "slant-eyed," "yellow-skinned devils" whose subterranean lair evokes the satanic dragon and paranoid psychic topography. Breaking up this white-slave trade, the hero himself is nearly killed. Saved by his comrades, he collapses from "the nervous strain" and wakes up in his own bed, shocked to discover in the mirror his post-traumatic self with "snowy white hair."

Late-Victorian themes resonate in "One Awful Night" and have surfaced again at the end of the twentieth century, more lurid than ever. The story conjures up terror and berserk rage, then achieves closure through the hero's dissociative "blackout," which is followed by a crippling, self-alienated numbness. Waking up in his bed senescent, with white hair (like Leo Vincey), the narrator has eliminated the Chinese sex fiends, but also his own drives toward rape and murder. The intrusive devils are cannibalistic like Tonga, but they also are businessmen, the combination evoking the monopolistic *fin de siècle* octopus ("gobbling up the girls by the wholesale").

No less strikingly, the story anticipates many of the imaginative materials that coalesced again fatally in American thinking about the Vietnam War, from the tunnels and the dehumanization of the "gooks" under the tyrannical "King Chang" to the subtexts of rape and loss of freedom, and the paramilitary nature of the American rescue. As the narrator of "One Awful Night" boasts, "Both being former Philipine Scouts during the Spanish-American war, we had little trouble to prove to the Chief of the Agency . . . that we had not purchased our expert riflemen's medals in some second-hand store."[52] The psychic crippling of the narrator evokes as well the expectation that while the "Agency" and the nation triumph, the ordinary trooper—the laborer, the young—will be sacrificed. Readers are not invited to recall that the "Agency" is presumably Pinkerton's, the mercenary enforcer for industrial lords such as Andrew Carnegie and Henry Clay Frick, who sent a private army of Pinkerton guards into Homestead, Pennsylvania, in 1892 to crush the last unionized steelworkers, in an undeclared war whose hardships and killing concretized the coercion euphemized in labor relations.

In "One Awful Night," victory culture still commands heroic conviction. But the closing image of self-sacrifice is formulaic yet unsettling. The story resorts to the contrived blackout to bring closure because it cannot imagine life for the narrator—the ordinary person—caught in the dangerous space between its triumphal and its persecutory ideation. Dynamically, the detective ends up at a characteristic late-Victorian dead end: impotent between messianic and self-sacrificing fantasies. As a soldier in Vietnam, his violence would be combat berserking, triggered by his intolerable position—of captivity or enslavement, as the psychiatrist Jonathan Shay puts it—between an enemy and a command structure that will punish or kill him if he does not fight.[53] In the aftermath of the Vietnam War the pat irony of the detective's white hair would become black comedy, like a detail out of Kurt Vonnegut's *Slaughterhouse Five*, and the psychic freeze would be explicitly post-traumatic. "One Awful

Night" can be read as an unconscious, euphemistic gloss on the traumatic experiences of recently returned veterans of World War I, even as the stricken detective and the drugged, commodified women victims presage the antiwar and feminist issues that crystallized in the Vietnam era.

Since the Vietnam War, veterans and feminists have used trauma to substantiate heroic counternarratives that repudiate victory (or patriarchal) culture. And that opposition has resonated widely across the political spectrum, so that even Michael Apted's *Thunderheart* (1992), a Hollywood movie about the American Indian movement, combines post-traumatic themes with an indictment of government brutality in a scenario that would have been unthinkable before the Vietnam War.

In the 1990s, victory culture had become like philistinism in the 1890s: a predominantly although not exclusively elite ideology, increasingly subject to ambivalence and irony. Even nihilism can be a thrilling opportunity. Oscar Wilde argued that an absence of *stories that matter* can be both a liberation and an injury. Which it is depends on your situation, as *De Profundis* wrenchingly demonstrates. In the pages that follow I try not to lose sight of the ambivalence of "storylessness," although in a book about trauma the freedom to reinvent the self gets less space than do widespread fears of a loss of subjectivity.

Two responses to storylessness begin to get at its threat to subjectivity. One response looks to the past; the other is postmodern. In John Sayles's film *Passion Fish* (1992), the star of a television soap opera is paralyzed by an auto accident in New York City. As May Alice wakes up terrified in the hospital, she ironically sees herself on television in her soap opera role as an amnesia victim. Here television literally models the injured woman's traumatic dissociation. Among other things, it implies that her real life in New York has been a fiction: that she has fallen victim to a cultural crash, in a numbed, alcoholic world that uses the camera and soap opera gimmicks to get illusory control over trauma. The medium models the "doublethink" of trauma. For a truly paralyzed victim, the onscreen story is a sham.

As *Passion Fish* develops, the crippled actress returns to her childhood home in rural Louisiana. At first she rages against her helplessness, but then she gradually rediscovers—like a recovering amnesia victim—the roots of her identity, renewed feeling, and solidarity with others. By the film's close we can appreciate that television has an oracular, riddling immediacy that tests the viewer's resources. In New York the tube made glitz and deception attractive to May Alice, even as it was displaying as empty soap opera the real, injured self she could only begin to acknowledge once she was in the hospital, actually stricken. *Passion Fish* proposes that trauma concentrates her mind on deep survival values, preparing the way for recovery—which turns out to be the recovery of romance with a hometown boy and the "lost" pastoral America of her Louisiana. Variations of this story abound in the chapters ahead, although in Hollywood treatments the traumatic city is often Los Angeles, and redemption lies in the hometown America merchandized by Disney.[54]

As it turns out, postmodern America reveals the same threat and recuperation of lost subjectivity. In a survey of "America's Blank Generation Fiction," for example, one of the most striking things about the generation and its fictions is that they are no more blank than "the lost generation" was lost.[55] The coauthors construe the novelists and their characters as survivors of a cultural crash, but behind the lyrical nihilism are predictably unconventional heroic projects.

Dennis Cooper's novel *Closer* (1989), for instance, features two car crashes. Elizabeth Young and Graham Caveney are enthusiastic about the hip "textual disjunctions wherein Cooper locates sublimity." But they summarize the smash-ups with an old-fashioned moral tidiness: "In the first crash, pornographic inauthenticity was shattered. In [the second] all the teen pop dreams are demolished. That is over." Describing an episode of sadomasochistic gay sex, they claim that "one of the differences between 1890s and 1980s decadence [is that] hysteria and emotionalism have been replaced by chilly cool." Yet chilly coolness is Dorian Gray's master fantasy, and in Cooper's novel that coolness turns out to be throbbing with unexamined sentiment. Finally, the two critics puff that "Cooper can be numbered among, in Barthes's words: 'the very few writers who combat both ideological repression and libidinal repression.'"[56] This "combat" tacitly makes Cooper an elite ideological warrior, with the blessing of the elite intellectual authority Roland Barthes. Postmodern desolation functions in the novel as an operatic backdrop for a familiar style of romantic rebellion.

High and low, academic and punk, postmodernism waffles ingeniously about the anguish and ecstasy of lost certitudes. Its rhapsodies about the freedoms of simulation and constructible identity hark back to Oscar Wilde's dream of multiple selves. But we need only substitute "staleness" for "storylessness" to be reminded that even for Sherlock Holmes, a century ago, the problem was already oppressive. And the Holmes solution—a voyeuristic immersion in thrilling, exotic cases, followed by a visionary, drugged collapse—has many echoes in the fashionable rhetoric of the 1990s. A recent article diagnoses in Generation X films a return of the neurasthenia of the 1890s, seen as "less a disorder of the person than a social malady, a pathology for a culture of slackers."[57]

Part II

Trauma as Story in the 1990s

Certainly Vietnam marked a definitive exit point in American history and the 1960s a sharp break with the past. . . . There, the war story's codes were jumbled, its roles redistributed, its certitudes dismantled, and new kinds of potential space opened up that proved, finally, less liberating than frightening. Americans had lived with and within victory culture for so long that no one left its precincts voluntarily. . . . The loss of boundaries beyond which conflict could be projected and of an enemy suitable for defeat in those borderlands meant a collapse of story. The post–Vietnam War years have so far represented only the afterlife of this societal crisis, the playing out of storylessness.

Tom Engelhardt, *The End of Victory Culture*

Unhealed combat trauma—and I suspect unhealed severe trauma from any source—destroys the unnoticed substructure of democracy, the cognitive and social capacities that enable a group of people to freely construct a cohesive narrative of their own future.

Jonathan Shay, *Achilles in Vietnam*

SIX

Thinking through Others

PROSTHETIC FANTASY AND TRAUMA

FEW IMAGES EVOKE the traumatic potential of modernism as powerfully as a plane crash or its late-Victorian antecedent, the train wrecks that indirectly contributed to the concept of traumatic neurosis. Chapter 6 begins with planes, trains, and cars because they are prosthetic extensions of us. They enable us to overcome our physical limits. We are virtuoso toolmakers, continually expanding ourselves through prosthetic engagement with the world. Although the word *prosthetic* usually signifies an artificial replacement for a missing or defective body part, I use the term to emphasize the way tools and relationships make up for our creaturely limitations. As in the story of Daedalus, the thinking animal is always seeking to make the body as unbounded as imagination is. Prosthetic relations may entail Faustian artifice, but they can also be symbiotic and are grounded in biology and the basic operations of culture.

Modernism is a period of radical prosthetic development in human identity. Only within the past century or so have we become creatures whose bare feet rarely if ever touch the ground, creatures who can see inside their bodies, artificially propagate themselves in petri dishes, walk on the moon. In this framework our prosthetic dimension calls into question the kind of animal we are. What is the ground of our experience? Where does the self stop and the tool begin? If a house or a piece of clothing functions as a shell, where does the self stop and the environment begin? And because other people can extend our wills as tools do, in a host of relationships from slavery to parenting, we sometimes need to ask where the self leaves off and the other begins.

Trauma reflects a disruption of prosthetic relationships to the world. By exposing the constructed and interdependent nature of our existence, it makes vivid how radically vulnerable and ephemeral we are. It follows that one way of looking at post-traumatic culture is to examine prosthetic relations.

Let me ground these propositions in the concrete experience of a particular child. One night when my daughter Vanessa was four years old, a dream woke her—a "good dream," she reported, meaning no devouring monsters. When I asked what it was about, she answered "You were teaching me to drive."

Ah, I thought: a dream about gaining autonomy. Lovely. I asked her where we were driving in the dream. Impatiently, she said "Oh, you weren't there."

"But you said I was teaching you to drive," I reminded her. She insisted: "Da-ad. You weren't there!" I asked the logical question: "How could I teach you to drive if I wasn't there?"

She puzzled over it, frowning. Finally, she gasped: "Oh, I know! It was like, well, I was holding the steering wheel and your voice was in my head. You'd say, 'Okay, step on that thing on the floor and the car will go. Good, good. Turn the wheel so we don't hit that tree. Good, good.' And that way I was driving."

We are, says Prospero, such stuff as dreams are made on. In Vanessa's dream, Freud might say, I am an introjected voice of cultural authority that she experiences as part of herself. On the one hand, my voice is teaching her, shaping her, authorizing her self-assertion. In Clifford Geertz's well-known formulation, "our ideas, our values, our acts, even our emotions are, like our nervous system itself, cultural products—products manufactured, indeed, out of tendencies, capacities, and dispositions with which we were born, but manufactured nonetheless."[1]

At the same time, though, in the dream I am an extension of herself, a tool the child is using to extend her reach and amplify her power. She is using me to account for herself. The dream points to a culturally authorized "voice in the head"—presumably one of many—to explain how she knows what she knows, and why she does what she does. The dream uses the voice of a parent—the representation of a parent—to locate the ground of her personality and to substantiate her in the world. It shows the child (literally) moving toward greater differentiation and autonomy, out of that earlier state in which, for example, two-year-olds may feel their own fingers to see if they are hurt when someone else cries.

As I read it, Vanessa's dream shows the child learning to think "through" other people. From a psychoanalytic perspective the relationship of child to parent resembles transference. The child projects power and control onto the other and then lets herself be directed by that reassuringly all-knowing figure. Although this seems to me true as far as it goes, transference usually implies regression, escape from anxiety, and the surrender of autonomy.[2] Vanessa's dream, however, also dramatizes symbiosis. The child imagines two wills working as one—with herself ultimately in control ("You weren't there!").

For her, the relationship is compensatory but also creative. She is "conceiving" a change in her own identity and appropriating the process of learning as she adapts to the future signified by the car and her place behind the steering wheel.[3] She trusts the world, and the car is the vehicle of her mastery in more ways than one. It is easy to see how symbiosis must accommodate increasing conflict and negotiation as a growing child strives for an expanding share of adult power. At about the age of three, after her first serious clash of wills with her mother, Vanessa dreamed that "a witch was beating me." But in the golden age of this dream, as it were, the child thinks through the internalized other.

To be sure, this is only one dream, by chance discovered, and as a young woman Vanessa now has no recollection of the dream at all. Still, as symbolically constituted animals, we live through ongoing efforts to ground the self in the world. Not so surprisingly, then, the process of internalization leaves telltale traces. The historical record is rich with vestiges of this process of cultural self-substantiation.

From one perspective, Western religious history is a record of shifting relationships to supernatural voices. In the Garden of Eden humankind directly communicated with God in the ecstasy of praise. With the Fall came an awakening from that ecstatic immediacy into self-awareness, the voice of the Lord now walking in the garden, alien and intrusive, defining the furtive, suddenly mortal Adam and Eve. Thereafter communication with God the Father required the mediation of prayer, although prayer might still take the form of intrusive voices. Popular culture has preserved a host of supernatural voices, from belief in angels and the occult counsel of psychics to anxieties about the insinuations of Satan. Children send letters to Santa Claus, who knows when you are sleeping or awake, when you are being naughty or nice. Victorian spiritualism used séances to catch reassuring voices from beyond. Schizophrenics often cannot screen out voices.

The archaic Greeks sometimes reported volition as the experience of a materialized voice.[4] In a moment of decision the Homeric warrior hallucinates the goddess Athena, who commands his limbs to act. The goddess objectifies cultural process; she is cultural control made user-friendly, as it were. The healing cult of Aesculapius brought patients into a temple to be healed by dreams in which the god "brought about their recovery by words alone or by manipulation at the site of the malady," in "a distinctly psychotherapeutic atmosphere."[5] Aesculapius anticipated Otto Rank, who explicitly conceived of the therapist acting as a prosthetic "helper ego" for troubled patients.[6]

By the time the goddess Diana materialized in Shakespeare's *Pericles* in early-modern Europe, ancient epiphany had become complexly naturalized and problematic. Shakespeare's theater used irony and parody to make the revelation equivocal, as in epilogues that mischievously blurred the boundary between sleeping and waking. This could be a risky strategy if parody shaded into mockery and threatened unconscious convictions about the ground of experience. After all, Renaissance witches aroused paranoid fury by supposedly mocking solemn rites such as the Mass. And people still try to protect supernatural voices from disenchantment, as in the death sentence decreed against Salman Rushdie for his novelistic insinuation that the lives of Islamic believers may be grounded not in the voice of God but in a voice out of fallible—and mortal—human history. With mind-boggling ingenuity, Christian "creationism" still labors to repackage the world as the personal handiwork of a divine parent.[7]

By relating the ephemeral self to the ultimate framework of thought, internalized cosmic voices provide substantiation for a creature faced with the prospect of final nothingness. Such voices constitute a suppositional or fictive ground for culture itself. In effect, like culture, they become a symbolic habitat for a symbolic creature always in need of shelter. The problem is, that habitat is finally as contingent as human life itself. Like the Victorians' fervor for spiritualism and fortunetellers, the 1990s fad for psychic telephone "networks" witnesses a need for uncanny voices to help shape everyday lives. On tape and in person, motivational speakers also perform a prosthetic service.[8]

One of the clearest illustrations of the link between traumatic death anxiety and prosthetic systems is a story that circulated on the Internet about a seven-year-old boy dying of inoperable cancer who wished through the Children's Wish Foundation for a million get-well cards so he could make the book of world records before he died. The appeal generated such a tidal wave of mail that the parents and the foundation implored people to stop the process as it continued spreading through the seemingly endless—immortal—reaches of the Internet. The dying child dreamed of a world of greeting-card voices sustaining him, and other mortals rushed to be part of that life-giving system.[9]

We aspire to autonomy, but we are literally made out of other people, so autonomy is bound to be conditional. For soldiers caught in the horror of World War I, writes Joanna Bourke, "it is clear that, on the whole, 'reality' remained firmly located back in 'dear old Blighty' and men continued to be engrossed in the day-to-day lives of their family and friends. . . . For most, home remained the touchstone of all their actions."[10] To preserve their sanity, soldiers concentrated on a prosthetic "reality," a "touchstone" by which to ground themselves. In Pat Barker's trilogy of novels about the war, centered on the British psychiatrist W. H. R. Rivers, some of Rivers's shell-shocked patients hallucinate the ghosts of fellow soldiers living and dead, who embody the moral and psychic crises "haunting" the traumatized survivors.[11] This hallucinatory thinking through others reveals the prosthetic network—the bonds—that supported individual soldiers in their extreme peril. But Barker also uses it to dramatize the soldiers' governing conviction that the network must survive, and that therefore they have a deep, irrational, organic responsibility to return to the front.

A Historical Application

Periods of unusual stress are marked by extraordinary efforts to devise a convincing ground for identity. In Shakespeare's day, for example, religious strife was, among other things, a competition to validate cosmic voices. Protestants and Catholics struggled over the ontological status of God's voice. Not only was the Word ambiguously alive on the page for many believers, but it could have a kind of comprehensive emotional authority difficult for modern imaginations to appreciate. When the famously playful Sir Thomas More repudiated Luther's heretical belief in individual communion with the divine voice, he mixed the ideation of fatherhood with oral and scatological imagery in an outburst of extraordinary horror and rage: "For as long as your reverend paternity will be determined to tell these shameless lies, others will be permitted, on behalf of his English majesty [Henry VIII], to throw back into your paternity's shitty mouth, truly the shit-pool of all shit, all the muck and shit which your damnable rottenness has vomited up, and to empty out all the sewers and privies onto your crown."[12] More's imagery evokes Satan, that other ruler, the vomiting father of lies, who is always threatening to displace the divine Father. In his fury More imagines expelling from his own body and from the body politic's "sewers and privies" the excremental essence of the false father. In developmental terms, he imagines a child expelling the internalized father and defiantly flinging "muck and shit" at him.

But More's violent dread is by no means unusual. The idea of a renaissance itself answers to anxiety about origins. To discover scraps of ancient lives is to face the traumatic possibility that whole worlds can vanish and leave not a rack behind. Hence the compensatory drive to resurrect the ancients' voices in imagination (and in the theater) in order to be situated in an expanded history, playing on a grander stage. Tudor propagandists did something similar in projecting various founding fathers for the state, including King Arthur; aristocrats paid to have their family trees traced back to the Garden of Eden and the first father.

As for Shakespeare, think of the many plays that begin with identity radically adrift—Viola shipwrecked in *Twelfth Night*, for example. Again and again the opening action is an effort to project an identity. As in the master trope of the period, that life is a play or a dream, the plays depict identity as an assertion— really an emergence—of will from the inchoate contingency of sleep or the tiring room backstage. In *A Midsummer Night's Dream*, Bottom's ecstatic union with the Fairy Queen burlesques the formation of personality insofar as Bottom is a bundle of infantile appetites and Titania enables him to reach into the world to gratify his needs and desires. Through her he acquires the commanding voice of a Renaissance lord. What's more, the relationship is reciprocal inasmuch as Bottom enables Titania vicariously to work through her obsession with the changeling child. In Bottom's dream cultural voices intermingle: parent and child; monarch and subject; divinity and mortal. They substantiate one another, offering a teasing glimpse of a ground or "bottom" to personality.

At its most literal, self-substantiation reinforces a wishful conviction of immortality. Anxiety haunts *A Midsummer Night's Dream*. The fairy monarchs' quarrel has endangered the harvest and, by analogy, crucial Athenian marriage plans. A "king of shadows," whose name suggests a lord of the underworld, controls the play world by imposing "death-counterfeiting sleep." By contrast, because "summer still doth tend upon [her] state" (3.1.155), the Fairy Queen personifies everlasting life. In this context, Bottom's dream replenishes an unconscious conviction of deathless well-being.

Patriarchy in the early-modern period functioned imperfectly as an immortality system.[13] It would be possible to examine the fairy king as a historical construction, a function of the patriarchal ideology that, like government and religion, supported convictions of security. As Theseus stipulates, to Hermia her father "should be as a god" (1.1.47). Ultimately the patriarch guaranteed the psychic life of all who depended on him. The poet Torquato Tasso confided in his patron "not as we trust in man, but as we trust in God. It appeared to me that, so long as I was under his protection, fortune and death had no power over me."[14]

Because patriarchy is a system of hero worship and only the privileged few can be lords, the Fairy Queen's love is also compensation. The lowly Bottom comes closer to supernatural vitality than do the aristocratic lovers, even though his bliss remains sublimely useless. Although the rebellious aristocratic lovers are struck down by a parodic execution, Bottom is harmless. He never threatens the economic marriages that underwrite the patriarchal fantasy of immortal posterity. On the contrary, the prosthetic nature of relationships in the play makes it appear that creatures can use one another to augment themselves without producing vicious rivalries.

Yet this is a comic treatment of historical stress. The Fairy Queen is able to mediate because Bottom has a big appetite but is not starving, and because he is an ass whose taste runs to bottles of hay, not flesh. In this Athens there is none of the bloodthirsty competition found in Shakespeare's histories. The poor and the upstart young are easily placated. Furthermore, the irrational potential of the patriarch is euphemistically split off in the figure of Puck, who is the one actually executing death-counterfeiting sleep on the mortals. But as Shakespeare's equivocation whispers, other configurations are equally plausible.

In fact, the other configurations may discover insanity and terror at the heart of things, for internalized voices can be a source of paranoia as well as ecstasy. Emphasize not Bottom's bliss but the delusion and manipulation at work, and prosthetic relations can signify a sinister entanglement. Marlowe's Dr. Faustus conjures a voice that promises to fulfill infantile wishes for omnipotence. But it is also a voice that, once inside, threatens to usurp and destroy his soul or essence. Yet the demonic voice is wondrously prosthetic, enabling the magician to extend his reach in space and time, to kiss the idealized queen, Helen of Troy, and humiliate the pope—the oppressive *il papa*. In the end of course this aggrandizement has its price: the demonic parent's annihilation of the child.

In Bottom's dream the internalized voice is maternal; in Hamlet, by contrast, the crucial voice is that of a poisoned father, who turns out to be not corroborative but nihilistic, so that the play dramatizes a desperate effort to ground the self—to be or not to be—in a disintegrated culture. Confronting the Ghost, Hamlet tacitly discovers the dreamlike, formative voice of the patriarch. Yet the voice imparts no conviction of immortality. On the contrary, trapped in the margin between life and final death, adrift in eschatological indeterminacy, the father-king is consumed by dread and rage. He cries out not only against Claudius and Gertrude, but also against his own unatoned sins, the decay of his body, and the weakness of his son Hamlet; he is unable to envision any positive role for his son or his people. He clamors not for renewal but for revenge, aggrandizing himself with his heroic torment and unspeakable secrets. If anything, the Ghost is more self-alienated and vulnerable than Hamlet; he literally disembodies the cultural guarantees necessary to sustain the living.

Hamlet meets his father's revelations by crying "O my prophetic soul!" (1.5.40) and vowing to purge his own identity so that "thy commandment all alone shall live/Within the book and volume of my brain" (102–3). Because he draws upon an implacably negative voice to substantiate himself, however, the result is naturally suicidal self-disgust. His famous delay expresses his ambivalence toward that destructive voice in him. Living through his son, the ghostly father would nullify him.

The play locates its only nurturant father in the graveyard. Peering at Yorick's skull, Hamlet recalls an affectionate father figure of "infinite jest." Like Bottom, Yorick was selflessly playful. But his skull disenchants the patriarchal promise of immortality with sickening force: "He hath borne me on his back a thousand times. And now how abhorred in my imagination it is! My gorge rises at it! Here hung those lips I have kissed I know not how oft" (5.1.187–89). The lips, the prosthetic voice are silent. The only ground is the grave, and Hamlet gags at this traumatic memory of intimacy: "And smelt so? Pah!" (200).

Peter Laslett emphasizes the social construction of identity in the early-modern period: people defined themselves through families, households, and groups. Shakespeare seems to see that interrelatedness as prosthetic.[15] In Ulysses' famous formula in *Troilus and Cressida*, "no man is the lord of any thing" until he is ratified by others (3.3.115). The plays and sonnets celebrate an ideology of friendship in which alter egos affirm and expand one another. The same is true of lovers. Romeo dreams that Juliet will make him an emperor with a kiss. In Cleopatra's doomed imagination, the superhuman Antony leads her on to apotheosis.

In Shakespeare's work, friendship and love are types of hero worship. As in Christianity, where the worshiper's surrender to God wins eternal life from him, Renaissance cultures liked to imagine symbiotic systems of hero worship. A "body politic" lives in and through the guiding will of a master. Talbot and his troops in *Henry VI* supposedly function with one superhuman will. A husband and wife are "one flesh," although the husband, like the king, is God's understudy on earth. We say parents "live through" their children, even into immortal posterity. Yet symbiosis was always as much prescription as reality. And as Hamlet—and Machiavelli—make plain, when not symbiotic, hero worship resembles the crudest prosthetic relation, slavery, in which a master lives parasitically through others. In effect, the master feeds his own immortality by subsuming the lives of slaves. Shakespearean drama readily identifies slavery with social death. The fear of that nullity registers in Hamlet's cry of self-disgust when he cannot invent a meaningful role for himself: "O, what a rogue and peasant slave am I!" (2.2.550).

Even the monstrous Caliban depends on uncanny voices. He hears delightful "twangling instruments . . . and sometime voices" that put him to sleep: "and then in dreaming, / The clouds methought would open and show riches / Ready to drop upon me, that when I wak'd / I cried to dream again."[16] These visions

shimmer with prosthetic energy, but their wishfulness and their flagrant strategic magic scarcely mask the underlying dissonance.

Anthropologically conceived, the theater I have described had much in common with today's movies and novels. Among other things, the theater was a
boundary-controlling institution. Like a church, it refocused imagination on the
edge of the conventional world and what lies beyond. It offered participants a
controlled exposure to the intolerable contradictions of the human situation in
ways that managed anxiety and even elicited energizing confidence. In effect,
audiences paid to probe the limits of conventional life and the profound emotions invested in fantasies about the ground of being. Although Christians expressed proprietary confidence in their own cosmic ground, some of them
flocked to hear an actor celebrate the infinite piece of work man is, gag at the
decay signified by Yorick's skull, and mime his own death. This suggests that theater augmented the dynamic, reality-testing dimension of religion, opening outward the often defensively homiletic formations of orthodox belief. Although
theater boasted no ultimate answers, it worked to structure imaginative experience and reinforce values whose popularity could be empirically measured at
the box office. Plays could allow audiences to explore the usually taboo margins
of experience and change, enlarging—and testing—the range of things they
could safely think about.

In this way the play itself could function as a prosthetic voice. In the theater
a play is an event in which the dramatist's, players', and spectators' imaginations
intermingle. Like other forms of storytelling, theater puts life-affirming voices
into the heads of the participating spectators, and is reciprocally shaped by the
spectators' use of those voices. Sharing in the voices of the play, an individual,
alienated consciousness can expand into a crowd or community—the collective
"you" Puck addresses in his epilogue. The play extends the individual's reach in
space and time, allowing an experience outside the unsettling accidents and inhibitions of conventional life. The voices of the play may bring onlookers into
the presence of kings and supernatural beings even as the play puts the words of
gods and kings into mortal ears. As the actors "put on" an expanded repertory of
behaviors and motives, audiences live in that scripted yet contingent space—in
effect, like my daughter, imagining autonomy, "learning to drive."

In this account, then, Shakespeare's audiences used drama to shape and re-
shape identity. A useful analogy for the process would be parenting. Although
epilogues defer to the "parental" judgment of the spectators, the play—like a
parent—actually provides materials for a heuristic engagement of identity. To
the extent that spectators construe their interpretive experience as a dream, as
Puck recommends, the play operates as Oberon does, through "death-counter-

feiting sleep." In effect, the play is a technology for evoking an experience—a frankly illusory experience—of the ground of being that fortifies imaginations to entertain new constructions of reality. Such a change can be understood as growth, but it is also an ideological adjustment of existing heroic values. It can increase social integration or control, or as the London city fathers complained, it may spawn anarchy—or a combination thereof. Prosthetic relationships affect particular individuals and subgroups differently, and the experience of internalized voices can be both individual and collective. Given these complexities and the limited evidence available in the best of circumstances, we can only recover that experience in an approximate manner. Yet patterns—traces—do emerge, and in sites such as Shakespeare's theater these patterns had already begun to take a usable form.

What difference could this viewpoint make for cultural studies? The idea of prosthesis emphasizes identity formation as a creative act, inherently social and systemic in its mutuality. Prosthetic relationships can provide a way for us to think about symbiotic qualities in family and cultural systems. Insofar as they invite us to think in terms of interdependent behavioral systems rather than individual conflicts, they open toward evolutionary and ethological perspectives. They foreground concerns that are apt to be deemphasized in criticism and psychology based on intrapsychic or interpersonal conflict. The new historicism and cultural materialism, for example, work to demystify given categories of power within culture, such as political, economic, and gender conflicts. But there is something potentially melodramatic and culture-bound about terms such as *contestation, subversion, appropriation, hegemony,* and so on. In a highly individualistic capitalist culture it can be difficult to appreciate how subtly natural a competitive ideology can seem to be.

Anxiety about the ground of being is a deep determinant of behavior. We can usefully ask not only how a particular text manipulates given cultural values, but also what that manipulation may reveal about efforts to compose a ground for identity in a particular historical situation. The effort to substantiate the self is a deep ideological activity. Analysis of prosthetic relations can open up that deep ideology and explore ways in which the self suffers and repairs traumatic damage.

Cultural Crash and Prosthetic Ground

As an enclosed man-made world suspended in space, an airliner makes a logical image of conventional reality. When the plane crashes in *Fearless,* the survivors are thrown out of that enclosed mental space. The protagonist, an architect named Max Klein, is both a victim and a visionary hero, as paradoxically small ("Klein") and larger than life ("Max") as his name. In the hellish chaos of the fuselage after the impact, the way out appears to Max as a shimmering tunnel of light like the glimpses of heaven reported in popular accounts of near-death experiences, and he leads other passengers to safety—back to life—crying, "Follow me to the light!"

Facing death, Max feels not terror but the same sense of invulnerability that may overtake soldiers during a combat breakdown. Dissociating, in a state of messianic calm, he rescues others from the wreckage. Yet afterward Max keeps reliving the crash, rediscovering his lack of fear, as if trying to reconnect with his missing humanity. He says "I thought I was dead." Now he looks into the magic circle of everyday life from outside, seeing through pretensions and denial, yet unable to understand his own disenchantment. He sees people hiding from life and compulsively substituting fantasies of power and prestige for love. America itself seems to have crashed. At the crash site a callous cab driver shoots home-video footage of the carnage. A crass lawyer bullies the survivors to lie for more compensation. Carla, the grieving mother, falls into a depression while her husband schemes to turn their child's death into a financial jackpot. Max's children play video games that naively counter death anxiety with fantasies of triumphal killing, and in disgust Max confiscates one of the games from them. Nobody else, neither the plodding psychiatrist nor Max's devoted wife, can share his awareness of the blind denial around him. After he finally agrees to distort his testimony about the accident in order to help his partner's widow, he dashes out onto the roof of the office building and faces down his panic by forcing himself to walk on the parapet. Trauma exposes not only the ultimate nothingness of the self, but also the sickening falseness of the social world. As Carla mourns, "The U.S. is falling apart."

How does the film put the survivors—and the spectator—back inside the conventional world? Since the crash wrenched her baby out of her arms, Carla has been paralyzed by guilt and shock. Her suicidal depression gives Max purpose. He visits her and experiences a profound, tacitly messianic love. And he saves her. In an effort to undo her guilt, he eventually reenacts the crash. To prove that nobody could have saved the baby, he straps her into the backseat of his car cradling a gift, a substitute child, and then he smashes the car into a wall. Unhurt, able now to appreciate her human helplessness and to forgive herself, Carla moves toward healing. The seriously injured Max in turn lets his idealized wife, Laura, summon him back from the brink to his family and the healing rhythms of everyday life.

This is movie psychology. Carla's flash of insight after the therapeutic car crash amounts to the sort of abreaction that Charcot and the early Freud thought could cure hysteria. And Max's wife stands for the wholesomeness of family. Because Max's therapeutic smash-up has gotten results, we forget that his behavior has been in reality suicidal, and even potentially homicidal. Still, this pat ending does have something to reveal about how the culture manages trauma.

Recall the Aliquippa disaster described in part 1 above. There, journalists countered death by focusing on two heroic roles played by the rescuers. The Federal Aviation Administration investigators, like Sherlock Holmes, were going to recreate the plane's last moments by studying its "black box" flight recorder. Through a sort of abreaction, they would make the "black box" of the traumatized psyche—another prosthetic voice—repeat and undo its imprinted fatal secret. Max, too, recreates a plane crash trying to release a lifesaving truth.

The Aliquippa story also spotlighted a minister who mourned a lost flight attendant and reassuringly pointed readers toward symbolic forms—marriage, a wedding ring—that imply immortality. This role is echoed in Max's behavior. He too plays the priest, not only by rescuing Carla from despair, but also by calming the other passengers as the plane crashes, and then commanding them, "follow me to the light."[17] His voice becomes the voice of a prosthetic will, compensating for others' paralysis. The journalists and screenwriters conjure up a vision of sacramental heroic rescue. Max is explicitly sacrificial. Christlike, he offers Carla forgiveness for her guilt, and then leads her through a play-death and resurrection in the car crash that returns her to innocence and nearly kills him.

The sacrificial heroism also subtly redeems the "fallen" world. At one point, banal decorations in a shopping mall falsify the spirituality of Christmas, whereas Carla is entranced by the sight of a living infant, a version of the Christ child, in another woman's arms. She pauses discreetly to savor the baby's smell. "Maybe I *am* a ghost," she murmurs. This is when Max conceives his scheme for the therapeutic crash that will restore Carla and motherhood to the world, like the symbolic wedding ring in the news story. He proposes that they "buy presents for the dead." And they do, imagining the wishes of Carla's baby and his dead father—the lost, prosthetic past and future. By this sacrificial offering they counter the selfishness of the people around them. With Carla in the backseat bearing a gift in her arms as a surrogate baby, Max steers them into that second, redemptive near-death.

This time Carla is unharmed while Max is seriously banged up, so the plot turns symmetrically, with the rescued mother urging the once-again-mortal hero to put aside his messianic role and go home: "You can't save everybody, Max. You have to try taking care of yourself." In a last twist of the plot, the conniving lawyer arrives with holiday gifts—morally tainted gifts. Since childhood, Max has been allergic to strawberries, symbols of life's most natural pleasures. His body's allergic revolt suggests childhood trauma. Yet since the plane crash, when he defied death, Max has been boldly relishing strawberries. Now, ironically, the forbidden fruit plunges him into anaphylactic shock and he experiences a final hallucinatory return to the plane crash and the beckoning tunnel of death, from which his wife's voice recalls him.

This melodramatic resolution argues that reentry into the conventional world is a moral negotiation. The lawyer's symbolically "poisonous" gifts trigger Max's final shock and set up Laura's rescue. Her intervention might remind us that a wedding ring not only signifies a wife and children, but also points back toward a mother and infancy. In the symbolic economy of the film, Max saves the "dark" ethnic mother, Carla Roderigo, and is in turn saved when she sacrifices her romantic love for him so that his faithful wife can mother him back to life. Both he and Carla give up their heroic gender roles of superhuman mother and messianic father. For Max, the return from trauma is a double recuperation. Not only does the allergic shock undo the shock of the airline crash; it also undoes the haunting death of his father, which Max witnessed at the age of thirteen, releasing him now to take over the father's role in his own family.

Hollywood reproduces the culture's ideological use of trauma. Injury exposes society's failures, even as the plane crash objectifies Max and Carla's unconscious distress over their malfunctioning social world and troubled marriages. Whether it is an earthquake, a shipwreck, or an abusive relationship, every trauma reveals the inability of the social world to protect the victim from harm. In fact, the event may expose society's active evil. The aftershock of disaster tests the sympathies of those around the survivor. Every trauma implies a criticism of life. Stunned, Max sees the everyday world's vanity with the sudden clarity of H. G. Wells's stranded Time Traveller. As a survivor, he is a potential renegade, a threat. In healing him, the screenplay also domesticates him again, using familiar comic and romantic conventions. But history never guarantees that comedy will prevail. The young Adolf Hitler was wounded in World War I and spent the rest of his life becoming first the savior and then the scourge of a people. This danger takes a playful twist in Steven Frears's film *Hero* (1992), which satirizes the hero-making mania spawned by a plane crash and an inadvertent rescue.

What remains powerfully mystified at the end of *Fearless* is the role of mother and wife, a role graphically exploited in a recent British Airways advertisement (fig. 6). Although the ad is pitched toward the harried executive whose first-class ticket entitles him to the airline's new sleeping accommodations, its underlying fantasy is voluptuously infantile. The executive is middle-aged, which sublimates the erotic bond between mother and child; the mother's photo is sepia-toned to evoke a lost but cherished era. The image evokes Rider Haggard's *She* and the heroic travels of Leo and Holly into the arms of an omnipotent, pro-

The new Club World cradle seat. Lullaby not included.

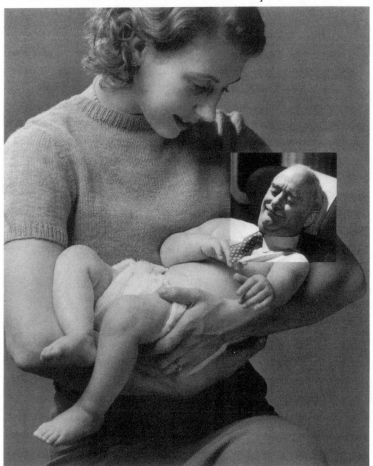

Fig. 6. Mother as prosthetic ground in an advertisement from the *New Yorker*, June 10, 1996. The caption says, "Introducing the unique new business class cradle seat. It doesn't simply recline but tilts as a whole, raising your knees and relieving your body of stress and pressure. Pity you may not be awake to enjoy all the other changes on new Club World."

tecting mother. It is what the ring stands for in the newspaper account of the Aliquippa airline crash. In the largest sense it projects a wished-for, reconstituted prosthetic relation. In effect, mother and son form a symbolic, supernatural life. The ambiguous executive child is in color and implicitly in control, like my daughter driving the car in the dream that opens this chapter, and Bottom in the arms of the Fairy Queen.

In its juxtaposed images, the ad alludes to travel as a paradoxical escape from, and exposure to, death anxiety. The airplane, that symbol of modernism's promise and peril, magnifies dread and summons up the need for executive aggrandizement and infantile reassurance. The cradled executive could be Carla's baby, rescued here by the motherly corporation standing in for "mother" nature. The photo elides all other passengers, including the "mob" in tourist class. So cropped, it screens out the competing community that might compromise its variation on Bottom's dream. The ad could be construed, then, as an instance of a core fantasy that the movie *Fearless* shatters and, in the saving voice of Max's wife, recuperates. The ad imagines not simply comfort but the bliss of survival in enfolding arms.

Prosthetic relationships imply economies. Parents "invest" themselves in their children, and the children traditionally repay the debt when the parents are old. *Fearless* satirizes the way the crash survivors exploit the airline's debts to them as victims by suing for compensation. Exposure to death anxiety tacitly justifies economic claims on the corporate "parent." The film is scornful about those claims, suggesting that although actual injury may support demands on others, the demands may be inflated. But this sort of exploitation is potentially far more pervasive and perverse than it might appear, for causality may flow both ways. Injury may justify demands on others, but demands on others may also tempt people to justify their demands by feeling aggrieved or injured. Corporate "parents" regularly fault workers for insufficient productivity and reliability as a way of rationalizing meager wages. In its extreme form, as I will argue in my reading of *Schindler's List*, this behavior was at the heart of the predatory Nazi economy.

The British Airways ad implicitly reflects a business as well as a psychic economy. The pampered executive "deserves" a prosthetic mother as the Japanese boss does a geisha, especially because his work exposes him to anxiety about literal and symbolic crashes. In effect, he has "earned" a servant-mother, just as Roman warrior-aristocrats "deserved" to be supported by a vast slave class formed from the ranks and descendants of defeated enemies. The airline makes use of sublimated death anxiety to energize the strong currents of pleasure and mastery dramatized in the ad. Nothing sells like survival.

When prosthetic systems fail, people may look for compensation in machines, as in David Cronenberg's 1996 adaptation of J. G. Ballard's novel *Crash*. The film is mannered and silly in many respects, but it systematically develops a vocabulary of post-traumatic images and themes. At the center of the story is a shadowy group whose leader, Vaughan, recreates legendary auto smash-ups for invited spectators, conjuring up primal experiences of cultural crash. The protagonist, coyly called James Ballard, becomes fascinated with Vaughan and the power of conjured death. The film depicts a 1990s society of stale affluence, choked freeways, unrelieved numbness, and cold, dissociated rage. Ballard and his wife Catherine are attractive people, oppressed by frigidity and an absence of purpose, childless and self-involved. The film opens in a hangar with Catherine becoming erotically aroused by caressing the engine cowling of a sleek private plane. The machine's promise of freedom, speed, and metallic invulnerability turn her on. As in *Fearless* and the British Airlines advertisement, airplanes can fly above—transcend—a deadened conventional world.

Crash follows the fictional Ballard's increasingly desperate fascination with death as an orgasmic release. Like Max Klein, he obsessively courts death, but finds it sexy. Yet the adrenaline rush of risk too easily screens out its compensatory quality. It may be that flirting with suicide is a source of tremendous psychic energy, but it also acts out self-hatred and suggests that everyday life is so grimly inhibited that only berserk impulsiveness can break out of its confines. The inhibition originates not in old-fashioned moral restraints but in the sort of obsession with style that came to imprison Oscar Wilde. Characters speak in a stylized, expressionless monotone, make love in the stylized interiors of automobiles, in sterile apartments and slab-sided parking garages. This is a world of sterile architecture and lifeless consumer styles, with no openings—no need—for new creativity. It presents the sort of frozen environment that paralyzes the knights in Burne-Jones's *Briar Rose* paintings.

Inhibition surfaces specifically in the film's sexuality. The characters are preoccupied with masturbation and couplings from the rear that evoke homosexual encounters, with no eye contact and suggestions of one partner servicing, or being dominated by, another. By seducing James Ballard, the bisexual crash "artist," Vaughan, crashes sexual distinctions together, just as he tries to blur distinctions between life and death by reenacting famous car crashes. Although he has attracted a number of female groupies, Vaughan embodies the misogyny and homosexual conflict that haunts (and sometimes muddles) the film.

In his crashes Vaughan resurrects and kills again the mythic heroes of an earlier America, including James Dean and Jayne Mansfield. His project expresses a post-traumatic era's radical ambivalence toward the prosthetic voices that shaped American identity after World War II, and toward the doomed rebellion and bosomy voluptuousness they represented. Vaughan claims his crashes "fertilize" sexual experience with the sexuality of the dead heroes, and recreate "the moment that created a Hollywood legend," as if myth is more potent than reality. Like Mephistopheles summoning Helen of Troy for Faust, Vaughan conjures a super-reality. And there are ancient precedents for his uncanny smash-ups. Martial describes Roman mimes in which condemned criminals played the tragic lead. At the climax of the story of Orpheus, for instance, real beasts would actually kill the mythic personage with a special touch of horror and awe for spectators in the amphitheater.

In trying to produce sensation in his numbed followers and spectators, Vaughan is viciously tackling a problem that faced Victorian specialists in traumatic neurosis. In language reminiscent of the neurological theories of the 1890s, Vaughan's concealed headquarters is described as "the nerve center." In reenacting past horrors, he behaves as if seeking some abreaction that could dispel primal terror and reintegrate personality. His project, he tells Ballard, is the "reshaping of the human body by modern technology." Such remarks conjure up the hopes and fears of late Victorian nightmares such as H. G. Wells's *The Island of Dr. Moreau.*

Crippled prosthetic relations take concrete form when Ballard makes love to Gabrielle, one of Vaughan's followers, in a wrecked car. Gabrielle wears a shoulder belt and leg braces from earlier injuries, and to reach her Ballard has to wrestle with this prosthetic apparatus. In this equivalent of kinky bondage gear Gabrielle is helpless, and Ballard dominates her, freed from sexual anxiety. The woman has become tacitly mechanical, and Ballard's desire is directed away from life as other characters' desires are when they kiss wounds and scars. If it is impossible to think through others, imagination fetishizes mechanical substitutes and turns to barely sublimated necrophilia.

Inevitably, death worship itself grows stale, demanding more real sado-masochistic actions. In the first of two climactic freeway crashes, the spurned Vaughan keeps slamming Catherine and Ballard's car from behind in a parody of anal rape. After Vaughan careens off an overpass and dies, Ballard and Catherine reenact Vaughan's highway rape. This time Ballard's bumper bashing drives Catherine's car off the road, and the film closes with husband and injured wife trying to make love at the crash site, trying to feel pain and survival ecstasy. The lovemaking fails to reach an orgasm, and Ballard murmurs "Maybe the next one." So the story ends with characteristic post-traumatic symptoms. The stunned couple will keep reliving injury and terror until they kill each other someday. As the traffic buzzes around them, the pair wait for an emergency vehicle, in the grips of some original violence they cannot remember or exorcise, in a tableau of smashed machinery and values, on the ambivalent verge of survival and suicide, love and assault, numbness and orgasmic rage. Immobilized. Quite alone.

SEVEN

Abuse as a Prosthetic System

The more children Reagan sacrificed, the more local newspapers discovered such group-fantasies as "an epidemic of child abuse sweeping the city."

Lloyd deMause, *Reagan's America*

THE ABSENCE OF prosthetic relationships can be terrifying. In his image of the factory universe, for example, Havelock Ellis describes a psychic isolation that is a form of social death for the homeless child. But to discover yourself living through other selves could be equally appalling if you came to doubt the adequacy or benevolence of others. The orphan Leo Vincey searches for a prosthetic mother figure who has been brooding on him for centuries and who watches him approach through a magic glass. Yet she turns out to be a sinister presence, capable of killing and enslaving as well as nurturing him. Dorian Gray feels his ancestors infecting his will as vampires would. The patriarchal Count Dracula seduces, then subsumes his victims. One of *Dracula*'s core anxieties is that proliferating vampires are always silently converting positive prosthetic bonds into spectral abuse.

Historically, the danger of this treacherous conversion has triggered episodes of panic, such as in the anticommunist paranoia of the Cold War and a periodic backlash against feminism. It has fueled recurring hysteria about Satanism and demonic possession, and shows up in clinical pathologies such as the delusional voices of paranoid schizophrenia, which are often experienced as uncanny and controlling, whether they emanate from animals, objects, or space creatures. Some great popular fantasies such as Stoker's *Dracula* brilliantly exploit the frightening ambiguities of such delusional thinking. The Count's kiss subverts the stability of prosthetic relations, so that the demure Lucy suddenly becomes "voluptuous" and fanged, blurring basic conceptual categories so unnervingly that the heroes eventually try to "pin her down" once and for all with a stake in her tomb, in a parodic, grisly gang rape.[1] Conservative fantasies that big government is a vampire sucking capital out of the economy presuppose a similar fear of subversion and hostile reaction, as in presidential candidate Steve Forbes's vow to "drive a stake into the heart of the Internal Revenue Service."[2]

The more a culture values autonomy and believes that people create their own destinies, the more disturbing it is to be reminded that our personalities are formed in unstable prosthetic networks that to some extent silently subsume us. The dynamics of domination are encoded in the atavistic categories of Western thought. Christianity, for example, envisions creatures not simply living on the earth, but "serving the Lord." And as history insists, that service can be insidiously converted to satanic possession, with traumatic results.

Cultures stabilize faith in prosthetic relations through a mix of institutional structures and traditional guarantees. The Catholic Church has ritualized and codified the practice of confession. Victorians who engaged in spiritualism sought guidance and reassurance from supernatural voices, ritualizing the social framework of the séance to regulate the transaction. Sitting out of sight behind the analytical couch, theorizing about transference, Freud tried to regulate the prosthetic interaction of psychoanalysis to ensure the analyst's neutrality. But the threat of subversion persists, as shown in the rash of 1990s scandals about seductive priests and therapists.

Because relationships are invariably charged with transference potential, the idea of autonomy, or even indifference, is to some extent always a will-o'-the-wisp. In creating his image of the homeless child in a factory universe, Havelock Ellis set out to describe a feeling of abandonment, yet his imagery implies prosthetic abuse insofar as factories reduced workers—often women and children—to machines that magnified the will of bosses or owners. His strategic argument and symbolic logic tread different paths. Or consider H. G. Wells's *Invisible Man*. The "homeless child" Griffin copes with his sense of abandonment and abuse by making himself invisible in order to command a prosthetic will that could dominate others, as when his terrifying voice booms in the mind of Mr. Marvel, the "homeless" tramp.

Wells reminds us that victimization converts to vindictiveness as fluidly as the central nervous system may turn flight to fight. Abandoned children can exploit exploiters, as the blackmailing "rent boys" did Oscar Wilde. Morlocks dine on their former masters. If retaliation keeps escalating, abuse moves toward the all-consuming feud or the Social Darwinist law of the jungle, the war of all against all. Abuse not only threatens sexual or psychic harm, but puts at risk the faith in others that enables people to live in society. The worldwide struggle over modernism and traditional values is in this sense a struggle to come to terms with prosthetic relations. Not only our ideas but even our basic cognitive categories—the raw materials of thought—come to us from other people and ultimately from cultural history. As a result, we are predetermined creatures in a changing environment. How can we not be ambivalent about that crux? Is it any wonder we keep falling for Faust's dream of magical mastery, overlooking its dependence on the shifty, prosthetic voice of Mephistopheles?

Abuse, one person's selfish use of another, is a predatory prosthetic relation. Like slavery, it is traumatic when it shatters the will and identity of a victim. Abuse can be self-evident—the rapist's violence indicts him, and that's that. Yet in a democratic, individualistic culture, exploitation can be difficult to map—witness the popularity of "codependency" therapy, which promises to sort out one's deceptive entanglements with family and others. No less perplexing is the range of responses exploitation can provoke. Fantasy children such as the traumatized, messianic Happy Prince and the murderous Tonga can represent different post-traumatic reactions to an exploitative world. In the 1990s, the comparable emblematic roles are the traumatized victim of child abuse and the "savage" youth running amok.[3] In this chapter I unpack some of the cultural fantasies encoded in the first of those roles, saving the second for chapter 11.

Abuse and Its Uses

In "The Vogue of Childhood Misery" (1992), Nicholas Lemann reports that there is "a vast new body of work about unhappy childhood in middle-class America."[4] He examines a group of novels, memoirs, and self-help books about the lasting effects of that unhappiness. Patti Davis's novel *A House of Secrets* (1992), for instance, is "about a woman in her thirties whose life is dominated by memories of the emotional hurts she suffered while growing up in an affluent, secure, two-parent household." The therapeutic books he cites—with titles such as *Forgiving Your Parents*, *Toxic Parents*, and *Divorcing a Parent*—amplify the theme of childhood victimization. Pointing to Huckleberry Finn, who makes the best of a bruising childhood, Lemann speculates that the recent sensitivity to childhood distress may be an outcome of the nineteenth century's historic recognition of the rights of slaves, women, and children. He links the preoccupation with childhood misery to the "recovery" movement, which, like traumatic sexual abuse, came to prominence in the 1980s and has focused on overcoming the aftereffects of "dysfunctional" families.[5]

Katie Roiphe has in effect updated "The Vogue of Childhood Misery" by zeroing in on incest, which "has become our latest literary vogue." As public interest in traumatic sexual abuse has surged, novels about the subject have proliferated.[6] The novels are often marketed with a titillating Gothic vocabulary—typical is a heroine "forced to come to terms with the dark secret of her harrowing past."[7] They take for granted that incest causes post-traumatic stress and lifelong injury. As a "dark secret," sexual abuse has the spellbinding power of the riddle that captured Oedipus. And as in myth and early psychoanalysis, insight and abreaction can break the spell. Heroines usually "find themselves" by unlocking the secret, which usually means repudiating a bad parent to achieve a new spirit of self-reliance. To identify this "secret" as a hackneyed fictional device is to beg the larger question of where it comes from and why it is apparently so compelling in the marketplace.[8] However widespread sexual abuse is in this culture, fiction apparently resonates with concerns that go beyond actual abuse.

Those concerns can be seen as an effort to account for the worries about compromised autonomy and impaired well-being that for a number of reasons are particularly strong today. Novels grounded in the "secret" of incest usually present damaged or absent prosthetic relationships in childhood. They can help explain why people in a relentlessly competitive and individualistic culture have —or think they have—difficulty thinking "through" other people.

In this context, the idea of trauma, now so vivid in the popular mind, accounts for the lost connection with a prosthetic childhood. In arguing that the concept of trauma in the 1990s has its ideological roots in the antiwar and feminist movements, Judith Lewis Herman depicts trauma as a direct route to visions of a ground of experience. After discussing combat trauma in Vietnam veterans, Herman calls the psychic consequences of rape "the combat neurosis of the sex war."[9] She asserts that "rape and combat might thus be considered complementary social rites of initiation into the coercive violence at the foundation of adult society."[10] Robert Zemeckis's movie *Forrest Gump* (1995) dramatizes the point by making Forrest's sexually abused childhood sweetheart follow a parallel course to the traumatized Vietnam War veteran, with a fatal outcome.

Assuming that these "rites of initiation" include childhood sexual abuse, the culture's unprecedented concern with abuse and stories about abuse also signifies a fascination with "the foundation of adult society" and of personal experience. The "coercive violence" at the core of social experience in America is the alluring monster in the heart of the labyrinth. It is the irresistible "secret" at the heart of the "literary vogue" of incest. Intimate sexual violence is compelling enough on its own terms. But as Herman's equation of rape and combat illustrates, it is also richly and inescapably figurative. Childhood abuse in particular evokes some of the most disturbing conflicts in American culture: gross inequalities in class and gender; predatory economic behavior (multimillion-dollar executives, minimum-wage workers in virtual peonage); the seductive glamour and treachery of patriarchal power, and more. Like abuse, these conflicts violate our proclaimed identity as a nation. We try to keep them a secret from the neighbors and from ourselves.

Because we depend on dissociation to tame large, terrifying conflicts in society, it is not surprising that dissociation should fascinate us as a symptom of sexual abuse. In the 1980s, traumatic amnesia surged to public attention in reports of "recovered memory"—incest victims' spontaneous recall of sometimes unverifiable incidents of abuse from years before. In the popular mind it is trauma's most important feature, dramatized uncritically on television, for example, in the show *Sisters*. Some therapists focused on recovered memories and the promise of definitive, abreactive insights as the keys to a host of disorders. "If you think you were sexually abused and your life shows the symptoms," Ellen Bass and Laura Davis claim in their well-known study, *The Courage to Heal: A Guide for Women Survivors of Child Sexual Abuse*, "then you were."[11]

In the 1990s, this sort of opening to suggestibility has produced bitter controversy, with many therapists outspoken in defense of apparently victimized clients, and not a few research scientists challenging the truth of recovered memories.[12] My interest here is not so much in the controversy as in the public's fascination with dissociation and the idea that we may carry around in memory, unawares, the influence or will of a sinister parent. It is as if people are haunted by the possibility of troubled imagination discovering a ground of personality that was fatally compromised long ago. Instead of learning to drive, as in my daughter's dream, the essential childhood project is revealed to be a secret, crippling subversion so dreadful that the victim cannot bear the memory of it.

As "perpetrator," the father is a sort of vampire usurping the will and vitality of the child, and it is probably no accident that a resurgence of vampire imagery and narratives has accompanied the culture's preoccupation with child abuse. Vampires in turn are the thematic offspring of Satan. Predictably, deformed prosthetic relationships readily take on the ideation of demonic possession. Although now undergoing a much-deserved critical debunking, some clinicians have associated child abuse with supposed satanic cults. Elaborating diagnoses of satanic ritual abuse, they have theorized a vast conspiracy of parent-cultists that has long used traumatic amnesia to silence children who have been subjected to, or witnessed, ritualistic tortures, infanticide, and other horrors.[13] This diagnosis itself resembles many self-confirming delusional systems in history. To my knowledge, police investigations have never produced any corroborating evidence for such cults (where are the bodies? skeptics ask). And the supposition that victims can be comprehensively programmed by the parent-cultists means that nothing victims report about the cult's existence (or nonexistence) can be trusted.

The belief in satanic abuse echoes disturbances well documented elsewhere in Western European history, most famously in the outbreaks of witchcraft hysteria throughout the early-modern period.[14] In this context, it is less surprising to find University of Utah Medical School professor Cory Hammond claiming that satanic cults are part of a global conspiracy masterminded by a renegade Jewish doctor named "Green," who had cooperated with Nazi scientists and now uses the CIA for his diabolical schemes.[15] Hammond's theory reads like a digest of this century's pulp fiction, with themes from the prophetic works of H. G. Wells and Fritz Lang's film *Spies* (1928) and kinship to the doctrines underpinning the right-wing Christian militia movement. Given Professor Hammond's belief that the satanic cult leaders seek to rule the world, his theory can be understood as a post-traumatic reaction to the industrial-scale, totalitarian horrors of the century .

As a fantasy of a subverted prosthetic relations, however, the idea of satanic abuse fits in well with other explanatory uses of trauma. The historian Norman Cohn points out that anxieties about Satan correlate with periods in which an ego ideal has become unusually demanding. When medieval Christians or Puritan reformers demanded of themselves an ever more perfect emulation of Christ, they came increasingly to need the irresistible influence of Satan to justify their failures. Such beliefs in no way rule out other possible motives for entertaining Satan, including fraud and profit. In the words of Philip Jenkins, "the whole ritual abuse scenario is utterly fictitious, founded on a sickening mixture of gullibility, avarice, self-promotion, and personal malice."[16]

Considered in terms of disordered prosthetic relations, the ideation of satanic abuse dovetails with larger cultural themes. The devil, after all, tempts his victims with illicit prosthetic power. In the wilderness he tries to seduce the son of God to rebellion by offering him a kingdom. In the Faust story, not to mention witchcraft lore, the devil promises a prosthetic transcendence of ordinary mortal limits. He enables flying witches to overcome time and space by smearing on their bodies an ointment prepared from the bodies of murdered infants.[17] There is the penalty of delusion and death to pay in the end, but the temptation is no less potent for that, as recent novels about incest half-naively illustrate. The Gothic taboo is traditionally not merely a threat but also an incitement to discover power.

In Mary Gaitskill's otherwise conventional novel *Two Girls, Fat and Thin* (1991), for example, incest unwittingly has devilish overtones reminiscent of historical witchcraft testimony and its Victorian offshoot *Dracula*. The invasive father possesses his thirteen-year-old daughter with his "deep smell produced by his particular combination of organs and glands and the food he ate. He pulled me against him, crushing my face into the chest hairs exposed by his open pajama top. I felt the power and insistence of his embrace. . . . My breath stopped. Arousal rose through my body and seized it. My excitement terrified me and made me feel ashamed because I knew it was wrong to be excited." The father's voice, like his smell and strength, is also uncanny: "'Yes,' he said, his voice crushed and strange. 'Yes.' He moved his hand away from my chest, not loosening his grip on my shoulders. Through the gown, he touched between my legs. Shock impaled my body."[18] What impales her is a penis "like the blunt, hairless limb of a medium-sized animal."[19] The traditional "medium-sized animal" of demonic persecution is the goat, and the imagery predictably implies a fear and loathing of our importunate and doomed biological bodies.

As Katie Roiphe notices, these fictional incest scenes regularly culminate in "literal images of radical detachment,"[20] as when Gaitskill's narrator reports that at the climax "my arms and legs flew from my pinned body to the corners of the ceiling, then back into their sockets, then back to the ceiling."[21] The bodily disconnection unwittingly draws on traditional fantasies of the devil's fury— recall that Faust is torn to pieces. But it also borrows the familiar descriptions of dissociation offered by abuse victims, especially those suffering from multiple-personality disorder, which one psychiatrist has named "the Osiris complex" after the Egyptian god whose sister Isis recovered and reconnected his scattered body parts after his murder—a myth supposed to be emblematic of trauma healed.[22]

In these fantasies of trauma, the prosthetic other merges with the child. The result, however, is not symbiosis but usurpation or, in the language of satanic fantasy, possession. Gaitskill imagines her young narrator gradually losing her will and her body to the invasive father: "Sometimes I would pretend I was asleep or ask him to stop, but he continued. I could not resist him anymore than that because with each visit my body seemed less mine and more his."[23] Her surrender is not merely passive; it is not a choice at all, but something uncanny. The supernatural mediates the harrowing cultural contradiction: that surrender brings her powerful sexual pleasure, but that her desire is wrong.

In Patti Davis's novel *Bondage* (1994), the narrator exacts a sadomasochistic revenge against her selfish, manipulative lover Anthony after her intimate friend Belinda has been raped and driven to suicide by a devilishly messianic religious healer so charismatic he could "take up residence" in her mind. The novel is an escapist bisexual pipe dream, but when it tries to fill in the heartless exploiter's motivation, it inserts a vision of his traumatic abuse. Sara has strung up Anthony in sadomasochistic gear and menaced him, particularly his genitals, with a nasty knife. But then "Sara stared at him, and saw the faint shadow of a seven-year-old boy, weeping confused tears at the torture of being forced to kneel in prayer while his father [a clergyman] towered over him naked, with an erection he neither touched nor used on his son. Was it sex or punishment? And what were the prayers supposed to be for? The child didn't know, and the man didn't either. But Anthony had spent years making everyone pay—especially women. They'd been paying for his mother's sin of sliding past the open doorway with blind eyes."[24]

Davis's climactic vision displaces the former lover's guilt onto an oppressive father whose penis comes to represent all male domination. The prosthetic medium imagined—the place where father and son merge—is the prayer the boy is forced to recite. The sinister tableau evokes the ideation of Satanism: the child made to worship the priapic demon father, their wills fusing in the uncanny prayer. Davis's narrator and the imagined son are angry at the father—and at the complicit mother as well—but they are both also compelled by the sheer display of the father's power. So there is a kind of magical undoing at work when Davis's narrator uses her own irresistible sexuality to seduce Anthony in order to tie him up. The superior power of her sexuality enables her to turn his lust against him. In this way she is binding up not only Anthony's, but also indirectly her own, father-demon, and at the close of the book she strides off in vindictive triumph, quite alone.

As in Gaitskill's story, not only the child but also the author and presumably the audience are fascinated by the father's magic wand, with its imagined power to conjure forbidden pleasure and destruction. These are fictional accounts and we are allowed to see into the characters' experience only through a narrow window. Behind the demonic masks, as individual people, the fathers scarcely exist. The psychic transaction in both these accounts is based on power, and power is cognitively magnified by taboo.

Vampire Abuse

To explore this alliance of demonic fantasy and power, let me turn to Cynthia D. Grant's *Uncle Vampire* (1993), a novel about traumatic incest for "young adult" readers available in local public libraries and bookstores. The book's marketing is a strong indication of how early in life children of the 1990s built ideas about sexual abuse into their basic views of social reality.

In *Uncle Vampire*, Carolyn and her twin, Honey, are model white upper-middle-class sixteen-year-olds. "We're pretty and smart. We've got a nice big house, a wonderful family, and our father drives a shiny new car."[25] Carolyn lists these blessings with bitter irony because, as the dust jacket warns, "Carolyn is hiding from a terrible truth." The truth is incest, but it is embedded in a cultural fantasy organized around familiar post-traumatic themes.

Throughout the novel Carolyn anguishes in strangled silence because her thirty-something live-in uncle, Toddy, is using her sexually. She thinks of him as "Uncle Vampire" and describes their sexual encounters in the lurid Gothic rhetoric of vampirism: "The walls have collapsed and my bedroom is gone. I am trapped in the world that my uncle has made. No air, no light. The wind shrieks in my ear. His teeth nibble delicately at my neck, tenderizing the flesh that he will tear" (*UV* 92). Her parents are in denial. Finally, in crisis, Carolyn reveals the "terrible truth" to a sympathetic teacher, and suddenly we recognize her traumatic symptoms. She has invented the twin sister, Honey; she is suffering from multiple-personality disorder.[26] A page or two later, Uncle Toddy is in prison and Carolyn is in therapy, living in Boston with her older sister Maggie, her parents repudiated.

At the heart of Carolyn's family is a vacuum. Her father is a self-involved insurance man driving a "shiny car" and given to anxious harangues about an impending cultural crash: "I mean, what's happening to this country? What's happened to our pride? Let's just come right out and admit it: The whole damned thing is going down the tubes!" (*UV* 127). With his fears of losing money and status, Carolyn's father is grindingly competitive toward his son Richie and his sister Marion. Toward Carolyn he is cold and controlling. Her mother also cannot relate to her family. Once hospitalized for "depression," she is a timid 1950s-style woman, still frozen in denial. Her breakdown was apparently traumatic, and her family constantly euphemizes life for fear of upsetting her.

In short, Carolyn's parents offer no prosthetic voice that could ground and empower a child. In parroting sex-stereotyped banalities, their voices have become false. A dead culture, like a vampire, has drained their personalities. It ventriloquizes through them. This is the small-town America of Sinclair Lewis's *Babbitt* and Evan Connell's *Mrs. Bridge*, with a touch of the zombielike conformity of Ira Levin's *The Stepford Wives*. Matthew Arnold, Oscar Wilde, and other culture critics of the 1890s would instantly recognize and excoriate its philistinism.

Carolyn's father's younger brother, Uncle Toddy, has moved in to fill the psychic space that her parents and middle-class culture have vacated. By Main Street standards he is a loser, a Jonathan Small who cannot hold a job or keep a girlfriend. But Uncle Toddy is a robust surrogate parent—as Jonathan Small is to Tonga. He fills a real need. Like Dracula looking after his guest in his castle, Uncle Toddy cooks the family's meals. He solicitously monitors Carolyn's health and grades, and he mediates family quarrels. He would be the ideal prosthetic father and mother were he not an interloper, promising Carolyn love and forcing sex on her.

Carolyn copes with her uncle's sexual intrusions by interpreting him as a vampire. He is stealthy, draining her vitality and self. Hickeys on her neck are signs of his bite. As the nurturant Uncle Toddy, he insists that he loves her and "he's nice." But in the moment of prosthetic conversion "his mask slides off. The eyes are bottomless, greedy" (UV 90). When she threatens to go to her parents and the police, he warns her that people will think she is crazy, and that her beloved "Grammy would die" (91). He begs, threatens, reasons, weeps. As they get closer to sex, her language becomes more Gothic, the experience at once obscure and demonic. At the moment of penetration (apparently), Carolyn has mentally "turned [her] back on him and [is] walking down a long dark hallway" (92) like the tunnel conventionally invoked in near-death experiences, not unlike the tunnel Max Klein finally escapes from in *Fearless*.

As Carolyn silently cringes and despises Uncle Toddy, nearly everyone worries about her decline in school and loss of appetite. By the time she finally spills her secret to a motherly teacher, her problems have become unmistakable traumatic symptoms. Most dramatically, we learn that in dissociated lapses in her own narrative Carolyn has presumably been acting out a blonde sister she calls Honey. In addition to multiple-personality disorder, she is suffering from anorexia, anxiety attacks, some amnesia, and alexithymia—a sense of being removed from her own life and only "as if" alive: "it feels like I'm watching myself in a play."[27] The author underlines the meaning of the symptoms for her young audience. In the last pages of the novel, Carolyn reports: "My therapist says that disguising my uncle as a vampire and inventing Honey were 'coping mechanisms,' defenses that enabled me to survive in an unpredictable and profoundly dysfunctional situation" (UV 170). We also learn that Carolyn has repudiated her family and moved in with her older sister Maggie, while "my uncle's going to prison. I never have to see him again" (169).

I am evaluating not the behavior of an actual child, but rather a public fantasy that models an experience of victimization. The novel reflects a climate of opinion, but it is also a formative discourse, in its handling of sympathies to some degree unavoidably didactic. For these reasons it makes sense to wonder what sorts of cultural materials the novel uses to construct its particular vision of abuse.

One source of its materials is a generic sort of moralistic Christianity that teaches righteous conformity, not self-reliance. Even the pious Grammy is too rigidly meek to face Carolyn's hints of trouble. Although Carolyn is supposed to be sixteen and learning to drive, she is as cowed by hellfire and conformity as she is by her vampire uncle. Nor is the connection accidental. Not only is the vampire another face of Satan, but historically, as Norman Cohn has shown, Satan has been most fearsome when severe idealism has left ordinary Christians feeling overwhelmed by guilt and helpless to resist the tempter. Like the vampire, Satan exposes self-doubt and a lack of groundedness. "God can't help you," Carolyn hears herself thinking. "You are such a dirty girl. You will burn in hell for the things you are saying, for the harm you have done your family" (160). The prosthetic voice in her head is a sinister sort of parent, part Uncle Toddy, part Satan. In bed, Carolyn wants to protest her uncle's advances, but the walls "collapse" and the bedroom vanishes; as in witchcraft lore, she is transported. Dissociation not only takes her out of herself, it makes her helpless and no longer responsible.

When Carolyn finally reveals her secret to her teacher, the book puts hellish imagery in her mind, not simply dramatizing guilty feelings but also hinting at a satanic rite: "My heart was pounding. I heard metal doors clanging. Voices were chanting the Lord's Prayer, backward. The chanting got louder and louder" (155). Grant is alluding to satanic cult fantasies, although she stops short of the claims for recovered memories of actual demonic family rites that have been discredited. Then Carolyn comes to her climactic revelation: "flames race toward me. The whole house is blazing. Fiery walls collapse around me. I crash through the glass that holds me in the burning room and plunge into space" (UV 158).

In this climactic crash, Christian themes dissolve into the imagery of traumatic disaster, as in *Fearless* and in Gothic horror tales. But the crash also evokes the window-shattering violence of countless action films, as if Carolyn is partly experiencing herself through the conventions of a gangster melodrama or war movie. Significantly, the explosion comes when the kindly teacher asks what her uncle has actually done to Honey and to her. The novel sets off the answer in a single-sentence paragraph meant to be final and mind-stopping: "I say: 'He fucks us'" (ibid.).

With this jarring bluntness, the author means to dramatize the shock of recognition as Carolyn reconnects with social reality. But Carolyn's "he fucks us" is peculiarly excessive. To put it in Vietnam War slang, in the context of the action-movie imagery of exploding rooms, the idea of fucking—the word— "blows her away." At the same time, her sudden verbal aggressiveness implies an action-movie toughness and knowingness in some part of her personality that conflicts with her helpless, tongue-tied innocence. We could conclude that in creating Carolyn's trauma the novel is dramatizing the old American clash between subcultures of violence (and violent entertainment) and puritanical religion. But the puzzles go deeper than that. For one thing, in the context of her religious guilt, Carolyn's climactic "he fucks us" is inflammatory—in her blazing imagination, truly "incendiary." Regarded this way, pulp fiction and pulpit reinforce one another. Religious hysteria about sex, hellfire, and damnation interacts with action-melodrama violence to fuel ever-higher levels of arousal and heroic meaning. Grant shows the taboo of sexual abuse providing Carolyn with a new means of using the banal, contradictory stuff of Middle-American culture and, in the end, with the help of school, the courts, therapists, and her older sister, creating a self-intoxicating, heroic purpose for her life. Having survived ambiguously superhuman psychic violence, she puts an evil vampire in prison. Like Samuel Richardson's devilishly desired and hounded Clarissa, Carolyn becomes a hero in a shallow world.

Lest I appear to be "blaming the victim," I want to emphasize my effort to see behavior and fantasy in the novel as parts of a cultural system. Grant darkly underlines Middle America's inability to provide people's lives with a life-sustaining purpose. Begin with this cultural sickness, and the critical question to ask becomes not simply "What are other people doing to this victim?" but "How is Carolyn going about improvising a meaning to live for?" Or more bluntly, "Why can't Carolyn speak up for herself? Why does she agonize so long in furious silence?" This line of inquiry leads away from easy blame and toward an uncomfortable realization that some of the basic premises of the book and its audience are part of the problem they are supposed to resolve.

The imaginative basis of Carolyn's trauma appears in a different light if we ask what her life would have been like without Uncle Toddy. We are told that Carolyn/Honey has been a superachiever in school, for instance, "so popular . . . pretty and smart" (UV 97). As Honey, Carolyn "is always the star of the show" (134), avid for glory and approval. Striving for the power and prestige of stardom is no small matter in American culture—the author herself has dedicated the book to several childhood girlfriends (apparently) and "the members of the Princess of Power Club,/May their tiaras twinkle all across the land."[28] To borrow Grant's metaphor, Carolyn/Honey is a princess in trouble, and was apparently in at least some trouble, given her unhappy family, even before Uncle Toddy turned vampire.

One proof is Carolyn's conflicted identity. Honey's striving for glory disgusts her. Yet the author herself is sharply ambivalent about stardom. She satirizes shallow "popularity" at school as Carolyn scorns Honey's eager-to-please nature, piano playing, cheerleading, and seductiveness. Yet just as Grant has a soft spot for her club of "princesses," so the novel fantasizes that when Honey "exquisitely" performs a Bach piano piece during a tense family holiday, "everyone stopped bickering and listened" (UV 78). The point is not that an adolescent should daydream about having magical power over an unhappy family, but that the daydream is assembled from Hollywood-princess clichés that displace the conflicts they seek to escape.[29] After all, in a competitive democratic culture, would-be princesses far outnumber willing servants. To be preeminent is to live off the approval and vitality of others, and this is a sort of vampirism—as Uncle Toddy confirms when he tells Carolyn in a nightmare that she too is a vampire (UV 59-61).

The striving to be a princess and a star implies a greedy wish for supremacy. Carolyn's father deviously grasps at the same supremacy when he snarls at American society and its trashy consumer products. Carolyn resents the falseness of Honey's motives. She knows that Honey is being seductive when she wears a miniskirt that arouses her driver-education teacher: "Her legs are long and curvy. She'd deny it but she likes people to notice her body" (67). Her seductive signals invite her teacher to pat her knee, just as they presumably influence Uncle Toddy. Yet the power they confirm also divides and weakens her. The adults dote on Carolyn/Honey when she performs as the star child, but they disconfirm the children's efforts at honest self-assertion. Bullying or ignoring the young, the parents alienate them (Carolyn, Richie) or infantilize them (Honey). In such a world, sexual manipulation offers a semblance of autonomy to the weak—the child, the weak uncle.

Sexual manipulation stands for false autonomy. But it is false autonomy partly because this society's codes make uncles and nieces illicit love objects. But the potential energy—the passion—trapped in this problem becomes evident the moment we recall that forbidden love is a tremendous motive force in literature. As ecstatic lovers, the same uncle and sixteen-year-old woman could be a Romeo and Juliet ("My only love sprung from my only hate!"), principals in a Greek tragedy or a Zang Zimou film of the 1990s, or simply a couple muddling through life like any other. In Uncle Vampire, this autonomy is false because uncle and niece are compromised. He loves her but greedily imposes on her. She is split between inviting an unconventional intimacy and, as the "good" child, despising it and suffering.

One reason Carolyn cannot speak up for herself is that she is divided against herself. Teachers and friends are solicitous about her symptoms, but she is unable to heed them even as her parents are numb to her. Dissociation allows Carolyn-as-Honey to deny the intimacy—and sex—she invites and condemns. Most important, dissociation enables her to screen out painful conflicts unrelated to incest, especially her self-contempt and her desperate ambivalence toward her parents. Part of her is still caught in childhood, striving to win over her unresponsive parents, trembling before mechanical religious authority, afraid of losing her will. Her climactic revelation to her teacher concludes with an interior monologue organized around the Lord's Prayer. Guilt ("You are an evil child") plays out in hellish, poetical imagery: "The voices scream. My ears are bleeding. I have fallen through a hole in the bottom of darkness, a drain through shadows into furred despair." The terror culminates in a version of the vampire's devouring: "Animals lunge at me, meat and teeth" (159).

The fear of being eaten is a fear of being subsumed; however innocently, adults are apt to croon to babies, "You're so cute I could eat you up." As in slavery and vampirism, this is a fear of soul stealing, of losing the self to a powerful other. The prosthetic voice Carolyn hears in her head sounds parental, but it attacks her: "You are an evil child" (ibid.). It lets her fall into darkness. The imagery of meat and teeth focuses her anxiety about the body, whose needs, anger, and desires may defy control. Teeth objectify the repressed anger in both her family and herself. And most threatening of all, as "meat" the self is destined to age and die. Carolyn fears that revelation of her "evil" will kill her grandmother and mother. She wants to grab her grandmother and shout "Don't get old! Don't die!" (79). But she fears aging and death for herself too (113), and in her nightmare she imagines Uncle Toddy telling her that she too is a vampire determined to escape death by sucking life from other people (59–61).

To appreciate the logic of Carolyn's nightmare, recall the generational antagonism of the 1890s. We have met this imagery before: the vampire, the Jekyll-Hyde split, the predatory (surrogate) parent and cannibal child. It is as if the ne'er-do-well Small is trying to seduce the abandoned Mary Morstan to become the cannibal Tonga and enjoy forbidden intimacy and criminal appetites. The striking difference is that the alliances by sex have been reversed: the homosocial bonds now tacitly unite women against inadequate men. But the villain is still a social failure threatening to drag down upwardly striving middle-class souls, and in the end, righteous violence finally banishes cannibal appetites. To put it in Wilde's terms, Carolyn/Honey tries to balance the tyranny of philistine morality and rebellious appetite through the "multiplication of personality," but an anxious society demands prison—literal prison for Uncle Toddy; the Foucaultian prison regimen of therapy for Carolyn/Honey. If this seems too subversive a claim, keep in mind that therapy not only heals Carolyn/Honey's trauma, it tames Honey's "hungry" and hunger-arousing sexuality. As Carolyn snipes at Honey's strapless prom dress, "I would never wear a strapless, my breasts served up. Please help yourself" (70).

In this deep-cultural context, Small's ambition to "show the folks back home" leads to criminal grasping at forbidden treasure, death anxiety (the crocodile), and an intimate discovery of cannibal appetites that must eventually be exterminated. If the absence of prosthetic supports makes a "Small" child an outsider and therefore "hungry" for confirmation, cannibalism or vampirism is the logical outcome—and anorexia becomes the logical way to avoid the guilt of it. Therapy will provide safe confinement in which the anorectic cannibal can learn to eat a safe diet.

Yet Carolyn's is only one life in a social network that was itself shaped by the 1890s. The novel overgeneralizes its social distress when, for example, it has Carolyn's older sister announce, "My psych professor says that most American families are dysfunctional, to one degree or another" (47). If Carolyn's father's "business is going down the drain" (68) and Carolyn plunges "through a hole in the bottom of darkness, a drain through shadows into furred despair" (159), the core fear is of falling. And this is the post-traumatic vocabulary of the 1890s: the cultural slide symbolized by the "down-going man." In *Uncle Vampire*, competition undercuts all sorts of prosthetic supports, from frigid parents to the wise guys who "torture" a fat schoolmate (69). As her brother Richie warns, echoing the free-market ideology of the 1980s and 1990s, "Just take care of yourself. . . . Everybody's on their own" (105). This ethos is not far from "every man for himself" and the vampire's greed. The novel foregrounds dog-eat-dog imagery in formulas such as "abuse is the dogs of hell" (171). If only the fittest survive, the seductive star Honey and the weight-lifting Uncle Toddy are striving to be among the fittest.

In this larger context, Uncle Toddy's sexual vampirism personifies a culturewide fear of emptiness and the prosthetic abuse of others that follows from it. From this standpoint, whatever the clinical reality and criminal statistics, the upsurge of concern about child abuse in the 1990s expresses a sense of traumatic disorder in the ground of social relations in American culture. *Uncle Vampire* plays out that widespread concern, but also plays to it, inviting readers to react in ways that exacerbate rather than respect the underlying dilemma.

In staging abuse as a crime melodrama, the novel ignores the disordered social ground. Instead it stresses themes of punishment and individual, therapeutic salvation. In the end Carolyn has triumphantly expelled her demon uncle, but her family has disintegrated, and she is "out of school, on independent study" (170), in a surrogate family of fellow "survivors" parented by "my therapist" (171). This medicalized resolution thinly disguises vindictive, triumphal themes that are really neither religious nor necessarily therapeutic. Although "Grammy says forgiveness is the soul of a true Christian," Carolyn is attracted to inflammatory, righteous anger: "But how can I forgive the unforgivable?" (78).

In Carolyn's world, forgiveness does less to support self-esteem than do the heroic escape from Satan's clutches and the righteous punishment of evil. Nothing in the book challenges Carolyn's assumption that sinners deserve hellfire, however weak, childish, or desperate they may be. "My uncle is in jail," she announces after her climactic revelation. "He's going to prison. I never have to see him again. He writes me letters that I won't read, telling me he's sorry and begging forgiveness" (169).

The premise that righteous rage makes you feel good resonates in a post-traumatic society in which many institutions silently induce a feeling of helplessness. In *The Courage to Heal*, the authors call anger "the backbone of healing" and encourage it: "Many survivors have strong feelings of wanting to get back at the people who hurt them so terribly. You may dream of murder or castration. It can be pleasurable to fantasize such scenes in vivid detail. Wanting revenge is a natural impulse, a sane response. Let yourself imagine it to your heart's content."[30]

The theory behind this advice is presumably that, given traumatic imprinting, central nervous system arousal can be transformed from a fright to a fight response, making good use of the feelings of invulnerability and power that often come with anger. If, as Judith Lewis Herman says, rape is "the combat neurosis of the sex war," then the encouragement of anger can be seen as a sensible means of hardening new recruits to fight "the sex war." How effective this strategy can be is an open question. Although some inhibited people need permission to assert themselves, everyone needs the ability to be strategic, and the difficulty is that righteous anger tends to be total and indiscriminate and to have no natural resolution (how much is enough?). Daniel Goleman calls the belief in the therapeutic effect of cathartic rage "the ventilation fallacy," and cites research showing that the venting of anger may feel satisfying but do little or nothing to dispel it.[31] The situation is even more worrisome when the culture itself is already disposed toward anger as a response to stress, for then anger readily becomes competitive and self-intoxicating. Like the urge to be a star, anger can be a swing from helplessness to wishful power.

To understand the dangers, it is worth remembering that as Honey, Carolyn has been provocatively seductive. With her driver-education instructor, "she twinkles and dimples and laughs at his jokes, and doesn't say a word when he pats her knee" (UV 64). This flirtation would be trivial were Carolyn not so disgusted by it. She understands perfectly well the signals Honey is sending to men: "I would never wear a strapless [dress], my breasts served up. Please help yourself" (70). Splitting here disguises Carolyn/Honey's affinity to the frigid princess, the castrating bitch, who is such a staple of melodrama. As the Salem witch trials long ago dramatized, it can be tempting for a young woman to gain power and stature by behaving—however unconsciously—as the devil's victim.[32] She is potentially the femme fatale, the fatal catalyst, arbiter of life and death, as in so many southern lynchings.

Uncle Vampire never acknowledges Carolyn's—and her society's—participation in a larger social drama, when the demonized Uncle Toddy is exorcised into prison. "He said he loved me, but he never did. He ate up my love and betrayed me. I felt like I was dying, but he kept me alive, and murdered me again and again and again" (*UV* 160). Substitute "I felt horrible" for "he murdered me," and you begin to see the inflammatory social story being constructed here. It is Carolyn's social world as much as Uncle Toddy that short-circuits her self-protective desire to protest. He never threatens physical harm, and in fact sometimes cries to get his way. A scream, or even just a shout, ought to be able to sweep away such a vampire like a cobweb.

How can Uncle Toddy be both a violator and a scapegoat? Grant's conception of him owes much to the psychodynamics of the romance novel. As Janice Radway has documented, following Nancy Chodorow's developmental theory, avid women readers seek in romance heroes an overwhelmingly intimate presence that can confirm and fulfill them the way mothers ideally corroborate their daughters.[33] Whereas boys grow up to marry women who can offer maternal support, girls usually find no replacement in marriage for that maternal bond. Romance heroes may supply that missing prosthetic presence. They simultaneously confirm the reader's individuation from the mother while projecting an idealized heterosexual bond that is so nurturant for the female protagonist that it amounts to an unconscious substitute for the mother's engulfing presence. Uncle Toddy's mothering makes up for Carolyn's lack of a caring parent. And to Carolyn's disgust, Honey denies or perhaps equivocally accepts his attentions.

The ambiguities multiply when we reconsider the cultural situation. Whereas Carolyn's father complains and bullies, his younger brother lifts weights, drives a pickup truck, and actively manages the family. Like the envious Jonathan Small, he infiltrates an elite world and steals a "treasure." The unemployed loser gets revenge against the successful insurance agent with the nice house, "shiny car," and model family. "But the truth about my uncle was too awful to bear. He was a parasite, sucking the blood out of babies. He was a cannibal, feasting on his family" (*UV* 167). He is also a rebel subverting the superficially patriarchal order. For Carolyn/Honey, at least before "he ate up my love and betrayed me" (160), Uncle Toddy was a solicitous outlaw offering forbidden fruits and a way to rebel against a suffocating family regime.

My purpose in reading Uncle Toddy's behavior this way is not to exonerate him or to shift blame to his victim, but to make plain the cultural fantasies masked by the trope of post-traumatic stress. In life it is the job of therapy to bring those formative cultural assumptions into the light. But therapy for Carolyn means separation from family, school, and friends. "Therapy is hard," she tells us. "It's like digging through mud, looking for bones, or weapons, or treasures" (171). This therapy echoes *The Sign of Four*, which is after all a search for treasure in Thames mud. The emphasis is on the possession of valuable goods—defenses and rewards. Given the vacuum in Carolyn's childhood, it would make more sense to encourage her to think realistically about her parents, family, and friends. Carolyn lacks not only parents but also a sense of what is crippling in her—and their—culture. She needs to understand that adults too can be seduced by glitz and smug conformity, because, like her, they have been injured and frightened by life. This sort of insight would entail not a chauvinistic repudiation of American middle-class life but a new understanding of its founding principles and the adaptive stress it faces in a skidding world. To put it more bluntly, Carolyn dramatizes the hysterical consequences of lying to children—and the children in ourselves—about the pressure of death and evil on good people, even in the suburbs.

What cripples the family—and the novel—is an inability to face up to evil and death. In a moment of dissociation at school, Carolyn writes about "a world ancient with sin." But exactly as her helpless mother might, she minimizes her own desperate concern: "It's just me going on and on about the sorrow and the suffering in the world, etc. Just me losing my mind on paper" (UV 103). She has been taught to see the immensity of evil, but given few cultural resources that could buck up her courage. Instead of teaching problem solving, compassion, and heroic self-assertion, her America encourages her to be a star, a "princess of power." Instead of solidarity and a tragic sense of human limits, she has overheated Christian rhetoric and a horror-movie mythos. In her world, moralism supplants morality, pumping up a hysterical simulacrum of heroic purpose. Uncle Toddy did not molest her, she insists; he abused her. "Molest sounds like something Chihuahuas do to your legs. Abuse is the dogs of hell" (171). The cute contrast here—Chihuahuas versus hellhounds (whatever they are)—ought to alert us to the rhetorical tricks being used on the reader, if not on Carolyn. Vaguely theological language is supposed to make Carolyn's sex with her uncle more horrific, but in fact it betrays uncertainty about what that sexual experience actually means. People, not diabolical fiends, hurt one another, and in the end we know next to nothing about Uncle Toddy as a person, and scarcely more about the girl's inner life.

Most unsettlingly, Carolyn's "dogs of hell" are self-aggrandizing. She is not outgrowing a painful experience with a despicable, muddled uncle, but rather overcoming cosmic evil. The dogs inflate her self-importance in accord with the demands of the ego ideal that elsewhere in the novel strives for grades, glamour, popularity, and applause. Even therapy promises a treasure hunt in the mud. As in the adventure romance, happiness lies not in a readjustment of the self but in a discovery of some gratification outside the self—in mother (treasure) or father (weapons). This externality is ominously reinforced by the ending, in which the uncle is socially destroyed and the family has been torn apart. Instead of being back among friends, learning to speak up for herself, practicing tolerance, and exploring the realities of desire and character, Carolyn now has a therapy group. "We share our histories and our hurts" (172). As for school and friends, "my life there seems like it took place on another planet" (171).

It seems to me that for group therapy to help, Carolyn ought to be learning about that "other planet," trying to understand how she got in trouble in the first place. The therapy group attempts to constitute the prosthetic network missing in Carolyn's life. It replaces Honey and the flawed family. But sharing "our histories and our hurts" (173) may not be the same thing as opening up to life and speaking freely in our own voices. Remember Carolyn's climactic revelation to her teacher, Ms. Johnson, who becomes the long-needed prosthetic voice capable of supporting Carolyn's truth. Unable to speak at first, Carolyn and Ms. Johnson write questions and answers on a pad of paper. Writing becomes the crucial prosthetic voice that mediates between self and taboo. The motherly Ms. Johnson and the voices on a page free the victim from her phantoms. The novel insinuates that its own voices on the page can be a liberating prosthetic medium.

Little wonder, then, that Carolyn has "been doing a lot of reading too." How liberating is the literature of sexual abuse? "Vampires like my uncle are as common as termites, infesting even the best homes. Their victims number in the millions" (172–73). The trope of infestation, with its carelessly grand "millions," repeats the inflammatory, aggrandizing gestures that surround abuse throughout the novel. Incest in this account is an inhuman force of nature that appeals to paranoia in its voracious, hidden subversion of even "the best homes." Carolyn and her creator still think in terms of "even the best homes": thinking like princesses.

The termite metaphor takes us back to witchcraft hysteria, projecting invisible demons against which our everyday senses and reason are helpless until the damage is already done, and relief from which can be found only in extermination. But the idea of invisible colonies undermining the houses of America has other social resonances that are closer to hand. The termite colonies suggest the ideation of anticommunism in the 1950s, which often equated Communists with invading insects, zombies, and other monsters.[34] No less relevant, given Uncle Toddy's status as a loser and a parasite, is the image's evocation of the sinister, proletarian Morlocks laboring away in the tunnels under the vulnerable, effeminate Eloi. In this fantasy, incest is not a solitary and tormentingly personal encounter between people, but rather the million-strong attack of "them" (men, presumably) on "our" elite.

This sort of rhetoric is post-traumatic in the familiar 1890s mode. It makes *Uncle Vampire* highly equivocal, because the effect on readers may be to narrow life space rather than reclaim and expand it for the "patient." After all, the novel imagines getting closure by excluding the uncle and his motives from further thought ever afterward. At the same time, the medicalization of their intimacy associates it with illness and a special, segregated group of fellow patients. This is neither a tragic nor an especially realistic view of life—no matter how prevalent child-rape is, adrenaline-charged visions of ubiquitous and insidious "termites" are more likely to lead to vigilant insecurity than to courageous resolve. After her long struggle to bring "a terrible truth" to light and a criminal to justice, Carolyn suffers a heroic collapse into therapy like Holmes nursed by Watson.

Whither Childhood?

Trying to account for the "vogue of childhood misery," Lemann connects it to "a world-wide historical awakening about child abuse" akin to the (historically recent) abolition of slavery. The recent preoccupation with abusive childhoods he sees as "in part a revisionist history of the Baby Boom years, written by the former babies; it gets much of its oomph from the idea that the heavily propagandized family life of the 1950s was actually often nightmarish. People who were intensely conscious while they were growing up that they were the most fortunate children in the history of the world . . . and who are raising their children in a time of very different social mores, are looking for a way to explain the disappointment and foreboding that they feel."[35]

The sharpened and disconfirmed expectations Lemann describes are a familiar component of post-traumatic imagination. Interpreted as trauma, childhood distress can justify adult failures and anxieties. By identifying with today's children, adults can also vicariously confirm explanations of the world that originate in ideas about their own early years. As a rule, concern for the well-being of children needs no explanation. But in the novels I have described, childhood serves many different ends. For one thing, it functions as it does in Rider Haggard's imagination, representing a lost ground of personality to be recuperated through mourning.

This sort of strategic mourning can be problematic. Not only may it all too readily drift from grief into grievance, but it makes a case based on evidence that continually recedes into history, in need of ever more resourceful attempts at reconstruction. Given the risks of false prosecution or simply overreaction, the post-traumatic symptom of "recovered memory" has understandably caused grave controversy among researchers, clinicians, and jurists.[36] Indirectly, the controversy reveals some of our basic ideas about ourselves to be weakly grounded, if not untenable. If we overestimate the influence of childhood experience on adult behavior, we are only following Freud, who made the recuperation of childhood central to his project of psychoanalysis as mourning.[37] Freud's great endeavor persists as part of the heroic project of our own era. Yet some research confutes the Freudian assumption that childhood experience strongly influences adult behavior. For every study confirming that childhood abuse causes lasting psychic impairment, there seems to be one that draws the opposite conclusion.[38] Like our thinking about grief—is it healthier to "let it all out" or to favor composure?—incompatible models of identity contend around us, and no closure is yet in sight. Is Carolyn exclusively the victim of an overwhelmingly evil uncle? Or is her distress also a result of learned helplessness fostered by a confused and conflicted culture?[39]

This confusion affects many critical issues in our culture, child-welfare policy among them. It can be seen in the startling irrationality of the Reagan era, which transformed the altruistic, parental government of Roosevelt and Eisenhower into the sinister "big government" that President Reagan vilified as a devouring, abusive monster even as he led the attack on support networks for children. Reagan cut "almost all of the funds for the highly successful National Center on Child Abuse and Neglect."[40] Since the 1980s, studies have repeatedly confirmed the increasing numbers of American children in poverty, with a widening gap between the rich and the poor ahead of them. In 1995 the government estimated that two thousand children a year die from abuse and neglect. The "number of children abused and neglected annually has more than doubled in the past decade—from 1.4 million to 2.9 million."[41] In 1996, the Department of Health and Human Services reported that "the abuse and neglect of America's young nearly doubled from 1986 to 1993, an increase so dramatic that it reflects a 'true rise' in the severity of the problem rather than one based solely on heightened awareness."[42] As families and communities groan under stress, the public mind embraces desperate contradictions, trying to reconcile an individualistic ideology with a belief in, and need for, generous public support for vulnerable neighbors. People are understandably fascinated—lured, appalled—by fantasies of disrupted prosthetic relationships because they express a suspicion that "good" parents have withdrawn from—have disinvested in or are "using"—families. In a "me first," dog-eat-dog culture, prosthetic relationships are apt to seem negative: a void to be filled up or overcome, a wound to be healed, a crippling spell to be broken.

Signs of this tension abound, and they are not confined only to discontented, "revisionist" baby boomers. Their children, for example, have been styled "Generation X," as if they had been abandoned at birth. Their preoccupation with electronic media, the great prosthetic trope of industrial civilization, suggests compensatory fantasies of uncanny parenting that have long haunted humankind (children raised by wolves and witches) as well as cybernetic dreams of perfect or perfectly ghastly parenting (the robots in *Star Wars*, the telescreens in George Orwell's *1984*). We speak of television "baby-sitting" the young, the ill, and the old, even as its manipulative venality evokes the specter of demonic agencies—such as vampires or those Orwellian telescreens—capturing the souls of "couch potatoes" and zombie consumers. This doubleness persists in the prosthetic promise of virtual reality, whose utopian hype is counterbalanced by the Faustian anxieties in novels by William Gibson (*Neuromancer*) and Neil Stevenson (*Snow Crash, Zodiac*) as well as such films as Bret Leonard's *Lawnmower Man*.

Yet these fantasies can seem tame and abstract compared to what has come to symbolize the ultimate prosthetic relationship: pregnancy. Among other things, technologies such as ultrasound have magnified the prosthetic interaction of mother and fetus. Artificial fertilization and surrogate motherhood have dramatized the fetus's use of the female body as its vehicle to life. From a different yet related perspective, that status as vehicle highlights the possibilities of strategic instrumentality in childbearing, and may bluntly demystify the culture's protective fantasies of inexhaustible mother love. No wonder, then, that these symptoms of a secular era, combined with the sorts of stress I suggested above, may contribute to extraordinary ambivalence about pregnancy and pregnant women. Like the Victorians,[43] we are of opposite minds about the prosthetic mother bond, perhaps most shockingly in the homicidal rage that religious antiabortion protesters sometimes express toward "infant-killing" mothers and doctors. The ambivalence resonates in the most unlikely places, as in William Gibson's *Neuromancer*, when his cyberspace "cowboy" hero, Case, penetrates a fortified corporate headquarters and steals a valuable cybernetic treasure by using virtual reality to "ride" inside the head of a prosthetically enhanced agent, the murderously powerful mothering girlfriend, Molly.

The painful paradox for young and old is that parents cannot be wished away. No matter how vivid the illusion, nobody is wholly self-created. We make ourselves out of—we swim in—other personalities. In post-traumatic phases, our culture seems unable to support those synergistic interconnections, and people begin to feel ungrounded and oppressed by survival anxiety. In the 1990s, as in the 1890s, all sorts of boundaries are shifting, with predictable effects on people's sense of moral order, communal integrity, and family coherence. Change means aroused expectations and inescapable anxiety.

More specifically, since the Vietnam War the country's leaders have turned away from the New Deal vision of the parenting or nurturant community, and have begun reviving Social Darwinist visions of the survival of the fittest. In countless ways, policymakers in business and government have not only shifted back from the carrot to the stick as a motivating tool, but they have rationalized the shift in ways that create serious emotional stress. The resulting insecurity, I think, shows up in the public's need for scapegoats and vindictive policies toward welfare, immigration, and crime. The wealthy nation that "cannot afford" health insurance or welfare can afford a massive peacetime military-industrial enterprise and one of the world's largest prison systems. When workers' "terminations" are justified by a need to "survive" foreign competition, the fear of death takes on fabulous euphemistic forms. Competitive capitalism is rooted in survival motives and dread. Even our sports sublimate survival ecstasy, as we unwittingly acknowledge when we envision a game going into "sudden-death" overtime.

In the present queasy historical moment, if this account is correct, the internalized voices of childhood may be changing. And our sense of them, too, may be changing. It is impossible to tell how superficial or enduring the changes may be. And this is hardly the first time the psychic ground of the culture has shifted—it would be more accurate to say that it is slipping and quaking all the time. Like Nicholas Lemann, however, I suspect that our recent inclination to see childhood as "unhappy, or at the very least fragile and imperilled, may reveal something about the condition we think the country is in, as well as about the lives of our children."[44] It seems safe to say that sensitivity toward the condition of children, women, and the poor has taken on a new moral force in the two centuries since the great democratic revolutions and campaigns against slavery. This suggests that in the current fascination with abuse, imaginations may be acting on a rising standard of justice and empathy, even as they blindly wrestle with shadowy cultural changes of a magnitude greater than we like to think.

However sensitive it may be, popular awareness of abuse is also radically irrational. It reflects some of the deepest prejudices of American culture. In ancient Athens as in the Globe Theatre, tragedy made the traumatic suffering of elite heroes an object of general empathy. Inside the Globe, the world witnessed and validated aristocratic pain. "Low persons" had to endure. In the 1990s the percentages have shifted, but as Jonathan Shay emphasizes in his study of combat trauma, "we must also bear in mind *the enormous advantage that the powerful have over the powerless in the conduct of griefwork.*"[45] Like the for-profit, individualized healthcare "industry," Hollywood and popular narratives of abuse such as *Uncle Vampire* serve upwardly mobile victims far better than they serve those on the bottom.

As a cultural construct, the approved model of abuse management acts to "institutionalize" the experience. In *Uncle Vampire*, with the best of intentions, "abuse therapy" strengthens scapegoat behaviors while not allowing or helping the victim to realize herself. To be herself, she needs not only the support of understanding fellow victims, but encouragement to stay in her world and work on accepting herself and others instead of withdrawing into a righteous therapy that is really a system of compensation. The psychiatrist Jonathan Shay expresses a similar misgiving: "I cannot escape the suspicion that what we do as mental health professionals is not as good as the healing that in other cultures has been rooted in the native soil of the returning soldier's community."[46]

Shay's rhetoric of groundedness ("rooted," "native soil") directly exposes the crux of trauma: how can a culture restore the integrity of its belief system after the terror of death has damaged it? He suspects that more-rooted communities more readily heal traumatic symptoms. This is the familiar protest against modernism. If more-rooted societies heal more effectively, they owe their efficacy to the power of communalizing to reabsorb the terrorized individual into the group—into the prosthetic womb of collective experience, as it were, where psychic rebirth becomes possible.

In class-riven cultures such as America in the 1990s, the professional womb of therapy is patently less open to the poor than to their betters. The public often will not, or cannot bear to, acknowledge the abuse of the despised and unpromising poor. Anyone who doubts this needs only to contemplate the numbers of criminals who have been brutalized as children—the tragic burden of Sister Helen Prejean's account in *Dead Man Walking* of the condemned murderer she counseled. Somewhere between the extremes of ideology therapy and practical neglect is a space for empathy that can heal injured souls. The construct of abuse in the 1990s promises an expansion of that empathy. But it also fosters a conviction that because trauma is "imprinted," every victim is going to be an "adult survivor." That split reflects the way the idea of trauma is reconfiguring death anxiety in a new era, and points to the rude existential challenges that radically complicate human motives.

EIGHT

Traumatic Triumph in a Black Childhood

> Black an' ugly
> But he sho' do treat me kind.
> I'm black an' ugly
> But he sho do treat me kind.
> High-in-heaven Jesus,
> Please don't take this man o' mine.
>
> Langston Hughes, "Lament over Love"

CYNTHIA GRANT'S *Uncle Vampire* argues that traumatic sexual abuse has "shattered" its victim. Yet Carolyn's disturbance is part of a cultural system that manages competition by praising individual initiative while insidiously fostering self-disablement. Like the smothering husband in Charlotte Perkins Gilman's story "The Yellow Wallpaper" (1892), Carolyn's uncle is only the most obvious source of her helplessness. At any point in the story Carolyn—or Gilman's heroine—could speak up for herself. What cripples her is her internalized fear and conflict. She is "afraid" to hurt or be hurt by nearly everyone around her, especially her family. She is also angry, and afraid of her anger. Her inhibitions and pain may be real, but they are not the products of demonic magic.

For blacks in America, traumatic abuse began before the first slave ship docked, and the vampire uncle has been Uncle Sam. The abuse has been violent, pervasive, and even today often institutional.[1] And yet however improbable it seems, trauma is not simply self-evident for black Americans, any more than it is for the white teenager in the "nice big house" (*UV* 97).

For one thing, slavery has taken many forms in history and, as the United Nations reports year after year, it still shackles some cultures. Roman slavery relieved the pressures of revolt and despair by evolving complex systems for working slaves toward manumission and citizenship. In the United States, it took a cataclysmic civil war to force emancipation. And for many freed slaves, Appomattox only sublimated the war, because what followed was a century of class and economic strife organized around racial hostility. Sherlock Holmes's vigilante execution of Tonga euphemizes the atrocious lynchings and assassinations that terrorized black Americans. In this atmosphere of economic and physical insecurity, blacks have good reason to feel the continuing impact of slavery.

If you feel disembedded in your own culture, which is how many blacks feel at one time or another about being Americans, then the need to substantiate your identity understandably leads to a search for a historical ground in religion or heritage. Like all remedies for disembeddedness, the search for roots is likely to be compensatory—as when Afrocentric historians try to make Africa not simply worthy but the wellspring of Western culture. To be sure, most American blacks have lost any personal connection to a particular African origin. But then, go back far enough—who were the Irish before they took over Ireland?—and all lives are adrift in mystery. Darwin exposed this queasy open-endedness by asking the questions he did. To complicate matters, the vast majority of American blacks are of mixed ancestry anyway—as are a great many other Americans. But when prosthetic relations in the immediate world are in trouble, history assumes a special significance.

Construed as a purifying ordeal—we speak of character "formed" in a crucible—slavery can substantiate identity by conferring moral authority and the magic of survivorship. As a traumatic injury, by contrast, it signifies lasting damage to selfhood—which is why Malcolm X repudiated his "white slave-master name of 'Little' [cf. Small] which some blue-eyed devil named Little had imposed upon my paternal forebears," substituting an "X" to symbolize "the true African family name that he never could know."[2] The post-traumatic effects of slavery also follow different interpretive arcs. A trajectory of berserk fury, for example, connects Nat Turner's slave revolt to the black rage associated with Marcus Garvey, Malcolm X, the Black Panthers, and the stylized threat displays of "gangsta rap" in the 1990s. A different theme, formed in traumatic numbness and withdrawal, passes through the moral teaching of passive resistance and sacrifice in black Christianity, and is writ large in American culture in figures such as Harriet Beecher Stowe's Uncle Tom and, with a sacrificial-messianic prophecy ("I have a dream"), in a figure such as Martin Luther King.

By making blacks either demonic or messianic figures, the popular culture has never stopped reinforcing this psychic split. Although Stowe canonized the saintly Uncle Tom, D. W. Griffith's *Birth of a Nation* (1915) pitted Saint George in a Ku Klux Klan hood against the black rapist run amok. In a more enlightened era, after the great civil-rights struggles of the 1960s, Hollywood's ambivalence was modulated. By the mid-1990s, for instance, screenwriters were fusing stereotypes of the terroristic gangsta rapper and the messianic black rebel. In *Strange Days* (1996), this hybrid figure is the musician-activist Jeriko, who has been gunned down by racist police officers in the closing days of 1999. In *Johnny Mnemonic* (1995), a hip-hop underground leader outwits elite industrial culture and broadcasts a cure for a disease similar to AIDS. These two films portray blacks both as the primary victims of the corporate state and as mythic saviors. Both films show Hollywood manipulating black identity with jarring effrontery. They tame the anger of the streets by promoting a black Saint George of the 'hood, who evokes Malcolm X but also happens to be, flatteringly, a star in a billion-dollar entertainment industry militantly sympathetic toward the humblest blacks.

In the real world, blacks have had to disarm that ambivalent image. Civil-rights leaders succeeded in the 1960s, for example, not only by marshaling their political resources, but also by strategically mirroring American ideals. In Tom Engelhardt's words, "Immaculate in suits and ties, polite and tolerant, blacks offered an audience of whites a minstrelsy of inclusiveness, a theatrical and incisive whiteface critique played out on black bodies. This disarming mirroring of the best the American tradition could promise threw into horrific contrast actual white acts . . . and turned whites—from Birmingham Police Chief Bull Connor to Alabama Governor George Wallace, from abusive students at the University of Mississippi to Klan bombers—into savages."[3] As a means of countering bigotry, Booker T. Washington had urged blacks to lead exemplary lives. The civil-rights era gave that idealized identity a dramatic global confirmation.

If blacks were no longer Manichean outsiders, then white ambivalence was awkwardly, even embarrassingly, inappropriate. One response has been to coopt and control the new image of blacks. Since the Reagan years, movies and advertising campaigns have been reimagining the black outsider as a special friend to whites. As Benjamin DeMott put it, "the nation's corporate ministries of culture churn out images of racial harmony."[4] Although the black buddy plainly makes a healthier stereotype than the crazed black rapist, DeMott emphasizes that this fantasy relieves white audiences of any guilt about the treatment of blacks. And this diminished responsibility has far-reaching economic consequences because it can be used to justify shifts in public policy. If there is no racial animosity or injustice in America, then with a clear conscience the majority can save tax money by cutting welfare, housing subsidies, and educational support for its lowest caste. The contrived imagery of racial friendship both justifies and sanitizes popular attacks on affirmative action and other measures intended to equalize competition in education and the work force. It rationalizes the Supreme Court's slackened concern about racial justice. It is as if Jonathan Small's friendship with Tonga guaranteed that the empire's blacks were wearing cravats and prospering.

Which brings us back to trauma. "Although there was scant popular awareness of it at the time (1977)," says DeMott, "the television miniseries *Roots* introduced the figure of the Unscathed Slave. To an enthralled audience of more than 80 million the series intimated that the damage resulting from generations of birth-ascribed, semi-animal status was largely temporary, that slavery was a product of motiveless malignity on the social margins rather than of respectable rationality, and that the ultimate significance of the institution lay in the demonstration, by freed slaves, that no force on earth can best the energies of American individualism."[5] The new amicability toward blacks, in short, can be used to dispel the reality of slavery, like Big Brother's historical machinations in 1984. Interviewed as a potential presidential candidate, General Colin Powell protested against this maneuver when he complained that he "'almost went crazy' reading a Republican newsletter saying affirmative action was no longer needed to combat 'vague and ancient wrongs.'"[6]

The following chapter, on Steven Spielberg's *Schindler's List*, examines in detail a similar process of rehabilitating slave labor through fantasies of special friendship, with painful economic implications for 1990s America. Here I want to suggest that heroic fantasies about freed slaves not only whitewash slavery, they deny that racism and the exploitation of labor are behavioral systems whose laws override individual heroism. Measurements consistently show a mocking skew between whites and blacks in the distribution of income, net worth, and prison sentences. In a business culture that prizes arbitrage, technological skills, downsizing, and the search for ever-cheaper labor abroad, African-American labor is actually worth less than it was in slavery. This equation means that attacks on social programs intended to protect the under- and unemployed are doubly damaging. Not only do they further jeopardize economically insecure people; they also seek to force them into a labor market where the legal minimum wage is not enough to live on—a sinister echo of slavery. Certainly this is not a problem for blacks alone. Yet as last hired/first fired, blacks take a disproportionate number of casualties.

If slavery is "social death," as Orlando Patterson says,[7] then its traumatic core is a threat to destroy the self. As in vampirism, a master usurps the slave's will and steals the living body. The regime of terror and disconfirmation sets out to extirpate supportive prosthetic relations among its slaves. Between master and slave it enforces distorted relationships, degrading the slave into an animal or a machine, or inventing an infinitely compliant superparent such as Uncle Tom or the mammy.[8] But in all these schemes, coercion and falseness are inescapable, and firsthand accounts of antebellum slavery regularly complain about how stressful all interpersonal life became. Like any other trauma victims, some freed slaves did heal and thrive during Reconstruction. Others faced continuing oppression, exclusion, and enforced helplessness, with a range of symptoms not always obvious in the historical record. As Frantz Fanon insisted in *The Wretched of the Earth*, the post-traumatic legacies of oppression are self-doubt and an impaired will.

A century after emancipation slavery still casts a sinister shadow. But at this point it is, after all, a shadow: a group memory that has to be reconceived and retransmitted. For blacks, one crucial problem is how to keep the idea of slavery's damaging effects from becoming a demoralizing and self-fulfilling prophecy. Even more challenging is how to sort out the poisonous aftereffects of slavery from the insidiously crippling influences operating in American culture today.[9] As I see it, no analysis of this problem can be complete unless, as in Carolyn's case in *Uncle Vampire* (granting the enormous difference of scale), we ask how injured people may be internalizing unhealthy aspects of their environment. Like Carolyn, black Americans are not simply victimized others, but Americans living in a society riven by competition, conflict, and fear. Given the pressure of conflicting historical models of identity, this can be a confounding inquiry. One way to begin is to look closely at a novel about a black childhood and a daughter who, like Carolyn, is trying to find a voice of her own.

Recovering Child Recovering Childhood

Not unexpectedly in a story marketed for young readers, the front matter of Virginia Hamilton's *Sweet Whispers, Brother Rush* (1982) promises the renewal of family: "Fourteen-year-old Tree [Teresa Pratt], resentful of her working mother who leaves her in charge of a retarded brother[,] encounters the ghost of her dead uncle and comes to a deeper understanding of her family's problems."[10] More exactly, this is an urban black family under stress in contemporary America. Tree copes with near-abandonment by her parents and comes of age witnessing her brother's death from the same inherited disease that has, as she discovers, killed several of her mother's brothers as well.

Although the novel overtly celebrates a young woman's hard-won autonomy, its plot dooms most of the male characters and marginalizes the girl's mother. In my reading, the novel's message of reconciliation and personal triumph projects suspect values. Far from being a feminist novel, as it might appear to be, *Sweet Whispers, Brother Rush* reinforces a covert fantasy of alienated, heroic survival.

Its apparent celebration of black solidarity overlies a regressive vision of relentless, sadistic competition. The novel's contradictions call attention to the way in which it manipulates cultural values, but also to how that manipulation itself may be a response to the deep determinants of behavior (such as traumatic death anxiety) that shape its cultural forms.

In the opening pages of the novel, Tree is returning from school, hugging her books to "hide herself"—her budding breasts—from "dudes" on the street who have begun paying attention to her (*SWBR* 9). Just at this point, as she is being reminded of adult sexuality, Tree sees a young man who turns out to be the ghost of her mother's dead brother. Dressed in seductively elegant "funeral clothes" (11), Brother Rush is the "stone finest dude Tree had ever seen in her short life" (12).

As it happens, the budding fourteen-year-old is already tacitly burdened with motherhood. Left alone in an apartment for days or weeks at a time while her mother works, Tree cares for her retarded older brother, Dabney. From time to time girls come home from school with Dab and sleep with him. But apart from her mother's periodic visits to replenish the groceries, and the Saturday visits of an ineffectual, elderly housecleaner, Miss Pricherd, Tree is radically isolated. She fills her time with artistic exploration. In a junk-filled "closet-room" where she draws pictures of houses and families (20), she again encounters the spectral Brother Rush, who leads her into a dream landscape that turns out to be her own repressed childhood. Yet as Tree sees more and more deeply into her own traumatic origins, her brother Dabney grows terrifyingly sick.

Tree's visions, such as the intrusive hallucination of Brother Rush, are classic symptoms of trauma. They recapitulate the past disintegration of the family. Innocently she rediscovers her mother, M'Vy, and her father, Ken, fighting; witnesses the young, exasperated M'Vy beating her retarded son, Dabney; and relives an afternoon in which Brother Rush let the children wander off alone while he fell tipsily asleep, and an auto accident in which Rush, mysteriously ill, let himself be killed.

At the novel's climax, Tree's mother returns with her new lover, the idealized, fatherly Silversmith, and rushes Dabney to the hospital and an offstage death. We then learn that an inherited disease, porphyria, doomed Dabney, Rush, and several of M'Vy's other brothers. Tree grieves violently and rages against her long-absent mother. In addition, she fears for her own life, although as a practical nurse her mother reassures her that even if Tree did suffer from porphyria (she does not), it is only fatal when complicated by blind efforts to escape the pain through drugs such as barbiturates (Dab) or alcohol (Rush).

No sooner is Dabney buried than Tree's life takes a drastic turn. Silversmith's attractive son Don takes her out on her first date, and her mother arranges for a suddenly invigorated Miss Pricherd to move into the apartment and care for the girl. M'Vy confesses her past inadequacies as a parent: "Call me a fool. Been so busy workin, makin our lives—I'll take a lot of the blame. . . . I mean to be a good mother one day. I love you so much, Tree" (214). The ghost vanishes for good, and "Granny" Pricherd concludes by doing "a little dance" (215).

For a reader identifying with Tree, *Sweet Whispers, Brother Rush* projects intense wish fulfillment. As in *Cinderella*, the child-mother Tree proves her mettle and is released from symbolic bondage. Like a fairy godmother, her mother M'Vy providentially returns to redirect the girl's destiny with new signs of power, including a new car and the sympathetic mate Silversmith. Although the sickly brother Dabney dies, the princely, collegiate stepbrother Don (Silversmith's son) gratuitously appears to take his place. Thanks to the ghostly Brother Rush, Tree can recognize and try to forgive M'Vy's failures as a mother and come to terms with porphyria. Able at last to account for the absence of kin, Tree finds a usable ground for her identity, a history that presumably can support a future for her outside the suffocating apartment.

The significance of the novel's wish fulfillment becomes clearer in the context of popular romances. As Janice Radway theorizes, for female readers romance simultaneously confirms their individuation from their mothers while projecting an idealized heterosexual bond that is so nurturant for the female protagonist that it amounts to an unconscious substitute for the mother's engulfing presence.[11] For many women, the reading of romances is a means of strengthening female identity. It allows women readers to recreate their relationships to their own developmental conflicts as well as to a problematic patriarchal culture. Radway's analysis shows the effects of romance to be highly equivocal: it is unclear whether in the long term the experience furthers or hinders the readers' efforts at self-realization—whether it makes readers less or more effective in shaping the world in which they live.

Like a romance, *Sweet Whispers, Brother Rush* projects a compromise solution to developmental dilemmas. At the outset Tree's growth is blocked. Locked into her mother's apartment by the criminal violence of the city, she lives on the edge of dreams, out of time. She is caught in paralyzing contradictions, prematurely forced toward self-reliance and adult responsibility, yet also kept chronically anxious about maternal abandonment, wondering if "M'Vy would come back before all the food was gone" (*SWBR* 38). One moment her mother is distressingly remote; the next, she is oppressively in charge. The woman who would force individuation on the child also represents a threat to take away (or a temptation to relinquish) all of Tree's hard-earned independence: "What did it matter that Tree couldn't breathe, planted as she was against M'Vy's breast? She would have grown again inside M'Vy if she could have" (90). Reunited with the girl, M'Vy "patty-caked Tree's hands. Not saying any words, Vy went through the motions of the rhyme of infants. Tree giggled. 'Makin me a baby!'" (91).

The novel's solution to these conflicts relates it to the romance genre. Don and Silversmith dramatize the promise of nurturant heterosexuality; they are competent in the world and yet conspicuously sympathetic to women's needs. Don "treated her the way she wanted to be treated, like a person worthy of consideration" (204). Father and son represent the possibility of a completely absorbing and satisfying heterosexual bond. And what of the mother—in Chodorow's view the unconscious, ambivalent ground of the young woman's needs.[12]

The novel projects an evasive solution: the mother is displaced by the grandmotherly Miss Pricherd, who promises to provide the nurture Tree has missed. Initially the old woman was lazy and parasitical—a competitor "hiding in the kitchen and sneaking . . . food" (48). By the last page, however, the new "Granny" is "honey-frying chicken in an ancient skillet she must have brought with her" (215). As a surrogate provider, Miss Pricherd eases the threat of maternal dominance over the child; Tree can safely rebel against her: "How you know anything, you old fool!" (191).

From another angle, Miss Pricherd also dramatizes the gratifications of vicarious motherhood. Caught up in Tree's lonely struggle, readers may not notice that the girl's arduous maternal role with Dab has afforded her extraordinary power. In M'Vy's absence Tree is the mistress of the house, making her own decisions, and Dab literally owes her his life. Like Tree, Miss Pricherd acquires a mother's heroic authority without the responsibility of motherhood. Once a destitute nobody wandering the streets, always in danger, suddenly the old woman is now secure and the stable center of someone else's life. In a way, Miss Pricherd takes over the conflicted but covertly rewarding role that Tree relinquishes.

The novel culminates in vicarious relationships. Tree is made to spell it out: "We all like a family—is it what a family's like? Talkin, bein close and laughin, always knowin they there? Me and Don are the kids; M'Vy and Silversmith, the parents. And Miss Pricherd. Granny Pricherd! Yeah, it feels all right" (208). But there is something hollow about this affirmation, inasmuch as the "family" is once again about to leave the daughter behind as they go back to their own lives across town. As in romance, the daughter's wish for a profound bond with her mother cannot be directly fulfilled. The difference is that romances offer a masculine substitute for the mother, while Tree stands alone imagining a tacit family in which intimacy remains peculiarly deferred.

Developmentally, a young girl usually individuates from her mother by turning to her father. By identifying with him, she distances herself from her mother's feminine traits, free to redefine herself. In Tree's childhood, however, men are emotionally numb if not absent. Her father exists in hazy memories. In some ways he is merged in the figure of Brother Rush, who "had to belong to her. She belonged to him the moment she saw him" (12). But Rush is a messenger of mortality. As a result, Tree's feeling for men is invested wholly in the feeble Dab, and when he dies—even though consolations appear—Tree blurts out her sense of loss: "'I want to find my dad,' Tree said, and began to cry like a baby." When her mother argues that Tree's grief for her father is compensation for the loss of her brother, Tree is not soothed. "'I want my dad!' Tree cried, sobbing." Her mother then offers the idealized Silversmith as a substitute, but Tree counters: "He may become your husband . . . but he ain't my dad!" She accuses M'Vy of having always "done did what you want," and then pleads, "Why can't you stay wit me? . . . I want *you*" (211). M'Vy apologizes for her past neglect but never does give a satisfactory answer to the question.

Dab's death inspires Tree's urgent wish to ground herself in a father and, beyond that, in her mother. When she learns of her father's desertion years before and her mother refuses to stay on with her, the girl panics. Her "eyes ran with terror and she burst into racking sobs." All at once she blurts out her fear of death: "When . . . porphyria, *me?* When I'm . . . When I'm goin *die*, like Dab?" (212). To reassure her, M'Vy gives an account of the inherited disease that has killed so many males in the family. In effect, the child's effort to ground herself climaxes in this traumatic vision of doomed males, and any explanation of the family must ask about the meaning of its crucial disease.

Blackness as a Traumatic Illness

To understand the family's disease is to unfold its symbolic logic. For a start, in this novel porphyria afflicts black males. "Ain't it strange," Tree exclaims, "black men get a disease where no light can touch their skin?" (*SWBR* 183). Given this pathological sensitivity to light, the disease becomes a metaphor for racial oppression, and finally for the trauma of African-American history. It "'come from Africa,' Vy whispered, 'Yea, way long time ago. It was a white man's disease. Traced to South Africa and a Dutch settler. Then, it became a *colored* porphyria and made its way to America probably through the slave trade'" (ibid.). Hence the scourge can be taken to symbolize the torment of slavery and the debilitating psychic pain transmitted from one generation to the next. Barbiturates and alcohol, which promise relief, actually cause the disease to flare up in a life-threatening form, as the deaths of Dab and Brother Rush confirm. By extension, an inherited disease tacitly comes to explain the destructive addictions of black males. Through a neat symbolic stroke, Hamilton evokes the historical oppression of blacks to account for self-destructiveness in black urban culture.

The novel insinuates that the porphyria sufferer's morbid sensitivity to light destroys identity. In confining Dab and his sister inside a dim apartment, for example, the disease metaphorically keeps the self obscure and unreal. Tree's impulse to hide herself from boys on the street turns out to be in part an expression of self-disgust and anxiety about being judged. Told by Silversmith that she is only "self-conscious" (157), she insists: "I thought I must be ashamed cause of my color" (158). Tree's sense of shame helps explain the pervasive repression in the family: repression that keeps her locked inside the apartment and yields only to her trancelike visions of her lost childhood. The repression originates in her mother's shame. M'Vy confesses to a sense of guilty inadequacy that made her cruelly scapegoat her retarded son: "I was so afraid. I was young. I didn't have no smarts—who did, back then? I beat that boy. I beat him, help me, I beat him. You won't forgive me. But I won't forgive myself. Maybe I thought if I beat him people would think he really bad, blame him, not me. . . . But really all the time I was afraid he might have the sickness, like my brothers. I was so afraid, Tree" (173). To the extent that M'Vy evades as well as accepts responsibility, Hamilton's translation of racial anxiety into the metaphor of disease serves to mask some of the story's most important concerns behind spurious givens.

Desperate for a sense of power and belonging, M'Vy has tacitly defined her "bad" child as an enemy to be punished. Although she acknowledges her malice, M'Vy is also partly a victim insofar as she is grasping for autonomy, which is morbidly scarce in the world around her. Logically enough, her daughter competes with her for power, imitating M'Vy's punishing self-aggrandizement, trying to compensate for her own crippling shame. As a toddler, Tree mimics the woman's aggression by regularly hitting Dab (107, 113). To intimidate him she threatens at one point to tie him up and leave him as her mother does: "'You want me tie you to the [bed]post? I can do it. I can be the woman, see?' She lifted the rope toward him. He swatted it out of her hand to the floor. His mouth turned down. His eyes filled with tears. Eyes wet and shining at her. The boy climbed up on the bed and covered his head with a pillow." Then he "cried and he cried" (75). As a scapegoat, Dab hides his head under a pillow in a gesture that suggests shame and suffocation. Denied by their parents, terrified, competing for scarce autonomy ("I can be the woman, see?"), children compensate by dominating those weaker than themselves, so that initial failures of nurture have crippling consequences in wider social relationships.

The competition to survive is deeply corrupting. Whites persecute blacks, as in the murder of the old Reverend (83); black street toughs terrorize other blacks. "Put Dab on the Street for one day and night, and Tree knew he would be dead, worse, a junkie, or a slave, stealing for somebody, by the next morning" (81). Within the family, men beat women (86). Tree and her mother beat the retarded Dab. Competition poisons even the smallest encounters. During Miss Pricherd's first housecleaning visit, Tree coldly monitors her: "Tree didn't take up the conversation. She glanced hard at Miss Pricherd to see if she might be thinking about swiping some things from the little room" (62). But then, Tree has grown up surrounded by broken or malicious spirits, in a network of fragmented prosthetic relations.

Even apparent victims may perpetuate the cycle of traumatic abuse. Although he has lost his entire family, Tree's childhood neighbor Mr. Simms spreads despair rather than sympathy; his eyes "told everybody that nothing was ever going to get any better" (26). Absorbed in his own pain, Brother Rush drunkenly nods off, letting Tree and her brother wander away down a dangerous road (108). M'Vy's grip on her daughter is protective, but it is also a narcissistic reflex because, as Chodorow notes, the mother tends to experience her daughter as an extension of herself.[13] In addition, M'Vy's possessive concentration on Tree enables her to "forget the boy for hours at a time" (*SWBR* 74).

Some of this inability to care for others results from economic and social oppression. Yet the novel also envisions alienation perpetuated in a generational cycle as parents wrest precious autonomy from children who grow up to deprive their own young. Tree remembers her mother beating the young Dab with a stick for intruding into the front seat of the car, although Dab "just wanted to see everything in front" because "he loves to hold the wheel" (69)—because he was playfully reaching for the autonomy that his mother coveted.

The novel never resolves its ambivalence about the struggle for selfhood: the struggle seems essential to personal happiness, yet it maims others. To use the imagery of cars, it promises freedom and produces catastrophe. Brother Rush drives with enviable, reckless confidence, yet he dies in an auto wreck. The crippled Aunt Binnie owns a mangled dog who has "been run down by a car" (31). Mr. Simms's family has been killed in a highway crash. Seen through Tree's uncomprehending eyes, it is men who own cars. She recalls her father and her uncle leaving her mother behind, promising to run errands for her. Although her father abandoned her mother ("Some say he went to Cincinnati"), M'Vy bitterly protests that "a woman, a mother of two kids, cain't just pick up and go hunting" (133). Hence the displaced rage with which M'Vy attacks her son when he reaches for the steering wheel. One reason M'Vy later neglects her children is so that she can buy the used car that in the end symbolizes personal freedom to Tree, and "the safest place in the world" (143). Significantly, a man (Silversmith) helped M'Vy buy the car.

In the repressed world of the apartment there is no rivalry between women and men. In her dream childhood, however, Tree rediscovers the parental quarrel over gambling that drove away her overworked father (75). Her mother later confesses that she had sacrificed her children in her pursuit of money—"I should've taken less money and stayed with you and your brother" (211)—even as she is once more about to leave her daughter behind. In effect, M'Vy's victory in the contest for selfhood has destroyed the family.[14]

Tree is likewise ambivalent. As a rival sibling, Dab has provoked her to bullying violence. In his last days, submissively ill, however, Dab elicits guilty love from his sister. By contrast, the novel's men weather abuses and misfortunes, yet they never lash out in protest. On the contrary, Hamilton imagines their anger turned depressively inward as disease. Their porphyria objectifies a rage turned against the self. The novel honors the men while making them moot. It invites sympathy for the women's loss while celebrating their triumphal survival. It masks the women's anger, preempting anxiety about (and criticism of) their aggressive feelings. Tree comes closest to acknowledging Dab's role as scapegoat when after his death she rages at her mother: "How come you didn't do something sooner? You don't even think of Dab, when all the mens die off. You killing him, can't you do something?" (SWBR 173). And after all, because Tree has overlooked Dab's addiction to barbiturates, she shares some of her mother's responsibility for the neglect that contributes to his death.

The point is not that the women are monsters or that the book is merely a covert assault on men, but that it tries to euphemize women's motives, excusing them from competition that can be especially cruel among poor blacks. In attempting to treat the hardships of the single-parent urban black family, Hamilton transforms terrifying "man problems" such as drug addiction, domestic violence, and desertion into a gratifyingly sorrowful mortality.[15] By a series of strategic illusions reassuring to white as well as to black readers, Hamilton deploys a heroic paradigm in which black males meekly perish and women bravely endure until idealized mates appear. As in the romance form, such a scenario screens out a crucial range of experience. It implies heroic values—and healing—that are largely unearned. The depth of that denial emerges in the novel's preoccupation with death.

Sweet Whispers, Brother Death

Death resembles play-death insofar as selves are not annihilated but are converted to ghosts, spirits, or angels. *Sweet Whispers, Brother Rush* makes use of such conversions. The fatally weak brother Dabney dies of his addiction and the robustly collegiate stepbrother Don suddenly appears to take his place. Whereas

Dabney is "good-looking almost to pretty" (SWBR 15) and indiscriminately sleeps with girls who like "that sweet, empty look that could take over his eyes" (16), Don potentially promises an exclusive, meaningful bond. Whereas Dab's vacancy uses up a woman's devotion, Don imparts to or releases energy in Tree. Given her insecurity about her color (158), Tree's ecstasy over the doomed Brother Rush evokes the patriarchal dynamics of the Langston Hughes blues poem that opens this chapter, in which the speaker corroborates her self-worth through "this man o' mine" and prays to "high-in-heaben Jesus" that he won't die. Let that corroboration fail or become oppressive, however, and the man's death reveals an ambivalent new aspect.

Tree herself undergoes play-deaths each time she follows the ghost into the traumatic dream landscape of her childhood where she loses her superficial identity and recovers a truer, dissociated sense of self. In various forms, fantasies of play-death serve to substantiate and reinforce the self. Yet to some extent play-death is compensatory as well: it allows imagination to relinquish conventional identity and frees it to experience reorganization and renewal, without responsibility. It allows an anxious, conflicted personality to break out of its defensive rigidity. To use Hamilton's symbolic language, Tree dies out of her suffocating apartment into life just as black males die out of the inherited psychic bonds of slavery into new identities. This imagery distantly evokes the gospel vision that sustained black slaves but also to some extent rationalized their suffering and preempted rebellion.

For much of the novel Tree is desperately balanced between self-reliance and dependence. Inside her mother's car, "the safest place in the world," she fantasizes that "no other power was like this power motor in a good car" (142). The car represents independence even as it enfolds her as a mother does a baby. The "power motor" suggests the prosthetic recovery of her mother's long-impaired will. In her dream memories Tree actually merges with her mother: "Tree was the child; she was also the woman. Yet she knew she was still Tree" (68).

What surfaces in these equivocal moments is a wish to be grounded in someone or something bigger, more powerful than the self. The wish becomes urgently problematic for the girl in the opening scene, when Brother Rush "hit[s] her in one never-to-be-forgotten impression: His suit was good enough for a funeral or a wedding" (10). The ghost defines anxious possibilities—marriage and death—making fertility and annihilation enticingly yet dreadfully equal. In effect, death makes this ambiguous brother-uncle-father-lover attractive by putting him beyond aggressive rivalry, outfitting him in the passive, idealized formality of a funeral costume. He is an object of contemplation, dissociated, both menacing and eerily harmless. Not illogically, the vision removes Tree's inhibitions so that she is free to follow the figure into the dream landscape. In that process of letting go, she "allows" her surrogate brother-son Dab to die and discovers her own desires. Going out into the city to bury Dab, she daydreams excitedly about driving lessons (143). She flirts with Don (207), and at a horror movie in his secure company she enjoys being "scared to death of the walking dead and the werewolves" (210). Thereafter the ghost vanishes for good, and in a surge of panic Tree becomes aware of her own basic human dread: "When I'm gone *die*, like Dab!" (212).

On one level Tree's dissociated states are a form of magical undoing inasmuch as she overcomes inhibition by imaginatively "making dead" the patriarchal figures in her family. This sublime aggression releases ambition and desire in her and "resurrects" Dab in the figure of Don. As in Victorian culture, sweet resignation can permit an escape from harsh workaday constraints. Victorian piety toward death often served to convert a horrifying necessity into a reward chosen and thereby tacitly controlled.[16] Fantasies of death promise to disarm the most formidable oppressor, as in Charlotte Brontë's *Jane Eyre*, where a fiery symbolic death and resurrection purge Mr. Rochester of his masculine hostility.

On another level, however, *Sweet Whispers, Brother Rush* acts out a traumatic discovery of death and a cultural construction of self in response to that dread. Usually we cope with that intolerable awareness by maintaining what Robert Jay Lifton calls a "middle knowledge" of death.[17] In this way, symbolic immortality systems not only relieve dread but also energize people. Hence Tree's first reaction to Brother Rush is to invest him with heroic glamour, primarily in the form of fancy clothes, just as she later denies Dab's death by imagining a glamorous funeral for him. She uses hero worship as she magnifies her mother, to secure herself in the world. Only in viewing her brother's corpse at the funeral home does she begin to acknowledge her terror. "Suddenly she knew something she had never suspected. Once dead, you were no longer yourself" (*SWBR* 201). As superficial heroism quickly loses its credibility, she discovers that Brother Rush's handsome face "was no longer a face; it was a skull, old and white. Roots of things began growing in it" (181). Terror grips her.

As Tree's uncle and imaginary lover, Brother Rush embodies the unspoken promises of the patriarchal family. In essence, Tree is seeing patriarchal heroism—the ancient system of security based on the strength and authority of the father—decaying before her eyes. Her horror comes not only from the discovery of death, but also from a recognition that in her world some of the most basic cultural defenses against death are deceptive and ephemeral. Her uncle's skull reveals that the cultural guarantees of her parents' world are hollow. Presumably her mother has also discovered this hollowness and has taken out on her son the anger she has felt toward the treacherously helpless males in her life—including the brothers killed (punished, we might say) by porphyria. In beating Dab, she is also raging against the threat of death: "But really all the time I was afraid he might have the sickness, like my brothers. I was so afraid, Tree" (173).

In this world children cry out to parents who themselves feel panic and dread and loss. The mythic basis of that loss surfaces in the storybook Tree reads to Dab, in which white fathers—rival patriarchs—murder the kindly black grandfather, the Reverend (83). But Tree's discovery of death is still more complicated. She awakens fatherless, not only within a troubled urban black culture, but also within a larger secular, industrial society that invests in a furious profusion of immortality symbols, from churches to capital. In the factory world money earned while neglecting your children can buy you a car that is "the safest place in the world." Moreover, this society is so influential yet alien to Tree that its insecurity about death can only be magnified in her.

To contain this terror, the novel deploys a familiar heroic scenario: the child's lonely struggle toward maturity. Not only does the child compete for a place in the value system that supports adults in the face of death, but also, as Ernest Becker reminds us, the competition has a larger cultural meaning: crying for freedom and human dignity, minority groups in present-day industrial society are really "asking that they be given a sense of primary heroism of which they have been cheated historically."[18] To be kept on the margins of symbolic immortality is to be silently terrorized, especially if your ancestors suffered the social death of slavery and were, in Lifton's phrase, "death-tainted." As historians of American slavery have made abundantly clear, poor whites helped defend the lordly plantation owners of the Confederacy in order to perpetuate a class of working people whose labor defined them as inhuman and thereby conferred heroic vitality on all those above them.[19]

In closer focus, Tree's role as a motherly Cinderella is plainly life-giving for her failing brother. She not only unconsciously mimics her mother's role as practical nurse but makes a more dedicated and caring nurse at that. Moreover, she has the courage to enter the forbidden territory of repression and retrieve a life-enhancing understanding of her parents and her traumatic past, whereas her mother has been frozen in denial. Despite setbacks and a storm of grief at Dab's death, Tree seems to move toward self-realization.

Yet *Sweet Whispers, Brother Rush* is more equivocal than a casual reading might reveal. By outliving so many male relatives, Tree incurs grief and fear but also proves herself. In Elias Canetti's bracing summary, "the moment of survival is the moment of power. Horror at the sight of death turns into satisfaction that it is someone else who is dead . . . and all grief is insignificant measured against this elemental triumph."[20] In fiction, where characters perish ultimately in play, the vicarious sensation of immortality is more readily guilt-free and hence a source of potent pleasure.

Socially conceived, porphyria becomes a way of dramatizing women's desire to be independent of unhealthy males while avoiding any grounds for personal antagonism. Fantasies of play-death make it possible for a woman to protest patriarchal restrictions and yet, in a host of ways, to be reconciled to them. In this instance, play-death acts out of a disguised attempt to "forget" one conception of men so that a new, more desirable image may take its place. Because these sorts of strategies evade responsibility in different ways, however, the self-substantiation they offer is bound to be limited. Figuratively speaking, they are apt to fill the survivor's mind with unquiet ghosts, like the walking dead before whom Tree quakes in the movies.

Because symbolic immortality is a conviction always potentially in need of renewal, the survivor's exaltation is especially apt to prove ephemeral. Literature abounds in survivors whose drive to intensify that conviction becomes a monstrous lust for immortality, from Shakespeare's Richard III and Macbeth to Bram Stoker's insatiable Count. In *Sweet Whispers, Brother Rush*, the rage for survival is by no means so maniacal, yet troubling implications haunt the outcome. From the start, Tree has usurped her mother's position. She runs the apartment and mothers M'Vy's son. Because the girl has been neglected, a reader can say she makes a heroic virtue out of necessity. From another angle, however, the mother's withdrawal also permits a latchkey child to take over the house and supplant her rival. But there is an implied retaliation as well. At the height of her alienation, Tree rages at her mother, "I hate you to death!" (SWBR 185).

This reading is poignantly corroborated in the final pages. Arguably, we are meant to regard Miss Pricherd's employment as a surrogate mother as a positive social strategy. Having been a homeless bag lady, "Granny" Pricherd can teach Tree how to survive the city's violence. It is she, not Tree's mother, who convinces the girl not to run away. She can recreate prosthetic supports for the child. Taken in off the street, however, the old woman now dresses as a servant, and much is made of her willingness to cook and clean and meet all of Tree's needs. Miss Pricherd professes to be so grateful for shelter that she will work for nothing or next to nothing. Lurking in this imagery is Tree's satisfaction at having risen above menial exploitation. No longer is she a nobody. Because Miss Pricherd stands in for M'Vy, the old lady's service indulges Tree in her childish fantasy of rising above a rivalrous parent. In this oddly unfeeling treatment of status, the novel innocently plays out a vindictive fantasy. Once captured, the remote and neglectful mother is turned into a good-natured Aunt Jemima. Not for nothing do we last see Miss Pricherd taking a break from her cooking chores to do "a little dance in her slippers" (215)—a motif associated with the witless, doomed Dabney. It is supposedly a spontaneous dance, yet it is all too clearly contrived to bring closure: a dance whose eagerness to please denies the alienation that the novel cannot dispel.

Self-Disabling Mastery

What does it mean for *Sweet Whispers, Brother Rush* to contrive this surreptitious triumph over trauma? To be sure, the novel depends on popular formulas, notably the Gothic romance heroine, who also endures parental abandonment in ghostly quarters. Hamilton's attraction to Gothic conventions for a tale of black childhood is easy to understand, especially considering the status of blacks as estranged stepchildren of the dominant culture. No less important are the constraints of the cultural moment. Given publishers' unadvertised economic and ideological requirements, and given the sensitivities of many groups of readers, a more forthright novel might never have seen print.

On another level, the novel worries the problem of a ground for identity into a symbolic zone where the threat of social death for black Americans blurs with existential death anxiety. The losses of her brother and the rest of her family bring Tree not to grief for them but to a spasm of self-protectiveness. The pressure of panic gives the book depth even as it produces Tree's compensatory supremacy. In embracing the novel's wishful resolution, readers unwittingly ratify some familiar ideological strategies. By valorizing Tree's autonomy, for example, readers may believe they are endorsing a hard-won feminist or African-American scenario, whereas the book's resistance to patriarchal bonds disguises a fantasy of heroic survival achieved largely by imagining away males and a dominating mother. Insofar as Tree is a fledgling artist, the novel asks us to believe that loss and alienation are the price she pays for the artist's commanding detachment—rather as loss gives storytelling authority to Zora Neale Hurston's protagonist in *Their Eyes Were Watching God*. But this vision of the artist as witness conflicts painfully with Tree's continuing isolation and the limited imaginative sympathy of her world.

The narrative arrives not at a liberation but at a sublimated imprisonment—in Chris Baldick's words, the "reactionary relapse into concealed feudal tyrannies imagined in Gothic novels."[21] In the end, what prevails is not cooperation or intimacy but resolute alienation. Tree's insights have not freed her to negotiate a future in society with a confident voice. Certainly she is better off having Granny Pricherd working for her, but she is still talking mostly to herself. And yet the fantasy of the self-made woman, the visionary survivor, can have a strong appeal—and to avowedly dissimilar groups of readers: not only feminists and blacks but also entrepreneurial individualists.

A more specifically African-American argument might defend the novel's closing compromise by appealing to "the acceptance of the supernatural" that Toni Morrison finds in black culture.[22] In "Rootedness: The Ancestor as Foundation," Morrison praises storytelling forms that can ground African-American identity. Chiefly she celebrates the oral authority of African-American writing and "the presence of an ancestor." In many black narratives

> there is always an elder there. And these ancestors are not just parents, they are sort of timeless people whose relationships to the characters are benevolent, instructive, and protective. . . . What struck me in looking at some contemporary fiction was that . . . the presence or absence of that figure determined the success or happiness of the character. It was the absence of an ancestor that was frightening, that was threatening, and it caused huge destruction and disarray in the work itself. . . . Whether the character was in Harlem or Arkansas, the point was there, this timelessness was there, this person who represented this ancestor.[23]

Brother Rush and Granny Pricherd qualify as ancestors. As substitute parents, they reconstitute a collapsed family. Like dream figures, they also objectify awareness and memories that were dissociated in Tree's traumatic childhood. They help Tree locate herself not only in the historical past but also in recovered experience, repairing her sense of disembeddedness and abandonment. They dramatize imagination's ability to recreate prosthetic networks by improvising surrogate caregivers in order to overcome fragmentation and loss. In these capacities the ancestors perform the transformational, restorative function of mourning.

But the ancestral spirit has its limitations. Toni Morrison advocates "the acceptance of the supernatural and a profound rootedness in the real world."[24] But presumably a feeling of rootedness depends on a connection between the "real" or conventional world and the "supernatural" or extrarational. And although the traumatic past is exactly what most impels American blacks to seek beyond conventional reality for ancestors and an ineffable black identity, that same trauma signifies unfinished business—the impossibility of rootedness. For post-traumatic imagination, rootedness is as urgently desirable as it is at best conditional. As for the supernatural, it requires more than "acceptance." Ancestors have to be created out of something. And because ancestors can be helpless or even vicious—because they may console you or they may destroy you—they have to be tested against experience, and continually retested.

In his way, Tree's self-destructive uncle, Rush, is as seductive and dangerous as Carolyn's Uncle Toddy. Brother Rush makes vivid the need to rise above a maimed past, even as his spectral intrusions keep ominously leading Tree away from the present. "Granny" Pricherd appears to be the more-benevolent "ancestor." Yet in the end she too represents a displacement of responsibility away from real relationships and into fantasy. Wearing Dabney's magical shoes in the last scene, Granny Prichard "fills his shoes," taking over his role as potential male provider. She substitutes for or resurrects the sacrificed brother, yet the substitution must remain disguised because Dabney himself was a supposedly harmless substitute for the absent father, and his self-destructiveness and faith-less promiscuity signal why the plot must kill off him and his father. The fairy godmother who survives in his shoes draws off all the insoluble and unbearable conflict in the world of the novel, even as she fulfills childhood dreams. For Tree she becomes an Aunt Jemima who can be wishful but must be kept at a distance as long as love might compromise her fragile autonomy.

Without minimizing the hardships facing blacks in America, let me recall the equivocal nature of mourning for Haggard and the many Victorians who also sought out ancestral support in séances and storytelling. As they provide consolation for deracinating change, ancestors keep attention on the past. To be spellbound by ancestors and roots can be like trying to run while constantly watching your feet: you may be more surefooted but you may also be running blind. Tree badly needs to live in the present in order to forge a role for herself in a demanding society. Mourning affirms her identity, but not without cost.

Toni Morrison gives the supernatural a defining place in black culture. She defends it in class terms, suggesting that "the press of upward social mobility would mean to get as far away from that kind of knowledge as possible" because the supernatural has been unfairly "discredited" as superstition.[25] To be "up-wardly mobile" is presumably to lose contact with your spiritual roots. But poverty is a major reason for the crippling scarcity of autonomy in the novel.[26] And Morrison's categories are needlessly exclusionary. Social climbers may or may not be shallow. Either way, their mobility says nothing about those left be-hind. In *Uncle Vampire*, social pretensions falsify adult life—but then the "ac-ceptance of the supernatural" robs children like Carolyn of their will and makes it easier for the "benevolent, instructive, and protective" ancestor Uncle Toddy to violate her. In themselves, categories such as roots and upward mobility have limited use, because all strategies for living have to be tested against the world.

Sweet Whispers, Brother Rush demonstrates how a drive to master trauma may unwittingly become self-disabling. To moralize about Tree's limitations would be beside the point. Trauma makes us aware that the effort to substanti-ate the self involves a deep level of symbolic, ideological activity. As a response to injury, that effort at self-substantiation may seem compulsive or intrusive long after the original terror has faded. At the same time the process foregrounds cul-tural forms—or the absence of cultural forms—that could support a healthier adaptation. Crisis forces both Carolyn and Tree to leave unsympathetic families. But no mentoring older sister awaits Tree, no sheltering clinic and no solicitous therapist. Outside her door lies the grueling poverty of the streets. Hamilton's book does not fantasize a nurturing fairy-tale culture as television so often does—Tree is no Cosby kid or Fresh Princess of Bel Air. At the same time the novel does not recognize the way in which its limited vision shades into and reinforces the post-traumatic conditions prevailing around it—not only in the formulas promoted by publishers, but also in the larger culture, the mass market, that they serve.

NINE

Traumatic Economies in *Schindler's List*

"The Age of Nerves of the nineteenth century has found its close with us."

Adolf Hitler, Proclamation at Nazi Party Congress, September 4, 1934

I am chairman of the department of Hitler studies at the College-on-the-Hill. . . . When I suggested to the chancellor that we might build a whole department around Hitler's life and work, he was quick to see the possibilities. It was an immediate and electrifying success. The chancellor went on to serve as advisor to Nixon, Ford, and Carter before his death on a ski lift in Austria.

Don De Lillo, *White Noise*

THERE IS SOMETHING bizarre about the recreated trauma and evil of the Holocaust "winning" seven Academy Awards. Protesting the honors lavished on *Schindler's List*, Jason Epstein argues that "a dramatic representation of Hitler's crime should leave us shaken and humiliated on behalf of our species, for the Holocaust raises the most serious questions about our collective sanity, to say nothing of our moral quality. . . . *Schindler's List* doesn't face these questions at all, nor does it ask its audience to face them."[1]

To be sure, the film does focus less on Nazi atrocities than on the peripheral Oskar Schindler and a tale of rescue. But the critic's scorn may be justified and yet complacent as well. After all, as the Duc de La Rochefoucauld said, no one can stare directly at death or the sun without going blind. Is it surprising that the idea of annihilation in a century of unprecedented mass murder compels us to blink? To put it bluntly: is it really possible to come to terms with catastrophic evil? We live by indirection, always compensating for what we finally cannot bear. Every culture invests in symbolic immortality. Immersed in the rules and rituals of cultural perpetuity, we compulsively tell stories that flatter our imaginative control.

One such story is that of heroic rescue. To give maximum meaning to Schindler's lifesaving actions, *Schindler's List* must frame the Nazi horror. In effect, it tames indescribable evil by trying to make it serve honorable narrative ends while preventing anxiety and despair from paralyzing the spectators. The problem, as Epstein understands, is that the effort to tame death may also domesticate evil, surreptitiously inviting audiences to deny dread through thrill-seeking voyeurism and even identification with the powerful Nazis. But however perverse the film, we can be sure it is trying to transform unmanageable terrors into heroic values, so it makes sense for critics to look for signs of that effaced terror for what they may tell us about the Holocaust and also about the culture screening the film.

"In a famous scene" from the film, Epstein writes, "a beautiful boy is up to his shoulders in a reeking latrine. His expression is troubled and angelic, an expression that denies the experience of being in a real latrine, as the film itself evades the real lesson of the Holocaust."[2] Whether or not the Holocaust has a simple "real lesson," this summary catches the scene's denial and evasion. But the denial itself is eloquent. For one thing, the "reeking latrine" epitomizes our animal nature. It reminds us that we live by compulsively killing and devouring other creatures and expelling them as disgusting waste, even as we too must finally die and rot away into foul waste. Fabulous rules and rituals usually mask that reality from us, yet the Nazis force the child to "lower" himself into it for shelter. The moment is poignant because it evokes and also, in the child's "angelic" face, denies our animal mortality. And more than that: it is a horribly perverse struggle for transcendence that fuels the Nazi viciousness, because the racial fanaticism that scapegoats Jews imagines that by destroying all bestial "filth" the killers can confirm their own deathless purity.[3] This is only one of the symbolic inversions in the scene. The demonic alter ego of the "angelic" child in the latrine, for instance, would be an ideal blond member of the Hitler Youth immersed in an ideological realm of superhuman purity that is actually a cesspool of evil motives akin to the excremental mire in Dante's hell.

Schindler's List sees everything self-protectively, not quite in focus. And the distortion applies not only to the things observed but to the observer as well. In the moviegoer's imagination, through the "angelic" composure sentimentally contrived by the filmmaker, the Jewish child in the latrine achieves the symbolic transcendence of death that the Nazis think to achieve through futile violence. This is a sort of magical undoing, a fantasy familiar to contemporary audiences from, among other things, fairy tales and cartoons. When the camera repeatedly discovers innocent moppets hiding from the Schutzstaffel (SS) in every cranny of the barracks, including the latrine, the perversely comic effect alludes to the many Hollywood cartoons in which intrepid mice and other surrogate children hide out from snapping jaws—cartoons that acknowledge our animal nature while covertly celebrating a triumph over its death-ensnared, devouring horror. The sequence frames reality. The tacit presence of a Hollywood filmmaker assures us of a controlled, even happy ending: such children will survive.

Culture disarms existential threat by putting it in familiar heroic forms, just as *Schindler's List* constructs its denial from materials out of Hollywood and American, sometimes specifically Jewish-American, life. To go through the muck and to survive by cunning is a comic commonplace in the movies, energized by anxieties about degradation and bad luck, and the source of countless jokes. Among other things, it reflects the nostalgic vision that has emerged among former immigrants who passed through humiliating poverty in America on their way to prosperity.[4]

But the scene in the latrine has another topical context as well: the distress over the wretchedness of many American children in the 1980s and 1990s. Hollywood films such as Chris Columbus's *Home Alone* give comic form to a dread of abandonment that in *Sweet Whispers, Brother Rush* is terrifying and in daily newspapers routine copy. The "angelic," plucky child in the barracks fends for himself because the adults' Europe has degenerated into predatory horror. Like the shocking percentage of American children growing up in poverty, the child competes for life against others who have already staked out a niche to hide in, and he finally plunges out of the genteel culture altogether, into bestial mire. Conceived in these terms, the film's denial may evoke anxieties and sympathies for the young outside the movie theater. In dunking the "angelic" child and insinuating a sort of symbolic triumph, the filmmakers deploy images that gesture toward, and moot, social responsibility. Is the film using a contemporary social crisis to support sympathy for historical victims? Or, in not confronting the Nazis' sickening extermination of children, does the scene quiet our concerns for the living victims around us?

Greed for Life

Like Schindler himself, then, *Schindler's List* in some ambiguous ways goes beyond its own intentions, recreating the past through present concerns. Given all the stories that could be told about the Holocaust, why are we moved at this historical moment by an account of a factory boss saving people from death by making them slave laborers?

Schindler's List invites us to see the German war machine as a business venture that uses conquest to produce land, cheap labor, raw materials, and warehouses of stolen treasure. The master plan puts German soldiers to work transforming other countries into factories where slave labor will produce foodstuffs and goods to feed German appetites, and soldiers will be bosses freed from drudgery and fear. The film's senior Nazis command the world like executives, flaunting luxuries like the parvenu robber barons of the Gilded Age. Even the lowliest Nazis behave like venal proprietors and brokers and consumers. This economic role-playing follows the emotional logic of wartime, in which fantasies of mastery and forbidden pleasures buy off the dread of death and the guilt of killing. Put it this way and the Nazis' profit is not just a sum in a ledger or even a mountain of goods, but a conviction of symbolic immortality.

In this economy SS bosses superintend the new factory states by using terror as a management tool to wring greater productivity out of conquered people. By mass-producing death, the war machine manufactures, as a by-product, an invaluable escape from death—life—that can be used to create willing slaves who can in turn produce more for the war machine. Of course to the extent that the machine only redistributes existing goods through conquest, the idea of production is a semantic trick, and the economy may eventually weaken or fail. But in existential terms the Nazis are producing for themselves a conviction of infinite vitality and mastery. For them, even apart from the mystical hocus-pocus of the "thousand-year Reich," conquest is a vast immortality project.

The film shows this economy at work in the behavior of masters and victims. As the storm troopers close in on the ghetto, the camera inventories cherished possessions in Jewish homes, and shows us desperate people evaluating their belongings to choose those that have the highest practical and symbolic survival value. Belongings substantiate us in the world; they may command respect and even facilitate our command over other people. Facing annihilation, terrified people reveal the magical potency they attribute to their valuables. The Nazis corroborate that magic in their greed for plunder. Once in possession of the goods, the war machine continues the process of intensifying their value by further appraising them, as we see in the endless lists—invoices, manifests, vouchers—that the Nazi regime uses to sort its loot. The same process evaluates the newly acquired human property too, repeatedly ranking and classifying captives for destruction or living slavery.

The center of the Nazi economy is the death camp. As factories, parodies of industrial process, the camps manufacture death with an illusion of total control and superhuman purpose.[5] In Otto Rank's words, "The death fear of the ego is lessened by the killing, the sacrifice, of the other." In a metaphor that points to the underlying economy, Rank adds, "through the death of the other, one buys oneself free from the penalty of dying."[6] As a form of group behavior, death anxiety can be epidemic, releasing synergistic rage and panic, and tightly regulated killing may create a conviction of godlike mastery.

"By victimizing another group and establishing it as death-tainted," Robert

Jay Lifton says, "one's own collective existence or symbolic immortality can seem to be affirmed."[7] Once associated with death, the victims "can be more readily killed, which makes them still more death-tainted. . . . Since they are historically and psychologically already dead, one may kill them arbitrarily, without the feeling one is taking a life."[8] In business terms, the Nazis expend "inferior" human lives to manufacture a healthy, superior society, and their profit is a sense of immortality. In this mentality, the application of mass-production technologies seems natural, for the more you kill, the more profit you earn. Until it runs out of living raw material or is shut down by hostile competitors, the "system" seems superhuman.

Rather than distance this economy from ourselves as "aberrant," it would be better for us to remember that most cultures sanction some predatory economic behavior. Historically, the great city-states of the Near East and Mesoamerica were grounded in sadistic triumphalism, perpetually warring with their neighbors, exacting tribute and slaves and exterminating captives. Mayan city-states produced more life for themselves through their sacrificial slaughter and ritual cannibalism of rival warriors, literally consuming the lifeblood of their enemies.[9] Our own benevolent economy euphemizes as healthy "competition" the ruthless economic behavior documented in Michael Moore's *Roger and Me* (1989), which smashed neighborhoods in Flint, Michigan, as surely as any blitzkrieg.[10] Dogging American culture, half-repressed, it is a well-documented history of the intimidation and murder used to control working people.

The Nazi economy evolved within existing cultural forms, intensifying its violent economic and military precedents. After all, World War I had acted out convulsive competition as neighbors sought to seize prosperity by force. Not only did the antagonists struggle for monopolies and markets—including colonies—but the war itself caricatured the industrial process. Once set in motion, mobilization in the West rolled on complex, interlocking railroad timetables, beyond any possibility of executive second thoughts, and industrial weapons such as the machine gun annihilated combatants on a dehumanized, corporate scale. Once underway, the hostilities increasingly tested each adversary's capacity to produce munitions and matériel on an unprecedented scale, so that defeat finally meant traumatic exhaustion.

From this perspective, the Nazi economy—like other value systems—functioned as an enabling fantasy, a means of energizing the will. Dreams of a master race and a prosperous millennial reign ministered to the trauma of German collapse in World War I, to the extraordinary futile slaughter at the front and the ghastly destitution of the early Weimar years. Nazi behavior can be understood as a form of post-traumatic violence: a compulsive repetition of an overwhelming breakdown, reenacted against others in an effort to undo it. Hitler and

Goering personally suffered the terror of combat and the death of the old Germany—Hitler wounded, both men decorated for bravery. In their subsequent lawless rage on behalf of a transcendent Reich, they acted out a desperate attempt to force the world and themselves into a safe "new order." Much of the haunted feeling of the Nazi era, including the inclination to speak of Hitler's "magnetism" and "spellbinding" oratory, registers the pressure of that all-consuming, unconscious struggle for conviction.[11] The nonentity who survived senseless death in a lost war and economic death in postwar flophouses projected a corporate self in the Germany ordained "lord of the earth" on the last page of *Mein Kampf*.[12]

And yet such a project is finally self-confounding. Sooner or later everybody dies. At every moment we are unthinkably vulnerable. The work of killing reminds even the most ecstatic killer of death. Violent dispossession may unsettle as well as exalt the conqueror, because the sight of victims stripped to a doomed nakedness may also reveal the pitiably ephemeral nature of all immortalizing cultural props, not just quotidian clothes and "everlasting" gold and diamonds. Like the heaps of useless eyeglasses and shoes at the extermination depots, suitcases stuffed with belongings insinuate that all our lives are improvised from shreds and tatters.

As a result of this instability, sadistic aggrandizement tends to be self-intoxicating, and leads to an ever-expanding economy. Grounded in delusion, helplessly obsessive, Nazi persecution demands constant reinforcement from ever more conquests and victims. Because the drive toward triumphal annihilation has no logical closure, it represents a form of the suicidal and apocalyptic imagination.[13] Accordingly, individual Nazis have to struggle to stay enchanted at all times. *Schindler's List* emphasizes the irrationality of the persecutions. The film's Nazis confidently invoke blueprints, rules, and rituals, yet again and again their behavior falters in caprice. Like their victims, they are creatures driven by wishes and fear, at the mercy of the baffling obstinacy of the real world, as when the SS officer Amon Goeth capriciously judges one of Schindler's workers incompetent and tries to execute him, only to be defeated by not one but two malfunctioning pistols. At that point he strikes his prisoner in frustration and then walks away to save face, implicitly routed, leaving his would-be victim to go back to work. Goeth suffers a tormenting ambivalence toward his Jewish housemaid and a depressive anxiety about the future, as we see during a medical examination. Persuaded by Schindler, he experiments with mercy, sparing some lives only to expose to himself and to us the appalling instability and emptiness of his convictions.

To emerge from a delusional system such as the Nazi economy would mean facing long-repressed terror and psychic death. Little wonder that the Nazis labor at self-intoxication. The officers reveling in stolen champagne and baubles are battening on gorgeous trash that cannot save them. Their greed becomes obsessive: no one can ever get enough. Like the mania moralized in medieval paintings of the miser despairing on his deathbed, and like the "undead" vampire's insatiable thirst, the Nazis' appetite for life paradoxically takes them into the shadowy margins of death. If Hitler was indeed traumatized in World War I, then even his timing of the extermination campaign takes on an unexpected logic as a form of berserking, because the Wannsee conference (January 1942) coincided with the army's terrifying losses in Russia and the first death throes of the Reich.

Slaves and Actors

Schindler enters this evil economy as a cheerful opportunist. Like the Nazis, he is reacting against lifelong failures. But whereas the Nazis are trapped in their predatory obsessions, the film's Schindler is a playful parasite. He improvises expansively, fashioning a precious bon vivant camaraderie out of materials—wine, women, and song—saved from the Nazis' bleak world. When the SS bosses hold business meetings, they display the totems of sociable luxury, but the spirit is missing. Because goods and pleasures always threaten to grow stale, Schindler is a valuable practitioner of enchantment. Whereas the Nazis numbly heap up valuables, Schindler gives them away with carnival abandon. As cynical as his gifts to the SS bosses may be, they are also a form of largesse, presented in shows of affectionate play that momentarily relieve the sadistic grimness of the war.

Schindler's revelry with the Nazis tacitly constitutes a form of therapy that briefly relieves their obsession with death. With his bonhomie and his bankroll, he creates a play space and encourages his Nazi clients to act out fellow feeling. The therapy succeeds because Schindler can be an actor-dramatist and use adventitious props to create scenarios of communal harmony. He can wheel and deal effectively because he is an entertainer and a showman, manipulating the wishes and illusions of his audience. Yet Schindler himself remains almost wholesomely disenchanted. His own conviction of immortality comes not from the sadistic investment of the SS but from amassing a bankroll and improvising social and erotic pleasures on a heroic scale. As the war goes on, he becomes increasingly aware of his therapeutic influence and its power to save lives.

Consider the fascinating conundrum at the center of the film: that slavery saves lives. "Slavery," says David Brion Davis, "is preeminently a relationship of power and dominion originating in and sustained by violence. It is a state of 'social death' substituting for a commuted physical death from war, capital punishment, starvation, or exposure."[14] To redeploy Lifton's term, as "social death" slavery is living proof of a given person's or group's "death-tainted" being. By dramatizing the master's power over mortality, the slave may allay, or substitute for, homicidal fantasies that, once aroused, have no logical stopping point.

Slavery can also be understood as a prosthetic aggrandizement of a master's will. In effacing their own volition, slaves become tools that express the master's wishes and extend his reach. They give the master many eyes and hands, magnifying his physical strength and stamina and his resistance to pain. In turn, the master becomes pure agency, an executive self that transcends his own vulnerable biological body, able to accomplish superhuman deeds. Yet even when slavery is stabilized as domesticity or sexual intimacy, the master remains a predator and lives by consuming other people's energy and spirits. Disguised in the figure of the vampire, this prosthetic relationship fascinated nineteenth-century European culture, perhaps in part because the great era of emancipation aroused a humanitarian sensitivity to slavery yet—until World War I—left untouched so many other forms of exploitation, from oppression in Russia to widespread domestic service in the West. Whether as a monstrous folkish revenant or Bram Stoker's supremely patriarchal Count, the vampire dramatizes not only the fear of death but also a fear of becoming infected by death in the desperate effort to stay alive by feeding on others.

A slave economy also substantiates immortality fantasies. In creating wealth, slavery creates extra, "free" time for the master—that is, more life. Working "for nothing," slaves produce "plenty" as if from thin air. They turn out goods that themselves, like slaves, aggrandize the owner by signifying more life. The suppression of individuality in slave labor led to rude versions of mass production as far back as late antiquity.[15] In Schindler's Polish factory, virtually anyone can learn on the spot how to run the machinery. Ironically, the anonymity of the industrial process enables it to shelter any number of technically unqualified workers. From this dehumanized energy comes the factory's stock of military mess kits that supports the Nazi project of conquest. Later, in Czechoslovakia, Schindler's workers produce artillery shells. Part of the magic of slavery is that it can be used to create the conditions for still more slavery, in a dream of infinitely available energy.

Captive sexuality likewise serves immortality fantasies. Although Jews are officially contaminated untouchables, Amon Goeth's anguished ambivalence toward his Jewish housekeeper dramatizes the cost of grounding personality in sadistic mastery. Throughout the war economy, dominance gives the SS elite access to pleasure through control over desirable bodies—youthful, "undying" bodies. Yet even as glimpses of pretty young women and breasts repeatedly evoke life and nurture in the film, they expose the numbness of the conquerors. Hoping to be selected for survival, women in a labor camp use drops of their own blood to rouge their cheeks to a stronger semblance of vitality. Playing desperately at makeup, parading naked as at a slave or livestock market, they endure a nightmarish industrial parody of mate selection, hoping to be selected for life by men crippled in their sexual feeling. Slavery tends to deform and subvert the social categories devised to control it, as in imperial Rome, where slaves played an astonishing variety of roles. A quality of theatricality may evolve in social relations as a means of stabilizing fundamental contradictions. Schindler's Jews impersonate skilled craftspeople to satisfy Nazi rules. When a real construction engineer reports a real technical problem to her SS boss, by contrast, he has her shot on the spot for stepping out of her assigned role as witless slave.

Predictably enough, the longer Schindler associates with his workers, the more fully they emulate his theatricality. Stern, for instance, uses his self-effacement to move through protean guises, including accountant, foreman, and advisor. The film imagines Schindler's factories gradually turning into play spaces in which Jews fool the SS to preserve life. From backstage, as it were, the workers equip Schindler, the master thespian, with props and even sexually beguiling actors to keep his Nazi audience spellbound. Like a harried but resourceful stage manager, Stern provides indispensable lists of gifts and bribes, and sets the stage for Schindler's wily comic scripts.

By the war's end Schindler himself has taken a moral stand against the regime and begun to use theater strategically. His business operations become more and more brazenly fictional. Following his lead, the workers in his Czech munitions plant are paradoxically able to restore healthy meaning to labor by deliberately turning out trash: dud artillery shells that will harm nobody. Like their boss, the businessman-playactor, the workers become artists of a sort, creating a parodic arsenal and facsimile weapons for a script that will ultimately triumph.

Economic Trauma

Sympathy and cinematic art make it easy to forget that *Schindler's List* is not simply an opening onto the past but also a product of the Hollywood "dream factory" in postindustrial America. Of all the possible stories about the Holocaust, why invest so much in this one?[16]

To begin with, the film's Schindler wishfully magnifies Hollywood's own virtues. His skill at illusion and entertainment creates a factory in which Jew and gentile cooperate to outwit tyrannical repression and foster brotherhood. This Schindler is at once noble and self-serving. Indirectly, the film is a nostalgic tribute to the role played by the entertainment industry during World War II, when it deployed patriotic scripts and stars such as Ronald Reagan to overcome fascism's threat to morale on the home front. In wartime scenarios little guys—usually including "ethnic types" like the film's Jews—invariably survive oppression through courage and cunning, team spirit and cooperation with their leaders.

But the film also plays out a more direct version of Hollywood's structural situation in American culture today. Schindler's life-giving theatricality combines idealism and the profit motive as the entertainment industry does in its equivocal restaging of actual catastrophes as uplifting (and profitable) docudramas and sitcoms. Sooner or later, nearly every nightmare of American life shows up on the screen, on the premise that inspired entertainment may indirectly serve crucial humane ends. This analogy can be strikingly particular, as in the case of the misery of America's black inner cities. Like Jews in the ghetto, poor urban blacks suffer social death. Facing high rates of infant mortality, homicide, unemployment, and health problems, the poorest Americans these days are supposed to be grateful to be chosen for the marginal jobs available to them, jobs that—because the minimum wage is not really a living wage—resemble slave labor. When rage and despair ignite uprisings such as the Los Angeles riots, the cameras roll. Before long, the screenwriters have recreated the struggle against social death as a situation comedy called *South Central*, set in the riot zone and featuring a winsome single black mother who relies on maternal magic and Schindlerian compassion to redeem her teenage sons from drugs and crime, because she has no resources with which to buy their safety.

Hitler's terror factory was far more horrific than America in the 1990s, yet we can recognize the same symbolic logic at work. Unwittingly, the film provides a lens through which audiences can explore in a safely disguised form the distressing situation of working people in postindustrial America. In its series on the "traumatic" effects of downsizing, the *New York Times* (March 4, 1996) used the metaphor of warfare in references to "battlefields" and "casualties," and in the subheading "War Stories." For the majority of workers, real wages have been falling since the early 1970s. Despite high profits, business has systematically undermined job security as well as retirement and health benefits. By contrast, the typical chief executive officer of a large American company twenty years ago earned about forty times as much as a typical worker, whereas "now he earns a hundred and ninety times as much."[17] Since *Schindler's List* debuted, anxiety about the social violence of economic injustice has begun to surface—as in the title of the article just cited, "Who Killed the Middle Class?" and its subhead: "The economy is fine, but most Americans are not—and the ideal that once defined how we lived is gone." This context gives special poignancy to Richard L. Rubenstein's remark that "the Jews of Europe became a surplus population [to be exterminated] not so much because they were unemployed but because they were competitors of a group that feared its own downward mobility and unemployment."[18]

The film's victims resemble superfluous workers in a system increasingly dominated by a powerful elite that hoards not only material wealth but also the scarce jobs that can give people a sense of primary worth, and then blames the "losers" for burdening—injuring—everybody else. Automation and marginal service jobs have displaced skilled workers, as corporate muscle has deliberately destroyed organized labor. Without compunction, Chrysler can announce a bonus worth millions for its chairman, Lee Iaccoca, and then, days later, the export of its K-car production to Mexico. Such decisions have gutted whole neighborhoods in places such as Flint, Michigan, and in effect deported the refugees to other regions to beg for work. Roughly a quarter of all working Americans earn salaries that put them at the poverty line, where survival begins. And when job prospects begin to improve "too much," the Federal Reserve openly acts to drive up unemployment in order to prevent inflation and stabilize the financial markets. In such a system "welfare reform" not only forces people to rely on jobs that do not exist,[19] but also creates more surplus labor, ensuring that wages and working conditions will stay depressed.

In *Schindler's List* as in postindustrial America, people menaced with social death equate jobs with survival. But there are always more people than there are adequate jobs. In the film superfluous labor becomes a ghastly threat when prisoners in the Plaszow labor camp are divided into two groups, the weaker group to be killed to make room for new arrivals from Yugoslavia and Hungary. The selection process dramatizes the use of surplus labor to terrify workers into increasingly desperate productivity.[20] The new inmates function like cheap labor in other countries recruited to lower the costs of labor and extract the maximum—frightened—productivity out of employees in America today, even as the SS boss plays the role of executive "hatchet man."

The Plaszow sequence has a number of disturbing topical associations. Like the Yugoslavs and Hungarians arriving in the camp, new immigrants to the United States arouse fears of lost employment. In the early 1980s, the Reverend Jerry Falwell used a fascist discourse to argue that unless Americans supported the Reagan administration's undeclared war against Nicaragua, we would suffer an invasion of displaced "foot people" from Central America who would take our jobs. More concretely—and this is only one of many examples—an analysis of the Los Angeles riots found that because recently arrived "brown" Mexican immigrants arouse less racial prejudice in white employers, they have been taking over many jobs blacks once held, with serious consequences for blacks and also for race relations.[21] "Illegals" generally have to work cheaply, submissively, and in the least desirable jobs.

The process of weeding out weaker inmates at the Plaszow camp could suggest the increasingly common use of selective layoffs to get rid of older and less robust employees who are more likely to draw costly health and retirement benefits. It also epitomizes the Nazi dream of eugenics as a pseudoscientific means of breeding a perfect human type. Eugenics itself is a mutation of a crude nineteenth-century Darwinism, in which slogans such as "survival of the fittest" link it to the "natural law" of capitalism that justifies unrestrained competition, whatever the individual human cost.[22]

In American business culture, executives justify the "termination" of "redundant" employees by appeals to "the bottom line," supposedly the measure of corporate "survival." And downsizing transfers survival terror to employees; one was quoted by the New York Times as referring to a "'Schindler's List' of employees who've got jobs with our new parent corporation."[23] However realistic or self-justifying it may be in any particular instance, this survival angst pervades the corporate world today as it did during the Great Depression, when it helped shape the war machine of the corporate fascist state. Even the Nuremberg race laws of 1935 construed the German people as a fragile community engulfed by a Zionist conspiracy of vast international might. In all-out competitive capitalism, survival dread justifies a paradoxical drive to expand while zealously streamlining production. As corporations expand they relentlessly force down the cost and status of labor, so a widening gulf between rich and poor may seem inescapable.

The deep systemic irrationality of this behavior surfaced in the middle of the Great Depression when, as the editors of Consumer Reports warned, "Nazi piledrivers [are] pounding the German workers into serfdom," while "in some of the large corporations of this country the techniques of Der Fuehrer and his cohorts are followed with avidity and approval and a feeling of 'why can't we get away with that too.'"[24] Henry Ford's paternalism, for example, had evolved toward a corporate police state of spies and enforcers, which became clear in 1932 when company and city police fired at laid-off workers demonstrating outside Ford's Rouge plant, killing four.[25] But even in the late 1920s Ford was already facing economic setbacks that baffled his naive theories and contributed to the fulminations about an international Jewish financial conspiracy that earned Ford's photograph a place on the wall of Hitler's office in Munich and his newspaper, the Dearborn Independent, a space on Hitler's coffee table. Ford reacted to the shock of the early 1930s by intensifying his prejudices, flogging the "lazy" work force to produce more for less pay. Drive down the cost of labor far enough, he and other leaders insisted, and prosperity would return. Yet it was not this deflationary elixir but Keynesian stimulation—justified by a world war—that finally revived economies—not increased executive control but wider participation in the creation and rewards of economic life.

Seen from this angle, the crisis in the Plaszow labor camp models a grotesque form of the downsizing that has become a commonplace survival strategy for business in the 1990s. Management slogans such as "lean and mean" project the values of an elite military force toughened by punishing training and selection in order to ensure the triumph of the top brass and the stockholders. We focus on the Nazis' malice, but the Plaszow sequence also dramatizes the inability of Depression-era capitalist cultures to imagine the means to enlarge the spheres of economic participation. Industrial economies needed either more customers for more workers or reduced costs—such as slave wages—for fewer customers. In a contracting economy, fantasies of "getting more for less" make some people nothing so that others can be exalted. When some of Schindler's workers are mistakenly routed to Auschwitz, Schindler rescues them by bribing an SS officer, who cannot understand Schindler's refusal to substitute other workers for his group.

The SS man expresses the industrial principle that workers are merely interchangeable parts in a machine that serves an all-important executive will. They are supposed to be absorbed in their task to the exclusion of all other awareness and feeling—German slang calls this *Fachidiotie*. When the female engineer at Plaszow interrupts construction to point out a serious flaw in the design of the barracks, she is summarily put to death. The woman acts as if her professional training gives her autonomy and responsibility, whereas the command system finds her insubordinate. Such problems of self-effacement and subordination are painfully vivid now when new workers living in a highly individualistic American culture need to submit to authority in the workplace. In the words of the supposedly fresh philosophy of "Total Quality Management," "The unwritten standard . . . is that if all personnel were suddenly replaced[,] the new people could continue making the product or providing the service as before."[26] As various studies have shown, the total number of new jobs in the United States may roughly match the number of people entering the work force, but the quality of jobs—judged by the amount of autonomy and freedom offered—is declining.

As in other areas of conflict between labor and management, when the processes of negotiation and renewal break down, extremes of individualistic and authoritarian behavior are liable to follow, with a likely resort to force. From the perspective of management, it may be desirable to export jobs abroad not simply because labor is cheap there, but because an authoritarian political culture and economic deprivation may make some foreign workers more tractable than their American counterparts. Instead of engaging in difficult negotiations with labor, corporations can pay a foreign manager who will contract to deliver labor in a cheap and trouble-free package, sometimes in the form of company dormitories, as in Taiwan, in which the level of control, by American standards, may suggest a labor camp. Logically enough, in this country labor camps usually house the most vulnerable, punishingly driven members of the labor force, migrant workers.[27]

The industrial mentality also surfaces in *Schindler's List*'s parody of time-motion studies when the extra foreign prisoners are about to arrive. The SS boss Amon Goeth clocks one of Schindler's workers as he makes a hinge, and the penalty for inefficiency is death. The scene dramatizes the mania of competition and the fantasy that efficiency can be endlessly increased. At the same time Goeth unconsciously plays out his own predicament, inasmuch as he labors under tyrannical commands in the SS hierarchy; for Goeth no less than for his victims, disobedience would mean death. Like an angry adult once abused as a child, he abuses others, compulsively reenacting his own domination.[28] In the culture of corporate downsizing, according to the *New York Times* (March 4, 1996), managers who must lay off workers are colloquially termed "executioners" and become prone to post-traumatic symptoms.[29]

Schindler's List's Jews challenge the Nazis' industrial ethos through their solidarity and adaptability. In the enamelware factory, for example, experienced workers quickly teach newcomers the necessary skills to qualify as essential to the war effort. This is the classic liberal democratic credo: that education and cooperation create a wholesome community. Although the screenplay shows some Jews trying to survive in the ghetto through black-market connivance and collaboration, once Schindler's factory provides a means of escape, we see that the Jews have organized a system of self-government that helps them make wise and compassionate executive decisions about who among them will survive.[30]

As dramatized, Stern's recruitment for the factory creates no conflict over favoritism or corruption. Stern himself is impeccably selfless, and the Jews seem instinctively to cooperate in a lifesaving network. Fifty years later, just such networks turned out to be crucial to political refugees seeking asylum in the United States, but also in a less drastic way to people seeking employment. According to the labor economist Paul Osterman, "most jobs are found through personal contacts," and employers rely a great deal on this informal network, especially if the contact is a relative. The lack of such contacts helps explain the shocking unemployment rate among young blacks in America's inner-city ghettoes.[31]

As for Oskar Schindler: in the context of American fears about employment, it is as if the callous Roger Smith in *Roger and Me* had wrestled with the angel of death on behalf of General Motors's autoworkers and emerged a redeemer. In its symbolic logic the film celebrates a reconciliation of labor, management, and ownership. In this scenario Jewish victims bring about through their sacrifices a rehabilitation of labor and a mystical union with the once-predatory boss. The union is consecrated by the gold band—very like a wedding ring—that

Schindler's workers cast from gold teeth they have personally sacrificed for the purpose. It is easy to forget that neither Schindler nor the filmmakers ever challenge the assumption that lives are exchangeable for gold and money. Equally easy to overlook is Schindler's extortion from rich Jews of the money necessary to open the factory in the first place. At gunpoint, as it were, the self-appointed boss rescues Jews from their stereotypical tight-fistedness.

In the actual postwar industrial world the marriage of labor and the boss has been a troubled one. After the bitterness of the Great Depression, American workers underwent a purgative initiation rite, as it were, in World War II, after which a grateful nation rewarded them with a steadily increasing share of postwar prosperity. Now those decades of job security and optimism are gone. As in Roger Smith's Detroit, automation and hostile management have routed organized labor, and once again business culture is dividing society into the poor and the very rich.

During the same postwar period management progressively usurped stockholders' control over companies, and a new myth of executive genius flourished, aggrandizing power at the top and bringing with it grossly bloated compensation. This fantasy of the entrepreneurial executive resonates strongly in Hollywood, and especially in Hollywood's Schindler. John Kenneth Galbraith sees this fantasy figure disguising "the bureaucratic tendency in the modern private corporation"—a term that might recall the supremely bureaucratic Nazis. The entrepreneurial executive is imagined to be "original, self-motivated, innovative, welcoming risk, [and] a creature of the market," the market that executive is often assumed to have discovered. "His counterpart, in fact, is the army general operating with a large and compliant staff behind the lines, who pictures himself as leading the tanks in fierce and unrelenting combat." In this atmosphere of fantasy, Galbraith concludes, "an entrepreneur can, indeed, fail, but he can do no wrong."[32]

Karl Albrecht's study of managerial stress subtly perpetuates this executive fantasy. While arguing for more "socially responsible" values, Albrecht makes "stress" an all-purpose nemesis, euphemizing the roots of predatory motives and the relative powerlessness of working people.[33] In his Foreword, Dr. Hans Selye warns that stress "can contribute to coronary heart disease, peptic ulcers, suicide, nervous disorders, migraine headaches, insomnia, pill popping, cocktail hangups, marital discords, child abuse, self-abuse, lack of confidence, allergies, strikes, picketing, and labor violence" (vi). This grab bag of symptoms lumps together personal executive discomforts such as "allergies" and "lack of confidence" with "strikes, picketing, and labor violence." The diagnosis blurs internalized, somatized disturbances and social conflict. In such a maneuver awkward questions—"Am I my brother's keeper?"—vanish.

But with the end of the Cold War, the master myth of the postwar period has disintegrated. In this context *Schindler's List* has a powerful ideological resonance. It celebrates a humane and all-too-human capitalist who teams up with willing workers to help defeat a totalitarian enemy that could be the Soviet "evil empire" of Stalinist atrocities and Siberian labor camps. In this scenario democratic, American-style business overcomes a rival economy paralyzed by dictatorial planning and a contempt for labor. And yet this triumph pays off like a military conquest, inasmuch as the demise of the enemy magnifies the virtue and vitality of the survivor. In reality, living standards for ordinary Americans appear to be slipping, and they are slipping far more drastically in the old Soviet world, where entrenched governmental corruption, wearing new masks, now routinely participates in "free market" business, and has earned the label "mafia" from a cowed citizenry.[34]

In reaction to economic trauma, the newly independent states have begun reenacting versions of the Nazi selection process, driving out minorities and seizing their jobs. The Bosnian Serbs have committed forthright atrocities in the service of "ethnic cleansing," fueling their self-righteousness with memories of the Croats' cooperation with the Nazis. At the same time, as Jason Epstein protests, capitalist trade representatives eagerly shake hands with the despotic rulers of the new quasi-capitalist China.[35] In this light, *Schindler's List*'s image of workers wedding the boss amplifies the propaganda emanating from corporate headquarters and governmental agencies throughout the industrial world. Toil selflessly and trust the boss and someday all will be well.

Yet as usual, Hollywood is equivocal about established power, offering the working poor a sympathetic wink too. Schindler finally owes his success to his canny and responsible Jewish employees. When he is cavalier about profits, they chide him. A vision of partnership begins to emerge. Yet no sooner do slaves and master ritualize their bond at war's end than the master vanishes, leaving behind a fleeting scene of brotherhood and moot questions about ownership and economic justice in the future. What could have been a populist or quasi-socialist partnership ends up characterized not by assertive solidarity but by escapism. The capitalist Schindler finally redeems himself by choosing harmless failure over profits. In the last months of the war he creates a subversive antifactory, deliberately manufacturing dud artillery shells. The epilogue tells us that after the war, Schindler failed twice more in business. His inability to exploit working people tacitly vindicates the critique of acquisitive business that is implicit throughout the story. The victims eventually thrive, presumably in business endeavors, but that takes place offscreen.

Magical Undoing

Schindler's List celebrates evil's defeat and the vitality of the survivors. But the film's affirmation depends on a rich network of subliminal supports, and like the unarticulated emotions that suffuse and motivate the Nazis' behavior, some of those supports can be teased out. Foremost among them is the screenplay's use of magical undoing to coax its storm of meanings and emotions toward closure. When the camera follows some of Schindler's workers into the gas chamber, under the shower nozzles, for example, the screenplay has fate deliver not death but water: not industrial poison but the biblical symbol of life. On most audiences, the effect is probably more complex than simple escapism, but the reversal does tame or contain the vision the camera sets out to discover.

And so in an inversion of the death camps' selection process, the epilogue marches victims past the grave of the dead Schindler in solemn tribute. Instead of ordaining doom, the now-empowered survivors give memorial life to the dead. Although Schindler remains personally as unknowable as ever, this ceremonial hero worship undoes the threat of Nazi annihilation by testifying to the importance of the individual. The story argues that a single resourceful imagination can prevail against the cold hatred of an entire nation. A lone voice can withstand the fury of the horde. As in lowly adventure tales, such a scenario can enable a moviegoer to convert a source of terror into a celebration of heroic vitality. Whereas Edward Lewis Wallant's *Pawnbroker* (1961) takes for granted that survivors are likely to suffer classic trauma symptoms long after the war, some recent studies report a high rate of healthy adaptation among the aging survivors.[36]

In its cultural context the epilogue mourns the lost leader it praises. In an era when American business executives make more grossly disproportionate salaries than executives elsewhere in the world—40 percent higher than their Japanese counterparts, for example—the business leader is an ambivalent figure. In Michael Moore's documentary, corporate brutality toward "GM families" leaves Flint, Michigan, looking ransacked, so business culture in that film more readily evokes *Schindler's List's* Nazis than its rescuers. Hence the need for a flawed but generous Oskar Schindler, an enigmatic and comic messiah, who can restore some faith in leaders without raising serious questions about any established power structure.

Schindler's workers, the film reports, have not only survived but multiplied, producing some thousands of offspring. Ancient and seemingly natural as this reverence for increase is, it also directly undoes the traumatic loss of life, making it possible for audiences to forget that the dead cannot really be replaced. On another level, this numerical prosperity on the screen could be taken as an eerie echo of the drive to produce and quantify that appears everywhere in industrial culture. In this respect it amplifies Schindler's last-minute lament that if he had only made more money, he could have saved even more lives, as if money or numbers were the key. Like other economic fantasies, the posterity count assumes that more means better—and more—life.

If magical undoing promises wishful prosperity, it also promises to satisfy righteous wrath. Amon Goeth tries to execute a victim at Plaszow, only to find that not one but two pistols will not fire. Lest the moviegoer miss the hint of uncanny providence at work, the epilogue invokes a magical, talionic inversion when it reports that Goeth was executed as a war criminal—and then shows us the hanging, a botched affair in which the hangmen have to kick a chair out from under him not once but several times, each kick comically splintering the chair. The theatrical ironies contrive a cosmically sanctioned punishment leavened with comic vindictiveness. In economic slang, Goeth is paying his debt and being paid back.

Finally, magical undoing attempts to reunite the cultural meanings that disintegrated under Nazi assaults. Through the sacramental ring, the screenplay tries to stabilize the meaning of Schindler's union with "his" people. After all, Schindler himself is both criminal and hero, predator and guardian angel, monstrously selfish and altruistic. "His" people had reason to hate as well as love him. In freely giving gold teeth for the ring, the survivors undo the coercion of slavery. Slaves and gold teeth are both prosthetic entities: one substitutes for another. Through the ring, the laborers undo the hideous death camp slogan *Arbeit Macht Frei*—work will make you free—gladly giving gold from their own bodies to marry their wills to the redemptive leader. At the same time the ring is meant to protect Schindler from punishment as a war criminal, so it rescues him as he rescued "his" people. The transformation of body parts into a symbolic ring also undoes the Nazis' murder for body parts and personal items—hair, gold teeth, glasses—that can be scavenged for reuse. The ring is a pledge of mutual faith in a tragic and chaotic moment, yet it also exists within a larger cultural economy of obligations, rewards, and wishes. The screenplay makes it a final, magical product of Schindler's factory, a device meant to bring closure to the horrors, and faith in the future—and not only for those who suffered and were there.

The Darkness off the Map

Jason Epstein wants *Schindler's List* to educate us about "the real lesson of the Holocaust." He deplores the way some "educated and humane" people cried out against Hitler's crimes and yet tolerated Stalin's crimes for ideological reasons. But Epstein goes on to lambaste American culture, with special ire for "the literary theory of deconstruction" in the universities, because "the plain fact is that we have taught ourselves and our children to regard the conventional discourse of our civilization with the utmost skepticism, so that from high culture to low—from Plato and Shakespeare all the way down to the White House . . . we now, as a matter of habit, dismantle everything, leaving only the most fragile spiritual and cultural ground beneath us."[37]

Epstein's anxiety about a "cultural ground" shows the trope of trauma at work. His indignation is as eloquent as it is self-contradictory. Goethe and Beethoven are among the noblest voices in "our civilization," and yet as Spielberg insists by having a storm trooper play a famous scrap of Beethoven on the piano as his squad liquidates an apartment in the ghetto, it is a commonplace to lament that not even the highest cultural values stopped the Nazis' predatory frenzy. Goebbels's image managers were able to warp all sorts of cultural discourse to Nazi ends, from the arts to philosophy.

But then, even the most venerated great books of Western civilization can be dangerous guides to conduct. In his study of combat trauma, Jonathan Shay comments "that the modern cultural habit of dehumanizing the enemy originates in biblical religion."[38] The text is forthright. God promises to reward Israel's conquests with plunder and slave labor. Pharaoh's erstwhile victims become righteous predators reflexively validated by their god. "As he announces his plans for the ethnic cleansing of Canaan," says Jack Miles, "the Lord does not, to repeat, seem angry with the Canaanites, but the effect is genocidal all the same, and there is no escaping it."[39] The Deuteronomic prescription makes plain the competition for resources and the determining categories of warrior-masters, slaves, and human "booty":

> When you approach a town to attack it, you shall offer it terms of peace. If it responds peaceably and lets you in, all the people present there shall serve you at forced labor. If it does not surrender to you, but would join battle with you, you shall lay siege to it; and when the Lord your God delivers it into your hands, you shall put all its males to the sword. You may, however, take as your booty the women, the children, the livestock, and everything in the town—all its spoil—and enjoy the use of the spoil of your enemy, which the Lord your God gives you.
>
> Thus you shall deal with all the towns that lie very far from you, towns that do not belong to nations hereabout. In the towns of the latter peoples, however, which the Lord your God is giving you as a heritage, you shall not let a soul remain alive. No, you must proscribe them—the Hittites and the Amorites, the Canaanites and the Perizzites, the Hivites and the Jebusites—as the Lord your God has commanded you, lest they lead you into doing all the abhorrent things that they have done for their gods and you stand guilty before the Lord your God. (Deut. 20:10–18)[40]

The Israelites were hardly unique in their predatory behavior. The disturbing truth is that any humans may get caught up in competition to the death.[41] Tragically, there is no neutral "conventional discourse of our civilization" guaranteed to be benign. Christianity was used both to condemn and to justify the Vietnam War, just as the courts have been used to oppose and to foster slavery and racial equality. Nobody can trust any particular package of values to make a reliable first-aid kit for all moral emergencies.

But Epstein's complaint about skepticism also masks a false solution. Do people tolerate a Stalin because they are uncritically committed to the wrong principles, or because "utmost skepticism" prevents them from acting? The painful truth is that evil thrives as readily on misguided noble commitment as on skepticism. It is possible to sympathize with exhortations to cherish particular heroic values—the unspecified "real lesson of the Holocaust"—and simultaneously to recognize that radical existential motives such as death anxiety and compensatory cultural chauvinism also greatly determine our ability to hear and to be taught. In this spirit, it seems important not just to regret that *Schindler's List* blinks at evil and death, but also to try to understand that reflex so we may be a little less compulsive. Granted, the film is a particular structure of denial and consolation: what can that structure tell us about our behavior?

Let me put *Schindler's List*'s affirmation in the historical context of Conrad's turn-of-the-century heart of darkness, where European business culture strives to enslave and reap. Kurtz goes berserk in response to the traumatic darkness he discovers. "Exterminate all the brutes!" he cries,[42] echoing the biblical command that "you shall not let a soul remain alive." Colonialism in the novel is nothing less than a precursor of the Nazi war machine, fueled by racism, greed, and a fear of the incomprehensible darkness that can be assuaged by feeding on the vitality of others. Kurtz's remote camp even suggests the death camps in its obsession with hoarding the precious body parts of slain elephants and, impaled on stakes, men.[43] Like Conan Doyle's "Small," Kurtz's name ("short") in German suggests inadequacy, and his mania for treasure, a compensation for inadequacy.

Conrad was reporting on the economy of death at the same time that artists and governments were redefining heroic values at home, cultivating the serenely organic forms of art nouveau in a campaign to humanize industrial society. Government buildings and apartment houses were dressed in conspicuous decorative motifs—voluptuous lilies and beautiful young women. Yet in the iconography of art nouveau, fecundity and desire play out familiar immortality themes, as in the State Opera House in Budapest and the concert hall of the Liszt Academy, in which bare-breasted black maidens form the pillars that support the balconies. In these lovely interiors, removed from the sordid streets, beauty ennobles the brute labor expended on it. European art transformed lethal slave labors into images of sexualized immortality. The admiring patron rarely appreciates that the artist's achievement actually depends on the anonymous laborers who mine raw materials, dig foundations, and heave brick and stone into place. The exotic colonial maidens epitomize fertility and pleasure, not unlike the "magnificent" keening black woman who has been Kurtz's lover and the "passionate soul" of the Congo's "fecund and mysterious life" (HD 60); they celebrate women's life-giving mysteries and the social dream of mastering those mysteries.[44] For the turn-of-the-century artists and patrons who devised those women, the project almost certainly had some life-giving and redemptive motive of its own. Yet however removed in time and circumstance, those literally uplifting black women, frozen in their laboring repose as architectural "pillars of society," are also not unlike Kurtz's faithful fiancée and even the young Jewish woman in Schindler's List whom Amon Goeth culls from the assembly line of death to become his symbolic housekeeper, mother, wife, and lover.[45]

In Weimar during the summer in which Germany was reunited, in that banal, fabled shrine touched by Goethe and Schiller and Bach, a short drive from Buchenwald, I was astonished to find a street of perfectly preserved Jugendstil houses from Conrad's day, their wrought-iron gates and window grilles floral, in their stucco facades the bas-relief faces of maidens, lifelike and yet as idealized as theatrical masks. It was, I thought, an impossible moment to sum up. The artistic urge had not stopped the Nazi mania; neither had it been destroyed by it. Hitler's propagandists shamelessly used aesthetic ideals to rationalize their extermination of "degenerate" lives. Guards in the death camps presumably felt a tug of piety when Goethe's name flitted to their attention. In Weimar I had no way of knowing what responses those sublime stucco faces now evoked in the neglected streets just awakening from the prolonged aftershock of the war. Not that art transcended the rampage of history; not at all. What struck me was the incalculable fluidity and fullness of meanings in those illusory faces—meanings that only exist, after all, if there is an observer to construe them. At that supercharged moment in German history, those dissociated, sphinxlike faces—those meanings—were potentially as sublime or as barbaric as carved stone in a desert, poised between renaissance and oblivion, depending on what the living imagination will make of them.[46]

I want to suggest how sublime—or treacherous, if you will—the connections are between horror and denial, hearts of love and hearts of darkness. It measures Conrad's achievement that he was able at least to sketch the complicity of the "pillars of society" in the exterminating economy of the Congo. As if in a premonition of Hitler, Conrad has a journalist praise Kurtz as potentially "a splendid leader of an extreme party," a party "on the popular side," (HD 74) even as the episode of the French cruiser anxiously bombarding the African coast expresses "the heart of a conquering darkness" (HD 75).

But Conrad also patiently unfolds the delusions in genteel, stupefied Brussels that keep the heart dark. When Marlow brings the news of Kurtz's death to his fiancée, she is possessive of Kurtz and inflates her love to make it a heroic value that can sustain a life deadened by gentility. "Ah, but I believed in him more than any one on earth," the woman cries, "more than his own mother, more than—himself. He needed me! Me! I would have treasured every sigh, every word, every sign, every glance" (HD 78). Love here is economic, a matter of "treasuring," of value making. In the fiancée's innocent and ruthless hero worship, Kurtz, like Hitler, becomes the means to the followers' apotheosis. Through their superhuman, criminal appetites the rest of us seize our immortality.

But there is something else. Conrad's Marlow has seen the dying Kurtz "on the stretcher, opening his mouth voraciously, as if to devour all the earth with all its mankind" (HD 74). Marlow could be looking into the open abyss of Nazi greed for life. But what is startling is less the brilliant evocation of that devouring rage than Marlow's reluctance to turn away. That need to witness and understand is itself a form of heroic value: a willingness to bear evil and the horror of death long enough to question it and, through it, ourselves. All too often a reflex condemnation of "others" turns out to be self-excusing. In culture, strange to say, that tolerance of dread and unknowing is as rare as it is crucial; even as I write those words I have a defensive urge to protest that I am in no way apologizing for Nazism. Like any other value, that tolerance can be perverted. It is no consolation for the enormity of real personal suffering, and no guarantee that wise judgment and resolute action will follow; yet it is finally the only way to connect the deep motives of the economy of death with living imaginations and moral will—which is, after all, the task before us.

TEN

Traumatic Romance /
Romantic Trauma

LET ME SHIFT the argument from World War II to what Judith Lewis Herman calls "the sex war." The combination of trauma and romance can be used to legitimate the predatory greed for life associated with vampires, slave masters, and *Schindler's List*'s Nazi economy. I focus here not on abused spouses but on Hollywood fantasies of traumatized heroes, especially princely executives, healed by romance—notably by a devoted prostitute who is at heart a princess. However insipid they appear, these fantasies model richly conflicted attitudes toward sex and class relations. They dramatize psychic economies just as *Uncle Vampire* and *Schindler's List* do. The hookers occupy the position of Amon Goeth's Jewish housekeeper, the black caryatids in *fin de siècle* opera houses, and the "naked negresses" ministering to Des Esseintes's mock-funeral party guests in Joris Karl Huysmans's *À rebours*.[1] In this way, deviously, the Hollywood fantasies shed light on our contemporary culture's irresolute efforts to control violent abuse. In their combination of mythic naiveté and rationalized violence, the films call attention to the stupefying centrality of dissociation in boardroom and bedroom and squalid back streets.

To be healed, post-traumatic stress needs to be shared in order to reestablish a sense of communal bonds. And, as Jonathan Shay noted, "we must also bear in mind *the enormous advantage that the powerful have over the powerless in the conduct of griefwork*."[2] As a cultural fantasy, romantic trauma can be used to justify the aggressive striving for privilege, and also to console us for the injuries that result. So innocuous do Disney films such as *Beauty and the Beast* (1991) appear that it is useful to remember that as Hollywood was celebrating the power of romance to heal the prince's traumatic fairy-tale curse, across town in South Central Los Angeles a different order of trauma was goading the poor to riot. Read with an eye for post-traumatic themes, the Disney film contains a revealingly distorted interpretation of that ugly civic convulsion.

Beauty and the Beast of L.A.

Written to edify genteel young ladies by Madame Le Prince de Beaumont in 1756, the early *Beauty and the Beast* celebrates love. Beauty ransoms her father from the Beast, who holds her captive in his palace, but then she comes to love the Beast, and love transforms him into a prince and a husband. Indirectly, the tale dramatizes love as part of a code of cultural values—the Christian ideology of *ancien régime* French aristocracy. Love according to this heroic code, says the tale, and the daughter of a merchant may redeem a "brutish" nobleman and make an ideal marriage.

The Disney film adapted the familiar love story for the 1990s and created a specific social world to justify its aristocratic code. Most strikingly, the film made love a function of class competition. The Disney writers invented a rival suitor (Gaston), whose abusive courtship of Beauty (Belle) climaxes in a riot when he leads a mob of villagers to storm the Beast's palace. In this crucial battle, the palace's animate furnishings—a talking candlestick, teapot, and the like—rout the mob as the Beast destroys the loutish rival. The film projects a caricature of the French Revolution, which traumatized the old aristocratic world, and then defeats it. For audiences unsettled by the latest aftershock of that revolution in the Los Angeles riots of 1991, the film showed princely values triumphing in the postindustrial world. How the Disney magic turned back the clock and the mob is worth a closer look.

The film begins with a traumatic curse. An ugly beggar, a decaying mother figure, puts a spell on a "spoiled" prince who denies her shelter in his castle. Symbolically, the "haggard" old woman arouses in the prince anxieties about death and the loss of nurture, as in Wilde's "Happy Prince" and in Haggard's *She*. Transformed by dissociation into a beast, the prince suffers numbness, depression, and intrusive rage, while the funereal palace objectifies his psychic freeze. To regain human form he must renounce his selfish arrogance and learn to love. The beggar disappears, but her threat persists. After all, poverty threatens to create a world in which starved people prey on one another—exactly like the wolves who terrorize the country outside Belle's village. But poverty also haunts Belle's neighbors. As the story opens, the girl sings of how boring her fellow villagers are, while the camera shows commonplace folks, amiable philistines, grinding away at their tasks, presumably—in the wisdom of slang— to keep the wolf from the door.

Belle is a bookworm, and a dreamer. She feels confined among her workaday neighbors, just as she will be a prisoner at first in the Beast's palace. She escapes a life of anonymous drudgery by reading, searching in romance adventures for more meaning in life. In rejecting her neighbors she might remind us of the selfish prince—or of Carolyn/Honey in Uncle Vampire—but the story protects her from criticism. Instead of rejecting a parent figure like the beggar, as the prince has done, Belle is devoted to her vulnerable father, and this devotion makes her ambitions seem innocent. To appreciate Belle's rejection of her working neighbors, we must keep in mind that in the end she will dominate society as the supreme woman in the kingdom. As Americans say, she wants to make it.

Belle's father represents a partial solution to her problem, because he invents a machine that chops firewood and that could free people from "degrading" work. The father is that familiar Disney type, the bumbling inventor, as harmless as he is endearing. He embodies the promise of industrialism without its cruel complications. His machine is quaint and personal: it involves no hoarded capital, no deafening assembly line, no pollutants, no labor strikes. The wood-chopper will provide limitless energy and eliminate meaningless drudgery. In addition, by losing his way in his effort to market his machine, the father leads Belle to the aristocratic palace of her dreams.

By contrast, Belle's village suitor would oppress her. Although we never see him actually working, Gaston caricatures working-class values. Vain, paternalistic, bullying, he would keep a wife in anonymous servitude. By threatening to subdue Belle, eventually chasing her out of the village and into the arms of the Beast, Gaston helps the film disguise Belle's motives. Instead of having to recognize the hero's self-aggrandizing progress toward the palace, we can sympathize with her plucky flight from victimization. As Gaston turns into an arrogant, Mussolini-like leader and the villagers degenerate into a vicious mob, we can forget that all along Belle has been striving for superiority. When at last she becomes a princess, the premier woman in the land, it seems her natural reward.

The palace first appears as a refuge. When Belle's father sets out to market his machine at a fair, he loses his way. Attacked by wolves, he finds shelter in the

Beast's palace. There is striking social and economic logic to this misadventure. The inventor must compete for a prize at the fair, and he also suffers the competitive hostility of his envious neighbors, who ridicule his genius and eventually persecute him by seeking to imprison him in an insane asylum. If the film stopped here, the story would be a scornful indictment of the free-market ideology touted in the 1890s and 1990s. As in Shakespeare, the wolves who beset the old man en route to the fair evoke the malice lurking in the villagers, the repressed rage for survival—the savagery that surfaces when the mob attacks the palace.

To put it in a historical context, the inventor is assaulted by predatory economic appetites the instant he leaves the regimented village, whose protective if boring inhibitions have barely kept under control anarchic, greedy envy. The traditional power of aristocracy offers the genius shelter, yet it also imprisons him. In a way this is the history of industrial America: the lone inventor captured by capitalists—the great robber barons—who ruled over the nation's economy like royalty. Meritocracy is forced to submit to established privilege. In this fantasy it takes the inventor's daughter to ransom him and humanize his captor. Significantly, the old man never recovers his creative energy, although his machine is later set in motion to rescue him and his daughter from the terror Gaston has unleashed. In the end, the woodchopping machine works, but it disappears from view, and its effects are far more complex and devious than they appear to be. In part this is because the magic of aristocratic love sublimates the economic realities of the machine and the village. But there is another, more disturbing aspect of this sublimation.

The prince and the rival lover Gaston present an archaic solution to the problems of competitive envy and anarchy. They dominate the crowd with the personal force of the ancient warrior-hero. Whereas the prince shows us the warrior-hero evolved into a lawmaking, aristocratic master, Gaston is the hero as hunter-provider, capable of violent command. Gaston is supremely self-confident and wolfishly aggressive, decorating walls with the horns of hunted prey. As the supreme male of the village, he demands Belle as his due: "Don't I deserve the best?" As a warrior-hero and a monster of narcissism, he is the man the young prince would have become had the beggar's curse not frozen his life.

Although the film ridicules him, Gaston is charismatic enough to command the crowd like a fascist demagogue. The film mocks him and yet fears him too. He is comically pink and clumsy, yet also homicidal. In this respect he resembles the villagers themselves, who are workaday folks and yet potential killers. The ambivalence is at work from the start. As Belle sweetly sings about the tedium of her neighbors in the opening sequence, for example, she pauses at the communal well to read a book the kindly bookseller has just given her. Down the street comes a herd of innocuous sheep, one of whom eats a page out of her book. The image neatly evokes the villagers, who are in Belle's eyes conformist sheep: apparently docile and yet in their natural appetite like wolves. Disapproving of idle reading, figuratively eating books, they devour the girl's dreams, "innocently" expressing an envy that will turn openly sadistic when they form a mob and storm the palace in an effort to force her into marriage with Gaston.[3]

When the Beast first releases Belle, she is attacked by wolves and symbolically can no longer return to the village. Once the Beast rescues her, his palace explicitly begins to embody her heroic dream. After all, the palace dominates the landscape in solitary splendor, full of symbols of cultural authority. Architecturally, it resembles an everlasting stone cathedral, with spires reaching toward heaven and a navelike interior. At the same time, the palace is an ambivalent place. Fortified like a castle, isolated and cold, it is a paranoid structure. It objectifies the traumatic numbness inflicted by the old hag's curse. Yet it is also a mysterious storehouse of power and love, because it houses not only the beast-prince and a colossal library of romantic adventures, but also a host of animated furnishings that act out affection and strength.

On one level, the animate furnishings form a magical, omnipotent family. They include a solicitous, avuncular candlestick and a motherly teapot with a British accent and a set of teacup children. Collectively, they offer Belle parental warmth and family solidarity. Unlike the ravenous wolves and the initially selfish prince, the servants feed the girl when she is first a prisoner of the Beast, singing about the joys of serving others. They stage a combination feast and floor show for her. This gustatory folly mimics a 1930s Busby Berkeley musical, a form that Hollywood invented to counter the miseries of the Great Depression. This calls us back to economics: the wolf at the door and the berserking of fascist mobs.

Here is where the film's social fantasy reveals its sinister core. While a Hollywood musical beguiles the hungry Belle inside the palace, in the village pressure is mounting for a crude sort of revolutionary violence. Gaston lusts to carry off the desirable Belle, and his followers lust for booty. In the climactic confrontation, the wounded Beast destroys the would-be usurper. The enchanted furnishings in turn form an army and rout the rampaging commoners. And as the traumatic curse is finally lifted, the Beast turns back into a prince, while the robotic furnishings turn into actual human servants who are not only relieved to be released from the spell, but positively glad to be human servants again.

As usual, this magic is only apparently uncanny. In fact, the servants and the villagers are two faces of the same common people: one group loyally subservient to an aristocratic master, the other dangerously preoccupied with economic survival and easily seduced by an evil buffoon into envious rebellion. The

battle for the palace acts out a psychic struggle in which good subservience sup-
presses ugly self-interest. In celebrating Belle's triumph, the film offers a fantasy
of lordly individualism that is supported by cheerfully self-sacrificing servants.

The fantasy disguises the hidden economy of aristocracy, which depends on
wresting fulfillment from a class of servile inferiors, just as it masks the human
costs of servitude by making the servants cybernetic and magically powerful.
They can destroy their counterparts from the village with no personal consequences. In this way they resemble the "smart weapons" advertised so vividly in
the Gulf War, which depersonalize killing and the responsibility for killing
while promising superhuman protection. The servants also suggest the manufacturing automatons in *Roger and Me* that achieved miracles of efficiency on
the automobile assembly lines and, while their corporate masters dined in regal
solitude, beggared Flint, Michigan. In their kindness toward Belle, the robots
defy their master's commands and become ambiguously superhuman: tutelary
spirits akin to Cinderella's fairy godmother. They are also in the position of the
poor Germans who were enabled by their participation in the Nazi war machine
to slaughter their poor neighbors for gain. Read against the plot of *Uncle Vampire*, it is as if Uncle Toddy plays the kind, nurturant good servant to his successful older brother–prince, while striving as the bad servants do to rape the
prince's bride-to-be.[4]

By winning the prince's love, Belle acquires not only the supreme husband
in the kingdom, but also the supreme house and—literally—an army of happy
servants. She acts out the superhuman bliss that the media conjured up in covering Princess Diana's wedding. Her success also plays out an ad man's dream of
corporate America. By overcoming her distaste for the ugly, hostile Beast, the little woman wins the prince and a house full of wish-fulfilling appliances. It is the
logical extension of her father's firewood-making machine into a utopia of creature comforts, with all human costs hidden. And it is typical of 1990s advertising
that this dream is given an attractive feminist gloss to coopt an audience certain
to include many women and their daughters.

The dark side of this gratification may be the most disturbing thing in the
film—certainly more frightening than the film's blustering, rather bovine Beast.
Belle achieves her preeminence by rejecting community for a vision of individual omnipotence. She too celebrates the righteous killing of Gaston.[5] With the
working world banished, she will be waited on and applauded by endlessly oblig-
ing inferiors. The servants' mechanical nature suggests the prosthetic ideal of
slavery: that slaves give a master more hands and stamina and indifference to
pain than any ordinary mortal could ever hope for. A master who can command
a potentially unlimited number of slaves becomes practically superhuman, an
undying demigod, like Dracula. Because the prince's servants spontaneously or-

ganize into a loyal and invincible army of smart weapons when attacked, they make the palace a fantasy of omnipotence as well as immortality.

Acting out their master's will, the servants euphemize the prince's heroic violence. They represent one of the many strategies by which the film tries to reconcile its dreams of power with an ethos of love. The Beast, for example, finally kills Gaston only when treacherously provoked, hurling the villain into the abyss beneath the castle like God casting Lucifer into hell. Wounded in this struggle, the Beast undergoes a sort of play-death that symbolically purges him of violence in dissolving his beastly shape. As a prince, he is also feminized, drawn with Michael Jackson–like androgyny.

The prince's euphemized power also serves a larger social purpose. The prince shows no rage against the attacking villagers, for that would acknowledge that the attack is in fact a revolution in which the villagers would place one of their own in charge of their most desirable maiden and the kingdom as a whole. Here is where the enchanted servants become crucial. Who routs the mob? Not an oppressive aristocracy with an arsenal of magic, but stalwart working folks. The jovial candlestick and teapot and their friends suppress the rebellion, but also they discredit the rebels so that movie audiences who are tacitly villagers will not sympathize with them as people like themselves. The film makes it easy to forget that these Praetorian servants are the armies, the national guards, the police, that defend a ruling elite from the resentment of their "inferiors."

In postindustrial America, where the idea of a service economy has its own magic, Hollywood functions as the palace does. The entertainment industry traditionally dresses up in the imagery of stars and royalty, but it also ambiguously uses its magic to serve the financial powers that direct the nation. Not surprisingly, the servants in the Disney studio staged a fairy tale in which righteous daydreams win princely glory as vulgar working people become villains because they begin to desire the love and loot that belong to their noble masters. Like the prince's servants, the Disney artists have made violence entertaining. And for good reason. Corporate America wants to be seen as solicitously paternal rather than domineering. The customer is always right.

The rulers of the country, corporations especially, like to play at serving citizens. But although they advertise humble benevolence, they fear beastly rage and riots too, particularly in labor conflicts and lawsuits over pollution and public accountability. They are prepared to put a would-be prince such as Michael Millken in federal prison when he becomes too flagrantly selfish a beast. Corporations have controlled strikes and protests through police action and, more than once in our history, through military force. In the late 1940s corporate Hollywood cooperated with the House Un-American Activities Committee to police movie industry labor and screenwriters. Lately, corporate leaders have been able to preempt many of these conflicts by exporting jobs to authoritarian countries where such problems can be policed without alarming the American public.

Which brings us back to Los Angeles, whose poorer villagers rioted when a jury excused police for beating an upstart black motorist named Rodney King with a force so superior it was tantamount to magic. The jurors identified with the palace, so to speak, as Belle does. Like the robotic servants, the police are protectors when seen from above, oppressors when seen from below. I am reminded of the high-tech prison in Flint, Michigan, which employed laid-off autoworkers to jail former factory mates who became lawbreakers after General Motors took away their livelihoods. The fortified prison is the other face of the impenetrable General Motors headquarters that Michael Moore tries so many times to enter in *Roger and Me*. The connection was revealed when the prison opened and Flint socialites paid a hundred dollars a couple to spend the inaugural night in jail. The guests danced to rock music and tried on handcuffs, playing at rebellion and punishment while enjoying a sense of mastery. In Disney terms, the guests were testing their own wolfish impulses with impunity while reassuring themselves of the palace's power to lock up troublemakers from below.

If everyone with the price of admission can see *Beauty and the Beast* and dream of marrying out of the village and into the palace, how can the resulting competition be regulated? One answer is the ethos of service. In the film, some poor people do not need to storm the palace: they work there. They love their master and gladly make room for Belle. But they also work to keep out competitors, by force if necessary. The beating of Rodney King in Los Angeles acted out the anger of (public) servants against an outsider, an unruly upstart they claimed had threatened them.

Such forthright hostility risks unleashing wolfish rage throughout society, so the film offers a balancing vision of love. The masters register none of the malice around them. As the prince leaves the Beast behind, the struggle for power vanishes into the glow of new love. The servants' version of romantic love is hero worship—like the relationship of the audience to movie stars. As the film closes, the servants admire their new masters. In the ballroom, watching the royal couple waltz, they are ambiguously both servants and guests, living vicariously, as if beholding the consummation of love on television. They reconstitute the village, with only a faint echo of the fratricidal confrontation persisting now in the mild, egotistical bickering of the servants who were once candelabra and clock—and without a trace of anger at the boss.

The film contrives to make masters, servants, and moviegoers alike innocent. After all, this is frankly a fairy tale. And yet this innocence is also the posture of Roger Smith, the sleazy chairman of General Motors, who evades Michael

Moore's efforts to have him witness the havoc his policies have wrought among his workers. *Roger and Me* closes with Roger Smith at a General Motors Christmas party, reciting Dickens's pious description of Christmas as a time of pure generosity with no competitive meanness. This is a corporate Christmas that promises endless consumer goods and services for free, thanks to a fatherly Santa Claus, whose elves, after all, are supernatural cousins of the magical appliances in the prince's castle.

By a nice coincidence, the September 14, 1992, issue of *Advertising Age* trumpeted a "record-setting $65 million holiday promotion" for the home-video release of *Beauty and the Beast*. Disney "will try by sheer dollars spent to blow away the competition with its campaign," presumably so that Santa would put a videocassette of the film under every twinkling tree. Combining Vietnam War and entrepreneurial heroism, the slangy vindictiveness—"to blow away the competition"—tells the tale. In the same holiday spirit, according to the *New York Times* (December 2, 1992), Disney's chairman cashed in stock options worth slightly more than $197 million. Fearing that Washington might eliminate executive pay as a corporate tax break, the timely chairman acted to "beat the taxman." In one stroke this clever accounting device, as rewarding as any wood-chopping gizmo, enabled Disney to lavish princely compensation on its chief servant even as the servant saved the Magic Kingdom roughly ninety million dollars in taxes that might otherwise have gone to rebuild South Central Los Angeles. In July 1995, Disney announced that it was acquiring the corporation that owns ABC broadcasting, massively advancing its influence over the stories Americans tell—and do not tell—themselves.

The more thoroughly moviegoers identify with *Beauty and the Beast*'s magic circle of admiring servants and waltzing lovers, the more limited their vision of society will be. After all, the jurors in the trial of the police who beat Rodney King were ordinary citizens who could not face the graphic evidence of police viciousness and could not see the human face of the suffering and rage in South Central Los Angeles. The film invites viewers, especially female viewers, to associate the Beast not with a spoiled elite but with an enraged and frustrated mob in the poorest streets of America. If they learn to love the prince and enjoy the righteous rout of Gaston's loutish male chauvinism, audiences will see a glorious cartoon horizon that fades to a close before anyone can ask what has happened to Belle's neighbors, and how the infantile, cozily ruthless world of the castle can ever relate to those neighbors in the future. Children thrilling to this romance will be innocently prepared for service in the corporate fortress, probably unaware that they have left the old neighborhood behind.

Beauty and the Breast of L.A.

To probe the cultural distress masked by fairy-tale wedding bells, let me turn to a romance that might be called "Beauty and the Breast of Los Angeles." Filmed partly in the Disney studios, Garry Marshall's *Pretty Woman* (1990) can be read as a gloss on *Beauty and the Beast*. It clarifies the way in which trauma as a trope in the 1990s opened up associations between the business culture and the survival anxieties seen in *Schindler's List*. As in the fairy tale, a beautiful nobody heals the post-traumatic symptoms of a prince—in this case, a lordly financier—and in return he makes her a princess. As a fantasy about the rehabilitation of a heartless capitalist by a girl of the streets, *Pretty Woman* recombines Victorian materials from stories such as Dickens's *Christmas Carol* and Shaw's *Pygmalion*. But the whore who heals a prince is a venerable figure; recall Marina in Shakespeare's once wildly popular romance *Pericles*. As a self-mocking chivalric romance, *Pretty Woman* dramatizes a Saint George who has defeated a paternal dragon, yet still needs a soulful maiden to release him from the dragon's spell. The plot goes like this:

In Los Angeles to buy a huge, vulnerable shipbuilding firm, a ruthless arbitrager named Edward Lewis stops on Hollywood Boulevard to ask a hooker named Vivian Ward for street directions, and ends up hiring her as an escort for a week and falling in love with her. The vivacious Viv tacitly lifts a childhood curse on the beast/prince, just as Edward becomes a princely Pygmalion making a princess out of her with the help of kindly servants such as the hotel manager, Barney Thompson. The hooker with the heart of gold turns out to be purely an amateur, a high-school dropout with sharp wits and impeccable hygiene from Milledgeville, Georgia, the home of Flannery O'Connor. In a sense Edward too turns out to be only playing at corporate piracy, inasmuch as he gives up cutting fiscal throats without a great inner struggle and apparently without any financial loss.

Despite the predictable Hollywood lard in this recipe, *Pretty Woman* attempted a critique of the 1990s whose insights and omissions justify a second look. Its central conceit is that in 1990s America, economic life had become a form of prostitution, with post-traumatic consequences that gripped all of society like an uncanny curse. As Edward quips, "We both screw people for money." Because prostitution dehumanizes and falsifies life, inviting numbness and dissociation, it radiates traumatic shock. The screenplay drives home the connection when Edward insists, "I can't let myself get emotionally involved in business." Viv retorts that hookers cannot get involved either. "That's why no kissing," she says. "It's too personal. It's like what you're saying, you stay numb, don't get involved. When I'm with a guy, I'm like a robot, I just do it." Edward then tries to close off this emotionally risky subject with the callous wisecrack, "You and I are such similar creatures, Viv. We both screw people for money." Moments later, though, she draws him out about the recent death of his abusive father, and Edward begins to resemble the Disney prince frozen by a traumatic childhood curse.

But in the film's Los Angeles, almost everyone is finally a servant, and the weaker must "suck up" to the stronger, with connotations of oral sex for hire. Even socially elite women try to "sell themselves" to the affluent, marriageable Edward. The tacit prostitution entails post-traumatic symptoms, not only numbness but also aggression, as we see when the boutique clerks on Rodeo Drive first rout Viv the way the palace servants "suck up" to Belle but maul the villagers. Out on the street, where a prostitute has just turned up murdered in a dumpster, the mix of numbness and rage is even more volatile. But the film astutely insinuates that we are looking at a social system. The screenplay allows us to see that Edward's business prostitution is also a form of post-traumatic rage. As Barlett and Steele have shown,[6] raiding and reselling industries can harm many more victims than turning tricks does. Although Edward and Viv "both screw people for money," "screw" here can mean both the fulfillment of sexual desires for pay and criminal injury to another person. Numbness falsifies the pleasure Viv peddles, but the transaction is presumably consensual. By contrast, Edward uses financial leverage to force intimacy (mergers), and this corporate rape can inflict collateral damage on whole cities.

The film acknowledges that Edward has an unsavory side. At first Viv mistakes him for a lawyer because he has "a sharp, useless look about him." When he explains arbitrage to her, she cuts to the crucial point: that he does not make or produce anything. "I buy companies," he says, "and break them up into parts. Then I sell the parts for more than the whole is worth."

"Sort of like stealing cars and selling the parts."

"But it's legal."

At this juncture we are uncomfortably close to the motives of the Nazi economy. Like *Schindler's List*'s Nazi bosses, Edward is puritanical and utilitarian, obsessed with rules and efficiency, his death anxiety focused in his phobia about heights. He is "all business," but also divorced and deadened to eros. He reduces other people to tools just as the curse in the fairy tale reduces the servants to furnishings. Like a Nazi strategist, he conquers and sacrifices workers. Given a slight twist in perspective, *Pretty Woman* could be shockingly sinister, with the avuncular hotel manager Barney playing Stern's role, invisibly sponsoring a "dirty," despised streetwalker in order to save her from ending up in a dumpster, like the Jewish corpses dumped into mass graves. What protects us from stumbling into this sort of horror are the invisible barriers of dissociation that implicitly define the post-traumatic syndrome in the screenplay, in American culture, and in ourselves.

With Barney's support, Viv operates as Schindler does. She restores Edward's ability to feel through her capacity for playfulness and camaraderie. On their first evening together she sprawls before the television set, chortling at an *I Love Lucy* rerun in which Lucy treads wine grapes in a vat. The television farce is purgative in the spirit of lower-class carnival. Lucy gawkily dramatizes the process of getting used to being at home in the absurd human body, literally making wine, the celebratory elixir of play and desire that serves Schindler and the endangered Jews so well. The television show is the Hollywood of wine, women, and song, the Hollywood of the servants' show business in the prince's palace, and Viv ingenuously uses it to soften up Edward.

At the same time, as in the Victorian scheme Freud outlined in "The Most Prevalent Form of Degradation in Erotic Life," Viv can reach Edward exactly because she is a hooker—an outcast, not altogether a real woman, and therefore she does not threaten him. As a whore redefined as a contractual employee, Vivian can be commanded. By contrast, women in elite society compete like cutthroat executives to win the affluent Edward as a prize. Edward himself is jealous of rivals for Viv, and with his lawyer, Philip Stuckey, envying him, he has good reason for anxiety. But then, competition and envy are fundamental markers of value in the culture of the film. Viv is transformed not by altering her soul but by learning the theatrical mysteries of class: fashion, manners ("stop fidgeting"), and that litmus test for sublime emotion, opera. In effect, she learns a semiotic code of caste and command.

Viv rises through a Darwinian social milieu—one front in the sex war—epitomized by the physically abusive Philip Stuckey. Not only is the lawyer's attempted rape of Viv emblematic of the predatory violence lurking everywhere in the film's America, it also recapitulates for us and for Edward the cause of Edward's post-traumatic symptoms: his father's cruelty. In the judgment of the honorable, fatherly Mr. Morse, whose shipbuilding company Edward covets, "everybody" thought Edward's father was "a bastard."

Edward's mother, we learn, was a piano teacher, the source of his artistic tastes, his love of opera and skill at the piano. Like Viv, she was a poor nobody, but she married the wealthy businessman Carter Lewis, only to be cast off by him. Stung by her premature death, Edward has made his career an obsessive struggle to undo this family violence by retaliation. In one of his earliest corporate raids, some fifteen years before the film opens, he bought his father's business out from under him. Yet even though he defeated his father, Edward is still in the grip of childhood injury. As he tells Viv, it "cost me ten thousand dollars in therapy to be able to say, 'I'm angry at my father.'" But his entire career of corporate buccaneering has been a form of berserking against stand-ins for the patriarchal brute—against scapegoats. The old man's recent death and Viv's openness allow Edward to begin to accept his past.

When Edward declines to close in for his current corporate kill—when Mr. Morse's "jugular is exposed"—his change of heart reflects his internalization of Viv's tacit critique of business as rape. He compassionately attempts to undo the past by bonding with a heroic father figure. "Men like my grandfather," says Mr. Morse's grandson, "made this country." Trying to counter Edward's depredations, Mr. Morse joins forces with his employees. He wants to build things and to foster solidarity, not to buy companies cheaply and liquidate them. To be sure, Mr. Morse and his history are idealized. But the screenplay is perfectly cogent about the damage that Edward Lewises have done to working people. And this is why, when Edward finally agrees to help Mr. Morse save his company, the film makes the old man a surrogate father whose grateful praise—"I'm proud of you"—presumably reconstitutes the prosthetic parental voice that was absent or had turned vicious in Edward's childhood.

In the Nazi economy, Viv would be one of Schindler's Jewish beauties, serving a masterful employer who would save her from social death. Sexuality buys her life. In the traumatic economy she functions largely as a surrogate mother to Edward. In their first encounter, Viv strokes and coddles him, undressing him and giving him pleasure, presumably orally, while he enjoys her with an admiring, passive, even infantile gaze. The Wall Street conqueror relishes not sexual conquest but maternal nursing that allays his death anxiety.[7] Later, he unburdens his traumatic childhood to Viv as she bathes him in the tub and encircles him with her arms and legs—which is, she teases, a therapy much cheaper than that which his therapist provides. One need not make a Freudian leap to associate this moment with the ecstasy of the womb and early infancy. Later that night, she finds him downstairs in the hotel's deserted ballroom. Unburdened now, he is playing the piano—his mother's métier—and he makes love to Viv atop the piano, her feet delicately playing a few comic, aleatory notes on the keyboard. As a mother figure, she fulfills a long-denied desire to nurse, merging sex and infancy. The lovemaking can be seen as a magic undoing of his mother's traumatic death as well as a sublimation of an Oedipal wish.

There is emptiness in Vivian's background too. "When I was a little girl and I was bad (and I was bad a lot) my mother used to lock me in the attic, and I used to pretend I was a princess trapped in a tower by a wicked queen. Then suddenly this knight on a white horse . . . would climb the tower and rescue me." In the absence of a knight, Viv has rebelled against the suffocation and punishment of home, striking out as Belle does for the palace. In Los Angeles she has defied her moralistic mother by becoming a reluctant hooker, the same way Carolyn in

Uncle Vampire unwillingly submits to her uncle's sexual advances but also—rebelliously—despises the coercive, phony moralizing of her parents' world. Yet like Edward, Viv is still looking for a mother's nurture. Hence the resonance when she says to her sugar daddy, Edward, at their first bittersweet breakup, "I think you have a lot of special gifts." "Gifts" here means not only his personal talents and the luxurious wardrobe he has bestowed on her, but also the nurture he has made available as a reluctant example of the substitute mother that Janice Radway finds in the idealized romance hero.[8]

Edward and Viv play at parenting each other. As lovers, they find in each other the prosthetic support withheld in childhood by their punitive and rapacious parents. In the fashion boutique on Rodeo Drive, helping Viv negotiate intimidating class barriers, Edward privately instructs the manager to boost her self-esteem. In the bath together, as Edward reveals his anguished childhood to her, Viv strokes his breast like a mother bathing a baby—but also, ambiguously, like a child enjoying her mother's breast. In different ways, insofar as the breast signifies psychic integrity, secure bonds, and generosity, the lovers can interchangeably take the roles of beauty and the breast of L.A. In the tenderness of this scene the screenplay tries to imagine behavior that could address imprinted injury. The symbolic logic assumes that as long as the characters labor under the spell of trauma, they cannot really change. The film suggests that debates about social values are less efficacious—less revolutionary—than is deep, remedial nurture.

This concept of trauma and the generous breast is a poignant but equivocal fantasy. Although it respects the irrational depths of private, individual motivation, it tends as well to render moot any immediate political remedies for social ills. If our past and private injuries must be healed before we can reform society, then we have little leverage against evil. The fantasy arguably displaces responsibility onto the indefinite past. This is one reason the film screens out real poverty and suffering: they might cry out for immediate action and make a mockery of self-involved romance. Paradoxically the film's fantasy of release from post-traumatic dissociation actually encourages dissociation on another front insofar as it concentrates on private individuals to the exclusion of the social interrelations that constitute the city. The bliss of love screens out other people.

Consider again the way in which a decision in Edward's palatial Hilton suite may radiate traumatic shock in all directions. People in different social positions experience different aspects of traumatic distress. As the *New York Times* (March 4, 1996) summarized, "White-collar, middle-class Americans in mass numbers are coming to understand first hand the chronic insecurity on which the working class and poor are experts." But trauma is inherently social, and so even "those who have not lost their jobs and their identities, and do not expect to, are also being traumatized. The witnesses, the people who stay employed but sit next to empty desks and wilting ferns, are grappling with the guilt that psychologists label survivor's syndrome" (ibid.). As "executioners," even lordly executives develop a psychic numbing and the somatic reactions typical of trauma. These developments undermine loyalties and trust in the workplace and in the community as well. The damage to trust was registered in the epic junk-bond and savings-and-loan scandals of the 1980s, which echoed the late-Victorian "taint in the air."[9] But the damage poisons private lives too, whether or not people directly face the underlying survival anxiety. In 1995 a Sunday newspaper cartoon depicted a teenage boy saying nervously to his middle-class parents: "Sure I'm insecure. . . . What if you guys decide to downsize?"[10]

The cartoon glances at the terror in Edward's childhood. Symbolically, "downsizing" your own children is infanticide or the psychic abandonment Havelock Ellis felt in the factory universe. Carter Lewis sacrificed his wife and son to feed his own hunger for immortality. In *Pretty Woman* the camera repeatedly reinforces this criticism by associating financial dominance with senescence and death anxiety, showing us snobbish, white-haired couples in the lobby of the Hilton who eye the sexy Viv with painful ambivalence, having sacrificed their youth and eros for chimerical security. At the opera she is genuinely moved, while the elderly lady in the next box turns out to be hard-of-hearing and primly conventional. Even Edward at first seems a bit mummified in his body language compared to the way Viv sprawls, squats, hunkers down on chairs, and eats like a young primate at home in nature.

By contrast, the seedy streets are full of mortal but vital young people. The film opens with Viv facing eviction because even with a respectable job she "couldn't make the rent" and her roommate has squandered on drugs the money she earned from hooking. In the street, Viv hears about a murdered prostitute found in a dumpster. If she escapes violence, time will eventually "waste" her beauty and make even hooking impossible. Viv's instinct for self-preservation is basically middle-class, as the film telegraphs in countless details: the snapshots of home in her room, her habit of flossing, her prudence about money. She is able to shift from the street to the penthouse because she brings with her the old-fashioned values of village America. Showing her assortment of condoms to Edward, she chirps, "I'm a safety girl."

If the film stopped here, Viv would be a sort of Schindler, thawing a grim Nazi and helping protect her precarious roommate Kit. But as she tells Edward, "I want more. . . . I want the fairy tale." Romance is about overcoming barriers to desire and fertility—barriers such as condoms, caste, and the baleful old man, Carter Lewis. Presumably the lovers will dissolve their personal barriers and produce two or three children who need not fear downsizing or resort to prostitution. Romances dream that love will conquer the fear of death and convert swords—the Nazi economy—to plowshares, as in Edward's rescue of Mr. Morse's shipyard and its workers. Yet romance also means to overcome terror and accept commitment. In renouncing further romantic or martial conquests, lovers (or knights) are accepting death.

But as Saint George's fate attests, even after saving the walled city the knight may be tempted into a still-greater—and fatal—crusade. Like the film, romances usually culminate in the magical undoing that rescue represents, screening out any anxious, post-traumatic hereafter. *Pretty Woman* acknowledges this by abruptly ironizing its happy ending. When Viv sighs wistfully, "Who does [romance] really work out for?" Kit's answer is nobody: "Cinde-fucking-rella." A moment later the savior-knight is scaling the fire escape—but then Darryl, the limousine driver, undercuts that resolution with a final twist that looks back toward *A Midsummer Night's Dream*. His voice-over becomes prosthetic speech, interpreting the world for us. "Hollywood, land of dreams," he elegizes. "Keep on dreaming."

This bittersweet close has the structure of equivocation. Cognitively, the screenplay beautifully patterns the world through magical undoing, and its use of trauma is a marker for this wishful symmetry. Healing tends to involve a reversal of polarities. Edward punches out his crass alter ego, the lawyer Philip Stuckey, who would abuse Viv and loves only "the kill." Having toppled his father, Edward converts his rage to cooperation through Mr. Morse. His mother returns from social death in the ascendant Viv. This symmetry can stand for heroic triumph or for mutuality, as when Edward asks what happens after the knight rescues the maiden, and Viv replies, "She rescues him right back." In one way, the magical undoing is escapist; in another it supports morale ("keep on dreaming"). Like *Beauty and the Beast*, the film gestures toward feminism while coopting it.

A number of cultural possibilities levitate in this precarious suspension. For one thing, the parodic recycling of chivalry (the knight scaling a fire escape with an umbrella-sword) was a familiar sign of storylessness in the 1990s. With the exception of the slimy lawyer Philip Stuckey, there are no more enemies who are safe to hate. And even Stuckey's evil is more evocative of shark-lawyer jokes than of any mythic resonance. The significant evil in the film is found in what I have been calling, for simplicity's sake, the survival economy. But *Pretty Woman* finally turns a blind eye to that greed for life, not simply because the film is a romantic comedy but because it wants to be heroic without cost. Edward is benevolent to kindly old Mr. Morse, but he is not about to leverage his politician cronies to blow the whistle on the cozy elite who own the palace.

The film never seriously challenges its narcissism. Cured of his numbness, cold rage, and phobia about heights, Edward is still the center of the world, god-like in his freedom to wave a financial magic wand. As Viv tells Kit, "It's easy to clean up when you have money." But the film never imagines how the mean streets might be improved. Nobody questions the boss's right to fiddle tax breaks to avoid his share of the city's upkeep. On the contrary, the film's use of trauma argues that both lovers deserve a reward for their earlier sorrows. And even rewards can be perverse; there is a latent vindictiveness in magical reversal. Turning the tables on one's adversaries, for example, may not remove the sting of past injustice but only perpetuate a cycle of aggression. Compelling clerks to "suck up" to you, as Edward makes them fawn on Viv, may soothe a past humiliation, but it may also foster resentment and more respect for credit cards than for realistic self-esteem.

That said, there are some balancing signs of an older, progressive social vision too. The screenplay takes pains to show that the lovers' generosity of spirit affects others. Viv, for example, passes on to Kit the morale boost and the urge to self-improvement she has received from Edward. At one point they joke about the "Edward Lewis scholarship," and the detail hints that Edward is capable of some modest empowering gesture of that sort. In an equally glancing fashion we are invited to surmise that in the future Edward will invest in corporations that produce something and that foster cooperation with workers. Rather than praise or sneer at these vaporous goals, I want to point out that the screenplay tries to imagine a way to defy post-traumatic assumptions. Granted, its magic lies in its argument that individuals can change, although Viv is the sort of "safety girl" who has all along been half-consciously preparing to move up. By implication we need Hollywood—those kindly palace servants again—to enable us to "keep on dreaming" that private change will shape public policy. But what is most striking in *Pretty Woman* is perhaps what goes unspoken. The film relishes the prospect of individuals overcoming injury, but it cannot imagine a society awakening from a traumatic curse into new life.

Beauty and the Prince of Tides

In one direction, the ambiguities of romantic trauma lead toward a film such as Barbra Streisand's *Prince of Tides* (1991), in which she plays a New York psychiatrist (Dr. Susan Lowenstein) who dispels the childhood trauma of a Carolina teacher and football coach (Tom) with an assist from Cupid. In this formula a feminist subtext reverses roles, making Tom unemployed and Dr. Lowenstein a prestigious urban professional. He may be a prince of tides, but she has the indispensable anodyne, and she bills for it. The screenplay's gentle chauvinism also asserts that the Holocaust gives Jews a special therapeutic empathy. For his part, Tom has suffered his father's abusive anger and also, for good measure, sodomy at the hands of three escaped convicts. The implausible episode of anal rape is significant not only because it crystallizes the latent threat of Tom's father's rage, but also because in Hollywood in the 1990s it had become a marker for vicious competition for status.

In *Prince of Tides*, the widening gulf between rich and poor is subtly yet shockingly literal. Tom's once-abused mother has gotten remarried, to an affluent southern hypocrite, but her post-traumatic numbness alienates her from her son. By contrast, the sensitive children have slipped toward social death. Having rescued his family from the escaped convicts, Tom's brother Luke became an activist fighting to preserve the environment and his heritage, and in despair killed himself. Tom's twin sister Savanna blocked out their childhood trauma. In choosing a pen name as a poet she has presented herself as a daughter of Holocaust survivors, an honorary Jew, and now needs Dr. Lowenstein and Hollywood to rescue her from attempted suicide. Like Forrest Gump's abused sweetheart Jenny, she is controlled by childhood injury.

In this social scheme the cosmopolitan Jewish female doctor is also Barbra Streisand, the actor-producer-director who uses Hollywood to heal traditional WASP America by coaxing out its shameful, traumatic secrets on the screen. But why is Hollywood ministering to the American psyche? One answer is that the machinery of traumatic romance maintains the status quo for the privileged people and institutions that actually govern America. On one level, *Prince of Tides* is a sort of ceremonial dance enacted to stabilize the forces affecting the tribe—although everybody knows that its efficacy wanes as the final credits start to roll. Outside the theater, laid-off teachers such as Tom are commonplace and as hapless as the rioters in *Beauty and the Beast* or South Central Los Angeles. The film, however, contrives a democratic-seeming economy. Nobody asks how a working man such as Tom could ever pay Manhattan-scale psychiatric fees. Tom is also a football coach, a princely athlete who repays Dr. Lowenstein by helping her son find his manhood, just as the doctor helps Tom recover his manhood by facing his memory of anal rape. To fine-tune the balance, the story has Tom married to a decent, unimpassioned doctor back home whose income will presumably cover the cost of his visits to Dr. Lowenstein. And spiritual equality is achieved when patient and psychiatrist become lovers.

The film's traumatic equations flatter Tom and his rescuer. What interests me is that the screenplay insists on the muted sorrows of these well-placed, contented people. When Tom has healed, he and Susan Lowenstein finally renounce their love, at which point she becomes a sacrificial Jewish mother to a needy brood. "I gotta find me a nice Jewish boy," she says. "You guys are killing me." In the voice-over that closes the film, Tom is back in the South. He tells us that he still goes home to his family every day reciting her name over and over "as praise, as prayer, 'Lowenstein, Lowenstein.'" The bathos here makes the doctor a prosthetic tutelary spirit, a mother-goddess. But her self-sacrifice and sorrows take attention away from her elegantly rewarded professional life. Measured in terms of freedom and luxury, autonomy and culturally validated heroic purpose, Susan Lowenstein is as supreme a princess as there can be.

The power of this formula became clear in the mass demonstration of grief for Princess Diana after her death in a car wreck in 1997. Just as the death of Prince Albert crystallized typically Victorian fantasies about the ideal paterfamilias, so Diana's death focused characteristic themes of the 1990s. Media and the public saw a feminist story about a shy nursery school teacher who married a prince, suffered betrayal, eating disorders, and divorce, but then became a respected mother and moral leader. Traumatic affliction gave substance to Diana's new moral stature, even as it helped to justify the enviable glitz of international stardom (she appeared forty-three times on the cover of *People* magazine). Women mourners seemed to show solidarity with Diana as with a victim of rape or abuse. As the *New York Times* reported, "Women in particular have swarmed to the various shrines where Diana is being remembered."[11] Like Marilyn Monroe, she became intensely desirable yet never found true love. Like Barbra Streisand's Lowenstein, she brought motherly solace to victims of AIDS, for example, and of land mines.

In Diana's story the trope of trauma supported fantasies that one good woman could help heal an injured world. But the trope also had reactionary possibilities insofar as it imagined an elite, ineffectual child becoming a "true" princess the way Shakespeare's shepherdess Perdita discovers her "natural," magical nobility. As in *Beauty and the Beast*, Diana's abuse at the hands of unfeeling royalty became the means of the royal family's renewal. Her death forced the royal family to protest its devotion to its divorced and alienated daughter-in-law to counter a widespread perception that the royals were being callous about her death—that is, abusive.[12] In a further irony, the outpouring of grief and adulation also expressed an ambivalent public's disavowal of its negative feelings about the princess. Until her unexpected death, the tabloids had been feeding an appetite for inflammatory stories about Diana's scandalous love life and missteps. In this respect, Diana's apotheosis follows the same mythic rhythm as *Pretty Woman*.

Beauty and the Beast of Las Vegas

Privileged self-pity is a gratifying daydream in *Prince of Tides*, but it harbors sordid possibilities. In Mike Figgis's *Leaving Las Vegas* (1995), a movie executive who has been traumatized by the loss of his wife and family—and by the emptiness of Los Angeles—supposedly drinks himself to death with the assistance of a hooker who is an unspoiled, devoted beauty like Belle and Viv. I say "supposedly drinks himself to death" because Mike Figgis's screenplay, based on a novel by John O'Brien, seems to me implausible. But it is exactly that implausibility that most starkly calls into question the meaning of the audience's willingness to believe and in turn suggests that the film is saying more than it knows.

"Oh, this movie is so sad!" laments reviewer Roger Ebert. *Leaving Las Vegas* is sad "not because of the tragic lives of its characters, but because of their goodness and their charity." Ebert's bathos implies a post-traumatic world in which goodness and charity are achingly absent. He speaks for many who were moved by the film, among them the Hollywood judges who awarded it Oscars. "Ben was a movie executive," Ebert explains. "Something bad happened in his life, and his wife and son are gone. Is he divorced? Are they dead? It is never made clear."[13] In narratives such as Vladimir Nabokov's *Lolita* (1955) and Nabokovian variants such as Jaco van Dormael's *Toto the Hero* (1991) and Patrice Leconte's *Hairdresser's Husband* (1992), a traumatic lost love in childhood shapes an adult "destiny." What is the "something bad" in Ben's life?

Ben is in an alcoholic free fall. He cadges money from other executives in a Los Angeles restaurant, guzzles, hits on women in bars, gets fired, lets a prostitute steal his wedding ring by sucking it off his finger, abandons his apartment and burns mementos of his family, drives to Las Vegas determined to drink himself to death, moves in with a beautiful, lonesome hooker named Sera, and spins increasingly out of control. After he alienates Sera, she leaves but blunders into a ghastly rape. She returns to find Ben suffering from delirium tremens, but she mounts him and brings him to a successful orgasm as he dies.

In this skeletal outline, *Leaving Las Vegas* inverts *Pretty Woman*. The faithful hooker fails to save the injured executive knight. He "dies"—with the usual Renaissance wordplay—in the arms of his grieving lady. And the film invites us to join in that grief. The goodness and charity Roger Ebert attributes to Ben and Sera are signs of their nobility in an overwhelming, evil world. The film announces the post-traumatic disjunction between that world and the incapable self as a soundtrack vocal asks if you ever feel that the world has left you behind and that you are losing your mind. The prosthetic voice is out there, yet in us as well, undermining the listener's self-confidence by insinuating that we are mad in a world out of control.

What does it mean if we regard Ben as the victim of a traumatic culture? The question bristles with difficulties. If trauma is an injury entailing interpretation of injury, what sort of interpretation is appropriate here? By any historical measure, Ben enjoys a princely life. Despite the predictable atmospheric bleakness of Los Angeles, for example, he keeps encountering sympathetic voices. What keeps him from responding? No matter how squalid the culture is, solidarity with even one or two others can be meaningful. Why does Ben bond with nobody? The few times people do abuse him, he has courted trouble. Nobody makes him squander his life. Why should he be so belligerently suicidal? What is wrong?

The film associates Ben's free fall with the traumatic loss of his wife, family, and career in an unbearable world. But the screenplay deliberately obscures the nature of the injury. When Ben explains it to Sera, he quips, "I'm not sure if I lost my family because of my drinking, or if I'm drinking because I lost my family." Roger Ebert comments that "the details would not help, because this is not a case history but a sad love song."[14]

But I think the details do matter. They matter because the film evokes a powerful mood of despair and grievance as well as pity. Its symbolic logic mounts an argument about the culture outside the theater that resonates with many moviegoers. Is the culture that kills Ben the same monstrous force that "Christian thrillers" dramatize as a dragon? Is Ben suffering from the disease Matthew Arnold called "modern life"? In the larger historical context, Ben resembles those relatively affluent patients who baffled late-Victorian physicians with symptoms of neurasthenia and traumatic neurosis. It would be wise to keep in mind the sensation in the press caused by the "suicide epidemic" in the 1890s, and the way in which neurasthenia feeds on unexamined feeling. Again: by any historical measure, Ben is enviably situated in life, and Sera is plainly a capable woman. No wonder their story is framed by her therapy sessions and groping explanations.

The puzzles also relate to the film's assumptions. Is Leaving Las Vegas an exceptionally honest confrontation with a sick America? If the sources of the characters' torment are unclear, is this a function of their symptomatic dissociation and denial, sharply dramatized by the filmmakers? Or is the film itself a symptom of a wider fantasy of a cultural crash? And if so, how is its global despair used? To the extent that the film takes trauma for granted, it orchestrates pity for the victims. And although that sentimentality could be richly satisfying, it would close off other responses worth exploring.

Let me put Leaving Las Vegas in the context of the other traumatic romances in this chapter. As if cursed like the selfish fairy-tale prince, Ben cannot love. In an astonishing analogue to the fairy tale, Ben behaves as if punished by an angry mother figure. In a Los Angeles strip joint, for example, the camera cuts back and forth between the stripper's inviting breasts and Ben, greedily sucking down a pint of whiskey like a baby at the nipple, unable to find fulfillment. In *Pretty Woman*, the breast is tactfully out of sight but everywhere a thematic presence. In *Leaving Las Vegas* the breast is on display, but Ben cannot relate well to women. The same eerie disconnection appears in an earlier scene when he tries to pick up a woman in a bar. He is both obnoxiously aggressive and vulnerable. "I really wish you'd come home with me," he pleads. "You're so cute. And I'm really good in bed, believe me." His anxiety about women is so clearly telegraphed that his aggressiveness is sympathetic—like the Disney beast's—and the woman exits, giving him a motherly pat. When his boss gently fires him, a female coworker comforts him like the motherly teapot in the palace. These moments prepare us for Sera's motherliness in Las Vegas. She takes Ben in, cleans him up, fondles him, buys him gifts, and nurses him.

In the "palace" of Las Vegas, the beautiful Sera tries to undo the curse on Ben, but dissociation and covert hostility undercut their intimacy. Ben calls her his "angel," keeping her idealized and impersonal, as in the saccharine barroom lament "Angel Eyes." And like a child governed by a taboo of silence in a fairy tale, she is forbidden to try to save him: "You can never, ever ask me to stop drinking." Although she explains that she is tired of living alone, and he has no sexual desire left, the film virtually never shows them in conversation together. It is impossible to overstress the screenplay's coyness about this. Supposedly they delight in each other's talk, yet at his death their lives are still nearly totally blank.

The film, I think, blames this personal numbness on post-traumatic Los Angeles and Las Vegas, whose servants and prostitutes seem to labor under the magic curse of numbness. Following the symbolic logic of *Beauty and the Beast*, they have been turned into animate objects or malicious rivals. Ben cannot get real with others. He makes insipid set speeches to bartenders and substitutes lame witticisms and campy movie dialogue for more-personal responses. Like a hooker's come-on, his effort to cadge money from acquaintances in the restaurant is scripted and calls for him to "suck up" to them. On the office telephone his business propositions are compulsive and as phony as a con man's pitch.

This is the nightmare disguised in *Beauty and the Beast*: if you cannot be a prince, how can you learn to tolerate being a servant? The Disney script resolves the conflict through romantic triumphalism and psychic splitting. Good servants repel upstart servants, and the prince kills the overreaching Gaston—which makes romantic solidarity possible. Among hookers and other servants, Ben behaves with princely extravagance, but he is not a prince. In a culture that makes service an industry and does not value it, he can find no meaning in any service role. This is a Tom Sawyer culture in which the smart trick is to get someone else to serve as fence painter. Princes command servants and escape their own obligations to serve. This polarization of society is what makes Ben's flailing confusion seem sympathetic.

Like many other post-traumatic narratives, the film implies that a failed prince faces social death. For Ben, suicide is preferable. Where does the motive energy for suicide come from in the film? Unlike Viv and the palace servants, Ben gets no relief from romance or psychic splitting. With love gone, he staggers drunkenly about, using numbness to contain his rage. In burning family photographs on his last night in Los Angeles, for example, he acts out repression. By "cleaning up" the past, he numbs himself. Yet he does not simply put away the memories; he incinerates them. This is a revenge against the past, not unrelated to newspaper stories about stealthy fathers who have slain their whole families as a desperate judgment on a tormenting, insoluble intimacy. The film foregrounds Ben's pain but leaves his more-disturbing motives unexamined.

Let me flesh out this point by following Ben to the bank to cash his severance check the next morning. His hand shakes so badly that when the imposing blonde teller asks him to sign the check, he fails. After tanking up at a local bar, he goes back to the teller's line with new confidence that is as obscene and deviously hostile as it is brash. Speaking to a miniature tape recorder as if working on some sort of movie speech, he appalls his audience of female customers. He improvises the monologue as if—but only as if—telling off the intimidating blonde teller who earlier humiliated him. Notice the way he uses sex and class to retaliate:

> Are you desirable? Are you irresistible? Maybe if you drank bourbon with me it would help. If you kissed me and I could taste the sting in your mouth, it would help. If you drank bourbon with me naked, if you smelled of bourbon as you fucked me, it would increase my esteem for you. If you poured bourbon on your naked body and said to me, "Drink this." If you spread your legs and you had bourbon dripping from your breasts and your pussy and said drink it here, then I could fall in love with you, because then I would have a purpose, to clean you up and that would prove that I'm worth something. I'd lick you clean so that you could go away and fuck someone else.

The monologue mixes abjection, jealousy, and vindictiveness. It could be argued that this scenario wishfully acts out in public, against a veiled scapegoat, the earlier revenge of burning up his wife and family. Sousing and licking a woman to make her desirable suggests a wish to humble a wife felt to be intimidatingly judgmental and haughty—as the bank teller tacitly is. On a deeper level it is an infantile fantasy of using booze to furnish a "dry" mother figure with love that he can orally enjoy. "Falling in love" with her—romance—would give him "purpose." No longer an abject servant, he would be "worth something"—in command. The triumph over impotence would also be a resurrection from social death.

The traumatic injury implied in this scenario may be extrapolated from the final crack of the fantasy whip: "I'd lick you clean so that you could go away and fuck someone else." To me this suggests that heroic purpose for Ben would be vindictively sacrificial: "You've betrayed me with other men, but in degrading you and then licking you clean—rescuing you—I vindicate myself, now willingly letting you injure me, proving yourself a whore and me worthwhile." The fantasy is a form of traumatic rescue, with the maiden become frighteningly treacherous and the route to glory sacrificial. This self-abnegating triumphalism is reminiscent of Oscar Wilde's prison ruminations about suicidal messianism. This is an analogue worth keeping in mind, because other signs of conflicted sexual identity appear in Ben when he reaches Las Vegas.

The rage under the surface of Ben's monologue also affects his behavior on the road to Las Vegas. He blazes down the highway with death-defying, drunken recklessness, so capable of killing people in a wreck that his mania qualifies as a form of berserking. After the depressive symptoms he exhibited in Los Angeles, these stirrings of aggression logically introduce him to Sera, who in many ways plays out the role of fantasy wife-mother-whore anticipated earlier. At first, romance appears to convert aggression to love, or at least to solace. But romance obscures deeper issues. The Disney prince overcomes the curse by splitting off and destroying his hostile alter ego Gaston, just as the servants split off and beat down their rebellious rage. Ben, by contrast, kills himself trying to kill off his rage. The sicker he gets, the more aggressively he acts. The screenplay uses Sera's pimp to make Ben look mild at first, but when Yuri leaves the film, Ben's dark side emerges; it culminates in his betrayal of Sera by bringing home another whore. This may be why his otherwise incredible orgasmic death has such emotional force. Extinguishing his own rage makes him able to relate to Sera. But love costs him his life.

From this angle, the film is tacitly about the motives of sexual violence. Its romantic energy draws not only on Sera's efforts to heal Ben, but also on her recuperation of his injured conception of women. She tries to defuse his misogyny by preempting his hostility. In his motel room for the first time, she spells out the psychic economy of prostitution based on dominance and servility. "For five hundred dollars," she says, "you can do whatever you want, up the ass, in my face." Unwittingly, she confronts his aggression and shames him. When she is unable to arouse him, asking if he is too drunk for sex, he replies, "I don't care about any of that. Just stay."

Sera does stay. And as in Freud's famous essay, Ben goes on to reverse the polarities, converting her from whore to "angel." But in this splitting, the anguished individual woman gets lost. To her therapist, Sera implies that in intimate moments with Ben she could be herself. But we never see those moments on screen. Practically speaking, the screenplay cannot show much intimacy between them without making Ben's suicidal obsession seem merely sick and Sera's tolerance morally irresponsible. Like Ben's vague past, this blackout blurs the film's attitude toward the characters.

If we think of Ben and Sera as traumatized, then their romance is a form of "postarousal bonding"—the bond created by release from stress. This is what draws Max and Elena together after the crash in *Fearless*, what sent Patty Hearst into the arms of her captors, and what helps bond a mother and her infant after the pangs of childbirth. Their mutual acceptance then appears to be less a generous respect for each other's autonomy than a strategy by which two gun-shy people can get closer without risking friction and further abuse. But this sort of self-protective acceptance is likely to be self-effacing or even servile. As a kind of role-playing (he does not really want her to peddle herself; she does not really want him to die), their tolerance is a form of alexithymia, the post-traumatic symptom of distancing or "as-if-ness." It is a crucial mark of the film's—and the 1990s'—post-traumatic assumptions that nobody on screen ever really challenges Ben and Sera's pact. Because they make a play space separate from the—presumably—oppressive culture around them, their acceptance can seem somehow admirable to us. Yet this defensive acceptance is limiting for lovers, because it precludes a creative entanglement in each other's lives. It is as if the dread of being used or overmastered is so strong in the culture that all prosthetic relationships seem tyrannical rather than symbiotic. The result is like the psychic freeze of the fairy-tale curse.

In this larger context Las Vegas dramatizes romance as a cultural anaesthetic. Rather than face social death in Los Angeles, the stunned executive escapes to Las Vegas, where he destroys himself playing the princely role that failed in Los Angeles. Las Vegas evokes the false merriment of those Nazi officers' orgies that Schindler services. Ben too is doomed, and for his partying he hires an abused prostitute who is at the same abject dead end as the Jews in Schindler's "escort service." Like Amon Goeth and his Jewish housekeeper, Ben has before him the life-and-death options of love and the phony immortality symbol of glitzy loot. Being too sensitive, Ben chooses a "sad" and vaguely noble suicide.

What keeps audiences from finding this death merely sick or absurd is the trope of a cultural crash. Presumably, Ben succumbs to a soulless world whose odds, like those of the casinos, are impossibly stacked. In the spectral city, money has corrupted marriage and betrayed posterity, even though polluted romance gives the city a treacherous allure. Sera acts to restore honest feeling but is defeated by the pull of death. The traumatic loss of family love has "understandably" broken Ben's will to struggle against the odds. Otherwise his death could strike us as monstrously selfish or demented, and Sera's tolerance as warped complicity. Yet the cultural crash in the film is a construction, an interpretation. As used here, it directs our attention to global grievances, away from more-immediate puzzles. If Ben chose Las Vegas so he could die in a blaze of princely self-aggrandizement, this childish compensation might make his pact with Sera less poignant than pathetic.

It seems to me that *Leaving Las Vegas* tries to be brutally honest about Ben's limits while also denying them. For example, the film consistently euphemizes Ben's alcoholism. Every time Nicholas Cage picks up a bottle, he makes drinking an endearingly clumsy comic shtick. And Ben's Falstaffian consumption seems as improbably excessive as his physical deterioration seems understated. More crucially, the film is of two minds about his anger and his failure. We never learn why his marriage ended. It makes a difference if he was betrayed, as his fantasies suggest, or if he mistreated his family. It is easy to overlook his arrogance. When the young woman in the neighborhood Las Vegas bar flirts with Ben to inflame her boyfriend's jealousy, for instance, Ben stands up to the "brute." That he humorously and only halfheartedly plays the southern gentleman defending the belle's honor disguises his impulse to play the movie hero who would usually dominate with his fists. The bottled-up rage finally erupts during an otherwise romantic evening with Sera at the gaming table, when Ben suddenly goes berserk and must be subdued.

But this is only Ben's manifest rage. More sinister is the pattern of misogyny and homosexual entanglement in Ben's fantasies about anal rape and domination. In her opening pitch to him as a hooker, Sera offers him sex "up the ass" for the price he is willing to pay. As lovers, he later gives her an earring and tells her "You'll be able to feel it sharp and hot in your ear as one of the brothers pushes your face down into one of the penthouse pillows." He apparently imagines an abusive male sodomizing Sera, anticipating the anal gang rape she actually suffers at the hands of the vicious young athletes who hire her to initiate their frigid buddy.

These allusions to anal sex dramatize a rage for dominance that became a commonplace public topic in the 1990s. Homosexual prison rape has become a conventional metaphor for the helplessness of low-status males in a ruthlessly organized, soul-annihilating environment. But as a metaphor, homosexual rape resonates profoundly in society. For the aggressor, it symbolizes supremacy of will and escape from death. It is an executive behavior, enacted upon a servile other.[15] Hollywood has made prostitution seem romantic and entertaining by identifying it with the harmless, infantile gratification of oral sex, as in *Pretty Woman*. By contrast, anal sex has come to represent the exploitation and dehumanization of "real" prostitution. Like women divided into angels and whores, prostitution tends to be divided into an acceptable recreational service and a repugnant atrocity.

Ambivalence toward prostitution is nothing new. But in the 1990s, as seen in *Pretty Woman* and *Schindler's List*, it often reflected the fear that the nation was splitting into masterful, elite survivors and prostituted, buggered losers. Ben, the film implies, prefers death by bourbon to the endless prostitution of his talent in Los Angeles. But the film also shows him more than once imagining giving "his" woman to other men to use sexually. In his spiel in the bank, he would "prove that I'm worth something" by licking the blonde teller clean "so that [she] could go away and fuck someone else." The moment shivers with unspoken motives. Possibly Ben is thinking of his wife, who left him for other men after he "cleaned her up." Certainly he is imagining the teller as a whore to be passed on to other men. This is symbolically what happens when he fights with Sera and she leaves. She falls into the clutches of jocks who sodomize and beat her, recording their dominance of her on videotape to prove that they are now initiates in a predatory elite.[16]

To give a woman to other men for them to use can be a submissive, placative gesture by a man cowed by those above him. The gesture expresses not only misogyny and self-hatred, but also a compulsion to appease predatory others and thereby to escape death anxiety. Ben "surrenders" Sera as he seems to have given up his wife. In this respect, the behavior is one more symptom of Ben's "giving up" and abnegation: one more sign that death is preferable to the post-traumatic world.

Read from another direction, however, Ben's behavior puts him in the position of a pimp "cleaning up" and training "his" woman to turn tricks for johns—such as Yuri, who uses Sera to try to pay off the Los Angeles gangsters threatening him. In this master-slave fantasy, anal sex also symbolizes a predatory prosthetic relationship. Breaking the "slave"'s will, the pimp becomes an executive self commanding other bodies—as in vampirism and the Nazi economy. Yuri "brands" Sera with knife-cuts on her buttocks as "punishment," terrifying her and then weeping in the classic pattern of abusers, epitomizing one form of traumatic romance. From this perspective, Yuri's situation is a grotesque variant of Ben's. No longer able to manage those (literally) under and above him, he too is a failing low-level executive in flight from Los Angeles and now, fatally demoralized, facing death. Ben can appear sympathetic to us because he subliminally resembles the pimp, but with his rage directed more against himself than against others. To clinch our sympathy, the analogy makes the Los Angeles hit men stalking Yuri stark examples of the cutthroat business that has implicitly broken Ben in Los Angeles and will soon kill him.

And Sera? A romantic reading can envision her as a devoted mate whose love is unrequited. To all appearances, Sera has suffered more abuse than Ben has, and she keeps returning to her abusers. How does she manage to survive and find therapy in the end?

In *Mighty Aphrodite* (1995), Woody Allen has his lovable prostitute say: "You know why I liked you right from the start? Because I'm always attracted to losers." She adds: "Yeah, you've got no confidence, it's sweet. I like that in a man. I can't stand these johns who come in here and . . . whip out a big dick and wave it all over the joint." The impotent Ben is a solution to Sera's justifiable terror of men. Whereas Yuri has been mechanically assaultive as a lover—a bully like Gaston or Philip Stuckey—Ben is boyish and apparently harmless. Sera acts out the familiar role of abuse victim, as seen in Joseph Ruben's *Sleeping with the Enemy* (1991), where the wife of a dictatorial stockbroker must fake drowning to escape her marriage, only to have her homicidal husband pursue her across the country. The husband's maniacal pursuit is a variation on Gaston's assault on the palace to reclaim Belle, and his rivalry with the prince is caricatured in the little bust of a pharaoh with which he identifies, a sign of his rule over his wife. Curiously, like Sara Waters in *Sleeping with the Enemy*, Sera finds refuge with a "gentle" man named Ben who is involved in theater or Hollywood and does not demand work from her. With Ben, Sera can boast, "I'm my own boss." As she tells her therapist, "I feel like me with Ben."

But Ben is gentle because he has given up on life. Not his nurture but his helplessness gives Sera autonomy and purpose. In an echo of the 1890s, she is a ministering "angel in the house," yet also a beautiful femme fatale who exploits men's weakness. I say this because Sera does abet Ben's suicide. The screenplay insists that she loves him. But the more helpless Ben becomes, the more purposefully heroic she can be.[17] She tries to fill his emptiness with gifts and the roles they imply, and with talk. When he comes home beaten up, she lavishes kisses on his bloody face. In effect, she licks his blood as he licks bourbon from his fantasy lover. In their deathbed love scene, Sera's crooning over him might suggest the gloating of a vampire. "You're so sick, so pale," she murmurs. "See how hard you make me, angel," he croaks with boyish pride. But "angel" now evokes the angel of death, because she could be phoning for emergency medical help. On the soundtrack a minimalist parody of Gregorian chant insinuates religiosity. Sera mounts him and he gasps, "You know I love you." As they reach their long-deferred climax, angelic voices swell on the soundtrack, and afterward Sera hugs him like a corpse until he dies and the undercurrent of misogyny in the screenplay is consummated.

"I accepted him for what he was," Sera tells a therapist in the traumatic aftermath, "and I didn't expect him to change." But of course she does try to change Ben, and she underestimates his rage. But the film supports her conviction that he is a fallen hero. "I loved him," she sums up. "I really loved him." This vow brings Ben's boyishly good-natured face onto the screen in a visual valediction that recognizes his unappreciated heroism. After all, it is Ben's sacrifice that has brought Sera to this therapeutic testimonial to love. In praising their goodness and charity, Roger Ebert concludes that Ben "was her redemption, and when it seems he scorns her gift, she punishes herself" by blundering into the gang rape.[18] But the word *redemption*, with its hints of messianic chivalry, invites another reading: that all along Ben has been a benevolent prosthetic support for her. According to this symbolic logic, when she walks out on him in disgust, she loses her knight, her "angel," her survival magic, and hence suffers the horrendous violation.[19]

"We both realized that we didn't have that much time," Sera tells the therapist, using the mood of cultural crash to explain their behavior. But there are other ways to explore this sense of doom. If death anxiety increases with lost self-esteem, then *Leaving Las Vegas* dramatizes some of the consequences of storylessness. As personalities, the lovers are unusually blank: we know almost nothing about them, and almost never overhear any intimacy. Were it not for romantic sentiment—wherever it comes from—we would be witnessing a traumatic collapse of subjectivity. Nothing outside himself interests Ben. When he becomes slightly animated, he is usually launching a line of movie-industry patter or a parody of bad movie dialogue. Even his drinking is such a pastiche of roles that it is a relief when a concerned and disgusted bartender interrupts one of Ben's wheedling set speeches and snarls, "Don't fuck with me."

But fantasies of injury such as Ben's resonate with wider cultural motives. For middle-class audiences in a time of worrisome economic and social slippage, not to mention family instability, Ben may objectify and afford some control over poisonous anxieties. At a time when sexual roles are in transition and everywhere affected by economic changes, the film offers women a fantasy of greater sexual freedom and autonomy achieved through the bittersweet loss of men— not unlike the ambivalent triumphs at the close of *Sweet Whispers, Brother Rush* and *Uncle Vampire*. In these stories of traumatic romance, women find the only facsimile of intimacy in the therapist's office. If mass-produced romance formulas seem lifeless, then the trope of romantic trauma can be both a structural innovation meant to revive conviction and an expression of the distress caused by narrative exhaustion.[20]

There is another reward system worth noting. In all the films analyzed in this chapter, traumatic romance also rationalizes the behavior and values of the culture's elite. Angelic women rehabilitate sorrowing princes and arbitragers. Ben's collapse explains why successful survivors must be ruthless, even as it gives public recognition to the post-traumatic symptoms they may have incurred themselves in beating others to the top. As in the 1890s, it is a middle-class or professional-class man under downward social pressure who attracts concern. The film excludes from sympathy the damaged nobodies in the mean streets; like the sneaky hooker who snags Ben's wedding ring, they tend to be crass predators. By contrast, Ben's boss expresses pity for a wounded employee that flatters the elite and coopts the angry workers in the audience. Ben is a prince too mild for Machiavelli, an Edward Lewis too kind for the corporate jungle. Instead of challenging the culture—where *has* subjectivity gone? what makes family, sex, and the future appear meaningless?—the film supports the status quo. However intentionally, it sacrifices the ambiguous Ben in ways that draw off the critical energy that for an audience could be the equivalent of Ben's rage and alarm.

In Nicholas Broomfield's BBC documentary *Heidi Fleiss, Hollywood Madam* (1995), Heidi Fleiss describes a sex job that sheds light on *Leaving Las Vegas* and Hollywood's fascination with prostitution. For a forty-thousand-dollar trick, Fleiss provided not only a hooker, but also a running fantasy narrative that she stayed around to improvise. The exorbitant fee was "for me to sit there and make all that stuff up, like: 'Bob, look at her. Aren't her tits beautiful? Isn't she just gorgeous? Isn't, look at her face, look at—she just loves you, there's love in her eyes. Oh look at what a slut she is.' It was a lunatic thing, it was so bizarre, it's hard to keep going for a couple of hours."

In this threesome, Heidi Fleiss was hired to be a prosthetic voice, interpreting imaginary sexual experiences to her client, verbalizing fantasies he was "impotent" to invent. She was hired to reinvigorate an "exhausted" script in which a nurturant hooker ("Aren't her tits beautiful?") worships the lordly client. The prosthetic role makes sense as an effort to convert commodified sex into intimacy for a jaded client who could buy anything. But Heidi Fleiss was also being paid to allow him to rediscover his desires; she provided focus and substance to someone overwhelmed by consumer possibilities and deceptive surfaces. In this moment of willed regression she externalized his voice, and he talked to himself through her, rather as a child talks out loud to himself in the voice that eventually—at school age, for example—becomes internalized subjectivity. The need to hire a compensatory voice suggests that the client felt numbed or overwhelmed—or insufficiently aggrandized—and was trying to become more "real." This psychic deficiency implies stress that the client may have experienced as injury: the basis for a sense of personal or cultural trauma.

Even more than the other romances in this chapter, *Leaving Las Vegas* eerily echoes turn-of-the-century fantasies surrounding women's emancipation and the story of overstrained manhood that Gail Bederman unfolds in *Manliness and Civilization*. In spirit, Ben's exhausted saturnalia has much in common with Sherlock Holmes's drugged fiddling on the edge of death. Unlike the Disney prince, who has an expedient mob of villagers to subdue, Ben faces the 1990s American dilemma of storylessness. He has no one to hate, no scapegoat who can carry off his guilt and rage. His boss is a soulful father who can finesse him into social oblivion with velvet management skills. The screenplay's gangsters conveniently dispatch the post-Soviet immigrant Yuri like the last figment of the Cold War. That leaves Ben to confront his own past failures, wounded narcissism, and careless rage. In this ragged moment of historical transition Ben acts out the disenchantment and despair that has always been the undersong of American ingenuity and triumph. That we feel for him says little in itself, because the question is, as always, where we go from here.

ELEVEN

Berserk in Babylon

[The] sense of absurd evil radiated outward from the actual killing
and dying, and . . . every American in Vietnam shared in some of
the corruption of that environment.

Robert J. Lifton, *Home from the War*

No one can be certain why combat trauma immobilizes one soldier and
launches another into a murderous frenzy. Self-protectively, we assume that a
freeze response in the face of death is more logical than a "senseless" rampage.
But "when a soldier is trapped, surrounded, or overrun and facing certain death,
the berserk state has apparent survival value, because he apparently has nothing
to lose and everything to gain from reckless frenzy."[1] Berserking is rooted in evolutionary physiology and conditioned by ancient cultural convictions that give
it a powerful, if often perverse, cogency. To go "baresark" or "bare shirt" is to
shed your armor and all other prosthetic supports and be possessed by a godlike
or beastlike fury.[2] "Going into" that frenzy, "going out" of his vulnerable mind,
the berserker gains access to extraordinary power through central-nervous-
system flooding and its psychic analogue, the intoxicating ideation of rage. The
killing frenzy can be related to ancient ideas of restoring order or "getting even"
through revenge, of mystically replenishing life through death—what Ernest
Becker in *Escape from Evil* calls a "death potlatch"[3]—and of annihilating death
itself through superhuman fury. In such fantasies creaturely compulsion (biting

289

aggression) and stress psychology (mania) come together with warrior culture. In Corinthians and in Handel's *Messiah*, the sublime battle cry promises that death will be "swallowed up in victory."

The trope of swallowing death—of devouring the devourer—unfolds toward ultimate cognitive frames such as the apocalypse, in which the conviction of godlike power can be given cosmic finality. But death is the ultimate loss of everything, forever, and its terror and fascination are potentially limitless, so millennial closure paradoxically promises to substantiate as well as to obliterate the self and its maddeningly volatile experience. The trope of swallowing death illustrates the striking correlation between central-nervous-system physiology and interpretive themes, because the abandonment of restraints crosses modalities. Soldiers gone amok report feeling a sense of godlike invulnerability, and in some cases they literally cannibalize a fallen enemy.

Off the battlefield, the dynamics of berserking appear in a range of behaviors from football hooliganism to "crimes of passion," from rampages in the workplace to the Long Island Railroad commuter massacre in December 1993. Cross-cultural evidence shows the berserk state to be culturally conditioned. In Indonesia, for example, the syndrome of running amok "essentially disappeared" when the Dutch colonial administration insisted that berserkers no longer be killed but rather taken into custody and sentenced to a lifetime of penal servitude.[4] After a string of workplace rampages in the 1980s and 1990s, the berserk United States postal worker became a popular symbol of post-traumatic job stress. In an era of "lean and mean" demands for total self-reliance, the practice of downsizing exposed employees to social death. Not surprisingly, management techniques in the 1990s increasingly emphasized ways to defuse the potential for violent retaliation when "cutting loose" an employee. In a cartoon published in the *New Yorker*, one executive says to another "We've got to get rid of some people, Cosgrove. Who are the least likely to come back and shoot us?"[5]

Berserking is charged with ambiguity because it may denote both chaotic madness and exemplary valor. Combat frenzy is often indiscriminately murderous, and if the berserker survives, the psychic damage may be permanent. Although Joseph Campbell defines the archetypal hero as a figure of "self-achieved submission,"[6] cultures the world over celebrate heroes for their daring and excess. Superman literalizes the aura of transcendence attached to the hero. When Clark Kent ducks into a telephone booth to put on the Superman cape, he dramatizes a psychic change similar to the onset of the berserk state. He crosses a threshold of arousal like the ancient hero swearing an oath and donning his armor. In the Indian film *God Is My Witness* (1992), directed by Mukul Anand, the contemporary Afghan hero must avenge the murder of his beloved's father in order to win her hand. He journeys into India on horseback and finally slays the killer after taking on with his sword a whole police garrison and an army of thugs. Although the film never uses the term, the father's murder functions as a trauma to be resolved through culturally sanctioned, "honorable" violence. In effect, the hero's undertaking is a codified form of berserking: frenzied vengeance organized through the rhetoric of heroic destiny, divine witness, and a sacramental family alliance. As propaganda, the film has the Afghan hero submit to the Indian justice system and to prison, but only after swearing a consoling pact of blood brotherhood with the chief police officer.

In many post-Vietnam Hollywood films, trauma resembles the traditional code of honor in authorizing do-or-die vengeance. This is the premise of Ted Kotcheff's *First Blood* (1982), in which Sylvester Stallone's John Rambo, "a vet with post-Vietnam shock[, acts] out the nihilistic rage of the forgotten man, among other things wasting a local police force contemptuous of war-torn vets."[7] Among Rambo's counterparts are the "everyman" vigilantes in revenge thrillers such as Michael Winner's *Death Wish* (1974) and Joel Schumacher's *Falling Down* (1993). The films renew the *fin de siècle* dread that civilization has sapped "manliness," suggesting that purgative violence can free the "pitiful, helpless giant" from its crippling inhibitions.

When the hero of *God Is My Witness* overleaps conventional boundaries, the meaning of his mayhem is never in doubt. In post-traumatic films, by comparison, the familiar distinctions blur. Even when the films glorify berserking as heroic daring, they insinuate its pathological character, sometimes with a thrilling ambivalence. Like Holmes's drug-addicted brilliance, berserking objectifies our fascination with illicit power. Behind the romantic injury of the hero lies the idea of the devil's pact. A good deal of the public complaint about Hollywood's sleaze seems derived from an anxiety that the industry weakens cultural restraints by flirting with the idea of berserk violence as a form of the devil's pact, even though that anxiety is an invigorating tonic and in demand at the box office. The hero's injury is symbolically the price—or sop—paid to justify his excess and to forestall the spectator's fear, envy, and condemnation.

As tropes, berserking and the idea of a cultural crash are closely related. If autonomy is scarce and the social order is in chaos, then survival is a violent gamble. This is a post-Vietnam mentality, shaped in no small measure by the peculiar atmosphere of the Reagan years, in which rhapsodies about prosperity mixed with paranoia about apocalyptic (nuclear) evil. In those years the nation threw off regulatory restraints and became intoxicated with gambling, lotteries, and the entrepreneurial speculation that exploded in the savings-and-loan scandals, which were a nuclear bomb compared to earlier bubbles. The wagering fever influenced the stock-market boom of the mid-1990s.[8] That mania also revealed an attitude toward identity, projecting a bravura ethos that held that only violent self-assertion pays off in an unstable world.

American slang is rich in terms that evoke the overthrow of inhibition and the dynamic limitlessness of trauma—expressions such as to "flip out" or "go off the deep end," or synonyms for being killed such as to be "wasted" or "blown away," to name only a few. In a culture that casually encourages people to "go for it," calls social fun a "blast," and honors "cutthroat" competition, we should expect ideology to favor the heroic violation of restraints and efforts at self-transcendence. In a wide range of public fantasies, from consumer plenty to cyberhype, Americans still believe that "the sky's the limit." The ancient Romans were awed by "the spirit of the gladiator," for it signified being "'without hope or fear,' i.e., fierce, unstoppable, irresistible."[9] Living beyond hope and despair, the gladiator killed or died unconquered—though he was sure to die. His fury responded to a sense of doom that was shared with—and that provided pleasure and edification for—the spectators. By contrast, the Vietnam War increasingly came to dramatize demoralizing limits. Yet the fascination with post-traumatic stress after the war reflected a great ambivalence about the historical moment, heightening our awareness of victimization but also, in the trope of berserking, giving new forms to the nation's venerable faith in raw power and deliverance.

Although my argument is centrally concerned with combat berserking, it gives only passing attention to the experience of Vietnam veterans because that subject is vast and much enlightening work on it already exists. A full-scale investigation of berserking might explore the popularity since the 1980s of the image of a "feeding frenzy," or analyze the media fascination with the self-aggrandizing "bad-boy" nihilism of the inner city and the predatory frenzy of youth gangs that has been dubbed "wilding." But the present chapter, alas, cannot throw off all constraints, and so I examine only a small number of films and novels in which berserking is a structural principle with implications all the more compelling for being routinely overlooked: for example, depictions of business aggression, gambling, and drug dealing. In Western culture, the ultimate berserk state is the apocalypse, the cosmic rampage of the Antichrist or "the beast"—kin to Saint George's dragon. The final chapter explores the link between berserking and millennial themes in futuristic movies such as Terry Gilliam's *Twelve Monkeys* (1995).

Berserk in the Culture of War

The Vietnam War divided America, sabotaged trust in the government, gutted social programs, and destabilized the economy. Yet the war was also simply another face of the culture back home. In Vietnam, for instance, the United States Army began to collapse under minimal pressure in part because the military command had been reorganized on the lines of corporate industrial management.[10] By the standards of World War II, the officer corps was top-heavy with beribboned rear-echelon executives. Instead of preparing men to face death and sharing their risks, the senior officers worked in air-conditioned offices, removed from the fighting. So many officers depended on experience in Vietnam for career advancement that their tours of duty had to be cut in half to fit them all in—which also abbreviated their contact with the soldiers serving under them. Feeling betrayed, some of those soldiers retaliated by killing officers. As the war dragged on, its justification becoming increasingly muddled and deceptive, "fragging" (assassination using fragmentation grenades) in the army became part of a class war with tragic roots in American society.[11]

The great strength of Jonathan Shay's study is his recognition that trauma is a psychocultural process. Specifically, he conceives of it as a form of abuse: "Bad leadership is a cause of combat trauma" (AV 196), because it destroys a soldier's faith in the culture that defines and sustains him. Shay uses the Greek word *thèmis* to refer to the integrity of a culture because it takes in "the whole sweep of a culture's definition of right and wrong," whereas "we use terms such as moral order, convention, normative expectations, ethics, and commonly understood social values. . . . A word of this scope is needed for the betrayals experienced by Vietnam combat veterans" (AV 5). Betrayal destroys our faith in our world—in *thèmis*—and thus damages the ground of the self, magnifying the terror of death, which reciprocally magnifies the sense of betrayal and evil. Because identity is a prosthetic construction, the self and its world disintegrate together. To lose faith in your culture is not simply to miss moral values or other content but to be stripped of a formative, prosthetic support for identity; this is a form of nakedness that can be taken as a precondition for a symptomatic immobility or the naked rage of berserking.

As an assault on psychic integrity, betrayal opens directly into the wider ambiguities of trauma in the culture. Like the Germans after World War I, many Americans felt betrayed after the Vietnam War. But with varying degrees of realism and in contradictory combinations they blamed officers, politicians, antiwar protesters, and apathetic citizens. Just as people construe death as the personal malevolence of some agent or other, so the abstractions and complexities of scale invite convictions of betrayal that may or may not be justified. This is why Shay's account of the existential position of the combat soldier is so compelling. In his trenchant phrase, "combat is a condition of captivity and enslavement" (AV 35).

> For soldiers in prolonged combat, war is the mutual struggle to paralyze or control the will of enemy soldiers by inflicting wounds and death and creating the ter-

ror of these. . . . The domination that a soldier seeks over his enemy is as total as the domination a master has over a slave, aiming for fear to so completely grip the enemy that he flees in panic, surrenders, or is too terrified to move, let alone resist. . . .

The struggle to dominate the will, however, is reciprocal. All the tools of physical warfare can be understood as attempts to create in the enemy the broken mental state of a slave. . . . The enemy's attempts to dominate the soldier's will are invariably met by counterdomination by his own side. The mind, the heart, the soul of the combat soldier become the focus of competing attempts to enslave. (AV 36)[12]

If you believe in your cause, you are heroic, even if you have been sacrificed. Lose that trust and you become a slave, and the idea of slavery as social death takes on a terrifying new meaning:

If a soldier flees the terror of the battle, it makes no difference in which direction he flees. He flees toward death or imprisonment no matter which direction he takes. If he flees toward the enemy he may be shot out of hand . . . or he may be imprisoned as a POW. If he flees toward his own rear, he may be summarily shot or imprisoned as a deserter. The front line is thus a narrow zone of fear and death lying between two prisons. In this narrow zone two massive social organizations compete to enslave the soldier. . . . Terror, mortal dependency, barriers to escape— these are characteristics of modern combat that mark it as a condition of captivity and enslavement as harsh as any political prison or labor camp. (AV 36–37)

Shay reads from the battlefield back to society, but the lens can be reversed. Military strategy in Vietnam called for industrial-scale firepower to obliterate the primitive Vietnamese enemy. For those in executive or support positions, the war could be a corporate campaign, with production targets to meet, input measured in Pentagon requests to Congress, and output measured in body counts. The officers managed personnel through industrial regimentation, and deployed "psywar" tactics derived from industrial psychology. Like assembly-line workers, soldiers were trained to run machines designed to maximize killing and minimize risk. In reality, the industrial might—all the bomb tonnage, firepower, poisonous defoliants, and filing cabinets—failed to break the enemy's will, and combat soldiers lived on the boundary between social death and physical annihilation. If you want to stop the war, they joked, shut off the air conditioning. The joke sees the machinery of prosperity (air conditioning) sheltering elite "rear-echelon motherfuckers" for whom the war meant career advancement and heroic status while also being "just a job," albeit a comfortable job. The casualty rates among officers were substantially lower than those in World War II.

For those at the top, the scope of executive command implied the Sherlock Holmes dream of encyclopedic omnicompetence. For the "Small" soldier sacrificed in the revolutionary cross fire of an alien client country, the army was like the factory universe Havelock Ellis envisioned, only more lethal. Just as India and England interpenetrate in Holmes's post-traumatic London, so Vietnam and the United States were and are enfolded. Ellis felt like a homeless orphan, but the adults and children who toiled in factories were not far removed from literal slavery in their fight for survival.[13] Conan Doyle disguises the berserk potential of those "Small" worker-soldiers by splitting them off in the Sikh (compare Vietcong) rebellion and in Tonga's childlike murderousness. London resembles a war zone as Holmes musters "his" street Arabs like native mercenaries and defeats Small-Tonga in a skirmish on the Thames.

The same concerns turned up in post-traumatic culture in the 1990s. *Schindler's List* shudders with displaced anxiety about an economy based on coercion and betrayal, in which "redundancy" or inefficiency on the job spells social death. *Roger and Me* records the sacrifice by General Motors of expendable worker-soldiers. In Flint, Michigan, this downsizing (or making Small) led to berserking in the form of the highest crime rate in the country. The film includes television news footage of police sharpshooters wounding an unemployed man who wore a Superman cape and carried a rifle in the streets. Like the paramilitary police, troops, and company goons who have killed other unemployed or striking workers, as at Ford's Rouge plant or Republic Steel during the Great Depression, the Flint police imposed military discipline on an economic battlefield.

Entangled fantasies of productivity and sacrificial killing power are made literal in America's military-industrial complex. Even as it has enriched the financial and technological elites, it has continually bled resources from social programs. Washington starved Great Society programs to pay for the Vietnam War in the 1970s. Reinflating the country's self-esteem after the defeat in Vietnam, President Reagan "hardened" the nation by cutting programs for those on the bottom and undertaking a trillion-dollar military buildup.[14] By 1995-96, the same year that Congress abolished federal welfare guarantees for the poor, the nation still had a wartime military budget but no enemies, the Pentagon spent five million dollars for a third golf course at Andrews Air Force Base,[15] and the same corporate military that had sent faulty M-16 rifles to Vietnam had spent some one hundred billion dollars on unworkable missile defenses projected to ward off ultimate nuclear annihilation.[16]

Military-industrial culture is expansive and powerful, and it creates symbolic potency and well-being for many Americans, especially those at the top. But that conviction of potency depends on the use of scapegoats to purge anger and guilty dread. Although the paranoia and baffled rage of the Reagan years began to look bizarre as the feebleness of our supposed enemies came to light in the 1990s, the nation was still obsessed with those demons, "waging war" on crime (but not poverty), drug "lords," welfare "abusers," and "international terrorism." As a trope, trauma grows prominent when the demand for sacrificial victims is so strong in our culture—and in us—that it threatens to consume not only "proper" scapegoats but some of us as well. This probably contributed to the emergence of traumatic abuse as a trope during the 1980s, when "supply-side" ideology was used to justify ever-increasing sacrificial cuts for those at the bottom; in media imagery President Reagan wielded a menacing budget-cutting sword or battle-ax, even as he promoted nuclear weapons and warned that the ultimate cut, Judgment Day, was nigh. As Lloyd deMause points out in his survey of media imagery, "those sacrificed were often seen as small as children."[17]

No one better articulated the unconscious premise of sacrificial killing than President Reagan. In directing the country's rage outward at hapless Nicaragua, for example, he sounded the theme of holy war. As the New Republic reported, "he thrilled his audience with the tale of a man who said that 'I would rather see my little girls die now, still believing in God, than have them grow up under Communism.'"[18] The threat to kill one's own children rather than let them live with (and worship) a "false," rival father makes the children implicitly soldiers to be killed if they refuse to fight the enemy to the death.

Growing up in a family and a generation disturbed by such infanticidal ideation, a child may well come to adulthood susceptible to the numbness or rage associated with trauma. President Reagan's apocryphal father expresses the instability of prosthetic conversion—that your parents may nurture you or kill you. The threat of conversion is a function of the father's projection: he attributes to the Communists the evil he fears in himself, and his little girls are caught in the middle. President Reagan often sounded exactly like his Communist and Islamic fundamentalist enemies, as in his vilification of the Soviet Union as the satanic "evil empire" and Muammar Qaddafi as a "mad dog."[19] Insofar as he spoke for America, Reagan unconsciously projected a family that could be troubling for children. To be sure, the sacrificial fantasy can be spellbinding. As long as the focus remains on the family's superiority over the Communists, the children are exalted soldiers of Christ, free of guilt, deathless in faith. But should that warlike spirit falter, the children become scapegoats, as doomed as the enemy— and as susceptible to paranoid rage as Rambo.[20]

When economic policies enrich those at the top by driving down wages and living standards, workers feel trapped and betrayed. And like soldiers, they may experience unrestrained rage. As in war, in communities such as Detroit and Los Angeles the most sensational reaction has been berserking: not only individual and gang rampages but also full-scale urban riots that have drawn a paramilitary response from the government and turned the streets into a battlefield. The rioters lash out like soldiers gone amok, and the authorities represent both the enemy and their own restraining, punishing officers. In John Singleton's

Boyz N the Hood (1991), the police helicopters patrolling the Los Angeles ghetto evoke Vietnam War gunships; this is not surprising, because in both zones the strategy favored cybernetic remote control over a more expensive and morally committed investment in personnel. In an era of tax revolts, Los Angeles economized on its police budget by favoring small, highly mobile tactical units— similar to the gunship-borne troops in Vietnam—that proved inadequate for such a large city.[21] Singleton's film shows young people in the ghetto caught between an alien, militarized government and local gang violence that resembles guerilla warfare. Like disaffected conscripts, they feel trapped and betrayed on all sides, and they are prone to rampage.

Which brings us back to the core ambiguity of berserking as a trope: is it ruinous or heroic? Although the clinician Jonathan Shay sees it as a pathology, he recognizes its vicious ambiguity: "The folk culture of the American military, especially during the Vietnam War, merged fighting spirit with being berserk. Leadership beliefs encouraged the conversion of grief into berserk rage as a militarily desirable consequence" (AV 200). But the problem is more fundamental than that. Soldiers may be victims. Yet we would do well to remember that some of them signed up to fight in Vietnam partly to share in a promise of glory (and reward) to be achieved by sacrificing the enemy. Their berserking can be understood not simply as a *reaction* to grief and terror but also as the *actualization* of rage latent in fantasy from the day of recruitment, or even from childhood.[22] This is why the massacre of innocents at My Lai is no less a cultural tragedy than atrocities in the inner city.

And this is why equivocation in Hollywood and the media toward berserking is unsettling. In the 1990s, for example, American culture developed the nihilism of urban youth as a familiar trope, in gangsta rap, in films such as Larry Clark's *Kids* (1995) and Spike Lee's *Clockers* (1995), and in the media fascination with gang violence. Even as the trope imagines that violent young people are beyond caring, it turns hair-trigger, "transcendent" rage into a role in a repertory of familiarized roles. It defines urban young people (as "bad boys," for example), magnifying their bravado and ignoring their actual complexities. In casting them as contemporary versions of Tonga, the trope expresses hostility toward the young, which hostility acquired new bite in the 1960s and a new legitimacy from the conservative right's attacks on social programs during the Reagan years.

Hollywood routinely equivocates about berserking, often construing it as a form of conversion experience—a fantasy of a new identity achieved by bursting inhibitions. In vigilante movies such as *Death Wish*, berserking stands for the recovery of manhood. The "Final Girl" horror films, beginning with *Halloween* (1978), imply that an initiation into annihilating ferocity gives women survival magic and helps them expand an otherwise constricted identity.[23] Such scenarios can be related to news stories and television docudramas about the woman who finally murders her abusive husband in a blind fury and at once frees herself and her self. Even in a secular culture conversion experiences often use religious forms such as the imagery of purification and rebirth.[24] Whether tragic or redemptive, the berserk state has always evoked rapture and possession. But religious transcendence is only one paradigm. Another, much favored at the turn of the century, envisions conversion as a return to nature and the recuperation of stifled instinct.

Instinctively Amok

I have described Ben's fatal drinking in *Leaving Las Vegas* as a form of berserk violence directed against himself. In a satiric comedy that echoes *Leaving Las Vegas* in many ways, but turns its berserking inside out—Mike Nichols's *Wolf* (1994)—another entertainment-industry executive loses his job and his wife and goes on a rampage, solaced by a rebellious and beautiful young woman.

Driving to see a client in Vermont, a Manhattan book editor named Will Randall hits a wolf on a dark, snowy back road. When he gets out of his car to investigate, the wolf bites him. As the days go by, the middle-aged editor begins to turn into a wolf, acquiring a superhuman wolf sensorium—including an uncanny sense of smell that allows him to detect closet alcoholics and his own wife's infidelity with his archrival in the publishing firm. Put out of his job as senior editor by an impending merger and a ruthless younger rival named Stewart Swinton, Randall retaliates with wolfish daring. Discovering Swinton's treachery in the firm and with his wife, Charlotte, he wins his job back, routs his rival, and cuts his ties to Charlotte. In confronting Swinton about Charlotte, Randall bites Swinton's hand, unwittingly spreading the wolfishness. Before long he has become lovers with the boss's headstrong daughter, Laura. The moon, however, has begun to turn Randall into a ferocious predator, and one night at his boss's estate he brings down a deer. The next night, near the Bronx Zoo, he is accosted by predatory muggers and bites off several of their fingers. By day, he is terrified of his new capacity for violence, and Laura begins handcuffing him overnight. Soon Charlotte is found dead in Central Park, and the police suspect Randall. The murderer is Swinton, as Laura realizes, and in a climactic struggle Randall kills Swinton to save her from him. The film closes with Randall gone back to nature and Laura, her senses suddenly growing keen, about to follow him.

Disney wolves signify mob appetite, far removed from aristocratic individualism. In *Wolf*, by contrast, wolves are individuals turned predatory by a savagely competitive civilization whose business culture is in truth the Social Darwinist's jungle. Its gentility masks the howling wilderness of wolves that Shakespeare's dying Henry IV fears will be England's destiny.[25] The wolf bite symbolizes the traumatic violence of business competition, and the werewolf transformation eloquently dramatizes the berserk state. And as Canetti, Becker, and others might have predicted,[26] the film shows the bite to be contagious. Once bitten, victims experience an "illness" whose outcome is feral disinhibition. They in turn bite others, producing a shadow world of anarchic predation. Whereas the Disney ideology polarizes the heroic individual and the wolfish mob, *Wolf* understands wolfishness to be the survival mania of anarchic individualism— hence its aptness for a decade in which libertarian and free-market ideologies frequently euphemized a dog-eat-dog Social Darwinism.

Wolf makes clear American ambivalence about berserking in the 1990s. The wolf has traditionally been an emblem of death and immortality.[27] We fear the wolf at the door, and we fear diseases such as lupus, named after the wolf. But the animal is also a totem figure, as celebrated in Kevin Costner's *Dances with Wolves* (1990), for example. And in the frenzy of the berserk state, wolfishness brings a sense of invulnerability, a self-intoxicating belief in the power of instinct to overcome all adversaries. Jack Nicholson plays Will Randall as a weary, middle-aged gentleman rejuvenated by the wolf bite. After some unaccustomed lovemaking, his wife praises his sexual potency by playfully panting, "You animal." Sought out for advice about Randall's transformation, the ethnologist Dr. Vijay Alezius confides that he is himself dying of cancer, and begs Randall to confer immortality by biting him.

And yet wolfish immortality is grounded in aggression. The werewolf fantasy makes clear the principle that the power to inflict death on others lessens one's own death anxiety. It is no accident that Nazi iconography favored the wolf as a totem figure. Shakespeare and the Victorians dreaded the irresistible momentum of disinhibition. Conan Doyle imagines the impulsive Tonga as humankind devolving toward an animal-child, which is the destination as well of Jekyll-as-Hyde and Dracula's bitten "creatures." As Dr. Alezius tells Randall, the wolf itself is neutral: the effect of its bite reflects the character of the victim.

But the film's wolfishness is derived from a particular form of 1990s post-traumatic culture. Randall's boss, Raymond Alden, is a cynical, unredeemed financier—an Edward Lewis whose pretty woman is a beautiful daughter who rejects him and his ruthlessness. At Alden's mansion on the evening when Randall is about to be forced out of his job, the guests wring their hands about the fate of the rain forests, and when Will Randall defines the situation as a cultural crash: "You could make the case that the world has already ended, is dead. We're exhausted. Instead of art we have pop culture and TV." His particular diagnosis fastens on storylessness, which is the "exhaustion" of desire or—to pick up the pun on his name—of "will." The publisher shows some interest in Eastern Europe, so we know this is the post-Soviet world, with Cold War aggression now devolving toward intramural struggles.

Wolf defines its cultural crash in the familiar way, as an unchecked obsession with rapacity. In sacking Randall, Raymond Alden concludes, "You're a nice person, Will. Thank God I replaced you." At a time of collapsing civility, Randall's "taste and individuality" are "drawbacks." But whereas Disney's *Beauty and the Beast* links a cultural crash to unfettered mob values, *Wolf* imagines the mob galvanized and even created by the corporate manipulation of mass markets. The mean streets spawn the muggers in Central Park, but business brutality created the means streets in the first place. From this perspective, storylessness is primarily a by-product of corporate capitalism's mania for monolithic control and immoderate profit. A Raymond Alden may praise the free market and heroic initiative, but he behaves with dictatorial rigidity.

The film defines its lovers by their shared contempt for business mania, but also—in an echo of *Leaving Las Vegas*—by their willingness to acknowledge the taboo of death anxiety that drives business. When Randall confides, "I don't have the courage to be jobless at my age," Laura challenges his fears: "Old guy, huh?" She shows him the lakeside spot where as a child she used to bury her pets and where she realized that one day she would die. Like their determined candor, their willingness to be open about death defines their special bond. Laura's courage enables her to open Randall to his own inhibited will, just as she is able to pick the lock on the handcuffs he has brought back to his hotel from a midnight scrape with the police. The film uses the handcuffs playfully to dramatize the lovers' willingness to spend the night together despite Randall's dangerous wolfishness. The threat of berserking makes Laura's control over Randall meaningful as well as gratifying, and enables the screenplay to dramatize her generosity and courage.

By contrast, business culture subsumes sexuality. The backstabbing Stewart Swinton steals not only Randall's job but also his wife. When confronted, Swinton keeps crooning "I love you, Bill." But the tag quickly begins to suggest a homosexual subtext of competitive domination, and when Swinton tries to rape Laura during his rampage at the Alden estate, he mounts her from behind, as if sodomizing and, in Hollywood's vocabulary, subjugating her. The affectionate stage "business" of the handcuffs counteracts the unwilling bondage of business.

As a trope for berserking, wolfishness is the logical outcome of a cultural crash. On that deserted Vermont road, civilization runs down nature, and the wolfish contagion is nature's revenge. The trope acts out the guilt Rank and Becker tell us to look for in humankind: the expectation of punishment latent in much pop environmentalism and apocalypticism. This is the latest form of the Victorian farmers' conviction that railroads deform livestock and blight crops. But in the 1990s, the trope bore complex layers of other meanings too.

If we read the film inside out, *Wolf* introduces the idea of a cultural crash as a fantasy therapy for a culture suffocated by obsessive control and a closed-off future. If you are Will Randall, a good servant of the firm on your way to beg a client for a contract, a collision with nature can be revitalizing. As they are in movies about cruel pimps and tough, vulnerable hookers, fantasies of a cultural crash can be exciting for women as well. Laura's command of the handcuffs in her love play with the volatile Randall is a calculated stimulant. A little peril makes the self seem more substantial—more "real"—even outside the movie theater. At the same time, the handcuffs outfit an enabling fantasy for women in a society—and in a world audience—growing more aware of inequality and violence between the sexes.

As a trope, the screenplay's wolf falsifies nature even as it offers satiric leverage on a cultural dilemma. Real wolves are social animals, with control mechanisms that allow individuals to fight for status without killing each other. In evolutionary terms, the most successful wolf is not the adult wolf famed for its predatory cunning, but its neotenic cousin, the dog. Like Randall's protégé in the firm, the dog is "a polished ass-kisser" but also a comfortable citizen of civilization, bound to humans by a web of prosthetic relationships that favor its childlike, care-soliciting status and willingness to serve. But like its masters, the dog must be able to figure out the hierarchy in order to flourish. And the 1990s were arguably no less ambivalent about neoteny than H. G. Wells was.

Wolf ends ambiguously, with Randall fleeing the carnage at the estate, presumably headed back to nature, with Laura not far behind. The ending suggests the sort of back-to-nature daydreams that anxious men relished in Tarzan stories at the start of the century. But there is another possibility to consider as well. In his contagious violence the wolfman is potentially a vampire. Wolf opens as the novel Dracula does, in a dark wilderness of wolves, with a citified businessman on his way to solicit a contract from a remote client. The film, however, never develops anything like Bram Stoker's hierarchical family of predators. For this reason, Wolf was a vision better suited to the libertarian 1990s, in which berserking led individuals out of the congested world into a nature as engulfing as an apocalypse.

Berserking as a Conversion Experience

Like Wolf, Joel Schumacher's Falling Down (1993) is ostensibly about economic trauma. Its protagonist, William Foster (Michael Douglas), is a missile engineer thrown out of work by the end of the Cold War. Caught in a traffic jam in stupefying summer heat, he abandons his car and marches across Los Angeles toward a showdown with his former wife, going progressively more amok as his frustration mounts. A minor dispute with a Korean convenience-store owner provokes him to trash the store with a baseball bat. In self-defense he shoots a Latino gang member. Desperate to get his former wife and his daughter back, he menaces them, drawing the police into his intimate nightmare.

Falling Down is a such a naive assemblage of post-traumatic themes from other movies that it vividly demonstrates how historically peculiar materials may be naturalized. Trapped in his car in the heat, for example, his agitated mouth and eyes in closeup, Foster looks like a hungry predator—a wolf—and beads of sweat show his stress. Like Ben in *Leaving Las Vegas*, he has lost his family and his career, and now moves toward social death in a depersonalizing urban maze. Throughout his rampage he will be known to the police only by his license plate: *D-Fens*.

The name locates Foster and the film historically. As a defense engineer he is only the latest male casualty of the Vietnam debacle. Alienated, misunderstood, a stalwart anticommunist obsessed with his own code of traditional values, he is unexpectedly in the situation of Stallone's Rambo in *First Blood* and the vigilantes in John G. Avildsen's *Joe* (1970) and *Death Wish*. His mission across the asphalt jungle echoes a patrol in Vietnam, but the racial others are now immigrant grocers and gang members armed with automatic weapons, while the military's sadistic streak resonates in the neo-Nazi surplus-store owner who tangles with him. On the phone, threatening his former wife, Foster sounds like a returning veteran: "I'm coming home, Beth."

But twenty years separate *Falling Down* from revenge movies such as *Death Wish* that kept magically undoing the Vietnam War. Roger Ebert catches the post-traumatic difference. Instead of inciting audiences to cheer vigilante violence against drug addicts and rapists, *Falling Down* encourages "viewers . . . to pick up on [Foster's] anomie—his soulsickness that has turned to madness, his bafflement at becoming obsolete and irrelevant."[28] Like Ben, but using his own aerospace vocabulary, Foster feels radically ungrounded, out of touch, like a space capsule "behind the moon," and his deepest motive is suicide.

The cultural crash has predictable features in this Los Angeles, from overcrowding to the decaying infrastructure under repair everywhere. In Foster's car the news buzzes as meaninglessly as the fly that pesters him. The film shows post-traumatic symptoms spread widely among whites and minorities. Foster's adversary is a canny detective (like Holmes), himself shaken by an earlier wound (like Watson) and the loss of his daughter to sudden infant death syndrome. Detective Prendergast is about to retire from the police force—or to quit—but his rescue of Foster's wife and daughter brings out the father in him and gives him the courage to endure. By facing down his own traumatized, hostile wife, he implicitly rescues her as well. Like his alter ego Foster, Prendergast strives to reclaim his lost masculinity, but he does it through heroic rescue rather than through berserk willfulness. It is a mark of the film's argumentative strength and weakness that it can only imagine two modes of adaptation to traumatic stress.

If we read these mirror opposites as two faces of the same personality, the plot shows its hero killing off his rage in order to be a parent again. Yet in truth, this is violence not extinguished but harnessed. Prendergast has suffered an abusive wife and boss, but he is capable of "manly" aggression. When he tells off his wife and yet slugs a malicious fellow officer to defend her dignity, the film argues that he is merely maintaining respect and order. Only Foster's death threats finally provoke Prendergast to kill him, but he does pull the trigger.

Hollywood's equivocation about violence is scarcely news. Wooden as it is, the film's conception of berserking registers tremors felt in many quarters of American culture in the 1990s. Put him in biblical robes and William Foster could be an Old Testament prophet stumping across ancient cities, decrying sin and folly.[29] When his wife pleads that he is sick and needs help, Foster retorts with prophetic conviction that it is society that is sick. The film gives him an ironic righteousness, as when he wreaks vengeance on the gang members and on the homophobic neo-Nazi store owner gloating over his Zyklon B canisters—a horror out of *Schindler's List*. As a prophet, Foster evokes the militant, disaffected religious groups that arose in the 1990s in repudiation of the unholy civil order. Among them were the heavily armed Branch Davidians in Waco, Texas, who withstood a shootout with federal agents before creating a cult of martyrdom through their self-immolation.

Like the religious radicals, Foster repudiates "big government." At a road-repair site in Los Angeles he argues with a worker that there is really nothing broken under the street, only a political contract scam at work. Summing up his career as a government missile engineer, he tells Detective Prendergast "They lied to me." Prendergast amplifies this: "They lie to everybody." This careless rhetoric—"they lie to everybody"—has an apocalyptic sweep. The screenplay contemplates not a nation of some two hundred million people whose leadership is bound to have failings and perversities, but a captive group—"everybody"—deceived by the prince of lies. Having lost control, "the people" feel like helpless, angry children tormented by a callous parent; in their final confrontation, Foster ironically dies while threatening the detective with his child's water pistol.

This regression accords with the pop notion of cracking under pressure. Like Ben in *Leaving Las Vegas*, Foster drops out of society. But we could also look at his behavior another way: as a form of conversion experience dramatized by the berserk state. When identity is stabilized by powerful social and internal inhibitions, and perhaps rigidified by traumatic anxiety, personal change can be difficult, even when stress demands it. Like Will Randall or even the Disney prince, Foster is an idealistic personality trapped in a claustrophobic role; if the prince had no conscience, for example, the curse would have no sting for him. Foster's possessive mother shows the police his monkishly neat room in her house. In Hollywood psychology, the berserk state can be a psychic convulsion—shock therapy, as it were—that permits change. Hollywood often shares pop psychology's faith that letting out anger can be therapeutic. Foster's conversion frees him from his rigid daily grind and patriotic platitudes. Finally he *acts*—but it kills him. Beneath his rigid public persona he is empty, and so in the end, unable to connect with his family, he provokes his own death. In this way the teetotaler Foster shares the mysterious, traumatic loss or impairment of subjectivity that kills Ben in Las Vegas.

Like William Foster, the hero of Michael Apted's 1992 film *Thunderheart* is a government servant, in this instance a young FBI agent named Ray Levoi. Because he is part Sioux, he is sent out by the FBI's Sensitive Operations Unit to the Pine Ridge reservation in South Dakota to solve a murder and to defuse factional strife between the corrupt tribal authority and ARM, the movie's version of AIM, the American Indian Movement. Trauma organizes the film like a strong magnetic current. In the deep background is the historical abuse of Native Americans, and in particular the United States Army's massacre of several hundred Sioux at Wounded Knee Creek in 1890.[30]

The massacre haunts Agent Levoi because his experiences at Pine Ridge precipitate post-traumatic flashbacks. He has intrusive visions of the massacre that express his repressed identification with the Indian victims, and also more-conventional recovered memories of his childhood, when he and his mother watched his Indian father, a construction worker, drink himself to death—not unlike Hollywood's Ben. Through the flashbacks, Ray Levoi rediscovers his childhood and the roots of his Indian identity. By the film's end, FBI Agent Levoi has repudiated the white man's myth system—the civil religion of government—and become the messianic warrior hero Thunderheart. The screenplay invites belief in a mystical notion of racial and cultural identity, reinforcing it with a faith that Levoi's post-traumatic memories of childhood hold the key to his authentic nature.

Levoi's conversion models the purification of Indian culture. By renouncing technological civilization, the film argues, the ARM reformers can get back into nature and live harmoniously in a timeless myth. The Indians' reform program would be a solution to the worldwide, centuries-old problem of modernism. But across the planet, mythic cultures are everywhere in retreat from the apparently irresistible dynamism of skeptical, restless, innovation-hungry Western cultures. For the world's billions to try to recuperate an atavistic way of life would probably be impossible at this stage, or even perverse, as it was during the Khmer Rouge horrors in Cambodia. This is not to disparage such cultures or the dream of regaining mythic composure, but to keep in mind that what sustains the present massive human population is modernism, from the great Victorian public-health projects to the agricultural revolution.

Ray Levoi's transformation can be understood as a cultural process, a conversion experience shaped by an engulfing ideological conflict. The death of a weak, socially disgraced father can leave a child desperately vulnerable. What better compensation than to identify with J. Edgar Hoover's invincible FBI? Assaulting the Indians in the movie, the FBI marches to a complex ideological anthem. As the agent in command puts it, "I feel for them. But they're a conquered people, to be dictated to by the conquerors." This is the unholy dream of victory culture, with its genocidal motto, once the vernacular wisdom of Hollywood Westerns, that "the only good injun is a dead injun." That dream climaxes in the movie's discovery of a government plot to steal Indian lands in order to mine uranium, that archsymbol of exterminating frenzy and Faustian immortality. The movie's federal officers evoke the cavalry at Wounded Knee and *Schindler's List*'s storm troopers. But they also evoke the Vietnam War in their use of helicopters, excessive firepower, and chaotic firefights in civilian neighborhoods—all signs of berserking. In the symbolic logic of the film, the officers are reacting to modern America's cultural crash by running amok among pastoral folk, trying to seize the demonic immortality of nuclear power.

The Indian reformers, by contrast, organize around a return to traditional myth and ecological sensitivity. Their spokesperson is a good-natured old shaman whose gently indulgent sense of humor is ironically modern, not only in its practical accommodation of Rolex watches and ancient wisdom but also in its detachment. The shaman's detachment throws into relief the misleading categories at work everywhere in the film. Insofar as the government and the Indians use ideology or faith to take power in a conflicted situation, they are caught up in similar contradictions. The officers want nuclear power as part of a myth system—a kind of magic in stark contrast to the shaman's benign lore. The government's industrial mentality is as ambiguously premodern as that of the Indians. For their part, the Indians espouse traditional myths but are also inescapably caught up in the ironies and contingencies of modernism, and they see a modern sense of identity as something that can be refashioned or rediscovered. Their discussions overlook their reliance on pickup trucks as well as the cruelties and suffering that were a part of ancient Indian ways.

Practically speaking, the film's enthusiasm for Indian spirituality distracts attention from the real evils besetting Pine Ridge. That torment comes into sharper focus in Michael Apted's 1992 documentary about the violence on the reservation in the early 1970s, *Incident at Oglala*. What the camera recorded was a community riven by exceptionally high rates of poverty and murder—some of the highest in the country. In one interview after another, eyewitnesses describe an atmosphere of despair and terror. In this post-traumatic "war zone," as Dennis Banks calls it, berserking was common. A member of the United States Commission on Civil Rights reports that the shooting of two FBI agents at Pine Ridge was not surprising "given the levels of fear, anxiety, and tension on the reservation."

From this perspective the turmoil at Pine Ridge is a dog-eat-dog competition for scarce resources, with the struggle over ideology and the attendant conversion experience working to reconcile gravely conflicted loyalties and values. The situation reflects the worldwide phenomenon of devolution in the 1990s, as national authorities in many places proved unable or unwilling to devise satisfactory means of sharing wealth. In the early 1990s, devolution began to fracture the Canadian polity as well as Yugoslavia and the old Soviet system. The Pine Ridge reservation followed a familiar pattern as one political faction captured electoral power, then used servile cooperation with the national government to manipulate incoming federal money, rewarding supporters and punishing opponents. In *Thunderheart*, the tribal leader, Jack Milton (historically, Dick Wilson), runs a Mafia-style regime. Although this crass factionalism is a form of colonial corruption, it is also typical of political machines, from Boss Tweed's New York to the Las Vegas depicted in Martin Scorsese's *Casino* (1995), not to mention the cities of the old Soviet world.[31]

Thunderheart's focus on goon squads, a uranium conspiracy, and ideology overlooks the familiar historical pattern. In postwar Westerns or detective thrillers, the hero restores order, but order is supposedly guaranteed by "the governor" or even by Washington. *Thunderheart*, by contrast, depicts the Indian nation and nature itself engulfed by predatory corruption that originates in Washington. Yet for all the rhetoric about living in harmony with nature, the reservation cannot be economically self-sufficient, and traditional values are not so robust that the wise shaman, Grandpa Sam Reaches, will forgo television and a Rolex watch. The violence on the reservation brings in the Indian reform movement, the FBI, goon squads, and the film crew. But the focus on berserking means the film gives less attention to the equally real failures of the political process and of negotiation.

Trauma rationalizes the young FBI agent's repudiation of the failures of his Indian father and the "great white father," supporting a fantasy of his ascendancy as the renegade-savior Thunderheart. Trauma shapes the argument in more-subtle ways too. The murder used to frame the Indian reformers turns out to be the work of a former convict who feigns paralysis in a wheelchair. The ironic unmasking functions both to exonerate the reformers—whose warrior ideology and anger plainly make them potential killers too—and to expose the way in which traumatic injury may disguise dangerous motives. The unmasking also reinforces the reformers' criticism of the role of helpless victim that developed in some Native American cultures after the traumatic closing of the frontier.

At the film's close, Grandpa Sam Reaches directs the now-renegade Levoi: "Run for the stronghold, Thunderheart. The soldiers are coming. They broke my TV." Cornered at the wilderness redoubt, the messianic hero seems destined for sacrifice, but then on the bluff overhead the ARM army materializes. On the screen, the opposing forces are symmetrical and neatly Manichean. The film fantasizes that a show of force—a spiritually superior force—can hold off a paramilitary siege by the dominant culture. Whether this is a cogent strategy or wishful magic like the "ghost dance" Sioux warriors once believed would ward off cavalry bullets is unclear.

On the soundtrack the initiated Thunderheart finally cries out, "This land is not for sale." He is referring to Washington's conniving at uranium-mining rights. But his defiance also sounds like a refusal to submit to prostitution, and hence is an unwitting gloss on those Hollywood films in which elite America ambivalently seeks to woo or subjugate servile hookers who are "for sale." In this framework the FBI's authoritarian structure resembles the corporate hierarchy that symbolically "buggers" underlings, and Thunderheart's refusal to sell out "this land" is not only about real estate but also about the threat of emasculation.

It is disquieting to watch *Thunderheart*'s closing footage substitute honorific gestures for a more prosaic but hardheaded dramatization of political conflict. I say this not simply because armed confrontations between staggeringly unequal forces tend to be quixotic, and because deflected rage may injure innocent bystanders, but also because *Thunderheart*'s symbolic logic resonates far beyond the reservation. For example, like Ray Levoi, Timothy McVeigh, the convicted bomber of the government office building in Oklahoma City in 1995, acquired military training from the government and then apparently underwent an ideological conversion influenced by the militia movement. Although the militia groups that coalesced in the early 1990s have no epic history of oppression and often disagree about ideology, they could read many of their grievances in the film's depiction of Native Americans crushed by a federal juggernaut.

Like the film's Indian reformers, people with the militia mentality feel oppressed by urban modernism. They mix libertarian tenets with paramilitary discipline, nostalgia for the small-town America of Shays's Rebellion, the warrior pastoralism of popular hunting and gun magazines, and a moralizing, sometimes racist worldview with many millennial ingredients. As a rule, militias envision "regular Americans"—Teddy Roosevelt's and Rider Haggard's displaced yeomen—rescuing the nation from tyranny through guerilla actions involving a Rambo-like reimmersion in nature and plenty of hoarded weapons. As in *Thunderheart*, the threat is "big government," an abusive, Orwellian "Big Brother" that was ironically made larger than life in conservative Cold War propaganda. On a more immediate level—as Rambo might argue—the enemy seems also to be the politicians and the bureaucracy that sent soldiers to die in Vietnam for hollow reasons.

However different their motives, the militias share with Hollywood a preoccupation with the trope of trauma. Their survivalist fantasies require a cultural crash and a cry for rescue, even an apocalyptic showdown such as the "run for the stronghold" at the end of *Thunderheart*. Radical right-wing groups were quick to give traumatic significance to the firestorm that leveled the Branch Davidian complex in Waco, Texas, construing the victims as martyrs and themselves as post-traumatic witnesses. The holocaust at Waco in turn gave a transcendent purpose to righteous rage against the "jackbooted" federal agents blamed for the debacle.

Is the ideation of trauma in this reaction purely self-intoxicating? Or are imaginations affected by this imagery already to some degree traumatized? I can see no easy way to sort out the causality, yet the pervasiveness of berserking as a trope makes the problem acute. In Mel Gibson's Oscar-winning *Braveheart* (1995), the dynamics of *Thunderheart* are made more crushingly simplistic. Shocked as a boy by the murder of his family, the Scottish hero Wallace (Mel Gibson) equates retaliation against the English with their extermination. In the midst of his rampage he is betrayed and suffers a messianic martyrdom. His execution on a cruciform torturer's bench ostensibly rallies all Scotland, but the betrayal confirms the Scots' fratricidal factionalism with a bitter logic, because Wallace's political vision consists of a single thrilling, empty slogan—"freedom"—that comes to sound like the "every man for himself" libertarianism of the 1990s.

A Generation Amok

In his final assault on Will Randall, the wolfish Stewart Swinton is no longer simply his young rival but also a figure of the cannibal child, literally fanged. In this section I want to explore berserking as an expression of generational antagonism in the 1990s. In Tony Scott's 1993 film *True Romance*, the young hero, a romantic bumpkin comically named Clarence, falls in love with a girlish hooker, goes amok, and survives the slaughter he precipitates. I read the film's use of trauma against four contemporary contexts: the Menendez brothers' murder of their parents in Beverly Hills, the post-traumatic aftershock of the Vietnam War, the economic injustices of the 1990s, and the environmental apocalypse implied by the solar fireball that closes the film.

In August 1989, at 722 North Elm Drive in Beverly Hills, Lyle and Erik Menendez murdered their parents in such a frenzy of shotgun fire that the bodies were nearly unrecognizable. This excess suggests the ecstatic rage of combat berserking. At first glance, the comparison seems bizarre. The Menendez brothers planned the assassination of their unarmed parents, a Hollywood executive and his wife. Afterward they systematically cleaned up, phoned the police, blamed "the Mafia" for the killings, and inherited a fortune. Yet the brothers apparently thought in terms of trauma, because in their defense they claimed their father, Jose, had sexually abused them over a "lifetime of terror, [a] lifetime of threats."[32]

In the brothers' scenario, the apparent victims were monsters, whereas the murderous sons were suffering, heroic victims who deserved to inherit the earth. Chances are, the brothers devised this story out of their own deep feelings and their sense of what people wanted to hear. After all, they lived in a scriptwriting culture, and Erik had earlier written a play in which a son murders his father for his money. While awaiting trial, they read Paul Mones's book *When a Child Kills: Abused Children Who Kill Their Parents*, "a study of true cases and how they were defended in court."[33] For them, traumatic violence was an emotional reality but also a strategic script.

The prosecution's story depicted Lyle and Erik as parasites and failures. Princeton had expelled Lyle for cheating, and at one point the brothers were in serious trouble with the police for burglarizing the houses of affluent family friends. Although Jose had shielded his sons from prosecution, he threatened to cut off their financial support. In the trial dramas, these stories of guilt and desperate innocence clashed in a life-and-death struggle for credibility. Each of the stories in its way had the power to turn reality inside out and point to fabulous motives invisible in everyday reality. Taken together, the clash of stories makes a sort of Greek tragedy of monstrous ambition and family collapse. But it also tells us something about economic strife and generational antagonism in the 1990s.

One way to get at the fantasies implied in that clash of stories is to read the Menendez murders against *True Romance*. The film opens in a decayed, industrial Detroit, where unemployed men warm their hands over a fire in a waste barrel. This cityscape evokes the poverty in Cuba that Jose Menendez escaped by struggling to the top in executive Hollywood, and the desolation of the Pine Ridge reservation. The dying city suggests the punishment awaiting those who fail in the competition for the American dream, and also, for the young, the dead end of postindustrial decline. In short, the film opens with Lyle and Erik Menendez's worst nightmare.

As "minimum-wage kids," a store clerk and a call girl, the film's young lovers teeter over the economic abyss with the romantic pluck of children in a Depression-era romantic comedy. When Clarence (Christian Slater) sighs that "the world seems to be collapsing," Alabama (Patricia Arquette) counters spunkily, "Sometimes it can go the other way." For the lovers, as for the immigrant Jose Menendez, escape lies in the direction of sunny, romantic Hollywood.

But in Detroit as in Beverly Hills, fathers seem to control destiny, and as a result sons are dangerously ambivalent. Clarence's feelings are divided among benign or monstrous father figures: his boss and his girl's pimp; his biological father and a Mafia godfather. Like Jose Menendez, Clarence's boss sells heroic dreams. He has provided Clarence with a working-class education through his comic-book store, a library of superheroes such as Spider Man, who were invented to uplift Depression-era landscapes like the film's Detroit. In the end the Menendez brothers failed to make it as Ivy League role models, and they turned to Clarence's shadow world of superheroes and "bad motherfuckers." When they failed to master their father's elite Hollywood, they identified with self-created heroes who thrive by destroying supercriminal father figures.

The problem with fathers is that sooner or later they weaken and die, and sons must take their place. Patriarchs traditionally cope with this threat by cultivating symbolic immortality, investing in sons who will carry them into posterity, just as Jose Menendez evidently dreamed of establishing a Kennedy-style political dynasty in Florida. But the transition is always precarious. Fathers may make their dreams so grand that their sons feel inadequate and resentful. For mediocre sons who have been expelled from Princeton or who sell comic books for a living, crime may seem to offer the only plausible way to attain that glory. In *True Romance* as in the polarized 1990s, hapless Detroit and fabulous Hollywood are so far apart that only a suitcase full of criminal loot can carry you from one place to the other.

But other dark motives can destabilize coming of age. Fathers have as strong an incentive to delay inheritance as sons do to hurry it along. Motives may be fatally mixed. Jose Menendez kept urging his sons to find women and settle down, trying to dictate their desires and buy posterity. In *True Romance*, the good boss hires a call girl as a birthday surprise for Clarence; when the paid sex turns romantic, the gift inadvertently produces a happy marriage. But such a gift makes a bitter parody of a traditional arranged marriage, because Clarence's "father" is not really willing to share his wealth and his name with the next generation. Appropriately, Alabama confesses to the birthday sex scheme as she and Clarence sit on the catwalk of a billboard after making love, caught in the blinding floodlights of commercialism.

The gift unwittingly confirms that the father owns everything, including the call girl, so that in making love to her the son is actually doing the father's will. In a sense the son is making love to the father through the prostitute. All the world becomes an expression of the father's will. This sublimated slavery assumes a nightmare face in the Menendez allegations of sexual abuse. In the film it locates an original violation that can explain the son's rebellious urge to go into the underworld and kill the girl's pimp, the vicious surrogate father, lover, and rival, Drexl. The symbolic logic of their confrontation is wholly apt. Drexl sneers threats of homosexual dominance with a menacing smile that captures not only the numbness but also the emotional disconfirmation of Clarence's childhood world.

At the extreme, in fear or rage, an aging father may turn against his children, trying to devour the children's vitality to replenish his own waning life. As in vampire fantasies, the children become the abuser's "creatures." In the Menendez sons' courtroom defense, this scenario culminated in Erik's claim, "I thought [my father] was going to kill me that night, and I thought he was going to have sex with me first."[34] In this statement, however fanciful it may be, sex and death go together.

This scenario puts the son in a heroic role. The threat of annihilation objectifies his fear of his own weakness and justifies not only self-defense, but heroic, superhuman rage. In confessing to the murders to his therapist, Lyle could have been characterizing one of Clarence's superheroes: "What Erik and I did took courage beyond belief. Beyond, beyond strength."[35] But what if the son exaggerates or invents the parental aggression? A child may be tempted to believe himself abused insofar as abuse makes his resentment heroic. The calculating Laius, after all, had the infant Oedipus put out to die. Much depends on the ambiguities of motive and responsibility. Clarence idolizes not only the noble Spider Man but also the "bad motherfucker." The opposites merge in Clarence's ultimate hero, Elvis. Elvis is the obedient son who submitted to military service with great fanfare, and also the renegade bad boy. At the same time Elvis fuses the roles of son and father, because he is both a rebellious son and "the king," a hallucinatory father-hero who watches over and advises Clarence at moments of crisis.

Elvis offers a troubled son a gratifying fantasy solution to father-son conflict. The solution imagines antagonism overcome by a radical erotic identification with the intimidating power figure. Although Clarence insists that he is not homosexual, he dreams about making love with Elvis. Sexual surrender to the king or father entices him because it promises a total merger, total approval, and direct participation in the king's greatness. But the bond is dangerously unstable. Submission can placate the older man's jealousy of the son as a potential rival who is destined to replace him. But sexual surrender also raises the dependent lover's fear of never becoming his own man.[36]

These conflicts help explain why, in fantasy, the father tends to split into opposites, and why traumatic violence may be needed for sons finally to break away. Clarence's marriage, for example, triggers a fatal reckoning. Whereas the boss has been benignly manipulating behind the scenes, he now tacitly appears as the vicious pimp who is the lover's "boss." In a hallucinatory encounter, Elvis reinforces Clarence's desire to face down the pimp. "You can count on me to protect you," Clarence pledges to Alabama, like a new patriarch. It is easy to forget that Clarence sets up and provokes the film's chain of killings. Supposedly he shoots the pimp in self-defense and "innocently" takes home his wife's suitcase containing a fortune in cocaine. In taking the cocaine, itself stolen from a Mafia godfather, Clarence is wresting an inheritance from evil father figures, the rightful patrimony that his boss, the deceptively good father, would have withheld. In effect, Elvis, the ambiguous son-as-father-king, authorizes Clarence to destroy the depraved father. As the pimp exclaims when he learns that "his" whore has wed Clarence, "Then we're just about relations." The wisecrack implies incestuous abuse between the pimp and "his" girl, but also between the pimp and this upstart, rival male. And this fantasy echoes in the Menendez brothers' allegations of abuse and humiliation.

In these on- and offscreen stories, ambivalent homosexual feeling surfaces whenever men are struggling together for power and identity—which is virtually everywhere. In a Los Angeles motel room, Alabama kills a Mafia hit man in an episode of hand-to-hand combat that is as brutal as anything we see in the film. "You have a lot of heart," the hit man says, praising her ferocity. At heart she is tacitly one of the boys. Despite some energetic lovemaking on screen, in the film—as in the brothers' stories—the survival struggle between men matters more than tenderness or eros.

As the plot develops, generational stress keeps returning in increasingly grotesque forms. On the run with his new wife and the contraband, Clarence turns for help to his biological father (Dennis Hopper). Once a cop and an alcoholic, this father abandoned his family and presumably left his son traumatized. Now he is a security guard, living alone, injured but wiser, self-sacrificing and nurturant. Having killed off a selfish incarnation of the father (Drexl), Clarence can be reconciled with a "real" father who is able to say "I love you." Yet almost at once another evil father—the Mafia godfather—emerges. No sooner do the lovers escape to Hollywood than gangsters come to the father's trailer, looking for Clarence and the stolen cocaine. Once again a symbolic father and son are in mortal conflict.

This time the aggressive son, Don Vincenzo Coccotti, serves an evil father, the offstage Mafia godfather. And this time a good father sacrifices himself to save a son he loves; Clarence's father provokes his own death so that the gangsters will not torture him into revealing his son's whereabouts. Specifically, he goads the Mafioso son into killing him by playing on his racism, shaming the Sicilian by invoking the historical conquest or "penetration" of Sicily by black Moors. The Moorish "niggers," he taunts, raped the ancestral mothers, so today's Sicilians, including the Mafioso, are racially mixed. This is one more fantasy of the predatory (fore)father, displaced into history, and Don Vincenzo reacts with murderous fury.

This historical rape is akin to the aggression of the pimp that has spurred Clarence to murder. Like Clarence reacting to the pimp, and like the Menendez brothers, the Mafiosi are sons outraged by the thought of paternal rape. But there is another dimension to this fantasy. Just as the Mafiosi violently deny their "black" origins, so Jose Menendez sought to deny the "black" inferiority of his Cuban origins by founding in the United States a dynasty of sons with Anglo-European names who would go to Princeton and transcend his background. Their failure to live up to that dynastic ambition threatened Lyle and Erik not only with a slide into a Detroit-style dead end, but also with a humiliating reminder of the family's lowly origins.[37] The film slyly mocks paternal pretensions to elite purity, even as it covets the supremacy a suitcase full of drugs can buy.

When the lovers flee to Los Angeles, Clarence acts as a sort of dramatist, scripting his caper as he goes along, and his dream of making a fortune by combining acting and crime echoes Erik Menendez's screenwriting and acting aspirations. In this way the plot justifies the drug scam by making Hollywood hopelessly corrupt. Clarence plots to sell the drug stash to a movie producer—a Hollywood executive as corrupt as Jose Menendez was alleged to be. The producer has clear affinities with the Mafia godfather, as we see when a car cuts him off and he threatens the other driver: "Don't give me the finger or I'll have you killed." The producer is another incarnation of the killer father. Although he is superficially ingratiating, his tyrannical nature is reflected in the sycophantic, self-abasing behavior of his assistant and surrogate son, Elliot Blitzer. As Clarence gradually cons and bullies Elliot into the drug deal, we are meant to see a cagey, independent son overcoming a spineless alter ego.

Picked up accidently on a drug charge, Elliot Blitzer is forced by the police to betray the producer-father. With Elliot wired to capture incriminating evidence, the police set a trap to catch the producer buying the stolen cocaine. But then the godfather and his soldiers unexpectedly intervene. Caught in the middle of the climactic shootout, Clarence slips free with a token wound; Elliot dies as punishment for his weakness in betraying the producer-father's drug lust to the authorities. This resembles the Menendez brothers' excuse for not having gone to the police about their years of abuse: supposedly Jose was so powerful he would have had them killed. On another level, as the bugged medium for his boss's incriminating confession, Elliot functions as Hollywood itself does, exposing other people's corruption for profit. In putting Elliot to death, Hollywood slyly mocks itself for its profitable exploitation of other people's sins, even as it scorns the self-indulgent producer.

One underlying fantasy is that the film daringly improvises an exploration of Hollywood's sleazy reality just as Clarence improvises gangster lines so persuasive they draw the naively crooked producer and others into playing parts in his play. Faking underworld experience, Clarence uses illusion—Hollywood's tool—to penetrate a shady realm where staggering riches are hidden from the gullible public. The wishful assumption is that everyone is acting, but the imaginative son is a natural actor, an effortless professional, able to play the role of master criminal without being tainted by it. If fathers and godfathers are finally alike, stealing from them is scarcely crime at all. This fantasy has an echo in the Menendez brothers' scheme to be gentleman burglars as well as killers.

In the earlier battles with the pimp and the hit man, Clarence and Alabama are caught up in a sudden spasm of violence and kill their adversaries. In the final shootout, however, the cross fire is an all-engulfing and yet sourceless maelstrom. It begins as a standoff. Equally armed and full of lethal suspicion, the parties are stunned to find themselves confronting one another in the hotel room. The implicit fantasy is that the moment of supreme tension reveals the deepest motives. Lee Donowitz, the sleazy producer, catches on to Elliot's betrayal. "I treated you like a son!" he screams, launching into a tantrum that triggers the holocaust.

By implication, the sham friendliness of Hollywood masks an underlying tension that resembles the atmosphere in a police state. Surveillance and entrapment are basic modes of operation for all the parties in the drug deal. Not only the police but also the Mafiosi and Clarence are driven by moralistic outrage. Combined with paranoid vigilance, that drive to punish poisons all relationships. Any break in the surface of life may trigger rage. Little wonder that Elliot can confide in no one. To survive here, a rebellious son needs to be "cool," like Clarence: meaning wholly dissociated.

The lovers escape with the loot to Brazil, where they romp on the beach, triumphant but alone. They have a son named Elvis, and they are founding a dynasty as Jose Menendez wished to do. But dominating the closing moments of the film is a setting sun as monstrous as an atomic fireball.

The final sunset might evoke Nevil Shute's doomsday scenario *On the Beach*, or even the nightmare shore at the entropic end of time in H. G. Wells's *Time Machine*. In the glib, lurid vocabulary of apocalyptic science fiction, that furious sun makes this the final couple, chased from a dying civilization like the parents of Superman, bearing little Elvis, the eschatological hero. The imagery alludes to environmental catastrophe and sums up earlier hints of a cultural crash. But if the raging sun signifies the ultimate menace, it also blazons the futility of self-restraint, delayed gratification, and cultural values. In this way the scene deviously reinforces and even inflames the assumptions about behavior that have been operating all along. An irrational, hostile, even doomed world demands a capacity for violent assertion and violent enjoyment in the available moment. The apocalyptic sun makes a striking image of the berserk state. It is emotionally dissociated yet a part of the beach holiday, just as rage is a dissociated part of Clarence, the cool hero, the new father.

On one level, the berserk state is a trick to bring closure to a screenplay in which the late-twentieth-century conventions of depersonalization and violence are so extreme that no particular action can seem climactic or even authentic. Only losing control, being cool in the grip of frenzy, conveys authenticity. In this respect berserking dramatizes an escape from the plasticity of 1990s culture, the glut of interchangeable, self-parodic stories that was Hollywood and mass entertainment. If everything is for sale, if computer simulation makes everything possible, then everything is arbitrary and therefore meaningless—poisoned by death anxiety.

Ecstatic violence represents an effort to escape death anxiety by using death against others, just as the Hiroshima fireball first promised strategists control over the principle of annihilation. It is only a short step to the Vietnam War, which brought berserking to the public eye in accounts of atrocities such as the My Lai massacre. This is one connotation suggested when the Mafioso calls Clarence's murder of the pimp a "massacre." It is coyly evoked in the sleazy producer's film about the Vietnam War, *Coming Home in a Body Bag*, which Clarence calls his favorite movie of all time, as if the war had been totally commercialized by this point, like any kung fu movie. The producer is working on a sequel, *Body Bag II*, which is in effect this movie, *True Romance*. Like the need for endless movie sequels, berserking represents an effort to impose narrative closure on a war that resists rationalization.[38]

By no accident the extravagant firepower of the industrial post-Hiroshima army evokes slang words for killing such as "vaporizing." The idea is that methodical excess, as in military fantasies about Vietnam and in the Gulf War, will not simply cripple but actually annihilate the enemy, eliminating the need for negotiation, compromise, and anticlimax. This is the dream of omnipotence that lurks in the ideas of nerve gas and the "clean" neutron bomb that would destroy masses of people but leave their property intact, like the Jewish apartments Germans took over during the Nazi period.

True Romance implies that social life is war, that the odds are against rational planning and negotiation, and that people only survive by abandoning themselves to the berserk state. The underlying conceit is that Clarence is a combat veteran. Among the veterans Robert Jay Lifton treated for post-traumatic stress is one who reported, "The most widely read literature among the guys that return from Vietnam, it's comics. Comic books and adventure stories. You know, *Male*: you see the picture of some guy killing somebody and the bare-breasted, Vietnamese-type Asian-looking woman. . . . These guys are just living in a dream world."[39]

But like Will Randall's wolfishness, Clarence's berserking also reflects a new disposition toward business. For Clarence as for the Menendez brothers, who began impulsively buying up businesses with their legacy, success means "making a killing." The connection is found in the trope of berserking, which implies throwing yourself into an action with controlled abandon. In these terms, the ultimate deal epitomizes an ethos in which life is a headlong, possibly suicidal gamble. This is a subtext that emerged in the Reagan 1980s, when institutional controls over business were relaxed and the buccaneering entrepreneur became a self-aggrandizing, self-declared culture hero. As the record-shattering savings-and-loan scandals proved, business took on some of the reckless, addictive qualities of gambling. Films such as *Casino* and *Leaving Las Vegas* localize in a mythic Nevada a mentality that has transformed post-Vietnam America, putting state-sponsored—and Indian-sponsored—gambling in tempting proximity to every paycheck.[40]

Berserking operates to inflate and to excuse ugly, predatory economic motives that look back to the ruthless Social Darwinism of the 1890s and to the new post-Soviet world. If traditional business safeguards are compromised, decisions are risky and fellow businesspeople cannot be trusted. "Berserking" objectifies that anxiety about lost control and offers some relief from the exacerbated tension of "the deal." In "innocently" stealing the cocaine, Clarence dramatizes the assumption that the corporate muscle that destroyed Detroit and that owns everything is akin to the Mafia. In effect, berserking is the only technique left to the "little guy" in his revolt against vicious fathers. To further excuse Clarence, the screenplay also makes him a folk type, the trickster, who fools his enemies into destroying one another. The trickster–business hero is cousin to the Hollywood illusionist and mythmaker, whose story we behold on the screen.

The apocalyptic sun and the businessman-trickster may seem poles apart, but berserking bridges that gap. And this may explain why the Menendez sons killed in a frenzy—because in split focus they both underestimated and overestimated their parents. Behind their pretensions, Jose and Kitty were contemptibly small, although their power over their sons seemed so vast that the sons felt that only superhuman violence could kill them. The brothers operated in a force field of images and assumptions much like those that carry Clarence and Alabama and little Elvis to that utopian beach at the end of livable life.

In its self-involvement, this cluster of images is a tricky mix of nihilism and posturing. The fireball sun expresses a fear of not being able to get back into the safety of conventional roles after a traumatic disenchantment with everyday culture. Life is then like combat, with the individual caught between an enemy other and punishing fathers.[41] But the survivor's reaction is rage against the rest of the world: everybody else dies. The screenplay makes Alabama say that if Clarence had been killed, she would have wanted to die too—implicitly dooming her baby. This seems to be more the voice of the screenwriter than that of a young mother. The apocalyptic wish is related to the exterminatory rage implicit in matter-of-fact Cold War plans for Mutual Assured Destruction, itself an outgrowth of the Nazi death camps and the terror bombing of World War II.[42] At the same time, Alabama is an elfin, sentimental lass, who can gush "You're so cool."

Like true Hollywood, *True Romance* is both opportunistic and equivocal. And like the hung juries in the first Menendez trials (the brothers were eventually convicted and given life sentences), the film is acutely ambivalent. It sympathizes with victimized young people while reinforcing the media's self-fulfilling prophecies that they are "superpredators" who will "take violence to a new level."[43] Through its hyped-up rhetoric—the verbal equivalent of berserking—the film "wipes out" the problem it attacks, tacitly apologizing for injustice and privilege in the status quo. The Brazilian beach is a cop-out, if only because in compensating for death anxiety, the fantasy of being supreme survivors is exactly what drives the cruelty and injustice of the dead world the survivors have fled.

The film challenges itself on a number of levels, primarily in order to protect the core values it most needs to move beyond. The proof of this, I think, is not so much what *True Romance* includes as what it leaves out—what it cannot think about. The obsession with berserking and "popular" apocalypse tacitly nullifies mother and child, nurture and desire, and in this way recreates and justifies the sort of brutal family that triggered the first killings on screen and also in the Menendez living room. Read this way, the film unwittingly dramatizes a cultural system. And the crucial question we need to ask is a systemic question, an ethological question: how to open up a cultural obsession as confining as the ruthless business frenzy that makes killers of young men such as the Menendez brothers and their counterparts in the film.

TWELVE

Amok at the Apocalypse

Let us, however, remember that more than 100,000,000 people have perished through human violence in this century. The apocalypse is not a future event conjured up by paranoids and religious fanatics. It has already happened to millions.

Richard L. Rubenstein, *The Age of Triage*

The only way to tell man from machine is by their screams!

Trailer for Christian Duguay's *Screamers* (1995)

WITH THEIR DRIVE toward exterminatory violence, the tropes of berserking and the apocalypse belong to the same sinister family of ideas. Norman Cohn links the belief in apocalyptic purification to a "collapse of the traditional framework of life and loss of faith in institutions, whether they be the sacred monarchy, the Catholic Church, or the modern state."[1] If that collapse is traumatic, then apocalyptic fantasy can be understood as symbolic berserking. Apocalyptic fantasy usually places the perfect society just over the eschatological horizon. In the foreground the warrior Christ confronts the Antichrist; Saint George's dragon becomes the revealed beast.

Like inconceivable death, the apocalypse occupies a cognitive category that must be filled with analogies or equivalents. As Cohn demonstrates in *The Pursuit of the Millennium,* the lineaments of the apocalypse can be found in Nazi and Communist ideology as well as in Christian belief. Correspondingly, millennial Christian cults such as David Koresh's Branch Davidians and Jim Jones's People's Temple may develop militarized, totalitarian organizations. This remarkable lability means that many kinds of cultural materials may be adapted to serve apocalyptic dynamics. This fluidity is essential because apocalyptic fantasies are ideas about death and, like any other death equivalent, they become subject to the mediation of terror management. President Reagan's pronouncements about doomsday quickly lost their power to shock the public. Like the threat of nuclear war, which was also often on the president's lips and eventually tamed in "Star Wars" visions of a "nuclear shield," doomsday became less literal as people diluted the threat. It became a form of half-knowledge, with a quality of tacitness or "as-if-ness" about it.

There is an aura of play about such ultimates, even when people mean to be deadly serious about them. This is not to deny their tragic potential. Like the Aum Supreme Truth cult in Japan, David Koresh's Branch Davidians stockpiled weapons for a supreme struggle. Their defiance of the United States government's overwhelming power magnified their heroic stature but also the likelihood of their doom. In such an excruciating atmosphere of exaltation and threat, categories may blur. The Branch Davidian leaders' decision to touch off a firestorm at a moment of crisis represents a numbing or blurring of distinctions as well as a perversely logical next step in a long chain of argument.

An apocalypse, then, is a trope: an argument. The sun at the close of *True Romance*, for example, insinuates doomsday and leaves a threat in the air. Although the impact is bound to vary with different audiences, some meanings seem clear enough. The swollen sun moralizes about the violent, greedy injustice the lovers have outwitted, but as an allusion to a nuclear fireball it also anticipates cosmic folly, if not divine judgment. In this respect, it can be read as a symbolic check on the wishful aggression dramatized by the lovers' triumph. As a cautionary sun, it attempts to break the escalating rampage in the film, implying that the lovers' transformation into a family may be unstable, and that if the threat is relaxed, a reversion to survival greed might follow. The problem is that reminders of mortality may exacerbate survival hysteria rather than tame it. Step back far enough and the final threat on the screen is a controlled provocation to elicit excitement in an audience paying for pleasurable stimulation.

Berserking as a Threat Display

True Romance is one of many films in which berserking functions as do threat displays among other primates. The film shows younger and older males trying to intimidate one another in a contest over resources, including women. In American cities in the 1990s, teenage males, notably young blacks, systematically developed threat displays—challenging eye contact in the subway, for example—into a social tool. Yet their behavior was part of a larger symbolic con-

frontation over resources in which the nation's governing classes tried to dominate by engaging in political chest-thumping about "getting tough on crime."
Like the menacing displays of hostile tribes or massed armies, this highly theatrical intimidation was intended to preempt actual bloodshed if possible. The
contest worked against an investment in crime prevention or social services, because the goal of the dominant group was less to assimilate the have-nots than
to reinforce the hierarchy. Cries of alarm or outrage are often threats of retaliation: "Criminal-justice experts have predicted the arrival of the superpredators—a generation of teens so numerous and savage that they'll take violence to
a new level. 'It's *Lord of the Flies* on a massive scale,' says Cook County State's
Attorney Jack O'Malley. 'We've become a nation being terrorized by our children.'"[2] The prosecutor turns "our children" into devilish savages like Tonga,
and *Newsweek* broadcasts his call to arms.

   True Romance is part of the rhetorical skirmish. It constitutes a threat display
admonishing an older generation to be more generous, while flattering young
viewers that their rebellious displays are risky but potentially effective. In this
context, the film is another phase of an argument that was already well advanced
when Tonga blew poison darts at Holmes—an argument that twisted through
the decade of Vietnam and counterculture rebellion, and the expanding childhood poverty and widening income gap of the Reagan years.

   In this contest of threats, images of berserking and the apocalypse advertise a
willingness to abandon all restraints on violence. They measure the escalation
of rhetorical hostilities that accompanies the post-traumatic mood. The media
culture's disproportionate emphasis on cops-and-robbers violence is one indicator of how lavishly developed threat displays have become. Another indicator is
a clutch of films such as *River's Edge* (1986), *Kalifornia* (1993), *Natural Born
Killers* (1994), and *Kids* (1995), which blazon the terrifying nihilism of youth.
Whereas the Menendez brothers and Clarence grasp at the fantasies that money
can buy, these films imagine young people injured and enraged beyond caring.

   Dominic Sena's *Kalifornia*, for example, matches up Brian and Carrie, an
ambitious yuppie writer and a photographer, with Early and Adele, whom Roger
Ebert revealingly classifies as "wretched white trash."[3] The yuppies plan to head
for California, stopping at famous sites of mass murders to photograph them and
write them up for a book. By chance, Early's parole officer has sent him to apply
for a janitorial job at the university, where he spots the yuppies' bulletin-board
ad for riders to share the cost of the trip. He and Adele sign on for the ride; then
he murders the landlord who has been harassing them for his overdue rent. The
trip is a vertiginous plunge into the berserk state. Early Grace becomes the classic drifter-psychopath, an object of middle-class fascination and horror, and the
plot culminates in his rape of Carrie. He abducts her and takes her to an aban-

doned nuclear test site, a ghost town called "Dreamland Ranch," where they hole up in a house full of store-window dummies. At the climax, Carrie stabs Early, and after a final man-to-man confrontation, Brian administers the *coup de grâce*.

Roger Ebert's review of the film illustrates how American culture "naturally" moralizes about violence. At the screening, a woman behind Ebert kept muttering about the movie's "depravity." Afterward, he tells us, "she admitted it was 'very well-made,' but that she feared 'the wrong people could see it and get bad ideas.'" He defends the film by concluding, "I think the point of *Kalifornia* is that it's altogether too comforting to believe that people need inspiration to hurt and kill. Some people, the movie says, are simply evil. They lack all values and sympathy. And they don't need anybody to give them ideas."[4]

The woman understands that the film is an argument, but she fears it will give "bad ideas" to "the wrong people." Ebert illogically counters by insisting that the killer in the film is inherently evil. Not only does the reviewer ignore the question of the movie's influence on viewers; his own moralistic anxieties leave him unable to appreciate the social prejudices that hold him (and the woman, and the film itself) in their grip. After all, who are "the wrong people"? And what does it mean to label someone "simply evil"?

In fact the film offers a detailed argument about class competition. Early and Adele live in a stereotypically trashy trailer, bullied by a demanding landlord. Adele is an uneducated child of television who justifies her submissiveness to Early by arguing that he will protect her from a rape like the one that apparently traumatized her at the age of thirteen. Early's parole officer dramatizes the nation's post-Vietnam hardness toward the poor. He has a hook hand, suggesting a traumatic injury, and he sneers as he sends Early to look for a job as a janitor, as if nothing could be worse than a low-status job. Early's rebellious reaction to that provocation motivates the cross-country survey of "mass-murder sites."[5] As it happens, at each of the sites, the murderer's story includes hints of traumatic abuse and economic exploitation that resonate with Early's character. One killer, for instance, had been an abused child working in a slaughterhouse since the age of eight. As Early becomes more violent, the film discovers more signs of injury in him, including a psychotic delusion that he can see "doors" to other realities.

Despite its sympathy for the poor, *Kalifornia* plays out conventional prejudices. Early is that old American bogeyman, the drifter-psychopath. Although they are both emotionally numb, the working-class Early and Adele are sexual animals, and their feral rutting in the backseat of the car fascinates the voyeuristic photographer Carrie, with grim consequences. Carrie becomes a fatally irresistible object of desire for Early, as Shakespeare's Miranda does for the "monster"

Caliban in *The Tempest*. The prejudices are echoed widely in films of the 1990s. Quentin Tarantino's *Pulp Fiction* (1995) dissolves its mockery of white trash in a sophisticated tonic of campy irony, but the audience is expected to share in the knowing condescension.[6] When Brian must kill Early in *Kalifornia*, he is symbolically destroying a barbarian rapist, not wrestling with a potential version of himself. And this is a definitive imaginative maneuver in a class system.

The coerciveness of class begins to stand out if we stop thinking of the two couples, white trash and yuppies, as opposites. After all, the yuppies are as much outsiders as their travel mates. They too are penniless migrants on the make; that is why they teamed up with Early and Adele in the first place. The difference is that these yuppies are ambitious for status and have sublimated their desires into an aesthetic voyeurism, while their alter egos supposedly still experience raw life. The actual antagonist of both couples is more plausibly the invisible elite that controls the punishing economic system—whose representative on screen is Early's snarling landlord.

Kalifornia could have dramatized a conflict between losers and the sort of stingy, self-righteous social climbers for whom the term *yuppie* was invented in the Reagan go-go years. Instead, the screenplay indirectly identifies economic violence with the military-industrial mind-set and the nuclear bomb. Fleeing from the police in a gathering squall of violence, Early takes the couples to invade the house of a retired atomic-weapons engineer in the desert. Later, Early abducts Carrie in a big Lincoln with an aerial bomb strapped to the hood, sealing his identification with America's—or, to use the 1960s spelling, Amerika's—militarism. In the post-Vietnam, post-Soviet era, the working-class psychopath has been marshaled into the role of a scapegoat Communist. The film annihilates him, but equivocally, insinuating that, like a post-traumatic combat veteran, Early has been driven amok by a militaristic society. In the imagery of the screenplay, Early neatly fulfills Jonathan Shay's clinical recipe for berserking: captivity (prison), enslavement (the contemptible janitorial job), and the threat of death on all sides.

Because Early is part of a system, the movie describes a society undergoing a slow-motion apocalypse whose source is the mania for dominance symbolized by the nuclear test site, now a ghost town in a wasteland, as squalid as Clarence's Detroit and the decaying infrastructure everywhere evident on the screen. This is the weakest part of the film's argument. The rampaging Early runs away with the film's otherwise cogent logic. We are left with a classic post-traumatic formula: at one extreme, an ambiguously victimized "forgotten man" gone berserk; at the other, demonized "big government" or "modernism." Instead of using Brian and Carrie to dramatize this conflict, the film has them play out Hollywood's—and the audience's—guilt at its voyeurism and exploitation.

Brian's and Carrie's urge to record famous victimizations is a variation on a familiar trope associated with berserking. As a prosthetic eye, the camera allows the vulnerable imagination to defy taboo and gaze on the terrifying sources of trauma—violation and death—through a dissociated or distancing medium, something like observing the retina-searing sun through smoked glass. Although Georges Battaile and others have mystified the violation of taboo as a form of sacramental ecstasy, the usual effect seems to me more prosaic and paradoxical. The camera's promise of superhuman power both stimulates and desensitizes the observer, as in slasher films or when the jocks in *Leaving Las Vegas* video-tape their gang rape of Sera.

Almost from the beginning, the camera has shown an affinity for vicarious berserking. In *The Cameraman* (1928), for example, Buster Keaton blunders into a maelstrom of gang violence in Chinatown. The ambivalence of the camera-eye trope came home in Vietnam War reportage, which "brought the war into America's living rooms," making it too real for comfort. Haskell Wexler drama-tized the heartless camera in *Medium Cool*, his treatment of media at the fate-ful Democratic National Convention in Chicago. *True Romance* mocks the slick movie producer who keeps repackaging the Vietnam War for avid con-sumers. In *Fearless*, the trope is used to dramatize numbness and cultural crash when survivors of a plane crash stumble past a taxi driver callously videotaping the disaster.

Although it is tempting for us to moralize about it, the camera may promote engagement as well as detachment. Likewise, the camera may be a means of substantiating rather than distancing the self. Like Clarence, both couples in *Kalifornia* are nobodies who dream of Hollywood as a utopian source of heroic self-expansion. Echoing *Wolf*, Early vows "We'll climb up to [the Hollywood] sign and howl at the moon." Yet like killing, taking a photograph stops life, turn-ing it into a trophy, which is why preindustrial people may fear being pho-tographed. In capturing life, in reducing it to a controlled facsimile of itself, pho-tography can evoke vampirism or enslavement or the evil eye. Early rejects Carrie's photos as "boring," and his final obsession with her makes sense as a symbolic struggle to overcome the deadness rapidly closing in on him in the wasteland. The berserker and the photographer-artist represent opposed solu-tions to the competition for scarce subjectivity. In this crisis the yuppie artists slay the overt criminal, although fittingly it is the crass Brian who strikes the final blow, after trying as a therapist would to engage Early in questions about his mo-tives. This struggle resonates in many futuristic visions of apocalyptic social crash in which cybernetic subversion through cameras and robots threatens to mechanize, numb, or attenuate subjectivity.

As in *True Romance*, these lovers too end up on a sinister beach, successful but numbed by the freezing water and the jolt of evil. Shown in a yuppie art gallery, Carrie's work can have little soul. In the final moments they listen to Adele's childlike voice on tape appealing to them not to "forget us in California. You're the only friends we got."

Early Grace's outbreak prefigures the killing spree satirized in Oliver Stone's *Natural Born Killers*. Whereas *Kalifornia* hints that traumatic abuse lies behind all the aggression on the screen, Stone's film is of two minds about abuse as an all-purpose explanation. His young killers, Mickey and Mallory, model symptoms of post-traumatic stress such as intrusive flashbacks. And Stone's black comedy can be affectingly complex, as when the soundtrack shows disconfirmation at work by synchronizing the sexual depredations of Mallory's swinish father with a situation comedy laugh track. The father updates ancient grotesques such as the incestuous King Antiochus in Shakespeare's *Pericles* or the maiden-devouring dragon opposing Saint George. As in Terrence Malick's *Badlands*, a young man's rejection of a demeaning job and his murder of his girlfriend's rivalrous father precipitate all the outrages to follow.

In this pattern, berserking is youth's rebellion against de facto slavery and social death. When the young killers become celebrities, it is tempting to moralize about the culture's lust for violence as if violence were an end in itself. But it seems more revealing to regard their depicted rages as threat displays, and the media frenzy as symptomatic of the nation's fascination, during a whirlwind of cultural change, with contests for dominance not only between generations but also, because Mallory is as ruthless as Mickey, between the sexes. Stone satirizes the way in which berserking acquires commercial value as a marker in symbolically charged cultural skirmishes. As renegades, Mickey and Mallory become hot properties, as did Pretty Boy Floyd during the Great Depression. The screenplay has Wayne Gale, a tabloid television host, hound the couple, exploiting them and yet increasingly being seduced by their wolfish power. In the end they turn on him and, before a running camera, to his astonishment, gun him down too.

Stone insists that in its violation of taboos, the media frenzy is itself a kind of vicarious berserking. This same transgression of boundaries gives a sinister dizziness to Nicholas Broomfield's 1992 documentary *Aileen Wuornos: The Selling of a Serial Killer*. Aileen Wuornos was a prostitute in Florida when the military men who were her regular customers left for the Gulf War. To support her lesbian lover, she began picking up strangers and, she says, killed seven of them in self-defense when they assaulted her. Convicted and sentenced to death under peculiarly prejudicial circumstances, the woman gives the ambiguities of berserking a painful immediacy.

Was Wuornos an opportunistic killer? The documentary sees Florida as a macho society inured to "the sex war," in which Wuornos found herself a half-willing combatant. After her conviction, allegations surfaced that law officers had tried to negotiate media deals to sell their inside story of the freakish woman serial murderer. In her account, she describes her sadistic customers not only inflicting pain but trying to crush her will. In these encounters, the men found much of their pleasure in using threat displays to reduce her to a sex slave. Because Wuornos had been a runaway teenager and was abused as a child, Broomfield plausibly suggests that she was a post-traumatic personality sparked to rage by her johns' brutality. Conceivably, her first experience of terror, killing, and survival ecstasy drew her into a pattern of killing. As a prostitute she seems to have been caught in a cross fire between the misogyny of some of her clients and the prejudices of the state. Yet the series of homicides that Wuornos describes has some characteristics of the rape-revenge narratives that mushroomed into feature-length films in the 1970s,[7] and there is a disquieting possibility that American culture was the model for her vindictive fury. In this situation, trauma opens up more questions than it answers.[8]

As Nicholas Broomfield reconstructs her life, Aileen Wuornos was another abandoned child in the factory universe. As a hooker, she earned a living by selling intimacy to military personnel. As a runaway teenager, she seems to have grown up deeply affected by parent-child conflicts. In mothering her lesbian lover, she was apparently also nurturing the dependent child in herself. On camera she seems to oscillate between playing parent and child, tough survivor and naively self-sacrificing waif. Self-effacement as a means of winning parental love became an appalling vulnerability when her case attracted the attention of a woman her own age who ingratiated herself with the imprisoned Wuornos by writing to her, legally adopted her as a daughter, and urged catastrophic legal advice on her in order to exploit her story for a windfall. Interviewed on camera, that woman combines a smarmy motherliness and a born-again Christian's paternalistic certainty with a palpable venality.

The Family Amok

In films like *True Romance* and *Aileen Wuornos*, parents turn out to be traumatized children; consider Mallory's parents in *Natural Born Killers*, who act out berserk rage and despairing passivity. I have suggested some of the historical circumstances behind this generational conflict. But its proximity to apocalyptic themes calls attention to an even larger context: neoteny in evolution. For although neoteny disposes humans to be lifelong juveniles, playful, care soliciting, and social, it also disposes them as parents to be rivals for nurture. And that limitation of reliable adult parenting contributes to the survival rage dramatized in the films. The problem has a bearing on cultural evolution, for instance, in H. G. Wells's fiction, which wrestles with a conflicted Victorian view of humans as both sociable juveniles and predatory adults. In this historical moment, at least, the idea of neoteny is a spectral presence in the culture, implicit in the obsession with youth, for example. But as in Wells's day, a century later the pressure of competitive survival dread makes it difficult for us to relinquish our traditional assumptions about humans as "natural-born" adult predators. The subliminal awareness of neoteny in such a conflicted context contributed to the sense of abandonment and doom in Wells's imagination. Much the same dead-end mood also lurks in modern films about parental abandonment, sentimentally tamed in *Home Alone* (1990), terminally grim in Tim Hunter's *River's Edge*.

River's Edge dramatizes a sensational news story about teenagers who for many days kept secret a friend's impulsive murder of a girl in their circle. The media played the story as an indictment of nihilistic young people.[9] But nihilism is a category whose nothingness gets filled up with symbolic equivalents. The young murderer in the film (coyly named Sampson) killed the girl (Jamie) on impulse because she "talked shit" about his dead mother. In a post-traumatic reaction to his mother's death—and his abandonment—Sampson impulsively discharges his grief and rage at Jamie. When the burned-out father figure, Feck, asks "Are you a psycho?" Sampson replies, "When I get in a fight, I go fucking crazy, you know. Everything goes black. Then I fucking explode, you know, like it's the end of the world and who cares if this guy wastes me because I'm going to waste him first. I mean, the whole world's gonna be blown up anyway. I got this philosophy, you do shit and it's done and you die."

Trying to imagine a teenager gone amok, the screenplay makes Sampson sound like a stricken Vietnam veteran, using combat slang for annihilation ("to waste") and evoking a Reagan-era nuclear Armageddon. To flesh out the idea of collateral traumatization from the war, the film depicts a small-town atmosphere of dog-eat-dog meanness—broken families, alienated children, and nasty police officers. The nominal parents all feel economically harried and demoralized. Fathers compensate for their social impotence with a macho rivalry that recalls the analogous pattern of homosexual conflict in *True Romance*—a pattern never confronted in *River's Edge*.

Although it means to represent social reality, the atmosphere of berserking and doomsday futility in *River's Edge* has much in common with the nihilism projected in futuristic fantasies such as *Strange Days* (1995) and *Twelve Monkeys* (1995). The crisis mentality of adolescence, especially in the teenage drug subculture, so fills the screen that we forget that a humdrum society surrounds the teenagers. The undertone of panic about emasculation and abandonment is only one sign of a pervasive anxiety about lost subjectivity. The town itself seems as stagnant as Holmes's London, its voices gesturing at meaning and purpose, but finally storyless. Neither the individual nor the family nor the community has a center; work is moot; and the only potent parent figures are authoritarian, like the police detectives, or burned out, like the high-school history teacher. As in Havelock Ellis's 1890s and Jean-Pierre Jeunet's aptly named *City of Lost Children* (1995), everyone is tacitly an abandoned child, the dead Jamie only the foremost among them.

As in Haggard's Kôr, the lost children are unconsciously transfixed by the need for a larger-than-life mother figure to ground them. Sampson killed Jamie when she "talked shit" about his dead mother as if she were trying—but unable—to take his mother's place. But Sampson's motives have a post-traumatic haziness and impulsiveness about them. And he is only one of the town's killers of women. The movie opens with a malicious boy, Tim, figuratively drowning his sister's doll in the river. The former biker, Feck, claims to have killed a girlfriend years before. Now he has a sex doll, a prosthetic, eternal woman-mother, to whom he complains about getting old, in a grotesque analogue of Sampson's relationship to his dead mother.

Symbolically castrated in a traumatic motorcycle accident that cost him his leg, forgotten by his brother bikers, Feck is a surrogate father to his family of teenagers, but also one more despairing rival for absent mother love. Other father figures exhibit the same mix of deprivation and antagonism. The police detective bristles with outrage at the boys, but shows no curiosity about anyone's motives. In effect, the detective and the traumatized former biker are split-off faces of the same futile manhood, a diminished echo of Holmes and the limping Watson. Whether it is the defeat in Vietnam or a motorcycle accident, the film needs some offscreen trauma to account for the town's drained will and dulled emotions. To the question "Why are you two such delinquents?" the teenagers breezily reply: "Because we had a fucked-up childhood." The town, and to a great extent the film, takes the answer for granted.

At the river's edge, the traditional prosthetic supports for identity have vanished. Even small-town America now walks mean streets. Hollywood's futuristic nightmares show cyberculture trying to reconstitute those prosthetic supports through technology, but with a high-voltage ambivalence. *River's Edge* shows mysterious, hysterical forces—drugs, youth culture, nihilism—turning people into robots as people literally do in scenarios such as those of Paul Verhoeven's *RoboCop* (1987) or Robert Longo's *Johnny Mnemonic* (1995). The fear of psychic deadness sounds clearly in Sampson's admission that in strangling Jamie, he "felt so fucking alive." Instead of construing the teenagers' reaction to one particular murder in terms of particular conflicted personalities, the film globalizes the incident as journalists did, so that the characters' diminished subjectivity is as much a function of American movie culture as of the California town it depicts. Like Max Nordau's *Degeneration* a century ago, the screenplay discovers a decadence that is in large part the shadow cast by its own moral hysteria and indifference to particulars.[10] As the list of song titles in the soundtrack credits reveals, the film—and presumably the audience—readily play up threat displays and let atmospherics insinuate an argument.[11] The fundamentalist coloration of apocalyptic berserking comes out in the cosmic sweep of titles such as "Evil Has No Boundaries." Paradoxically, as these globalizing habits of mind ratchet up moral urgency, they diminish moral pain by diluting personal experience. This, too, I think, contributes to our forebodings about a robotic subversion of subjectivity.

Vampire Families Amok

Among the great precursors of cybernetic perversity are Frankenstein's monster and Count Dracula. Vampires resemble robots inasmuch as their uncanny powers depend on dissociation from daylight and feeling, and on compulsive feeding. In Kathryn Bigelow's *Near Dark* (1987), a family of 1980s vampires marauds through rural Oklahoma and Texas landscapes that allude to the Dust Bowl. Led by an undead Confederate soldier named Jesse, the vampires prowl the earth in a recreational vehicle. In one direction, like many post-Vietnam scenarios, this fantasy hints that macho violence in society is a post-traumatic effect of war, and that Jesse's ongoing depredations are revenge for a harrowing defeat.

But like Dracula, Jesse has recruited a new generation to form, in an era of broken homes, an alternative, predatory family. The vampires are dispossessed proletarian renegades, with hints of counterculture and cult. The children, Homer and the teenage Mae, have been enticed away from repressive mainstream culture by the lure of immortality and transgressions from sex to car theft to serial murder. In their turn, Mae and Homer try to seduce the innocent Caleb and Sarah away from their farm family, so a clear cultural opposition emerges. Whereas Caleb's father is the yeoman farmer idealized by Teddy Roosevelt and Rider Haggard, Jesse's family is the latest incarnation of the vagrants who terrorized rural imaginations in nineteenth-century America.[12] When they wreak carnage in a local bar, the vampires recall outlaw gangs in Westerns, in motorcycle films such as *The Wild One* (1954), and in 1990s inner-city lore. At the same time, *Near Dark* identifies vampirism with atavistic instincts in modern industrial life. The camera shows virgin landscapes being despoiled by oil derricks. The analogy becomes explicit when the seduced Caleb feeds on Mae's blood while oil derricks pump relentlessly in the background. The film contrasts this greed for energy with the ecological harmonies of the family farm.

Caleb's initiation makes vampirism a form of conversion experience. He joins the criminal family in what amounts to a religious rite. In "turning," he suffers a physical crisis akin to Leo's fever in *She* or to drug withdrawal, and he completes the transformation by nursing on blood from Mae's wrist. The gesture has meanings that are echoed in berserking. Nursing on a surrogate mother, the motherless Caleb is compensating for a loss of identity and cultural ground. As a prosthetic transfusion, his feeding on Mae's blood is a sublimated form of cannibalism that will cause him to go berserk once his appetite is aroused. At the same time the transfusion implies that the vampire's rage for life is contagious, like a "drug epidemic" or a disease like AIDS.

This infection is silently defined by class. The vampires prey on white-trash muggers as well as marginal folks such as a trucker, assorted girls, and blacks. The havoc in the roadside bar begins when Mae dances with a terrified local teenager and Caleb cuts in to kill him. Although Caleb lacks the stomach to finish off his rival, the family's confrontational threat displays provoke an explosion that consumes the place. Whereas Dracula preyed on the aristocratic Lucy, a century later vampires regularly woo the audience's sympathy by carrying out a eugenics program against social undesirables. Jesse's menage exterminates nasty losers just as, in John Landis's witty *Innocent Blood* (1992), a beautiful French vampire feasts on mobsters.

In its chase toward closure, *Near Dark* uses Bram Stoker's device of a father-to-child transfusion to reconvert Caleb (and through him, Mae). The vampires' climactic mayhem borrows the conceit of the unkillable killer popularized by James Cameron's *Terminator* (1984), whose robotic assassin (played by Arnold Schwarzenegger) appears unstoppable. The gimmick neatly dramatizes the conviction of invulnerability that berserking confers. No less allusive are the firestorms of sunlight that finally annihilate Jesse's family. The individual conflagrations can evoke Renaissance witch burnings, Vietnam (the famous photograph of a girl engulfed by napalm), and the nuclear fireball sun in *True Romance*. With an apocalyptic finality, the vicious Homer springs out of the car after his escaping victim, explodes in purifying flame, and, along with the rest of his family, is vaporized.

Near Dark assumes that susceptibility to vampirism originates in combat trauma (Jesse) and in forbidden sexual desire (Caleb). What links the two etiologies is a greed for life—the survival panic that underlies much misogyny and macho aggression. Seduction, for Caleb, means blood-fusion with a dangerous mother-substitute and an escape from the monotonous family farm into a midnight zone of violent appetite. The same fantasies careen out of control in

Robert Rodriguez's bizarre *From Dusk till Dawn* (1996), but with a misogyny and class snobbery that shed light on the conservative subtext of Hollywood's apocalyptic berserking.

The film begins as a conventional crime spree. An escaped convict, Seth, and his psychopathic brother, Richie, take a family hostage, and in their commandeered recreational vehicle they go berserk on their way over the Mexican border, where they rendezvous with a criminal who is supposed to hide them. As in *Near Dark*, the conventional family is a widowed father, a former pastor named Jacob Fuller, his son, Scott, and his teenage daughter, Kate. At the Titty Twister Café, a Mexican roadside nightclub-bar "for truckers and bikers," the screenplay swerves into supernatural territory. In the course of the night, tensions mount until the fugitives and their hostages discover that everyone in the bar—road types, a black Vietnam veteran, rock musicians, waitresses, and go-go dancers— is a vampire. The resulting frenzy ends in a holocaust that only Seth and Kate survive.

A camp sensibility governs this holocaust and the audience's response. It suspends imagination between horror and mockery. Like Oscar Wilde's work, with its equivocal poise, the film wants to thrill the audience but also to offer a wink of superiority. Seth is an outlaw Dorian Gray, strategically aloof and selfish. Goading the former pastor to drop all restraints in battling the demons, for example, Seth demands, "Which are you? A faithless preacher or a mean motherfucking servant of God?" The ambiguity gives the smartass criminal the voice of a radically militant Christian while justifying his murderous fury: he mocks involvement as he urges it. Like Clarence and many another outlaw hero of the 1990s, Seth achieves total autonomy through pure violence. In the obligatory lip service it pays to feminism, the screenplay also allows the pastor's sly daughter, Kate, to survive the onslaught because, like Seth, she can shrug off her pious inhibitions and kill with abandon—and then distance herself afterward as if beyond shock.

As in *The Picture of Dorian Gray*, ironic detachment promises to master death anxiety. But when irony flags, the personality is threatened by obsessive survival greed—the intrusive cyber-rage represented by zombies, vampires, and Dorian's ghastly portrait. Seen in this light, *From Dusk till Dawn* is an American variant of the story of Jekyll and Hyde. The mocking criminal individualist escapes from a heartland prison of inhibitions, only to confront his own death anxiety and forbidden appetites on the border of the mind in the form of vampires. The conflict reveals his suppressed vampire underside—the equivalent of Dorian's evil portrait—which embodies all of his suppressed death anxiety and rage for life. The vampires mirror Seth's criminality in the loot they have stolen from travelers and hoarded in the cellar. But they also mirror the Middle-American family. Since his wife's traumatic death, the pastor has lost his faith. The vampire strippers burlesque Kate's seductiveness. Fighting for her life, she can go berserk as Seth does, and in the aftermath want to team up with him.

As a cultural fantasy, the film presents a demoralized, moralistic America—the faithless preacher's family—kidnapped by escaped criminal desires. Exposed to temptations—liquor, blasphemy, ear-splitting rock, and in-your-face sex—the nation-family is torn apart by its own dissociated, predatory rage. The survivors, an outlaw and a teenager, overcome the vampires by abandoning civilized restraints in a purifying firestorm that leaves them burned out—cauterized but alive. The conclusion superficially mocks the moralistic piety that split off the vampires in the first place. Yet the survivors triumph by exercising a superior rage that leaves them more hardened than ever. After the slaughter, Kate asks Seth if he "needs some company." "I may be a bastard," Seth replies, "but I'm not a fucking bastard." The campy repartee, with its misogynistic, possibly gay punchline, does not dispel the film's moral hysteria. Like Oscar Wilde released from prison, the survivors face an ominous, constricted future. Rising above the smoking ruins, the camera discovers that the café sits on the edge of a bluff at the top of an ancient Mesoamerican temple pyramid, insinuating that a menacing, occult evil, the spawn of traumatic human sacrifice, will outlast the present age.

One way to approach this moralistic pessimism is to look beyond its obvious source, the preacher's family. Given a Christian gloss, the café's spectacular depravity alludes to Sodom, Gomorrah, and the millennialism of the Noah story. The titillating last-days-of-Babylon nightclub scene is a regular feature of apocalyptic films. But what is doomsday damnation actually made of? The sins on display in the Titty Twister Café appeal to a "bad-boy" misogyny that suggests Dr. Jekyll's conflicted sexuality. The name flaunts an infantile rage against the bad breast, the provocative, ungiving mother. The climactic erotic dance number, for example, features an updated 1890s femme fatale sporting the clichéd snake of sleazy striptease. She commands the gawkers to "bow your head, worship at the feet of Satanico Pandemonico." Pouring whiskey down her leg and into Richie's open mouth, she plays bitch-goddess to his infantilized manhood, echoing Ben's fantasy in *Leaving Las Vegas* of licking booze from the body of a whore-goddess. She orders Seth to eat dog shit, sneering "Welcome to slavery." He replies, "No thanks, I already had a wife." In *Leaving Las Vegas*, the executive Ben also suffers because he "already had a wife." As an elite figure, Ben invites audiences to identify upward, and in his masochistic psychosexual slumming he is safely distanced from us by his fabulous alcoholism. *From Dusk till Dawn* plays out a sadistic, tacitly homosexual reaction to sexual menace, summed up in Seth's exhortation to the pastor to "take a cross and shove it up these monsters' asses." Seth himself uses a power-driven stake as a weapon, so killing becomes a parodic, cybernetic rape. The jokes about homosexual rape drive home, so to speak, the film's preoccupation with domination and submission.

Slavery, lest we forget, is social death. And what "Satanico Pandemonico" threatens is not sexual depravity so much as status collapse. The astonishing thing about the café's enticements is how swinish, depersonalized, and predatory they are. They appeal less to erotic desire than to a vicious appetite for power. It might be possible to argue that the spectacle represents some sort of polymorphous perversity. But it makes more sense, I think, to read the scene as a whole, in which case the nightclub's temptations are suspiciously mechanical, and the real excitement lies in the payoff: the freedom to run amok against the vampires. That battle, like the psychosexual slumming that passes for sin, is a paranoid fantasy of class warfare. Dr. Jekyll splits into queasy respectability and lower-class vice—which turns out to be, at least on the printed page, not sex but rage. The Hyde who stomps the little girl and beats Sir Danvers Carew to death is less a sensualist than he is a berserk terrorist from the slums of social death.

The film's nominal Mexico seems to be populated mostly by white trash. Their gross pleasures are Hollywood's—and conservative America's—idea of working-class vices. Like the loutish villain, Gaston, whom Disney invented for *Beauty and the Beast*, and the barroom louts slaughtered in *Near Dark*, the vampires embody the fears and snobberies of affluent America. They are the misfits and losers whose misbehavior excites American news headlines; there is not a white-collar criminal among them. There is an emblematic Vietnam veteran, however, a black man who in 1972, at the war's treacherous end, lay in a ditch "listening to the enemy laugh" at their victory. He went berserk, he tells us, slaughtering an entire Vietcong squad, "blood and chunks of yellow flesh clinging to my bayonet." He too turns vampire and burns up in the final holocaust, releasing any residual American guilt about the war's lasting damage to its veterans.

The brute pleasures in the café mock white-trash tastes in hell raising, but they also justify the fear and loathing that are kept safely distanced by the film's campy irony. As seen by an audience identifying upward, that flaunted pleasure is actually a working-class threat display intended to fascinate and appall the gawkers in the movie theater as well as those in the bar. It also provokes—and justifies—the righteous combat that annihilates nearly everyone. Even a sophisticated, campy sneer is a form of threat display, with evolutionary roots in a facial gesture that curls lips and bares teeth.[13]

As in *Dr. Jekyll and Mr. Hyde*, which associates forbidden pleasures with the persecutory respectability of Victorian culture—ultimately, the gallows—so in *From Dusk till Dawn*, pleasure exists not for its own sake, not as play and a celebration of life, but as a resource to be guarded with homicidal vigilance. Pleasure is another form of the loot the vampires have stashed in the cellar, a degraded sign of a social competition whose obsessiveness registers as the compulsiveness—the supernatural robotics, as it were—of vampires. Like *The Time Machine*'s Morlocks, a lower-class underworld appears to be the source of the anarchic competition endangering mainstream America, and sex and generational clashes as well. Not only do men fight to the death, they also fight off liberated female vampires.

In a still-larger framework, these underclass types evoke the teeming scum of the earth that crowded in on America's borders in the globalized 1990s, like the hordes that the 1890s dreaded. As the night's havoc unfolds in the film, the vampires begin physically to resemble alien refugees. At one point, the heroes are besieged in a tunnel by mangy, starved-looking vampires who caricature the swarms demonized in the xenophobic alarums of this century raised by Teddy Roosevelt and Hitler and Jerry Falwell.[14]

This global threat reinforces the millennial imagery. During the vampires' assault, Pastor Jacob makes a cross with the bartender's bat and an automatic rifle, brandishing it as a symbolic and literal weapon against the aliens. And at least one of the vampire bikers metamorphoses into a snarling beast with apocalyptic connotations on his way to annihilation. Underlying the combat is the sickening assumption that wavering Christians can revive their faith through the total commitment of berserking. Paranoid self-defense reinflates militant faith, to the tune of an ersatz Gregorian chant on the soundtrack. That this homicidal fantasy ministers to an underlying death anxiety becomes clear when the pastor is finally bitten by a vampire and he asks his family to kill him rather than let him turn into a "lapdog of Satan." In the ecstasy of killing others he can face his own death with resolve. The secular complement is Richie's death, eased by his hand-holding exchange of vows ("I love you") with his brother Seth.

Despite the film's campy jokiness, it is difficult to screen out echoes of Nazi blood brotherhood and Hitler's post-traumatic sense of Wagnerian doom. The scum-of-the-earth vampires occupy the place of the sneaky, swarming Jews in Nazi propaganda films such as *The Eternal Jew*. In their other roles, as the bloodsucking owners of the café and seductive performers feeding on trapped customers, the vampires evoke the Jew as businessperson. These projections silently played out for 1990s audiences fears of economic exploitation akin to those afflicting the Germans—fears of economic meanness so unsettling that they must be safely deflected onto demons, just as they are associated with the Nazis in *Schindler's List*. As a business, after all, the café advertises consumer pleasures, masking its real obsession with loot, blood-sucking enslavement, and human sacrifice. Even the clever incidental details fit this logic. In the midst of the burning corpses, for example, the vampire rock band uses a partly dismembered body as a guitar—a prosthetic use of another person akin to ultimate slavery and reminiscent of the death camps' reduction of victims to heaps of hair and eyeglasses and gold teeth.

This cluster of grisly associations is thrown into sharper relief by the cannibalistic murders committed by Jeffrey Dahmer and Dennis Nilsen, in which vampire berserking appears to be a traumatic response to threatened subjectivity. Both men reported shattering childhood encounters with death. In his biography of the implacably ordinary-seeming Nilsen, Brian Masters calls attention to the shock the five-year-old Nilsen suffered when he was brought into a parlor to view the drowned, disfigured corpse of his fisherman grandfather. Jeffrey Dahmer's obsessions seem to have originated in a childhood fascination with death; his father reported that Dahmer eviscerated animals that had been killed in the road.[15]

Jeffrey Dahmer's compulsion to anatomize and pickle parts of his victims has many echoes in world culture, from ancient Egyptian mummification rites to the cult of relics in medieval Christianity. The behavior seeks to master death by opening up its secrets, breaking mortality down into manipulable and, in the case of bones, indestructible parts. The conviction of mastery may entail infantile fantasies of social omnipotence (total control over a dead body) and oral incorporation (appropriating the victim's vitality). It seems likely that all these motives are implicated in Dahmer's murders, just as in horror films they are rehearsed in play. In a sense, the paintings of Saint George function as horror films do insofar as they excite a measured fear in viewers while modeling the defeat of the dragon to reinforce the viewers' self-control. Carpaccio's Saint George, for example, shows the vampirelike dragon surrounded by dismembered body parts.

Dahmer's compulsion to anatomize may be akin to the obsessive thoughts about the ground of the self that Louis Sass reports in schizophrenia.[16] According to Sass, schizophrenia often involves a hyperreflexive consciousness that cannot stop thinking about—cannot stop anatomizing—itself. In this view, the frantic effort to secure the sense of self contributes to its fragmentation and to the emergence of delusional systems. Like the act of dismembering a corpse to find its lost life or the secret of death, an obsessive awareness disintegrates its object. Dahmer and Nilsen seem to have tried to ground the self in others—namely, in homosexual intimacy with their seduced or kidnapped victims, followed by magical efforts to control and merge with the other, culminating in the literal union of cannibalism. Dahmer described killing as a way of maintaining an ecstatic sense of closeness with his victims, which suggests a desperate attempt to substantiate his own subjectivity through fantasies of containing an other.

Ingesting blood, the vampire could be considered a cannibal. Jeffrey Dahmer acted the part of the vampire as well. At one point he attempted to lobotomize a boy he had kidnapped in order to gain absolute mastery over his slave. The victim would become a living sex doll, one of the "living dead," a combination of Jamie's unburied corpse and Feck's sex doll in *River's Edge*. Dahmer's father described his son as a young man at one point in possession of a handmade wooden box that had apparently contained the head of one of his victims. As in mummification, the behavior suggests an effort to impose stability on the unfathomable boundary between life and death; to enclose and preserve lost life. It tries to objectify the fascination—the blinding, fixated surrender and compulsion—of death.

Absolute domination of another person is tantamount to omnipotence, and it is one of the most desperately infantile defenses against death anxiety. Like Tonga's intimacy with Small in *The Sign of Four*, Dahmer's homosexual practices imply tremendous fear and guilt as well as desire. Even Small's relationship is rooted in fantasies of healing, because he has saved the cannibal child from a near-fatal illness and in return been rescued from his prison island by Tonga. Jeffrey Dahmer's predatory love also was tacitly a fantasy of being rescued into an ecstatic state that he wished would go on without end. This need for an absolute, magical merger with another suggests a terrified child reacting against a sense of the abyss, killing in a desperate attempt to fill himself up with other people. Not coincidentally, *From Dusk till Dawn* ends with the camera withdrawing into the sky to take in the ruins of the café atop a sacrificial temple whose steps descend into the abyss of a canyon. In paintings of Saint George, the knight faces not only the dragon but also the demon's cave—which is tacitly the mouth of hell and the doorway to the abyss.

Read in this way, Dahmer's atrocities are a desperate effort at self-substantiation. "For the fascinated," says Carlin Barton, "all categories dissolve, including those by which he or she defines the self. The victim of fascination enters a world beyond (or lost to) symbolic representation and systematic categorization, a world that can only be hinted at through paradox, where satisfaction cannot be distinguished from hunger, presence from absence, self from other, beauty from hideousness, the pious from the obscene."[17] Dahmer's project can be construed in the context of the late-Victorian dread of self-dissolution in "nervous breakdowns." It is not only the stigma of homosexuality that spurs Dorian Gray to murder and a plan to demolish the corpse of a former lover, but the uncanny subjectivity associated with a multiplied or fragmented self and Dorian's fascination with mirrors and the abyss. Wilde evokes in Dorian an autistic sort of inability to relate to others that is not unlike Jeffrey Dahmer's psychic isolation. Both concretize unbearable thoughts in bodies and body parts. Parallels could also be drawn between Dorian's obsession with his death-infected portrait and Dahmer's morbidity. As forms of berserking, even the murders they commit share some affinities; each foray is more recklessly desperate than the one before. Stupefied by death awareness and guilt, trapped between the potential outrage of victims and respectable society, both Dahmer and Dorian throw off constraints as if they were soldiers breaking out of the enslavement of combat by going amok. But berserking is itself a form of stupefaction and compulsion, and a paradoxical reciprocity means that the two states of self-loss, captivity and violence, may keep sliding into one another, so that the berserker can reach no outcome, no repose short of dying. In the categories of post-traumatic stress, this reciprocity shows up as chronic hypervigilance and the endless, intrusive return of intolerable memory.

Although berserking involves a breakdown of cultural constraints, it is not necessarily incoherent. Like Dorian Gray or a soldier running amok, Jeffrey Dahmer was out of control and yet strategic in his predation. This sort of doubleness fascinated Wilde and his audience, and for good reason. We still cannot reliably make our categories fit such protean phenomena. Berserking, like many other aspects of trauma, points to a zone in which categories such as freedom and evil, neurophysiology and narrative logic, seem always to be dissolving into one another.

Berserk at the End of the Self

Vampire berserking was one reaction to the dread of self-loss that plagued the *fin de siècle*. In the twentieth century, that fear has behaved as if it were a mutating flu virus, ebbing and flowing across the planet as feverish change has transformed social possibilities. The dread is primarily a thematic symptom of adaptive stress, akin to Haggard's fear of barbarians overwhelming the civilized self. But it should also remind us of the structural limits of subjectivity that show up clearly in some forms of mental illness, with a sense of apocalypse as a prominent symptom. In schizophrenia, says Louis Sass, "an extreme loss of self is not . . . likely to occur in total isolation from the patient's experience of the rest of the world. In fact, it is common . . . for profound disturbances of self-experience to be accompanied by a well-recognized symptom called the 'World Catastrophe' delusion, an awesomely disconcerting experience in which the very being of the universe seems to be undermined or even destroyed."[18] Yet the self is as ephemeral as life, and therefore always a source of psychocultural dread. H. G. Wells made his name by projecting "world catastrophe" in *The Time Machine*. As I see it, Wells was part of a larger project of exploring and taming this "schizophrenic" potential in modern culture. Something comparable seems to be going on in Hollywood's end-of-civilization-as-we-know-it movies in the 1990s.

The 1890s projected a cannibalistic threat onto aliens such as Dracula and Tonga. In Kathryn Bigelow's *Strange Days*, the threat to subjectivity comes from cyberculture and a terminal degeneration that recalls Max Nordau.[19] The film returns us to Los Angeles for the forty-eight hours before New Year's Eve, 1999. Crowds throng the mean streets, burned-out hedonists haunt the back streets, and anarchic criminality prevails. Characters mutter "It's over"—meaning civilization as we know it. A former police officer, now a corrupt security man, says "The whole planet's total fucking chaos." What trauma has racked the world?

It appears that "big government" has warped into a police state. Hair-trigger police brutality has killed the rap star Jeriko One, "one of the most important black men in America," during a routine traffic stop. The coverup by the Los Angeles Police Department plays to the sort of conspiracy sentiment O. J. Simpson's defense exploited. After Jeriko's assassination, the city has exploded in riots. At the close, we learn that the corrupt former police officer, Max, and his boss, the sinister rock impresario Philo Gant, created much of the mischief. And when the protagonist entrusts his evidence about the rapper's assassination to "the Assistant Commissioner," the official magically redeems the police department and the government, arresting the city's terminal plunge.

As in *From Dusk till Dawn*, the screenplay's incoherence turns out to be an ideological maneuver. Robbed of their hero, Jeriko One, the mob protests against police brutality as real rioters have done in such cities as Los Angeles, Miami, and (in 1996) St. Petersburg, Florida, when police have killed unarmed black motorists. Thematically, the film sympathizes with the city's underclass. But as depicted on the screen, the crowds are nearly as alien as Mexican vampires. They choke the streets and fill the screen with a swarming anonymity. As the hero, Mace, tries to escape rogue police assassins at the climax, she must fight her way through a tangle of milling bodies. Just then the Assistant Commissioner materializes and takes charge of the scene. With a wave of his hand, as it were, he makes the menacing riot cops benign, disarming the assassins and saving Mace's life. As white executive authority restores order, the crowd becomes a tableau of personalized and tame faces—our neighbors now, not the berserk villagers storming the prince's palace in Disney's Los Angeles.

This exemplifies elite Hollywood's usual split focus on the downtrodden and democracy. But *Strange Days* unexpectedly clarifies the ambivalence. The film's protagonist is a former vice officer named Lenny Nero who is now peddling illegal Squid technology. Developed to improve government eavesdropping, a Squid is a brain-wave transmitter put on as if it were a skullcap. It enables the wearer to "jack into" another person's tape-recorded experiences and experience them as his or her own. In the opening sequence Lenny offers a sample run in which the camera has recorded the last moments of a burglar's life. The audience and the customer see what the criminal saw: a nighttime robbery gone awry, a panicky flight, and a headfirst, fatal plummet off a rooftop.

The film depicts this software as illegal and quasi-pornographic in its violation of taboos. The Squid fusion of self and other in virtual reality is another variant of the vampire fantasy—another means of making someone "your" creature. It taps a number of fears pricked by digital technology: loss of privacy, cybernetic expropriation of inner life, the sale of subjectivity (prostitution) to any upscale creep with a credit card. But Squid technology is sinister mostly for ancient reasons—because it can be used against people. Otherwise it is only an intriguing, high-tech example of what I call "prosthetic thinking through others," and it dramatizes some of the anxieties aroused by prosthetic bonds.

The Squid opens vistas of endless self-expansion and self-loss. In Lenny's fervent sales pitch, "This is not like TV, only better. This is life. A piece of somebody's life." This radical fusion offers conservative, elite customers a way to violate laws and inhibitions without personally risking anything, as in the burglary sequence. "It's about the forbidden fruit," Lenny insists. "I can get you what you want [in software]. I am your priest, your shrink, the magic man. The Santa Claus of the subconscious." The fruit is forbidden knowledge. But in a distrustful, puritanical society it also compensates for missing or jaded experience, especially lost intimacy. It allows the human animal to exercise social instincts without the risk of drowning in the sea of anonymous humanity teeming in the city's streets or on the Mexican border. The world's billions of humans swamp our powers of imaginative sympathy: how can we trust our ability to read or intuit the unique inner life of an other who is one of billions?

Likewise, as a regulated exposure to trauma, Squid is a potent anodyne for death anxiety. On demand, the customer can summon up the eternally preserved spirits of other people, much the way séances in the 1890s allowed the living to mingle with the not-really-dead. Like television—which is only a box emitting light and sound waves—Squid conjures a subjectivity that feels real. In another sense it presents vicarious trauma, safely distanced and for sale. We can try out "our" deaths just as the Time Traveller's trip to the end of the cosmos allowed late Victorians to "try out" the annihilation modeled for them in the new science.

But another sort of flirtation with transcendence is also implied here. Recall the Roman mimes I described in chapter 6, in which condemned criminals actually died enacting the story of Orpheus, for example, in order to give spectators in the amphitheater a sensation of horror and transcendent reality. This sort of illusionism, high-tech in the days of the Coliseum, is a precursor not only of

Squid but of Hollywood itself, where special effects and a fascination with transcendence—aliens, cloned dinosaurs, vampires—supplant interest in character. What the 1990s hyped as virtual reality is only the latest stage of an ancient effort to create "magical" art.[20] The 1890s equivalent was the sybaritic illusionism that enthralled Oscar Wilde. When Huysmans's Des Esseintes retreats to his mansion and loses himself in sensory stimulants and props, "he was able to enjoy . . . all the sensations of a long sea-voyage, without ever leaving home; the pleasure of moving from place to place . . . without fatigue or worry. . . . Travel, indeed, struck him as being a waste of time, since he believed that the imagination could provide a more-than-adequate substitute for the vulgar reality of actual experience."[21]

In *Strange Days* subjectivity is everywhere flattened into type. The world as we know it ends not in fire or in ice but in noir stereotypes. The hero, Lenny, carries a torch for a singer seduced by the villain. The real villain, Max, supposedly has "some kind of tumor," some 1890s-style traumatic lesion on the brain, that accounts for his sick behavior. But these motives are perfunctory. The film's apocalyptic mood stresses the exhaustion and oppression of character. As in satanic-abuse hysteria, gratuitous evil controls life. Allusions to 1984 abound, from the jackbooted Los Angeles police officers to the gigantic outdoor telescreen on which mobs watch the millennial carnival. Nowhere are there signs of personal pleasure: not in the obligatory degenerate nightclub scene, and not in intimate moments.

The meaning of this mood is condensed in the movie's central moment of cruelty. In silencing the one witness to the police officers' murder of Jeriko One, a woman named Iris, the evil Max kills her after wiring her to a Squid receptor. As a result, she dies seeing herself raped and put to death through his eyes, her imagination flooded by his sadism. For all its potential contradictions (wouldn't this be a kindness, because Iris would feel his sadistic pleasure, not her own suffering?) the scene is revelatory. It shows a victim helplessly turned against herself, compelled to share in her own execution. This a graphic instance of prosthetic conversion in which mingled thoughts turn terrifyingly subversive as murder is experienced as self-hatred and suicide. This is Satan's modus operandi, and it also expresses the dynamics of child abuse. Used in this way, Squid technology reconfigures the intrusive, abusive telescreen visage of Big Brother in 1984. It is the fear of being manipulated into a self-confounded paralysis that Shakespeare memorably identified in *Hamlet*.

Superficially, this self-loss originates in villainy. A more substantial explanation lies in the film's Los Angeles. All the people there seem to live vicariously through telescreens, "playback," or parasitical property crimes. Their relationships are organized around dominance and submission. Instead of intimacy, there is an obsession with fellatio and rape. The economic equivalent is the flattening of creativity and craft into a service industry. It is as if the vast servant class dissolving in the 1890s were coalescing again in the equally anxious 1990s. In this Los Angeles, the black "supermom," Mace, chauffeurs a wealthy elite through the anarchic streets in an armored limousine, playing out without satiric bite the antebellum dream of an aristocracy coddled by the loyal Aunt Jemima.[22] Politics in this imploding future consists of threat displays and heroic bromides. Hassled by the Los Angeles police, the revolutionary rapper Jeriko protests with threats about "my lawyers" and boasts, "You'll be sorry." The film nods to the victimization of the underclass, but handles its black celebrity "spokesman" with ambivalence. He blusters and dies in a hail of police bullets, only to be vindicated when safely dead by the avuncular, white Assistant Commissioner as the closing credits roll.

In *Strange Days*, Lenny is a police officer turned black-market peddler of vicarious life. In Robert Longo's *Johnny Mnemonic*, based on a short story by William Gibson, the time is the second decade of the twenty-first century and the Lenny figure is a courier who smuggles life-giving information past corporate goons. A group of Asians has stolen the secret cure for an epidemic similar to AIDS from a ruthless global corporation named Pharmakom, which is withholding the cure because it makes more money treating dying patients. The anarchist-thieves hire Johnny Mnemonic to take the formula to Newark. He is a partially cybernetic person, implanted with silicon chips that make him one of the "elite agents who smuggle data in wet-wired brain implants."

Like Sherlock Holmes's genius, the implants transform Johnny into a superhuman data bank. Because the bootleg medical cure he carries constitutes an information overload, he suffers the sort of stress that drives Holmes to drugs. The epidemic disease, "nerve attenuation syndrome," also harks back to the 1890s in its suggestion of neurasthenia or traumatic neurosis. And the screenplay invokes trauma as the operative connection. Johnny has been traumatized by the implant of silicon in his brain for courier work. (Why technology must use the human brain at all is unclear.) Now he wants his native memory restored through surgery, because he has lost his childhood and is ungrounded. After harrowing escapes from corporate thugs, he manages to download his data, symbolized on screen as an uprushing, life-giving cloud much like sperm. In the process Johnny has post-traumatic flashbacks to his childhood in a late-Victorian house in Hollywood's usual hometown America. Once self-centered, Johnny has become a reluctant virtual messiah conveying the cure for the epidemic, suffering and self-sacrificing. Like Ben in *Leaving Las Vegas*, and like Lenny Nero, he is a surrogate for Hollywood itself, because he delivers life-giving stories to cure a "nervously attenuated" subjectivity.

Johnny's trauma implies a family broken by a corporate state as predatory as the Nazi economy in *Schindler's List*. By exploiting the traumatic symptoms of nerve attenuation for profit, the corporation "attenuates" people as vampirism or slavery would. But because technology has made slaves expendable, the practical result is that the corporation exterminates people for profit in a version of the Nazi economy. As in *Strange Days*, the screenplay imagines that a proletarian resistance has organized around urban blacks, "LoTeks," who are hackers, data pirates, and thieves in the "info wars."[23] The rebel leader, a black hip-hop disk jockey like Jeriko One, broadcasts the cure for the attenuation disease for his listeners to capture on their videocassette recorders.

The term *info wars* suggests both data piracy and the wholly propagandized public reality of 1984. But nobody on the screen works for a living. This is a vision of group dissociation: everybody either manipulates "info" or lives in a state of squalid social death. The LoTeks have supposedly improvised technical equipment, including a captive telepathic dolphin, but on the screen, again, that labor is a given. Heroism instead consists of delivering other people's "info." In this sense both Johnny and the celebrity–entertainer–resistance leader are media figures. The LoTek triumph, the dissemination of the cure, is literally a broadcast. Nobody ever asks how isolated poor people are going to use videocassette recorders to transform the dangerous overload of data Johnny was carrying into an actual pharmaceutical substance.

In this future, as in 1984, people drift disembodied in a sea of "info." This is the world prefigured by 1990s media capitalism, which hyped a communications revolution in cable, satellite, and computer technologies as commercial forces split information into hyperspecialized, hermetic formulas and mass-market trivia. In theory the media have never been so richly diverse. In reality, the news increasingly emulates tabloid or lifestyle entertainment, not only "dumbed down" but also ever more disconnected from any direct citizen action. Like Oscar Wilde in prison, this future sensibility fears a terminal breakdown because, in Neil Postman's phrase, "amusing ourselves to death" attenuates our subjectivity, dissipating our will and desire even as it appears to gratify them. "Info" or virtual reality in these films is a post-traumatic symptom that attempts to compensate for a diminished sense of public reality. It has historical antecedents in Holmes's encyclopedic alienation, but also in the Time Traveller's terror of being stranded in the future, amid the attenuated subjectivity of the Eloi and the decaying "encyclopedic" knowledge in the porcelain palace, always menaced by unseen industrial predators.

Squid tapes offer a black-market subjectivity something like the voices sought in late-Victorian séances. A more direct echo of the 1890s is found in the telepathic support Johnny Mnemonic receives from the founder of Pharmakom, who has been forced out in a coup and imprisoned in virtual reality. She appears as a prosthetic voice, a sort of hotline psychic or "angel" who resembles Rider Haggard's Ayesha in her dissociated, mournful power and evokes memories of lost mother love. With his flashbacks to childhood, Johnny's orgasmic delivery of the spermlike data amounts to a wishful consummation.

The film's climactic threat combines berserking with apocalyptic images. The corporation's Japanese Yakuza thugs dispatch a street preacher to hunt down Johnny and his messianic "info." As a pseudo-Jesus, a druggie prophet, the assassin is a type of Antichrist. The movie uses the figure to parody the sort of paramilitary fundamentalism found in Pat Robertson's novels, as well as the hypocrisies of preachers such as Jimmy Swaggart. In the final crisis, the LoTeks' prosthetically enhanced dolphin kills this Antichrist by telepathy, incinerating him as if he were a Renaissance heretic burned at the stake, or a vampire. The charred corpse of "Jesus" is now "garbage" and is contemptuously dumped into the ocean.

In the parodic religiosity of this conclusion, traditional religious categories dissolve into one another, producing exactly the sort of "info" that unmoors subjectivity. The killer, "Jesus," is spectacularly turned into "garbage," trash, or—as Johnny calls the data he carries—"shit." Even in this hectic exorcism there is no vision of personal happiness or confrontation with personal evil, but rather a 1984-like scenario of traumatic desperation given nominal closure by the vocabulary of berserking and apocalypse.

In these fantasies, apocalypse is a trope, a mood like the foreknowledge of doom in the Saint George story. The imagined end tends to be a process of termination rather than a cataclysm followed by a blank screen. In this sense, the apocalypse is another expression of fears of degeneration and entropy, as in Max Nordau's work and the terminal reaches of *The Time Machine*. Consider two futuristic fantasies in which the foreground berserking and apocalyptic mood leave the movie audience in an eschatological limbo, a post-Wagnerian twilight of the gods.

William Gibson's novel *Neuromancer* opens with "the sky above the port . . . the color of television, tuned to a dead channel."[24] Like Gibson's damaged hero, Case, with his prosthetic implants, the scene shows dead technology usurping nature. The novel is an old-fashioned quest romance in cyber-dress, and it climaxes with Case's infiltration of a funereal virtual-reality castle in search of the futuristic equivalent of the Agra treasure. As a site of cryogenic immortality, the fortress resembles Haggard's Kôr and the Palace of Green Porcelain in its decay. Case views the room in which its master, a corporate patriarch something like Howard Hughes, died. The founder is "Victorian" (N 263), and his castle's decor sports touches of Victorian orientalism. Because the decadent patriarch murders young women to arouse himself, the atmosphere shudders with the 1890s outrage at aristocratic sexual predators that brought down Oscar Wilde.

The retro details of the novel bring into focus its peculiar emptiness. Gibson's characters are cartoonlike. Their partially cybernetic bodies are emblematic of their generic personalities and the video-game feel of the plot, but they also dramatize an attenuation of subjectivity. Nearly every character is motivated by some past trauma. In structural terms, subjectivity has been diluted into cyberspace. Virtual reality in the novel is actually a kind of externalized psychic topography. In response to the emptying out of traditional verities, says Peter Homans, the mourning Freud created psychoanalysis to fill interior psychic space with compensatory meaning and vitality.[25] *Neuromancer* imagines a post-traumatic world that reacts against an inner deadness by volatilizing the psychic life into a cyberscape. The resulting scenario has an allegorical quality to it—the ego messenger navigating between the corporate superego and the instinctual proletarians—but the allusiveness dissipates toward a final twilight. There are moments of horror, as when Case's bodyguard-girlfriend Molly describes murdering a sadomasochistic john in her earlier life as a prostitute, but the incident exists more to provide pulp sensation—as information—than to express personal experience.

The soulless quality of the novel reflects the pressures of mass-market entertainment in an era of storylessness. Gibson's fantasy of cyberspace arises out of the post-traumatic trope just as 1990s Internet hype showed the imprint of late-Victorian dreams: of an omnipotent "world encyclopedia" (H. G. Wells, Conan Doyle), yet also "pandemonium" (Henry Adams)[26] and an endlessly degenerating subjectivity (Nordau). As the media rhapsodized about the "information superhighway," authorities fanned a moral panic about its sinister infestation by pornographers, neo-Nazis, and hacker-terrorists. Cyberspace came to stand for the Faustian reach and infinite bounty of the industrial revolution as it substantiated our fears of terminal anomie.

Whatever else it is, in short, cyberspace is a fantasy. Its cultural origins matter in this argument because they reveal survival dread as well as creative euphoria. I have in mind not just the video game's use of cyberspace to stage extermination exercises, or the dread of a massive system collapse—of an act of sabotage or an engineering failure that could leave civilization helpless, and not simply the ego's fear of being lost in a globalized, tacit wilderness. Rather, I am thinking of the post-traumatic ideation of the 1890s that was implicated in the century's great catastrophes: World War I and then the Nazi era. The techno-future that Gibson dreads has many of the Wagnerian qualities that obsessed Hitler, from the aristocratic "founder's" crepuscular Valhalla in virtual reality to the quasi-fascist fantasies of corporate immortality. "Power, in Case's world, meant corporate power. The zaibatsus, the multinationals that shaped the course of human history, had transcended old barriers. Viewed as organisms, they had attained a kind of immortality. You couldn't kill a zaibatsu by killing a dozen key executives; there were others waiting to step up the ladder, assume the vacated position, access the vast banks of corporate memory" (N 203). The corporation, like the fascist state, subsumes individuals into an immortal group organism. As an abusive father figure, the dying founder of the corporate organism in the novel evokes Hitler or the sort of decadent aristocrats allied with fascism in Europe and South America.

Trying to personify an antagonist, *Neuromancer* imagines a shadowy cousin of Orwell's Big Brother, descended from pulp-fiction masterminds such as Ian Fleming's Dr. No and Sherlock Holmes's archenemy, Dr. Moriarty. The hero and his friends are freelance entrepreneurs who make a killing by carrying out computer raids as if they were post-Vietnam "smart weapons." Because they model warrior fantasies elaborated from video games, and because their autonomy is more important than loyalties or any vision of the future, they are as reactionary as their parental adversary. Although they pay lip service to creativity and technological possibilities, they are numb to self-awareness and intimacy. They act out the self-involvement of the computer nerd in a costume drama of entrepreneurial daring whose ultimate goal is to serve a hazy mother figure and be "credited with large amounts [of money] in numbered Geneva accounts" (N 268).

The infantile roots of "cyberpunk" and the link to traumatic-abuse ideation appear in the Oedipal family Gibson projects. As in *Johnny Mnemonic*, corporate brutality has usurped a nurturant mother figure, the patriarch's wife, Wintermute. Seeking immortality, Wintermute has been punished with a form of play-death and displaced into a funereal tacit reality—exactly the fate of Haggard's She-who-must-be-obeyed. Now, like Ayesha monitoring her crystal ball, she presides over the hero's redemptive penetration of the family fortress, the data structures stripped of all feeling and aptly named "ice." After the hateful father's death, the mother's prosthetic voice merges with the hero-child. Wintermute "meshed somehow" with Case's alter ego, the alienated wizard-child Neuromancer (ibid.). Freedom and vitality are restored. Reinvigorated by his Geneva bank account, purged of toxic implants, Case bids goodbye to his tough warrior sidekick Molly.

This Oedipal scheme maps the familiar disturbances of post-traumatic culture: a retreat from generational and status conflicts; isolation as an orphan in a factory universe. The attenuation of the self matches the exaggerated importance of prosthetic relations, social and technological, and of the phantom mother figure. But these compensations all prove inadequate or treacherous. This is why the climax of the novel, Case's raid on the corporate treasure and his creation of revolutionary change, is the achievement of berserk rage. "'Hate'll get you through,' the voice said. . . . 'Now you gotta *hate*.'" Beginning his attack, Case "came in steep, fueled by self-loathing." But "then—old alchemy of the brain and its vast pharmacy—his hate flowed into his hands. In the instant before he drove Kuang's sting through the base of the first tower, he'd attained a level of proficiency exceeding anything he'd ever known or imagined. Beyond ego, beyond personality, beyond awareness, he moved, Kuang moving with him, evading his attackers with an ancient dance, Hideo's dance, grace of the mind-body interface granted him, in that second, by the clarity and singleness of his wish to die" (*N* 261–62).

Despite the rhapsody about dance, the passage is really about an effort to feel rage. It is a self-intoxicating war cry directed against abstract enemies and against the deficient self ("fueled by self-loathing"). In its greed for transcendence ("beyond . . . beyond . . . beyond") and righteous annihilation, the conjured fury is apocalyptic. The pathos in this tantrum lies in the suspicion of infantile weakness, deprivation, and self-loathing behind it. Imagination commands superhuman mastery, but the self feels vague. Like a victim of abuse, Case is divided against himself as if partially under the influence of the "father" he is attacking. Only exterminatory rage can purify his will.[27] But in life as in fiction, rage is not a reliable therapy. Like Sherlock Holmes shooting cocaine in "stagnant" London, Case ends up in a world without social feeling, affluent enough to take a holiday from his warrior-entrepreneurialism, under the same "dead" sky, "the color of television, tuned to a dead channel" (*N* 3).

Although its subjects are cyberspace and renewal, *Neuromancer* is as deeply conservative as its 1890s ancestors. Struggling to extricate the greyed-out self from the factory world, self-intoxicating violence produces more of the deadness it fights against. This is the morbid irony in Terry Gilliam's *Twelve Monkeys*. A rogue virus has poisoned the earth and driven the survivors underground. With a time machine, they send a prison "volunteer" back into the past—into our present—to discover and disarm the source of the plague. In the underground future, James Cole is apparently in prison for berserk behavior connected with a recurring nightmare about a childhood trauma. Reluctantly, he enters the past on a messianic mission, to save humankind. But with the future at least provisionally ordained, his mission is actually a form of traumatic rescue. Mistaken for a madman, he is committed to an asylum, and in one of many ironies he nearly blunders into the source of the viral plague. His quest leads him to the moment he has been, and will be, dreaming about, in which he is killed trying to stop the plague terrorist.

Twelve Monkeys ends in a radically equivocal moment. James Cole seems destined to be trapped in a cycle of post-traumatic suffering. Haunted by flashbacks to his own death, he will go berserk, be imprisoned, return to the past in search of the originary world trauma, blunder again into his own death, awaken haunted by flashbacks, and so on. This is a bold statement of the cycle of trauma and detection in which the addicted Sherlock Holmes is ensnared, and a succinct image of post-traumatic culture.

Apocalypse Management

The fear of being swallowed into an infinite regression, as in *Twelve Monkeys*, assumes that life is a prison. Like traumatic flashbacks, recurring episodes of evil and grief intensify the pressure for apocalyptic relief through a final annihilation. The dynamic is hysterical, like the terror of being buried alive. Judeo-Christian culture thinks of the Last Judgment dividing humankind—"man"—in two, immortalizing the good half and dissociating the damned to outer darkness. All the fury of Armageddon leads to this fantasy that climactic judgment can free the self of "man" of its guilty, discordant, damned "impurities." The critical ambiguity in such thinking is that it posits a force of cosmic necessity, but in practice it tends to be self-intoxicating. As a result, it is no easy matter, as the history of psychology shows, to evaluate internal controls. We are high-strung primates who fear death yet also carefully model it in racing accidents, headline disasters, and crime dramas to stimulate and police ourselves. In sports and games, with buttered popcorn, we continually rehearse warfare.

Ideas of the apocalypse are tools for restructuring particular lives. Nuclear Armageddon was not only a realistic threat but also an argument for military-industrial investment and cuts in social services. Corporate survival rhetoric justifies personnel triage and wage cuts. By contrast, the hero's berserk raid on corporate patriarchy in *Neuromancer* has a pseudofeminist subtext centered on the exiled mother figure and Case's tough ninja girlfriend Molly, even as it acts out a form of conversion or coming-of-age experience for a symbolic son. Yet instead of imagining new ways of living, the novel combines familiar quest-story conventions with fantasies of computer prowess, using its do-or-die apocalypse to reinforce the status quo.

This use of the apocalypse as a threat and a stimulant can become a conventional gesture. Max Nordau's *Degeneration* extravagantly rages against extravagance in its defense of wholesome propriety. The buoyant Walt Whitman is "crazy." His "'goodness,' which is in reality moral obtuseness and morbid sentimentality, frequently accompanies degeneration, and appears even in the cruelest assassins."[28] Nordau strikes a pose of magisterial gravity, but his rhetoric wages a battle against cosmic doom. Mystics, for instance, "but especially egomaniacs and filthy pseudo-realists, are enemies to society of the direst kind. Society must unconditionally defend itself against them" (N 557). To defend "unconditionally" is to wage total war: it is the definition of berserking. A century later, similar jeremiads follow Nordau's flight path. The Christian right has relied heavily on apocalyptic excitement, and in the 1990s, as overexposure dulled their edge, the conventions became as oddly dissociated as they are in Nordau; witness failed Supreme Court nominee Robert H. Bork, whose rage in *Slouching towards Gomorrah* is pure Nordau.

The judge sees corporations and prisons stabilizing a Christian nation corrupted by vile "liberals" and is pitching headfirst toward doom. Like Nordau and such cosmic shootouts as Hollywood's *Independence Day* (1996), Judge Bork conjures up a righteous anger that supplants curiosity about the way people are actually living. Apocalyptic imaginations are out of sympathy with the humble projects of making a living, paying the rent, raising the children, and coping with old age. Instead, these arguments promote a sensation of personal coherence achieved (or grounded) through a momentous attack. The exalted righteousness sacrifices the faulty—mortal—everyday self. As Jonathan Shay says, "the berserker also feels like a god."[29]

Judge Bork anchors his argument in a traumatic moment at Yale in the 1960s, when he came across a pile of books on the sidewalk burned in an act of vandalism or perhaps—he never considers other possibilities—as a protest against the Vietnam War by powerless young people reluctant to die for a cause they did not believe in. Decades afterward, their assault on "civilization" still outraged the judge. Does his diatribe deserve to be called berserking? After all, his attack is a rhetorical assault rather than a bayonet thrust. Despite his adjectival incontinence, he is strategic. He blasts ideological straw men, bowling over proper nouns and zapping abstractions as if they were enemies in a video game. In his eyes "affluence" is ruinous, for example, but affluent people like him and the institutions they dominate are happily above all suspicion. He takes a perfunctory swipe at "Hanoi Jane" Fonda but ignores Henry Kissinger's manipulation of peace negotiations for selfish political ends.[30] However, as his title makes plain, Judge Bork uses survival panic to incite authoritarian passions, and his argument functions as a threat display meant to cow readers, even as it offers them an injection of righteousness if they submit to his views. What makes this threat display tantamount to berserking is its call for the punishment and death of "enemies."

In Vietnam, says Page Smith, the United States behaved as Great Britain did during the American Revolution. "Declaring to the world our devotion to international justice, to self-determination, to democracy, we undertook to check the progress of 'Godless Communism' in a small country half a world away. . . . And in our rage at not being able to win, we—enlightened democratic nation that we profess to be—embarked on a policy of senseless devastation, that most bankrupt of policies, the punitive. If we could not defeat our enemy, we would punish him severely."[31]

This assessment applies with breathtaking fitness to rhetorical fire like that of Judge Bork. As in the psychiatrist's account of combat berserking, the judge felt betrayed by a breakdown of cultural integrity or *thèmis*. He acted out a "rupture" between "the social realization of 'what's right' and the inner *thèmis* of ideals, ambitions, and affiliations."[32] And after his failed Supreme Court bid he felt personally injured. His title makes his—and everybody else's—everyday life a battle against looming death. Reasonable minds can disagree about how realistic he is, and reactionary voices are not the only ones that may run amok with their morals blazing.

In the context of this book, what matters is the dangerous ambiguity of the judge's behavior and his inability to think critically about it *as a behavior*. After all, Gomorrah and the implied day of reckoning are fantasies of extermination. His rage is a battle cry, a call to crush "enemies." Implicitly it is a group experience, affecting others just as one soldier's berserking influences comrades—and enemies. And like many other examples of post-traumatic thinking in these pages, his cry of injury and apocalypse mingles self-serving calculation with visceral—as it were, somatized—conviction. As a call for the restoration of righteous health, by government force if necessary, the judge's war cry is not only a symptom of historical turmoil, and not simply a unique effort to rally morale, but also a technique for managing an unruly world, a handy rhetorical weapon, a *style*; this is, after all, why interpretation always needs to go beyond injury.

Epilogue

AS A TROPE, trauma has adapted to frame the experiences of individuals and nations. It can be formulated to relieve suffering and to adjust the scales of justice, but it can also rationalize dependence or aggression. Neuroscience may one day clarify the processes that govern particular expressions of trauma. But even then, because neurological events do not take place in a vacuum, we would still need criticism to evaluate the stories that shape us. In one expert view, the popularity of trauma theories may be "still growing rapidly."[1] But the opposite may also be true: "As the veterans of Vietnam age and fade, and their patrons in government adopt new priorities, a chapter in the history of the traumatic memory draws to a close."[2] The trope is still in motion.

And so a highly placed judge published a tract defining the nation's character in the 1990s. Distressed by events beginning in the 1960s, armed with the rhetoric of the religious right, he called for "unconditional" war against "enemy" Americans, and threatened divine extermination. On December 8, 1993, a Jamaican immigrant obsessed with racial injury used the notion of a biblical apocalypse and a pistol in a "holy war" that killed five commuters in a Long Island

Railroad coach. Although Colin Ferguson appears to have suffered from classic paranoid schizophrenia, familiar post-traumatic cultural themes also shaped his behavior. After a sheltered, affluent childhood in Jamaica, he suddenly lost both his parents. The *New York Times* focused on his "unrealistic" expectations, his career failures in the United States, and his "long slide from privilege to slaughter."[3] In late-Victorian terms, he was a "down-going man," and in 1988 his wife divorced him, administering "what acquaintances called a crushing blow to a psychologically fragile man." He was forced to leave Adelphi University, was arrested for harassing a subway passenger, and was injured at work but unable to collect "what he felt was a rightful worker's compensation settlement." Afraid of his growing incoherence, his (also black) landlord evicted him, "threatening his last refuge." As the traumatic stress mounted, "night after night he had read aloud from a Bible and handled a gun and brooded over what he saw as the implacable racism of the United States."[4]

And what of the cultural categories that structured Ferguson's tragic rage? In effect, his need for deliverance led him to think in terms of an Armageddon on the model of "ethnic cleansing." In his room he chanted "mantras all night about 'all the black people killing all the white people.'" According to his landlord, after he bought a pistol "he talked in the third person about some apocryphal-doom [apocalyptic] scenario."[5] But while he was acting as a messianic deliverer, Ferguson was also probably influenced by headline stories in the 1980s and 1990s of distraught employees gone amok with firearms in the workplace. And in methodically arming himself, he seems to have modeled his "mission" on the berserking of combat soldiers or post-traumatic veterans. For a while, it appeared that his legal defense would be based on a post-traumatic concept of "black rage." At his trial he referred to himself in the third person, although the extent to which this dissociation was a conscious strategy to evade criminal responsibility is unclear. In acting as his own trial counsel, he seems to have modeled his behavior on melodrama—this time, courtroom scenarios.

For this reason it is poignant to read Ferguson's torment against a post-traumatic fantasia such as John Frankenheimer's 1996 remake of H. G. Wells's *Island of Dr. Moreau* (1896). The film opens with a cultural crash when an airplane bearing United Nations peace negotiators goes down in the Pacific. In the life raft, two of the survivors kill each other while competing for the last canteen of water. The third, Douglas, is rescued and taken to Dr. Moreau's island, where he discovers the former Nobel Prize winner (played by Marlon Brando) trying to "perfect" humankind by crafting hybrid "beast-people" through genetic engineering. Like the immigrant from Jamaica awaking from a privileged childhood, Wells's narrator wakes from a crash on a prison island, among psychically disembedded, traumatically abused beast-people. As he watches, the victims become aware of their abuse and finally, going berserk, trigger a holocaust.

Moreau's island is a symbolic immortality system based on hero worship. But as in *Schindler's List*, the system turns out to be a vampire/slave economy. The doctor's hybrid people are "his" creatures, extensions of his will, like dehumanized colonial "children," concentration-camp Jews, black slaves, or the robotic servants in *Beauty and the Beast*. Overtly, Moreau is a paternalistic father-creator, and Brando shrewdly plays him as a kindly, self-deluded figure with good manners and a taste for Chopin. But Moreau dominates "his" children, raising them in his heroic aura but also feeding on their vitality, manipulating their genes to substantiate his own Faustian aggrandizement. He moves among them in a military utility vehicle rigged up like the "pope-mobile" in which the pontiff—"il papa"—makes personal appearances, and the image brilliantly evokes the ambivalent potential in hero worship. As a prosthetic voice, Moreau is "implanted" in his children's bodies in the form of electroshock sensors that allow his verbal commands to stun them into submission with a remote-control button. The device dramatizes not only the prosthetic voice's potential for treacherous conversion from nurture to tyranny, but also the shock of trauma. It acts out a radical confusion of agency and identity akin to psychosis. In the crisis of self-awareness that precipitates the beast-people's uprising, they plaintively ask the doctor, "What am I?"

There it is: the question Colin Ferguson must have asked when American social realities disconfirmed his sense of himself. "What am I?" Ferguson began life in an elite Jamaican family, identifying with white privilege. Like one of the beast-people who form Moreau's inner circle—one of whom is actually given dreadlocks—he seems to have lived a life in split focus. And like that elite Praetorian Guard, Ferguson felt himself drawn into an all-consuming class war (recall the mantras about "all the black people killing all the white people"), just as the island's final explosion corresponds to Ferguson's "apocryphal-doom [apocalyptic] scenario." The man may well have been psychotic, but he formed his psychotic fantasies out of familiar cultural materials.

The story of Dr. Moreau offers several overlaid explanations for the insurrection. As in apologies for social hierarchy going back through colonialism, *The Tempest*, and Saint George to the ancients, one answer is that lowly creatures such as the beast-people "naturally" degenerate toward a dog-eat-dog anarchy unless an elite hero governs them. Even Moreau's beautiful feline "daughter" Aissa needs maintenance injections of "serum" to keep her from regressing. The Victorian ethos of paternalistic technological progress grew out of this moralized aristocratic science—literally so, because the "fathers" of modern science came mostly from the upper classes. But whereas Dr. Moreau rhapsodizes like the Holmesian Hamlet about human perfectibility, the crash survivor Douglas condemns him for concocting a scientific pact with the devil. Douglas voices the other Victorian tradition, that of hostility toward modernism. Faustian efforts to improve life seem to him demonic; they unleash primeval rage (which is the moral of Steven Spielberg's *Jurassic Park*). Like many fundamentalists today, he seems to side with exploited "bottom dogs," yet his deepest faith is in the "natural" status quo—which would preserve a caste system.

These are arguments that Colin Ferguson could have used in interpreting his situation. The terms—heroic self-improvement, satanic treachery, poisoned will, prophetic wrath—would have suited his biblical fixation on "apocryphal doom." What is limited in *Moreau*'s and Ferguson's imaginations is a capacity for stories that can make something of the question—the core problem of modernism—"What am I?" In the end, nobody on the island is able to think about that question. Whether humans are perfectible or inherently tainted by primeval rage, people need purpose, a conviction that their lives matter, that the strongest dog need not always devour the other dogs down to the last bark. Moreau tries to offer his awakening creatures a benevolent answer, but their question threatens his status. "You are my children," he tells them. "But the Law is necessary." The law forbids their rebellion but also, like the Nazi order, freezes an oppressive social hierarchy in place. Moreau's law legitimizes the predatory immortality system. Supposedly, the beast-people's accidental discovery of the satisfactions of killing and eating meat (rabbits) breaks Moreau's fundamental taboo and unleashes a cannibalistic competition. But the law itself cannot resist killing. As Moreau tries to discipline and forgive the first carnivore, one of his elite guards impulsively shoots the offender, and this vigilante execution traumatizes the assembled "family."

This is the sort of prosthetic conversion that shatters trust in the world, and ultimately it destroys the island. With the beast-people's self-awareness comes the realization that Moreau's fatherly voice in them can turn shockingly vicious. With his remote-control stun gun, he personifies techno-tyrants such as Orwell's Big Brother. The beast-people's awakening is like Douglas's discovery that while he was injured, unconscious from the plane crash, Moreau experimented on him, medically abusing him. The healer is Dracula in a lab coat, and nobody on the island can make sense of this inner reality. None of the characters thinks in terms of prosthetic interrelations. Neither does the screenplay. Nobody is curious about the peculiar subjectivity of the beast-people. The island is funded and run by an invisible, absentee, paternalistic foundation, and by Moreau's elite professionalism. It is like a Sherlock Holmes case, centered in one "genius," without curiosity, play, or desire. Instead of fostering creative initiative in his "children," Moreau inculcates reflex obedience. Poignantly, he only introduces his creatures to music as a trick to soothe them when they start to rebel.

At heart, this is the 1890s' nightmare family of predatory parent and cannibal child, just as Moreau's lab, with its steel cages and human infants floating in specimen jars, is the factory world that orphaned Havelock Ellis and the high-tech prison rising in Flint, Michigan, to manage its beast-people on their "long slide from privilege" to jobless criminality. Moreau himself resembles paternalistic empire builders such as Andrew Carnegie and Henry Ford, each of them responsible for an infamous massacre of employees. The slaughtered rabbits that bring out the crazed carnivore in the beast-people are related to the bunnies *Roger and Me* associates with sacrificed autoworkers, to the Jews shipped to slaughter in cattle cars in *Schindler's List*, and to the victims of Nazi and Japanese military doctors, some of them killed by vivisection, fulfilling the worst Victorian nightmares about medical science.

Once the cycle of survival competition begins, the story argues, it engulfs everything. But what triggers the competition in the first place? As in the world of modern technology, food and shelter need not be in short supply in Moreau's island paradise, but autonomy is. Heroic purpose is. When subjectivity is hoarded at the top, as scarce as drinking water on a life raft in a sea of social death, people will kill each other. Like America's underclass, Moreau's "half-breeds" know they are missing something. They cope with demoralization through the doctor's escapist drugs, "carnivorous" crime, and when all else fails, a version of the urban riots dramatized in so many 1990s films, not to mention South Central Los Angeles. The moment the boss is killed in the havoc on the island, his lieutenant (Montgomery) usurps his role, voice, costume, and all, only to be overthrown in turn. But the desire to be a messianic dictator that turns the island into a parody of Jonestown is rooted in a survival terror that consumes nearly everyone before it burns out.

From the vantage point of this book, those moral flames on the screen burn up not only the island's society but also its fund of unexamined stories. In the end the film itself leaves a post-traumatic imprint on imagination insofar as the climactic annihilation of stories constricts the range of responses available to us. The beast-people's prophet figure, the "Giver of the Law," ruefully sums up the conflagration to the departing Douglas: "We have to be what we are." He seems not only to warn us against overreaching as Faust does, but also to confirm the status quo: "Perhaps four legs is better anyway." This implies that class is biological destiny, and the half-breeds and beast-people of this world had better get used to not walking upright. Like blacks as conceived by the *Bell Curve* polemicists, the beast-people are "naturally" deficient in intelligence and culture.[6] Therefore the doctor needs gently to keep them in their places so that unrealistic aspirations do not frustrate them and cause a regression toward primal violence like Colin Ferguson's "long slide." In leaving the traumatized Douglas and the audience with this summation, this "last judgment," the film could be said to model numbness and avoidance of the holocaust it has just presented. It narrows rather than expands the options for thinking about that horror. Its conspicuously balanced judgment masks its limited capacity for empathy. In this way the film reinforces the status quo, serving the Moreaus of the 1990s, the unaccountable Roger Smiths and the other "benevolent dictators" who exploit "beast-people" all over the globe, from China to Mexico to Flint, with genteel logic, secret police, and a thumb on the stun gun.

Colin Ferguson tried to understand his conflicts as a post-traumatic story. A black man injured on the job and in a racist society cannot collect compensation, cannot get the white "doctor" to acknowledge him as a man, and so he runs amok. To an indeterminate extent, mental illness presumably restricted Ferguson's story options. If other stories had opened for him—in a psychiatric, neighborhood, or intimate context, for example—they may or may not have forestalled his rampage; nobody can say for sure. What I want to point out is the scarcity of narrative resources in the cultural moment. Colin Ferguson could have seen his inner anguish writ large on the screen of public fantasy in *The Island of Dr. Moreau*, but he would probably have had no way of sharing that experience. Like Douglas, like Wells's Time Traveller, the immigrant Ferguson felt victimized in what was supposed to be a paradise, but nobody would believe him, and his voice grew into an intimidating biblical rant that choked off all relationships. His landlord listened. He could read his tenant's growing stress. But apparently he could not find a useful way to involve friends and neighbors, let alone the overstrained social-service bureaucracy of New York City. Chances are the landlord felt that involving the police was out of the question. By what story logic could he get his paranoid tenant to a psychiatrist, even if antipsychotic drugs were guaranteed to save half a dozen lives? In retrospect, Colin Ferguson's story was clear enough as a drama of "degeneration," but the surrounding culture had few stories through which to relate to him—few stories that people were able to hear.

The *New York Times* coverage is symptomatic. It recognized post-traumatic qualities in Ferguson's story, especially in his claims for compensation. But the *Times* in 1993 also wanted to show that it was not naive and could not be fooled into "bleeding-heart" sympathies. The newspaper was caught up in a typically American competition. When it could find no traumatic racial victimization in Ferguson's past—no shocking abuse—the *Times* story concluded that Ferguson was not one of "us," but was deluded. This is something like *The Island of Dr. Moreau*, polarizing life into beast and human being, the four-legged and the two-legged, with no subjectivity in between. After all, racial injustice is a fact of life in the United States and elsewhere, and it has been exacerbated by the economic dogfight of the "lean and mean" decades. Ferguson's America not only saw President Reagan introducing apocalyptic rhetoric on the six o'clock news, it also witnessed increasingly bold attacks on the historic gains made in the 1960s and 1970s in civil rights. Such a harsh climate breeds distortions on all sides; at a summer camp for inner-city children in Chicago, counselors are instructed never to physically restrain the campers, even if provoked, because the children have learned that such an "injury" may give them grounds to sue for "damages."

Colin Ferguson was prepared to justify his bloodbath by invoking "black rage," a concept charged with a vague yet irresistible authority. But in an aggressively competitive culture, his paranoia is not so much illogical as disproportionate. Neuroscience could have much to tell us about his tragic lapse of self-control, but in the end we still need criticism to decode the cultural relationships through which, and despite which, the man fashioned his identity and actions. The *New York Times* could see a 1990s tale of a "slide from privilege to slaughter." But in an era when the scale of human life is mind-boggling, when democracy's responsible citizen is a trivial mote among the billions on the planet, and great social predators scoop up small fry and hype the feeding frenzy in press releases and the media pipeline, the *Times* has nothing to say about Colin Ferguson's inner life save that he "slid" and was "crushed" when his wife left him. And somehow this post-traumatic soap opera left five people shot to death.

Let me close by revisiting Kazakhstan, half a world away, on the morning I mentioned in my preface, where a local teacher I will call Tatiana was also thinking about biblical deliverance and being told she was crazy. As we talked about the post-Soviet shake-up in the Peace Corps workshop that morning, Tatiana volunteered that in a recent dream she had seen Christ. Her messiah was a handsome Russian-looking young man, and when she asked if he was truly "the God," he had assured her he was indeed the real thing. When she told her husband about her dream, Tatiana said wryly, "He told me I was crazy."

Everyone in the workshop chuckled at this wink of domestic comedy and reality testing. The sensible, motherly, blonde Tatiana was not about to enlist in a holy war. I do not know if she had ever heard of post-traumatic stress; like Vietnam, the Soviet defeat in Afghanistan had produced many stressed combat veterans. Tatiana's dream caught my attention partly because it showed post-traumatic dynamics at work. She had grown up in a nominally Islamic family, in another corner of the Soviet Union, and the prosthetic voice in her dream seemed to offer her a sense of groundedness after a psychic jolt. And for good reason. For some local teachers who were not ethnic Kazakhs, the breakup of the Soviet Union was a cultural crash. After lifetimes of stringent stability, they expected to be eased out of their jobs in the new Kazakhstan and forced to join the flood of emigrants displaced as the autoworkers were in *Roger and Me*. At the same time shock waves of ethnic violence were rippling through the post-Soviet world from places such as Bosnia and Azerbaijan, where ancient injuries had become an interpretive frame for political power plays and personal ambitions. Nobody had been raped or put to death where Tatiana lived, but her world was coming apart. The "new millionaires," "mafia," and some politicians were thriving, but for many ordinary folks the new order threatened a slide toward social death. The once-revered Lenin had vanished from city parks everywhere, and as a prosthetic voice he now seemed to many people a source of abuse.

In this situation, Tatiana's dream of deliverance seemed to be a therapeutic effort, a sort of do-it-yourself version of the ancient cult of Aesculapius, in which the god appeared in dreams to heal people. Because the dream is finally Tatiana's, her Christ fills the role of prosthetic "helper ego" that Otto Rank prescribes for the therapist.[7] In practical terms, her messiah seemed to be helping her decide to identify with Christian Russia if the cultural crash forced her to choose a new identity. Quite apart from any evangelical implications, her vision has echoes in 1990s America. In a popular fantasy about a "near-death experience," for example, a surgical patient's heart stopped for a moment and she saw Christ beckoning to her in a tunnel of light.[8] In a more secular epiphany, *Fearless* makes the wrecked fuselage of the airliner appear as a tunnel to Max Klein— and to the movie audience—as he commands his fellow passengers, "Follow me to the light."

What strikes me about these visionary deliverances, even Colin Ferguson's "mantras," is how private they are. They call to mind Otto Rank's central insight: that we tend to live for our immortality projects rather than in our actual lives, the more vulnerable for our fear and mistrust of the mortal world and mortal people. This is one reason why I was moved that Tatiana wanted to share her "crazy" experience that morning. The old Soviet regime, like factory systems everywhere, had discouraged openness and sharing. Even now I could sense resistance in some of the teachers. Still, most of them joined the young Peace Corps volunteers in reflecting on Tatiana's dream with her. Looking back, it seems to me that the imaginative sympathy of the group was like the grooming behavior of other primates. Intuitively, the group formed a prosthetic network, carrying out the dream's initiative, the work of substantiating the self, and trying to make up for a flustered family ("He told me I was crazy"), imperfect national leaders, and contested mythic epiphanies.

As I see it, this potential for relatedness, whatever form it takes, is the critical zone in which the interplay of injury and interpretation engenders post-traumatic themes or enables the self to get on with life. However much we venerate autonomy, we are social animals. We literally take form out of the genetic and psychic stuff of other people. But in periods when the scale and pace of life rapidly change, self-esteem comes under pressure, with its resultant anxiety and aggression, and the ability to keep renewing forms of relatedness becomes if anything even more momentous. The cruel irony is that stress may rigidify behavior, creating predators and victims just when we most need adaptive flexibility.

The globalizing 1980s and 1990s saw a worldwide retreat from large-scale institutions and cultural systems: a withdrawal toward a local, private, and personal scale. The idea of trauma, with its emphasis on grounding the self by mastering a past injury, may be one expression of that retreat. Yet it would be easy to misjudge this most adaptable of tropes. Although it has been a source of mischief, as in satanic-abuse scenarios, it can also be a useful if imperfect tool for thinking about violence, victimization, and cultural morale.

Every culture must find ways of taming predatory appetites and rationalizing hierarchies. Historically, most complex societies have been organized around a warrior-priest aristocracy, scapegoats, and slaves. As a recently emerged idea, trauma implies a world in which it is at least possible to think about some elemental questions. Can we reconsider our Darwinian worship of superior fangs and survival ecstasy? How do we distinguish between healthy, adaptive stress and stress that cripples? Should we prefer the carrot to the stick? How can we prevent the extermination of the weak? At this transitional moment, in this spectacularly conflicted world of cybernetics and child labor, stealth bombers, consumer magic, and slum trash-pickers, what kind of animals are we? Such questions cry for attention in this momentary lull, while the gears and drives grind quietly in the background, in the factory universe we have inherited, where interpretation is always working overtime to keep up with the production of injury.

Notes

Preface

1. The fourth edition of the psychiatrists' diagnostic manual (*Diagnostic and Statistical Manual of Mental Disorders*, or *DSM-IV*) now contains in excess of three hundred mental disorders, more than three times the number in the first edition (1952). See Stuart A. Kirk and Herb Kutchins, *The Selling of DSM: The Rhetoric of Science in Psychiatry* (New York, 1992). For a bracing appraisal of the excesses and improbabilities of the manual, see L. J. Davis, "The Encyclopedia of Insanity," *Harper's*, February 1997, 61–66.

2. Frederick Leboyer, *Birth without Violence* (New York, 1975); Otto Rank, *The Trauma of Birth* (New York, 1929).

Introduction

1. See George Frederick Drinka, M.D., *The Birth of Neurosis: Myth, Malady, and the Victorians* (New York, 1984), 108–22. In *The Social Unrest* (New York, 1903), J. C. Brooks reports ten thousand fatalities and eighty thousand serious injuries in the United States in 1890, five times England's accident rate. See Otto L. Bettmann, *The Good Old Days—They Were Terrible!* (New York, 1974), 171.

2. Donald L. Barlett and James B. Steele, *America: What Went Wrong?* (Kansas City, Mo., 1992); Paul Krugman, "Long-Term Riches, Short-Term Pain," *New York Times*, September 26, 1994; Christopher Lasch, *The Revolt of the Elites and the Betrayal of Democracy* (New York, 1995).

3. Kirk Johnson, "In the Class of 70, Wounded Winners," *New York Times*, March 7, 1996.

4. Katherine S. Newman, *Declining Fortunes: The Withering of the American Dream* (New York, 1993), 3, 199. See also Paul Krugman, *The Age of Diminished Expectations: U.S. Economic Policy in the 1990s* (Cambridge, Mass., 1990).

5. "A respect for international opinion would have spared the United States the trauma of defeat in war and the disruption of its economy and the unity of society." Donald W. White, *The American Century: The Rise and Decline of the United States as a World Power* (New Haven, Conn., 1996), 436.

6. See John Cassidy, "Who Killed the Middle Class?" *New Yorker*, October 16, 1995, 113–24.

7. John Kenneth Galbraith, *The Culture of Contentment* (New York, 1992), 118.

8. Tom Engelhardt, *The End of Victory Culture* (New York, 1995).

9. Dean Ornish, M.D., *Eat More, Weigh Less* (New York, 1993), 21.

10. Kevin Phillips, *Arrogant Capital* (New York, 1994), 61.

11. See Norman Cohn, *The Pursuit of the Millennium* (New York, 1961).

12. According to the Associated Press, Harold Camping has written two books predicting the end, *1994* and *Are You Ready?* In mid-July 1994, annual giving to his company, Family Radio, was reported to be "up 20 percent this year to $12 million."

13. Lewis H. Lapham, "Balzac's Garret," *Harper's*, May 1996, 9–10. Lapham marvels that in less than a year Pat Robertson's novel sold 275,000 copies.

14. G. M. Young, *Victorian England: Portrait of an Age* (London, 1936), 165.

15. Karl Beckson, *London in the 1890s: A Cultural History* (New York, 1992), xiv.

16. Judith Lewis Herman, *Trauma and Recovery* (New York, 1992), 33.

17. Nancy C. Andreasen, "Post-traumatic Stress Disorder," in *The Comprehensive Textbook of Psychiatry*, edited by H. I. Kaplan and B. J. Sadock (Baltimore, 1985), 919.

18. See, e.g., Irvin D. Yalom, *Existential Psychotherapy* (New York, 1980), 41–43.

19. Herman, *Trauma and Recovery*, 44.

20. Neuroscience has generated a vast and rapidly expanding literature of trauma research. Daniel Goleman offers a lay overview of this research, though not of its controversies and lacunae, in *Emotional Intelligence* (New York, 1995), chap. 13 and appendix C.

21. Allan Young, *The Harmony of Illusions: Inventing Post-Traumatic Stress Disorder* (Princeton, 1995), 5. For attempts to assimilate ethnocultural perspectives into an overview of PTSD, see Derek Summerfield, "Addressing Human Response to War and Atrocity," in *Beyond Trauma: Cultural and Societal Dynamics*, edited by Rolf J. Kleber, Charles R. Figley, and Berthold P. R. Gersons (New York, 1995), 17–29, and *Ethnocultural Aspects of Posttraumatic Stress Disorder*, edited by Anthony J. Marsella et al. (Washington, D.C., 1996).

22. Young, *Harmony of Illusions*, 13.

23. Drinka, *Birth of Neurosis*, 114.

24. Doug Stewart, "The Curse of the *Great Eastern*," *Smithsonian*, November 1994, 66.

25. Quoted in Reinhard Kuhn, *The Demon of Noontide: Ennui in Western Literature* (Princeton, 1976), 26.

26. Drinka, *Birth of Neurosis*, 118.

27. Ibid., 129.

28. In *The Laws of England*, railways and tram companies figure prominently in the cases cited in the statutes governing negligence and damages. The terminology that would come to define trauma was already emerging at the beginning of the nineteenth century, as in number 807, which stipulates that "special damage may be recovered for pecuniary loss sustained . . . or for any other loss or injury actually suffered which follows in the ordinary course of things from the negligent act." A footnote specifies that

"this includes damages which result from nervous shock causing physical injury, whether the incident creating the shock was accompanied by physical impact or not, and whether the injury results directly from the shock or from a cause of action induced by shock." Legal precedents cited begin with a case from 1816 (*Jones v. Bayes*). The ambiguities in this footnote gave rise to the perplexities that called the concept of trauma into being. See The Earl of Halsbury, *The Laws of England* (London, 1912), 21:483.

29. Young, *Harmony of Illusions*, 17. Young notes that in the year following the liberalization of the act, "juries awarded over three hundred thousand pounds to people injured on the railways" (ibid.).

30. The standard history has been Ilza Veith's psychoanalytically oriented *Hysteria: The History of a Disease* (Chicago, 1965). Perhaps the best-known feminist study of hysteria in the nineteenth century is Elaine Showalter, *The Female Malady: Women, Madness, and English Culture, 1830–1980* (New York, 1985). More recent is Showalter's *Hystories: Hysterical Epidemics and Modern Media* (New York, 1997), which examines alien abduction delusions, chronic fatigue syndrome, satanic ritual abuse, recovered memory, and multiple personality syndrome. For an up-to-date overview of hysteria studies with a useful bibliography, see Mark S. Micale, *Approaching Hysteria: Disease and Its Interpretations* (Princeton, 1995).

31. See Micale's survey in *Approaching Hysteria*, 75–88.

32. Showalter, *Hystories*, 3–5.

33. Richard S. Lazarus, "The Costs and Benefits of Denial," in *The Denial of Stress*, edited by Shlomo Breznitz (New York, 1983), 1, 9–10. Lazarus quotes Ernest Becker's *The Denial of Death* (New York, 1973).

34. Ibid., 238.

35. Janet Oppenheim, *Shattered Nerves: Doctors, Patients, and Depression in Victorian England* (New York, 1991).

36. Abram Kardiner, *The Traumatic Neuroses of War*, appeared in 1941, followed after the war by A. Kardiner and H. Spiegel, *War, Stress, and Neurotic Illness* (New York, 1947).

37. See Robert Jay Lifton, *Home from the War* (New York, 1973), and Jonathan Shay, *Achilles in Vietnam: Combat Trauma and the Undoing of Character* (New York, 1994).

38. Oppenheim, *Shattered Nerves*, 103.

39. Allan Young (1995) analyzes the negotiations that created *DSM-III*, and documents the process by which its central categories took shape.

40. Herman, *Trauma and Recovery*, 1.

41. Nancy Ann Jeffrey, "Disability Claims Mirror Rising Job Cuts," *Wall Street Journal*, November 21, 1996. The article summarizes American Management Association and Cigna Corp. reports.

42. Herman, *Trauma and Recovery*, 140–47.

43. In *Regeneration* (New York, 1992), her novel about the psychiatrist W. H. R. Rivers and the Craiglockhart War Hospital in World War I, Pat Barker has Wilfred Owen explain the analogy of shell-shocked patients to Antaeus, who is too strong for his adversary Hercules until his feet leave the ground, rendering him helpless. Psychi-

atry "thinks we—the patients—are like Antaeus in the sense that we've been ungrounded by the war. And the way back to health is to re-establish the link between oneself and the earth, but understanding 'earth' to mean society as well as nature" (123).

44. One therapist, for example, has proposed the fuzzy category of "insidious trauma" that would encompass the psychic damage caused by chronic fear of sexual assault in a misogynistic culture. See Maria P. Root, "Reconstructing the Impact of Trauma on Personality," in *Personality and Psychopathology: Feminist Reappraisals*, edited by L. S. Brown and M. Baillou (New York, 1992).

45. See, e.g., Bessel van der Kolk, "The Body Keeps the Score: Memory and the Evolving Psychobiology of Posttraumatic Stress," *Harvard Review of Psychiatry*, January–February 1994, 253–65.

46. See Robert Elias, *The Politics of Victimization: Victims, Victimology, and Human Rights* (New York, 1986), chap. 1.

47. See "Witchcraft Beliefs as an Explanation of Suffering and a Means of Resolving Conflict," in A. D. J. Macfarlane, *Witchcraft in Tudor and Stuart England* (New York, 1970), 192–207.

48. Herman, *Trauma and Recovery*, 7.

49. Ibid., 9.

50. Ibid., 28.

51. Ibid., 1.

52. Cathy Caruth, ed., *Trauma: Explorations in Memory* (Baltimore, 1995), 6.

53. Kali Tal, *Worlds of Hurt: Reading the Literatures of Trauma* (New York, 1996), 9–16.

54. Among innumerable examples of such films are *True Romance* and *The Professional*; in the latter, a girl persuades a professional assassin to train her in what the film coyly calls "cleaning."

55. "Harper's Index," *Harper's*, April 1996.

56. An article in the *Toronto Star* (September 20, 1993) reports that auto mishaps are the biggest cause of traumatic stress disorder. It cites a study in the *British Medical Journal* that found that 25 percent of motor vehicle accident victims have severe psychological disturbances lasting a year or more, and mentions a study published in the *Journal of Consulting and Clinical Psychology* in June 1992 that discovered post-traumatic stress disorder in 11.5 percent of accident victims.

57. C. R. Whittaker, "The Poor," in *The Romans*, edited by Andrea Giardina (Chicago, 1993), 273.

58. Becker, *The Denial of Death*, 2.

59. Richard L. Rubenstein, *The Age of Triage* (Boston, 1983), 161.

60. Kai Erikson, "Notes on Trauma and Community," in Caruth, *Trauma*, 198.

61. See Ernest Becker, *Escape from Evil* (New York, 1975), and René Girard, *Violence and the Sacred* (Baltimore, 1977). See also Jeff Greenberg, Sheldon Solomon, and Tom Pyszczynski, "Terror Management Theory of Self-Esteem and Cultural Worldviews: Empirical Assessments and Conceptual Refinements," *Advances in Experimental Social Psychology*, edited by Mark P. Zanna, vol. 29 (New York, 1997), and

the same authors' account of terror management in *Psychological Inquiry* 8, no. 1 (1997): 1–20, 59–70.

62. Associated Press story in the *Daily Hampshire Gazette* (Northampton, Mass.), September 10–11, 1994.

63. Machines are supposed to work infallibly, Becker points out, "since we have to put all our trust in them [to control nature]. And so when they fail to work our whole world view begins to crumble—just as the primitives' world view did when they found their rituals were not working in the face of western culture and weaponry. I am thinking of how anxious we are to find the exact cause of an airplane crash, or how eager we are to attribute the crash to 'human error' and not machine failure." *Escape from Evil*, 9.

64. *Daily Hampshire Gazette* (Northampton, Mass.), September 10–11, 1994.

65. See William Walters Sargant, *Battle for the Mind: A Physiology of Conversion and Brain-washing* (New York, 1971).

66. Ellen Bass and Luise Thornton, eds., *I Never Told Anyone: Writings by Women Survivors of Sexual Abuse* (New York, 1983), 22.

67. In *On Death and Dying* (New York, 1969) Dr. Kubler-Ross studied the process of dying with refreshing empirical boldness. Then during the 1970s, as if increasingly traumatized herself, she apparently underwent a sort of conversion experience, promulgating doctrinaire fantasies of an afterlife that have naively reinvented late-Victorian spiritualism and helped shape New Age beliefs.

68. Charles Perrow, *Normal Accidents* (New York, 1984). Although it cost millions of dollars, the investigation of TWA Flight 800's explosion off Long Island in 1995 could only arrive at probable causes. The investigators had to counter persistent rumors of terrorist malice, government conspiracy, and other popular moral-agonistic explanations.

69. Sociologist Diane Vaughan examines NASA's culture in *The Challenger Launch Decision* (Chicago, 1996).

70. Trevor Gambling, "Magic, Accounting and Morale," *Accounting Organizations and Society* 2, no. 2 (1977): 150.

71. This phenomenon is called risk homeostasis. Improvements in safety may perversely encourage people to push their limits. Recent risk theory is the subject of Malcolm Gladwell's "Blowup," *New Yorker*, January 22, 1996, 32–36. Gladwell reports on studies of the Three Mile Island nuclear accident, among others.

72. For example, in A.D. 14, in what is now Westphalia, Roman soldiers exterminated a people called the Marsi in order to teach their neighbors an unforgettable lesson.

73. See Elaine Scarry, *The Body in Pain: The Making and Unmaking of the World* (New York, 1985), 27.

74. See Shay, *Achilles in Vietnam*, 3–4.

75. See Linda Schele and Mary Ellen Miller, eds., *The Blood of Kings* (Fort Worth, Tex., 1986); see also Richard Castillo's recent pair of articles in *Culture, Medicine, and Psychiatry* 18 (1994): 1–21 and 141–62.

76. In "Hysteria: A Neurobiological Theory," in *Archives of General Psychiatry* 27

(1972): 771–86, A. M. Ludwig proposes that hysterical reactions to traumatic threat follow two neurobiological patterns, violent motor reaction and a sham death reflex that I associate with play-death. Kay H. Blacker and Joe P. Tupin sketch some reservations about Ludwig's hypothesis in *Hysterical Personality*, edited by Mardi J. Horowitz (New York, 1977), 108–9.

77. John C. Danforth, *Resurrection: The Confirmation of Clarence Thomas* (New York, 1994), 208. Danforth worried that Thomas would be "shell-shocked" during his testimony (121); he claims that Thomas's counsel, Ken Duberstein, "felt shell-shocked by the [political] system" (196). Among the commentators to have referred to trauma is Jeffrey Rosen: "A less self-pitying justice might have begun to recover from the trauma of his hearings by now." See "Confirmations," *New Republic*, December 19, 1994, 33.

78. See, e.g., Alan M. Dershowitz, *The Abuse Excuse and Other Cop Outs, Sob Stories, and Evasions of Responsibility* (New York, 1994). The provocative righteousness of Dershowitz's title mirrors the manipulative righteousness he scorns. A cautious effort to sort out these issues is found in Donald Alexander Downs, *More than Victims: Battered Women, the Syndrome Society, and the Law* (Chicago, 1996).

79. During her imprisonment Mary embroidered these words in the Oxburgh hangings (1569–84), now in the Victoria and Albert Museum. The motto is not simply a sentimental consolation and Petrarchan convention, but also a self-empowering threat, as Mary's cousin Queen Elizabeth recognized by having the headsman put an end to her rival's "thriving" in a judicial murder as devious as the motto (1587).

80. Cathy Horyn, "Absolute Cindy," *Vanity Fair*, August 1994, 72.

81. "Episode 23: 'Bart Gets Hit by a Car.'"

82. Young, *Harmony of Illusions*, 17. See also Oppenheim, *Shattered Nerves*, 97–100.

83. March 2, 1993. Described in Michael Yapko, *Suggestions of Abuse: True and False Memories of Childhood Trauma* (New York, 1994), 159.

84. See Elizabeth Loftus and Katherine Ketcham, *The Myth of Repressed Memory: False Memories and Allegations of Sexual Abuse* (New York, 1994).

85. See, e.g., Lester Thurow, "The Rich: Why Their World Might Crumble," *New York Times Magazine*, November 19, 1995, which explores analogies between the 1990s and the decline of Rome (78).

86. Charles Sugnet, "For Polite Reactionaries," *Transition* 69 (Spring 1996), 26. Sugden shows that "anarchy" in this context lumps together global, class, and gender anxieties.

87. Aor. Konrad Brendler, "Working Through the Holocaust: Still a Task for Germany's Youth?" in Kleber, Figley, and Gersons, *Beyond Trauma*, 249.

88. One sign of this is the number of movies and novels that recreate the 1890s and that era's stories, from remakes of *Dracula, Dr. Jekyll and Mr. Hyde*, and the ubiquitous Sherlock Holmes to novels such as Caleb Carr's *The Alienist* and E. L. Doctorow's *Waterworks*, Stephen Poliakoff's film *Century*, and the BBC/PBS television serial *Bramwell*.

89. Micale, *Approaching Hysteria*, 75–88.

90. Lynn White Jr., "Death and the Devil," in Robert S. Kinsman, *The Dark Side of the Renaissance* (Berkeley and Los Angeles, 1974), 25–46.

91. T. Walter Herbert, "Mozart, Hawthorne, and Mario Savio," *College English* 57, no. 4 (1995): 403. Herbert quotes Henry Adams, *The Education of Henry Adams*, edited by Ernest Samuels (Boston, 1973), 433.

92. Rubenstein, *Age of Triage*, 1. Rubenstein proposes that the Enclosure Acts, which drove whole peasant villages out of existence in Renaissance England, were among the first signs of that triage mentality.

93. I. F. Clarke, *Voices Prophesying War*, 2d ed. (Oxford, 1992), 84.

94. A succinct and cogent argument of this sort is found in Sean Wilentz, "Un-golden Age," *New Republic*, April 1, 1996, 20–21. A more elaborate version of the thesis appears in Phillips, *Arrogant Capital*.

95. Louis Uchitelle and N. R. Kleinfield, "On the Battlefields of Business, Millions of Casualties," *New York Times*, March 3, 1996, sec. A. The seven-part series in the *Times*, "The Downsizing of America," repeatedly uses the vocabulary of trauma to describe the economic dislocations of the 1990s.

96. Michael J. Sandel, "America's Search for a New Public Philosophy," *Atlantic Monthly*, March 1996, 59, adapted from Sandel's *Democracy's Discontent: America in Search of Public Philosophy* (Cambridge, Mass., 1996).

97. See Christopher Lasch, *The Culture of Narcissism* (New York, 1978). More recent and polemical are Robert J. Samuelson, *The Good Life and Its Discontents: The American Dream in the Age of Entitlement, 1945–1995* (New York, 1996); William Damon, *Greater Expectations: Overcoming the Culture of Indulgence in America's Homes and Schools* (New York, 1996); and Charles Sykes, *Dumbing Down Our Kids: Why American Children Feel Good about Themselves But Can't Read, Write, or Add* (New York, 1996).

98. A *New York Times* poll (March 5, 1996, sec. A) reported that 35 percent of all middle-class respondents felt "at risk of falling out of the middle class." The number rose to 53 percent among those affected even indirectly by layoffs.

99. David Cannadine, "The Brass-Tacks Queen," *New York Review of Books*, April 23, 1987, 31.

100. Anthony Storr, *Human Destructiveness* (New York, 1991), 105.

101. Gail Bederman, *Manliness and Civilization* (Chicago, 1995), chap. 1.

102. Havelock Ellis, *The Dance of Life* (London, 1923), 199.

103. H. G. Wells, *The Island of Dr. Moreau* (New York, 1988), 98.

104. Ibid.

105. Ibid., 136.

Chapter 1: Traumatic Heroism

1. Max Nordau, *Degeneration* (1895; reprint, Lincoln, Nebr., 1968, 1993), 2–3.

2. This phrase is from Roger L. Williams, *The Horror of Life* (Chicago, 1980).

3. John Davidson, *A Full and True Account of the Wonderful Mission of Earl Laven-der* (1895), quoted in John Stokes, *In the Nineties* (Chicago, 1993), 26.

4. See *American Scientist* 81, no. 3 (1993): 235. Koch's vaccine failed.

5. George Frederick Drinka, M.D., *The Birth of Neurosis: Myth, Malady, and the Victorians* (New York, 1984), 62–64.

6. Stokes, *In the Nineties*, 26.

7. *Punch*, December 1881. Reproduced in Wolf Von Eckardt, Sander L. Gilman, and J. Edward Chamberlin, eds., *Oscar Wilde's London* (Garden City, 1987), 172.

8. This tableau is found, for example, in Renaissance paintings by Rogier van der Weyden, Vittore Carpaccio, Tintoretto, and Paolo Uccello. In a painting reproduced in my *Play, Death, and Heroism in Shakespeare* (Chapel Hill, 1989), David Vinckboons depicts Death, reinforced by Father Time, assaulting a throng of citizens who are try-ing to defend the gate of their walled city (93).

9. See, for example, the mummers' play of Saint George in *Chief Pre-Shake-spearean Dramas*, edited by Joseph Q. Adams (Cambridge, Mass., 1924), which was still being played in Leicestershire in the 1860s (355).

10. Dante Gabriel Rossetti painted Saint George more than once; Sir Edward Burne-Jones labored over his dead King Arthur for nearly twenty years (1881–98). Her-bert James Draper's *Lament for Icarus* (1898) gives defeat and death an erotic, pubes-cent glow.

11. The sociologist Edward A. Ross, who coined the term "race suicide," warned that "the same manly virtues which had once allowed the 'Superior Race' to evolve the highest civilization [i.e., excessive self-discipline and sexual self-control] now threat-ened that race's very survival." See Ross, "The Causes of Race Superiority," *Annals of the American Academy of Political and Social Science* 18 (July 1901), 67–89, quoted in Gail Bederman, *Manliness and Civilization* (Chicago, 1995), 200.

12. Frederick Wedmore, "Some Tendencies in Recent Painting," *Temple Bar* 55 (July 1878), quoted in *The Grosvenor Gallery: A Palace of Art in Victorian England*, edited by Susan P. Casteras and Colleen Denney (New Haven, Conn., 1996), 84. For other samples of critical anxiety about morbidity, see 81–86.

13. The best survey of the genre is I. F. Clarke, *Voices Prophesying War*, 2d ed. (Ox-ford, 1992). Although Clarke finds continuity in the genre across the nineteenth cen-tury, in *War Machine: The Rationalisation of Slaughter in the Modern Age* (New Haven, Conn., 1996), Daniel Pick notes that "at other points [Clarke] acknowledges that 1870–71 marked a watershed" (118). Clarke and Pick provide detailed accounts of the panics that recurred in Britain until 1914.

14. In a speech at Whitby on September 3, 1871, Gladstone inveighed against alarmist stories like Chesney's that "make us ridiculous in the eyes of the whole world. I do not say that the writers of them are not sincere—that is another matter—but I do say that the result of these things is practically the spending of more and more of your money. Be on your guard against alarmism. Depend on it that there is not this aston-ishing disposition on the part of all mankind to make us the objects of hatred." Quoted in Clarke, *Voices Prophesying War*, 34.

15. Arthur Machen, "The Bowmen," quoted in ibid., 92.

16. Ibid.

17. Shakespeare, *Richard II*, 3.2.60.

18. The term is from Tom Engelhardt, *The End of Victory Culture* (New York, 1995).

19. Bederman, *Manliness and Civilization*, 200–201.

20. In mystical Judaism the vessels broken at the world's creation are restored in the divine communion of *tikkun*. See Gershom Scholem, *Kabbalah* (New York, 1974), 142–43.

21. See Robert Pattison, *The Child Figure in English Literature* (Athens, Ga., 1978), 74, and also Lloyd deMause, ed., *The History of Childhood* (New York, 1975), chaps. 1 and 2.

22. Cardinal Newman, *Apologia pro Vita Sua*, edited by Martin J. Svaglic (Oxford, 1967?), 218.

23. Georges Louis Leclerc, Comte de Buffon, quoted in Norman Cohn, *Noah's Flood: The Genesis Story in Western Thought* (New Haven, Conn., 1996), 101.

24. In *The Uncertainty of Analysis* (Ithaca, N.Y., 1989), Timothy J. Reiss points out that the libertarian faith of "New Right" thinkers and extreme evangelical fundamentalism both "seem predicated upon a quasi-Rousseauesque notion of socialization as a Fall from Edenic grace and of religion as an offer of (political and cultural) redemption." He adds that "such demagogues as Pat Robertson, Jerry Falwell, and the rest are busy elaborating abstract myths that serve not only as concealing receptacles for despair but as simplifying mystifications of real sociocultural praxis in all its complexity. A similar phenomenon is at work, it would appear, in *some* feminist and/or psychoanalytic views of the socialization of the individual as a fall from *its own* wholeness (the Platonic myth of the undivided complete being is seemingly tenacious)." Reiss finds this dynamic in Hélène Cixous, Jacques Lacan, Julia Kristeva, and Jacques Derrida (139–40). Romantic love proposes that eros is a response to traumatic origins, because in Plato's myth the union of lovers recreates the original four-legged human animal that the gods had sundered in a stroke of originary violence.

25. For a comprehensive survey, see Joseph Fontenrose, *Python* (Berkeley and Los Angeles, 1980), which is centered on the combat of Apollo with the dragon Python in the origin myth of Apollo's Delphic shrine. As for Christ, John Bale envisions him at Calvary defeating "the great Dragon, or captayn of all the vnfaithful sort, that olde croked serpent which deceyued Adam." John Bale, *The Image of Bothe Churches* (1548?), sig. e vii.

26. "Consider the argument that group-living intensifies reproductive competition between individuals and requires continual pressure from some outside selective forces such as predators to persist. It implies that human society is a network of lies and deception, persisting only because systems of conventions about permissible kinds and extents of lying have arisen." Richard D. Alexander, "The Search for a General Theory of Behavior," *Behavioral Science* 20 (1975): 96. Although Alexander goes beyond this bleak vision of society in his account of human motives, the vision has a grain of truth.

27. See the entry "Trauma" (and those for "Traumatic Neurosis" and "War Neuro-

sis") in *Psychoanalytic Terms and Concepts*, edited by Burness E. Moore, M.D., and Bernard D. Fine, M.D. (New Haven, Conn., 1990). Freud discusses trauma in *Moses and Monotheism*, in the Standard Edition, 23: 3–137 (reprint, New York, 1975). See also "Psychic Trauma," in *Psychic Trauma*, edited by S. S. Furst (New York, 1967), 3–50.

28. Drinka, *Birth of Neurosis*, 114–15.

29. Ibid.

30. Nordau, *Degeneration*, 3.

31. "Psychologically, the father-figure occupies a place analogous to that of the dragon, as does the monster in the story of Oedipus. In slaying the dragon and re-deeming the kingdom, Redcrosse puts to death the Old Adam." James Nohrnberg, *The Analogy of the Faerie Queene* (Princeton, 1980), 185.

32. And what of the maiden? In the folk tales, the rescuer marries her, assumes the throne, and becomes the next lord. In the Christian story the Virgin Mary mourns for her crucified son. In a painting by Hans Baldung Grien, "Mary and Angels Weeping for Christ as Man of Sorrows" (1513), she grieves for her suffering son in heaven, mon-itored from a distance by the faintly visible Father, while from the infinite horizon, flowing into the foreground as if released in fertile abundance by the sacrificial death of Christ, come swarms of infantile putti, fecundity released by obedient death. Sacrifice in the service of the Father earns the Son his mother's love. In effect, the mother validates the sacrificial compact with tears that ambiguously reinforce the Fa-ther's dominance and her own emotional bond to her son. This is one expression in Christian Europe of the misogynistic suspicion that women always have divided loyal-ties. It also confirms the trauma of the Edenic curse: that new life means the death of the old.

33. For a history of millennialism, see Norman Cohn, *Pursuit of the Millennium* (New York, 1961) and *Cosmos, Chaos, and the World to Come* (New Haven, Conn., 1993).

34. See Nohrnberg, *Analogy of the Faerie Queene*, 139–41, 184–85. In *The Faerie Queene*, Saint George appears as Redcrosse.

35. William Blake's preface to *Milton* epitomizes the call to otherworldly idealism:

> I will not cease from Mental Fight,
> Nor shall my Sword sleep in my hand:
> Till we have built Jerusalem,
> In Englands green & pleasant Land.

The Complete Poetry and Prose of William Blake, edited by David V. Erdman (Garden City, N.Y., 1982), 95.

36. In the antebellum historical romances, southerners such as George Tucker and William Gilmore Simms use a recurring plot in which a young planter rescues a planter's daughter from an "enemy" of her class. See Susan J. Tracy, *In the Master's Eye: Representations of Women, Blacks, and Poor Whites in Antebellum Southern Lit-erature* (Amherst, Mass., 1995).

37. In Andrew Carnegie's smarmy prose, the gospel of wealth calls upon the mil-

lionaire to "sell all that he hath and give it in the highest and best form to the poor by administering his estate himself for the good of his fellows, before he is called upon to lie down and rest upon the bosom of Mother Earth." He will thus be incalculably enriched by "the affection, gratitude, and admiration of his fellow-men, and . . . soothed and sustained by the still, small voice within, which, whispering, tells him that, because he has lived, perhaps one small part of the great world has been bettered just a little." Andrew Carnegie, *The Gospel of Wealth and Other Timely Essays* (Cambridge, Mass., 1900), chap. 2.

38. Horatio Alger composed an epitaph that assembles a mock-apotheosis for himself out of the titles of his novels: "Six feet underground reposes Horatio Alger, *Helping Himself* to a part of the earth, not *Digging for Gold* or *In Search of Treasure*, but *Struggling Upward* and *Bound to Rise* at last *In a New World* where it shall be said he is *Risen from the Ranks.*" See the introduction to Horatio Alger, *Ragged Dick and Mark, the Match Boy*, edited by Rychard Fink (New York, 1962), 15.

39. Shakespeare is full of jokes about chivalric pretensions, as when the absurdly shipwrecked Prince Pericles finds his father's rusted armor washed ashore and uses it to wow a hostile father-in-law in a jousting tournament. Then there is Montague, whose wordplay describes the lovesick Romeo as "an artificial night" (*Romeo and Juliet*, 1.1.140).

40. In the Lady Lever Art Gallery is a fatuous silver table centerpiece by Edward Onslow Ford, which depicts the saint standing atop the slain dragon with his sword raised in a stilted pose suggesting a military parade.

41. Mary Midgley, *Beast and Man: The Roots of Human Nature* (Ithaca, N.Y., 1978), 264.

42. In *Art of Darkness: A Poetics of Gothic* (Chicago, 1995), Anne Williams notes the role of Saint George in Dracula (133–34) and associates it with the "antifeminism" she finds in what she calls "the Male Gothic" (135–36).

43. See Judith R. Walkowitz, *City of Dreadful Delight* (Chicago, 1992), chaps. 3 and 4. On both sides of the Atlantic the saint's walled city is a model for Victorian rescue homes for fallen women, including Angela Burdett Coutts's interestingly named Urania Cottage, which Dickens managed for more than a decade. See Amanda Anderson, *Tainted Souls and Painted Faces: The Rhetoric of Fallenness in Victorian Culture* (Ithaca, N.Y., 1993), 68–79. See also Sally Mitchell, *The Fallen Angel: Chastity, Class, and Women's Reading, 1835–1880* (Bowling Green, Ohio, 1981).

44. See "Knights Errant," in Douglass Shand-Tucci, *Boston Bohemia, 1881–1900* (Amherst, Mass., 1995), 415–55. *Parsifal*, claims Richard Mohr, became the "shadowy center of a world of male homosexual attractions." See Mohr, *Gay Ideas* (Boston, 1992), 223.

45. For example, the heroine of Garry Marshall's film *Pretty Woman* (1990) vows that once rescued by her knight, she would "rescue him right back." See chap. 10 below.

46. Ernest Becker, *Escape from Evil* (New York, 1975), 1.

47. Quoted in Casteras and Denney, *Grosvenor Gallery*, 90.

48. See, for example, Spiro Agnew's famous "nattering nabobs of negativism." See also the discussion of President Reagan's response to storylessness in the Reconnaissance, below.

49. Holden Sampson, *Daily Chronicle* (London), August 18, 1893; quoted in Stokes, *In the Nineties*, 120.

50. Stokes, *In the Nineties*, 120.

51. Ibid., 121.

52. Frank Peretti, *The Oath* (Dallas, 1995).

53. See chap. 7 below. In Robert Zemeckis's comic recuperation of the story, *Back to the Future* (1985), a son travels back in time from the 1980s to the 1950s and saves his father from the traumatic bullying that would otherwise make him the emasculated, harried patriarch of the 1980s we see at the start of the movie. The son, that is, saves manhood from the fate that the *fin de siècle* dreaded.

Chapter 2: Empty Treasure

1. Arthur Conan Doyle, *The Sign of Four* (1890; reprint, London, 1934), 4 (hereafter cited as *SF*). Cf. Oscar Wilde's Dorian Gray: "I wish it were [not *fin de siècle* but] *fin du globe*. . . . Life is a great disappointment." *The Picture of Dorian Gray*, edited by Donald L. Lawler (New York, 1988), 138.

2. Shakespeare, *Hamlet*, 1.2.133–34. Quotations throughout are from *The Riverside Shakespeare*, edited by G. Blakemore Evans (New York, 1974). Hamlet provided the Victorians a robust vocabulary for traumatic anguish. An unsigned commentator in *Gentleman's Magazine* (December 1878), for example, borrowed the Prince's eloquent rage to attack Zola for injuring the public with reminders of our evolutionary origins and mortality. Unlike French writers, "English authors will not leave a celestial bed to prey on garbage" ("publication in our columns," quoted in Karl Beckson, *London in the 1890s: A Cultural History* [New York, 1992], 293).

3. Shakespeare, *Hamlet*, 1.2.304–8.

4. For an account of the Ghost's oppressiveness, see my *Play, Death, and Heroism in Shakespeare* (Chapel Hill, 1989), 65–66.

5. Christopher Marlowe, *The Tragical History of Dr. Faustus*, in *The Plays of Christopher Marlowe*, edited by Leo Kirschbaum (Cleveland, 1962), 1.1.38–42.

6. Hugh Kenner, *Dublin's Joyce* (London, 1953), 170.

7. Marlowe, *Dr. Faustus*, 1.1.14. Urging himself to "Be a physician" (like Watson), he despairs that despite all his triumphant cures, "Yet art thou but Faustus and a man. / Could'st thou make men to live eternally / . . . Then this profession were to be esteem'd" (1.1.13, 21–24).

8. The detective story is thus a strikingly transparent form of what Otto Rank calls an "immortality ideology." Rank holds that all people, at every stage of history, have felt that their own rightness about the world has special permanence and in turn profoundly substantiates them. Because such an ideology expresses humankind's deepest innate hunger, "every conflict over truth is in the last analysis just the same old strug-

gle over . . . immortality." See Otto Rank, *Psychology of the Soul* (New York, 1961), 87. "If anyone doubts this," adds Ernest Becker in *Escape from Evil* (New York, 1975), "let him try to explain in any other way the life-and-death viciousness of all ideological disputes. . . . No wonder men go into a rage about fine points of belief: if your adversary wins the argument about truth, you die. Your immortality system has been shown to be fallible, your life becomes fallible. History, then, can be understood as the succession of ideologies that console for death" (64). Symbolically, a detective story is a contest of ideologies. By annihilating a "criminal" mentality, the detective preserves the life-giving beliefs of his own client culture. In Faust's terms, righteousness is life and "sin is death" (1.1.38).

9. Marlowe, *Dr. Faustus*, 1.1.77.

10. In *Victorian People and Places* (New York, 1973), Richard D. Altick identifies one source of this anger: "In the big factories . . . the master . . . typically was rich, remote, and arbitrary. The worker . . . became no more than a name on a wage sheet. Under these conditions, the very word 'master' lost its former connotation of an amiable relationship in which loyal acceptance of social inferiority on one side was met by human decency on the other, and acquired the connotation of petty tyranny. In the fiction of the time, apologists for the factory system, anxious to neutralize the wicked stereotype of radical propaganda, regularly portrayed mill owners as men who retained the humane virtues" (244). Mr. Abel White offers just such an apology, yet the mutiny argues that unconsciously Conan Doyle had a far more complex attitude.

11. By 1890, the controversy over Governor Eyre's retaliatory massacre of black Jamaicans in 1865 had made people aware of the severely conflicted morality of imperial rule, which split public opinion because—as with Jonathan Small—"there [was] no middle way." See Edward Said's account of the debate (Thomas Carlyle, John Ruskin, and Matthew Arnold justifying repression; John Stuart Mill, T. H. Huxley, and Lord Chief Justice Cockburn opposed), in *Culture and Imperialism* (New York, 1993), 130.

12. Following Norman O. Brown's *Life against Death* (New York, 1959), Becker's *Escape from Evil* analyzes money as an immortality ideology (73–90). The thing that connects money with the domain of the sacred is its power. "We have long known that money gives power," he says, adding appropriately that "power means power to increase oneself, to change one's natural situation from one of *smallness*, helplessness, finitude, to one of bigness, control, durability, importance" (81, emphasis added).

13. "Aggressive creatures are commonly ones that want space around them, and once they have got somebody else out of it they are usually content to forget about him. Certainly killing him is one way of doing this, but in natural conditions it is a comparatively rare one. Much commoner is requiring his submission. An animal that gives way to a mild attack often does not need actually to vanish, provided that it makes itself *small*. It marks its submission by bowing down in some way, so that it does not intrude upon the space surrounding the victor." Mary Midgley, *Beast and Man: The Roots of Human Nature* (Ithaca, N.Y., 1978), 55; emphasis added.

14. Karen Horney would see the relationships among these four characters as intrapsychic conflict within a single personality given over to self-idealizing fantasies of

mastery. See "The Appeal to Mastery," in *Neurosis and Human Growth* (New York, 1950), 187–213.

15. The cannibal caricatures not only the potential failure of the hero's sublimation—"what a terrible criminal [Holmes] would have made had he turned his energy . . . against the law," Watson shudders (*SF* 98)—but also the risk to the hero-worshiper. Although Watson is devoted to Holmes as Small is to Tonga—"No man ever had a more faithful mate" (274)—he is also "irritated by the egotism which seemed to demand that every line [Watson writes about Holmes] should be devoted to his own special doings" (7). Watson resents the way his hero would tacitly devour the devotee.

16. See Becker, "The Mystery of Sacrifice," in *Escape from Evil*, 100–108. One reason "Darwin shocked his time," Becker notes, is that he showed so comprehensively that "life cannot go on without mutual devouring of organisms. If at the end of each person's life he were to be presented with the living spectacle of all that he had organismically incorporated in order to stay alive, he might well feel horrified by the living energy he had ingested. . . . To paraphrase Elias Canetti, each organism raises its head over a field of corpses, smiles into the sun, and declares life good" (2). This is precisely the haunting, inadmissible truth about human life projected onto Tonga and thrillingly "performed" by him at fairs.

17. See Robert Pattison, *The Child Figure in English Literature* (Athens, Ga., 1978).

18. David M. Lubin, *Picturing a Nation* (New Haven, Conn., 1994), 226. Lubin reprints Lewis Carroll's photograph of Alice Liddell posing as a saucy "beggar girl."

19. After the major's death, his son becomes as obsessed with the treasure as Small is. Like Holmes, Bartholomew has a laboratory at home. With Holmesian ingenuity he locates the treasure by calculating the dimensions of the house. His brother caricatures Watson's sentimentality and hypochondria (*SF* 7), and Holmes's aesthetic withdrawal. Where the detective retreats from the commonplace to his violin and syringe, Thaddeus shrinks "from all . . . rough materialism" (53), compensating with his art collection and hookah. The brothers are intermediate figures between heroes and villains, their conventional status defined by inhibition and ineffectuality.

20. The tiger was a well-known symbol of Indian resistance to colonial rule. In the Victoria and Albert Museum is "Tippoo's tiger," a life-sized automaton made for a rebellious Indian rajah and captured from him in 1799. The sculpted tiger is devouring a prostrate European in 1790s dress, and the figures emit groans and roars when an operator turns a crank to activate the organ works inside.

21. In this light at least, the novel is unconsciously a sort of *Everyman* in which the narrative imagination seeks out attitudes and values that might help Everyman answer to death and the life-poisoning awareness of death. In the play, Death himself uses terms that resonate in the novel, because he will "cruelly out-serche both grete and small," including the savage who "lyveth beestly/Out of Goodes lawes," and "He that loveth richesse." Like Knowledge, Holmes will "be thy gyde," and "Good Deedes" finds clear form in Miss Morstan, who renounces her worldly legacy, the Agra treasure. I point out the resemblances not to reduce the novel to allegory, but to emphasize how anxiously it conforms to orthodox paradigms and tries to reach a secure, subliminally devout conclusion.

22. See John Kucich, "Death Worship among the Victorians: *The Old Curiosity Shop*," *PMLA* 95 (1980): 58–72.

23. Horney characterizes compensatory striving for power and glory as "tyrannical," and argues that it produces overt or repressed self-hatred. "The realization that they are inseparable is an ancient one. . . . [It is] best symbolized by the stories of the devil's pact," in which an evil force promises infinite potency and the "price to pay . . . is the loss of the soul." Horney, *Neurosis and Human Growth*, 375–76. The connection of *Faust* with Holmes, then, speaks for itself.

24. According to Steven Marcus in *The Other Victorians* (New York, 1966), a state of enervation was commonly diagnosed as "spermatorrhea." Although it was associated with loss of sperm, the term was a "catch-all," often "allied with the various forms of impotence." Enervation "can be the result of sexual excess, but then it can just as well be the result of intellectual excess, mental exertions having apparently the same consequences" (27). It seems likely that to a Victorian doctor Holmes's final limpness would have suggested a sexual etiology.

25. Philip Rieff, *Freud: The Mind of the Moralist* (New York, 1961), 348.

26. In this way Conan Doyle shares some concerns of the greatest Victorian novelists. For example, Thomas P. Wolfe describes a scene in George Eliot's *Daniel Deronda* in which Gwendolyn is helpless, "looking at herself in a mirror . . . in a sad kind of companionship." She wishes that Deronda were God and thinks, "I wish he could know everything about me. . . . I wish he knew that I am not as contemptible as he thinks me—I am in deep trouble, and want something better if I could." Gwendolyn relates to Deronda as Watson and Miss Morstan relate to Holmes. But as Wolfe notes of Gwendolyn's self-appraisal, "the tender generosity here shown by the self toward the self has been painfully earned. Gwendolyn is for the moment the victim neither of impossible demands for godlike performance nor of virulent self-hatred." That is, the self is not driven toward the aggrandizement of Holmes or toward the guilty punishment of Small and Tonga. See Thomas P. Wolfe, "The Inward Vocation," in *Literary Monographs* 8 (Madison, Wisc., 1976), 46.

27. In most of the paintings the knight's horse is not merely a vehicle but an alter ego, a character "personally" attacking the dragon in its own right. Raphael depicts the horse actually twisting about at the crucial moment to make eye contact with the knight like a partner.

28. "The Criminal Registrar noted in 1901 that, since the 1840s, 'we have witnessed a great change in manners: the substitution of words without blows for blows . . . ; an approximation in the manners of different classes; a decline in the spirit of lawlessness." H. C. G. Matthew, "The Liberal Age," in *The Oxford Illustrated History of Britain*, edited by Kenneth O. Morgan (Oxford, 1984), 497.

29. Angus McLaren, *A Prescription for Murder: The Victorian Serial Killings of Dr. Thomas Neill Cream* (Chicago, 1993), 140. Contrast this anxiety with the patrician smugness Barbara Tuchman describes in the opening chapter of *The Proud Tower: A Portrait of the World before the War, 1890–1914* (New York, 1962).

30. Hobson quoted in Beckson, *London in the 1890s*, 4.

31. Concern over social unrest, especially in association with the Trafalgar Square

"riots" of 1887, resonates in William Morris's *Dream of John Bull* (1888), which feelingly revisits the doomed Peasants' Revolt of 1381.

32. Morgan, *Oxford Illustrated History of Britain*, 516.

33. "Stagnation" may reflect the conflict between the ideology of progress and actual conditions. "Contrary to popular belief," says Paul Thompson, "chances of social mobility have not much improved during the past hundred years." The ordinary Edwardian "had some hope of some social mobility, if slight. . . . This conclusion challenges complacent assumptions about social progress. It also helps to explain why more drastic change has not been demanded." Thompson, *The Edwardians: The Remaking of British Society* (New York, 1992), 164, 166.

34. Shearer West, *Fin de Siècle* (Woodstock, N.Y., 1994), 16.

35. See C. R. Whittaker, "The Poor," in *The Romans*, edited by Andrea Giardina (Chicago, 1993), 272–99.

36. To bring these abstractions closer to actual lives, it is worth noting how much Conan Doyle's story resonates with the case of the "Tichborne claimant" in the 1860s, "probably the most famous nineteenth-century attempt at fraud." A butcher's son nearly passed himself off "as the missing claimant to the Tichborne fortune. At the time the dramatic appeal of a shipwrecked prodigal son returning home after years of exile drew many to his side. The haunting specter of a legitimate heir possibly being deprived of his rightful due obviously hit a nerve in Victorian society; the case dragged on for years, splitting many English families into two warring camps." McLaren, *Prescription for Murder*, 88. Small, too, fantasizes about being a traumatized (shipwrecked) prodigal son "deprived of his rightful due," only in his case a spurious "son" invisibly hounds a fraudulent "father" (Sholto) for a deceptive treasure.

37. Roosevelt to Haggard, June 28, 1912, in H. Rider Haggard, *The Days of My Life* (London, 1926), 2:186.

38. Beckson, *London in the 1890s*, xvii.

39. In 1890, Tuchman reminds us, "the last armed conflict between Indians and whites in the United States took place at Wounded Knee Creek and the Census Bureau declared there was no longer a land frontier." Tuchman, *Proud Tower*, 130.

40. Elisée Reclus, "The Evolution of Cities," *Contemporary Review*, February 1885, 246. In 1891, Rosebery evoked the city's cannibalistic or dragon's appetite by comparing it to a "tumour, an elephantiasis sucking into its gorged system half the life and the blood and the bone of the rural districts." Quoted in E. Howard, *Garden Cities of Tomorrow* (London, 1902), 11. In William Morris's "Art and Socialism," London is a "spreading sore . . . swallowing up" the landscape. Morris, *Selected Writings*, edited by G. H. Cole (London, 1934), 657. Raymond Williams describes the cities' shocking rate of expansion in *The Country and the City* (New York, 1973). In 1598 John Stow was complaining about "incroching" new development and poisonous pollution in his *Survey of London*, edited by C. L. Kingsford (Oxford, 1908), 2, 72. A century later the city was already a monstrous, diseased body. See Lawrence Manley, "From Matron to Monster: Tudor-Stuart London and the Language of Description," in *The Historical Renaissance: New Essays on Tudor and Stuart Literature and Culture*, edited by

Heather Dubrow and Richard Strier (Chicago, 1988), 347–74. See also H. J. Dyos and Michael Wolff, eds., *The Victorian City: Images and Realities* (London, 1976).

41. Carol Dyhouse, "The Condition of England, 1860–1900," in *The Victorians*, edited by Laurance Lerner (New York, 1978), 81.

42. See Thomas Edward Jordan, *Victorian Childhood: Themes and Variations* (Albany, N.Y., 1987).

43. John Stokes, *In the Nineties* (Chicago, 1993), 99–100.

44. Although he is polemical and much criticized, Lloyd deMause squarely confronts the adult use of children as a "toilet" for projections throughout history. The Victorians were no less stunningly ambivalent and incoherent in their attitudes toward children than are contemporary Americans. See Lloyd deMause, ed., *The History of Childhood* (New York, 1975), 10. In *Child-Loving: The Erotic Child in Victorian Culture* (Berkeley and Los Angeles, 1993), James R. Kincaid demonstrates in detail the way in which Victorians attributed to children a range of impossibly contradictory qualities.

45. Kincaid, *Child-Loving*, 124–25.

46. "Just as [the colonies] were useful places to send wayward sons, superfluous populations of delinquents, poor people, and other undesirables, so the Orient was a place where one could look for sexual experience unobtainable in Europe." Edward Said, *Orientalism* (New York, 1979), 190. Bargaining with his son "Bosie" to separate him from Bosie's lover, Oscar Wilde, the Marquess of Queensberry offered his son "money to go to the South Sea Islands, where 'you will find plenty of beautiful girls.'" Richard Ellmann, *Oscar Wilde* (New York, 1988), 496.

47. "In Afghanistan and in the frontier," George MacMunn says in *The Underworld of India*, "the shameless proverb runs, 'A woman for business, a boy for pleasure.'" Quoted in Lewis Wurgaft, *The Imperial Imagination: Magic and Myth in Kipling's India* (Middletown, Conn., 1983), 50. In *Sexual Anarchy* (New York, 1990), Elaine Showalter surveys the relationship of Victorian homosexuality to what Richard Burton called "the Sotadic Zone" of exotic locales that included India (81–89).

48. *The English Malady* (1733), quoted in George Frederick Drinka, M.D., *The Birth of Neurosis: Myth, Malady, and the Victorians* (New York, 1984), 33–34. Dr. Cheyne construed "nervous" illness as a function of gender, class, and national identity. Gentlefolk have heroically developed interior lives and sensitive nerves, while the poor suffer a lower order of afflictions. Women, predictably, are more susceptible to nervous infirmities than are men. Like health-food zealots today, Dr. Cheyne served up moralized theories of nutrition, specifically warning against rich and spicy "foreign" food.

49. John Dickson Carr, *The Life of Sir Arthur Conan Doyle* (New York, 1949), 258.

50. See Clarke's account of the inflammatory pamphlets produced in 1882 during debates over a Channel tunnel, in I. F. Clarke, *Voices Prophesying War*, 2d ed. (Oxford, 1992), 95–99.

51. Le Queux was a proto–G. Gordon Liddy, eager to exploit public anxieties in public relations coups such as the deployment of sandwich-board men dressed as German soldiers to advertise a new invasion story. His novels include *A Secret Service* (1896), *The Great War in England in 1897* (1892), and *The Invasion of 1910* (1906).

52. See McLaren's illuminating account of the medical profession in the 1890s in *Prescription for Murder*, chap. 9, as well as his chapter on detectives, chap. 10.

53. Writing in the shadow of World War I, just as fascism was threatening Europe, the historian Esmé Wingfield-Stratford sounded the post-traumatic note: "The Victorian Age was, to adopt a phrase of its own prophet, one of shams." Its tragedy was the "failure to get at the root of any one of the main problems before them." Her decent, troubled voice fantasized about the ground of experience (roots) and empty chests (shams). See *The Victorian Aftermath* (London, 1933), xii.

54. Stokes, *In the Nineties*, 116.

55. Ibid., 120.

56. For a study of midcentury sources of this tension, see Alex J. Tuss, *The Inward Revolution: Troubled Young Men in Victorian Fiction, 1850–1880* (New York, 1992).

57. Stokes, *In the Nineties*, 187.

58. Ibid., 140.

59. A. Alvarez, *The Savage God: A Study of Suicide* (New York, 1970), 101.

60. Stokes, *In the Nineties*, 140.

61. Ibid., 126.

62. Thomas Hardy, *Jude the Obscure*, edited by Patricia Ingham (Oxford, 1985), 355. Suicide in Hardy's novels is the focus of Frank R. Giordano, *"I'd Have My Life Unbe": Thomas Hardy's Self-Destructive Characters* (University, Ala., 1984).

63. Stokes, *In the Nineties*, 126.

64. DeMause, *History of Childhood*, 6–21.

Chapter 3: Post-traumatic Mourning

1. Letter of June 28, 1912, in H. Rider Haggard, *The Days of My Life*, 2:186 (hereafter cited as *DML*).

2. Ibid., 2:104. During the Franco-Prussian War, the foretaste of industrialized slaughter had alarmed Queen Victoria, who worried that "the peoples will become extinct!" *Queen Victoria in Her Letters and Journals*, edited by Christopher Hibbert (Harmondsworth, England, 1985), 220. As the end of the century neared and German militarism expanded, Herbert Spencer and others began to worry about the dangers of "extinction." See Daniel Pick, *War Machine: The Rationalisation of Slaughter in the Modern Age* (New Haven, Conn., 1996), 87.

3. Peter Homans, *The Ability to Mourn* (Chicago, 1989), 3.

4. Possibly Haggard knew of the Capuchin catacomb in Palermo, where the dead were interred in positions that reflected their social rank, and are still on view to visitors, in air so dry it has naturally mummified them.

5. Norman Etherington, *The Annotated She* (Bloomington, Ind., 1991), xxxii.

6. Quotations are from the Penguin edition: H. Rider Haggard, *She* (Harmondsworth, England, 1982), hereafter cited as *She*. Ibid., 221.

7. Sandra M. Gilbert and Susan Gubar, *Sexchanges*, vol. 2 of *No Man's Land: The Place of the Woman Writer in the Twentieth Century* (New Haven, Conn., 1989), 10.

8. Shakespeare, *Antony and Cleopatra*, 2.2.234–35.

9. In *Denial of Death* (New York, 1973), Ernest Becker calls transference "The Spell Cast by Persons"; see chap. 7, esp. 148–58, and Becker, *Escape from Evil* (New York, 1975).

10. "Subsumed" is Peter Laslett's term in *The World We Have Lost*, 2d ed. (New York, 1973), 20–21. For contemporary views of the nurturant patriarch, see Deborah Shuger, *Habits of Thought in the English Renaissance: Religion, Politics, and the Dominant Culture* (Berkeley and Los Angeles, 1990).

11. Etherington, *Annotated She*, xxi–xxii.

12. Shakespeare, *A Midsummer Night's Dream*, 3.1.160.

13. In a fascinating dream he recorded in 1597, the astrologer-physician Dr. Forman "waits on" and "weights on" (that is, makes pregnant) the supremely powerful Queen Elizabeth I, who was at the time also a childless "little elderly woman" in need of an heir to guarantee stability beyond her encroaching death. See Louis Adrian Montrose, "'Shaping Fantasies': Figurations of Gender and Power in Elizabethan Culture," *Representations* 1, no. 2 (1983): 63. In *Play, Death, and Heroism in Shakespeare* (Chapel Hill, 1989), I analyze Forman's fantasy as a reaction to his traumatic past, especially the ghastly plague epidemic he survived in 1593 (201–6).

14. Haggard's manuscript identifies Ayesha with the Iron Chancellor, Bismarck. See Etherington, *Annotated She*, 234, n. 22.

15. Like many of their readers, both writers struggled mightily to believe in some plausible form of immortality. Conan Doyle reported that after his death Haggard, as prearranged, reported back to him in a séance from the undiscovered country to confirm life after death. Conan Doyle could be risibly gullible about spirits, as when two girls faked a photograph of fairies on a lawn, which Conan Doyle exultantly showed to a painter friend, who instantly saw that the light on the figures was coming from a different source than the sunlight on the grass but did not have the heart to disenchant Conan Doyle.

16. Homans, *Ability to Mourn*, 8.

17. Ibid., 4.

18. *DML* 1:248. Following Morton Cohen, *Rider Haggard* (New York, 1960), 24, Gilbert and Gubar distort this episode into a nightmare more personal than the one Haggard, at least, recalls (*Sexchanges*, 26).

19. Etherington, *Annotated She*, 222.

20. *DML* 1:23. The manuscript of *She* depicts Leo as a "red hot conservative," jokes about hot-potting Gladstone, and complains about Liberals "plundering" wealth by redistributing it. Ibid., xx.

21. John Bowlby, "The Role of Childhood Experience in Cognitive Disturbance," in *Cognition and Psychotherapy*, edited by Michael J. Mahoney and Arthur Freeman (New York, 1985), 184.

22. On the other hand, "with all the world explored and exhausted, I feel sorry for the romance writers of the future, for I know not whither they will turn without bringing themselves into competition with the efforts of dead but still remembered hands and exposing themselves to the sneers of the hunters-out of 'plagiarisms.'" *DML* 2:91.

The fantasy goal here for young writers is not to win a competition against dead predecessors, but to sidestep struggle altogether. Failing that, the creative impulse feels doomed.

23. *Times* (London), October 12, 1863. Gilbert and Gubar, among others, recognize Victoria as a model for Ayesha (*Sexchanges*, 45).

24. Elizabeth Darby and Nicola Smith, *The Cult of the Prince Consort* (New Haven, Conn., 1983), 92, 93, 101.

25. Ibid., 102.

26. Ibid., 105.

27. According to Lytton Strachey in *Queen Victoria* (New York, 1921), she "filled her diary for pages with minute descriptions of her mother's last hours, her dissolution, and her corpse, interspersed with vehement apostrophes, and the agitated outpourings of emotional reflection. . . . It was the horror and the mystery of Death—Death, present and actual—that seized upon the imagination of the Queen" (291). Her mother's death exposed her own vulnerability and increased her reliance on Albert. At the moment of his death "she shrieked one long wild shriek that rang through the terror-stricken castle—and understood that she had lost him for ever" (296). "In the first dreadful moments those about her had feared that she might lose her reason" (302). Strachey himself was a virtuoso of operatic mourning. In his account, Ayesha's wail and the keening of the "savage and superb, wild-eyed and magnificent" African woman for Kurtz in Conrad's *Heart of Darkness* are scarcely more extravagant than the cry of Britain's overweight, motherly queen.

28. Letter of December 24, 1861, in Hibbert, *Queen Victoria in Her Letters and Journals*, 157.

29. Ibid.

30. Strachey, *Queen Victoria*, 303.

31. Ibid., 306.

32. Queen Victoria's journal, November 30, 1864, quoted in Darby and Smith, *Cult of the Prince Consort*, 27. It is difficult to know what to think of this suicidal-sounding expostulation coming from a woman who nearly forty years later would ask to be buried in her bridal veil. Cf. Holly's fascination with "empty chambers that spoke more eloquently to the imagination than any crowded streets. And over all, the dead silence of the dead, the sense of utter loneliness, and the brooding of the Past! How beautiful it was, and yet how drear!" (*She*, 252).

33. Strachey, *Queen Victoria*, 400.

34. A revealing precedent for this frustration is the later reign of Queen Elizabeth I. In *The Aspiring Mind of the Elizabethan Younger Generation* (Durham, N.C., 1966), Anthony Esler describes how a cohort of younger courtiers chafed at their exclusion from economic and political advancement, compensating by seeking glory in daring expeditions abroad—precisely the pattern played out by Small, Haggard's heroes, and many others.

35. See Stanley Weintraub's corrective appraisal in *Victoria: An Intimate Biography* (New York, 1987).

36. Themes from *She* resonate in Queen Victoria's life as romanticized in John

Madden's film *Her Majesty Mrs Brown* (1997), which movie posters pitched as a fantasy of an empire revitalized by maternal omnipotence that sublimated, forbidden eros has released from morbidity:

> Queen Victoria, the World's Most Powerful Woman
> John Brown, a simple Scottish Highlander.
> Their extraordinary friendship transformed an empire.

37. For example, "The Captains and the Kings depart" and "Lo, all our pomp of yesterday/Is one with Ninevah and Tyre!" See *Rudyard Kipling's Verse: Inclusive Edition, 1885–1926* (Garden City, N.Y., 1927), 379–80. In *Sexchanges*, Gilbert and Gubar touch on "Recessional," as does Eric Hobsbawm in *The Age of Empire: 1875–1914* (New York, 1987), 82–83. What I associate with post-traumatic mourning, Hobsbawm construes in conventional moral terms, seeing empire as "vulnerable to the erosion from within of the will to rule" (83).

38. Curiously, Ayesha's collapse echoes Conan Doyle's symbolic language: "*Smaller* she grew, and *smaller* yet, till she was no larger than a monkey" (*She*, 280; emphasis added).

39. Karl Beckson, *London in the 1890s: A Cultural History* (New York, 1992), xi.

40. Etherington, *Annotated She*, xxxiv.

41. Cf. René Girard's theory of mimetic violence in, for example, *Violence and the Sacred* (Baltimore, 1977) and *Deceit, Desire, and the Novel: Self and Other in Literary Structure* (Baltimore, 1965).

42. Strachey, *Queen Victoria*, 409–10.

43. Terry Davidson, *Conjugal Crime: Understanding and Changing the Wifebeating Pattern* (New York, 1978), 108, 110. See also James Hammerton, *Cruelty and Companionship: Conflict in Nineteenth-Century Married Life* (London, 1992).

44. *She*, 251. Ayesha's diet also gives her a moral edge on those wealthy Britons who "ransack" the world to "gorge" their appetites, as in Dr. Cheyne's complaint quoted in note 48, chap. 2 above.

45. Gilbert and Gubar, *Sexchanges*, 21.

46. Cf. Haggard's *King Solomon's Mines* (1885) and *The Heart of the World* (1895). As late as 1918, in *When the World Shook*, he was still dreaming of a woman who would give her life rebelling against death and oppression in a sepulchral kingdom: this time a daughter (Yva) who submits to a consuming fire controlled by a father-magus (Oro).

47. Victoria can be seen using Albert to meet her needs for mothering in the way Janice Radway sees women doing when they become compulsive readers of romances. Following Nancy Chodorow's developmental paradigm, Radway theorizes that for female readers, romance simultaneously confirms their individuation from the mother and projects an idealized heterosexual bond that is so nurturant for the female protagonist that it amounts to an unconscious substitute for the mother's engulfing presence. See Radway, *Reading the Romance: Women, Patriarchy, and Popular Literature* (Chapel Hill, N.C., 1984). I consider this phenomenon in detail in chap. 8 below.

48. Angus McLaren, *A Prescription for Murder: The Victorian Serial Killings of Dr. Thomas Neill Cream* (Chicago, 1993), 83.

49. Ibid., 78.

50. Ibid., 79.

51. Frances Swiney, *The Bar of Isis: The Law of the Mother* (London, 1907), 17.

52. Gareth Stedman Jones elaborates on the widely accepted theory of urban degeneration in *Outcast London* (London, 1984), 127–29. The theory is central in H. G. Wells's imagination.

53. For some women this lore of the traumatic mother had a patriarchal counterpart. Frances Swiney specifically counters the apocalyptic vision of maternal degeneration by repudiating Eve's role as the mother of original sin and promoting "the divine mission of motherhood." She attributes the crucial role to fathers. "The 'real cause' of degeneration was the fact that men insisted upon making love to women too often—particularly when they were pregnant, menstruating or breast-feeding. The male sperm 'poisons' the womb." She combines anxiety about hereditary taint with an imagined form of sexual abuse taking place even before birth yet doing lasting, deforming damage as a sort of "poison" or pathogen, as syphilis would. The poison she envisions is parental—primarily men's—sexual desire. "They [children] are often conceived in iniquity, of drunken, lustful parents; and, developed in the rankest poison, they become stunted, malformed, diseased, and prematurely old before they see the light." Swiney, *Bar of Isis*, 26.

54. Becker, *Escape from Evil*, chaps. 2 and 8, esp. 104–6.

55. The interplay of skepticism and suggestibility persists today in supermarket tabloids that trumpet wishful immortality in an ambiguously self-parodic spirit. Compare the tabloid headline "Baby Describes Heaven before Birth" with the séance attended by Robert and Elizabeth Barrett Browning at which a twelve-year-old spirit named Wat "tugged at Elizabeth's skirt and offered to play the accordion." On a graver level the same volatile mix is present in today's controversy over post-traumatic "recovered memories" of abuse.

56. Robert Pattison, *The Child Figure in English Literature* (Athens, Ga., 1978), 70.

57. Ibid., 72.

58. See, e.g., Henri F. Ellenberger, *The Discovery of the Unconscious* (New York, 1970), 98–101. My account here relies on George Frederick Drinka, M.D., *The Birth of Neurosis: Myth, Malady, and the Victorians* (New York, 1984), chap. 4.

59. See Virginia Lieson Brereton, *From Sin to Salvation: Stories of Women's Conversions, 1800 to the Present* (Bloomington, Ind., 1991).

60. Drinka, *Birth of Neurosis*, 93.

61. Ibid., 102.

62. Ibid., 89–91.

63. Ibid., 88.

Chapter 4: Traumatic Prophecy

1. H. G. Wells, *The Time Machine* (New York, 1982), 34 (hereafter cited as *TM*).

2. Angus McLaren connects the "fear of a reversal of evolution" with "the anxieties

felt by an elite faced with disturbingly new gender and class challenges," and with the efforts of criminologists such as Cesare Lombroso to make criminals genetic aberrations rather than products of social ills. See Angus McLaren, *A Prescription for Murder: The Victorian Serial Killings of Dr. Thomas Neill Cream* (Chicago, 1993), 126.

3. Harry Geduld, *The Definitive Time Machine* (Bloomington, Ind., 1987), 174.

4. Norman MacKenzie and Jeanne MacKenzie, *H. G. Wells: A Biography* (New York, 1973), 443 (hereafter cited as *HGW*).

5. This prediction was made in *The World Set Free* (London, 1914). I. F. Clarke drily observes: "A quarter of a century before Einstein wrote his letter to warn President Roosevelt that the discoveries of the nuclear physicists had made possible the development of 'extremely powerful bombs of a new type,' Wells had already given the term 'atomic bomb' to the English language." I. F. Clarke, *Voices Prophesying War*, 2d ed. (Oxford, 1992), 90.

6. See Gail Bederman, *Manliness and Civilization* (Chicago, 1995), 20–31.

7. To appreciate the depth of the analogy, see "The Ape in Eden"—which reads Edenic iconography in terms of human evolution without reference to *The Time Machine*—in Robert Hughes, *Heaven and Hell in Western Art* (New York, 1968), 104–5.

8. See Clarke's comments on Wells in *Voices Prophesying War*, 81–90.

9. Moved by Ida Wells's antilynching campaign in 1893, the British *Christian World* protested that American lynch law "would disgrace a nation of cannibals." See Bederman, *Manliness and Civilization*, 67.

10. Kathryn Hume, "Eat or Be Eaten: H. G. Wells's *Time Machine*," *Philological Quarterly* 69, no. 2 (1990): 233–51.

11. Cf. the examples of the self-justifying "defensive" aggression of Columbus and others that Stephen Greenblatt itemizes in *Marvelous Possessions* (Chicago, 1991), esp. chap. 4.

12. *TM* 53. "The chief business of the upper-class girl was to dance and dine until she married." Paul Thompson, *The Edwardians: The Remaking of British Society* (New York, 1992), 60.

13. For example, the young plumber recently converted to socialism who explained his suicide attempt by protesting against "the battle of life" and asserting that "for many years I have had the opinion that the life of the wage earner, under the present economic conditions, was not worth living." From the *Pall Mall Gazette*, January 21, 1895, quoted in John Stokes, *In the Nineties* (Chicago, 1993), 187. Wells was writing pieces for the *Gazette* at about this time, including his symptomatic essay "The Extinction of Man," September 25, 1894.

14. *TM* 29. One of Charcot's patients was a former soldier who responded with traumatic symptoms to a thunderclap, which, the doctors reasoned, he associated with cannon fire and death. The Time Traveller appears to come out of the sky in a thunderclap like a god; Drinka calls Charcot's theory about the relationship of fright to neurosis "the Zeus myth." See George Frederick Drinka, M.D., *The Birth of Neurosis: Myth, Malady, and the Victorians* (New York, 1984), 110.

15. In "Wells as Edwardian," in *H. G. Wells: A Collection of Critical Essays*, edited by Bernard Bergonzi (Englewood Cliffs, N.J., 1976), William Bellamy maintains that

Tono-Bungay (1908) describes the alienation of "'post-cultural' man" (102). He quotes the passage in which George Ponderevo describes steamboats named *Caxton*, *Pepys*, and *Shakespeare* "wildly out of place, splashing about in that confusion. One wanted to take them out and wipe them and put them back in some English gentleman's library" (103). The moment echoes Huck Finn's encounter with the wrecked steamboat *Sir Walter Scott*.

16. HGW 17. Unless otherwise noted, quotations from Wells are from Norman MacKenzie and Jeanne MacKenzie's biography, *H. G. Wells*.

17. The footprints emerge from a "pit like the 'area' of a London house" (*TM* 82–83), suggesting both his mother's half-basement room at Up Park and the subterranean kitchen beneath his father's shop in Bromley from his earliest childhood. See Geduld, *Definitive Time Machine*, 2, 111 n. 8.

18. Darko Suvin, *Metamorphosis of Science Fiction: On the Poetics of and History of a Literary Genre* (New Haven, Conn., 1979), 239–40.

19. See, e.g., H. G. Wells, *The Science of Life* (Garden City, N.Y., 1931), 2:1241.

20. *The Outlook for Homo Sapiens*, in HGW, 416.

21. H. G. Wells, *Experiment in Autobiography* (New York, 1934), 73. In his screenplay for *The Man Who Could Work Miracles* (1937), Wells makes the messianic, mousy George Fotheringay—the haberdasher his mother wanted Wells to become—conjure up a gigantic pantheon-derived palace such as Hitler designed for Berlin (so large, Albert Speer reported, that clouds would form inside its dome). Fotheringay is a tame Jonathan Small, and is made to say "I was born small and grew small. Nobody likes being small." Significantly, his utopian wishes actually revert to the authority of an imperial past, with Roman monuments and Renaissance thrones.

22. In many details the "demonstrator" Griffin resembles the harassed and impoverished Wells during his several years studying science at South Kensington.

23. See Daniel Pick's enlightening chapter "The Biology of War" in *War Machine: The Rationalisation of Slaughter in the Modern Age* (New Haven, Conn., 1996), 75–87.

24. Andrew Carnegie, *The Gospel of Wealth and Other Timely Essays* (Cambridge, Mass., 1900), chap. 2. For the debate over Darwin's possible reliance on metaphors of free enterprise liberalism in his conception of natural selection, see Robert. M. Young, *Darwin's Metaphor: Nature's Place in Victorian Culture* (Cambridge, 1985) and Peter J. Bowler, *Evolution: The History of an Idea*, 2d ed. (Berkeley and Los Angeles, 1989), chap. 6. A recent attempt to ground free market ideology in evolutionary biology is David M. Wilkinson, "The Economics of Extinction," *The New Scientist* (April 12, 1987), 46.

25. Roy A. Rappaport, "The Sacred in Human Evolution," *Annual Review of Ecology and Systematics* 2 (1971): 35.

26. This is Ernest Becker's crucial premise. In Australia on the eve of World War II, Wells pronounced "all the reasons for believing that the human species was already staggering past the zenith of its ascendancy and on its ways through a succession of disasters to extinction." When he "finished this prophetic exordium, the chairman . . . led the singing of the national anthem. Then, said Wells, 'we shook off the disagreeable vision, and lifted up our voices in simple loyalty to things as they are'" (HGW 415). As

Becker would have predicted, the threat of death triggered the group's immediate reaffirmation of its cultural immortality system in the united strains of the ritual anthem.

27. In his study of the serial murderer Dr. Cream, whose choice of victims was apparently influenced by eugenics, Angus McLaren points out that in the 1890s Wells had attacked eugenicists for wanting to tamper with nature's complexity. See McLaren, *Prescription for Murder*, 121–24.

28. H. G. Wells, *The Shape of Things to Come* (New York, 1936), 422 (hereafter cited as STC).

29. "The Encyclopaedic organization, which centres upon Barcelona, with its seventeen million active workers, is the Memory of Mankind. Its tentacles spread out in one direction to million of investigators, checkers and correspondents, and in another to keep the educational process in living touch with mental advance." Ibid., 420. In Wells's *Anatomy of Frustration* (1936), the encyclopedia is tacitly a heroic protagonist, the "hope of our species" (*HGW* 403). Concepts such as that of a "world brain" make the encyclopedia a cosmic Sherlock Holmes and presage the messianic coloring of some panegyrics about computers in the late twentieth century.

30. In *Ontogeny and Phylogeny* (Cambridge, Mass., 1977), Stephen Jay Gould argues that neoteny has occurred in the evolution of many species, genera, and orders. Among primates, humans seem to be the outstanding example.

31. Raymond P. Coppinger and Charles Kay Smith, "A Model for Understanding the Evolution of the Mammalian Behavior," in *Current Mammalogy*, edited by Hugh H. Genoways (New York, 1990) 2:335–74. I am indebted to Kay Smith for exploring cultural implications of neoteny with me.

32. Raymond P. Coppinger and Charles Kay Smith, "Neotenic Evolution and the Origin of Human Nature: An Abstract," *Cybernetics* 1, no. 1 (1985): 38.

33. Ibid., 37–38.

34. Pick, *War Machine*, 87.

35. This is the final flourish of T. H. Huxley's "On the Relations of Man to the Lower Animals" (1863), reprinted in *Darwin*, edited by Philip Appleman (New York, 1979), 241. Cf. Sherlock Holmes's allusion to Hamlet's definition of man as "like a god," yet also "the paragon of animals."

36. Cf. Matthew Arnold, who "argued in his most popular work, *Literature and Dogma* (1873), we must read the God of the Bible 'in a scientific way,' that is, as an impersonal natural force, a 'not ourselves, which is in us and in the world around us.' But he needed to add that this was a natural force which 'makes for righteousness,' thus at a stroke deconstructing his painstaking 'scientific' case against anthropomorphism. He had to keep the human spirit at the center of things; nature as moral (righteous) is, after all, an 'ourselves.' Needless to say, Arnold was not alone in his moralization of the new god nature." Peter Allen Dale, "Realism Revisited: Darwin and Foucault among the Victorians," *Review* 12 (1990): 311. Darwin himself embraced a consoling idealism at times, as in the closing paragraph of *The Origin of Species*: "From the war of nature, from famine and death, the most exalted object which we are capable of conceiving, namely, the production of the higher animals, directly follows."

37. See "The Evolution of Childhood," in Lloyd deMause, ed., *The History of Childhood* (New York, 1975), 1–79. Although deMause's controversial argument needs qualification, its account of stressful living conditions in the past strikes me as bracingly realistic.

38. Paul B. Sears, *Charles Darwin: The Naturalist as a Cultural Force* (New York, 1950), 74.

39. James R. Kincaid, *Child-Loving: The Erotic Child in Victorian Culture* (Berkeley and Los Angeles, 1993).

40. Christopher Wood, *The Pre-Raphaelites* (London, 1994), 130.

41. See Priscilla Robertson, "The Home as a Nest," in deMause, *History of Childhood*, 423, and David M. Lubin, *Picturing a Nation* (New Haven, 1996), chap. 5.

42. The most distinctive exponent of these notions was Dr. G. Stanley Hall in the United States. "Key to all his formulations were evolutionary theories of racial recapitulation, the process whereby children relived the primitive evolutionary stages of their ancestors. By constructing savagery, with its plentiful supplies of nervous force, as a characteristic of youth, Hall was able to argue that civilized men could develop powerful reserves of nervous force by having a healthfully savage boyhood. Moreover, adolescent boys could develop the powerful manhood necessary to move the race toward the 'super-man' by taking advantage of the racial variations of their primitive ancestors. Hall believed that by applying racial recapitulation to white boys' education, he could solve problems of overcivilized effeminacy and lead American civilization toward a millennial racial perfection." Bederman, *Manliness and Civilization*, 119–20.

43. David J. Lake highlights some of the inconsistencies in Wells's understanding of evolution: "If the Eloi are made decadent by a too easy life, why should the subterranean workers be made decadent by a hard one? Would not their grim conditions in fact lead to selection for intelligence, for survival of the cunningest?" See "The White Sphinx and the Whitened Lemur: Images of Death in *The Time Machine*," *Science Fiction Studies* 6 (March 1979): 81.

44. In conceiving of the Morlocks, Wells probably had in mind the technologically superior, subterranean creatures called Vril-ya in Edward Bulwer-Lytton, *The Coming Race* (1871). As I. F. Clarke points out, "Lytton's parting shot comes straight from the *Origin of Species*: 'If they ever emerged from those nether recesses into the light of day, they would, according to their own traditional persuasions of their ultimate destiny, destroy and replace our existent varieties of man.'" Clarke, *Voices Prophesying War*, 49.

45. *TM* 55. Cf. Small's flight from his angry family and Holmes's identification with Hamlet, who is oppressed by a vindictive parental ghost. *She* depicts an obsession with—and flight from—an underground world of mummified, ghostly parents.

46. See Stanley Edgar Hyman, *The Tangled Bank* (New York, 1962), 134, 107.

47. Karl Beckson, *London in the 1890s: A Cultural History* (New York, 1992), xv.

48. Robert Pattison, *The Child Figure in English Literature* (Athens, Ga., 1978), 11–20. Pattison considers Victorian childhood in chaps. 4–6.

49. An even more exact analogy would be the way in which popular American magazines in the 1990s such as *Vanity Fair* and *Time* sentimentalized the sorry fates of self-indulgent and self-destructive celebrities, the decadent "aristocrats" of consumer democracy.

50. Androgyny had fashionable esoteric meanings in the 1890s. Cf. Wells's use of the sphinx in *The Time Machine* with Josephin Péladan's novel *L'Androgyne* (Paris, 1910), which fantasizes about evolution: "Esoterically, he [the androgyne] represents the initial state of man, which is identical to his final state. . . . The sphinx incarnates the complete theology with the solution of origins and finalities. . . . The sphinx smiles at his divine enlightenment; he will reconstitute a day of his original unity, because he is man and god, in the same measure of involution and evolution," 16–17, quoted in Shearer West, *Fin de Siècle* (Woodstock, N.Y., 1994), 81. Painters commonly used the sphinx to stress the spiritual significance of androgyny and to link that with religion and mysticism. See West, *Fin de Siècle*, chap. 5, esp. 81–82. Péladan's theory is ultimately misogynistic and homosexual—interesting in light of Wells's angst about homosexual decadence.

51. Ellis added: "You quote the saying of Hobbes, 'Homo homini lupus.' But as Shaftesbury pointed out two centuries ago, the saying is not valid, since we cannot compare the attitude of an animal to its *own* species with that to *another* species. If man is like the wolf, then, said Shaftesbury, we have to remember that 'wolves are to wolves very kind and loving creatures.' The impulse of aggression is, fundamentally, a manifestation of the impulse of mutual help. We are aggressive towards those whom, we think, threaten those we love. If we view aggression biologically, this seems to me its only explanation." See Phyllis Grosskurth, *Havelock Ellis* (New York, 1980), 393.

52. See J. Percy Smith, ed., *Bernard Shaw and H. G. Wells* (Toronto, 1995), 148.

53. These terms are from Stephen Jay Gould, *Ever Since Darwin* (New York, 1977).

54. Eric White, "The End of Metanarratives in Evolutionary Biology," *Modern Language Quarterly* 51, no. 1 (1990): 71.

55. For example, Gillian Beer, *Darwin's Plots: Evolutionary Narrative in Darwin* (London, 1983).

56. Davydd Greenwood, *The Taming of Evolution: The Persistence of Nonevolutionary Views in the Study of Humans* (Ithaca, N.Y., 1984), 69.

57. Richard Dawkins, *Climbing Mount Improbable* (New York, 1996).

58. HGW 395.

59. H. G. Wells, *The Invisible Man* (New York, 1983), 100.

Chapter 5: Post-traumatic Style

1. Richard Ellmann, *Oscar Wilde* (New York, 1988), 495–96 (hereafter cited as OW).

2. Oscar Wilde, *De Profundis* (hereafter cited as DP), in *The Complete Works of Oscar Wilde* (hereafter cited as CW), edited by Vyvyan Holland (London, 1966), 896.

3. A reviewer in the *Pall Mall Gazette* (May 12, 1891) complains that "his method is this: he takes some well-established truth . . . and asserts the contrary." See Karl Beckson, ed., *Oscar Wilde: The Critical Heritage* (London, 1970), 92. It galled critics that he worshiped originality but often operated as a literary magpie.

4. Wilde and Conan Doyle met at an authors' luncheon in 1889 at which J. M. Stoddart commissioned both *The Sign of Four* and *The Picture of Dorian Gray* for *Lippincott's Monthly Magazine*. See OW 313–14.

5. Walter Pater, *The Renaissance*, edited by Donald L. Hill (Berkeley and Los Angeles, 1980), 190.

6. Oscar Wilde, *The Picture of Dorian Gray*, edited by Donald L. Lawler (New York, 1988), 61 (hereafter cited as *PDG*).

7. In his self-justifying memoir *Oscar Wilde and Myself* (London, 1915), Alfred Douglas credibly describes Wilde's insecurity, and reports him "always as eager to know how he had 'gone down' as a *debutante*" (52). Douglas is scathing about his former lover's social pretensions: "That he should have persistently pretended to noble birth is . . . fairly contemptible" (54–55).

8. As friends were trying to whisk Wilde off to Calais, beyond prosecution, Lady Wilde "declaimed to Oscar in her grand manner, 'If you stay, even if you go to prison, you will always be my son. It will make no difference to my affection. But if you go, I will never speak to you again" (*OW* 468).

9. Melissa Knox, *Oscar Wilde: A Long and Lovely Suicide* (New Haven, Conn., 1994), 12.

10. Although the clinical term scarcely applies to Wilde, many commentators have remarked on his fragmentation. See, e.g., Barbara Charlesworth, *Dark Passages: The Decadent Consciousness in Victorian Literature* (Madison, Wisc., 1965), 53.

11. Max Nordau, *Degeneration* (1895; reprint, Lincoln, Nebr., 1968, 1993), 318.

12. In *Slouching towards Gomorrah* (New York, 1996), Robert H. Bork uses virtually the same rhetorical stick to beat *his* stand-in for Wilde: "liberalism" or "the 1960s." See chap. 12 below.

13. Oscar Wilde, "The Happy Prince," in *The Annotated Oscar Wilde*, edited by H. Montgomery Hyde (New York, 1982), hereafter cited as "HP."

14. Letter to Robert Ross, April 1, 1897, quoted in Hyde, ed., *The Annotated Oscar Wilde*, 464–65. The phrase is echoed in his letter of March 24, 1898, to the *Daily Chronicle*: "One of the tragedies of prison life is that it turns a man's heart to stone," (*CW* 968).

15. For a detailed demonstration, see chaps. 1 and 2 in my *Shakespeare's Creation* (Amherst, Mass., 1976).

16. For a provocative elaboration of these dynamics, see Sigurd Burckhardt, "The Poet as Fool and Priest," in *Shakespearean Meanings* (Princeton, 1968).

17. Oscar Wilde, "The Soul of Man under Socialism," *CW* 1081.

18. Wilde is a striking example of the economic maneuvering Pierre Bourdieu outlines in *Distinction: A Social Critique of the Judgment of Taste*, translated by Richard Nice (Cambridge, Mass., 1984).

19. See, e.g., Raymond Williams's positive words about "The Soul of Man under Socialism," in *Culture and Society, 1580–1950* (New York, 1983), 170–72.

20. Richard Ellmann, *Golden Codgers* (New York, 1973), 74.

21. This makes Wilde a therapeutic voice in relation to the disenchanted young people of the suicide "epidemic" of 1893. Consider the suicide note (printed in the *Daily Chronicle* of August 16, 1893) of Ernest Clark, who spoke like an aesthete despairing at a philistine world. "I resolved long ago that life is a sequence of shams [cf. masks]. That men have had to create utopias and heavens to make it bearable; and that all the wis-

est men have been disgusted with life as it is. Carlyle and Voltaire advise hard work, but only as an anaesthetic. . . . Only the transcendental and aesthetic in life are worth our thought. Only a life following beauty and creating it approaches any degree of joyousness, but the ugliness and vile monotony in my life have crowded beauty out" (John Stokes, *In the Nineties* [Chicago, 1993], 116).

22. Beckson, *Oscar Wilde*, glosses some of the play's "Uranian" double entendres (186–91).

23. See Louis A. Sass, *Madness and Modernism: Insanity in the Light of Modern Art, Literature, and Thought* (New York, 1992), chap. 1.

24. This fear took memorable form in Mary Shelley's *Frankenstein*, whose monster is a forced assemblage of body parts and horrifies the conventional people he meets. Chris Baldick analyzes the implied fear of anarchy in *In Frankenstein's Shadow* (Oxford, 1987).

25. Janet Oppenheim, *Shattered Nerves: Doctors, Patients, and Depression in Victorian England* (New York, 1991), 87.

26. Charlotte Perkins Gilman, *The Yellow Wallpaper and Other Writings by Charlotte Perkins Gilman*, edited by Lynne Sharon Schwartz (New York, 1989), 4.

27. Cardinal Newman, *Apologia pro Vita Sua*, edited by Martin J. Svaglic (Oxford, 1967), 216.

28. "A limited death is better than the real death," as Irvin Yalom puts it. "One need not fear death if one is dead anyway." *Existential Psychotherapy*, 151. See also my *Play, Death, and Heroism in Shakespeare* (Chapel Hill, 1989), chap. 3.

29. Letter to Robert Ross, April 1, 1897, quoted in Hyde, ed., *The Annotated Oscar Wilde*, 464–65.

30. See "Self-effacement and Autonomy," in my *Play, Death, and Heroism in Shakespeare*, 13–35.

31. In *De Profundis*, Wilde makes Christ the mouthpiece for his own mixed feelings about charity: "The cold philanthropies, the ostentatious public charities, the tedious formalisms so dear to the middle-class mind, [Christ] exposed with . . . scorn" (932).

32. In various versions of the story the saint is sawn in two, boiled in molten lead, and beheaded—all scenarios of submissive mutilation.

33. In *De Profundis*, Wilde pontificates with adjectival absolutes, "of course" invoking the "whole," the "entire," the "supreme," the "perfect" this or that. His relationship with Bosie, he wrote, was "entirely destructive of everything fine in me" (881). "There was no pleasure I did not experience" (922); therefore his penitence would have to be boundless.

34. "She dragged herself about the house in uncouth misery with drawn blotched face and hideous body, sick at heart because of our love. It was dreadful. I tried to be kind to her; forced myself to touch and kiss her, but she was sick always, and—oh! I cannot recall it, it is all loathsome. . . . Oh, nature is disgusting; it takes beauty and defiles it; it defaces the ivory-white body with the vile cicatrices of maternity; it befouls the altar of the soul." Frank Harris, *Oscar Wilde: His Life and Confessions* (New York, 1930), 337–38. This sounds to me like the voice of a doctor's child, sensitized to, and terrified of, the body's horrors.

35. Holmes has much in common with Dorian Gray: opium and cocaine experimentation; anxiety about stagnation; rage at mediocrity; a fascination with science; a mania for collecting. Both novels feature a moment in which a nemesis peers through a safe upper-class window (*PDG* 153). Conan Doyle also caricatures Des Esseintes' withdrawal in the "oriental" apartment of Thaddeus Sholto, and Joris Karl Huysmans's hypnotic fascination with precious objects resembles Conan Doyle's preoccupation with the Agra treasure.

36. Cf. the "secret" nursery in the attic with Dr. Jekyll's lab, that other site of psychic splitting marked by punitive rectitude, taboo homosexual feeling, fear of aging, child revolt, and suicide.

37. Wilde's prosecution epitomized the late-Victorian touchiness about reputation. Queensberry was pugnacious and homophobic, but he was also a creature of his culture. In Angus McLaren's words, "in the preindustrial world aristocrats who enjoyed a secure, ascribed status could be largely indifferent to what was said about them. Even in the nineteenth century the duke of Wellington responded to extortionate threats with his famous 'Publish and be damned' challenge. But less-favored Victorians viewed with increasing anxiety any threat of exposure of private matters. Judges agreed with them and continued to reduce the level of threats they believed the 'firm and constant man' could withstand. Reputations in a nineteenth-century careerist, mobile, middle-class society were increasingly important and fragile." Angus McLaren, *A Prescription for Murder: The Victorian Serial Killings of Dr. Thomas Neill Cream* (Chicago, 1993), 92.

38. Linda Dowling, *Hellenism and Homosexuality in Victorian England* (Ithaca, N.Y., 1994), 4.

39. Ibid., 8.

40. DP 882. In *De Profundis* there is every sign that Wilde half-recognized the justice of Queensberry's censure of his son, because Wilde also paid dearly for Bosie's callousness. Bosie not only bragged to Wilde that he "could beat [his] father 'at his own trade'" of abusive insults (939), but he also lashed the "loving" father Wilde more than once.

41. See Judith R. Walkowitz, *City of Dreadful Delight* (Chicago, 1992), 81–134. Stead's reportage was skewed to scapegoat bad mothers in ways that bring to mind Haggard's correspondence with Roosevelt. McLaren's account of this misogyny in *Prescription for Murder* is richly circumstantial.

42. In his memoir Douglas reports that at one point during their trip to Algiers, Wilde was mistaken for Douglas's father. Douglas teased an irritated Wilde about it. Douglas, *Oscar Wilde and Myself*, 204–5.

43. Charlesworth, *Dark Passages*, 55.

44. Cf. the plausible report that Tchaikovsky was formally pressured into suicide at about this time when his homosexual involvement with a young aristocrat caused a scandal that provoked the censure of the czar.

45. Cross-class sex ("'trade' as it is sometimes called, deriving from the feelings of so many upper-class Anglo-Saxons that sex cannot be without inhibitions within one's own class and is more spontaneous outside it") excited Wilde. Douglass Shand-Tucci, *Boston Bohemia, 1881–1900* (Amherst, Mass., 1995), 41; see also Karl Beckson, *London*

in the 1890s: A Cultural History (New York, 1992), 194. Cf. the situation in Franz Schubert's early nineteenth-century Vienna: "That the young men of the Schubert circle loved each other seems amply clear. And . . . it is reasonably probable that their primary orientation was a homosexual one. By finding sexual release with anonymous partners in Vienna's *Hallowett* [cf. Wilde 'feasting with panthers'], they were apparently able to maintain idealized, passionate friendships with each other and to infuse those friendships with some stability." Maynard Solomon, "Franz Schubert and the Peacocks of Benvenuto Cellini," *Nineteenth-Century Music* 12 (spring 1989): 202.

46. "I shunned sorrow and suffering of every kind. I hated both" (*DP* 919). "My only mistake was that I confined myself so exclusively to . . . the sunlit side of the garden, and shunned the other side for its shadow and its gloom. Failure, disgrace, poverty, sorrow, despair [and other miseries]—all these were things of which I was afraid" (922).

47. Gilman, *The Yellow Wallpaper*, 10.

48. Ibid., 12.

49. Wilde's prosecution was probably influenced by fears of a homosexual scandal surrounding the suicide of Queensberry's oldest son, who may have been vulnerable to blackmail over his relationship with the foreign minister, Lord Rosebery. See Ellmann's account of the trial in *Oscar Wilde*. Wilde's conduct of his defense was also determined by his wish to protect Alfred Douglas from prosecution. Given Douglas's ruthless self-vindication and repudiation of Wilde in his 1914 memoir, it is likely that he personally pressed Wilde to protect him.

50. Wilde, "Soul of Man under Socialism," *CW* 1099.

51. Shakespeare is plainly modern in his conception of, for example, Macbeth's terminal emptiness.

Reconnaissance

1. Tom Engelhardt, *The End of Victory Culture* (New York, 1995). See also Richard Slotkin's *Regeneration through Violence: The Mythology of the American Frontier, 1600–1860* (Middletown, Conn., 1973).

2. Engelhardt, *End of Victory Culture*, 38.

3. See the legal scholar John T. Noonan's account of the United Fruit Company's long tentacles in *Persons and Masks of the Law: Cardozo, Holmes, Jefferson, and Wythe as Makers of the Masks* (New York, 1976).

4. This is undoubtedly one reason why, in covering the 1996 Olympics in Atlanta, the networks tried to turn all the action into narratives, with thumbnail biographies of major contestants and boasts of American supremacy naively reminiscent of the Olympic vainglory that Leni Riefenstahl filmed for Hitler.

5. Engelhardt, *End of Victory Culture*, 15.

6. Fred Block has analyzed this neoconservative imagery of a "vampire" government devouring the "lifeblood" of capital in *The Vampire State and Other Myths and Fallacies about the U.S. Economy* (New York, 1996).

7. See Lloyd deMause, *Reagan's America* (New York, 1984), 3. Though sometimes

tendentious, deMause's book is a striking compendium of the easily forgotten imagery of injury, doom, and sacrifice that Reagan promulgated during his presidency. See also Garry Wills, *Reagan's America* (New York, 1988).

8. Metromedia News (July 11, 1982), cited in deMause, *Reagan's America*, 115.

9. The guilt of withdrawal from parental roles is neatly finessed in the Disney film *A Little Princess* (1995), adapted from the book by Frances Hodgson Burnett. A soldier suffering traumatic amnesia in World War I "forgets" his motherless daughter, plunging her into poverty and disgrace. In this scenario, war "explains" the orphan in the factory universe.

10. *New Yorker*, July 19, 1982, 24; William Martin, "Waiting for the End," *Atlantic Monthly*, June 1982, 31–37; and *Esquire*, November 1982, 16; quoted in deMause, *Reagan's America*, 104. As Robert Scheer has shown, President Reagan wanted to expand civil defense policies, believing that the nation could engage in, and survive, a nuclear war. Robert Scheer, *With Enough Shovels: Reagan, Bush and Nuclear War* (New York, 1982), 105–9.

11. DeMause, *Reagan's America*, 154.

12. As he widened the Vietnam War by invading Cambodia, President Nixon argued that the "most powerful nation on earth" would otherwise be reduced to a "pitiful helpless giant" (*New York Times*, May 1, 1970). For Reagan, the American defeat seemed to fulfill that threat.

13. George Gilder, *Wealth and Poverty* (New York, 1981), 114.

14. *Soho News*, December 22, 1981, 16, quoted in deMause, *Reagan's America*, 63.

15. *New York Post*, October 5, 1981, 3, quoted ibid.

16. This was J. Edgar Hoover's McCarthy-era epithet for Communist spies.

17. Glenn Hodges, "When Good Guys Lie," *Washington Monthly*, January–February 1997, 30. To point out the puritanical element in the hysteria is to invite charges of insensitivity to child welfare, but its 1890s equivalent was the fear of upper-class predators that scapegoated Oscar Wilde, and the panic about "white slavery" often directed at immigrants, as in the 1919 story "One Awful Night," discussed below.

18. Jonathan Shay, *Achilles in Vietnam: Combat Trauma and the Undoing of Character* (New York, 1994), 81.

19. Carrie R. Leana, "Corporate Anorexia May Wind Up Being Fatal," *The Los Angeles Times*, November 8, 1995. See also James L. Tyson, "'Ready-fire-aim' Layoff Strategy Backfires on Corporate America," *The Christian Science Monitor*, February 6, 1995.

20. "Feminazis" is the coinage of media polemicist Rush Limbaugh.

21. See, e.g., Zillah R. Eisenstein, "The Sexual Politics of the New Right: Understanding the 'Crisis of Liberalism' for the 1980s," *Signs: Journal of Women in Culture and Society* 7 (1982): 567–88.

22. Gail Bederman, *Manliness and Civilization* (Chicago, 1995).

23. Angus McLaren, *A Prescription for Murder: The Victorian Serial Killings of Dr. Thomas Neill Cream* (Chicago, 1993), 87.

24. Gilder, *Wealth and Poverty*, 114, quoted in deMause, *Reagan's America*, 63.

25. McLaren, *Prescription for Murder*, 83.

26. Hodges, "When Good Guys Lie," 38. One scientific source of fertility fears is

Theo Colborn, Dianne Dumanoski, and John Peterson Myers, *Our Stolen Future: Are We Threatening Our Fertility, Intelligence, and Survival? A Scientific Detective Story* (New York, 1996), whose title implicitly threatens annihilation.

27. Ronald Reagan, *Where's the Rest of Me?* (New York, 1965), hereafter cited as *WRM*.

28. See, e.g., deMause's analysis in *Reagan's America*, 36–50.

29. To use Wilde's vocabulary, it is as if in *King's Row* Reagan-Drake wakes up to find himself the "too happy" Prince in the process of giving his body parts to the poor. (In the film, victimized by the banker's embezzlement, he gives himself to working-class life and a poor but faithful girlfriend.) Wilde's Prince scorns the city fathers and in death joins the idealized heavenly Father. Reagan-Drake follows a compromise melodramatic version of the scenario, vowing to become a real-estate developer and build housing for workmen. His career will be a traumatic sacrifice in the service of a triumphal identification with the parent-rulers of the palace and city. The movie scenario is a version of the story I have traced in Reagan's presidential speeches.

30. It may be that if Reagan had been the sort of person who could confront and talk about those childhood disturbances in himself and others, he might have helped demystify them somewhat, but perhaps at the cost of losing some of the personal magnetism that audiences found mysteriously attractive in him.

31. Cf. Louis Uchitelle and N. R. Kleinfield, "On the Battlefields of Business, Millions of Casualties," *New York Times*, March 3, 1996, sec. A. In February 1996, the United States Department of Health and Human Services' Center for Mental Health Services convened a "prevention workshop" in Washington, D.C., titled "Minimizing Trauma and Violence during Downsizing and Layoffs."

32. The increase in stress is concretized in two studies in the *British Medical Journal* that correlate the sharp increase in income inequality in the United States since the early 1980s with "a breakdown in social cohesion, increased competition for scarce resources and greater levels of stress and frustration," and in turn poorer health. The studies find that the greater the income gap, the higher the death rate. See Alison Bass, "Income Inequality, Mortality Linked," *Boston Globe*, April 19, 1996. The article cites studies by Bruce Kennedy, director of public-health practice at the Harvard School of Public Health, and George A. Kaplan of the California Department of Health Services in Berkeley, published in the *British Medical Journal*.

33. Karl Albrecht, *Stress and the Manager* (New York, 1979), 1, 285, 292, 297–99.

34. It is symptomatic of the underlying conflicts in American life that few people ever realize that, by law, "every nonunion employee in the U.S. is an 'employee at will.' He can be fired for any reason, good or bad." Thomas Geoghegan, *Which Side Are You On?* (New York, 1991), 271.

35. Adam Walinsky, "The Crisis of Public Order," *Atlantic Monthly*, July 1995, 39. Like Reagan, Walinsky thinks "misguided" welfare policies caused "the collapse of the black lower class" (54), as if there had once been a golden age for poor blacks. He faults "stupidity and cowardice" in "the entire governmental apparatus" for abandoning the black ghettos, overlooking the windfall reaped by the affluent Americans whose tax revolt directly increased squalor in the streets, as John Kenneth Galbraith demonstrates

in *The Culture of Contentment* (New York, 1992). Walinsky prescribes as many as five million new police for his buildup.

36. Lewis Lapham, *Hotel America: Scenes in the Lobby of the Fin-de-Siècle* (London, 1995), 158–59. "In the name of virtue and the interest of municipal security," says Lapham, Trump "invites his fellow townspeople to reduce themselves to a howling mob"—that is, to go berserk (159).

37. Novels such as Frank Peretti's *The Oath* (Dallas, 1995) identify that demonic enemy as Saint George's dragon. The conservative Christian magazine *First Things* has insinuated that righteous Christians should revolt against the illegitimate United States government, a sentiment delicately echoed by the right-wing opinion makers such as Op-Ed columnist Cal Thomas.

38. William Leach unfolds the history of consumer capitalism from its late-Victorian invention to 1930 in *Land of Desire: Merchants, Power, and the Rise of a New American Culture* (New York, 1993).

39. Ernest Becker, "Letters from Ernest," edited by Harvey Bates, *Christian Century*, March 9, 1977, 227.

40. The concentration of media ownership appears to have increased standardization and conservatism in the stories America tells. Obeying "market forces," newspapers, movies, and novels emulate television, even as television emulates the dissociated sound bites and jabbing visual effects of advertising. A Hollywood film is a global marketing event with elaborate product tie-ins. According to Sidney Schanberg, between 1986 and 1996 "nearly 150 papers have shut their doors. . . . Most of our large cities have been reduced to but one newspaper—which means only one voice, one opinion, one view of the world. Meanwhile, 80 percent of the papers that have survived are chain-owned." Sidney Schanberg, "The Murder of *New York Newsday*," *Washington Monthly*, March 1996, 31. Thomas Whiteside has traced the corporate takeover of trade publishing in the 1970s and 1980s in *The Blockbuster Complex: Conglomerates, Show Business, and Book Publishing* (Middletown, Conn., 1981). Recent changes are surveyed in Andre Schiffrin, "The Corporatization of Publishing," *Nation* 262, no. 22 (1996): 29–32.

41. See Neil Postman, *Amusing Ourselves to Death: Public Discourse in the Age of Show Business* (New York, 1985).

42. Consider Henry Adams's awareness of "a 'subconscious chaos' of multiple inward selves, described by a 'new psychology' that had 'split personality not only into dualism, but also into complex groups, like telephonic centres and systems.' For Adams, the coherence of individual identity became a precarious balancing act, not a given." T. Walter Herbert, "Mozart, Hawthorne, and Mario Savio," *College English* 57, no. 4 (1995): 403.

43. Zygmunt Bauman, *Mortality, Immortality, and the Life Strategies* (Stanford, Calif., 1995).

44. Lapham, *Hotel America*, 233.

45. The media coverage of Christopher Reeves's (Superman's) traumatic paralysis in 1996 used the moral authority of the injured hero as a basic mode of consolation for the nation no less than for the injured actor.

46. Richard A. Gabriel and Paul L. Savage, *Crisis in Command: Mismanagement in the Army* (New York, 1978).

47. See, e.g., Peter Charles Hoffer's account of social and environmental stresses in Salem at the time of the witch trials, in *The Devil's Disciples* (Baltimore, 1996).

48. Toni Morrison, *Playing in the Dark: Whiteness and the Literary Imagination* (New York, 1993), 35.

49. David M. Lubin, *Picturing a Nation* (New Haven, Conn., 1994), 83.

50. I. F. Clarke, *Voices Prophesying War*, 2d ed. (Oxford, 1992), 42–43.

51. *True Confessions: Sixty Years of Suffering and Sorrow*, edited by Florence Moriarty (New York, 1979), 2–5.

52. In the *Nation* (July 10, 1920), Herbert J. Seligman, a staff member of the National Association for the Advancement of Colored People, reported on a visit to Haiti, where he found United States Marines, ostensibly there to stabilize the country, calling Haitians "Gooks" and treating them "with every variety of contempt, insult, and brutality. I have heard officers wearing the United States uniform . . . talk of 'bumping off' (i.e., killing) 'Gooks' as if it were a variety of sport like duck hunting." The epithet persisted in the Vietnam War, where the killing was no longer mere talk. See Robert Jay Lifton, *Home from the War* (New York, 1973), 200.

53. Shay, *Achilles in Vietnam*, 35.

54. This was literally so in 1996, when Disney was building a planned housing development in central Florida meant to recapture bygone America.

55. Elizabeth Young and Graham Caveney, *Shopping in Space: Essays on America's Blank Generation Fiction* (New York, 1994).

56. Ibid., 252, 250, 252–53.

57. Edward A. Gamarra Jr., "Generation X and Neurasthenia: Cultural Pathology in *Reality Bites, Singles*, and *Spanking the Monkey*," in *Pictures of a Generation on Hold*, edited by Murray Pomerance and John Sakeris (Toronto, 1996), 57.

Chapter 6: Thinking through Others

1. Clifford Geertz, *The Interpretation of Cultures* (New York, 1973), 50.

2. Erich Fromm, for example, conceives of transference in terms of idols. See Ernest Becker's useful definition of transference, "The Spell Cast by Persons," in Becker, *Denial of Death* (New York, 1973), 142–48.

3. Cf. this report from a young European friend of mine: "I had a dream very similar to that of your daughter. Only, I must have been way older then. I was driving a car although I didn't have my dad's permission and that gave me a horrible feeling while on the road. I only realized after waking up that I didn't know how to drive at all. I didn't have problems with that in the dream, though. Anyway, I am not sure how the dream ended."

4. If we can believe Bruno Snell, *The Discovery of the Mind* (New York, 1960), and Julian Jayne, *The Origins of Consciousness in the Breakdown of the Bicameral Mind* (Boston, 1976), intrusive voices were a fundamental feature of mental life in the archaic world.

5. Ilza Veith, "Four Thousand Years of Hysteria," in *Hysterical Personality*, edited by Mardi J. Horowitz (New York, 1977), 17.

6. See Otto Rank, *Will Therapy* (New York, 1978).

7. Jack Hitt, "On Earth as It Is in Heaven: Field Trips with the Apostles of Creation Science," *Harper's*, November 1996, 51–60. One link between creationist and apocalyptic fantasies lies in the story of Noah. See Norman Cohn, *Cosmos, Chaos, and the World to Come* (New Haven, Conn., 1993).

8. In the 1920s, the popular Émile Coué had clients talk to themselves "face-to-face" in the mirror, chanting "Every day, in every way, I am getting better and better." It seems likely that this zany exercise corroborated—or perhaps filled in for—a self-monitoring, usually self-encouraging voice partially internalized from prosthetic parental voices in childhood.

9. The appeal took on a life of its own, the identity of the boy mutating from one incarnation to the next. Because the story has been going around the Internet for years, it qualifies as a sort of crowd delusion. The original child apparently survived his illness.

10. Joanna Bourke, *Dismembering the Male: Men's Bodies, Britain, and the Great War* (Chicago, 1996), 22–23.

11. Pat Barker, *Regeneration* (New York, 1992), *The Eye in the Door* (New York, 1994), and *The Ghost Road* (New York, 1995).

12. Sir Thomas More, *Responsio ad Lutherum*, edited by John Headley, translated by Sister Scholastica Mandeville, in *The Complete Works of St. Thomas More* 5:1 (New Haven, Conn., 1969), 305–7.

13. See Kirby Farrell, *Play, Death, and Heroism in Shakespeare* (Chapel Hill, 1989), esp. chap. 8.

14. Torquato Tasso, quoted in Muriel Bradbrook, *Shakespeare: The Poet in His World* (London, 1980), 73.

15. Peter Laslett, *The World We Have Lost*, 2d ed. (New York, 1973).

16. Shakespeare, *The Tempest*, 3.2.137–43.

17. The rhythm is as ancient as oracles. Shakespearean drama offers a peculiarly vivid incarnation of it because the plays commonly use a fool to explode conventional meanings and values with wordplay, riddles, and mockery, and then give to a priestly figure enigmatic, visionary language that promises to knit the world back together. (See Burckhardt, "Poet as Fool and Priest," 22–48.) Naturally, Shakespeare thought in terms of the ritual figures of early-modern culture. In the secular world of *Fearless*, those ritual figures are combined in the well-meaning, impotent psychiatrist. But the structural rhythm is similar. King Lear is expelled from the conventional world, staggers about in traumatic chaos, and dies trying to reconnect the world he knows to the mystery beyond. In a comedy such as *As You Like It*, traumatic expulsion leads to the healing confusion in the Forest of Arden and the reintegration of marriage vows—with Rosalind explicitly playing the priest at the close.

Chapter 7: Abuse as a Prosthetic System

1. Christopher Craft, "'Kiss Me with Those Red Lips': Gender and Inversion in Bram Stoker's *Dracula*," in *Dracula: The Vampire and the Critics*, edited by Margaret L. Carter (Ann Arbor, Mich., 1988), 182–84.

2. Quoted in John Judis, "Budget Chicken Littles," *Washington Monthly*, December 1996, 58.

3. See, e.g., Peter Annin, "Superpredators Arrive: Should We Cage the New Breed of Vicious Kids?" *Newsweek*, January 12, 1996, 57.

4. Nicholas Lemann, "The Vogue of Childhood Misery," *Atlantic*, March 1992, 119.

5. "First-person memoirs of painful childhoods have become commonplace in our tell-all time. Chronicles of trauma and abuse are told as purifying rituals; redemption stories; all-American tales of the underdog beating back the beasts of his or her past. . . . They show little sympathy or understanding for anyone but the teller. And while they frequently end with resolve, they rarely allow room for further reflection, much less reconciliation of any sort." Maureen Dezell, "Facing Down the Ghosts of Childhood," *Boston Globe*, December 14, 1995.

6. For a convenient tally of such novels, see Katie Roiphe, "Making the Incest Scene," *Harper's*, November 1995, 65–69. A cogent account of the emergence of child abuse in industrializing nineteenth-century America is John Demos, *Past, Present, and Personal: The Family and the Life Course in American History* (New York, 1986), 68–91. Ian Hacking describes the history of the idea of child abuse in "The Making and Molding of Child Abuse," *Critical Inquiry* 17: 253–88.

7. Roiphe, "Making the Incest Scene," 65.

8. "Sexual abuse," Roiphe writes, "is everywhere splashed across the culture, wept about on talk shows, endlessly reported in the news. And writers of fiction have followed along; incest has become our latest literary vogue." Ibid., 65.

9. Judith Lewis Herman, *Trauma and Recovery* (New York, 1992), 28.

10. Ibid., 61.

11. Ellen Bass and Laura Davis, *The Courage to Heal: A Guide for Women Survivors of Child Sexual Abuse* (New York, 1988), 22.

12. See Elizabeth Loftus and Katherine Ketcham, *The Myth of Repressed Memory: False Memories and Allegations of Sexual Abuse* (New York, 1994). Frederick Crews appraises books about recovered memory in "The Revenge of the Repressed," *New York Review of Books*, November 17, 1994, 54. Researchers challenge the validity of this sort of amnesia on historical grounds, pointing to late-nineteenth-century studies of hysteria that were compromised by iatrogenic effects when patients "learned" to be disturbed in ways that met the physicians' subliminal expectations. But they also draw on experiments that indicate memory does not work in the simple fashion that is assumed in cases of recovered memory. We are apparently still far from a definitive understanding of such crucial phenomena as dissociation and suggestibility. A substantial recent study is Daniel L. Schacter, *Searching for Memory* (New York, 1996).

13. The epidemic quality of such beliefs comes boldly to light in folklore studies.

See Jeffrey S. Victor, *Satanic Panic* (Chicago, 1993). Debbie Nathan and Michael Snedeker persuasively debunk satanic abuse in *Satan's Silence: Ritual Abuse and the Making of a Modern American Witch Hunt* (New York, 1996). Elaine Showalter's *Hystories: Hysterical Epidemics and Modern Media* (New York, 1997) has a useful overview of the emergence of satanic ritual abuse fantasies in the 1980s (171–89).

14. It is hard to see how this paranoid lore could convince anyone who has read Norman Cohn's study, *Europe's Inner Demons* (New York, 1975), for example, or John Demos's psychoanalytic account of New England witchcraft delusions in *Entertaining Satan* (New York, 1982).

15. See Richard Ofshe and Ethan Watters, *Making Monsters: False Memories, Psychotherapy, and Sexual Hysteria* (New York, 1994), 188–95.

16. Philip Jenkins, "Out of Whole Cloth," *Chronicles*, April 1996, 29.

17. Anthony Storr, *Human Destructiveness* (New York, 1991), 126.

18. Mary Gaitskill, *Two Girls, Fat and Thin* (New York, 1991), 122.

19. Ibid., 124.

20. Roiphe, "Making the Incest Scene," 67.

21. Gaitskill, *Two Girls, Fat and Thin*, 71.

22. Colin A. Ross, M.D., *The Osiris Complex: Case Studies in Multiple Personality Disorder* (Toronto, 1994). Imagery of flying is especially common when the trauma involves dissociative disorders. In the etiology of multiple-personality disorder, which was once exceedingly rare, Ross envisions "two basic psychological manoueuvres. . . . First, the little girl who is being repeatedly sexually abused has an out-of-body experience: detached from her body and what is going on, she may float up to the ceiling and imagine that she is watching another little girl being abused . . . and the child is buffered from the direct impact of the trauma. Second, an amnesia barrier is erected between the original child and the newly created identity. Now not only is the abuse not happening to the original little girl, she doesn't even remember it" (vii–viii). The latest diagnostic manual, *DSM-IV*, has become more cautious about the syndrome, renaming it "dissociative identity disorder," and there is a growing body of research that holds it to be purely a cultural construct. See, e.g., Nicholas P. Spanos, *Multiple Identities and False Memories* (Washington, D.C., 1996), and its substantial bibliography.

23. Gaitskill, *Two Girls, Fat and Thin*, 123.

24. Patti Davis, *Bondage* (New York, 1994), 314.

25. Cynthia D. Grant, *Uncle Vampire* (New York, 1993), 97 (hereafter cited as *UV*).

26. The psychic violence of vampirism produces a sort of multiple-personality syndrome even in *Dracula*, when the infected Lucy develops two personalities, the demure maiden alternating with the fanged femme fatale.

27. Ibid., 99. *Alexithymia* is a psychoanalytic term from work with Holocaust survivors, coined by Henry Krystal in "Trauma: Consideration of Severity and Chronicity," in *Psychic Traumatization*, edited by H. Krystal and W. Niederland (Boston, 1971).

28. We will meet these tiaras again in Disney's *Beauty and the Beast*, where the vampire threat is put off onto wolves and rebellious villagers, creating a repressive political allegory masquerading as lighthearted romance.

29. Anxiety about sexual and economic aggrandizement strongly shaped the media

excitement over "the brutal killing of pageant princess JonBenet Ramsey, 6, [which] shocks the nation—and raises troubling questions." *People*, January 20, 1997. Even as media stories clucked about exploitative (that is, abusive) parents and their seductive, tacitly predatory child femme fatales, they plastered page and screen with photos of the miniature showbiz "princesses" in their glitzy regalia, also using the children.

30. Bass and Davis, *Courage to Heal*, 128.

31. Daniel Goleman, *Emotional Intelligence* (New York, 1995), 64.

32. See Demos, *Entertaining Satan*.

33. Janice Radway, *Reading the Romance: Women, Patriarchy, and Popular Literature* (Chapel Hill, N.C., 1984).

34. See, e.g., Frank J. Donner, *The Age of Surveillance: The Aims and the Methods of America's Political Intelligence System* (New York, 1980), 105–6. In David Helpern Jr.'s documentary film *Hollywood on Trial*, Jack Warner can be seen telling the House Un-American Activities Committee, "Ideological termites have burrowed into many American industries, organizations, and societies." In his testimony, Warner offered to help "exterminate" the infestation.

35. Lemann, "Vogue of Childhood Misery," 124. This may help explain why so many voters in the 1980s were enchanted by the fatherly image President Ronald Reagan (Patti Davis's father) projected. Although his administration began the attack on governmental paternalism that escalated in mid-1990s cutbacks in welfare, educational assistance, healthcare, and the like, Reagan always appeared to guarantee that the prosthetic family networks of the 1950s were still intact.

36. Courtroom and legislative struggles over recovered-memory and child-abuse allegations have been substantial and have evolved toward greater safeguards in the 1990s.

37. Peter Homans, *The Ability to Mourn* (Chicago, 1989).

38. See, e.g., David Finkelhor, *Child Sexual Abuse: New Theory and Research* (New York, 1988). In their *Sourcebook on Childhood Sexual Abuse* (Beverly Hills, Calif., 1986), Finkelhor and his coauthors conclude "from studies of clinical and nonclinical populations" that "the findings concerning the trauma of child sexual abuse appear to be as follows: In the immediate aftermath of sexual abuse, from one-fifth to two-fifths of abused children seen by clinicians manifest some noticeable disturbance. . . . When studied as adults, victims as a group demonstrate more impairment than their nonvictimized counterparts (about twice as much), but less than one-fifth evidence serious psychopathology. These findings give assurance to victims that extreme long-term effects are not inevitable. Nonetheless, they also suggest that the risk of initial and long-term mental health impairment for victims of child sexual abuse should be taken very seriously" (164). For contrary conclusions, see Martin E. P. Seligman, *What You Can Change and What You Can't* (New York, 1995), esp. chap. 14. See also Michael R. Nash et al., "Long-Term Sequelae of Childhood Sexual Abuse: Perceived Family Environment, Psychopathology, and Dissociation," *Journal of Consulting and Clinical Psychology* 61 (1993): 276–83; and Thomas J. Bouchard and Matthew McGue, "Genetics and Rearing Environmental Influences," *Journal of Personality* 68 (1990): 263–82.

39. See Christopher Peterson, Steven F. Maier, and Martin E. P. Seligman, *Learned Helplessness: A Theory for the Age of Personal Control* (New York, 1993).

40. Says deMause: "Article after article was written during the winter of 1981–2 on the rise in infant mortality in areas hardest hit by budget cutbacks and unemployment, on the over one million additional children on the poverty rolls, on the six million children who had lost health coverage because of layoffs of their parents, of the half million children who had lost health services because of the closing by the government of 239 community health centers, of the hundreds of additional children who would be battered to death because of Reagan's cutback of almost all of the funds for the highly successful National Center on Child Abuse and Neglect—in all, over twenty million children suffering needless pain, hunger and death with barely a mourner in sight." Lloyd deMause, *Reagan's America* (New York, 1984), 80.

41. David Stoez and Howard Jacob Karger, "Suffer the Children," *Washington Monthly*, June 1996, 21.

42. Deb Reichmann, "Abuse of Children Increases 89%," *Springfield Union News*, September 19, 1996: "Renita Davis, a case manager at an early childhood program in Laurel, Miss., said she thinks unemployment is partly to blame for a rise in abuse and neglect. 'The jobs that you get pay little or nothing' . . . and that leads to stress in the home, which leads to violence."

43. See, e.g., Angus McLaren, *A Prescription for Murder: The Victorian Serial Killings of Dr. Thomas Neill Cream* (Chicago, 1993). McLaren lucidly recaps the violent passions directed at women who sought increased control over their lives through birth control and abortion.

44. Lemann, "Vogue of Childhood Misery," 127.

45. Jonathan Shay, *Achilles in Vietnam: Combat Trauma and the Undoing of Character* (New York, 1994), 56.

46. Ibid., 194.

Chapter 8: Traumatic Triumph in a Black Childhood

1. See Irving M. Allen, "PTSD among African Americans," in *Ethnocultural Aspects of Posttraumatic Stress Disorder*, edited by Anthony J. Marsella et al. (Washington, D.C., 1996).

2. Malcolm X, *The Autobiography of Malcolm X* (New York, 1966), quoted in Tom Engelhardt, *The End of Victory Culture* (New York, 1995), 91.

3. Engelhardt, *End of Victory Culture*, 108.

4. Benjamin DeMott, "Put on a Happy Face," *Harper's*, September 1995, 33. Good examples of such compensatory friendships are found in the films *Forrest Gump* and *Pulp Fiction*. DeMott expands the argument in *The Trouble with Friendship: Why Americans Can't Think Straight about Race* (New York, 1995).

5. DeMott, "Put on a Happy Face," 38.

6. Henry Louis Gates, "Powell and the Black Elite," *New Yorker*, September 25, 1995, 76.

7. Orlando Patterson, *Slavery and Social Death: A Comparative Study* (Cambridge, Mass., 1982).

8. Cf. the mother in the British Airways ad in chap. 6 above.

9. After the great achievements of the civil-rights era, racism has returned wearing velvet gloves, as in the pseudoscientific polemics about the alleged mental limitations of blacks in the 1990s. For a sensible critique, see Steven Fraser, ed., *The Bell Curve Wars: Race, Intelligence, and the Future of America* (New York, 1995). The polemics revisited the unwholesome eugenics arguments of the 1920s. See chap. 9 on *Schindler's List*.

10. Virginia Hamilton, *Sweet Whispers, Brother Rush* (New York, 1982), hereafter cited as *SWBR*.

11. Janice Radway, *Reading the Romance: Women, Patriarchy, and Popular Literature* (Chapel Hill, N.C., 1984), shows that romances, for many women, can vicariously relieve fundamental anxieties about identity. Radway follows Nancy Chodorow's developmental theory, which maintains that the difficulties of trying to separate from a parent of the same sex dispose girls to experience themselves as less differentiated than boys, with a need for nurturance and attachment that persists into their adult lives (135–38). If a relationship with an adult male fails to fulfill that need for completion, a woman may turn to mothering as a way of establishing the necessary relationality. By identifying with her child, she imaginatively regresses to that state in which all her needs were anticipated and satisfied without any exertion on her part. Chodorow argues that men are emotionally constituted by female mothering in a way that makes them unable to nurture women, so women often resort to mothering as a source of vicarious nurturance.

12. Nancy Chodorow, *The Reproduction of Mothering: Psychoanalysis and the Sociology of Gender* (Berkeley and Los Angeles, 1978), 127–29.

13. Ibid., 166.

14. To keep the mother's behavior in historical context: in the years following emancipation, as Jacqueline Jones explains, black families were ridiculed and disparaged for attempting "to remove their wives and mothers from the workforce to attend to their own households. In contrast to the domestic ideal for white women of all classes, the larger society deemed it 'unnatural,' in fact 'evil,' for black married women 'to play the lady' while their husbands supported them. In the immediate postwar South, the role of menial worker outside their homes was demanded of black women, even at the cost of physical coercion." Quoted in Evelyn Brooks Higginbotham, "African-American Women's History and the Metalanguage of Race," in *Revising the Word and the World*, edited by Veve A. Clark, Ruth-Ellen B. Joeres, and Madelon Sprengnether (Chicago, 1993), 100.

15. Compare Darryl Pinckney's observation that in Alice Walker's *The Color Purple*, "the black men are seen at a distance—that is, entirely from the point of view of the women—as naifs incapable of reflection, tyrants filled with impotent rage, or as totemic do-gooders." Recognize the inward rage symbolized in porphyria, and it becomes evident that Hamilton's novel, *Sweet Whispers, Brother Rush*, subtly shares Walker's tendency to change "the color of the villains . . . from white society to black men." Darryl Pinckney, "Black Victims, Black Villains," *New York Review of Books*, January 29, 1987, 17.

16. See John Kucich, "Death Worship among the Victorians: *The Old Curiosity Shop*," *PMLA* 95 (1980): 58–72.

17. Robert J. Lifton, *The Broken Connection: On Death and the Continuity of Life* (New York, 1983), 17.

18. Becker, *Denial of Death*, 5.

19. For an account of this ideology, see Lacy K. Ford Jr., *Origins of Southern Radicalism: The South Carolina Upcountry, 1800–1860* (New York, 1988).

20. Elias Canetti, *Crowds and Power*, translated by Carol Stewart (New York, 1978), 229.

21. Chris Baldick, *In Frankenstein's Shadow* (Oxford, 1987), 78.

22. Toni Morrison, "Rootedness: The Ancestor as Foundation," in *Black Women Writers (1950–1980): A Critical Evaluation*, edited by Mari Evans (New York, 1984), 342.

23. Ibid., 343.

24. Ibid., 342.

25. Ibid.

26. The 1994 *Statistical Abstract of the United States* (Washington, D.C., 1995) shows that in 1992 those living in poverty included 11.6 percent of the white population, 33.3 percent of the black population, and 29.3 percent of the Hispanic population. Many of the poor were children. For example, half (51.4 %) of the 27.3 million people receiving food stamps were children, and 21 percent of all children in the United States lived in families in poverty (table 232).

Chapter 9: Traumatic Economies in Schindler's List

1. Jason Epstein, "A Dissent on 'Schindler's List,'" *New York Review of Books*, April 21, 1994, 65. David Mamet echoes Epstein's indictment: "Members of the audience learn nothing save the emotional lesson of all melodrama, that they are better than the villain." This "lesson," Mamet says, "is a lie. The audience is not superior to 'Those Bad Nazis.' Any of us has the capacity for atrocity—just as each of us has the capacity for heroism." Mamet, *Make-Believe Town* (New York, 1996), 142.

2. Epstein, "Dissent on 'Schindler's List,'" 65.

3. This is a connection Wilhelm Reich noted as early as 1933 in *The Mass Psychology of Fascism* (reprint, New York, 1970), 334–36.

4. See, e.g., *Maus: A Survivor's Tale*, Art Spiegelman's comic-book saga of the Holocaust (New York, 1986), in which the Jews are clever mice, the Poles are pigs, and the Nazis are cats. Even apart from its sentimental origins and implicit expectations, the imagery is disturbing insofar as it unintentionally confirms Nazi notions about the "reality" and separateness of racial categories.

5. In *Modernity and the Holocaust* (Cambridge, 1989), Zygmunt Bauman sees the death camps as "a mundane extension of the modern factory system. . . . The raw material was human beings and the end product was death" (8). See also Daniel Pick, *War Machine: The Rationalisation of Slaughter in the Modern Age* (New Haven, Conn., 1996).

6. Otto Rank, *Will Therapy* (New York, 1978), 130.

7. Robert Jay Lifton, *Home from the War* (New York, 1973), 213.

8. Ibid., 198. "The pattern goes back at least as far as the ancient Egyptians: in the Pyramid Texts, the pharaoh's eternal life is repeatedly acclaimed, and (as Breasted puts it, 'the word death never occurs . . . except in the negative or applied to a foe.') . . . Victimizing others can thus be understood as an aberrant form of immortalization" (199). Lifton's use of the word "aberrant" is poignantly wishful in this definition, because whole cultures have been founded on institutionalized slaughter and sadistic triumphalism.

9. See, e.g., Linda Schele and Mary Ellen Miller, eds., *The Blood of Kings* (Fort Worth, Tex., 1986), and Octavio Paz's incisive essay on the book's findings, "Food of the Gods," *New York Review of Books*, February 26, 1987, 3–7. In *The Sorrows of the Ancient Romans: The Gladiator and the Monster* (Princeton, 1993), Carlin Barton demonstrates how murderous competition was complexly assimilated to the contradictory values of Roman culture.

10. When Michael Moore, in *Roger and Me*, shows an unemployed woman slaughtering a rabbit from a crowded hutch, he dramatizes the dog-eat-dog mentality of the new economic order. The analogy between rabbit cage and concentration camp speaks for itself.

11. See Robert L. Waite, *The Psychopathic God: Adolf Hitler* (New York, 1978).

12. Hitler was produced by the tragic legacy of Kaiser Wilhelm, whose vainglorious posturing was a compensatory reaction to his traumatic humiliation as a poorly coordinated, "unmanly" child with an arm crippled during his breech birth. For more on Hitler's personal compensation for traumatic dread, see Rudolph Binion, *Hitler among the Germans* (New York, 1976).

13. For the millennial ingredients in Nazi and Soviet ideologies, see Norman Cohn, *The Pursuit of the Millennium* (New York, 1961).

14. David Brion Davis, *Slavery and Human Progress* (New York, 1984), 11.

15. Roman slave factories, for example, produced monotonously uniform pottery during the empire. Scholars have debated whether the depersonalized use of slaves in late antiquity prefigures the scientific management of the work force or represents a regression, given the sacrifice of the individual slave's creative sophistication to demands for machinelike control. For a useful summary of the debate, see *The Romans*, edited by Andrea Giardina (Chicago, 1993), 147–49.

16. David Mamet relays a sardonic quip he heard in Israel that tacitly protests the "use" of the Holocaust: "There's no business like Shoah business." Mamet, *Make-Believe Town*, 142.

17. John Cassidy, "Who Killed the Middle Class?" *New Yorker*, October 16, 1995, 113–24. Barlett and Steele survey some of the forces creating the new burgeoning underclass in Donald L. Barlett and James B. Steele, *America: What Went Wrong?* (Kansas City, Mo., 1992).

18. Richard L. Rubenstein, *The Age of Triage* (Boston, 1983), 26.

19. See Joel F. Handler, *The Poverty of Welfare Reform* (New Haven, Conn., 1995).

20. Cf. the slogan on a bumper sticker I saw in Massachusetts in 1992: "More money makes the rich work harder; less money makes the poor work harder." Political and

technological changes are bringing low-wage workers from places such as China, India, and Latin America into the international labor market in staggering numbers—by some estimates, as many as four billion people. According to the *New York Times* (June 10, 1996), the system that paid an Indonesian woman $2.00 a day for a pair of athletic shoes it then sells for $160.00 is now shifting plants to Vietnam, where wages are $30.00 a month.

21. See Jack Miles, "Blacks vs. Browns," *Atlantic*, October 1992, 41.

22. Dignified as a "science," eugenics enjoyed considerable prestige in America in the first decades of this century. Its abuse in the United States has been widely documented. In a letter to the *Boston Globe*, May 14, 1994, Kevin J. Dotson put it succinctly: "The works of leading American eugenicists were translated into German and devoured by German academics. . . . Such 'scientists' as Charles Benedict Davenport, . . . professor Lothrop Stoddard of Harvard, . . . and Lewis Terman . . . were widely honored at German universities for their work in isolating the gene for pauperism and helping bring to worldwide attention the dangers of allowing the blood of what Davenport called 'beaten men from beaten races' to mix with pure, superior Nordic blood. . . . It may be difficult for us to face, but American science in the early '20s played a great role in the development of Nazi racial purification policies and practices."

23. Louis Uchitelle and N. R. Kleinfield, "On the Battlefields of Business, Millions of Casualties," *New York Times*, March 3, 1996, sec. A.

24. *Consumer Reports* 2, no. 6 (1937): 32. "It is a matter of utmost importance to remember that the wages of labor do not decline without a corollary decline in the economic life of the entire nation (its *fuehrers*—for a while—excepted)." Ibid.

25. In effect, Henry Ford was drawn back to the regime of spies and paramilitary force that Andrew Carnegie and Henry Frick had developed in the steel industry in the 1890s.

26. From a Du Pont manual, "ISO 9000 Is Here! The Answers to Your Questions," from the Du Pont Quality Management and Technology Center, 1991. The utopian- (or totalitarian-) sounding fantasies implicit in the rubric "Total Quality Management" are noteworthy.

27. In part 2 of Henry Hampton's PBS documentary "America's War on Poverty," a migrant worker named Hector de la Rosa describes a "terrible" migrant labor camp in Soledad, California, in 1966, which had been a prison camp during World War II for German prisoners of war. The apparent ironies deserve a moment's reflection.

28. It is worth recalling that the corporate state evolved in Germany through murderous internal competition, such as the struggle to the death in 1933–34 among the army, Roehm's storm troopers, Himmler's SS, and paramilitary forces such as Goering's personal police force, the Landespolizeigruppe General Goering.

29. In *Stress and the Manager* (New York, 1979), Karl Albrecht deplores "the effects of executive health breakdown, which can be much more costly on a person-to-person basis and which is often much more severe for the individual, than in the case of lineworker health problems. When the executive 'crashes,' he usually does it dramatically and often irreversibly" (45). In this lament, class prejudices give the executive's ("his")

health melodramatic importance. In his Foreword to Albrecht's book, the well-known stress expert Hans Selye, M.D., uses language which naively reflects the same cultural distortion: "Occupational stress forms a major category in the International Institute of Stress library collection of more than 120,000 publications on stress and related subjects, but very few of these references are of any direct use to the driving force in Business and commerce—the executive and manager" (v). Luckily for "the driving force," Albrecht's book "has captured and synthesized the very essence of our vast store of knowledge about stress" (v–vi).

30. Not surprisingly, the reality was less ideal: "Survivors testify to the importance wealth, for example, played in helping you survive." Anne Karpf, "My Mother's Story," *Guardian*, February 17, 1994.

31. Paul Osterman, *Getting Started: The Youth Labor Market* (Cambridge, Mass., 1980), 143.

32. "In the early days of the great American S & L scandal, the principal official of the regulatory authority involved spoke in exculpatory terms of Charles Keating, the most notorious figure in this concerted attack on the public interest and pocketbook. He was, it was said, 'a very entrepreneurial businessman.'" John Kenneth Galbraith, *The Culture of Contentment* (New York, 1992), 75.

33. Albrecht, *Stress and the Manager*, 290.

34. "KGB generals and colonels now sit on the boards of commodity exchanges in Russia and on the boards of some of the largest financial and business enterprises." Henrik Bering-Jensen, "Russian Spies: Lean, Mean, and Ready for Profit," *Insight*, May 16, 1994, 7.

35. The "admirers of Spielberg's film in their Academy Award chatter have said nothing about China, whose crimes are no less evil than Hitler's" (Epstein, "A Dissent on 'Schindler's List,'" 65). In the meantime, Washington has altogether "de-linked" the issues of human rights in China and trade privileges, confirming Epstein's point.

36. See, e.g., William B. Helmreich, *Against All Odds: Holocaust Survivors and the Successful Lives They Made in America* (New York, 1992).

37. Epstein, "Dissent on 'Schindler's List,'" 65.

38. Jonathan Shay, *Achilles in Vietnam: Combat Trauma and the Undoing of Character* (New York, 1994), 104.

39. Jack Miles, *God: A Biography* (New York, 1996), 117.

40. Ibid., 144–45.

41. Richard Rubenstein calls his chapter on the Holocaust "The Unmastered Trauma" and demonstrates that competition between Jews and others was central— and is readily overlooked today. Rubenstein, *Age of Triage*, 128–64.

42. Joseph Conrad, *Heart of Darkness*, edited by Robert Kimbrough (New York, 1963), 51 (hereafter cited as *HD*).

43. The Belgian commission of inquiry sent in 1904 to the Congo Free State confirmed the abuses that reformers had bitterly deplored, yet in deference to business, the commission accepted forced labor as the only possible means of exploiting the country's riches. The first twentieth-century concentration camps were probably the

crude compounds the British constructed in the campaign against the Boers as Queen Victoria was dying. Interned Boer families died of disease in scandalous numbers, which caused an outcry in England and in Europe.

44. In the context of European imperialism, as Sandra Gilbert and Susan Gubar summarize, "women = 'outlanders'/'barbarians' = colonized peoples, and hence colonized peoples = women, a point that Freud emphasized when he defined female sexuality as a 'dark continent' and to which Ashley Montagu implicitly addresses himself when he reminds us of the 'Victorian saying that the last thing man would civilize would be woman.'" Gilbert and Gubar, *Sexchanges*, vol. 2 of *No Man's Land: The Place of the Woman Writer in the Twentieth Century* (New Haven, Conn., 1989), 36; see also 44–46. Lewis Wurgaft details the British association of colonial India with sexuality in *The Imperial Imagination: Magic and Myth in Kipling's India* (Middletown, Conn., 1983).

45. The perversity is explicit in Joris Karl Huysmans's À *rebours* (1884; Harmondsworth and New York, 1987), which deeply aroused Oscar Wilde. The novel imagines the decadent Des Esseintes staging a fabulous "funeral feast to mark the most ludicrous of personal misfortunes," the guests "waited on by naked negresses wearing only slippers and stockings in cloth of silver embroidered with tears" (27). Despite the decadent irony, the larger cultural fantasy is perfectly clear: exotic, degraded women comfort and heal morbid, elite males. To observe the same formula in 1990s Hollywood films about executives rescued from death anxiety by good-hearted hookers, see the following chapter.

46. To compound the ironies, those art nouveau forms recall the works of the peaceable Decadents of the 1890s, including Wilde, although in *Fascism: Past, Present, Future* (Oxford, 1996), Walter Laqueur remarks on the transformation of world-weary dandies such as Maurice Barres and Gabriele D'Annunzio into advocates of superpatriotism and antiliberal ideas "that came close to fascism" (234).

Chapter 10: Traumatic Romance/Romantic Trauma

1. See chap. 9, note 45 above.

2. Jonathan Shay, *Achilles in Vietnam: Combat Trauma and the Undoing of Character* (New York, 1994).

3. A tendency to scapegoat the poor shows up in other Disney films of the 1990s. The villain of Tim Burton's *Nightmare before Christmas* (1993) is a jive-talking Cab Calloway caricature named Oogie Boogie, who kidnaps a white, magically generous Santa Claus. In *The Lion King* (1994), Disney gives the villain's hyena accomplices the patois of urban black children. In *A Little Princess* (1995), the hero is persecuted by a snobbish schoolmistress and befriends a black servant girl—but the ending makes plain that happiness lies not among working people but in the friends' escape into gentility together.

4. Like the good servants, Uncle Toddy shares in the prince's traumatic curse inso-

far as he is a failure at life, his creative will frozen. As a usurping servant, he is a predator (vampire) like the hunter Gaston, vain about his strength (he lifts weights), and finally hurled to destruction while pursuing the princess.

5. So innocent can Disney ideology seem that a well-known feminist editor of the *Nation* dismissed my reading of the film, claiming, with a naiveté complicated by curious class prejudices, I thought, that Gaston is just a buffoon, more like a silly fraternity man than a fascist mob leader. But nobody would need to kill a silly fraternity man. The editor seemed to join Belle in siding with the palace against the loser Gaston, but also in making him jejune in order to sidestep qualms about caricaturing (and scapegoating) ordinary men as macho brutes. The significance of this maneuver is explored below.

6. Donald L. Barlett and James B. Steele, *America: What Went Wrong?* (Kansas City, Mo., 1992).

7. Edward is thus the executive type targeted by the British Airways ad analyzed at the close of chap. 6. Also, recall the prominently buxom black caryatids in opera houses and the "naked negresses" waiting on the "mourners" at the mock-funeral feast in Huysmans's *À rebours* (see chap. 9, note 45 above).

8. See Radway, *Reading the Romance.*

9. G. M. Young, *Victorian England: Portrait of an Age* (London, 1936), 146.

10. "Laugh Parade," by Bunny Hoest and John Reinet, *Parade Magazine*, January 29, 1995, 11.

11. *New York Times*, September 4, 1997.

12. "Royal Family, Stung by Critics, Responds to a Grieving Nation," (headline) ibid.

13. Roger Ebert, *Chicago Sun-Times*, November 10, 1995.

14. Ibid.

15. This is a running gag on the television show *The Simpsons*, whose corporate villain, Montgomery Burns, dominates a servile and sexually craven underling named Smithers. See also Mark Crispin Miller's analysis of the sexual anxiety in an ad for deodorant soap, in *Boxed In* (Evanston, Ill., 1988), 42–49.

16. The trope of videotaping violence to master it through voyeurism gained powerful force in the Vietnam War, in which television cameras again and again recorded American atrocities, arousing ambivalent excitement and horror at home. Haskell Wexler's film *Medium Cool* (1969), for example, explores this trope. But with its connotations of post-traumatic coping through dissociation, the video camera also makes a good prop to dramatize a cultural crash, as in the scene of the taxi driver callously filming the plane wreck in *Fearless.*

17. A lovely gloss on a theme that looks back to the ancient world through Shakespeare's *All's Well that Ends Well* and *The Winter's Tale* is Victor Erice's *Spirit of the Beehive* (1973), set in the post-traumatic aftermath of the Spanish civil war, in which a young girl sees another young girl befriend the monster in *Frankenstein*, and then secretly adopts a political fugitive hiding outside her village, with traumatic consequences when her rescue fails.

18. Ebert, *Chicago Sun-Times*, November 10, 1995.

19. By the same symbolic logic, concomitantly, the film punishes her for abandoning the wounded hero by having her raped.

20. Romance and cultural crash are not a new combination; witness Hemingway's postwar, post-traumatic *Farewell to Arms* and *The Sun Also Rises*.

Chapter 11: Berserk in Babylon

1. Jonathan Shay, *Achilles in Vietnam: Combat Trauma and the Undoing of Character* (New York, 1994), 79 (herafter cited as AV).

2. "Berserk," says Shay, "comes from the Norse word for the frenzied warriors who went into battle naked, or at least without armor, in a godlike or god-possessed—but also beastlike—fury" (AV 77, 97). The OED derives the term from "baresark," meaning "bare shirt," without armor. The uncontrolled violence of the berserk state is often called "berserking." According to E. L. Maguigad, *amok* derives from *amoq*, the Malay word for furious warfare. See "Psychiatry in the Philippines," *American Journal of Psychiatry* 121 (1964): 21–25.

3. Ernest Becker, *Escape from Evil* (New York, 1975), 103.

4. Kay H. Blacker and Joe P. Tupin, "Hysteria and Hysterical Structures: Developmental and Social Theories," in *Hysterical Personality*, edited by Mardi J. Horowitz (New York, 1977), 113. See also H. B. M. Murphy, "History and the Evolution of Syndromes: The Striking Case of Lateh and Amok," in *Psychopathology: Contributions from the Social, Behavioral, and Biological Sciences*, edited by M. Hammer, K. Salzinger, and S. Sutton (New York, 1973); and Lydia Temoshok and C. Clifford Attkisson, "Epidemiology of Hysterical Phenomena: Evidence for a Psychosocial Theory," in Horowitz, *Hysterical Personality*.

5. Cartoon by Leo Cullum in the *New Yorker*, January 27, 1997, 32.

6. Joseph Campbell, *The Hero with a Thousand Faces* (reprint, Princeton, 1972), 16.

7. Pat Aufderheide, "Good Soldiers," in *Seeing Through Movies*, edited by Mark Crispin Miller (New York, 1990), 105.

8. "As for business [in the 1990s], previously respectable transactions were now conducted in the spirit of the gaming table." John Stokes, *In the Nineties* (Chicago, 1993), 7.

9. Carlin Barton, *The Sorrows of the Ancient Romans: The Gladiator and the Monster* (Princeton, 1993), 17.

10. Richard A. Gabriel and Paul L. Savage, *Crisis in Command: Mismanagement in the Army* (New York, 1978).

11. See Howard Zinn, *A People's History of the United States* (rev. ed., New York, 1995), esp. chap. 18. "The Pentagon reported 209 fraggings in Vietnam in 1970 alone." Ibid., 486. For detailed casualty figures, see Gabriel and Savage, *Crisis in Command*. For a tactful dramatization of the way in which class differences blindly precipitated the murder of officers, see Tim O'Brien's novel *Going after Cacciato* (New York, 1975).

12. "During the Vietnam War, the more elite the unit, the more its training incorporated the psychological techniques of coercive control used on political prisoners. In

particular, incessant demands for proof of obedience and loyalty, and intense pressure to ally with the power-holder by forcing recruits to sacrifice and victimize other recruits, seem to have been common features of Marine and airborne training. . . . Organized techniques of disempowerment and disconnection were employed to 'break them [recruits] down and then build them back up again'—what veterans often quote as the basic goal of military training." AV 151.

13. The association of slavery, poverty, and menial work is deeply ingrained in Western cultures. Consider ancient Rome: "In the final analysis, the slave's most lasting characteristic . . . was the fact that the mass of slaves always belonged to the lower classes of society. The most fundamental definition of that mass was that it was set to servile tasks. However, all who were forced to sell their physical strength in order to live performed those same tasks. Cicero was right when he connected wages and servitude: *merces auctoramentum servitutis*; their pay is 'a pledge of their slavery.'" *The Romans*, edited by Andrea Giardina (Chicago, 1993), 173. "[The] social evolution that began toward the end of the early Empire . . . soon so diminished the real difference between free men and slaves that the juridical distinction between them was clearly meaningless. This happened in two ways. First, the privileged minority of slaves became increasingly integrated into the free population, thus prefiguring their social power once they were legally freed and demonstrating that no wealthy man could really be a slave. . . . Second, the situation of poor free men increasingly resembled that of the mass of the slaves." Especially in rural life, "they were in the same state of dependence, and the arbitrary division between free and nonfree was wiped out by social realities." Ibid., 172.

14. Anyone who doubts or misremembers the punishing cruelty of the Reagan years should consider the plentiful evidence in Lloyd deMause, *Reagan's America* (New York, 1984), which analyzes the hostile imagery in Reagan's speeches and in the media as they moved through fantasies of sacrificial killing and rebirth from month to month in the early 1980s.

15. "Harper's Index," *Harper's*, June 1996, 13.

16. Michelle Cottle, "May the Force Be with You," *Washington Monthly*, September 1996, 14.

17. DeMause, *Reagan's America*, 80.

18. *New Republic*, April 4, 1983, 7.

19. *Today Show*, NBC-TV, December 18, 1981, quoted by deMause (76). The American air attack on Tripoli in April 1986 apparently killed an adopted daughter of Qaddafi's. *Time* (April 28, 1986) reported that the Libyan leader "raged at Reagan and British Prime Minister Thatcher as 'child murderers.'" The magazine then pointed out that Qaddafi had praised a terrorist incident in which a child had died (18). In the same issue *Time* observed that Reagan's thoughts were "fixed" on Qaddafi "as a symbol of virtually everything he hates" (23). The previous issue (April 21, 1986) approvingly quoted Egyptian President Anwar Sadat's comment that Qaddafi "is 100% sick and possessed of the devil." *Time* concluded menacingly that Qaddafi "will not rest until he has struck back [at America] or been struck down" (29).

20. Who can forget the doomed Hitler's self-consoling determination to sacrifice the Germans—his "children"—rather than let them "grow up under Communism"?

21. Tax revolts in the 1980s reduced the size of police forces all over the country, especially in financially strapped cities where they were most needed. Although crime rates remained fairly constant, fluctuating with economic conditions, the decrease in police personnel may well have contributed to a public perception of greater insecurity.

22. Although the children in the Reagan anecdote have been trained to hate, Irvin D. Yalom points out in *Existential Psychotherapy* (New York, 1980) that "many children, especially boys, engage in feats of reckless daredeviltry" in an attempt to taunt or defy death (100).

23. See Carol Clover's discussion of the films in *Men, Women, and Chain Saws: Gender in the Modern Horror Film* (Princeton, 1992), 53.

24. See Virginia Lieson Brereton, *From Sin to Salvation: Stories of Women's Conversions, 1800 to the Present* (Bloomington, Ind., 1991).

25. Shakespeare, *Henry IV, Part 2*, 4.5.136–37.

26. The central premise of René Girard's theory of violence (cf. *Violence and the Sacred* [Baltimore, 1977]) is that humans have no natural, hard-wired mechanism to stop a cycle of retaliation once it has started. Elias Canetti makes a similar point in *Crowds and Power*, translated by Carol Stewart (New York, 1978).

27. "The wolf, as seen in many legends, became as much a metaphor for death as the Ancient Adversary or as the gaping jaws of hell." Franco Cardini, *Europe, 1492: Portrait of a Continent Five Hundred Years Ago*, translated by Jay Hyams (Milan, 1989), 160–61.

28. Roger Ebert, *Chicago Sun-Times*, February 26, 1993.

29. See Herbert Schneidau, *Sacred Discontent* (Berkeley and Los Angeles, 1974), chap. 1.

30. See Robert W. Robin et al., "Cumulative Trauma and PTSD in American Indian Communities," and Spero Manson et al., "Wounded Spirits, Ailing Hearts: PTSD and Related Disorders among American Indians," in *Ethnocultural Aspects of Posttraumatic Stress Disorder*, edited by Anthony J. Marsella et al. (Washington, D.C., 1996).

31. The use of goons by such regimes is a staple of crime fiction such as Dashiell Hammett's *Red Harvest* (1929) and Francis Ford Coppola's *Godfather* films (1972–90).

32. Dominick Dunne, "Menendez Justice," *Vanity Fair*, March 1994, 114.

33. Ibid., 112; see Paul Mones, *When a Child Kills: Abused Children Who Kill Their Parents* (New York, 1991).

34. Dunne, "Menendez Justice," 117.

35. Ibid., 119.

36. These issues pervaded American culture in the 1990s; in a *New Yorker* cartoon by Barsotti, one king says to another, "No, I wasn't abused but I cut off my father's head anyway."

37. The father's murder, it is worth noting, involved a direct blast to the face, the way the brothers annihilated their mother. The violence dramatizes an effort to obliterate personal (mortal) origins.

38. See, e.g., Kali Tal, *Worlds of Hurt: Reading the Literatures of Trauma* (New York, 1996), 64.

39. Robert Jay Lifton, *Home from the War* (New York, 1973), 204. The comic-book hero acts out a poignantly crude form of traumatic rescue fantasy.

40. In *Where's the Rest of Me?* (New York, 1965) Reagan describes a bout with pneumonia when he was blocked in his career in the late 1940s. In a "Freudian delirium" he hallucinated playing scenes with Humphrey Bogart, "always with a furtive air of danger in the surrounding darkness." Reagan felt suicidally depressed and saw his struggle against his own death wish as a winner-take-all gamble: "This was evidently the night—'Big Casino, bet or throw in.'" Though finally he decided he'd "be more comfortable not breathing," a "nice and persistent nurse" coaxed him through the crisis (195). Lloyd deMause plausibly construes Reagan's suicidal "gamble" as a crisis in his lifelong Oedipal struggle against his abusive, alcoholic father (*Reagan's America*, 26).

41. Cf. the *Rambo* films, in which the betrayed son is trapped between evil Asian and treacherous American "fathers" who threaten death either way.

42. Tom Engelhardt, *The End of Victory Culture* (New York, 1995), 54–58.

43. Peter Annin, "Superpredators Arrive: Should We Cage the New Breed of Vicious Kids?" *Newsweek*, January 12, 1996, 57. For an assessment of the revived myth of vicious youth, see Michael Males, *The Scapegoat Generation* (Boston, 1996).

Chapter 12: Amok at the Apocalypse

1. Cohn quoted in Damien Thompson, "Apocalypse Soon," *Sunday Telegraph*, January 7, 1996.

2. *Newsweek*, January 12, 1996, 57.

3. Roger Ebert, "Kalifornia," *Chicago Sun-Times*, September 3, 1993.

4. Ibid.

5. The same convention motivates the cross-country murders in Terrence Malick's *Badlands* (1973), where Kit's job as a garbage collector is a source of humiliation.

6. See Gareth Cook, "The Dark Side of Camp," *Washington Monthly*, September 1995, 10–14, and Benjamin DeMott, *The Imperial Middle: Why Americans Can't Think Straight about Class* (New York, 1990).

7. See Carol Clover, *Men, Women, and Chain Saws: Gender in the Modern Horror Film* (Princeton, 1992), 138–40. More recent is Mary Celeste Kearney's useful overview, "Girls Just Want to Have Fun? Female Avengers in '90s Teenpics," in *Pictures of a Generation on Hold*, edited by Murray Pomerance and John Sakeris (Toronto, 1996), 97–105.

8. See "The Problem of Human Motivation," in Donald Alexander Downs, *More than Victims: Battered Women, the Syndrome Society, and the Law* (Chicago, 1996), 158–81.

9. Reviewers drooled over the teen violence. In blurbs for the video, *LA Magazine* clucked that "everything that happens onscreen could be done by the kids next door." Another blurb for the video release praised "a raw honest look at teenage alienation, where values have been twisted beyond adult comprehension."

10. As it unfolds, Roger Ebert's review of the film grows hysterical right before our eyes: "'River's Edge' is not a film I will forget very soon. Its portrait of these adolescents is an exercise in despair. Not even old enough to legally order a beer, they already are destroyed by alcohol and drugs, abandoned by parents who also have lost hope. When the story of the dead girl first appeared in the papers, it seemed like a freak show, an aberration. 'River's Edge' sets it in an ordinary town and makes it seem like just what the op-ed philosophers said: an emblem of breakdown. The girl's body eventually was discovered and buried. If you seek her monument, look around you." *Chicago Sun-Times*, May 29, 1987.

11. The titles advertise teen aggression and rebellion: "Kyrie Eleison," "Captor of Sin," "Tormentor," "Die by the Sword," "Evil Has No Boundaries," "Lethal Tendencies," "Let Me Know," "Fire in the Rain," "I'm Gonna Miss You." The rock groups include Slayer and Agent Orange, and the soundtrack was put out by Blade Records.

12. See, e.g., Carl Bridenbaugh, *Vexed and Troubled Englishmen* (New York, 1968), and Michael Lesy, *Wisconsin Death Trip* (New York, 1973).

13. Stephen Jay Gould, *Eight Little Piggies: Reflections in Natural History* (London, 1993), 255–56.

14. For a report on the unspeakable conditions the "free market" has created in the *maquiladoras* on the Texas-Mexico border, see Charles Bowden, "While You Were Sleeping," *Harper's*, December 1996, 44–52.

15. Lionel Dahmer, *A Father's Story* (New York, 1994).

16. Louis A. Sass, *Madness and Modernism: Insanity in the Light of Modern Art, Literature, and Thought* (New York, 1992).

17. Carlin Barton, *The Sorrows of the Ancient Romans: The Gladiator and the Monster* (Princeton, 1993), 99.

18. Sass, *Madness and Modernism*, 25.

19. James Cameron, *Strange Days* (New York, 1995).

20. Renaissance aesthetics called this sense of magical transcendence *admiratio*, or "wonder." Artisans fashioned automatons and funerary statuary with movable limbs and real clothing. Cf. Shakespeare's sly praise of the hyperrealist sculptor Julio Romano in the last scene of *The Winter's Tale*. I have explored this motive in *Shakespeare's Creation* (Amherst, Mass., 1976) and *Play, Death, and Heroism in Shakespeare* (Chapel Hill, 1989).

21. J. K. Huysmans, *Against Nature* (Harmondsworth, England, 1959), 35.

22. Cf. Virginia Hamilton, *Sweet Whispers, Brother Rush* (New York, 1982), in which Tree rhapsodizes that "no other power was like this power motor in a good car" (142)—her mother's car, "the safest place in the world" (143).

23. In the familiar symbolic vocabulary of the 1990s, the film associates the disease with poverty, and blacks become the stereotype of a quixotic, marginal political opposition.

24. William Gibson, *Neuromancer* (New York, 1984), 3 (hereafter cited as N).

25. Peter Homans, *The Ability to Mourn* (Chicago, 1989), chap. 1.

26. Henry Adams, *The Education of Henry Adams*, edited by Ernest Samuels (Boston, 1973), 433.

27. Let me repeat the call for "healing" violence in *The Courage to Heal: A Guide for Women Survivors of Child Sexual Abuse* (New York, 1988). Ellen Bass and Laura Davis encourage anger: "Many survivors have strong feelings of wanting to get back at the people who hurt them so terribly. You may dream of murder or castration. It can be pleasurable to fantasize such scenes in vivid detail. Wanting revenge is a natural impulse, a sane response. Let yourself imagine it to your heart's content" (128).

28. Max Nordau, *Degeneration* (1895; reprint, Lincoln, Nebr., 1968, 1993), 231.

29. Jonathan Shay, *Achilles in Vietnam: Combat Trauma and the Undoing of Character* (New York, 1994), 84.

30. See H. R. Haldeman, *The Haldeman Diaries: Inside the Nixon White House* (New York, 1994).

31. Page Smith, *A New Age Begins: A People's History of the American Revolution* (New York, 1976), 2:1828.

32. Robert H. Bork, *Slouching towards Gomorrah* (New York, 1996), 37.

Epilogue

1. *Beyond Trauma: Cultural and Societal Dynamics*, edited by Rolf J. Kleber, Charles R. Figley, and Berthold P. R. Gersons (New York, 1995), 11.

2. Allan Young, *The Harmony of Illusions: Inventing Post-Traumatic Stress Disorder* (Princeton, 1995), 290.

3. Robert D. McFadden, "A Long Slide from Privilege Ends in Slaughter," *New York Times*, December 12, 1993.

4. Ibid.

5. Ibid.

6. Richard J. Herrnstein and Charles Murray, *The Bell Curve: Intelligence and Class Structure in American Life* (New York, 1994).

7. As described in Otto Rank, *Will Therapy* (New York, 1978).

8. Betty Eadie, *Embraced by the Light* (New York, 1994).

Index

Library of Congress Cataloging-in-Publication Data
Farrell, Kirby, 1942–
    Post-traumatic culture : injury and interpretation in the
nineties / Kirby Farrell.
        p.   cm.
    Includes bibliographical references and index.
    ISBN 0-8018-5786-4 (alk. paper). — ISBN 0-8018-5787-2 (pbk. :
alk. paper)
        1. American literature—20th century—History and criticism.
2. Psychoanalysis and literature—United States—History—20th
century. 3. English literature—19th century—History and criticism. 4. Motion pictures—United States—History and criticism.
5. Wounds and injuries in literature. 6. Literature—Psychological
aspects. 7. Psychic trauma in literature. 8. Eighteen nineties.
9. Nineteen nineties. I. Title.
PS228.P74F37 1998
810.9'353—dc21
                                                            97-44042
                                                               CIP